Echo of the Unconscious in Painting

A Case Study

Naum G. Itkin, MD, PhD ◊ Susanne Schuenke, PhD

A.R.T.E. PRESS LLC

Book Design by Susanne Schuenke and Sagaponack Books & Design

ISBNs

978-1-7322205-0-8 (softcover)
978-1-7322205-1-5 (hardcover)
978-1-7322205-2-2 (e-book)

Library of Congress Catalog Number: 2019910934

Summary: An exploration of the role of unconscious processes in artistic creativity. Includes bibliographical references and art index.

PSY026000 Psychology / Movements / Psychoanalysis
PSY051000 Psychology / Cognitive Neuroscience & Cognitive Neuropsychology
ART016030 Art / Individual Artists / Monographs
SCI090000 Science/ Cognitive Science

A.R.T.E press, LLC
Ponte Vedra Beach, Florida

First Edition
Printed in the United States of America

A picture is worth a thousand words

Proverb

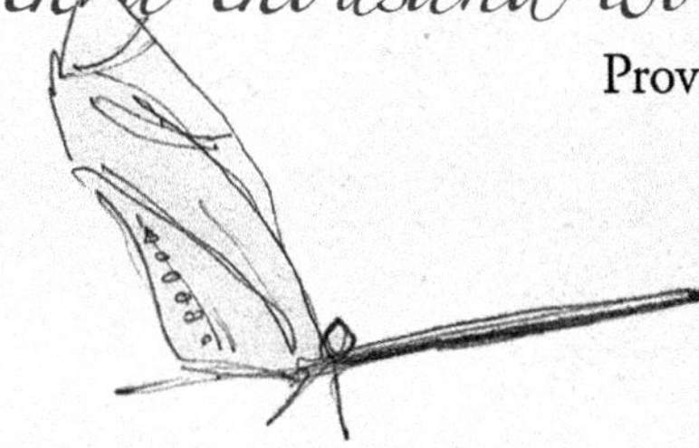

Contents

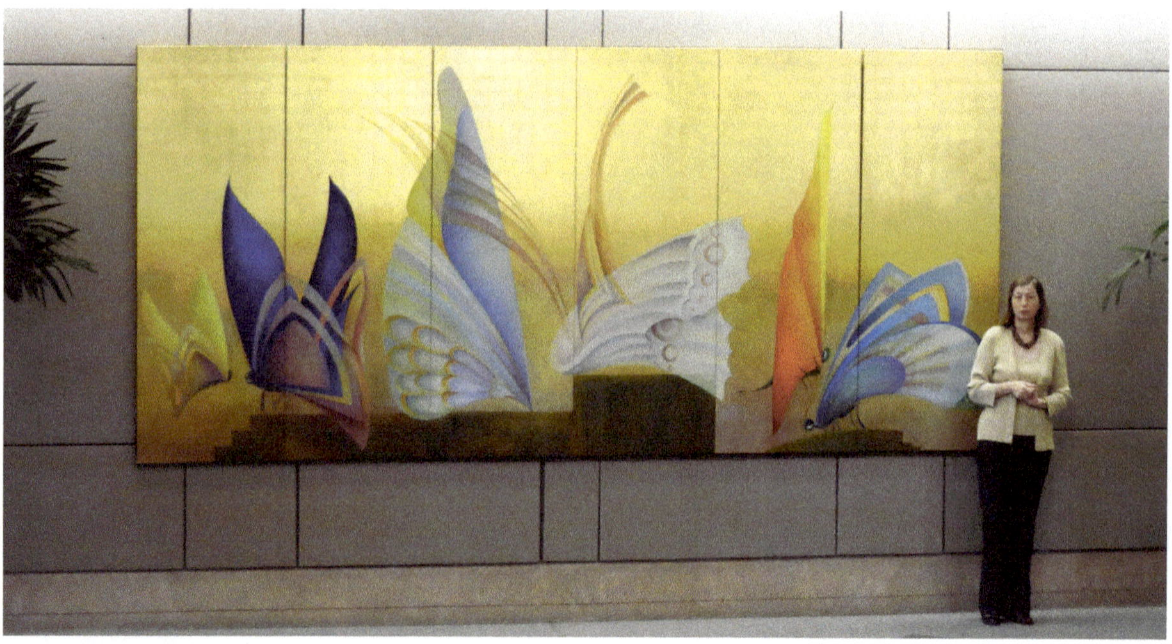

Give Me Wings! and the artist in its location.

Prologue

The artist had designed and created her painting *Give Me Wings!,* thinking that she had done it all at a conscious level but, as psychoanalytically orientated research later showed, she had not been aware at the time of creation and execution that her unconscious mind was fully involved in the process and cloaked "its voice" in imagery. In a painting, a "voice" cannot be heard, but can be discerned only by those searching "eyes" equipped with the knowledge of the unconscious. Furthermore, one month after completion of the painting, the artist had spontaneously written a private commentary, referred to as "Poetic Commentary," about the images of her work *Give Me Wings!,* still unsuspecting of any involvement of the unconscious. This addendum to the painting in written form has been fully integrated into the analysis of her creation.

It was a great advantage for this study that the artist agreed to provide authentic personal data through free associations. Access to essential information about her significant emotional experiences, supporting documentation, biographical facts, and discussions for clarification led us to discoveries of metaphorical meaning underlying the images of this painting.

We invite the reader to join our journey through the surprising territory of the unconscious and to walk with us along the way paved with unexpected keystones to a new outlook on the process of creativity and personal iconography.

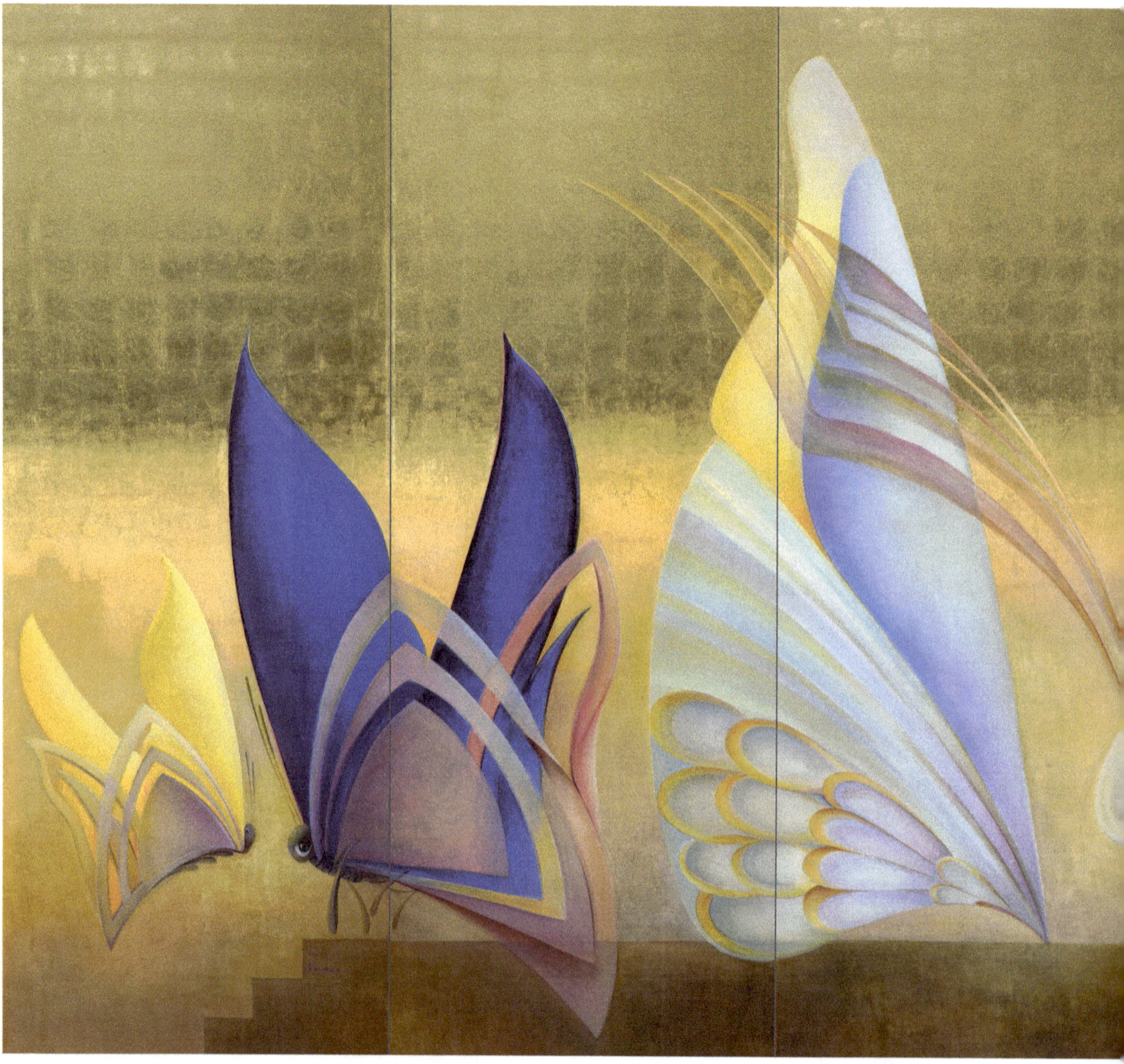

Susanne Schuenke, *Give Me Wings!*, 2004. Oil and gold leaf on canvas (six panels), 79 x 177 in (200 x 450 cm).

The Poetic Commentary

(written by the artist as "Seven WE's" in autumn 2004, about her oil painting *Give Me Wings!*)

"If you hear, if you only could hear what the antennae vibrate, the broadcast in the busy society of seven butterflies, their community chatter at the short gathering. Sometimes they come hungry for news, open to gossip, eager to speculate, hesitatingly to learn; other times they long for a rest from the noisy world, the media too thick to breathe your own thought, to clear the collective brains, to sip fresh purity—to be themselves again.

Little Why lives her nature to the fullest—questioning endlessly her minority role and significance—copying big True Blue in despair to reach one day his adapted aloofness and royalty.

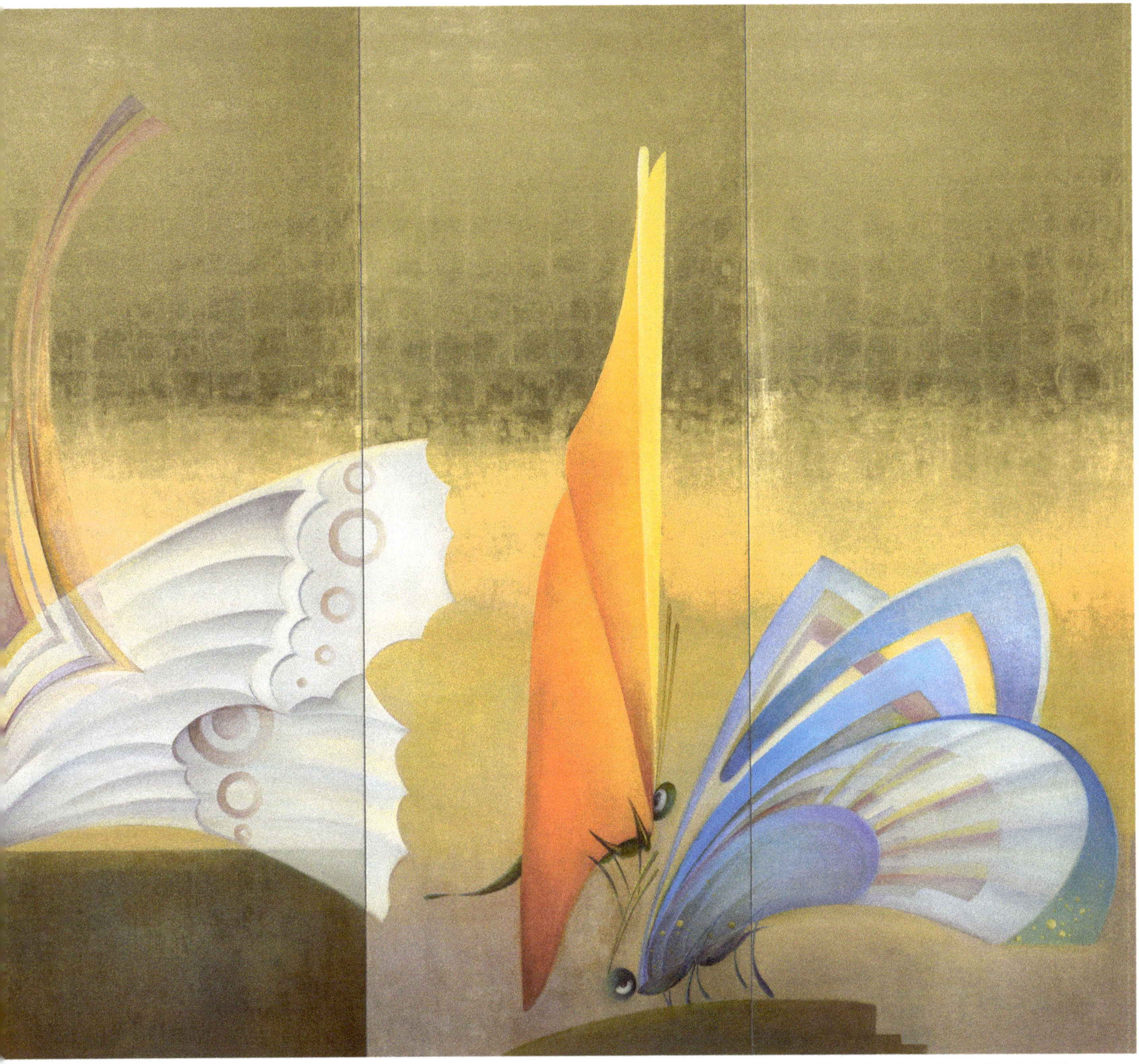

Mayo Clinic, Jacksonville, Florida

Little Why is torn between her admiration of the sapphire glow and the recollection of the values in her own lemony clarity. Little Why jumps up whenever she thinks someone will threaten her painfully fought success to approach the podium —but she herself is the only one who really anchors this position.

Firebird sometimes looks for camouflage in a bird of paradise, but he is much too choleric to restrain his trembling opinion. Having a miraculous range from purest white to deep burning orange, he is not even aware of the unbridgeable contradictions in his soul: From pure ideological goodness to ravishing anger and hate. In his bipolar temper, he will risk himself to rescue the friend in need, but a moment later he might condemn the same one as his blackest enemy and swear eternal warfare on him. His enormous range, the potential for the extraordinary, has turned into his greatest deficit, isolating him from the others.

Fanning Everything seeks approval under all circumstances, gracefully twisting diplomacy into a charade of shallow loveliness to cover high-quality opportunism. Dancing at every wedding, Fanning Everything is nowhere at home. In the display of countless alternatives, she thins down her integrity to tasteless chatter.

Touchless Misty pretends fragile daintiness, which hides his strict, structured strength underneath the elegant, polished white surface. Smoothly groomed rewards in academia and gliding weightlessly on the political parquet let him spread pleasant luster wherever his shadows dare to fall.

Pale Moonlight is much larger than her vaguely defined talents: her sketchy acknowledged qualities, and her barely illuminated brilliance. Her essence is concentrated at the core from which all her strength, beauty, endurance, and courage stream out, radiating in spiraling loops or in graceful bends, and sharply marking the division between "here" and "there." A glimpse of orange within the innate, energetic nucleus lets you wonder what could be when uncapped and let loose.

In the absence of true understanding, the one in the middle was nicknamed "Air," and the others couldn't even decide on the gender so it stayed an "it." "Air" is bridging between them, it is with them, but not of them, just visiting, hovering for an ephemeral moment before its unpredictable disappearance. With the light mirroring on its wings, "Air's" iridescent qualities will charm you away.

Little Why has no time for it, True Blue is too much involved with himself, and Firebird never had a chance to look at it. Touchless Misty and Pale Moonlight feel attracted, searching, but missing the point where they thought they would meet.

True Blue relies on status to declare the status quo, defending his territory, governing the richnesses and the options, the rules and the enforcements, the system, and its holiness."

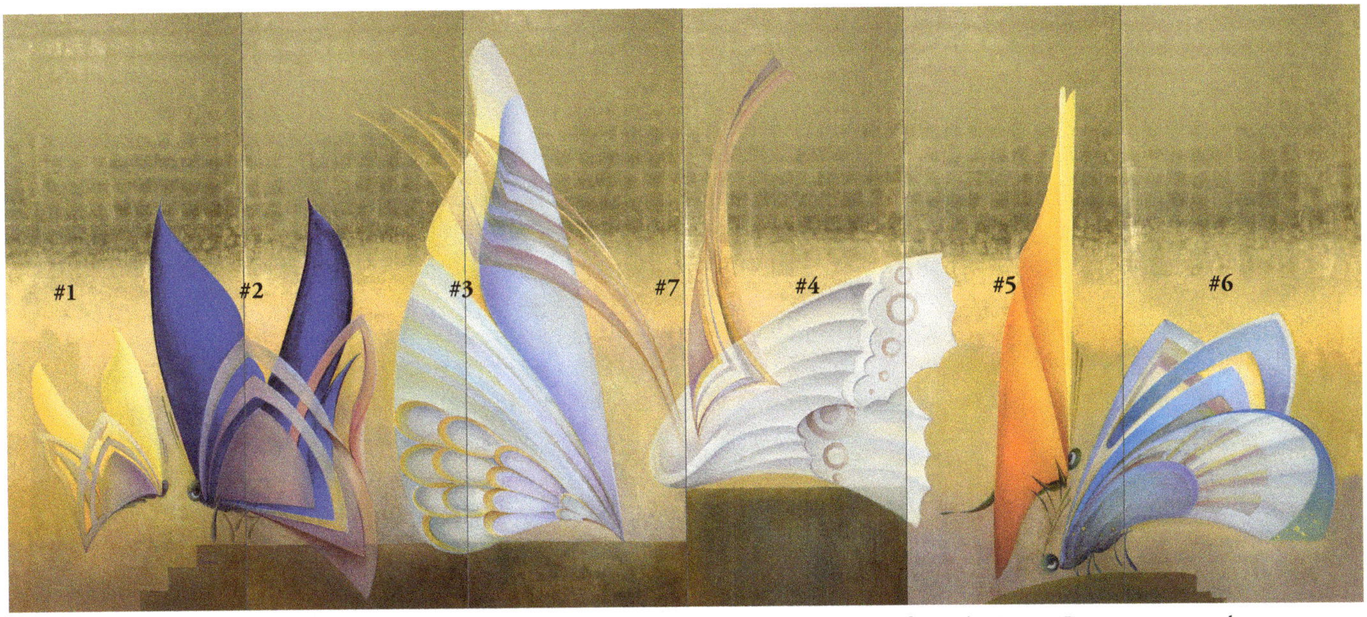

Fig. 1.0. References to numbers assigned to the butterflies, as given by the artist, sobriquets from the Poetic Commentary, and personifications of the butterfly images as used throughout the book.

1 *Little Why*	2 *True Blue*	3 *Pale Moonlight*	7 *Air*	4 *Touchless Misty*	5 *Firebird*	6 *Fanning Everything*
Susanne as child	Father/ Friend(s)	Susanne as adult	Spirituality	Susanne as adult	Father	Mother

Chapter 1

Introduction

1.1 In the Beginning—Sharing Personal Information

Psychological and psychiatric studies by researchers on famous painters (such as Leonardo da Vinci, Salvador Dalí, André Masson, Max Ernst, Pablo Picasso, Marcel Duchamp, Gustav Klimt, etc.)[1], as well as critical expositions of their lives and works by art historians and critics, are based primarily on secondhand historical and biographical data. The information is often patchy, anecdotal, and contradictory, leaving major gaps in the data concerning the artists' most formative years—childhood and early adulthood. Many painters have provided autobiographical material and commentaries on their works that facilitate the analysis of psychological aspects of their creativity. Rarely do researchers have the good fortune of direct access to the artists themselves and of conducting an extensive, evolving dialogue with them to receive confidential information. Even though legends and folklore of those famous artists reflect some degree of truth, had the artists been studied firsthand in their lifetimes by analysts with a psychoanalytic approach, we would have a more comprehensive insight into an analysis of the psychological processes that were instrumental in the creation of their art.

Imagery is assumed by an artist to have been created solely by the conscious mind. Through full cooperation with an analyst, an artist, in the process of sharing personal information, becomes aware of the involvements of the unconscious in the formation of images. Before analysis, these implicit messages are unrecognized and unanticipated. Obviously, the facts received from the artist can significantly assist the study in shedding light on the many puzzling phenomena

1 Freud 1989, Lomas 1979 and 2000, Ades, Cox, Hopkins 1999, Kandel 2012

and mysteries of creativity. Thus, these data are of inestimable value and great scientific interest. Unfortunately, the vast majority of studies done on painters from the past suffer from a lack of relevant records and an abundance of questionable clues regarding the artists' significant emotional experiences, particularly in their early years.

Recognizing the need for a comprehensive study of artistic creativity, the painter Susanne Schuenke agreed to provide private information continuously, which enabled the research to proceed and attain its fruition in discovering traces of the unconscious in her paintings.

Openly sharing the details and nuances of one's private life is rarely easy for a subject. The researcher usually encounters strong resistance and defense mechanisms from the person under analysis. Neurotic reactions and their convoluted development, as well as heightened individual sensitivities and the irrational responses to them, are often associated with highly talented people. These inclinations envelop the person like a swarm of mosquitos. They can be recognized in the figurative language of metaphors, symbols, and allegories that are embedded in hidden or open signs, when the person is engaged in a creative activity.

When the artist freely discloses personal information, the researcher can find firmer ground to present more meaningful interpretations of the artwork from multiple perspectives. Such was the case with the painting *Give Me Wings!* by Susanne Schuenke, co-author of this book, in which stylized butterflies were the subjects studied. At first glance, the butterflies appeared to be a simple exhibition of beauty. However, during the analysis, we uncovered expressions of peculiarities of the artist's psyche in their images, bringing some of its numerous facets to the surface. Furthermore, we were able to follow the traces of the unconscious, decode the formation of many personal symbols, and gain insight into the creativity of the artist's mind.

We believe the discovery of the psychological mechanisms behind Susanne's creative process will be a helpful addition to the existing literature in interpreting and discovering the hidden psychical underpinnings of the works of other artists for whom we have insufficient personal data.

1.2 The Innocuous Butterflies – Distinct Personalities

In 2004, the German-American artist Susanne Schuenke created *Give Me Wings!*, a monumental oil painting measuring 6 ½ x 14 feet (2 x 4.5 meters) on six panels, featuring seven stylized, gigantic butterflies (Fig. 1.0). Initially, prior to presenting the design of *Give Me Wings!* to the painting's future owners, Susanne had given the project her own working title, *Before the Flight* [2] as an intimation of humanity's eternal dream of flying beyond our earthly bounds. The painting's central butterfly as a representation of spirituality and the golden background, which rises behind and above the figures in the foreground, metaphorically signify the striving to ascend to a higher realm.

The artist, filled with enthusiasm for the work, became very fond of these seemingly innocuous butterflies. Over many months, Susanne watched them "hatching" under her brush and coming into existence with surprising contents unforeseen by her. For the artist, these butterflies were never merely cute and colorful little insects. In the first of three creative drawings,[3] she perceived them as powerful entities having much to say about themselves. She even experienced them as higher beings possessing distinct personalities.

Soon after completing the oil painting, Susanne became spontaneously inspired to write a short narration (known hereafter as the poetic commentary) as free associations commenting on the images in the painting. She endowed the butterflies with peculiar core qualities, which she expressed with appropriate poetic monikers[4] as they came to her spontaneously.

Finishing the commentary, the artist summarized her feelings and invented the unusual appellation *Seven WE's* for the title. Writing only to herself, she was unconcerned about who might ever read it. Following a subliminal desire to reinforce the collec-

2 The working title *Before the Flight* was written in pencil on a watercolor sheet. The final name for the painting, *Give Me Wings!*, was suggested by the client, who commissioned the work as a donation to the Mayo Clinic. The Mayo Clinic Board of Trustees endorsed this choice of title. The painting has hung in the entrance lobby of the Davis Building in the Mayo Clinic, Jacksonville, Florida, since October 2004. (Mayo Clinic 2014, pages 86-87)

3 The artist uses this term in a more technical sense, as in German "Kreativzeichnung," which stresses the more inventive aspect of the drawing process. See chapter 2 for more details.

4 Only one name existed before, "Firebird." It came to her spontaneously during the painting process (see chapter 4 for details).

tive aspect of its meaning (i.e., the collective presence of seven personified butterflies), Susanne capitalized the first-person plural word *we* (WE); she then pluralized it by adding "s" ("WEs"). But she still felt dissatisfied, so she changed it into an apostrophized *s* ('s), thus yielding "WE's." By the addition of the word *Seven*, the title became "Seven WE's," meaning each WE, seven in all, belongs to a group of WE's. This "WE's" construction conveys a sense of unity for the seven butterflies, emphasizing that they all belong to the group separately—and together.

In describing the butterflies and their personalities in the poetic commentary, the artist (as the narrator) felt herself among them, unconsciously expressing her self-identification with their personifications. Beside "personally" being in the group, Susanne's enigmatic coinage, "WE's," carries a manifold group identification, such as exemplified in the famous phrase "We the People," being a collective member of a family, society, or country. It also indicates "We are One," meaning the ultimate unity of mankind, although, in our contemporary world, this unity continues to escape our grasp and remains a utopian ideal.

Throughout this book, either the nickname and/or an assigned number[5] will refer to each individual butterfly, as follows (see Fig. 1.0).

Butterfly No. 1–*Little Why*
Butterfly No. 2–*True Blue*
Butterfly No. 3–*Pale Moonlight*
Butterfly No. 7–*Air*
Butterfly No. 4–*Touchless Misty*
Butterfly No. 5–*Firebird*
Butterfly No. 6–*Fanning Everything*

Susanne intentionally gave each butterfly a gender, with the same number of male (No. 2, 4, and 5) and female (No. 1, 3, and 6) subjects. She assigned a neuter, "it", to the center butterfly (No. 7).

1.3 Methods Applied to the Analysis

In 2007, three years after the creation of the painting, using the method of free association (first extensively developed by Sigmund Freud), Naum Itkin and Susanne Schuenke began analyzing the painting *Give Me Wings!*. Their objective was to reach a deeper understanding of her creative process. In the Freudian technique, the subject is asked to verbalize spontaneously every thought that comes to mind. This includes perceptions, feelings, emotions, beliefs, ideas, wishes, urges, drives, fantasies, images, and any kind of experience. The subject is encouraged to speak of all associations in the sequence in which they appear, while staying away from any selectivity and preexisting preferences. Value judgments such as "good" and "bad" are also discouraged, thus avoiding any moral evaluation or ethical predisposition. Nor should any consideration be given to the relevancy or even repugnancy of the content. The subjects must thus overcome personal resistance and relinquish their censorship's control.

For over a century, this psychoanalytic technique has proven reliable for exploring the unconscious. It has done so by uncovering the manner by which the unconscious encodes and manifests messages in various psychological phenomena such as dreams, Freudian slips (slips of tongue and pen, mishearing, misreading, forgetting, mislaying and losing objects), neurosis, neurotic reactions, etc.

In creating her painting *Give Me Wings!* and the poetic commentary "Seven WE's," Susanne unknowingly facilitated the process of free association without any previous knowledge of psychoanalytic and psychoanalytical practice. Her painting presents "manifest content" comparable with dreams. In the commentary, she articulated her associations with the images. That, together with the above-mentioned method of free association in direct dialogue with the analyst, gave us the foundation for interpretation of the "latent content" of her creative works. In this way, we were able to discover various aspects of the unconscious messages and their allegorical, metaphorical, and symbolic meanings, condensed into visual and verbal forms.

By following her intuition, by her own revelations, and by discovering multiple layers of meaning, she recognized many facets of references to past experiences in the details of her paintings. Directed by her unconscious mind during the analysis, she had many pivotal associations that revealed a kaleidoscope of her inner reality. This, in turn, provided a broader base for deciphering the unconscious meanings of her images. As a result, many messages of her personal and the universal unconscious came to the surface.

---

5 The numbers were assigned by the artist in 2007 for the purpose of reference in this research. She insisted in numbering the central image as "No. 7," stressing its unique significance for her (see chapter 10).

1.4 Approaching Metaphorical Meaning of the Images

We focused carefully on the details of every butterfly regarding lines, shape, color, and position, as well as composition, and how these elements relate to each other. Fashioning more precise descriptions and definitions of the details, we discovered numerous peculiarities that broadened our scope of observation. Thus, we identified additional facets essential for our interpretation that widened the basis of our assumptions. As a result, all the combined data became the foundation for understanding the modus operandi of the unconscious and its influence on the process of creativity.

By following the developmental transformations of the various elements of the images from the primary sketches, creative drawings, composition drawing, and the watercolor to the final oil painting (see chapter 2), we could either confirm our earlier presuppositions or find new interpretations. Moreover, Susanne's initial associations, as expressed in her poetic commentary, and the approach we employed above, led us to decipher the substantial connections between the painting's details and Susanne's life experiences. We found that no image, detail, word, or nuance came into existence by accident. They were imbued with layers of meaning rooted in her emotionally charged past events, memories, motivations, concepts, and attitudes.

We realized, step by step, the connection between the painting's peculiar details and Susanne's relevant feelings, significant emotional experiences, and thoughts. That enabled us to decode the underlying metaphorical implications of the images. The interpretation of their allegorical messages unraveled the structure of a symbolic language, which she had developed on the basis of her intellect, education, and experience. The code employed a wide variety of analogies far beyond the scope of this explicit iconography. In this context, we analyze the appearance and formation of the artist's unconscious symbolism rooted in the biological foundation of existence (instinctual drives). Gradually, we offer elucidation of how both aspects, expressed in the imageries, mirrored the artist's perception of herself and her world.

After the metaphorical content of certain details became evident, the influence of the unconscious on the artwork became well-founded. Progressively, we understand that the visual components of the paintings (form, line, color, and composition) reflect a multitude of latent meanings. This correlation was not known to the artist before the analysis. Gradually, we gained factually-based data that provide evidence to support such an interpretation. With increased numbers of perceived particulars and further associations, we uncovered more traces of the unconscious in the imagery. It became evident that almost every detail of the painting's design had definite links to the implicitly coded information. Deciphering its specifics in accordance to their origin led us, like the navigation markers, to the recognition and interpretation of the unconscious symbolism. This process was an important step toward tracing how an artist's creative mind transforms unconscious forces into art.

This research allowed the artist to recall specific personal information which, when correctly interpreted, enabled us to discover the specific ways by which the unconscious works to send its messages to the conscious surface. For us, the attempt to decode the metaphors and translate the symbolic signs of imagery into ordinary language became an adventurous journey, a voyage deep into the artist's psyche. Like the pieces of a jigsaw puzzle coming together, the innumerable details and interpretive meanings gradually formed a picture supporting our assumptions about metaphorical manifestations of the unconscious in the images of the painting. This general conclusion was confirmed by a series of important discoveries, which we will cover in the following chapters.

1.5 Phenomena of Personification

After starting our analysis with butterfly No. 5, "Firebird," we had our first breakthrough. A network of associations with the image's forms, coloration, and naming (see chapter 4) brought us to the hypothesis that the image of this butterfly could relate to a significant emotional subject. This was confirmed, especially, with the discovery of a specific shape in Firebird when seen from a certain angle. That configuration could be visualized as the raised index finger of an authoritarian person, which then was correlated with the familiar gestures of Susanne's lecturing father. A wide array of relevant details rich in symbolism sufficiently supported this interpretation, and from that came the revelation that butterfly No. 5 is coded unconsciously as the personification of the artist's father.

This recognition caused a sudden, unexpected turn as we began to identify further signs of the personification process in the other butterflies. After delving deeply into the task, we were rewarded with many more epiphanies, finding other personifications in accordance with an assortment of pertinent meanings in every butterfly. Analyzing numerous facets of each figure, we finally came to the interpretation that the images of the seven butterflies unconsciously represent personifications[6] of Susanne, her father, and her mother. The following table gives each butterfly's name,[7] reference number, and the identity of the family member personified by the butterfly (see also Fig. 1.0).

Butterfly No. 1–*Little Why*: Susanne as child
Butterfly No. 2–*True Blue*: Father/Friend(s)
Butterfly No. 3–*Pale Moonlight*: Susanne as adult
Butterfly No. 7–*Air*: Spirituality
Butterfly No. 4–*Touchless Misty*: Susanne as adult
Butterfly No. 5–*Firebird*: Father
Butterfly No. 6–*Fanning Everything*: Mother

1.6 Insight into Creativity

After discovering and accepting the phenomena of the personification and identification in the painting as a new insight, Susanne asked: "I wonder, if everything coming out from one person (saying, drawing, writing, etc.) on a conscious level is always a reflection of what is deeper inside, in the person's unconscious strata? Are all characters the author invents also facets of his/her personal unconscious structure, as in fiction? I was thinking—are some or all of the described characters' features also in me?"

In connection with this reflection, Susanne had a vision, which she described as follows: "I was kind of asleep and looked, with my eyes closed, straight ahead: To my right side, there was an image of the butterfly painting, and I observed with a detached attitude, like an observer standing by, how something like a small vertical shadow with a vague outline went out of me and entered the painting, then returned to me. I would call it the back and forth of a shadow, and I had the inner understanding that I identified myself with the painting. I was in it, out of it, among the butterflies, in the butterflies, and a part of them."

In 2005, long before the analysis commenced, the artist was questioned about the process of creating the butterfly painting. By coincidence, she wrote down her impression of the creative process in response: "Drinking from memories, that is how they pour out from me, how the lines flow into their expressions, without words. The curves playfully define their state of resting, catch their aspirations, or describe their eagerness before they take off. This smooth, continuous stream of lines comes in a way, which I can only describe with the word 'translation': First, I was in the butterfly conservatory in New York, and I attempted to follow as closely as possible the real event in front of my eyes with my naturalistic pencil drawings. After this, later, in my 'own' way of drawing, I stylized that repertoire of forms in sketches, impacted by impressions, memories and, I suppose, much more than I know, and brought forth a new synthesis. Something else always happens during this stylization process: The guidance comes out of somewhere deep in the brain, from the still unknown dwelling place of creativity, to follow a certain direction, not named, not defined yet, but still I follow, and the result is suddenly a genuine scene, a topic, a content."

This subjective experience matches the concept of "automatic writing and drawing" as defined in the *Manifesto of Surrealism* by Andre

---

6 A short explanation of the word "personification" might be necessary. In the arts, a personification is often used to describe something that looks like a human being, but which is actually intended to represent an abstract concept. A good example is the Statue of Liberty in New York Harbor: What we see is a mature woman with an aureole of rays around her head, draped in an antique garment, clasping a book, and holding a torch. From the cultural context in which this artwork was created, we know that this is not an ordinary female with a couple of accessories, but the personification of the principle of "Liberty." Her halo, as well as her classical Greek garment, readily identifies her as noble of spirit. The book adds a sign of wisdom, and the torch symbolizes the guiding light of this lofty concept - "Liberty."
In psychology, the term "personification" may be used in a slightly different way. It can indicate that certain human qualities are attributed to any object or non-human being. In the painting and in the poetic commentary, the artist attributed human characteristics to the butterflies.

7 For the sake of clarity, Susanne's monikers for the butterflies are also used by the researchers for analyzing the corresponding images found in the first drawings, the creative drawing, the watercolor, and the oil painting, although these names were invented by her only after the painting's completion, while writing the poetic commentary.

Breton in 1924.[8] He regards surrealism as a "pure psychic automatism" and that the images revealed by the artists were representations of the unconscious, following "obedience to this magic dictation."[9] His declaration is an analogy to the Freudian statement that "dreams are the royal road to the unconscious."[10] This goes along with the doctrine of psychic automatism, formulated by Pierre Janet ("*automatisme psychologiques*"), which became one of the fundamental postulates for interpreting and analyzing the creativity of the surrealist painters.

Those views can be reconciled with the Freudian model of the unconscious, from which automatic writing and drawing are derived. The unconscious—as the source, generator, and reactor—determines the free flow of energy toward its discharge. The energy is transmuted into dreams, obsessive compulsive dictates, phobias, automatic writing and drawing (visual images), etc. In automatic drawing, many significant experiences from the past, which unconsciously were displaced by new scenarios, find their expression in visual metaphors that encapsulate specific meanings from the previous emotionally charged episodes. These mental processes direct the artist's hand into a tangible realization of the unconscious content on paper, canvas, etc.

David Lomas, in his psychoanalytic study of a select few surrealist painters,[11] follows the Freudian concept in his summary of the effects of the unconscious on spontaneous creativity. He writes that, depending upon the context, the same shape could be, for example, a sign for a head, an egg, or a sun. A line, shape, color, or composition can deliver information coded by the unconscious. The line-configuration, approaching the condition of the linguistic sign, becomes equivalent to the word. This is in accordance with Jacques Lacan's[12] statement that "the unconscious is structured like language." Moreover, before the child has acquired linguistic competence, he/she perceives the surroundings through the senses (vision, hearing, smell, touch, taste). These perceptions remain imprinted in the unconscious—especially as visual memory. By the mechanisms of repression, visual memory becomes subliminal, but it can find its representation in different phenomena, including images in paintings. In the post-verbal stage, latent thoughts and fantasies, having been structured by the psychological mechanisms of condensations and displacements, manifest in different forms. Verbal and nonverbal experience become imprinted and encoded in various signs within the interacting stratifications.[13] These mechanisms have close affinities with metaphors, allegories, symbols, metonymies, etc.

"Memory traces," which are left in our brain as permanently imprinted records of perceptual events, could be expressed through the automatic drawing that brings them fragmentally to the conscious surface, coded in personal symbolism. These are hieroglyphs of the inner processes that reflect real life situations and their records, which we can reconstruct or even re-experience. Freud believed that memory traces are unavailable for the conscious due to repression. However, they can express their presence through psychic automatism. Through the artistic creative imagination, the unconscious transmutes different elements of past perceptions into new scenes, altering them in startling ways. The original situations are partly reassembled, manifesting the spectacular re-entrance of the repressed. This idea was expressed by Lomas in the following: "Automatic writing, as the trace of a voice emanating from another scene, the unconscious, was seen as displacing the authorial subject from its position as origin."[14]

1.7 Personal Preferences in Colors

One of the impressive results of our research was uncovering how, beneath the artist's conscious selecting and combining of colors, the unconscious guides the choices. Susanne's preferences were obviously connected with the familiar symbolic

8 Breton 1924

9 Breton 1922, 1: 274

10 Freud 1913

11 Lomas 2000

12 Lacan 1977

13 Freud 1938: page 32

14 Lomas 2000: page 21

meanings of the colors, developed throughout the history of western culture. However, in her artistic work, her personal bias toward certain hues and nuances of colors dominates, and on these preferences, she has built her own iconography.

We have tried to understand her iconographic partialities, and it has been intriguing to search Susanne's artistic oeuvre for the origins of her canon of favored and rejected hues and color combinations. At this point, we mention only a general outline. The detailed analysis will be in the following chapters.

An array of different parameters (cultural, political, religious, commercial, natural, etc.) determines the choices on the conscious and the unconscious levels. Such criteria include the painter's individual perceptions of beauty, an intuitive feeling of harmony, and insights into the interplay of the colors within a composition. When choosing a tone, the painter considers how the hue plays out with the shape and contributes to the content (i.e., what potential meaning it might harbor).

Susanne in her art is quite scrupulous and adamant as to which colors she likes or dislikes, and the same principles also rule her life. The following is a sampling of her personal color canon, established long before she began *Give Me Wings!*.

The artist's best-loved color has always been crimson red, considered by her the epitome of vibrant beauty. Most shades of reds and a selection of greens also rank among her favorites. On the other hand, she has an aversion to yellow and violet, particularly the combination of the two. Through her youth and early adulthood, blue was to her a boring color, which she came to appreciate only later in life. Greens are split into two ranks: The "yellowish greens" (like olive green) are cozy for her, whereas the "bluish greens," like turquoise, she finds repellent. Orange has always been a negative hue, which cannot please her in any way.

The painter claims that she is, in some measure, consciously aware of those preferences during the designing process for her works. From our study, we can attest that the harmony in her paintings is a result of the coalescence of conscious and unconscious factors.

The painter gives a rational explanation for her choice of colors, citing mainly "compositional reasons" and "personal liking." We made some impressive discoveries of the interactions between the conscious and unconscious processes that determine selection of the coloration in the painting. Many of her color preferences are rooted in her childhood and youth, when she lived in an atmosphere filled with visual stimulants provided by the parents, being artists themselves. Those were toys, richly illustrated story books, art books with manifold reproductions, her parents' workshop, and the artistic surroundings in the home, all enhanced by the parents' steady homage to their cultural traditions. This colorful environment furnished Susanne with some specific details, especially from certain artworks. Her psyche drew a connection between the color and a particular meaning associated with a life episode, which would provoke in her a strong emotional reaction, either pleasant or frightening, based on the nexus. We found that in some cases a particular hue would enter into her mind and trigger the associative affect. This color nuance becomes a symbolic, unconscious signifier for that emotion. This process predominates in the artist's approach to specific colors in her works, and unconsciously conveying potent inner messages of her psyche.

Coloration enters Susanne's artwork in most cases after the completion of the compositional drawing. The decisions in choosing colors are for her a more complicated process, in comparison with the flow of drawing lines and shapes. The artist explains: "…lines and shapes are for me comparable with words, describing thoughts. And the colors are like the emotions and the timbre with which the words are spoken." Following this analogy, the colors emerge as an impulsive expression for Susanne. The artist experiences them as complementary to the shapes, giving her the emotional satisfaction of completion.

The main hues in a painting come to Susanne's mind, in most cases, spontaneously. Then she selects the subordinate colors to support these dominant tones, supplying captivating variations and contrasts to her work and further strengthening the spatial arrangement of lines and shapes. The artist had been convinced that she was absolutely free in choosing her color schemes, but the present research found multiple indications that the unconscious consistently makes a strong contribution to the choice. Our analysis uncovered different and unexpected (i.e., consciously unknown) root causes, embedded in the artist's mind as to why she employs such disfavored colors.

The results of the research show that it is well worth going back to the sources of her negative attitude in the original situation. From this, we can form an interpretation of how every experience in her life is registered, processed, and activated by the artist's unconscious mind. The same approach, furthermore, can shed light on Susanne's assessment of established color "temperature" schemes (as expressed by many color theories[15]), which she finds to be "labels, artificially laid on the nature of color." Susanne does not share a certain established perception of color temperature. For example, she considers yellow in most cases as a cold color, in opposition to mainstream opinion. Her deviation from the conventional evaluation could be determined by emotionally loaded experiences in the past (detailed analysis in chapter 6).

The collection of the concrete data in this case study regarding the artist's predisposition toward the choice of colors is of special importance. As we have pointed out, reliable personal information on the artists of the past on this matter is woefully inadequate. Thus, our above findings of unconscious determination of color preferences elucidate some perspectives.

1.8 Life Experiences Reflected in the Images of the Butterflies

During the analysis, it became evident that the imagery of each butterfly reflected the following factors in various degrees:

- significant emotional experiences and events in the artist's life, particularly in the childhood and later formative years
- relationships in the artist's family
- philosophical and ideological concepts and attitudes
- existential issues of life as perceived and experienced by the artist
- the artist's adjustment to the environment, people, community, and society
- the artist's coping strategies for various issues and circumstances
- facets of the artist's character, patterns of behavior and personality problems
- psychological sensitivities, complexes, and various psychoneuroses and neurotic reactions

We have observed that those factors nurtured the artist's imagination and proclivities. In the following chapters, we will discuss how they were transmuted into the images of the butterflies in the painting, and manifested in the poetic commentary that was written to accompany the painting. Many aspects of Susanne's life, such as her professional training in art, a doctorate in art history, and her broad intellectual interests in the sciences, as well as in philosophy and religion, will be touched upon and accounted for in the analysis. The data and their interpretations will show how the psychodynamic factors and the psychological structure of complexes and repressed tendencies have played critical roles in the development of the artist's singular art style. We will analyze how these aspects subliminally permeated her imagery, disguised in specific forms, compositions, and colors, revealing the artist's unconscious symbolism.

The discovery of traces of the unconscious in the artist's paintings and the metaphorical expressions of significant emotional experiences in the images have had a positive impact on Susanne's condition. Over time, as the research progressed, it has become noticeable that bringing the latent meanings to awareness initiated a healing process. Susanne began to deal more successfully with many of the psychological problems with which she has been struggling all her life.

Learning about the unconscious and its various manifestations in her own life and art, Susanne started to perceive the outside world with more tolerance. Soon, changes in Susanne's behavior, attitudes, and neurotic reactions had become quite apparent to those who had known her long before the research was undertaken. Her friends now greet a calmer, happier, more patient and light-hearted Susanne who laughs much more and cries far less. Furthermore, it has become clearly noticeable to Susanne that there was a considerable decrease in the daily intrusions of her phobias that used to debilitate her psychologically and physically, which is a remarkable outcome, even though she still has a long way to go in becoming free of them. We consider that the analysis has freed the mental energy formerly bound to phobias, anxiety, and various repressed tendencies, and the artist now experiences increased stamina in her daily life

15 For example: Zelanski/Fisher 2010, page 39-40.

and activation in her creativity. The outcome of the analysis has surpassed all expectations.

Recognizing and evaluating the large assortment of significant emotional events in her life, we begin to see the critical role that those have played in the articulation of Susanne's artistic creativity. Our study makes no claim to having completely unraveled the secrets of how the interplay of the artist's conscious and unconscious selects particulars from the accumulated mental database, transforming and weaving them into an artwork—a visible story. Nevertheless, certain significant observations and inferences can be made from a careful and discerning application of a psychoanalytic approach that has been developed and refined for over a century in uncovering the *modi operandi* of the unconscious.

In conducting our research, careful attention was paid to restraining ourselves from making assumptions and jumping to hasty conclusions that would be the result of the authors' personal and professional bias and predispositions. The authors raised questions without pretense that their answers would be complete. We accepted the challenge of sifting through thickets of data, false leads, and speculations before arriving at a reasonably cogent understanding of the psychodynamic process at play regarding our subject of inquiry. We are aware that the findings of this study could not reach the level of objectivity that is called for in the natural sciences. Thus, doubts about the completeness and finality of the inferences we made will remain, pending further verification. The interpretations in this study are presented as hypotheses and assumptions, and have varying levels of validity. Our findings are providing numerous illustrations of manifestation of unconscious processes in painting.

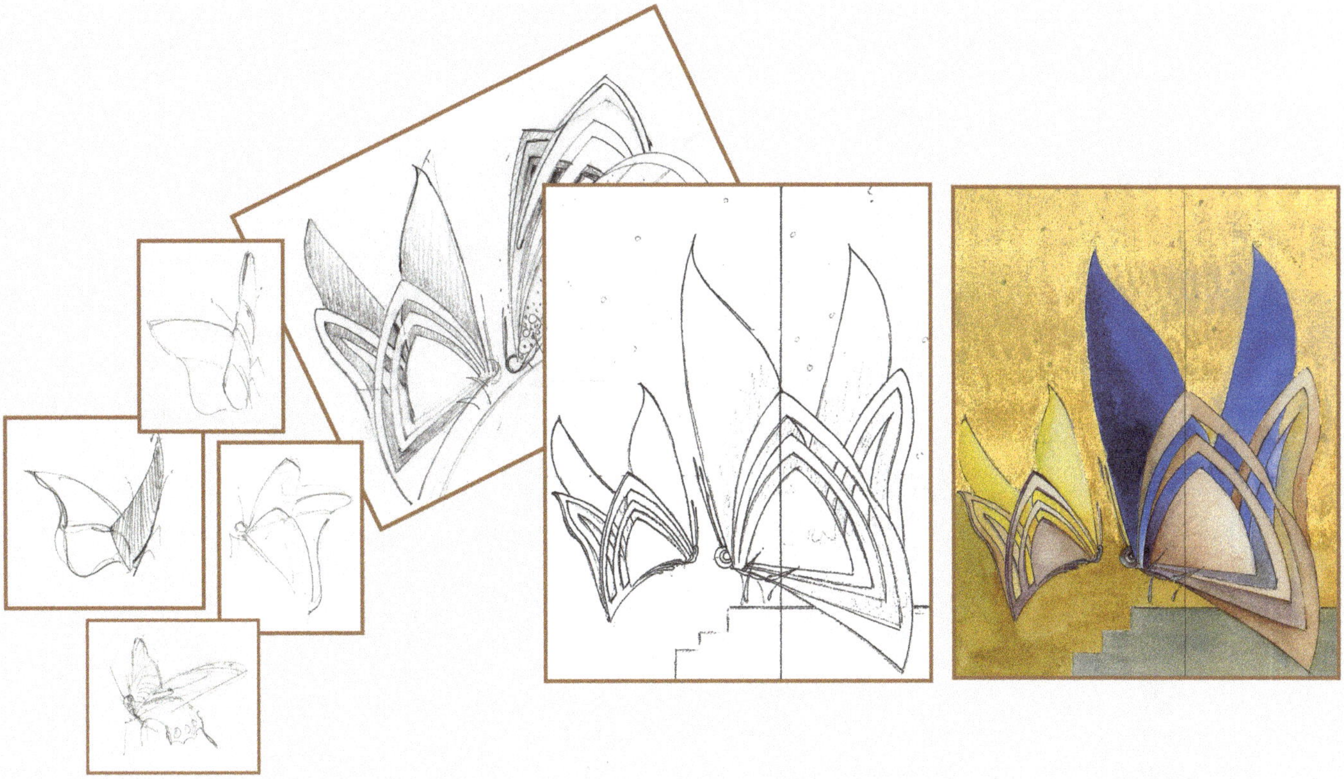

Fig. 2.0. Collage of selected stages of the development.

Chapter 2

Stages of Development

From sketches to the oil painting

Tabula rasa: On Dec 9th, 2003, by chance the artist, Susanne Schuenke, toured the American Museum of Natural History in New York City and discovered its Butterfly Conservatory. There, she was captivated by the mesmerizing beauty of the flying creatures that greeted their enchanted visitors. Observing the butterflies from various perspectives, she became so spellbound by their exquisite colors, elegant wing contours, and seemingly effortless aerial movements that she had a strong desire to draw them. She hurried to the museum gift shop to purchase paper and pencil. Then, the artist eagerly began sketching the creatures to capture those extraordinary moments. The lasting impression of her fascinating visit to the Conservatory was carried out over the next weeks and months and reflected through the various developmental stages of her masterpiece, *Give Me Wings!*. The artist categorizes[1] those stages as sketches, creative drawings, the compositional drawing, the watercolor, and the final oil painting. The stylization of certain essential elements of the butterflies in the finished work can be traced back through these various progressive phases.

---

1 The artist has her own vocabulary to denote specific elements or steps in the development of her artwork. The term "sketch" she reserves for quick, observational studies. Based on the German terminology "*Kreativ-Zeichnung*" (or "*Entwurfszeichnung*"), Susanne calls a drawing in which she freely invents her own shapes and topic as "creative drawing," in contrast to a study drawing or descriptive drawing. The term "compositional drawing" is used by Susanne in the traditional sense, as it involves the merging of various independent elements and designs into a coherent whole.

2.1 The Sketches

At the museum, the sketches had to be drawn quickly, often in only a matter of seconds, as the flying subjects were moving rapidly, quickly changing their positions in an unpredictable manner (Fig.2.1a-g). In such a situation, with her mind focused on the dynamic movements immediately in front of her, one can reasonably assume that the artist gave little conscious consideration to the details of the subjects' shapes and lines as the sketching rapidly progressed. Contrary to the realistic depictions of the subjects to be expected from purely conscious efforts, these quickly executed sketches show structural patterns such as deviation, stylization, invention, or omission that are dissimilar to the features of the natural models. Through the course of analysis, we have recognized this could stem from implicit tendencies in the painter's psyche intervening in the sketching process.

For example, a butterfly image on the top right-hand corner of Fig. 2.1f (for enlarged details, see Fig. 7.1) could illustrate how the artist replaced the natural ramification of the veins on the butterfly's wings by forming a radial line arrangement with an additional circle segment that enforces the perception of a fan. It might be due to the image of the fan that is symbolically associated with her mother (see subchapter 7.2.1).

This "fanning" attribute does not mirror the natural feature of the original model under her observation. It could also have been initiated by Susanne's unconscious mind as a displacement of the butterfly's veinal details presumably caused by her underlying aichmophobia.[2] Another example illustrates how Susanne's perception of the thin legs of the insect as being repugnant influenced the design of the butterflies. The butterfly possesses three pairs of legs that can be clearly seen, but in her drawings, this feature is either omitted or very faintly rendered. Among the sketches from the Conservatory, we find only half of them depicting the insects' legs. Moreover, they are often drawn incomplete with pencil strokes barely visible, lacking her usual vigorous, clear articulation (Figs. 7.1 and 7.2).

This tendency carries over into the next stages of the design (creative drawings, watercolor, and oil painting). In the oil painting, we can observe that only three (Nos. 2, 5, and 6) out of seven butterflies display legs, and the fourth one (No. 1) has legs tightly tucked under, making them almost invisible. The artist depicts the stylized limbs of butterflies No. 2 and No. 6 with exaggerated obclavate, club-like shapes in the lower parts. In contrast, butterfly No. 5's legs taper into sharp endings. The explanation for this exceptional aspect of butterfly No. 5, Firebird (a personification of the father), began to emerge once Susanne disclosed her arachnophobia. This topic came up when she alluded to similarities between the sharp-ending legs of Firebird and those of the spider. Moreover, she recalled her father's frequent reference to dialectical traps as his "spider's web" that he used to gain the upper hand during family disputes. This association led us to the insight that the spider per se could be construed in Susanne's psyche as a personification of her father. Apparently, the spider as a potent personification of him was established within the depth of the artist's unconscious well before the creation of *Give Me Wings!*. (For more on Firebird, see chapter 4.)

The artist might have avoided attributing similar needle-sharp legs for butterflies Nos. 2 and 6 (the idealized personifications of her father and mother, respectively) by making their extremities obclavate, formed like an oblong teardrop. With this design, she stayed away from rendering sharply tapering configurations, which in her iconography would have been considered as threatening. It could also be posited that the choice of obclavate legs for butterflies Nos. 2 and 6 was the result of her impression of similar limbs of the beloved Sabino Butterfly glass sculpture, which was one of the favorite art objects in her parents' home (see chapter 9 and Fig. 9.5). The absence of legs in butterflies Nos. 3, 4, and 7 is possibly because they are, unlike the others (Nos. 1, 2, 5, and 6), more abstract renderings of the insects, which lack the creature's head, body, and legs. This particularity had been preserved from creative drawing I onward.

---

2 Susanne's aichmophobia is highly idiosyncratic: hearing, or reading the word *vein* (English) and its German equivalent *Vene* would cause her to react immediately with the visualization of the vein being pierced by sharp instruments (syringe needles, blades, etc.). See chapter 9.

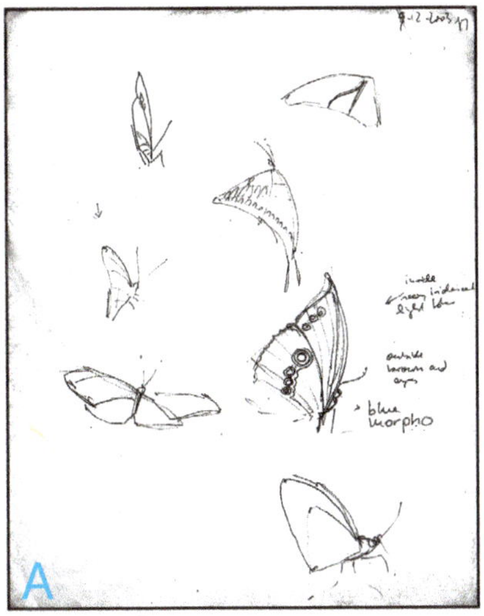

Fig. 2.1a Front

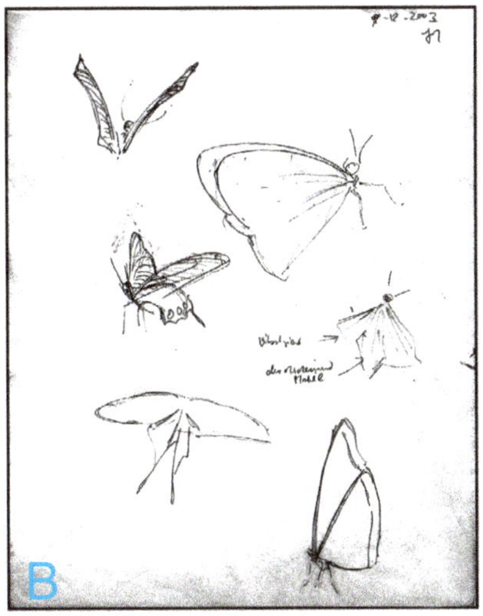

Fig. 2.1b Front

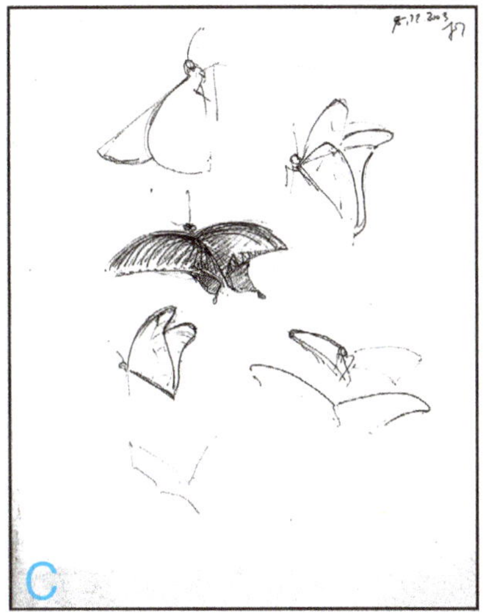

Fig. 2.1c Front

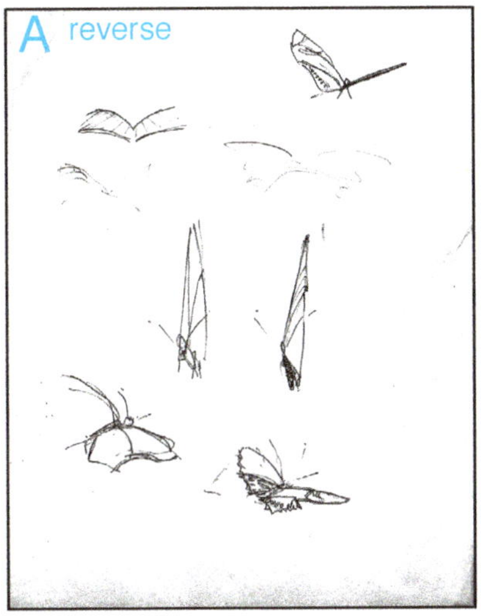

Fig. 2.1d Reverse

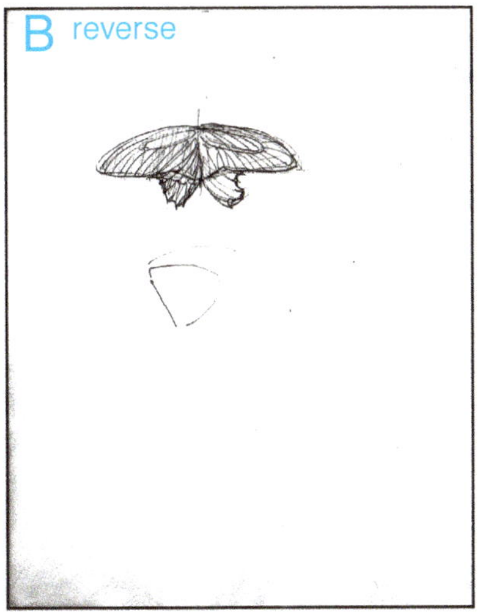

Fig. 2.1e Reverse

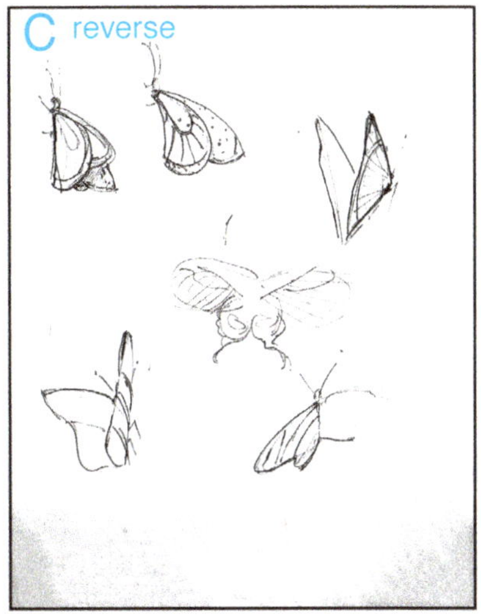

Fig. 2.1f Reverse

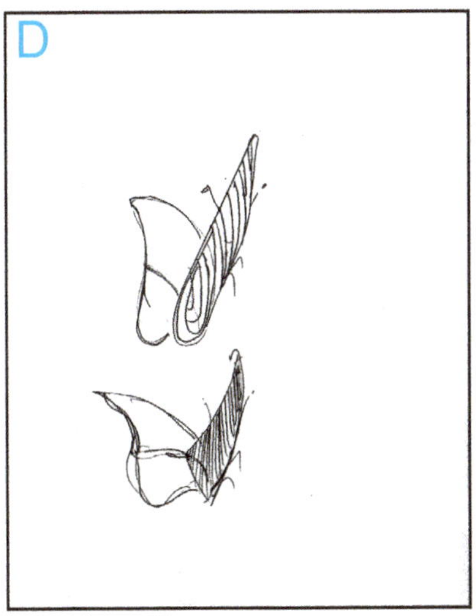

Fig. 2.1g Front

Fig. 2.1a-g. Susanne Schuenke, sketches, Dec. 9, 2003. Pencil on paper, 12 x 8¾ in (30.5 x 22.5 cm) each.
Collection of the artist.

Four sheets (shown front and reverse sides) of the primary sketches of the butterflies from Dec. 9, 2003, as drawn at the Butterfly Conservatory of the American Museum of Natural History, New York.

Note: There is no reverse side to the last sheet.
The letters (A-D) used for these pages are for identification purposes only, and there is no chronological sequence implied.
(Sheet D has only two sketches, and the page is shown cropped.)

The absence of these body parts in the afore-mentioned three butterflies could be a metaphorical fulfillment of the artist's wish to present the immaterial essence of being as a more desirable state of existence. It is possible that this abstractness in the portrayal of these butterflies, which we surmise are personifications of Susanne's self, might reflect her high aspirations to represent the spiritual aspects of life rather than the material.

During the analysis, we became aware that even the sketches of life models, executed rapidly with hardly any deliberation, contain peculiar shapes, drawn presumably through "pure psychic automatism." Those were the markers of past life situations whose significant emotional impact caused the formation of different neurotic reactions, and were instrumental in shaping Susanne's artwork. The deviation from the real models gave us clues to the sensibilities and workings of the artist's brain and mind, reflected in her artworks. Her sensory perception might be transformed by the unconscious as the effects of displacement, condensation, and secondary elaboration. These processes point to the presence of some underlying complexes exerting their influence.

2.2 Creative Drawings I, II, and III

On December 20, 2003, eleven days after her experience in the Butterfly Conservatory, Susanne created three pencil-drawn designs: creative drawings I, II, and III (Figs. 2.2, 2.3, and 2.4). She was recovering from minor surgery and had a strong desire to draw after having been away from her work for a while. She glanced over her original sketches from the museum visit, then laid them aside and started to draw with a pencil, feeling that she had by now "all the time and freedom to do what she wished to do," without any necessity to follow the natural models that she saw at the conservatory. In this session, the artist enjoyed reliving her exciting encounter with the enchanting butterflies and letting her impulse rule as those

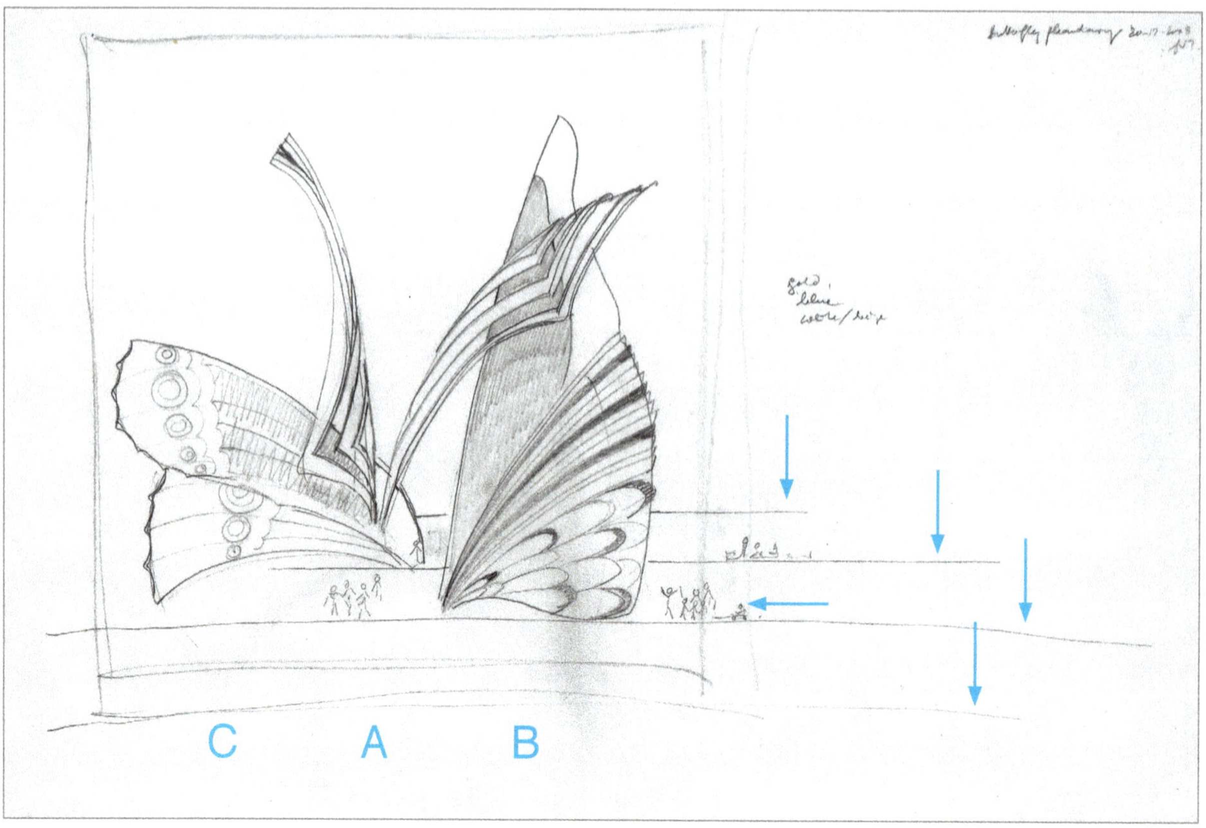

Fig 2.2. Susanne Schuenke, creative drawing I, Dec. 20, 2003. Pencil on paper, 11 x 17 in (28 x 43 cm). Collection of the artist. A group of three butterflies with stick figure people on a stage. The letters reflect the chronological sequence (to the best of the artist's recollection) in which the butterfly figures were drawn. There are two penciled notations. In the upper right corner: "Butterfly phantasy 20-12-2003 Sus." The date of December 20, 2003 follows the title, and "Sus" stands for her shortened signature. On the drawing at the right side: "Gold, blue, white/beige"

creative drawings gradually emerged.[3] During that afternoon, the artist had no vision or compositional plan for a monumental painting that was to come into being later.

These drawings are another invaluable source for the analysis, and they can illustrate the process of "automatic drawing" as an expression of the realms of the unconscious. Highly significant metaphorical meanings, rooted in the unconscious, were embedded in these spontaneously created images.

We look at them not as isolated artistic designs but as a dynamic and sequential reflection of the unconscious, which eventually manifested fully in the oil painting *Give Me Wings!*. The symbolic undertone in the characteristics of the butterflies will be untangled in the following chapters, each of which is dedicated to a particular butterfly.

In creative drawing I (Fig. 2.2), the artist drew the butterfly in the center first, which she depicted only by a stylized pair of wings, seen from behind (labeled –A– in the figure). This perplexing configuration of lines appears later in the oil painting, and was named "Air" in the poetic commentary written by the artist after the completion of the work. The creature mirrors the essence of the artist's most memorable emotional response to her experience in the Butterfly Conservatory of being awed and dazzled by the sight of the fast-flying butterflies around her. To catch the specific characteristics of the butterflies' nearby movements was not possible. The flapping of wings was too fast for the human eye to differentiate. Yet, as Susanne drew the image –A–, she intended to visualize on paper her impression of the nearly invisible fluttering wings and the ever-changing, whirling motion of the butterflies. Creating such an imaginative representation occurs on a mental level the artist cannot anticipate, plan for, or deliberately choose. Nor is it possible to give a rational explanation for its sudden advent.

After completing image –A–, the artist designed two more butterflies, B and C, in profile facing each other and placed to the right and left of the first butterfly (Fig. 2.2). This arrangement gives a focus to the middle butterfly, emphasizing its leading position in the triad. It is clear from this drawing that butterflies B and C constitute the prototypes for butterflies No. 3 and No. 4 (Pale Moonlight and Touchless Misty) in the final painting.

The size of the creatures in the drawing was larger than the life-size models from nature, measuring approximately 6" tall on an 11" x 17" sheet of paper. Initially, the artist had no conscious intention to express any specific meaning associated with the images, as she only followed the sense of harmony emerging from the lines and shapes she was drawing. As the images formed, she felt they were far more significant and potent than mere "dainty little butterflies." She intuitively discerned that something was missing in the design. Her artistic mind began to search for a way to present the butterflies' intrinsic qualities, which she sensed were not yet fully realized.

Accordingly, she concentrated her efforts on properly positioning the butterflies in space by providing them an appropriate stage. She accomplished this by drawing four parallel horizontal lines located beneath or behind the butterflies, conveying depth and perspective (note the four lines that are marked by the vertical arrows in Fig. 2.2). By these means, the butterflies were anchored in their places.

Moreover, she impulsively embellished the scene with tiny stick figures, the abstract representation of people in various postures, including a family group with a child in a wagon at the far right (see the horizontal arrow in Fig. 2.2). This way the butterflies were transformed into large-scale entities. Although the images of the butterflies the artist had drawn were nearly three times larger than the true size of the actual insects, they nevertheless remained "small" in the artist's perception until she introduced the human stick figures. At once, the three butterflies had become enormous, compared to the humans. Through this dramatic change in scale, Susanne's explosive imagination had changed the whole schema. The magnified butterflies were no longer harmless creatures but powerhouses of characters, status, and personalities, disguised by the butterflies' innocuous outer appearance. Therefore, the artist's creativity had sprung these miniscule human figures onto the scene, transforming the butterflies into signifiers of something fundamental, monumental, and even heroic.

At that point, the artist did not know yet what these imposing winged creatures might actually represent in a painting. She began to wonder

3 The artist estimates that the session lasted from 30 to 40 minutes. She remembers being exhausted and feeling that she somehow left creative drawing III unfinished.

if this trio of butterflies could stand for beings who possess superior qualities of wisdom, higher knowledge, and spirituality. Might not these creatures epitomize futuristic beings, who would be capable of governing the world without abusing their power?

The sudden appearance of the stick figures among the butterflies, not planned for, gave her an inkling that those winged creatures in her creative drawing were meant to be figurative representations of someone larger-than-life, even of a spiritual entity. In Susanne's artworks, diminutive stick figures, standing for human beings, often exemplify and emphasize the stark contrast between earthly and spiritual beings. The spiritual beings are shown to possess unlimited potential and supernal powers, whereas the Lilliputian stick figures are pictured as average human beings, sometimes even with reference to the faceless masses. This motif has been firmly established in the personal iconography of the artist and makes its appearance in many of Susanne's paintings before the inception of her major work, *Give Me Wings!* (see chapters 6, 7, and 10.)

As mentioned above, we came to a realization of the intricacy and the full extent of the personification schema already woven into the imagery of creative drawing I. She titled the drawing "butterfly phantasy" (scribbled at the top right-hand corner in Fig. 2.2), and, upon finishing the drawing, jotted down a reminder to herself as to a possible color scheme of "gold, blue, white/beige" (written next to the right frame line). After finishing creative drawing I, she was intrigued by the lines and the possibility of playing with the images of the magnified butterflies, and she continued to work, eventually producing two additional creative drawings (Figs. 2.3 and 2.4).

In creative drawing II, two imposing butterflies (D and E in Fig. 2.3), positioned on a slope, confront each other face to face, as if they are rivals struggling for hierarchical advantage. Our analysis revealed butterfly D as the forerunner of butterfly No. 2, True Blue (personification of the artist's father: see chapter 5) and also butterfly No. 1, Little Why (personification of Susanne: see chapter 6). Similarly, we identified butterfly E as the precursor of butterfly No. 6, Fanning Everything (personification of Susanne's mother, see chapter 7). From these identifications, we infer that the latent content of the artist's unconscious was already manifested symbolically in the imagery of the creative drawings, denoting her familial situation.

In creative drawing III (Fig. 2.4), we can envision another confrontation, reminiscent of the one in creative drawing II. But this time there is clear designation: Figure H is the "winner," signifying his triumph by hovering over the prostrate figure F, who is the "loser." The theme of winners and losers, as a consequence of conflicts, carries a particular relevance in Susanne's psyche, as the following recollection exemplifies. She recalls an event at the age of about ten. After having witnessed a rather heated argument between her parents, she made a cardboard sign and placed it on her father's large tripod-mounted camera. The message read "*Achtung, Kriegsgefahr*!" ("Attention, war danger!"). The child's distress was quite explicit. She did not want to be caught in the middle of the quarreling parents. This, as well as other traumatic emotional experiences of conflicts between her mother and father, could unconsciously have determined the confrontational postures in the imagery of creative drawings II and III. Asked during our analysis—why, unlike creative drawing I, drawings II and III lack the stick figures representing people—Susanne commented that "those little figures would not be appropriate, being exposed to the danger of the fighting giants." Therefore, the absence of the miniature people in these two drawings quite likely originated in Susanne's unconscious that expressed avoidance to be exposed to the conflicts and become victimized by them.

2.3 Building a Composition

While drafting the creative drawings, as mentioned earlier, the painter did not intend for an extensive composition that would include more butterflies, nor a very large-format painting. There were no preconditions to her creative freedom: No future plans, no conceptual restraint—the joy of drawing was her only guide. Three days after completing these creative drawings, the artist suddenly recognized their potential for a very large painting to be installed in a medical building for public viewing. As it turned out, Susanne had a pending commission by a wealthy donor, calling for just such an installation to be given to a medical institution in Jacksonville, Florida. Up to this time,

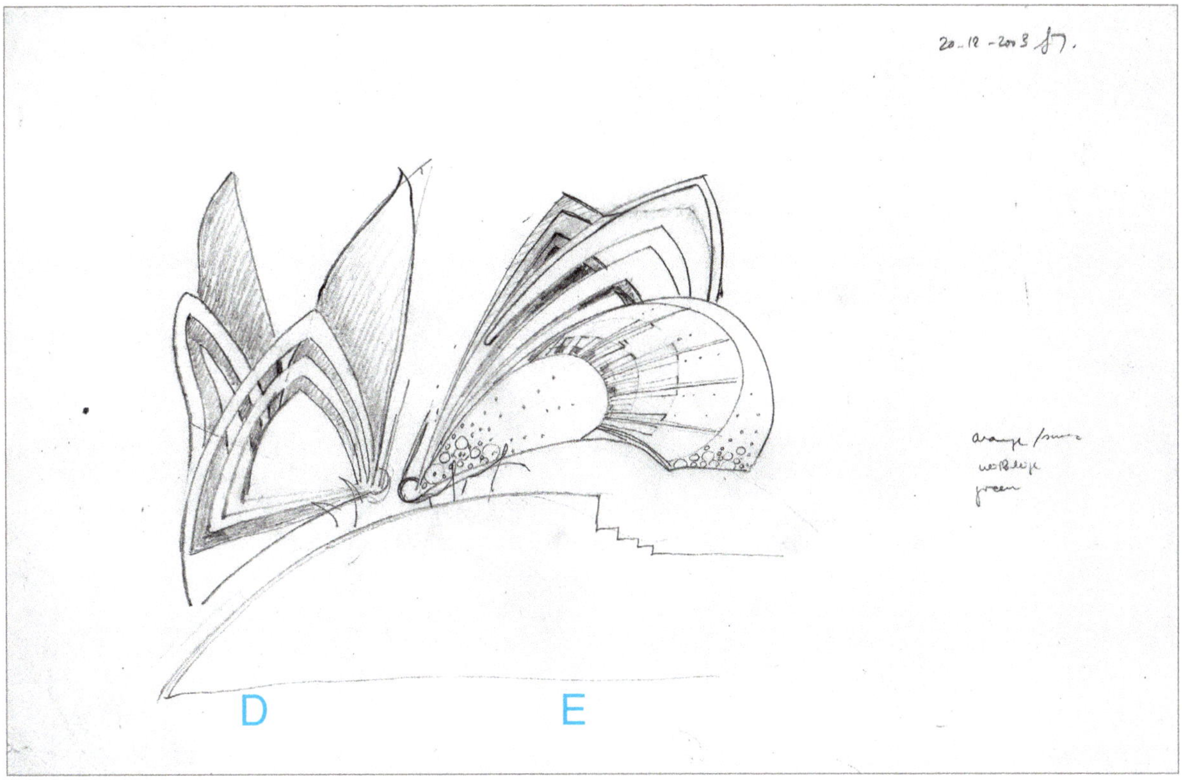

Fig. 2.3. Susanne Schuenke, creative drawing II, Dec.20, 2003. Pencil on paper, 11 x 17 in (28 x 43 cm). Collection of the artist. Two butterflies on a curved slope. The letters reflect the chronological sequence (to the best of the artist's recollection) in which the butterfly figures were drawn. The penciled notation is as follows: "20-12-2003 Sus." [The date of December 20, 2003 is followed by her shortened signature.] On the drawing at the right side: orange/Schwarz (German; English: orange/black) weiß beige (German; English: white beige) green.

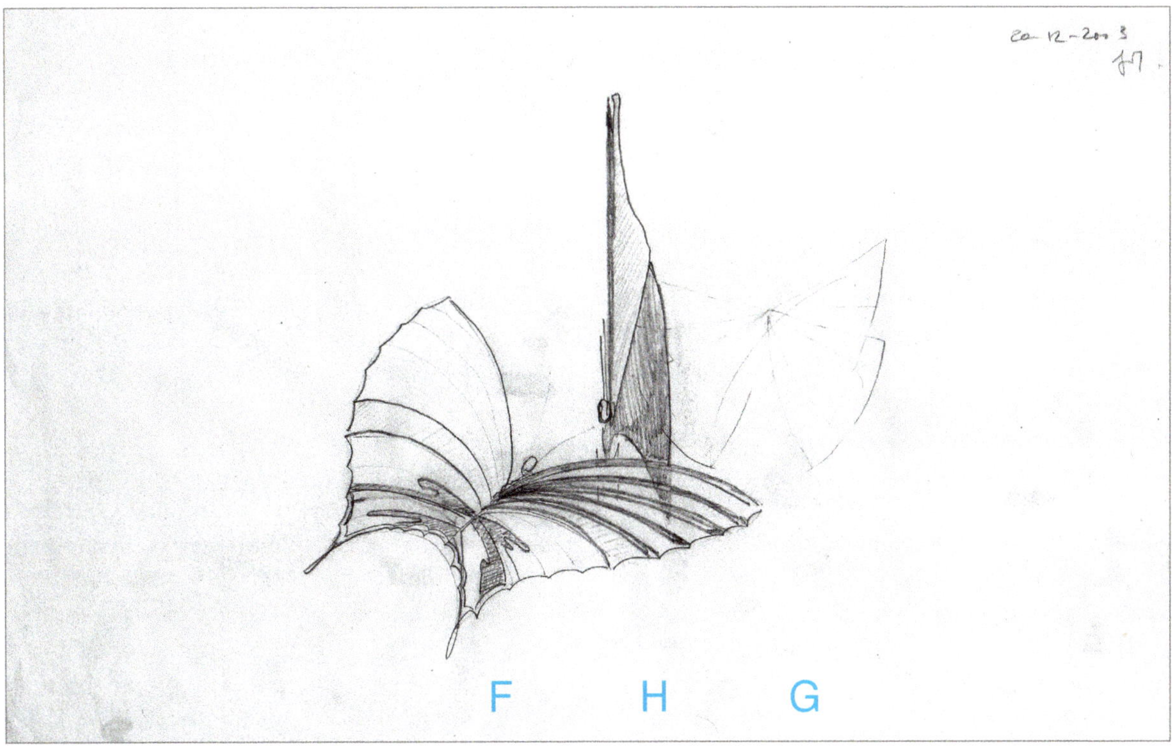

Fig. 2.4. Susanne Schuenke, creative drawing III, Dec.20, 2003. Pencil on paper, 11 x 17 in (28 x 43 cm). Collection of the artist. The three original butterflies (F, G, and H).
G was discarded and erased (traces are still visible). The letters reflect the chronological sequence (to the best of the artist's recollection) in which the butterfly figures were drawn.

the artist had not made any connection between the butterfly drawings and their potential use for the commissioned painting.

Looking at the creative drawing I with the appearance of the stick figure people, a new perspective came to the artist's mind in realization of her pending project on a large scale. She began in earnest to consider transposing the butterflies' grand postures into a monumental painting. She anticipated that using butterflies as the theme would be right, meeting the general specifications spelled out in the project's briefing. Aside from the considerable size[4] of the artwork, there were stipulations concerning the nature and potential repercussions of the imagery. The painting had to be free of any provocative or depressing content that might trigger negative emotions in the onlooker. The painting must evoke positive thoughts and feelings so as to enhance the healing environment of the clinic. Confident that she would meet the framework specified, the artist decided to transpose and modify the three drawings into a single, unified design—the compositional drawing—as the basis for the future painting (Fig. 2.11).

To accommodate the extraordinarily large dimensions of the proposed painting, the artist prepared the watercolor paper for the compositional drawing by marking vertical lines on the sheet to divide it into six equal sections. As the composition evolved toward the final design, Susanne adjusted the precise placements of the butterflies, using the dividing lines to select the locations of the butterflies on the canvas panels of the future oil painting. Next, she decided not to include the stick figures from creative drawing I to conform to the prerequisites given to her by the project committee. She thought the miniature size could easily be misunderstood by the public as a disparaging representation of the common people as being small, powerless, and negligible in their importance. Furthermore, the hospital's patients, already negatively impacted by their health issues, might assume pessimistic perspectives of their medical situations through such metaphoric perceptions.

Recognizing the potential importance of her artwork in improving the patients' psychological outlooks on their medical circumstances, Susanne aimed to turn the exalted beauty of the butterflies into a symbol of tranquility and healing harmony. This would be in line with the health institute's mission, subtly reassuring the patients and recalling the considerable resources with which the hospital took care of its patients. The artist wanted these sublime creatures to project a sense of radiance, airiness, and hope toward those who stood in front of them and experienced their metaphoric presence.

Susanne chose the splendid trio (butterflies A, B, and C) from creative drawing I as the core of the new painting, considering its expansion to both sides. She saw butterfly B's massive size (Fig. 2.2) as a hindrance to the compositional development of the scene to the right and solved this by flipping the entire group horizontally. Butterfly B was now situated to the left of the center (Fig. 2.5).

Expanding the scene, the artist selected butterfly D (precursor to butterfly No. 2) from creative drawing II to be located to the left of butterfly No. 3. However, the direct transfer of butterfly D's posture turned out to be unacceptable to the artist, as it made the butterfly look toward the central trio, facing the back of butterfly No. 3. The artist felt that this arrangement gave butterfly D the impression of being subservient to butterfly No. 3 (Fig. 2.6). This situation was intolerable, and she resolved it by flipping butterfly D horizontally so that it would face the left edge of the scene, allowing it to turn away from the central group, particularly the overpowering butterfly No. 3. By providing butterfly D with a strong, independent position and mien, the creation of butterfly No. 2 was accomplished (Fig. 2.7). We will point out the implicit motif behind the artist's action later, when our analysis reveals the unconscious personifications embedded in butterfly No. 2 (personification of the artist's father, see chapter 5) and butterfly No. 3 (personification of the artist, see chapter 8).

In order to balance the composition, Susanne widened the scene to the right by intentionally introducing a contrasting element. She achieved this with placing there the slim and towering butterfly H from creative drawing III, juxtaposed to the spreading shape of butterfly No. 4 and the verticality of No. 3. As butterfly H was inserted into the arena, she changed its original orientation to allow the figure to face the empty space towards the right margin. This image became butterfly No. 5, whose prominent, vertical presence dominated the right part of the composition (Fig. 2.8).

4 The presentation of the first detailed design to the project committee for approval was scheduled for spring 2004. From the very onset, the word "large" characterized the task, and a minimum width of about 10 feet (2.5 meters) was discussed.

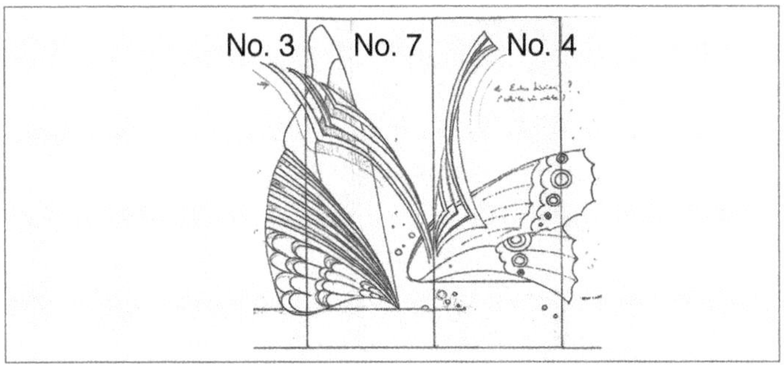

Fig. 2.5.
Development of a composition: phase 1, leading to the complete compositional drawing. (Reconstructed for this publication.) The artist's notations found in this and the following figures (Figs. 2.5-2.10) are explained in the caption to Fig. 2.11.

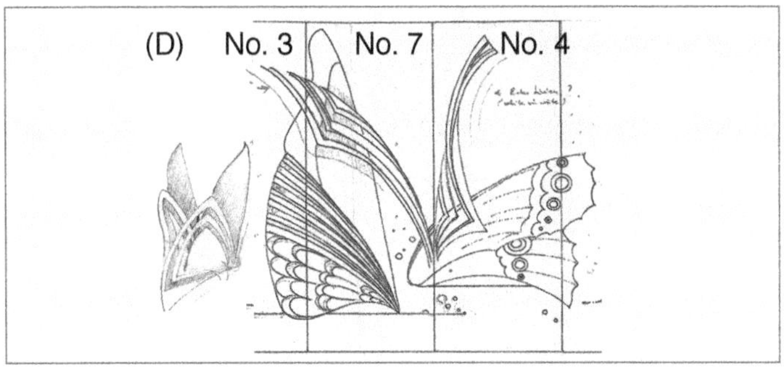

Fig 2.6.
Adding D to the center group: how it would have looked before turning D (No. 2) to the left. (Reconstructed for this publication.)

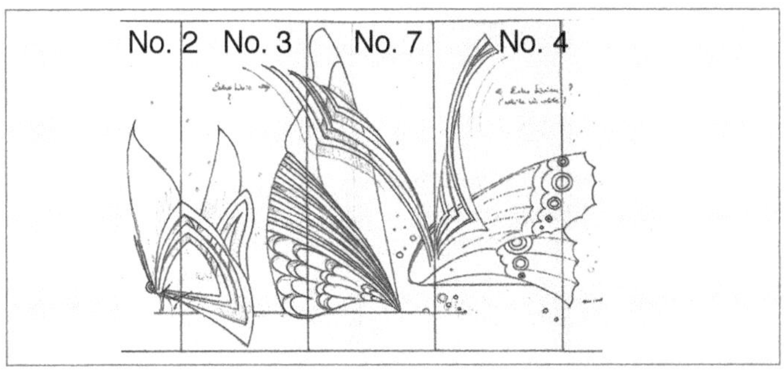

Fig. 2.7.
Development of a composition: phase 2, turning D to the left, leading to the complete compositional drawing. (Reconstructed for this publication.)

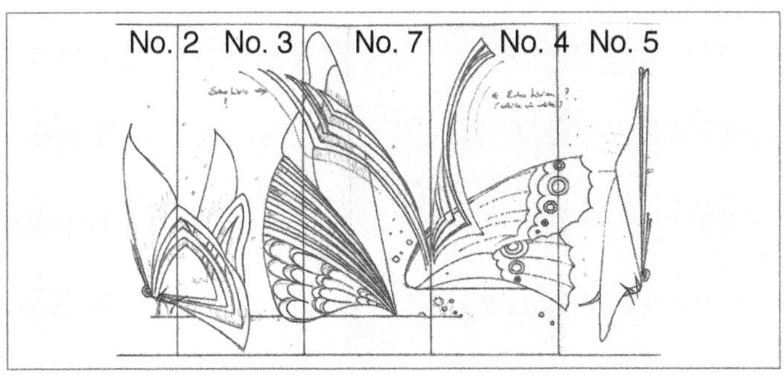

Fig. 2.8.
Adding H (No. 5) at right to the center group: phase 3 leading to the complete compositional drawing. (Reconstructed for this publication.)

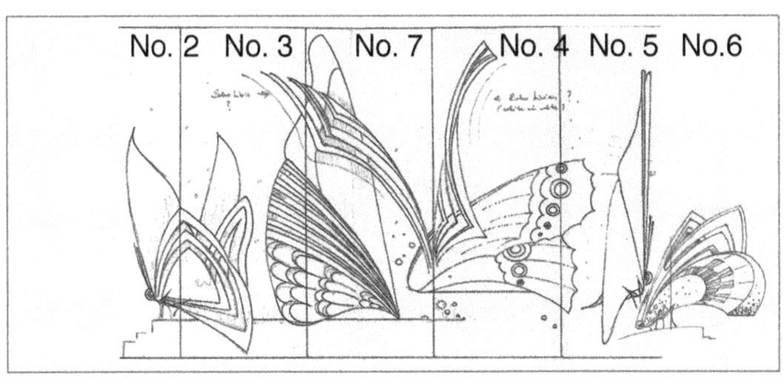

Fig. 2.9.
Adding E (No. 6) to the far right. (Reconstructed for this publication.)

The change, however, made the artist feel a palpable sense of incompleteness. It compelled her to mitigate the deficiency by filling the void with another butterfly (E) from creative drawing II, placing it opposite butterfly No. 5, face to face. This introduction of butterfly No. 6 completed the right half of the composition (Fig. 2.9).

A gap remained between butterfly No. 2 and the left edge of the compositional space, which called for a solution (Fig. 2.9). Susanne still had two butterflies available from drawing III, but she could not accept the thought of using either the "defeated" butterfly F or, worse, the "erased" butterfly G for the task (Fig. 2.4: more about this in chapters 7 and 9). The artist contemplated an alternative. She pondered taking advantage of the attractive design of butterfly No. 2, but she was concerned about the repetition. In the end, she consciously chose this, as she put it, "less original option" based on her artistic judgment, and she created butterfly No. 1, an "offspring" of butterfly No. 2, derived from him with various deliberate modifications.

The artist began the transformation by first copying butterfly No. 2 on a tracing paper (Fig. 2.10 "Step 1"). Then she flipped the sheet horizontally to make the butterfly face right (Fig. 2.10 "Step 2"). After that, she shrank the size of the butterfly and rotated its orientation a few degrees to the left. This gave the impression that the butterfly was in an ascending flight (Fig. 2.10 "Step 3"). Satisfied with her changes, Susanne transposed this new design into the compositional drawing to the left of butterfly No. 2 (Fig. 2.10 "Step 4"). This way, butterfly No. 1 entered the scene with a dynamic leap. (See Fig. 2.10 for the graphic explanation of the entire sequence described above.) In chapters 5 and 6, we will examine the unconscious-driven nature of this transformative process further, in which butterfly No. 1 is recognized as a personification of Susanne as a child, and butterfly No. 2 as a personification of her father.

Pleased with the arrangement of the butterflies in the pictorial space, Susanne now drew two horizontal lines as the bases to anchor butterflies Nos. 2, 3, and 4 (Fig. 2.11). Those lines were adjusted to different heights (a lower one for butterflies Nos. 2 and 3, and a higher one for butterfly No. 4). Subsequently, she added three steps at the left end of the lower line. All this created the prototype for the major part of the podium structure for the butterfly assembly.

Next, for the base for butterflies Nos. 5 and 6, she used the shallow platform with a convex slope and a set of steps on the right side of creative drawing II with minor modifications (Fig. 2.3). This constitutes the right part of the podium structure. Finally, on a whim, she sprinkled an assortment of little bubbles onto the setting. This completed the compositional drawing. (Fig. 2.11).

A careful inspection of the completed compositional drawing reveals yet another butterfly—the eighth butterfly behind butterfly No. 5 and above butterfly No. 6 at the far right. It is conceivable that this butterfly's design was influenced by one of the figures that she drew at the Butterfly Conservatory in New York (for example, the top left sketch in Fig. 2.1d (A reverse)). Certain circumstances made us pay special attention to butterfly No. 8 in the context of our research. First, there is its disappearance from the next phase of

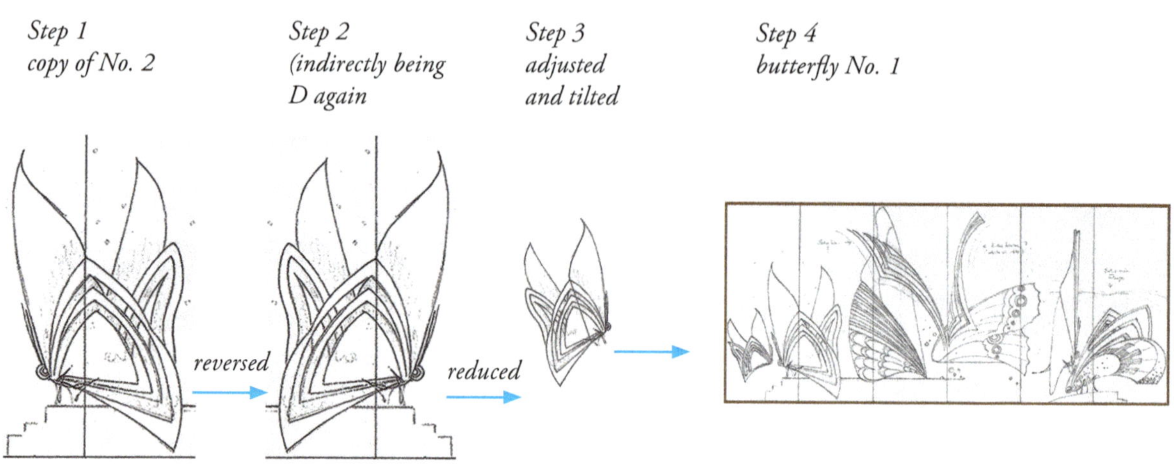

Fig. 2.10. The graphic explanation of the development of butterfly No. 1 from butterfly No. 2. (Reconstructed for this publication.)

the design. Second, its existence was forgotten by the artist. Lastly, there is the association of the date of compositional drawing with the day of her mother's death. Those facts together led us to assume the presence of a possible significant unconscious meaning (latent content) for this metaphorical image. (See chapter 11.)

The original of the final compositional drawing in pencil and ink, which shows the butterfly No. 8, is no longer available, as it disappeared under the aquarelle paints. However, we were able to use a photocopy of this drawing, which the artist made before she transformed the drawing into a watercolor painting on the same day.

In building the composition, the artist made significant changes to the figures taken from the three creative drawings. She selected, modified, flipped orientations, altered relative positions, and added two more butterflies. She also created a unified podium, a stage upon which the butterflies' roles and actions appear as a metaphorical manifestation, reflecting her biographical drama. All these modifications gave us a rich ground and numerous hints for discovering specific unconscious motivation behind Susanne's artistic decisions in the design process. Hence, we revealed unconscious tendencies of her psyche, which were recognized through the analysis of the individual images and their multiple relationships in the oil painting. We shall touch more on this in the following chapters.

2.4 Coloration

As listed in the caption, the compositional drawing (Fig. 2.11) was accompanied by the penciled scribbled comments of the artist's

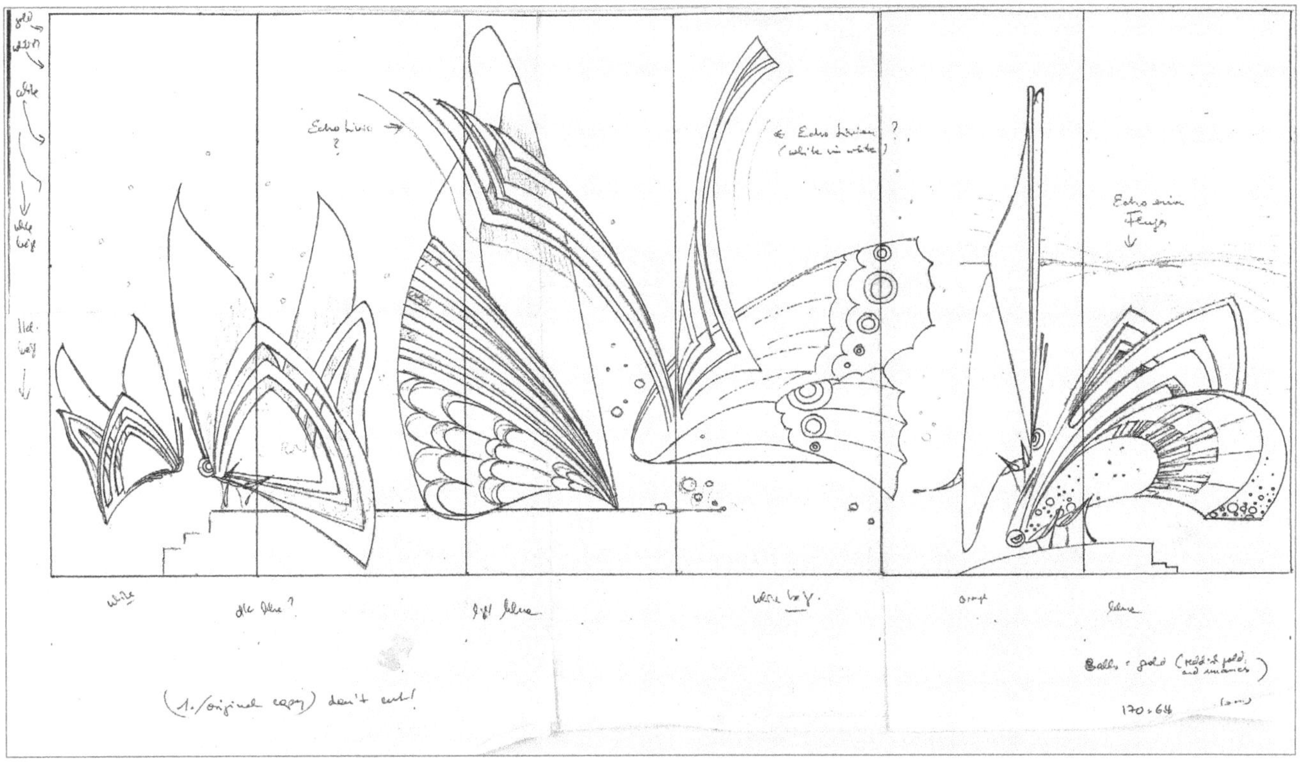

Fig. 2.11. Susanne Schuenke, compositional drawing, Dec. 23, 2003. Pencil and ink on paper, 10½ x 25 in (24.8 x 62 cm). Collection of the artist

The penciled-in notes are as follows (the original in italic; English translation in parentheses, if applicable):

Inside the drawing (from left to right): Echo Linie? (Echo line?), Echo Linien?(white in white) (Echo lines (white in white)), Echo eines Fluges (Echo of a flight).

Underneath the drawing (from left to right):
First line — White, dk blue? [dk for dark], light blue, white beige, orange, blue.
Second line (far right) —Balls: gold (reddish gold and nuances).
Third line —1./original copy) don't cut; and (far right): 170 x 64 (384) [the numbers are for measurement purposes].

At the left margin (moving from top to bottom): Gold, whitish, white, white beige, dkl.beige (dkl. stands for dunkel (English: dark) in German).

preliminary color schemes. These were jotted down automatically without premeditation. They became the base for her decisions for the watercolor study (Fig. 2.12).

The notes already reflect the principal symbolic meanings that these colors carry for the imagery, which was later recognized by our analysis. The watercolor paints were applied to the compositional drawing (the individual butterflies and the setting) in a single session focusing on chromatic harmony. To the best of the artist's recollection, the sequence of the color assignment in the watercolor painting was as follows (for a schematic presentation, see Figs. 2.13 (a through f)).

First, a dark blue for the front wings of butterfly No. 2 (later named in the poetic commentary as True Blue) was chosen (Fig. 2.13 (a)). This was motivated by her impression of the splendid blue of the Blue Morpho butterfly in the Butterfly Conservatory (Fig. 9.14). Second, she opted for white with shades of mainly gray modulation for butterfly No. 4 (Touchless Misty) (Fig. 2.13 (b)), a color which she associated with the blue morpho's underside. Next, she applied an array of light blues to No. 3 butterfly (Pale Moonlight) that she related to some subtle gradations from the blue morpho's scintillating wings (Fig. 2.13(c)). Then, Susanne assigned a strikingly vivid orange to No. 5 (Firebird) (Fig. 2.13(d)) that she intended as a counterweight to the dominant blue of No. 2. The orange coloration was quite familiar to her from the monarch butterflies in her garden. After this, she chose yellow for the front wings of butterfly No. 1 (Little Why) (Fig. 2.13(e)), with which she averted the orange of No. 5 from being an isolated color amongst all the blues. Furthermore, by adding yellow accents in No. 3, the artist counterbalanced the yellow of butterfly No. 1. The coloring of No. 6 (Fanning Everything) turned out to be a difficult challenge because Susanne did not wish to introduce a new color. Therefore, she combined the various dominant colors that were already in place in the other butterflies (blue, white, yellow) (Fig. 2.13(f)). She felt intuitively that butterfly No. 6's assortment of colors had some underpinnings. (Their implications will be analyzed in chapters 7 and 11.)

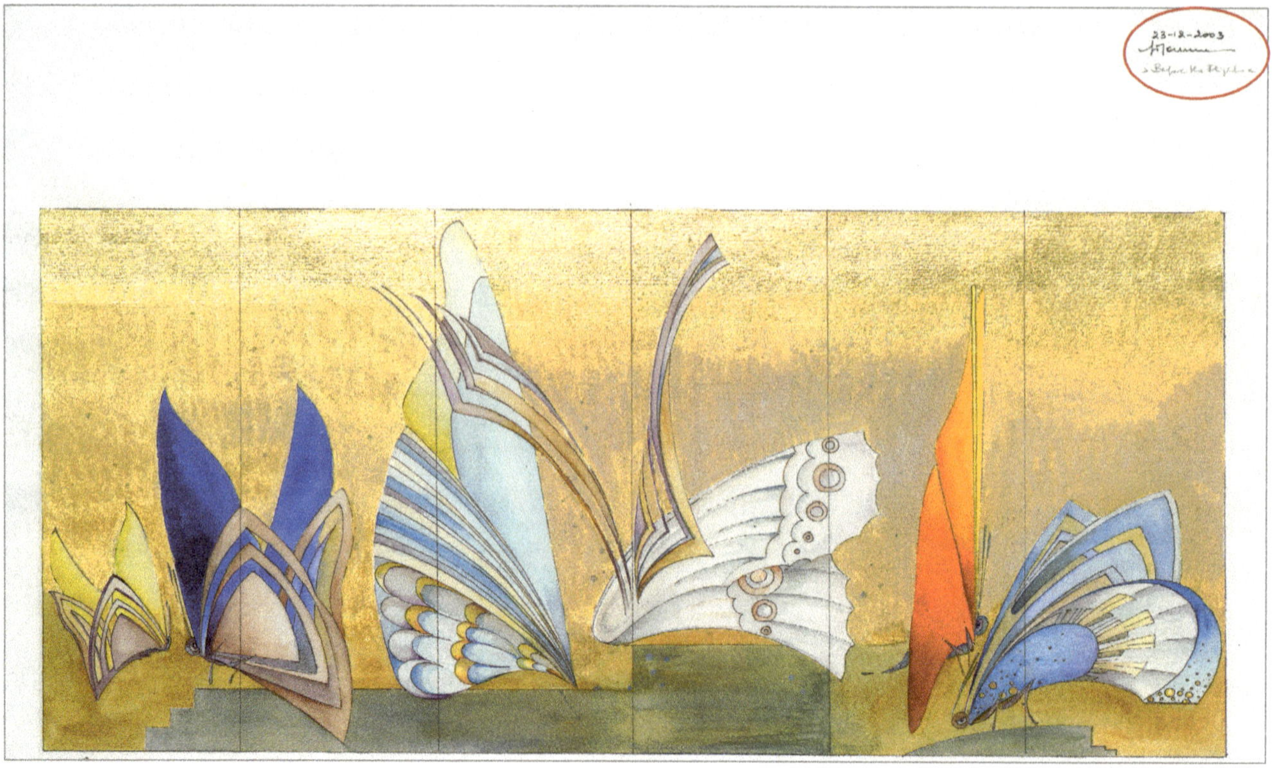

No.1 *Little Why* | No.2 *True Blue* | No. 3 *Pale Moonlight* | No. 7 *Air* | No. 4 *Touchless Misty* | No. 5 *Firebird* | No. 6 *Fanning Everything*

Fig. 2.12. Susanne Schuenke, *Before the Flight*, Dec.23, 2003. Watercolor, ink and gold leaf on paper, 19¾ x 25¼ in (50 x 64 cm). Collection of the artist. Watercolor of the design from Fig. 2.11. The encircled note at the top right-hand corner as follows: Dec.23, 2003, [the signature of the artist]; Before the Flight.

After this, the artist completed butterflies Nos. 1 and 2 with light violet-brown for the hind wings. For the rings of No. 4, she applied light brown, intentionally avoiding a new color for this detail. Her choice of coloration of No. 7 (Air) was ochre and soft violet to blend into the background, which was covered with an overlay of gold leaf (Fig. 2.12). Over the lower area of the gold, she spread a layer of translucent white to soften the transition from ochre at the very bottom of the painting to the shiny gold surface that dominates the upper part of the watercolor composition. On the gold and the thin coat of white, she reinstated the multiple little bubbles (the earlier drawing of them had disappeared under the layer of gold), painting them in light blue. Mostly bluish-gray hues were applied to the podium. At this point, all the necessary chroma designations were accomplished and the artist signed, dated, and titled her work, *Before the Flight.*

On this foundation, the artist developed her oil painting on six panels (whose dimensions became approximately 770% larger than her watercolor) with the refining of certain nuances. We observed that subtle but important modifications took place in some of the colors, which turned out to underscore and strengthen Susanne's conscious intentions as well as her unconscious messages. The specific changes in the coloration were found in the following: The hind wings of butterflies Nos. 1 and 2 were tinted with more violet hues. The rings in butterfly No. 4 gained a more brownish cast in their color. The tips of the front wings of butterfly No. 5 were whitened. The hind wing of butterfly No. 3 received certain deep orange accents. Butterfly No. 6 was embellished with pinkish nuances, and the podium turned from gray to brown. In addition, noticeable design changes were observed in the disappearance of the blue bubbles and butterfly No. 8 under the golden background. More attention will be given to these developments and their importance for the analysis in the upcoming chapters.

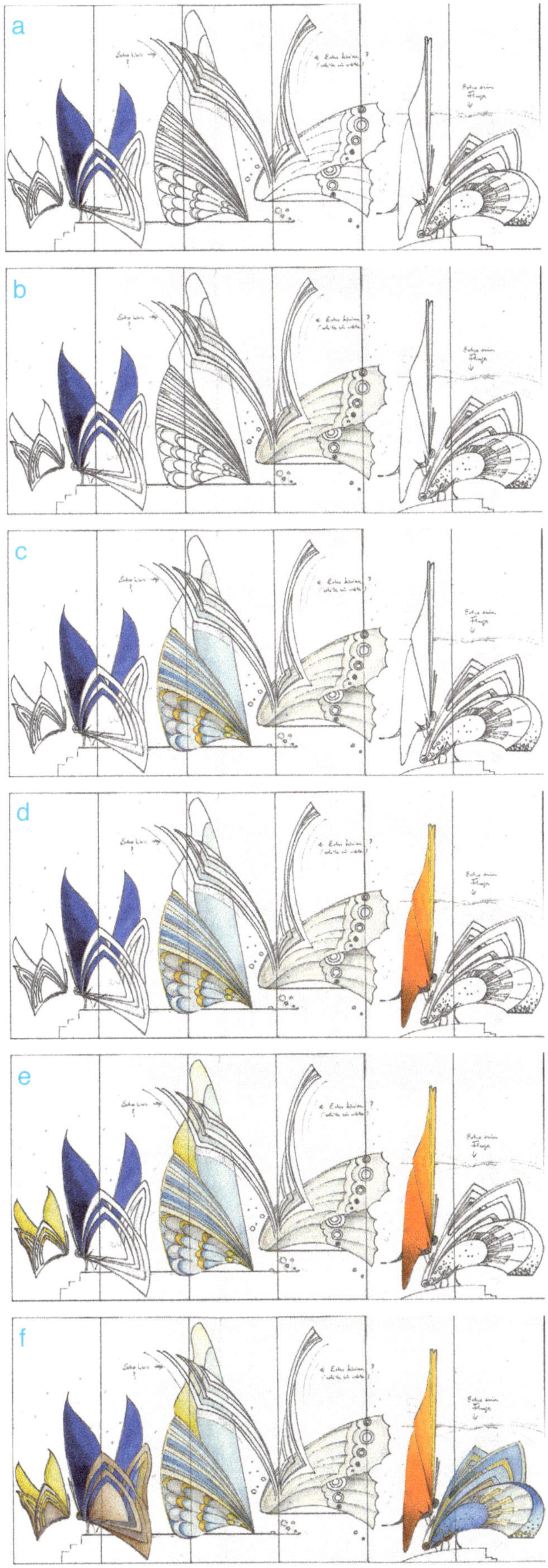

Fig. 2.13.
Building the color composition:
An approximate schematic reconstruction of the sequence in the application of colors before coloring the podium and applying the gold leaf to the background. Note that the central butterfly No. 7 is not colored until after the application of the gold leaf. (For the final stage of the coloration, see Fig. 2.12.)

By analyzing the above phases of the painting's development and comparing various relevant nuances therein, we were able to extract valuable information. It confirmed many assumptions concerning the symbolic expressions of the unconscious that were woven out of the artist's significant emotionally charged events, as well as thoughts and fantasies from her childhood onward. Our analysis revealed the impact of the unconscious on the process of artistic creativity in the guise of the artwork's peculiar imagery. As with the construction of shapes and composition, the influence of the unconscious processes can be demonstrated in the selection and execution of the color schemes in the artwork. In the following chapters, we will analyze the particular configurations, structures, colors, and their latent meaning. Moreover, we will pay attention to the spatial relationships of the images and their interactions in the composition. All these observations and information lead us to explore a plethora of symbolic and metaphoric implications as they manifest in the imagery.

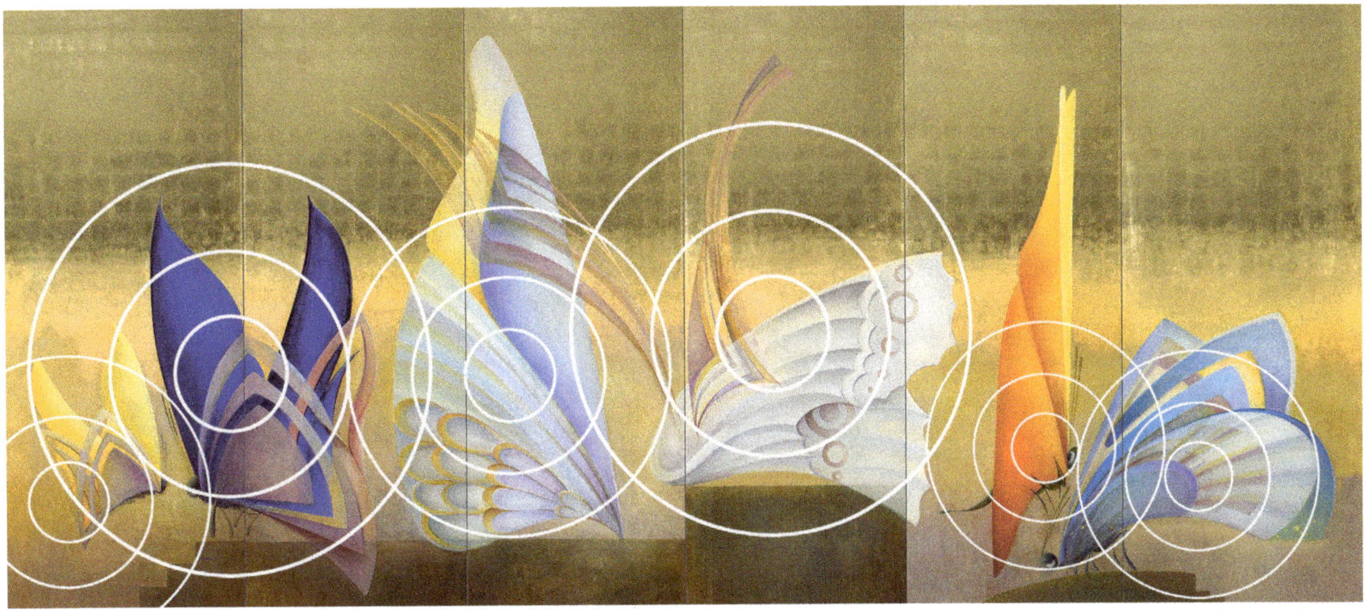

Fig. 3.0. An illustration to the poetic commentary's statement: *The broadcast in the busy society of seven butterflies...* (designed for this chapter)

If you hear, if you could only hear, what the antennae vibrate, the broadcast in the busy society of seven butterflies, their community chatter at the short gathering. Sometimes they come hungry for news, open to gossip, eager to speculate, hesitating to learn—other times they long for a rest from the noisy world, the media too thick to breathe your own thoughts—to clear their collective brains, to sip fresh purity— to be themselves again.

—From the artist's poetic commentary, 2004.

Chapter 3

Searching for Clarity: **"The Chatter"**

The beginning of Susanne's poetic commentary sets the tone for the scene before the butterflies are individually introduced. With her initial remarks, the artist reflects her attitude, thoughts, views on society, and outlook on the world on the conscious level, by turning into writing what she has captured in the painting: the individual characters of the seven monumental butterflies and their interactions. Through these images, the artist metaphorically records her emotional responses to such human themes as ambition and pride, drives and tempers, success and failure, and liberation from worldly concerns. She assigns each butterfly positive as well as negative qualities. On the unconscious level, the description mirrors the contradictory conditions Susanne experienced in her family as she was growing up. A remark like "too thick to breathe your own thoughts" points to Susanne's perception of her childhood experiences.

Starting from three original drawings of two or three butterflies, putting them all together, and extending the group to the final powerful seven images, the artist lays the groundwork for a hierarchical relationship among them, manifested by their placement, size, and orientation in relation to one another. The stage consists of a podium, a whitish fog, and the golden background where the seven butterfly players perform their roles in a miniature replica of family and society—and when color is added, everything "comes to life."

In *Before the Flight,* the atmosphere around the players is filled with thick media. Restrictions, oppressions, ambitions, and power struggles pervade the reality, and everybody is dragged into the wasteful game of manipulation, lies, and jostling for advantage. The smog of political correctness suffocates the mind. However, behind the smothering fog above the podium, the golden background rises, pointing the way to the spiritual realms of life some of the participants may reach. The artist associates the golden background with humanity's ultimate dream of transcending the harsh realities of life and ascending the enlightenment that liberates mankind from all earthly fetters.

Entering from the left, Little Why (butterfly No. 1) has still to climb to the podium, and she marshals all her energies toward arriving at the first elevated stand. Eager and ready to do what she is told, she faces the "big guy," True Blue (butterfly No. 2), who "has arrived" and defends his success in an imperious parade of power. His importance may lie in his membership in the "good old boys' club" or could be the result of unscrupulous manipulations. There is a tragic irony in the fact that Little Why is a miniature copy of True Blue, whom she is keen to imitate now, but hopes to challenge and replace later. At the opposite end of the stage, the embodiments of two different fates, isolated from the main group, share a single stand. Firebird (butterfly No. 5) and Fanning Everything (butterfly No. 6) are in a power struggle. It ends well for Firebird, and he forces obedience on the loser. Fanning Everything must resign herself to sacrificing her dream of self-realization.

A pair at the center, Pale Moonlight (butterfly No. 3) and Touchless Misty (butterfly No. 4), are enthroned in their dominant positions and engrossed with control of their territories, turning their backs on the rest of the group. Pale Moonlight, for example, might manipulate others to secure her success by a marriage of convenience to a powerbroker, assuring her a nearly-free ride to a chairwoman's seat. Touchless Misty has been polished by law school and will probably abuse his degree in politics and international affairs. His steely mind allows him to singly occupy the strongest position and influence the course of events to his group's benefit.

In the midst of this busy, noisy struggle for a supreme rank in the hierarchy, there is a place of silence. Here, Air (butterfly No. 7) hovers effortlessly, nearly unnoticed. Air is free of all anchors, rising above the ground. It may leave the group at any moment, unless the other butterflies can muster some higher values to entice Air to stay.

The word "chatter" in her text expresses Susanne's critical attitude toward superficial conversations, fake gestures of affection, and the widespread waste of time and human energy in the world as she sees it, from the supermarket to the doctor's office, from the sherry party to the party convention—and sometimes even inside the Church and academia.

"Hesitating to learn" alludes to the hypocritical pledge to social progress that politicians declare in their questionable affirmation of themselves as sole keepers of the true path. Only time and history will reject their dogmatic precepts and indoctrinations. This, according to Susanne, is how societies and their politics slow down progress due to their self-promoting actions.

Likewise, the family acts as a miniature model of society. Looking back, Susanne is troubled by the countless hours wasted in family discussions, where her father's over-dominance preoccupied everyone. Her mother suffered endlessly from the inactivity forced upon her by her husband during those sessions. Susanne and her two sisters reacted by either obediently following their father's lead or rebelling against his several-hours-long theoretical odysseys.

Susanne has been brought up on a mixture of exceptional freedoms and unequivocal restrictions. On the one hand, her self-employed parents were a constant presence, and scheduled time was not an ironclad rhythm in the household. On the other hand, her parents were subtle but strict in setting standards. With their unchallenged judgments, they dictated proper behavior, imposed their preferences of style and attitudes, and actually isolated the family from the outside world. This experience taught Susanne to recognize the same negative patterns pervading in society.

The artist's pessimistic outlook has, besides her negative family experiences, also intellectual and philosophical underpinnings. "Not free to breathe" can be understood as a metaphor for *all restrictions*, even though, at the time, the child had not perceived them as great sacrifices. It remains uncertain whether the most suffocating of the dictates imposed on Susanne came from inside or outside her family. In the painting, six of the butterflies seem destined to remain bound to the ground, whereas one is free of all constraints and ready to fly into the sky. This situation bears on her self-identification and appears as a metaphor of the artist's struggle to overcome many of her restrictions.

Yet, during the painting process, Susanne was not aware of the butterflies' existential condition. On the contrary, she thought she presented them as privileged, in her words "on a silver tray,"[1] and commended this with a majestic presentation on the podium. But unconsciously, the artist's depiction of the podium reflects the rules and values that her family imposed on her. During free association, Susanne explained that being bound to the podium had other connotations for her. The podium restrains the butterflies, as if it were covered with glue, impeding any movement toward liberation. Susanne figuratively expresses the situation in the following self-descriptive passage: "For many years my wings have been weighed down, and I could not take flight in spite of my wish to do so." A few weeks after completion of the painting, she participated in a personal-growth seminar. Susanne chose a role-play to illustrate her progress and used the analogy of a "butterfly bursting from the cocoon." She wrapped herself tightly in a shawl, from which she gradually freed herself, and finished with the triumphal statement: "Now, I can fly." She went on to say that the best way for her to free herself is creativity—her window into freedom, where she can be herself again.

"The media too thick to breathe" is an allusion to the "smog" of the news media, which add their own share of vain gossip and mind-numbing, noisy chatter. The antennae vibrate, "hungry for news," but not for truth. "The media too thick ..." is Susanne's own, idiosyncratic reaction to radio, the newspapers, and television. Her family allowed her to watch television only in adolescence, from approximately the age of 15 onwards. The radio was no favorite of hers, despite her sisters' enthusiasm for it. She despised newspapers and rarely read magazines, and in her adulthood, she openly rebelled against the news media as a wasteful and unwanted distraction of her mind and mood.

She feels "her antennae" bombarded and her senses overwhelmed by the abundance of aggressive advertisements and irrelevant information that intrude and shred to pieces any uninterrupted contemplation during reading, listening, or viewing, thus, not allowing her to "breathe" with her own thoughts. She considers this intrusion so thick that it not only threatens her freedom but also stifles the whole world. Nevertheless, she is engaged actively with the world, keeping herself well-informed, and allowing relevant and useful information to be filtered through to her.

During the analytic discussion, Susanne figuratively called "restriction" as "weights on the wings" that curb the essential freedom of flight,

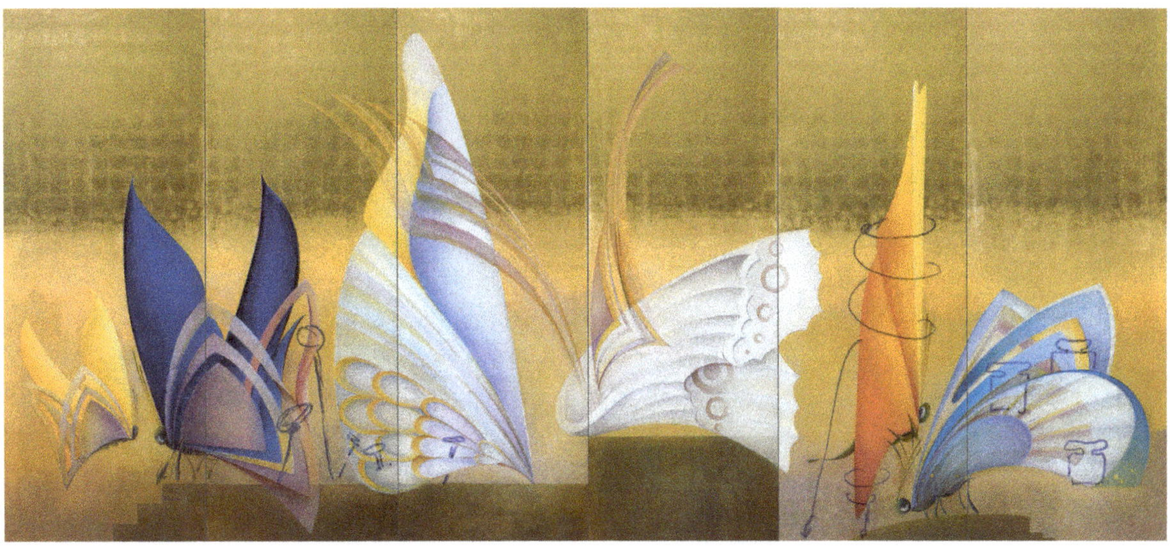

Fig. 3.1. A print of *Give Me Wings!* with details added by the artist in pencil (2009).

1 The watercolor (Fig. 2.9) shows the podium in varying hues of gray, a common way of representing silver, which could confirm her later comment about "presenting on a silver tray." In the oil painting, the artist changed the color into a muted brown that reflects a different meaning (see chapter 12).

and she demonstrated this with a sketch (Fig. 3.1). She took a pencil and, on a photocopy of the painting, drew heavy weights on butterfly No. 6, binding ropes on No. 2, nails through the wings of No. 3, and spiral ropes around the choleric No. 5. Only No. 1, too young, and No. 7, unreachable, (and No. 4, somehow forgotten) were spared the painful shackles.

Facing those added details, particularly the cruel nails, she had a strong reaction of disgust and a recurrent, tormenting phobia of having nails driven through her hands. This image triggered her whole gallery of horrors: Images of scissors, knife blades, and a pair of tongs attacking different areas of her body.

Susanne calls these horror-imaginations, against which she has no protection, her personal "Pandora's Box." These frightening images have latent meanings that manifest the imperatives of biological drives (sexual and aggressive) that determine her own complexes, reflecting the collective and personal unconscious.

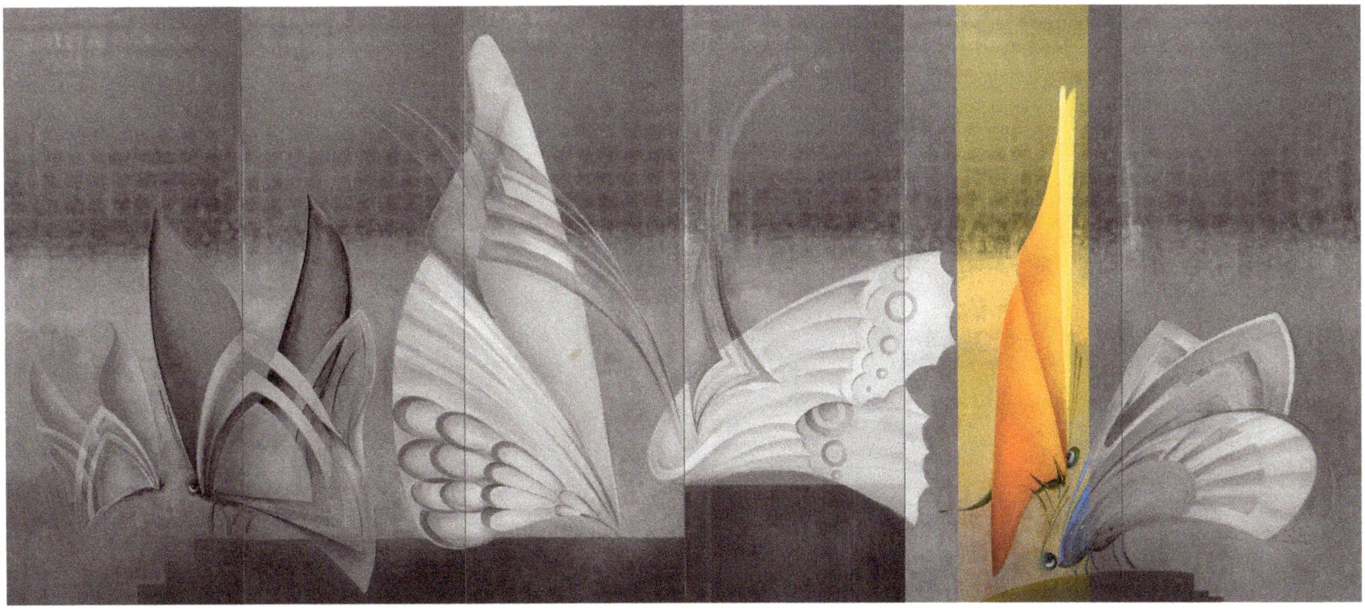

Fig. 4.0. *Give Me Wings!* with butterfly No. 5, Firebird, highlighted.

> *Firebird sometimes looks for camouflage in a bird-of-paradise* [flower], *but he is much too choleric to restrain his trembling opinion.* [*Although*] *having a miraculous range [of colors] from purest white to deep burning orange, he is not even aware of the unbridgeable contradictions in his soul: from pure ideological goodness to ravishing* [1] *anger and hate. In his bipolar temper*[*ament*], *he will risk himself to rescue a friend in need, but a moment later he might condemn the same one as his blackest enemy and swear eternal warfare on him. His enormous range, the potential for the extraordinary, has turned into his greatest deficit, isolating him from the others.*
> —From the artist's poetic commentary, 2004. The insertions in brackets were added later for clarification.

Chapter 4

Choleric **Butterfly No. 5 — Firebird**

A temper tantrum

4.1 Placement Among the Group

Butterfly No. 5, named Firebird, dominates the right side of the painting *Give Me Wings!* His elongated wings are tightly folded, rising straight up like a pair of steeples before the golden background and dipping deep down toward a sloped, lower segment of the podium. He is presented in a narrow, constricted profile that makes him appear the most compact and angular of the butterflies (Fig. 4.0). Firebird's rectilinear wing contour stands out from the serrated outline of his neighbor to the left and the shallow curves of the one to the right. The butterfly's spiking form adds a dominant vertical element to the right half of the compositional drawing, and with his fiery orange hue, he emerges even more preeminent in the final painting. Firebird appears to anchor himself on another butterfly, and his posture signals a domineering, unyielding nature. He towers over nearly everyone. With an inflated sense of self-importance and superiority, he turns his back to the rest of the assembly. In doing so, he is moving toward a position of separation. The artist's poetic commentary states this succinctly: "... isolating him from the others."

Looking for the origin of this butterfly's appearance, we find his prototype in two of the

1 The artist used the word "ravishing" in an archaic sense for rape.

sketches that Susanne made in the Butterfly Conservatory at the American Museum of Natural History in New York (Fig. 2.1d, or Fig. 4.1), which were then further stylized in creative drawing III that emphasized the striking verticality of the image (Fig. 2.4).

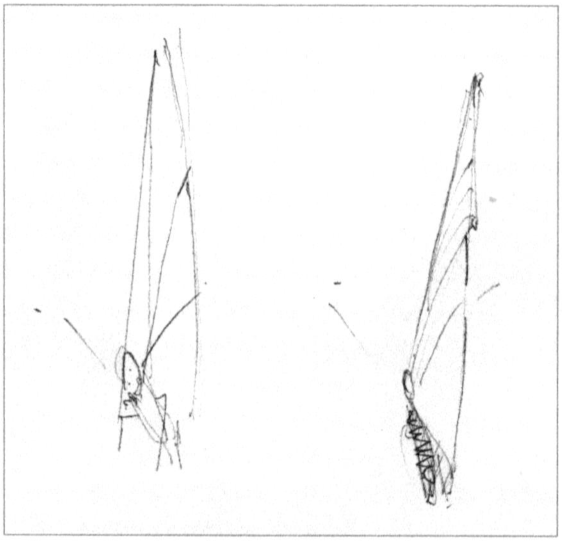

Fig. 4.1. Detail sketches from nature (from Fig. 2.1.d).

To achieve visual diversity in the composition and to underscore the individuality of each butterfly, Susanne considered many elements that could distinguish them from each other. As mentioned in chapter 2, working on the composition for the painting and having already drawn four butterflies, Nos. 2, 3, 7, and 4 (Fig. 2.7), the artist had an urge to add a strongly contrasting shape to the group. The solution was found by horizontally flipping over the image of the upright contour of a butterfly from her creative drawing III, which then became butterfly No. 5 (Fig. 2.8). Later, during the coloration phase of the final composition, Susanne assigned the colors that would emphasize butterfly No. 5's specific traits (Fig. 2.12). She clad this shape in orange and yellow, in spite of her avowed dislike of these hues. Situated between the expansive wings of butterfly No. 4, Touchless Misty (in white to the left) and butterfly No. 6, Fanning Everything (in light blue to the right), the flaming glare of butterfly No. 5's orange color stands out radiantly in contrast. Firebird became the focal point of the right half of the painting, balancing the powerful dark blue of butterfly No. 2, True Blue, at the left of the canvas. The peculiarities of shape and the variations in the intense chroma of butterfly No. 5 will be interpreted in the following analysis. For the identification of the structural features of butterfly No. 5 and references to specific colors, see Fig. 4.2.

4.2 Recognizing the Phenomenon of Personification

As mentioned briefly in the introduction, butterfly No. 5 played a key role in the discovery of the phenomenon of personification, which led to a systematic and wide-ranging analysis of the entire painting. An interwoven set of associations referring to Firebird's details, including his specific colors, brought us to this perspective. When Susanne verbally expressed her thoughts and attitude toward butterfly No. 5 in the poetic commentary, she was thoroughly convinced of the accuracy of her specific characterizations of Firebird as a personality. But she was not aware at that time that this image was a personification of her father.

Notably, the discovery of the personification phenomenon of the butterflies began with the understanding of this metaphorical meaning behind the fiery coloration of Firebird. Susanne recalls: "While I painted the transitions from the bottom in dark red-orange to the light tips of the wings, I thought of the changing colors of iron being heated in fire. When I was little, one of my favorite books was *Geboren im Feuer – Stahl* (*Born in Fire – Steel*) which belonged to my father.[2] It was a steel-industry public relations publication with many large, full color photographs of mines, coal-sorting, steel-cooking, steel-rolling, and hot iron bubbling and sparking like fireworks. I often went through the pages and was fascinated by the incredible range of reds and yellows and even white—called 'white heat'."[3] The dust jacket of the book shows those glowing colors (Fig. 4.3), and they can be thought of as anticipating the coloration of Firebird four decades later.

When assigning colors to butterfly No. 5 in the watercolor design, the artist chose light yellow for the right edge of his right front wing. However, when using oil colors for the final painting, the artist deviated from this color scheme. While working on the canvas, she impulsively brightened the intensity

2 Stachelscheid 1956

3 This color stage begins when the metal is heated up to temperatures higher than 1,300° C.

(a) Tips of the front wings (like a slightly opened pair of scissors)

(b) Tip of the left front wing (association with the scalpel)

(c) Right front wing

(d) Edge of the right front wing

(e) Edge of the left front wing

(f) Right hind wing

(g) Lower tip of the right hind wing (association to a raised finger)

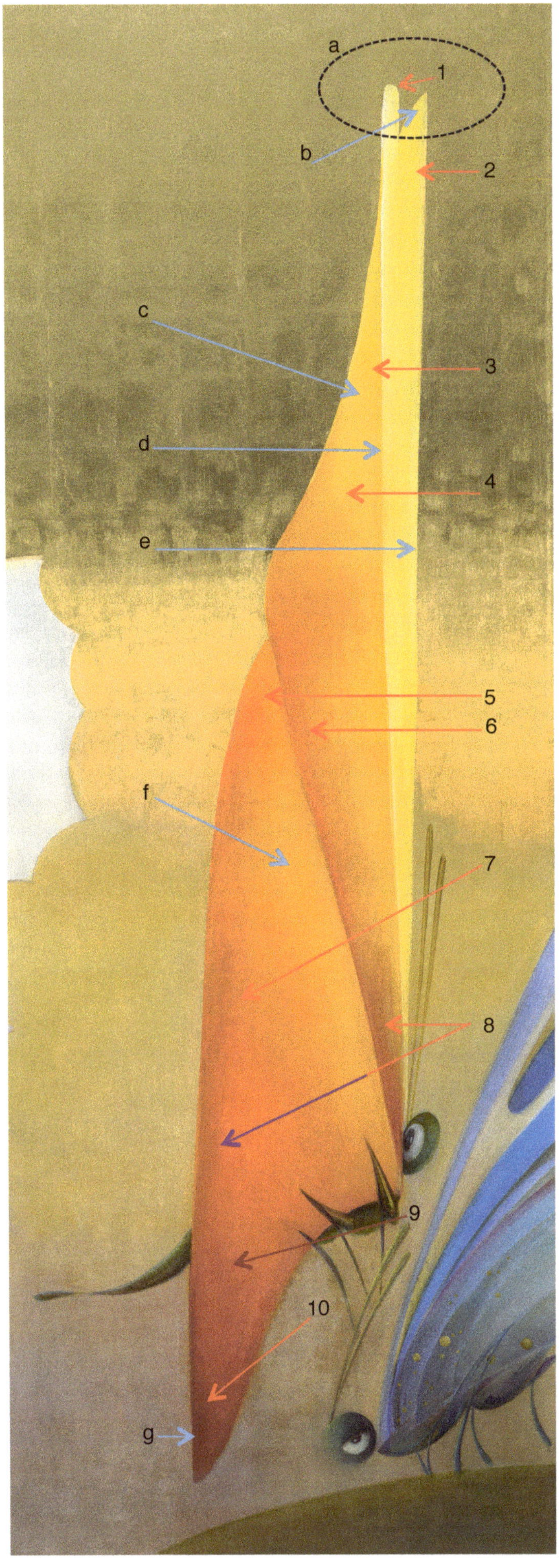

(1) White glow

(2) Light yellow

(3) Bright yellow

(4) Saffron yellow

(5) Orange

(6) Fold of orange

(7) Dark orange

(8) Burnt orange

(9) Orange-red brown

(10) Dark brown

Fig. 4.2. Structural features of butterfly No. 5. (left column) and references to specific colors (right column).

of this yellow hue, ending up with an all-white tip (Fig. 4.2 (1)). Seeing the result, the expression "*Weißglut*" (German for "white heat") sprang up in her mind, as a word that was also used in a metaphorical description for someone's emotionally heated mental state. That German idiom was well known in Susanne's family because, when her father worked himself into a temper tantrum, he was apt to angrily hurl the following rebuke at his daughters: "*Du bringst mich zur Weißglut*!" (English: "You bring me to white heat!").[4]

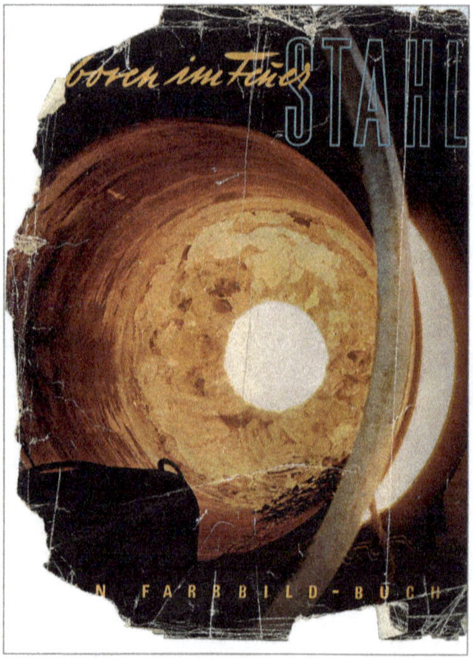

Fig. 4.3. A damaged dust jacket from the book *Geboren im Feuer STAHL* (Stachelscheid, 1956).

Thinking of the fiery vibrant colors in butterfly No. 5 and correlating them as equivalent to a range of human moods, Susanne perceived this butterfly as if it were a human being capable of assorted emotions and felt that was the essence of this creature. The artist was astonished when she was asked if this image could be a fitting portrait of her father. She immediately had to agree, amazed that she had not made the connection herself, even though she had fleeting thoughts of him while painting those "choleric colors" (Susanne's metaphor). This sudden revelation was confirmed by the artist's characterization of her father: "… he had a wide range of moods. He could be calm, peaceful and likeable, but when anger struck, it was frightening to witness how he 'heated' himself up, starting from annoyance, moving into anger, and then reaching the raging crescendo of loud screaming and extreme hostility. This was like the range of colors I painted."

The father's innate choleric temperament was unpredictable. It was not possible to determine what might trigger his next tantrum. The family learned how easily his annoyance could be provoked by the slightest of occasions, sometimes even without any apparent cause. His anger would quickly slide into a devastating avalanche of rage expressed in a quivering voice—an event dreaded by everyone. The father's deportment finds a terse portrayal in a line from the artist's poetic commentary annotating Firebird's attributes: "much too choleric to restrain his trembling opinion." The first part of the quote captures clearly the reality of her father's precarious temperament and correlates it with the butterfly's sharp shapes and colors in the painting. But the second part contains an unusual phrase: "trembling opinion." Susanne explains that this was her spontaneous way to most succinctly describe a person who in a highly agitated state of mind would utter words in an angry, trembling voice. Whenever describing such an individual with her choice of phraseology, she is reminded of her father in his rage. During a family discussion, the father dominated the entire session. He would not tolerate any interruptions, and whenever someone broke in, he felt incredibly insulted. He reacted with a sudden outburst of fury accompanied by trembling hands, disgruntled facial expressions, and wide-open staring eyes. Susanne remembers well her father's sudden fits of temper and the hollow feeling in her stomach that she would often get after such an outburst.

From the above context, "trembling opinion" can indicate one of the most memorable aspects of her father's character—his volcanic temper that determined a specific family situation. The speaker (the father, "the epicenter") would begin to shake in outrage, while the listeners (the rest of the family, the recipients of his "seismic waves"), whose minds now shivered with despair, sat still with no idea as to what to do with this "human earthquake." Being fearful, no one uttered an opinion as the head of the family grumbled on. Thus, for Susanne, the word "trembling" has a potent meaning that signifies patriarchal authority. Her father's proclivity was inscribed into her mental archive and became an alert signal of potential conflict.

4 German idiomatic expression to imply bringing someone to extreme anger.

The image of butterfly No. 5 (personification of the father) pressing down butterfly No. 6, Fanning Everything (personification of the mother) into a submissive posture in *Give Me Wings!* provides a further verification of the family dynamics.

The above observation is substantiated by the artist's choice of Firebird's striking, "choleric" color combination that could be characterized as "changing to extremes." The basic orange hue gradually alters its appearance from darker shades at the bottom of the wings to lighter tints at the top. There is a wide fluctuation, which quite likely delineates metaphorically the range of his personality traits: light and dark, cheerful and gloomy, friendly and hostile. Her father exhibited them quite readily in unpredictable turns, and it points to Susanne's perception of her father's emotional instability and inner tension. The outstretched antennae of butterfly No. 5 are poised to vibrate (i.e., "tremble") at any moment. Metaphorically, this reflects Susanne's explicit grasp of her father's emotional strain and its potential for a sudden outburst. Another notable characterization of Firebird's appearance is his eye. Susanne depicted it as a considerably protruding eyeball, which was perhaps modeled unconsciously after the bulging eyes of her father in paroxysm (Fig. 4.2). She, by rendering the mentioned peculiar attributes of this butterfly, unconsciously symbolized her father's temperament which he manifested whenever his precarious emotional stasis was disturbed.

The artist endowed all the butterflies in the poetic commentary with very specific personalities as though they were human beings. However, she had not thought of them as personifications of identifiable people, such as her parents, much less her self.[5] Susanne remembers that she had fleeting thoughts of her father while painting butterfly No. 5, and later when writing the corresponding part of the poetic commentary. She says: "I saw my father as an example of someone I had seen 'hot in anger.' In this way, Firebird and my father were comparable, but I never consciously thought about the butterfly's identity, that Firebird could be a personification of my father." Firebird's peculiarities did metaphorically correspond to the volatile aspect of her father's personality as seen through Susanne's eyes. Through our analysis, the personification phenomenon became apparent to her. After this original discovery, we subsequently also recognized this phenomenon for the other butterflies. In retrospect, her fleeting thoughts were no coincidence. They were telltale signs of the unconscious having been involved in her artistic creation, beyond the artist's awareness of such influence.

On the one hand, the first impression of Firebird is of a brilliant chromatic fire with gradually changing hues. These colors give this butterfly a dazzling and exquisite appearance. The artist's father, personified by this butterfly, possessed a charming personality with a friendly, kind, and helpful attitude—his public persona by which most people knew him.

On the other hand, Firebird's features include numerous sharp angles and pointed shapes, inflexible and vertically shooting lines, a harsh separation of the wings, and striking extremes in colors. These all hint at his other nature hidden underneath. These peculiarities are metaphorical expressions of her father's authoritarian nature concealed under the pleasant façade. Susanne aptly captured this perception in the poetic commentary: "Firebird sometimes looks for camouflage in a bird-of-paradise." This verbal statement correlates the form and colors of the butterfly with the blossom of the bird-of-paradise flower (Fig. 4.4), a connection which we will discuss further below (subchapter 4.3).

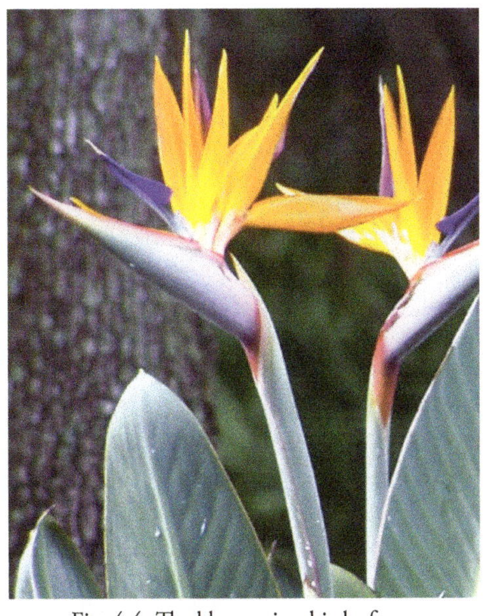

Fig. 4.4. The blossoming bird-of-paradise plant.

5 We can assume that the artist unconsciously prefigured personification of the butterflies as early as in creative drawing I (see chapter 2).

The essence of her father's fluctuating disposition was metaphorically captured by the irreconcilable contrasts between both the shapes (gentle vs. sharp) and the colors (dark vs. white) of Firebird. Correlating further, Firebird's characterization from the poetic commentary—"... he is not even aware of the unbridgeable contradictions in his soul: from pure ideological goodness to ravishing anger and hate"—matches the divergence in her father's psyche quite tellingly. For example, his "pure ideological goodness" was apparent to Susanne whenever he was passionately and selflessly engaged in giving assistance to others out of his personal principles. As she wrote: "He will risk himself to rescue a friend in need ... ," but it was also conceivable that "... a moment later he might condemn that same friend as his blackest enemy and swear eternal warfare on him." The antipodal nature of the father's psyche, in its darkest extreme, the artist enunciated in the poetic commentary as "ravishing anger and hate." Here Susanne employs "ravishing" as a synonym for committing rape in a metaphorical sense. Thus, the phrase connotes "psychological rape," which accords with her mother's idiosyncratic phrase "*Psychoterror*" (German for "psychological terrorism") that she often used to accuse her husband of his misbehavior.

The "ideological goodness" finds its visual representation in the shaft of glorious yellow light, streaming at the edges of the front wings down toward his head (Fig. 4.2 (2), (d), and (e)). This could be an illusion,[6] as if the light were originating from the golden background, which, in Susanne's symbology in this painting, stands for spirituality (see chapters 10 and 12). Moreover, the light yellow is spreading to the left, shifting into a saffron yellow hue (Fig. 4.2 (4))—an intimation of respect for the Buddhist faith. Susanne's general admiration for the virtuous life of Buddhist monks might have unconsciously been metaphorically transposed by the mellow, yellow hues onto the figure of Firebird as the signifier of her father's altruistic tendencies. This aspect of her parent, she acknowledged as "ideological goodness" in her poetic commentary describing this personified butterfly.

The contrasting aspect of "ravishing anger and hate" finds its expression in the butterfly's murky, dark orange that develops via orange-red brown into a dark brown at the very bottom wing tip (see the area (g) and colors (7–9) in Fig. 4.2). Its shape is evocative of the pointing index finger of the artist's father (Fig. 4.6 (b)), which was an indicator of escalating danger and an oppressive atmosphere during a typical family discussion. Firebird's front wings are tightly folded together with a narrow gap between them. The configuration is comparable to a barely open pair of scissors. This potentially hostile shape, in combination with the "white glow" of the right wing's apex, also signifies anger and threat.

Later in chapter 5, our analysis will reveal that the personification of Susanne's father in the imagery of *Give Me Wings!* is not limited to Firebird, as we will identify butterfly No. 2 (True Blue) as another personification of her father. Furthermore, we will show that this butterfly's attributes exhibit a congruence with those of Firebird. Both signify certain notable aspects of Susanne's father's character. The analysis, likewise, will illustrate how well the visual images of both butterflies and their characterizations in the artist's poetic commentary correspond with her perception of the father's personality.

4.3 Possible Sources for the Name

During the time Susanne was painting butterfly No. 5's fiery, vigorous hues on the oil canvas, "Firebird" spontaneously sprang to her mind as a fitting name for this tempestuous butterfly. This was the only one that received a moniker during the painting process. Everything discussed in the previous section analyzing various eminent aspects of this butterfly points to the appropriateness of the word "fire" in the compound name "Firebird."

Foremost, we find a correlation between the coloration of butterfly No. 5 and that of iron ore during the melting process, which she remembered vividly from the book (*Geboren im Feuer*) which her father possessed. A comparable range of colors, from dark red to brightening orange, yellow, and white, is represented in Firebird's wings. The right front wing culminates in white at the apex—the visual equivalent to the common saying "to bring a person to white heat" that her father used as a metaphor to characterize his increasing anger and frustration. Those associations could play the decisive role in triggering the fleeting thoughts of him which came into her mind during the

6 This illusory effect is more convincing in the actual painting than in the illustrations found in this book, as the specular gloss of the gold-leafed background is nearly impossible to reproduce in print.

painting process. Susanne's perception of the varying coloration of Firebird as blazing, flaming, glowing, chromatic fire that she names "choleric colors" is an appropriate description of the temper of her father. These aspects are epitomized in the word "fire," a code word with which the artist unconsciously associates her father.

Regarding the second constituent of the sobriquet "Firebird," the frequent appearance of birds in her father's creative work, as a graphic artist and painter, must be given due consideration. In the artwork of Susanne's father, Heinz-Günter Schünke (1924–2010)[7], birds and their eggs carry various significant, symbolic roles. In describing his fascination with the egg, one of the fundamental remarks that Susanne's father would make was that "everything that lives starts from an egg." He often equipped the eggs with a pair of eyes as a metaphoric representation of people.

In his oil painting, *Der Gewichtheber* (English: *The Weightlifter*), 1978 (Fig. 4.5), the egg-heads mostly represent society's powerbrokers—politicians, kings and aristocrats, military leaders, cardinals, bankers, industrialists, etc., identifiable by their attire and headgear. Their staring eyes are focused on the central figure of the painting, a monumentalized weightlifter with exaggerated musculature in dominant orange-red. His head is replaced by a highly polished Nautilus shell,[8] which hints at his existence as having been reduced to an inhuman state. He stands in front of an enormous barbell, which he is expected to lift. He holds an open birdcage, from which he has just released a robin that now sits on the barbell.

The father commented[9] on this detail that the weightlifter gives the bird the freedom which he has dreamed of. He cannot act according to his own mind because he has been manipulated and commanded by others, who hold power over him. Their oppressive social coercion is obvious. The big tears rolling down from the weightlifter's eye (see Fig. 5.17) illustrate his suffering because the masters demand a superhuman performance from him.

On the ground below, underneath the barbell, a moorhen chick has just hatched out of its eggshell. It is surrounded by monsters rising from the bubbling swamp mud—a possible allusion to the precarious nature of being born into the world with all its potential dangers. *The Weightlifter* is rich with metaphors and symbols, some of which will be further explicated in chapter 9. At this juncture, what should be noted is that Susanne was well aware of the importance of the bird motif in her father's paintings, and thus it is quite plausible that the bird became one of the metaphors by which her father was represented in her unconscious.

The following discussion covers several other associations and recollections in the artist's life concerning "fire" and "bird"—the two components of the name that might have further contributed unconsciously to the christening of the butterfly. Through her studies and reading, Susanne knew about the traditional belief, held throughout antiquity and the Middle Ages, that the "bird has symbolized the human soul ...".[10] In some cultures, the butterfly[11] represents the soul, mainly because of its weightlessness, beauty, and ability to fly, as well as the mystery of its transformation from caterpillar (larva) to pupa (chrysalis) and its rebirth as a winged being (imago).[12]

This metamorphic process is reflected in the religious concept of resurrection, which underpins the legend of another flying creature, the phoenix, said to achieve immortality in an eternal cycle of self-immolation, followed by its resurrection to a new life out of its own ashes. As teenager, Susanne had listened to one of her father's records with the orchestral concert suites of *The Firebird* by Igor Stravinsky. She found the music disharmonic and remembered hearing shrieking sounds as if a bird were being immolated.[13] This imagination of a bird on fire was troubling to Susanne, and she memorized it as a traumatic scenario. She did not

---

7 We refer here not only to his oil paintings but also to hundreds of graphic and digital designs.

8 When a Nautilus shell's outer layer is polished off, its underlying, shimmering mother-of-pearl surface is revealed.

9 We refer to the commentaries from the daughters on this topic.

10 Murray 1998: page 58.

11 Murray 1998: page 69.

12 The New Encyclopedia Britannica: Vol. 2, 1987: page 686.

13 Stravinsky's ballet is based on the mythical Firebird that appears in various popular Slavonic folktales. The phoenix belongs to Greek mythology. There is no connection between the two legendary narrations.

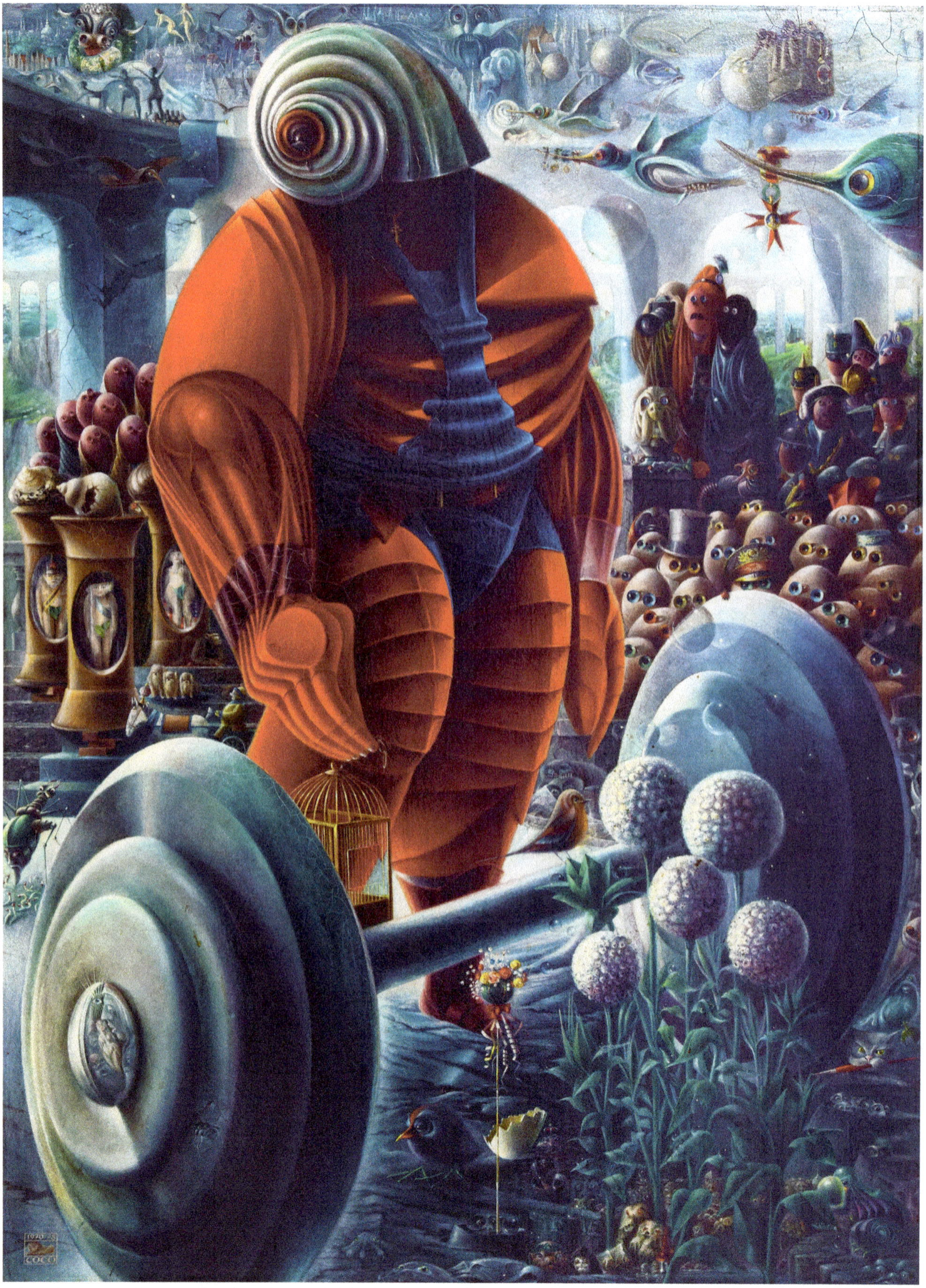

Fig. 4.5. Heinz-Günter Schünke, *The Weightlifter* (*Der Gewichtheber*), 1978. Oil on wood, 38.5 x 29 in (98 x 74 cm). Collection of the artist's family, Germany.

know anything about the story line behind the music and thought "firebird" was the English (and German) word for the Greek phoenix.

Fire has a particularly negative connotation for Susanne, because she associates it with a vision of human limbs being thrust into fire, and houses set on fire and their inhabitants incinerated. The imagery reminds her of the evils that humans do to their own kind with such savagery, malice, and inhumanity. In high school, she was required to read Grimmelshausen's *Simplicius Simplicissimus*,[14] written approximately 20 years after the end of the Thirty Years' War. The author detailed horrific descriptions of atrocities committed by the warring parties, including one particular torture technique that had stuck in the young Susanne's mind: that of putting "feet in fire." The distress she suffered reading this book was so severe that even recalling the episode over 40 years later would still make her cringe at such graphic accounts of inhumanity and barbarism. Learning about the Holocaust and World War II had been an equally distressing experience for her, with the records about the concentration camp crematoriums and the firebombing of cities.

Evidently, fire in Susanne's mind represents not only its potential for physical harm but also embodies the human being's destructive tendency to inflict pain and suffering on others. By her sensitivity and superior imagination, when Susanne is reading or hearing about atrocities, she instantly projects herself into the scene, feeling herself as the victim.

Another possible influence in the naming of the butterfly might have come from Susanne's recognition of her temperamental affinity with her father. When she and her classmates were studying Roman mythology in high school, her fellow students nicknamed her "Volcanus" (Vulcan—the Roman god of fire and metalworking) for her occasional outbursts of choleric temper. Her mother picked up on this moniker and used it for many years to admonish her daughter whenever Susanne misbehaved with angry irritation. Her mother saw the similarity in temperament between her husband and Susanne, which she characterized as having the inclination to "explode like a volcano," and presumably spew out fire. Thus, the word *fire* plays a significant role in defining the irascible disposition of a person.

In a discussion concerning the origin of the second part of the butterfly's name, the artist recalled comparing Firebird to the exotic bird-of-paradise flower. This had crossed her mind while working on the butterfly. She noted this association in her poetic commentary which was written after the painting was finished. When she first saw this tropical plant in Florida, she was quite taken by the blossom's unusual shape, strange sharpness, and intense orange color. During analysis, she pointed out the resemblance between the peculiar configuration of the flower's petals and the wings of Firebird (Figs. 4.4 and 4.0). The similarity between the two images was even more cogent by the orange-yellow coloration shared by both. She thought that this likeness, together with the mythological "firebird," might have led her to the sudden idea of "Firebird" as an amalgam created by her unconscious.

In summary, it became apparent to us that the moniker the artist assigned to the butterfly was not due to happenstance but quite likely the symbolic manifestation of her unconscious. The reasoning of this statement can be substantiated by multiple references to her emotionally charged experiences with her father as analyzed above. The probe into the possible sources for the name "Firebird" has provided numerous clues toward identifying who is personified in the imagery of this butterfly. These hints are strong enough to point to a specific person in Susanne's life—her father. It would be shortsighted to assume that this presupposition came about only through the analysis of the compound name "Firebird." Our starting point of this assumption was based on the comparison of the artist's selection of colors for this butterfly which are similar to the dust jacket of her father's book *Born in Fire–Steel* (see subchapter 4.2). We found associative parallels of the specific coloration of Firebird—orange, burnt orange, yellow, etc. including white glow—typical for fire. Susanne called them "choleric colors," which are metaphorical signs of peculiarities of her father's temperament that could develop to a condition characterized by the idiom "white heat." As we will see, the basically spiky configuration of the butterfly's image, which was already in place before the

14 Hans Jakob Christoffel von Grimmelshausen (1621–1676). Der Abentheuerliche Simplicissimus Teutsch, or Simplicius Simplicissimus. 1669 (English translation: The Adventurous Simplicissimus. 1912, and others)

artist accentuated it with the mentioned hues, also confirms the unconscious personification of the father in butterfly No. 5. The next section explores the possible unconscious meaning underlying specific shapes associated with Firebird.

4.4 The Peculiar Shapes and Their Metaphorical Meaning

4.4.1 A Spiky Shape

The three-quarter profile of butterfly No. 5 is an irregular triangle, with its two acute angles defining the top and bottom vertices (Fig. 4.2), while the body of the butterfly is nestled in the area of the obtuse angle. The sharp, spike-like tips of the wings are emphasized by a gradation of color, having the lightest at the top (white) and the darkest at the bottom (dark brown). The spiky appearance of Firebird can be interpreted as a metaphor alluding to the artist's perception of specific facets of her father's personality. Susanne remembers well her father's argumentative voice, the barbed, scathing words that he cast with accusations and name calling. All that was accompanied by exaggerated hand gestures and the movement of his index finger pointing toward the person like a spike. Whenever he felt the need to assert himself, his response was firm and overwhelming, with his light blue eyes staring down at the transgressor. The family felt as if they were forced to stand on pins and needles. Susanne's mother had a choice word for her husband's sharp comments and tirades: "*Nadelstiche*" (English: "pin pricks").

Susanne spent countless hours in the parents' workshop from the day she could crawl, and seeing her father at his large desk working with various precision instruments was quite familiar to her. There were cutting knives with their diverse blades, compasses with their needle ends, scissors, technical pens and pencils with sharp tips, tacks and staples, as well as metal drafting triangles. Those and other acute instruments were his tools, and she was repeatedly instructed not to touch them because of the danger of mishandling them and getting hurt. Their elongated shapes and dangerous endings are imprinted in her memory. They could have become unconsciously identified as a metaphorical analogy for certain features of her father's character. We can see how the details of the painted images not only represent the peculiarities of the father's behavior, but they also manifest the characteristics of various objects, which the artist's unconscious incorporated into her psyche as symbolic activators of Susanne's phobias. As mentioned in the introduction, she developed various phobias of sharp objects, such as knives, syringes, etc., including pointed fingers (aichmophobia), also of spiders (arachnophobia), and navels (omphalophobia) between the ages of eight and thirteen, and she has continued to suffer from them throughout her life.

Her aichmophobia, especially of syringes, turned each of her medical exigencies into a traumatic experience, triggering a more severe phobic reaction with each incident. In her 40's, she had concluded that those stressful experiences and her severe reactions to syringes and other procedures involving needles and injections had their source, as she stated, in "something that had power over me."[15]

In our analysis, special attention was paid to the contents of her phobias. The sharp forms that activated them might have been processed into particular unconscious symbolism on the basis of appropriate predisposition and individual experiences. These configurations emerge in specific ways in her imagery as markers of a danger. As mentioned before, the minute detail of the two apexes of Firebird's wings reminds us of a barely opened pair of shears (Fig. 4.2 (a)), one of the basic tools regularly used by the father in his workshop. Looking closely at the shape of the tip of the left front wing, we can picture the blade of the graphic designer's scalpel (Fig. 4.2 (b)). The presence of such cutting tools is not singular to Firebird. As it will be shown later, the front wings of butterfly No. 2 (True Blue) carry a remarkable resemblance to the shapes of blades and scissors. These artistically created forms can be a metaphorical expression of the peculiarities in Susanne's perception of her father's personality, and a manifestation of unconscious symbolism linking her phobias with the father complex (see chapter 5).

As touched upon above, certain spiky configurations of butterfly No. 5 bring to mind some objects of Susanne's fears, and our analysis

15 The state of being subjected to someone's "power" in accordance to hospital situations will be discussed in chapter 5. Her recurring thought of being subjugated could be traced back to her early childhood sexual fantasies (age 5 and onwards), where Susanne projected herself in a role where males had power over her (chapter 8, footnote 73).

shows this is no coincidence. The artist presented this butterfly in his right profile. His wings are tightly closed in a narrow, compressed shape with an acute perpendicularity. This formation makes butterfly No. 5 the most slender figure among all the butterflies depicted. The choice appears to be intentional, as Susanne wanted to place such a tall butterfly on the right side of the painting to introduce a vertical element for compositional balance. But, on the unconscious level, her decision might well have come under the influence of significant emotional experiences in her past, corresponding to her specific attitude toward her father. That could have led her to implicitly choose the prominent, elongated vertical form of this butterfly (personification of the father) that towered over nearly all other butterflies[16] (except for butterfly No. 3). She reinforced its significance by adding the appropriate colors later. Firebird's erect shape, dominant position, and brilliant coloration could signify Susanne's idealization of her father as the locus of her world. But in the same image, Firebird's spiky configuration can also indicate the connection between her phobias and their origin in the artist's transferential relation toward her father as the object of her childhood incestuous sexual desires that were censored, repressed, and transmuted into irrational fears.

On the one hand, specific pointed shapes and their coloration manifest as metaphorical signifiers for the personality of the artist's father. On the other hand, such shapes, especially various vertically elongated configurations, can symbolize the phallic function, that harbors the potentiality of penetration, reflecting the deep-rooted unconscious tendencies and drives with their appropriate symbolism, which were coined by Susanne's psyche. In chapter 9, which deals with Touchless Misty, this symbolism will be given further coverage in subchapter 9.4 (Optical Illusions).

4.4.2 Pointing Index Finger

The hind wing of Firebird tapers down toward the podium like a pointer. If we rotate the image of the butterfly by about 135 degrees clockwise (Fig. 4.6 (c)), the repositioned contour of the image evokes another significant analogy embedded in the imagery: the semblance of an imperiously pointed index finger of her lecturing father[17] (Fig. 4.6 (a) and (b)). This gesture awakens memories of his typical body language, including lively gesticulation during conversation, when he used his salient index finger to authoritatively underscore his points.

In the watercolor, *The Letter of the Law* (1995; Fig. 4.7), the artist used this hand gesture with a tapering, magisterial finger pointing with absolute authority to a reference in a book (Fig. 4.8). Whenever Susanne was in emotional disagreement with her father's logical arguments, his favorite threat and verbal chastisement was the prediction that she "would experience many blows to the neck dispensed by life" ("*Du wirst noch so viele Nackenschläge im Leben erhalten*"), which Susanne translated to imply that "life will punish you."

The repeated prophecy of pending calamities was absorbed by the artist's sensitive mind and unconsciously visualized, for example, in the watercolor *Diplomat's Cocktail* (1987: Fig. 4.9),

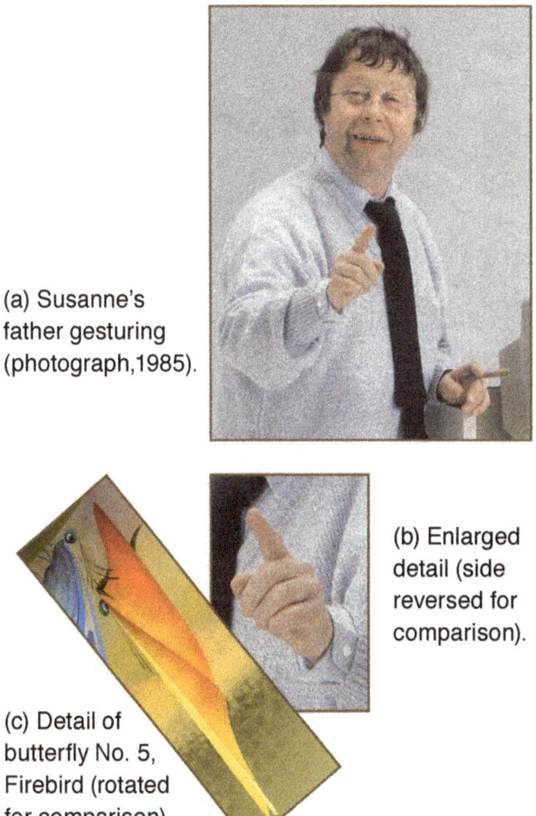

(a) Susanne's father gesturing (photograph,1985).

(b) Enlarged detail (side reversed for comparison).

(c) Detail of butterfly No. 5, Firebird (rotated for comparison).

Figs. 4.6(a)-(c). "Pointing finger": collage for comparison.

16 A commanding height is for Susanne one of the symbols to express power, superiority, and levels of accomplishment.

17 Susanne has only one photograph of her father. It shows him with a raised hand and a pointing finger. She kept this picture for years, long before painting "Firebird."

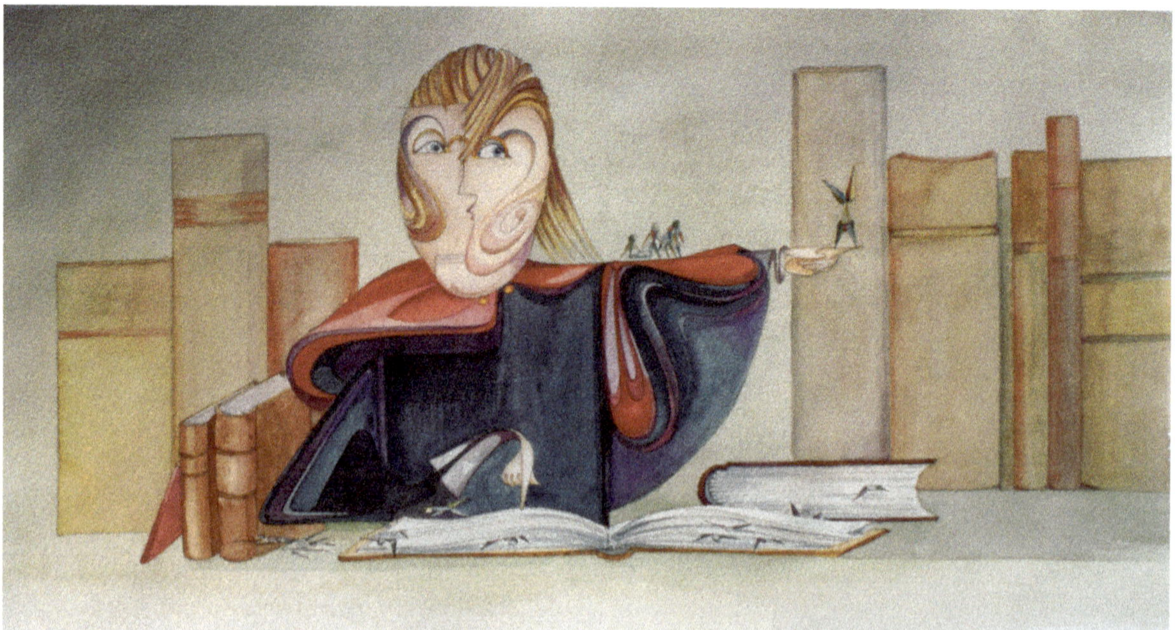

Fig. 4.7. Susanne Schuenke, *The Letter of the Law*, 1995. Watercolor, 13 x 20 in (33 x 50 cm). Private collection, Jacksonville, Florida.

where scissor blades and pointing finger are merged into one threatening configuration. The intriguing politician depicted in the painting looks in the opposite direction, averting his eyes while clipping a thread with his scissors-like fingers, which the artist clearly intended to symbolize the act of severing others' lives.

With this symbolism, Susanne unintentionally ties her design to the Greek goddess of fate, Atropos,[18] whose task is to end a life by cutting its thread with a pair of shears. Susanne knew of the three goddesses of fate from her study of Greek mythology in her youth, but she was not consciously aware of the reference when she was creating the work. A drop of blood running down the side of a cocktail glass confirms this interpretation, alluding to nameless victims. The color of blood is intentionally repeated in the politician's decoration, his dagger-like bow tie, and in the red lettering. The formation of the scissors-like fingers in this watercolor corresponds to a specific detail of Firebird. His front wings split open at the apex, resembling the tips of a barely opened pair of shears. Both particulars could be interpreted as symbols of a lurking threat (Fig. 4.10).

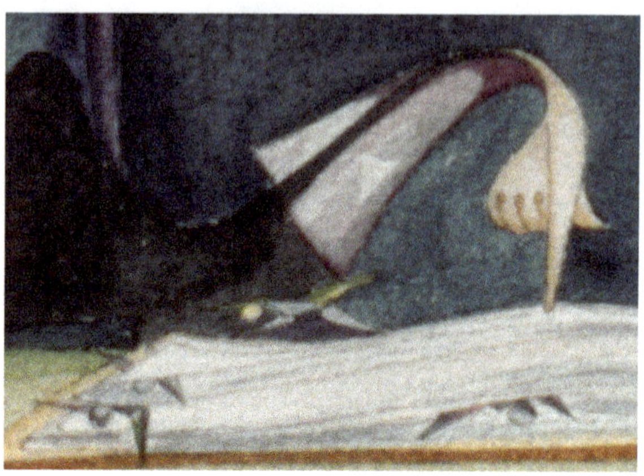

Fig. 4.8. Detail from Fig. 4.7 (note the figures of dead people lying between the pages).

In this context, there is another significant parallel found in the specific trait of Firebird's upper wings' tips. They look like a miniature version of the much larger configuration formed by the two front wings of butterfly No. 2, True Blue. Their appearance is reminiscent of a wide-open pair of scissor blades (see chapter 5). The similar layouts for both butterflies' wings could be perceived as a metaphor for a looming threat. Any sharp configuration, or analogous elongated item harbors a palpable latent threat for Susanne. To observe this, one only needs to aim a pointed object (finger, blade, or even pencil) unexpectedly toward her face or, worse, her navel and watch her panicked reactions.

18 Atropos is the oldest of the three Moirai (the three goddesses of fates).

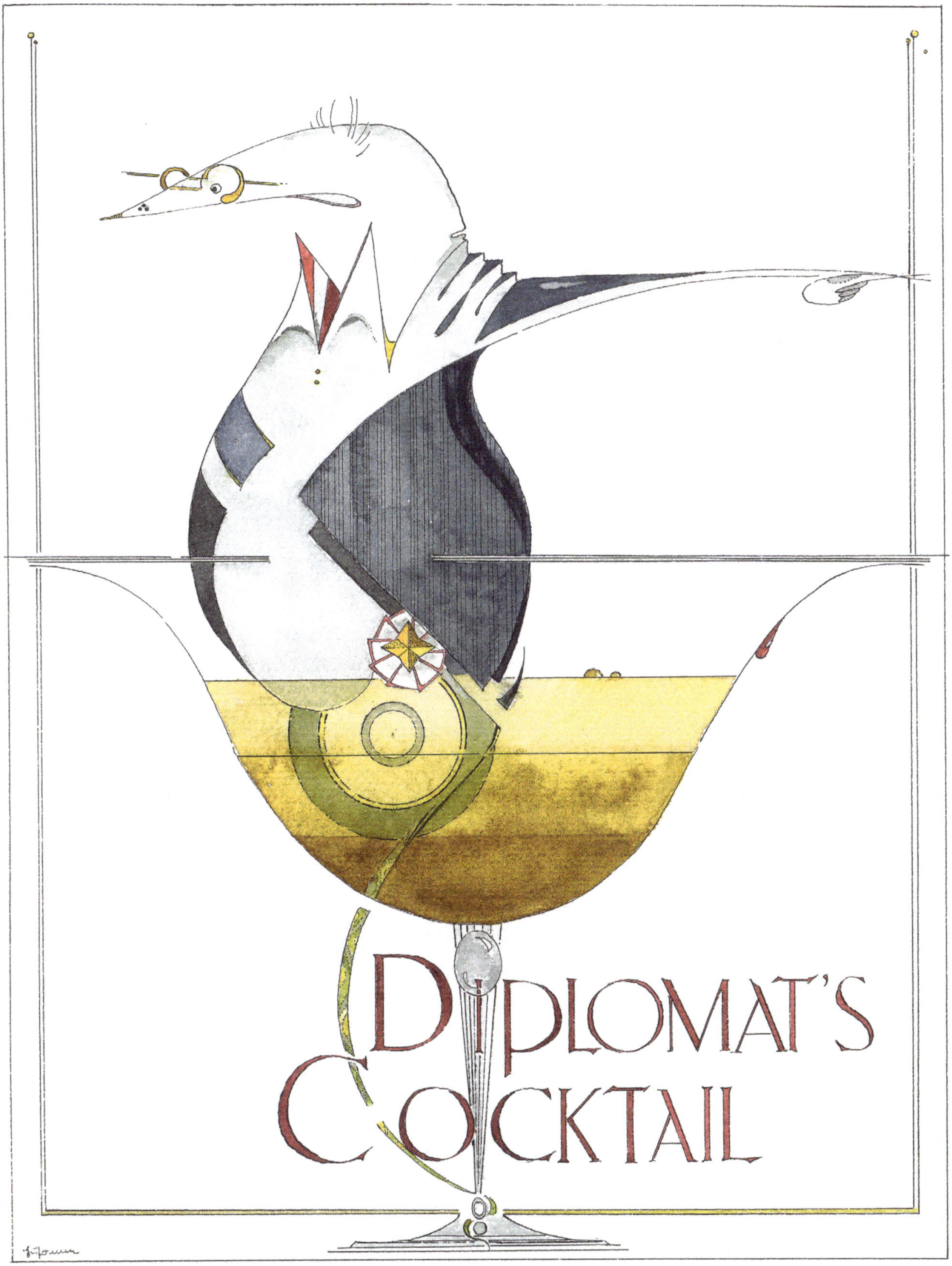

Fig. 4.9. Susanne Schuenke, *Diplomat's Cocktail*, 1987. Watercolor, approx 14 x 11 in (34 x 27 cm). Private collection, Jacksonville, Florida.

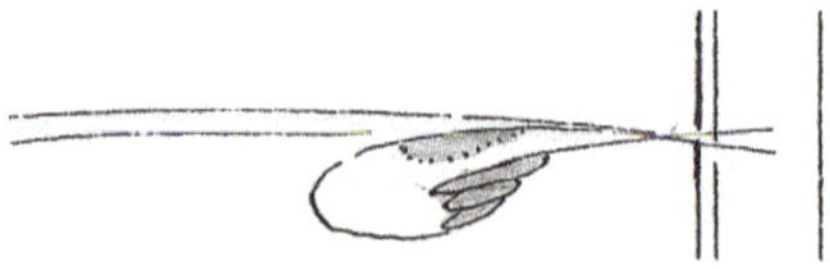

Fig. 4.10. Top: Detail from Fig. 4.9.
Bottom: Firebird's split-open top (for comparison).

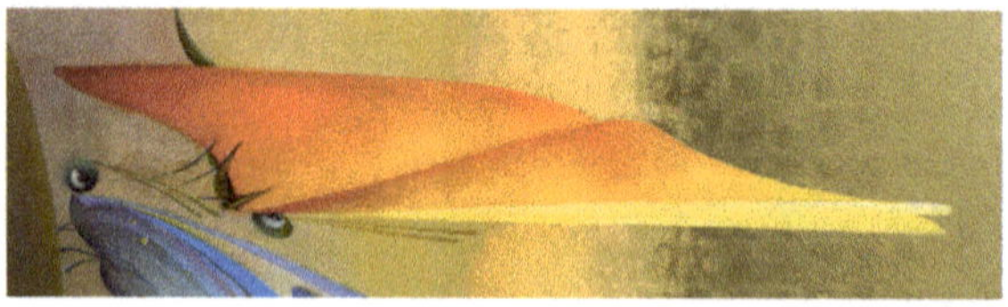

Even if the person merely accidentally points at her with such an object, her response is similar. Most people would react with surprise (changes in facial expression, slight body movements, etc.) to such a sudden move with a pointed object directed at them. Susanne's response is more extreme, manifesting her phobic reaction. Previously in subchapter 4.4.1, we noted that the sharp and spiky objects and configurations were represented by the artist unconsciously as phallic symbolism. The same symbolism, according to the above analysis, could be extended to the autocratic index finger of the father.

The metaphorical meaning of the pointing index finger can be traced back to one of Susanne's early oil paintings, completed two years before *Diplomat's Cocktail*, called *Ideology* (1985, Fig. 4.11). A member of the clergy is depicted with a raised finger in a doctrinaire gesture. In this symbolic bust portraiture, the upper torso is formed by a conglomeration of architecture, including a row of battlements at the top of the figure's shoulder. A closer inspection reveals blood-covered roofs and tracery featuring emblems of numerous dominating ideological concepts, both religious and secular, of the past and present. The cleric's upright index finger terminates with a narrow yellow strip that runs horizontally from the fingertip to the left edge of the painting. With this sharply defined, straight linear shape, the artist intended to express the unyielding stance of a dogmatic extremist. The thin shape appears again, like a ray that originates from his ice-blue eye. His eyes are portrayed with white pupils which remind Susanne of a ghost.

With these particulars, the artist metaphorically conveys her attitude toward a sickened authoritarian power structure and its outdated dogmas and judgments. Moreover, Susanne remembers, when designing the anemic, bluish-pale face combined with turquoise green and light violet hues, colors that are personally repellent to her, she aimed to symbolically underscore the degradation and decadence of a social system that had turned into a lifeless automaton. The sky, once blue on the right side of the painting, has turned dark as a night of persecution. Stick figures climb up the cleric's hand and challenge the authoritarian power. They slip on the oily surface of the upright finger and fall into the abyss, where they join the previous victims whose blood is spread on the ground below. The artist shows the lecturing finger, the piercing cold eyes bare of all emotions, imagining zealous preaching of the dogma, the absolute conviction of his unerring way, and the ardor for punishing those who disobey. We assume the artist integrated her partial perception of her father in this metaphorical portrait 30 years ago at a time of a very negative attitude toward him. She had no inkling that the grotesque attributes that she ascribed to the clergy figure indirectly could also reflect her subjective evaluation of her father in the past.

4.4.3 Hurtful Euphemism: "*Spitze*" versus "*Spritze*"

Continuing the topic of finger-gestures, one of Susanne's father's favorite expressions of praise was to form a circle with his thumb and index finger while pronouncing his judgment: "*Spitze!*" This German expression of high admiration (literally, "top", meaning "top quality") is also a common noun with a wide range of meanings, such as implying tip, peak, apex, point, head, spike, end, and so forth. The word "*Spitze*" happens to sound very much like "*Spritze*," the German term for a syringe, an item loathed by Susanne. This causes all the negative associations evoked by "*Spritze*" and her phobia of syringes and needles to be transferred to "*Spitze*," as a sharp tip. When Susanne's father used the word "*Spitze*" to praise her endeavors, it provoked in her mostly negative reactions, due to its association with "*Spritze*," one of the activators of her phobia. How certain words affected Susanne's mind can be found in a couple of dictionaries she still owns, where, decades ago, she blotted out phobia-inducing words with a black marker, among them, predictably, "*Spritze*."

We can hypothesize that the meanings of some of these words are also metaphorically embedded as unconsciously processed symbolism in specific

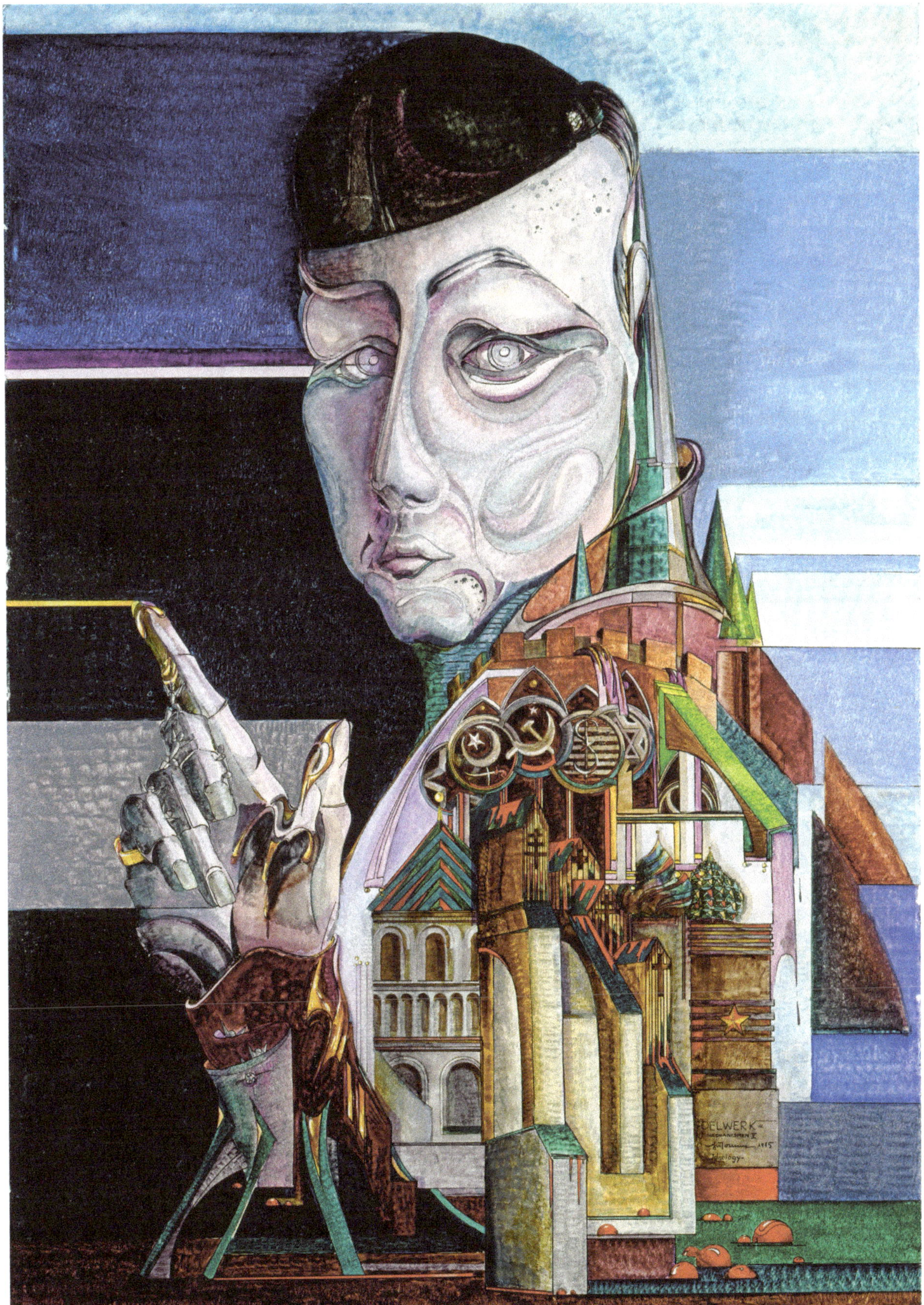

Fig. 4.11. Susanne Schuenke, *Ideology*, 1985. Oil on board, 28 x 20 in (70 x 50 cm). Private collection, North Carolina

configurations of Firebird's imagery: the upper wing tips resemble a pair of scissors, the hind wing is shaped like an index finger, and there are the spidery legs and needlelike antennae.

The artist's sensitivity to assonance has manifested itself in a variety of contexts. Her younger sister seized on this weakness by playing on the similarity in pronunciation between the word "*Puls*" ("pulse" in English)—a phobic word to which Susanne reacted painfully—and the word "*Pilz*" ("mushroom" in English). The sister would torment Susanne while avoiding their mother's admonition by cleverly substituting "*Pilz*" for "*Puls*." In that way, Susanne would respond to the word with a phobic reaction almost as badly as with the real phobic word ("*Puls*").

4.4.4 Spider Legs

In the analysis of Firebird, the recognition that this image represented the father's personality was the watershed moment. Next came the discovery that the specific spiky shapes (scalpel, scissors, pointing finger) of this butterfly harbored metaphorical meanings and could trigger some of the artist's phobias. In the context of sharp objects, Firebird's legs present another surprise in our research. In *Give Me Wings!*, there are only four butterflies out of seven depicted with legs: No. 2, True Blue (father); No. 5, Firebird (also father); No. 6, Fanning Everything (mother); and No. 1, Little Why (Susanne). On close inspection, unlike the other butterflies, the lower segments of Firebird's legs taper to needle-sharp points (Fig. 4.12).

The artist came to realize that this configuration was a close match for a spider (Fig. 4.13), like the one she had portrayed eleven years earlier in a painting titled *The Takeover* (Figs. 4.14 and 4.15). Susanne has been tormented by arachnophobia since her childhood. Spiders horrify her and cause irrational panic and uncontrollable reactions in her when she sees them, regardless of whether they are real or mere images in publications, movies, or paintings.

Despite her phobia, Susanne had rendered that tiny, almost invisible spider[19] from a photograph in the above-mentioned painting, in spite of her feelings of psychological distress. The similarity found in the painted legs of butterfly No. 5 and those of the spider (for comparison, see Figs. 4.12 and 4.13) leads us to a significant insight. If Firebird with his spidery legs is a personification of Susanne's father, then the spider itself could also be construed as a representation of him in her psyche, presumably forming a basis for her arachnophobia.

The unconscious link between the father and the spider could have developed in her childhood, perhaps as early as age nine. Her father used to compare his stratagem against

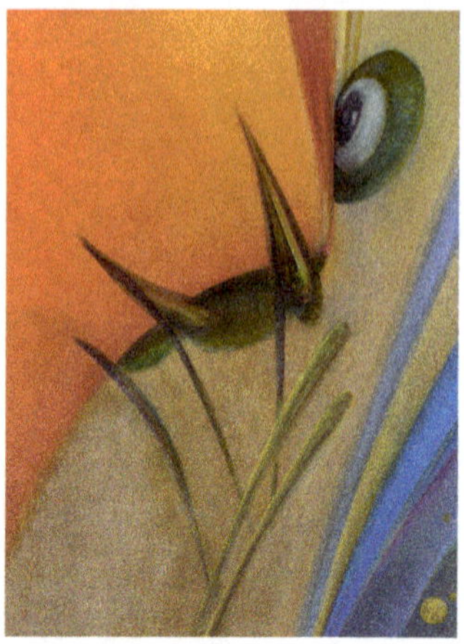

Fig. 4.12. Detail: the legs of butterfly No. 5.

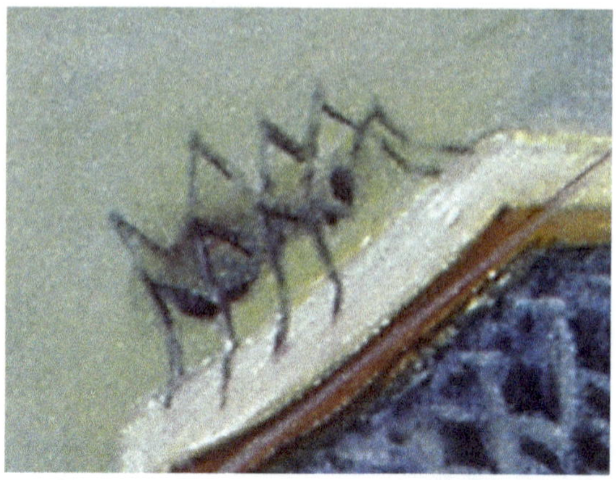

Fig. 4.13. The spider (detail from Figs. 4.14 and 4.15). Size is approx. 300% larger than original.

19 The artist explains that after she had depicted the ground plan of the Pentagon near Washington, D. C. in *The Takeover* (Fig. 4.15 see white arrows), she had the spontaneous association of the line arrangement comparable with a spider web, recognizing the symbolic meaning of it. In this context, she extended this figuration with additional web lines in the center (dashed white arrow in Fig. 4.15) and added a spider close to the bottom left corner of the canvas (the spider is red encircled in Fig. 4.15).

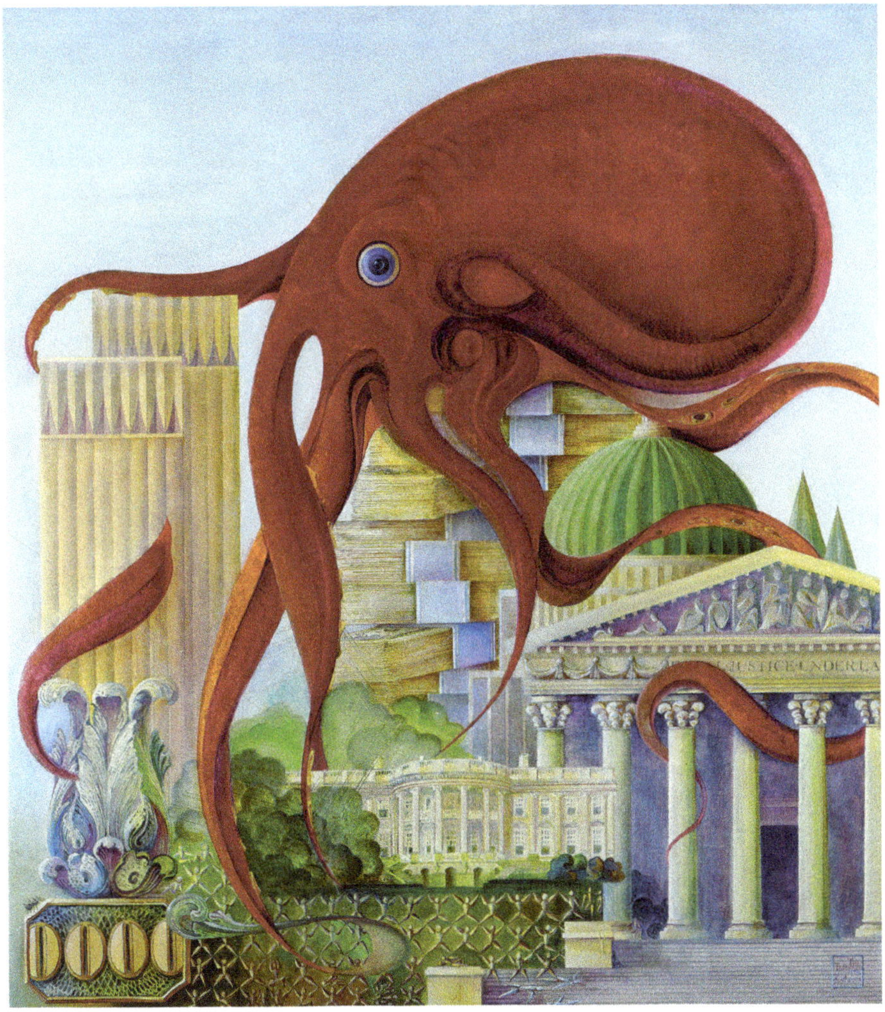

Fig. 4.14. Susanne Schuenke, *The Takeover*, 1997. Oil and palladium leaf on canvas, 44 x 40 in (110 x 100 cm). Corporate collection, Jacksonville, Florida.

his opponents with the weaving of a spider's web. Whenever he succeeded in making his point, he would triumphantly exclaim: "You fell right into it!" His metaphor could have activated Susanne's idiosyncratic imagination which identified herself as a spider's potential prey.[20] As such, the image of the spider became associated with her father. In accordance with transferential aspects rooted in early childhood toward her parent, the suppressed erotic and aggressive fantasies, including incestuous desires for him, could make Susanne's panic attack in the face of spiders explicable. Also, we must take into account the possibility of a conditioned response, acquired through the numerous adverse encounters with her father that her mind had construed to be threatening. The phobic fright of the spider could have become a replacement for the fear of her father.

4.4.5 Extraordinary Potentials and the Shadow Side

The frontal contours of Firebird's wings extend into the golden background with unbending vertical lines; no other butterflies in the group can match this. Although they are tightly closed, the pair of wings still reveal their impressive size. Their coloration exhibits a spectrum that consists of: white, bright yellow, saffron yellow, and glorious orange, radiating their energy in front of a golden background. The metaphoric meaning of these features reflects the artist's perception of her father. Susanne admired him throughout her childhood and youth, and in her adulthood she came to recognize and appreciate his considerable achievements in his profession, where he

20 Susanne loathed the haunting association, imagining to have her head caught in a cobweb and even worst, a spider crawling in her hair. This scenario was a rather realistic possibility to her in the cellar or attic of her parents' home in the past.

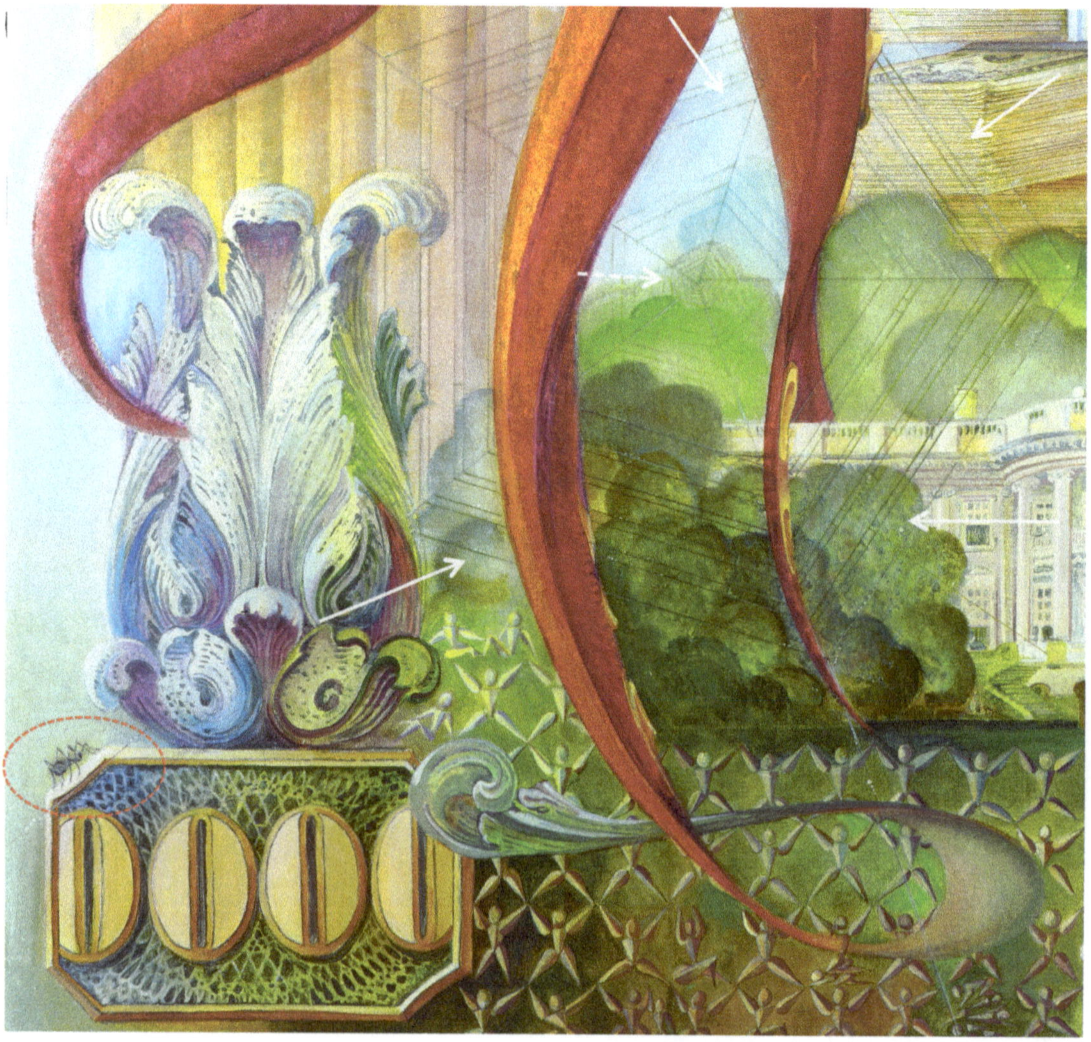

Fig. 4.15. Detail from Fig. 4.14. White arrows point to the Pentagon floor plan; the dashed white arrow points to the spiderweb in the center; encircled in red: spider (enlarged in Fig. 4.13).

displayed a high level of talent, discipline, and creativity as an artist.

Moreover, she saw that her father's personal excellence extended beyond art. She became aware of his wide-ranging and passionate interest in music, various cultural and civil activities, and intellectual discussions on a wide range of topics. He was equally adept at dealing with various organizational and transactional issues in a corporate environment. He also showed a great appreciation for both the wild and cultivated beauty of nature.

In contrast to the virtues and achievements just mentioned, Susanne's father had a shadow side that was dominated by his choleric temper, despotic demands, and intolerance. With this behavior, he gradually detached himself from a once-wide circle of friends and jeopardized his relationship with his wife and daughters. Accordingly, Susanne came to consider that "his enormous range, the potential for the extraordinary, has turned into his greatest deficit, isolating him from the others."[21]

In her opinion, her father's great talent as a painter had never been fully realized. In his long life, Heinz-Günter Schünke created a scant dozen oil paintings, mostly done between his 40th and 60th years, which were never exhibited and thus unknown to the public. This could have given an additional impetus to the shaping of Firebird's wings, with their impressive, folded appearance as an apt metaphor for the artist's father's unrealized potential. He had lacked sufficient opportunity to unfurl his "wings."

21 Poetic commentary

Susanne learned only during her later adult years that her father was full of turmoil and suffering that were rooted in the traumatic experiences of his past, especially the war years spent serving in the German armed forces with lasting consequences. It can scarcely be guessed what might have haunted him, as he was careful to keep his inner torment to himself. He was absolutely tight-lipped about the relationship with his own parents,[22] and he was equally veiled concerning the source of his strange superstitions and his thanatophobia (fear of death). These circumstances might also find their metaphorical illustration in the securely folded wings that do not allow any view inside.

Susanne's father imposed various injunctions on his family members that limited their freedom in relation to a broad range of topics and activities. For example, while bringing up three girls, her parents, led by her father, continuously discouraged their daughters from attempting to leave the tightly knit family circle, and they actively obstructed the children's friendships with their peers. Furthermore, her father's blunt and appalling comments concerning heterosexual friendship made the possibility of dating virtually unthinkable for the daughters. The issue of sexuality itself was very negatively judged by the parents. Susanne's father, in unison with his wife, invariably pushed it immediately into the field of carnal lust and social disgrace, and mostly avoided and suppressed topics pertaining to sexuality in their conversations. However, the parents' collection of the works of other artists contained some paintings and sculptures with sexually charged themes, and his own paintings also depicted outright erotic images.

4.5 The Coloration of Firebird

Firebird appears to be a vividly colored orange butterfly. However, a closer look reveals the complexity of its hues. The rich orange color transitions to a dark brownish tone at the bottom wing tip, while another gradation ascends the upper right wing tip to a pure titanium white. The vertical edge of the right front wing, leading to the top, is painted a light yellow (Fig. 4.2 (1)). Light yellow is also the color of the left front wing that is barely visible behind the right wing. Most of the right front wing and the upper part of the hind wing share the same rich, saffron yellow (Fig. 4.2 (4)). The separating crease area between the right front and right hind wings shows highly saturated orange (Fig. 4.2 (6)), which also dominates much of the hind wing. In the lower part of the hind wing, the color shifts into orange-red brown and terminates in a dark brown at the bottom wing tip.

The seamless transition of hues from light at the top to dark at the bottom is a singular characteristic of Firebird. Mentioned colors are of interpretive importance, as they are laden with potent meaning. The gradation from shining light to gloomy darkness metaphorically reveals the full spectrum of the artist's father's personality as reflected in the imagery of Firebird. The contrast in Firebird's colors serves as the signifier for the peculiarities of this image, which Susanne sees as closely mirroring his choleric temperament. The dramatic differences in the coloration of this butterfly are analogous to the wide spectrum of emotional states of the father—ranging from being amicable (i.e., kind, jovial, and peaceful) to destructive (i.e., angry, hateful, and unjust).[23]

As described in a previous section, we identified the correlation between the hues of butterfly No. 5 and those of molten iron heated in a blast furnace (see section 4.2). Furthermore, the highest temperature, "white heat," was recognized as a metaphor for a person who is "hot with anger." The artist had followed her impulse to whiten the tip of the front wing,[24] and counterbalanced the ascent of the orange into pure white with a descending

22 Susanne never met her paternal grandparents. Her paternal grandmother died before she was born, but, unbeknownst to her, her paternal grandfather lived until she was about 23 years old. It was a great surprise to her when Susanne's mother told her in her early twenties that her paternal grandfather had recently died.

23 From early childhood onward, Susanne observed the frequent inconsistencies in her father's judgments of others. The recipient of his cutting remarks could be a soccer player in a televised game, or a politician speaking in the parliament, etc. To her, his quick change of mind did not seem to be the result of any logical reasoning, but rather the outcome of emotionally charged impulsive reactions toward anything that he disapproved of, or thought erroneous.

24 As far as the artist can remember, the impulse to whiten the tip came while blending the hue of light yellow by adding more and more zinc white to the paint on the canvas. Once she had recognized the significance of the whitish tone at the tip, she consciously enforced it with the purest of white paint available to her in oil paint: titanium white, a completely opaque "immaculate" white.

gradation of the orange into a darker realm. She pondered and finally chose an orange-red brown hue toward the lower end of the hind wing. This selection of colors and the need to balance them might have been rooted in the artist's unconscious, as the highly contrasting "light and dark" coloration is one of the signifiers denoting personification of her father in Firebird's imagery.

In this context, the analyst asked, why did the artist not end the lower tip of Firebird in black instead of "dark brown"? Her first association in answering this question was that black would be unbearable for her, being too extreme in its uncompromising negativity. The rejection of pure darkness could be considered as Susanne's implicit assessment of Firebird (as personification of her father). Blackness did not reflect the full spectrum of the father's character.

We assume that the artist unconsciously repressed black as a choice and settled for darker tints of red-brown orange, including a specific hue called "burnt orange." The unconscious symbolism signified by this hue of orange in Susanne's paintings will be further explored when we analyze Pale Moonlight's "glimpses of burnt orange" in chapter 8, and in Air in chapter 10. The future discussions of the hue "burnt orange" as a reflection of the realm of biological drives in subsequent chapters (see subchapters 8.2.5 and 10.6) help us to understand the basis of the unconscious preferences and selection of hues, as we have begun to recognize this in analysis of specific colorations of Firebird.

As we have noted previously, Susanne has her personal preferences for colors. For example, she considers saffron yellow a sympathetic tone, very different from the cold lemon-yellow used in butterfly No. 1, Little Why (see chapter 6). Saffron yellow, known in oil painting terminology as Indian Yellow, has a strong association with the Buddhist faith for Susanne, due to the saffron-colored robes that the monks wear. This deep yellow hue carries for her positive meaning—a sense of admiration. It could reflect the daughter's respect and affection for the father. However, in her artistic sensibilities, Susanne tries very hard to avoid saffron yellow shifting into orange, for she does not like orange ("garish"). Her first impression of orange is "ugly," and she has often consciously employed this hue in her palette as a negative color, symbolizing threat and danger.

An example of the artist's established attitude toward orange is her painting *Terminator* (1985, Fig. 4.16) which depicts a modern-day warrior with an orange helmet and inhuman eyes, utilizing the same negative color. Looking at this picture, Susanne recalls what she had associated with the orange hue in this painting. In the late 1960s, she learned in school about Agent Orange, one of the defoliants used during the Vietnam War, and how it devastated the Vietnamese countryside and adversely affected the health of the people who were exposed to it. (See also page 195.)

Aside from this association, it should be noted that orange is widely used throughout the world as the preferred color for signage to warn of potential dangers. It is a relatively common usage of the color, which Susanne's mind may have adopted in her chromatic iconography to indicate something ominous. Regarding Susanne's selections of the color scheme for *Give Me Wings!*, she does not remember having any explicit intention to denote a negative significance in this painting when she chose orange "for compositional reasons" in the watercolor version (as mentioned in chapter 2). Only when Susanne began to darken the coloration in the upper part of the hind wing (Fig. 4.2 (7 and 8)) and the back edge of the right front wing (the area of "fold," Fig. 4.2 (6 and 8)), she perceived these hues as menacing tints, intuitively sensing them as anxiety-inducing colors that signaled lurking dangers. Then, she modified coloration of the lower bottom of this wing into "orange-red brown" and "dark brown" (Fig. 4.2 (9 and 10)). The artist perceived these two chromatic nuances as even more negative, judging them as particularly muddy, ugly, and threatening.

Across human cultures, a full range of orange colors has been used for various symbolic expressions, and those hues, to which Susanne displays such marked antipathy, could well be pleasing to others. In her personal view, the spectrum of orange is different. By some conscious and unconscious determination, she associates these tones with threatening aspects of existence. These hues, together with the imagery's details, reveal significant unconscious content. As noted above, in the context of the hostile spiky wing shape combined with orange-red brown, it becomes apparent that this butterfly's outline could remind Susanne of her father's index finger,

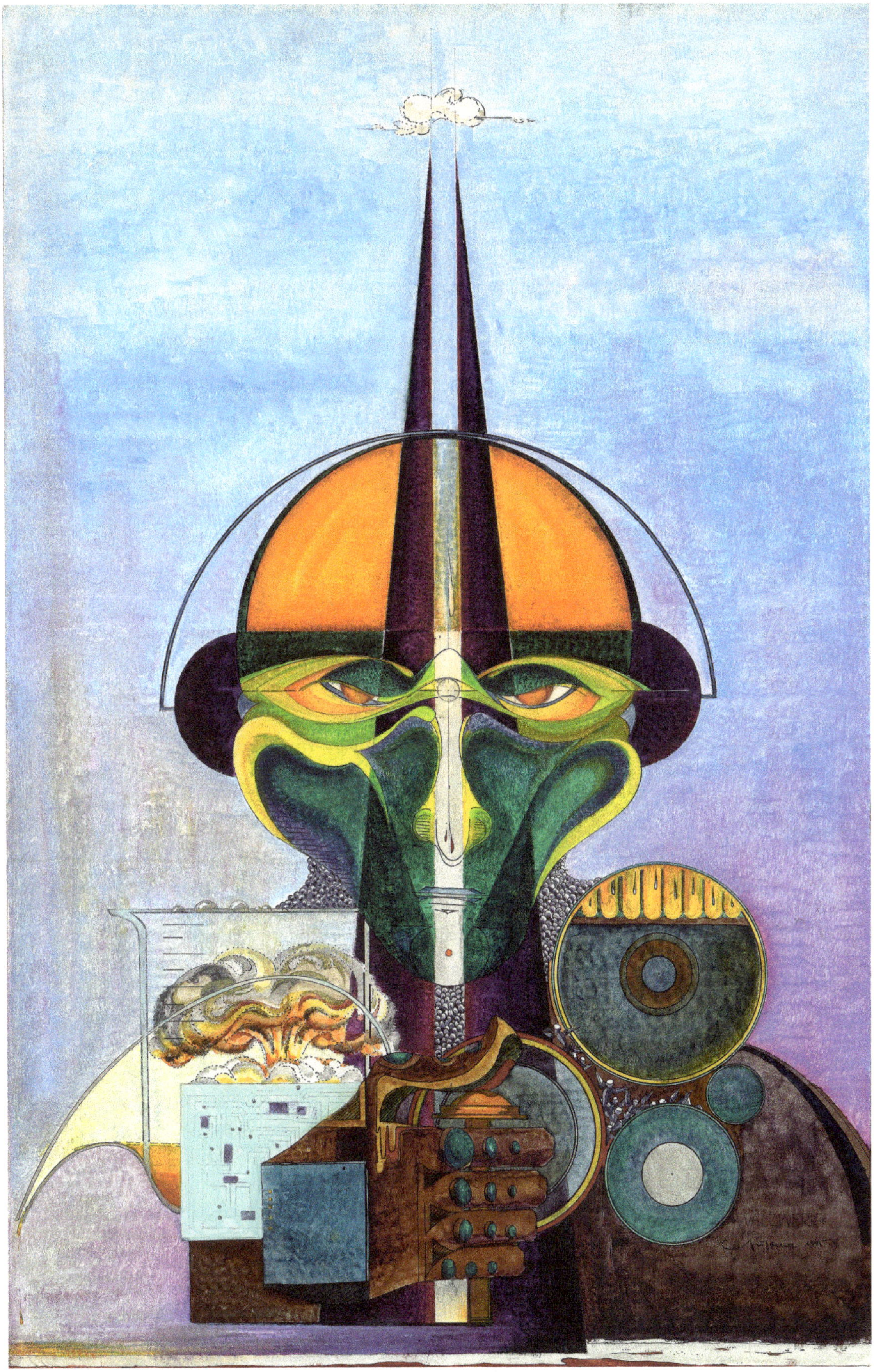

Fig. 4.16. Susanne Schuenke, *Terminator* (*War*), 1985. Oil on board, 24 x 16 in (60 x 41 cm). Collection of the artist.

often aggressively pointed at her during heated family discussions. Thus, the lower region of the wings—shaded in a perilous "burnt orange," "orange-red brown," and "dark brown"—becomes a metaphorical analogy of the father's highly charged, barely restrained parental aggression, epitomized by his pointed finger.

These frightening and emotionally upsetting signs from the patriarch of the family were instilled and incorporated permanently into Susanne's psyche. Hence, for her, the sight of a "pointing finger," as well as needles, pens and pencils, knives, syringes, and other pointed objects suggestive of cuts, punctures, and bloodletting might have become triggers for different phobias. Furthermore, we conjecture that the "index finger" became a metonymic reference to the ever-present influence of the father himself in her mind constituting unconscious symbolism with latent sexual and aggressive undertones. The shades of colors—combined with this specific, pointing form—echo and reinforce the strength of the message from the artist's unconscious.

4.6 Identification

We have argued that the details of Firebird's forms and his wide color range match Susanne's father's personal characteristics quite well. Some of these attributes, symbolized in this butterfly's imagery, are also applicable in describing the artist's own temperament and tendencies. During a detailed analysis of the butterfly, the artist reluctantly admitted that she, too, shared some of Firebird's qualities and, by extension, of her father, represented by this butterfly.

The artist's specific similarities with the father's personality could show, beside the genetic predisposition, the importance of his example on the formation of her character, setting some of her behavior patterns. It seems apparent that many facets of her father's character were imprinted through significant emotional experiences in his interactions with her. Our analysis of the traces of the unconscious, as manifested in the imagery of *Give Me Wings!*, particularly of Firebird, offers insights into Susanne's personality and tendencies (see chapters 6, 8, and 9). The daughter's strong attachment to the father in childhood was like "a hotbed"[25] for Susanne to acquire many of the habits, behavior patterns, and proclivities of his individuality.

The impact of her father's influence on Susanne is further substantiated when we evaluate the implications of the details, separately and together, of Firebird and True Blue (butterfly No. 2—another personification of the father). Furthermore, the details that are correlative between these two butterflies are also shared with some of the other butterflies personifying Susanne (see chapters 6, 8, 9, and part of chapter 7) in their essential metaphoric meaning. This confirms the presence of the psychological process of identification symbolically expressed by the forms, colors, and composition of the painting.

Susanne's father imparted his attitudes toward the world at large and his ethical and principled judgments concerning specific issues of daily life to the family. The child's early perceptions were mostly dominated by his worldview. He was the "creator of her universe," and she absorbed his explanations, ideas, and aspirations without question.

Her parents did their best to direct Susanne's socialization process by instilling in her the appropriate patterns of behavior and attitudes that would meet the expectations of society. Rules, concepts, mores, customary behaviors, and appropriate attitudes were instilled in the child's mind. The father's authority, and his beliefs and rules gradually tightened into a tailor-made suit that she wore to promote her social and professional success in the way he saw fit. Susanne's world was mainly "father-made," one which she was expected to conform with according to its maker's rules and expectations.

The artist was once described by a family friend as the true "son of her father"—an acute observation likely based on Susanne's streaks of *animus* behavioral patterns. The overlapping similarities between father and daughter were very strong in Susanne's childhood. All of her life her family has recognized this. The father's enormous influence on her was confirmed by the relatively objective assessment of her close friends. Our study contends that her unconscious mind channeled, displaced, and coded this impact into an ample variety of images, personal symbols, and metaphors

25 It is interesting to observe that when constructing this sentence, Susanne suggested replacing "basis" with "hotbed." As a child, Susanne slept in her parents' bed from time to time until the age of eight. The strong possibility of the unconscious implications of the use of this term by her cannot be ignored.

that are found in her paintings. In the following chapters, we will continue our study by analyzing how a rich spectrum of parental influences is metaphorically embedded into the details of other butterflies' images.

In summary, this chapter has shown that analysis of the shape, size, color, and relative position of butterfly No. 5 reveals multiple connections between Firebird's visual attributes and Susanne's perception of the personality traits of her father. The artist's poetic commentary contributes greatly to this assessment, as we find many relevant hints and supporting statements in her verbal presentation that correspond with the visual imagery of the painting. The close observation of the details of the painting, along with the analysis of the commentary, gives us sufficient "forensic" evidence to form a reasonably coherent case that butterfly No. 5 is a metaphorical portrait of her father, which the artist drew and painted under the influence of her unconscious.

Upon considering Firebird as a personification of her father, the artist was amazed at how the various details from her past experiences, memories, and perceptions were condensed into the images of the painting, and into the words of the poetic commentary as well. Every detail from the image of Firebird was found to carry specific meanings, expressed by the artist unconsciously in a metaphorical manifestation of her father's multi-faceted personality, as well as her attitude toward and perception of him. An abundance of clues discovered through the process of analysis proves to us the existence of the deep connection to the past that the artist still retains. The imagery of the painting metaphorically corroborates the process of identification as a signifier of parental influence.

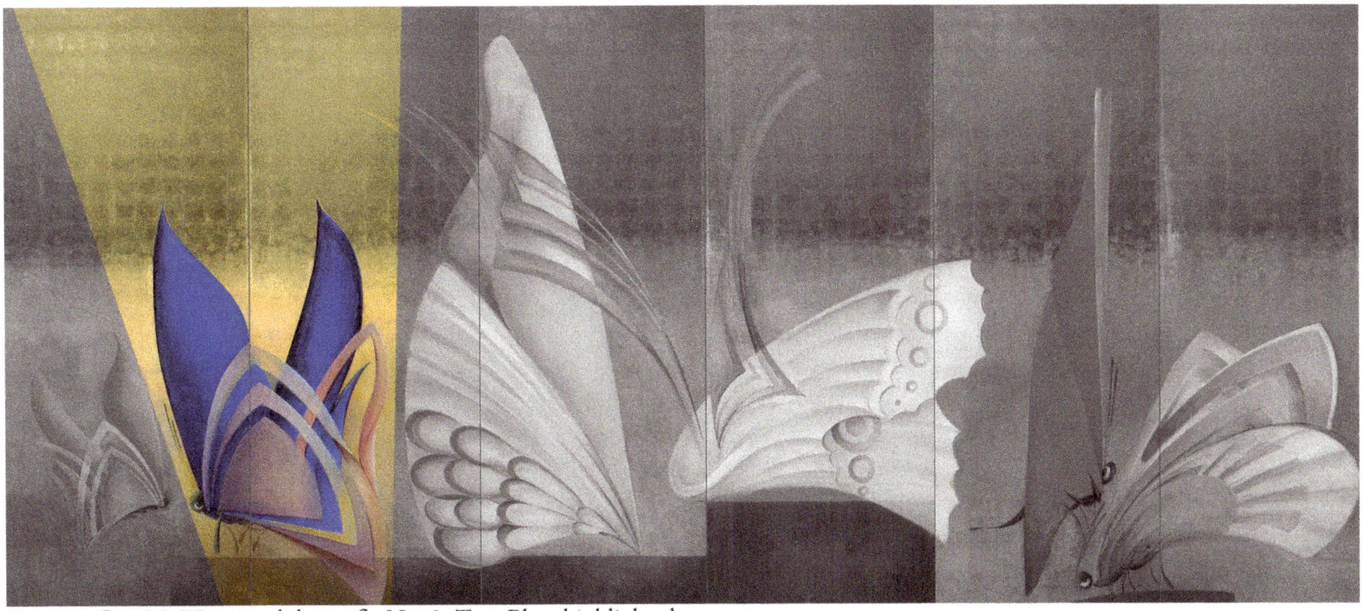

Fig. 5.0. *Give Me Wings!* with butterfly No. 2, True Blue, highlighted.

... True Blue ... his adapted Aloofness and Royalty ... sapphire glow ... True Blue relies on status to declare the status quo, defending his territory, governs the richness and the options, the rules and the enforcements, the system, and its holiness.

—From the artist's poetic commentary, 2004

Chapter 5

The Grandiose **Butterfly No. 2 — True Blue**

But it is not true

5.1. The Name

The artist considers butterfly No. 2, True Blue, with his impressive blue wings, to be the most striking figure among the assembly of butterflies, dominating the viewer's first impression of the painting (Fig. 5.0), even upstaging Firebird. The brilliant coloration of the blue morpho species had been for her the all-compelling color she had seen on her visit to the butterfly conservatory in New York. After having been inspired by observing the natural models, Susanne brought the butterfly's hue to its strongest, most exuberant realization by applying pure ultramarine, an intensively energetic shade of blue. She chose butterfly No. 2 as the first of the seven butterflies to be colored in the watercolor painting. Susanne desired to represent the enchanting chromatic quality of the blue morpho butterfly in her painting. With the use of modern synthetic ultramarine paint, she had the means to closely imitate the dazzling beauty of the natural model. Therefore, the word "true" as a modifier for "blue" in the butterfly's name might have been inspired by all the magnificence of the morpho species that was transferred onto the majestic appearance of True Blue as an assumed projection of the image of the father. This impression was emphasized verbally in the poetic commentary.

Witnessing the shimmering iridescence of the butterfly at the conservatory was a deeply fascinating experience for Susanne. At the beginning of our study, we assumed that her excitement in seeing the splendid blue morpho in nature could have formed the basis for her choice of coloration for butterfly No. 2. However, further analysis revealed that the artist's actual perception at the conservatory was also affected by the unconscious reactivation of emotionally significant experiences from her past (see subchapter 5.3). This realization was invaluable in clarifying why the artist felt the need to associate the word "blue" with the adjective "true" in the name. "True" is an important part of the sobriquet, and the analysis of its latent meaning in this butterfly's appearance will turn out to be an exploration full of surprises, with many unforeseen twists and turns.

First, the artist's choice of the adjective "true," which adds a certain value judgment to the color and the name, could have been influenced by her knowledge of the natural ultramarine (*ultramarinus*, a medieval Latin word for "beyond the sea," alluding to the main ingredient of the paint "coming from far away") that was traditionally obtained from grinding the gemstone lapis lazuli into genuine ultramarine pigment. For centuries in European art, this was the most expensive blue pigment. There had been times when ultramarine was worth its weight in gold. In many records of painter's contracts with their patrons prior to the nineteenth century, the expenses for ultramarine were listed separately from their overall work and were closely scrutinized to prevent the use of a cheaper substitute pigment.

Since 1826, nearly all ultramarine paint pigments have been synthetically produced, giving their vivid chromatic hues an intensity far superior to the gemstone-based pigments, while costing considerably less. However, the traditionally admired natural ultramarine remains in Susanne's hierarchy of color values at near the top rank. This coloration encapsulates an unconditional attitude and signifies absolute trustworthiness.

Secondly, Susanne's preference for ultramarine among the blue hues is rooted not only in her interest in art history but also in her personal fascination with the starry night sky, which she has depicted in many of her artworks as small details or large backgrounds. For representing the dark depths of interstellar space, she chooses ultramarine blue as the dominant color, often combining and reinforcing it with a variant of ultramarine-violet to bolster the impression of the cosmos's infinite extent. Taken in the context of its literal meaning ("beyond the sea"), "ultramarine" alludes to a vast distance. Figuratively, the artist has often used this color to depict some unfathomable aspects of the universe in her art, for example, the sky studded with stars.

We may remark, Susanne's attraction to the dark depths of the universe and its artistic realization in the chromatic metaphor of ultramarine might have its origin in one of her fantasies from her youth. She dreamed of traversing the vast distances of intergalactic space, prompted by the inexplicable urge to "go home to the stars," particularly to the star systems in the constellation of Orion (we will have more to say on this topic in chapters 9 and 10). As an adult, she came to recognize that her childish fantasy was a beautiful illusion. Nevertheless, she does not completely dismiss such fantasizing as delusional. This daydreaming leaps radically beyond the rational mind. However, by fully immersing in the flight of imagination, she allows her "unreasonable" thoughts and perceptions to be expressed in the images of her paintings without constraints.

Thirdly, in European art before the nineteenth century, natural ultramarine was used traditionally for the robes of the Blessed Virgin Mary, an outstanding example of which is found in the Wilton Diptych (circa 1395) at the National Gallery in London. Susanne knows this painting well from her numerous visits to the museum, and she counts it as one of her personal favorites amongst many artworks she has come to appreciate. Another influential experience with ultramarine occurred when the whole family visited the Mauritshuis, an art museum specializing in Dutch painting from the Golden Age in The Hague, Netherlands. Here Susanne shared the experience of seeing Jan Vermeer's *The Girl with a Pearl Earring*[1] with her father, who told her that this portrait was one of his favorite artworks. The canvas features a girl in a prominent headscarf that is painted in a strikingly natural ultramarine.

Lastly, her father was fond of using ultramarine regularly for a strong, clear blue in his paintings (for example, *The Street,* Fig. 8.38). This might have played a part in Susanne's creating the term "True Blue" for butterfly No. 2 as an unconscious metaphorical manifestation of a specific meaning connected with the father. It could indicate Susanne's projected ideal of her father as a good, desirable, brilliant, successful, and invincible parent, which correlates with the artist's

1 Jan Vermeer (1632–1675). The painting is assumed to have been created around 1665.

childhood idealization of him in real life. In this context, he is a "true father" which is analogous to the psychoanalytic concept of the "good father."[2] During a session with an American editor, both authors learned that the term "true blue" is used traditionally in English since the 17th century to describe an individual with unwavering loyalty to a person or belief. Although it is startling how closely this meaning matches the unconscious message in butterfly No. 2, we consider it as probably coincidental, since Susanne had no knowledge of this figure of speech.

The artist presents the visual image of a butterfly that, together with her references to such phrases as "sapphire glow" and "adapted Aloofness and Royalty" in the poetic commentary, clearly creates the perception of True Blue as an all-powerful figure in the eyes of the butterfly Little Why. This is in accordance with how Susanne as a child perceived her idolized father. In the depicted grandeur of True Blue, as expressed by his position in composition and dominant color, we recognize a characterization of the artist's father and the hierarchical situation that existed in the family.

Like most West German citizens, he and his wife had to start with literally nothing in the years following World War II, and they truly achieved their financial independence and upper middle class social status through their professional success in the field of graphic design. With a record of solid accomplishments, he sometimes displayed his sense of self-pride by engaging in boastful exaggerations.

In creating the sobriquet for butterfly No. 2, the artist vacillated between "True Blue" and "Royal Blue"; she even tried "True Royal Blue," but the name was eventually deemed too pompous. She abandoned "royal" as part of the name, although kept this association by using "royalty" to describe True Blue in the poetic commentary, reflecting on her father's public reputation as exhibiting a multifaceted and lofty persona. Susanne remembers that sometimes, especially when the father acted in too grand a manner, her mother would call him the "big show maker," or she would acquiesce to his bidding with barely concealed sarcasm: "You are the king." This further strengthens our interpretation that True Blue is a personification of the father. Since Susanne as a child and teenager placed her father on such a high pedestal, the epithet "royal" would have also been appropriate to describe him.

However, during analysis, Susanne made the following spontaneous comment: "Grandiose Butterfly No. 2, True Blue, but it is not true!"—which was later used as a subtitle for this chapter. This remark appears to contradict our prior assertion that True Blue metaphorically represented only a "good father." With this comment, the artist unconsciously not only reiterated her childhood admiration for her father but also mixed it with the painful emotional experiences that she had with him. That made us wonder what the word "true" in the butterfly's name really meant. We began to examine how much of this adulatory modifier "true" was not actually true. As we proceeded, we found a surprising confirmation of the contradictory nature of True Blue's name in the peculiarities of the butterfly's image, which are metaphorically congruent with her father's personality and Susanne's perception of him.

5.2 Details of True Blue and Their Metaphorical Meaning

Butterfly No. 2, True Blue, is presented in left profile, almost turning away from the observer and facing butterfly No. 1, Little Why, who takes up a spot at the left margin of the painting. He towers over Little Why, being approximately twice her height, and occupies the left end of the elongated platform with his hind wings partially hanging over the podium. Due to his overwhelming chromatic energy that dominates the scene, True Blue is the focal point of the left half of the painting.

There are some significant details in the structure of the front and hind wings of butterfly No. 2:

- The sharpness (front wings)
- The cut-out design (hind wings)
- The thorny spike (right front wing)
- The flip-over effect (both hind wings' outer frame elements)

In the ensuing subchapters, we will discuss and try to interpret these surreal details (Fig. 5.1) of butterfly No. 2 in the context of their possible metaphorical and symbolical meanings.

2 Melanie Klein 1975, page 223.

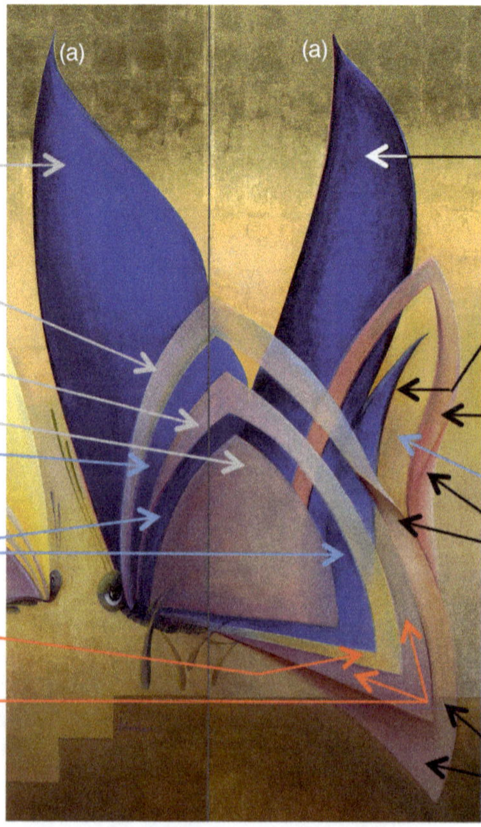

Fig. 5.1 Butterfly No. 2, True Blue.

5.2.1 The Sharpness of the Front Wings

The contours of True Blue's front wings are drawn out upward into tapering, needle-sharp points, which contrast with the golden background (Fig. 5.1(a)). The boldly designed wings are shaped as prolonged, slightly curved formations, like a pair of knife blades or open scissors. A comparable configuration (i.e., like a pair of unfolded scissors) can be observed at the top of butterfly No. 5, Firebird (a personification of the artist's father; see Fig. 4.2 (a)), although in much smaller proportions. Furthermore, the same characteristic shapes can be found in the wingtips of Little Why (which is a personification of Susanne as a child), but they stand out much less against the beige color of the foggy background, and their tapering end points are not so sharply pronounced (for the interpretation, see chapter 6). In another personification of Susanne (butterfly No. 4, Touchless Misty), the butterfly's sickle-shaped wing contour gives a serrated appearance to its image (Fig. 9.7), but its sharpness is considerably less striking than the wingtips of True Blue.

As Susanne was typing the above paragraph, it became obvious that she was suffering intense discomfort. Her facial expressions of disgust and fear were accompanied by hand and body movements that seemed to be trying to protect different parts of her face and body from an imaginary threat. On being asked what had happened and to write it down, Susanne blurted out sounds of fear and words of protest, expressing her desire to escape from the situation in which she found herself. She informed the analyst with great reluctance that she was in the grip of one of her "horror visions,"[3] which involve sharp objects—knives, blades, glass shards—attacking her tongue, eyes, wrists, breasts, or abdomen with threatening consequences.

This episode demonstrates that sharp configurations frightening for her. The content of the vision indicates idiosyncratic sensitivities, which could encapsulate expectations of destructive actions. As mentioned in chapter 4, Susanne had unlimited access to the parents' studio and its

3 Although the artist calls these overwhelming and involuntary imaginations "horror visions," she does not have a vivid visualization of them in her mind when they are triggered.

implements from very early childhood. The tools that they used were not only pencils and brushes, but also sharp cutting knives, razor blades, and pairs of scissors.

Recalling the details of those tender years evokes associations of positive emotions in Susanne. She was close to her parents and allowed to draw and play in their immediate presence. Nevertheless, such recollections include the items that might have triggered Susanne's horror visions. We assume her imaginary scenarios of being assaulted could be grounded in the actualization of her early childhood's repressed tendencies that are likely embedded in fantasies with aggressive content, of which we have only glimpses. She remembers in her teen years an abhorrence toward her mother's best kitchen knives, which were old but had very sharp spotted steel blades. She would sometimes hide those implements from her mother, whose patience was tested as she searched for them. These were also the years during which Susanne had to undergo multiple ear surgeries which were highly traumatic experiences for her.

Sharp blades are associated in Susanne's mind with the guillotine, which reminds her again of her father's choice phrase signaling his explicit disagreement with his daughter during some of their heated debates. As introduced in the previous chapter, his dubious prophetic pronouncement to Susanne was, "You will still receive many blows to the neck in your life." Susanne imagined often that these "blows to the neck," which her father promised, would be delivered by a hand acting like a blade on a person's neck. This was probably her own visualization because she saw this karate-like movement only as an adult in the movies. The father's repeated dark predictions built up appropriate expectations. The memories of them hold the potential for triggering her subjectively developed visions of the reification. The threatening sharpness of the shapes lurking in butterfly True Blue, which is akin to that of Firebird, could be linked symbolically to the facets of her father's personality, marking Susanne's conscious and unconscious perception of him. For example, the honed blade of True Blue's front wings could signify the father's sharp tongue "cutting" his interlocutor metaphorically with the choice of hurtful, even sometimes deeply insulting words.[4] Her father's aggressive verbal assaults left their imprint on Susanne's psyche. Following his model, she is quite capable of turning a sharp tongue on any adversary. Her imitative behavior could be based on her own latent inclinations, as well as her unconscious identification with her father as aggressor. These kinds of situations predispose Susanne to have her pent-up anger and aggression explode in the open. But most times, she suppresses this reaction.

Throughout her adult years, Susanne has been beset by involuntary daydreaming, when threatening thoughts of potential dangers have captivated her mind with speculations that often led to a cataclysmic fantasy. She imagines the deaths of innumerable people and the devastation of a widespread area brought about accidentally or intentionally by different causes. This destructiveness has no apparent rationale for its actualization. Her imagination could be due to the presence of the instinctual aggressive drive, which is rooted in her psyche and whose origin might go back to the universal unconscious with its differentiation through the evolutionary process. Susanne is ashamed of these destructive fantasies, and she wishes to be free of them, particularly the sense of guilt that lingers afterward.

As a child, Susanne was immersed in fantasies and reveries, in which she fabricated various situations and games, imagining having personal power over others and exercising it freely, often in oppressive ways. She still remembers that she was able to conjure up on demand various images by just closing her eyes. But as she grew up, according to the artist's vague memory, she lost this ability, perhaps before or around the age of ten. However, during the last few years, this "inner seeing" has begun to return, although only rarely and unpredictably.

When Susanne is quite upset, sometimes she fantasizes scenes of her death and the probable reactions of her family members and friends. During a discussion concerning these episodes, she also recollected an exceptional fantasy from

4 A couple of examples of her father's peculiar, acerbic sense of humor can be mentioned here. In arguing with her father, Susanne would often start by saying in her defense, "I only thought … ," which would usually be retorted by the father with, "You should leave the thinking for the horses because they have bigger heads than you!" Another typical criticism was "You are as stupid as the cow on Sunday," which was a typical expression of disapproval unleashed by him for Susanne's failure at a task.

her childhood, when she speculated about what would happen if she had been responsible for the simultaneous deaths of her parents.[5]

Most of these involuntary fleeting thoughts of death and destruction involved anonymous, faceless victims and equally unspecific localities. Such fantasies were very disturbing for her. To this day, they continue to be a burden. Whenever such fantasies occur, she applies different mental techniques to think of something positive.

To sum up, the blade-like front wings with their pronounced sharp tips, embedded in her artistic designs, can be considered Susanne's personal iconography of aggressive tendencies (unconscious symbolism). They reflect various facets of her father's personality and his periodically aggressive behavior as well as her identification with him as an aggressor. They also signify her own repressed aggressive drives in the different periods of her life. We will revisit the topic of sharpness as a symbol of aggression in chapter 9.

5.2.2 The Cut-out Design of the Hind Wings

The configuration of True Blue's left hind wing is made up of three segments: an "outer frame element," a "middle frame element," and an "inner element" (Fig. 5.1 (b, c, and d)). As the artist imagined it, the transparent areas ("see through" spaces, Fig. 5.1 (e and f)) of the wing are caused by those sections having been "cut out." The three remaining segments are what is left after the "removal" procedure. They all share the same pointed-arch shape and are nested together, separated by the empty spaces between them. Toward the bottom right hand corner of the left wing, we can observe that the middle frame element seems to have dissolved and, in its place, the foggy background can be seen (Fig. 5.1(i)). Next to it, the outer "see-through" space (Fig. 5.1(e)) appears to be solid toward the bottom. We notice a texture, which suggests that this zone is no longer empty space (Fig. 5.1(g)). The overall arrangement of the wing reminds us of openwork, where the presence of the openings is an integral element of the artwork, which resembles a typical Gothic window with its pointed arch and tracery design. We assume that this openwork configuration of the butterfly may have been created in accordance with the artist's extensive knowledge of medieval architecture, which she acquired as part of her doctoral studies. Her unconscious creative mind, expressing a specific symbolic message, might have transfigured a Gothic design into that of True Blue's left wing.

Turning our attention to the right hind wing, we find that it also has an anatomical defect. It has been drastically hollowed out and only an outer frame element remains (Fig. 5.1(j)). Because this outer element surrounds the thorny spike of the right front wing like a frame, the emptiness of the right hind wing might easily go unnoticed at a cursory glance (to identify this appearance in question, see Fig. 5.1 (j), (k), and (l)). Obviously, both hind wings are cut out to the point that butterfly No. 2 cannot be expected to fly. Thus, despite its overall majestic look, we may consider True Blue to be injured and severely handicapped, which could well be the unconscious message behind the creation of a dysfunctional wing configuration.

The anatomical deficiency of True Blue's hind wings could be appropriately correlated with some details of her father's biographical background as far as those were known to Susanne. Her father, Heinz-Günter Schünke, was born in Dortmund, Germany, in 1924 as the second son in a family of six children to an unbearably choleric and despotic father. As the second child, Susanne's father lived in the shadow of his older brother and was often mocked and bullied for his short stature and disproportionately large head.

He was totally devoted to his mother, and when she died in her early 50s, the loss was devastating. At the age of 16, he was drafted into the army and sent immediately to the Eastern Front in World War II as a soldier serving in the tank corps. He was severely wounded twice, but he recovered well enough to be sent back to the Eastern Front. In 1945, he became a prisoner of war in a British camp for a short period. Susanne recollects that her father rarely talked about his experience in the war, other than mentioning occasionally his war scars gave him pains. His wartime experience made him a fervent pacifist, and he forbade his

5 This particular fantasy involved a "what if" scenario, in which Susanne had taken her father's rifle to carry out the fantasized violence. The weapon had been acquired by her father with the specific permit to hunt muskrats (ondatra zibethicus) that were causing damage to the banks of the lakes on the family's property. In reality, however, the rifle was secured under lock and key by her father.

family members from handling any weapons. Susanne was given so little information about her father's past that it took her several decades to understand her mother's cryptic remarks, which she heard as a child about his inability to carry a suitcase[6] or to come to the hospital (when the daughter was ill). All this was most likely rooted in his fear of evoking traumatic memories of the war.

Only after the father's death did the daughters come to know the extent of his sufferings during the war. This occurred when his best friend disclosed to them that, in his early 30s, Susanne's father opened up to him and revealed some horrifying scenes from the war: of the dead bodies, the screams, the smells, the unfathomable horror of lying in the cold water of the Don River with his kidney shot waiting to die, of escaping from certain death by being airlifted out of besieged Stalingrad with a serious head wound, and horrid events in the military hospitals. He was, by all considerations, heavily traumatized by nearly five years of battlefield experience, and his extreme fear of death could have been caused by the exposure to events that were exceptionally brutal and tragic. After receiving this information, Susanne came to the full realization that her father must have suffered from deeply ingrained wartime trauma (nowadays known as posttraumatic stress disorder (PTSD)) from which he never recovered.

After the war, Susanne's father enrolled at the Fine Arts Academy of Düsseldorf to study art and graphic design, where he met his future wife, Ruth-Eva Fietze, with whom he had three daughters (Susanne being the middle child). Although he was a highly talented painter (with a strong proclivity for cubism), he never pursued a career of being an artist, as he fully embraced his responsibility to provide for the family after marrying Ruth-Eva in 1951. He was a successful graphic designer, and he and his wife worked together to apply their artistic talents to commercial art, which eventually afforded them a comfortable, upper middle-class life. However, this creative work was always for short-lived advertisements, forgotten as soon as they had outlived their usefulness. His true ambition of realizing his large painting projects never found their fulfillment.

He began to create oil paintings in his spare time when he turned 40, more than 15 years after he completed his studies at the art academy. He managed to create only 20 fine oil paintings over the span of 30 years.[7] The paucity of output had become a source of bitterness, as he regretted in his old age that he had not realized his potential due to the priority of the responsibility to support his family. In addition, he made no secret in his later years of his disappointment that his daughters had refused to follow the path he had made for them. Feeling betrayed of his hope to pass along his values, ideals, and aspiration to his children, he convinced himself that all the sacrifices that he and his wife made for their daughters had been in vain.

We assume that this attitude was metaphorically visualized in the posture of True Blue in *Give Me Wings!*, where he is seen turning away from Pale Moonlight and Touchless Misty, both of which represent the adult Susanne. Heinz-Günter Schünke passed away in 2010 at the age of 85, leaving behind a small oeuvre of paintings of remarkable inventiveness and intriguing visual metaphors, which, unfortunately to this day, have never been publicly exhibited. Susanne feels deep compassion and sympathy for her father for sacrificing his aspirations and chances to unfold his artistic gift fully as an independent artist in favor of providing his family with a prosperous life.

The cut-out design of True Blue's hind wings could metaphorically signify the physical and psychological wounds that life inflicted on the artist's father. The next section will introduce another anatomical defect, the thorny spike, as an appropriate visual metaphor that expresses fate's painful "incisions" from which her father suffered deeply.

5.2.3 A Thorny Spike

From the outer contour of the right front wing of True Blue, a shape similar to a thorn separates (Fig. 5.1(k)). The wedge-like gap suggests that there is a tear in the front wing, which has formed

---

6 Susanne was told by her mother that during his military service her father had marched miles and miles with heavy equipment, and this was the reason he would not carry a suitcase, for it would bring back memories of those war years.

7 Susanne's mother, in an attempt to encourage her husband to paint more, once told him that "you produce for the wastebasket," meaning that the commercial brochures and advertisements he was creating would have only a short shelf life.

this spiky shape. The outer element of the right hind wing (Fig. 5.1(j)) overlaps the front one in a way that gives the illusion of framing the thorny shape and adds emphasis to this feature.

A discussion during analysis about the metaphorical meaning of the thorny spike and its possible message of a painful injury triggered in the artist a fleeting thought that she had once painted such a spiky form as an indicator of a wound. She went through her records and found in the painting *Hypocrisy* (1988)[8] a comparable configuration, which she recalled having designed intentionally as signifying an inflicted injury (Fig. 5.2 and details in Fig. 5.3).

The painting in question depicts in three-quarter profile the bust portrait of a woman in a nurse's uniform, who rises out of a lush green mountainscape. She looks down on the once-serene landscape, which a plane is carpet-bombing (Fig. 5.3 (1)). On the left slope of the peak, we can observe that the bombs have blasted a huge cavity in the greenish rock. The contour of the gaping hole displays two spike-shapes to the right, with more below (Fig. 5.3 (2, 3 and 4)), which can be likened to the thorn-like shape in the right front wing of True Blue. The ragged outline of the cavernous bomb crater against the whitish sky in the background is further dramatized with a red glow surrounding the jagged edges as the result of the searing heat from the explosions.

A closer look reveals that other damage has been inflicted. For example, at the lower right side of the summit, a deep fracture threatens the whole mountain with collapse. The hollow area near the fissure is filled with pink vapor, reflecting the fiery glow of destruction. She explains that these are metaphorical details of the "bleeding wounds" suffered by the beautiful, victimized mountain. Susanne

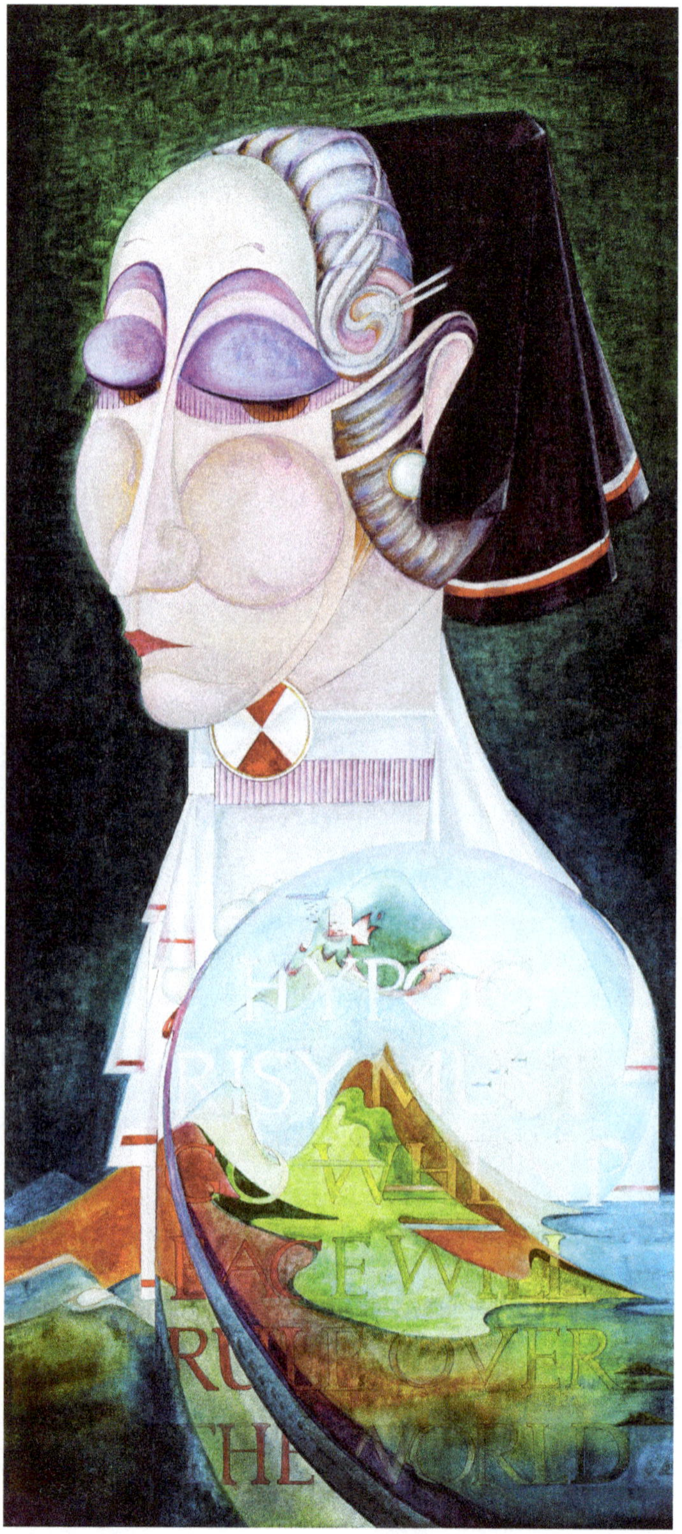

Fig. 5.2. Susanne Schuenke, *Hypocrisy*, 1988.
Oil on canvas, 34 x 16 in (86 x 40 cm). Private collection.

8 In contemplating the countless wars that have plagued mankind, including the ongoing ones today, the artist speculates that certain character flaws ("sins"), which are common in humans, have been responsible for the conflicts and divisions among humanity. To underscore this, she painted a watercolor series titled Seven Modern Sins (1980), consisting of Ambition, Intolerance, Greed, Lack of Education, Hypocrisy, Fanaticism, and Stupidity, of which three (the second, third, and fifth) were later painted in oil.

remembers that this painting was intended to express her grief at, criticism of, and protest against the senseless and brutal warfare that humanity has been waging, bringing terrible devastation upon itself and nature. The analyst identified in the odd configuration of the mountain top in question an optical illusion suggestive of a stylized human head in right profile with a protruding nose[9] (Fig. 5.3 (5)) and a chin-line (Fig. 5.3 (6)), which is surrounded by reddish vapor, indicating the fire caused by the bombardment. We noted that the letter "O" of the word, "Hypocrisy," incorporated into the painting, emphasizes this fire glow by functioning like a frame (see Fig. 5.3).

The visual perception of the mountaintop as an anthropomorphic head was strengthened by two critical details: A piece of red debris (Fig. 5.3 (7)) ejected from the explosion, which could appear to be an eye in this profile, and a dark fissure that could be imagined as a mouth (Fig. 5.3 (8)). Susanne had no awareness that she might have been creating a visual metaphor for an anthropoid head when she was painting it, which points to her unconscious as the source of this imagery. It should also be remarked that the metaphorical meaning of this "hidden" image had already surfaced unintentionally in her comment when she characterized the detail as a "wound in the mountain." This metaphor signified that she was thinking of the mountain as a humanized object.

There is no human victim depicted explicitly in this scene of aerial bombardment, but the anthropomorphic mountain-head could metaphorically visualize the traumatic injuries of the

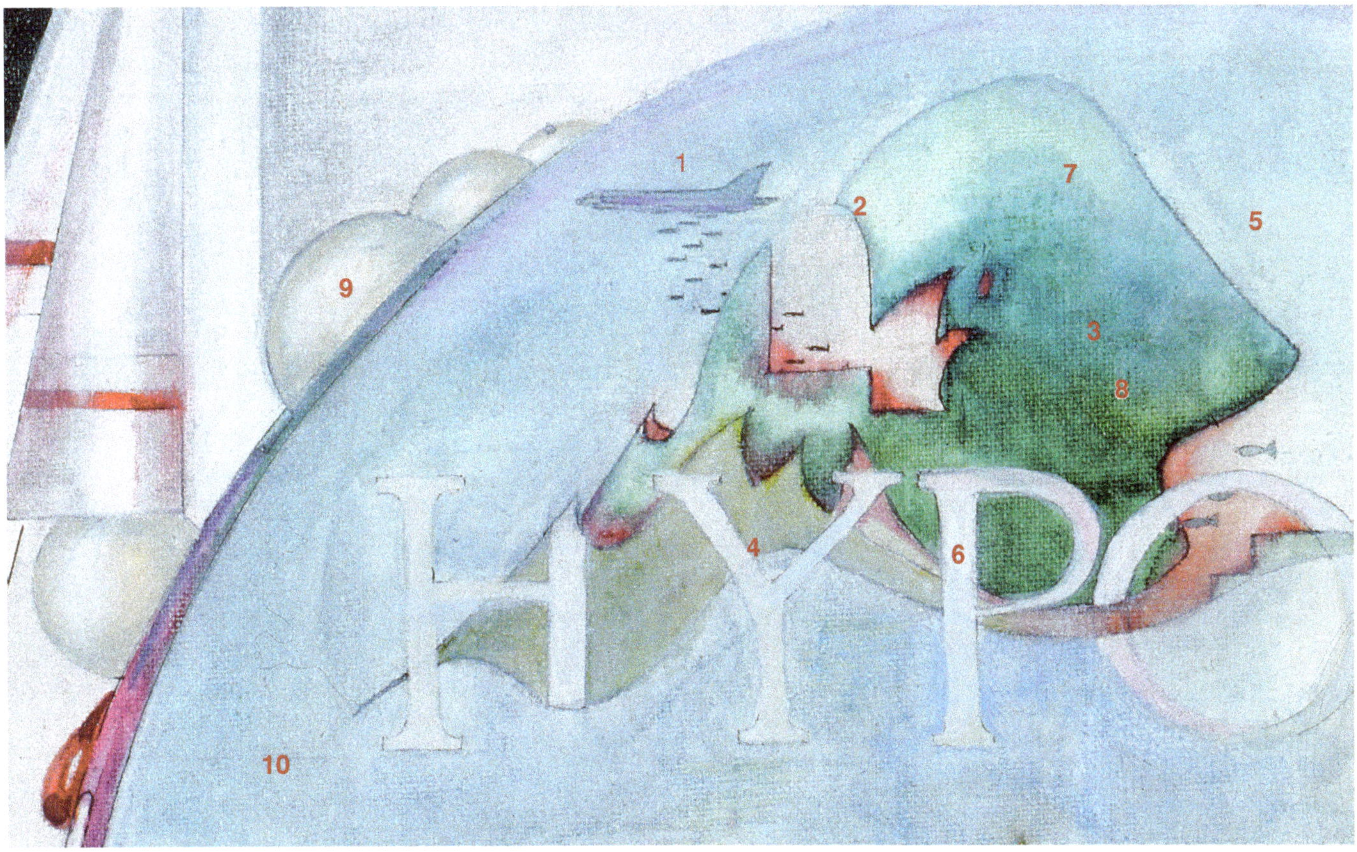

Fig. 5.3. Details from Fig. 5.2 with the following features:

(1) Plane. (2) and (3) Shapes in the mountain that are comparable with "thorny spike." (4) More spikes in the lower left of the mountain. Arrows pointing to reveal the optical illusion: (5) Tip of "nose." (6) "Chin." (7) "Eye." (8) Location of a "mouth."
Further details: (9) Pearls. (10) A drop of blood.

9 In this context, we point to chapter 9.4, where we discuss in detail the optical illusion situated in the negative space between the butterflies Nos. 4 and 5 as a human profile with a big protruding nose that we named "Big Face" and identified as a representation of the artist's father.

war. This unconscious metaphor could well reflect the father's head wound and the tormented state of his psyche. As a combat soldier, he was subjected to bombardment and strafing on the Eastern Front for nearly five years, particularly at Stalingrad.

It can be noted that the mountaintop approximately resembles the shape of the World War II German steel helmet, particularly in the rear, with its grayish green hue. Furthermore, there are some whitish areas on the mountain top, which could be comprehended as the color of the helmet (white) during winter warfare. The interpretation of this mountain configuration as an unconsciously created optical illusion could be considered as speculative. But when the artist started to paint the imagery of the mountain being destroyed by bombs, we assume this devastation might have related to her father's experience during the war. She realized from her mother's enigmatic short comments about some of his physical conditions that something terrible had happened during his military service. Although Susanne was not aware of the extent of the horror that her father had undergone in World War II, she had compassion in accordance with his injuries, particularly the head trauma. Therefore, his wartime head wound being metaphorically represented by the implicit optical illusion of a damaged Wehrmacht helmet is quite an apt hypothesis. It bears mentioning that the optical illusion in this painting is not an isolated occurrence. Additional cases of such unintended illusions in her oeuvre bearing equally remarkable messages (which we will present in chapters 8 and 9) confirm that the modus operandi of the unconscious transforms past experiences into visual allusions and metaphors of extraordinary inventiveness.

The portrait of a nurse in uniform as a personification of hypocrisy (thus the naming of the painting as *Hypocrisy*) conveys important personal symbolism that can stem from the artist's traumatic, emotional experiences. Susanne still remembers that, when she was around the age of five, her mother took her to a hospital for a tonsillectomy, where nuns in long white habits and headgear tried to prepare her for the outpatient procedure. As little Susanne saw the nurses approaching, she ran away from the surgical chair but was quickly caught by one of them, who deftly anesthetized her on the spot with a cotton sponge drenched with an anesthetic.

When she was 11, another dreadful episode reinforced her horrifying experience from six years earlier. For the first time in her life, she was staying in a hospital[10] alone without the usual presence of her mother, which made her anxious as she was to undergo a surgery. In preparation for the operation, Susanne was given an injection she had never experienced before. The nurse who was administering it assured her, "It will not hurt." However, it was extremely painful, and she screamed loudly in shock—but to no avail. The child was left alone in the room as the nurse exited, and no one came to comfort her during this ordeal.

The psychological consequences of these situations were dominated by her feeling of betrayal, which broke her trust in any nurse for decades to come. Surgery after surgery followed over the next few years, each time deepening her trauma and distrust, and eventually she resolved not to go to any doctor—forever. She held onto that vow for some years, for she had come to perceive medical professionals, especially nurses, as the signifiers of invasion, suffering, and horror, and, as such, to be avoided at all costs. With these disturbing experiences with nurses and nuns, it is understandable that, when Susanne aimed to design a metaphorical portrait of hypocrisy, she merged both vocations into one image. So, she drew a nurse capped with a black head veil as an allusion to the cloister. Furthermore, the sister's outer décor flaunts humility. Her gray hair is tightly brushed under the firm cap, which is held immaculately. Her facial expression is dominated by modestly lowered eyelids and a haughty expression on the firmly closed, thin lips. The high collar is meticulously clasped with a badge (Fig. 5.4), which was created by the artist as a stylized design that combines elements from the Red Cross, the Maltese Order, and the Swiss flag (Fig. 5.4 (1–3)). All three were transformed and condensed creatively into a new emblem, which alludes to these established symbols that are considered as representing humanitarianism and peace. Susanne's creation of the badge has a correlation with reality in the artist's life. Her aunt, Hella, was originally trained as a pediatric

10 The institution belonged to the Dominican order with the nuns dressed in black and white.

nurse, and a family photograph shows the young woman in a nurse's uniform, wearing a Red Cross badge and small white hood. Aunt Hella's role as the source of some of Susanne's traumatic experiences in her childhood will be covered in the subsequent chapters. The artist's highly negative perception of nurses might have found an expression in the imagery of *Hypocrisy* and could have been unconsciously reinforced by the adverse events connected with the aunt.

In the painting, underneath the regalia of humanitarian compassion, the artist created a very contrasting image, exposing numerous particulars that are inconsistent with the attributes expected of a nun/nurse. The details, which were intentionally incorporated by the artist, are as follows: heavy eye make-up and a sharp, slanted glance lurking from behind a curtain of eyelashes; a cold and forbidding mouth, tightly shut and ending in a needle-sharp point; a coquettish curl of hair loosened in a luscious curve; and a pearl fitted in gold peeking from the earlobe, with more pearls underneath the ruffles of the collar adorning the lower neck. With these contradictory characteristics, Susanne attempted to unmask hypocrisy allegorically as predatory behavior that exposes itself as a wolf in sheep's clothing. Ominously, a single drop of blood runs from the nurse's ruffles (Fig. 5.3 (10)). Keeping in mind that this painting was created consciously as a critique of the falsehood in the world that has often led to wars and destruction over the millennia, we conceive this drop of blood as the artist's simplest and most condensed symbol for the suffering of the countless victims of human depravity.

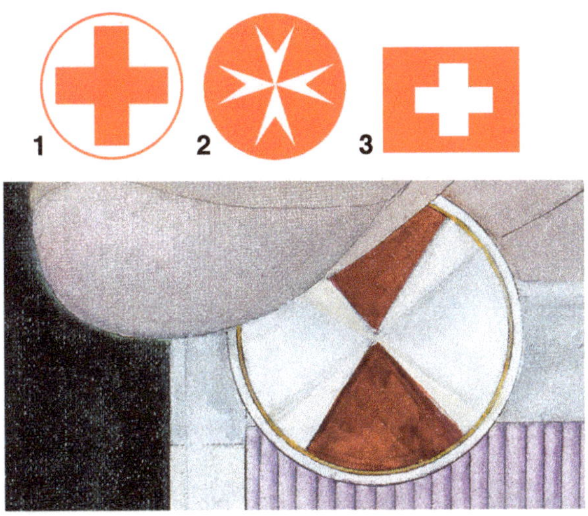

Fig. 5.4. Detail from Fig. 5.2: The nurse's badge and sources for transformation and condensation. (1) Red Cross symbol. (2) Maltese Cross. (3) Swiss flag.

Looking at the symbolism of the blood droplet, we recall Susanne's watercolor, *Diplomat's Cocktail* (1988) (Fig. 4.9), where a solitary red gutta spills from the glass that contains the intoxicating drink. It signifies the hidden aggressive tendencies associated with the hypocritical aspect of diplomacy. A comparable single drop of blood, Susanne rendered as a piece of ear jewelry in her earlier work, *Revolution* (1985), that turned into the red-tinted sea at the bottom of the painting (Fig. 9.43b). In Susanne's iconography, a scarlet drop has become a symbol of the wholesale destruction and bloodshed that have stained human history so disastrously. In *Hypocrisy*, the artist employs this symbolism in combination with the explicit negative image of the nurse and aerial bombardment to represent the victimization of individuals and nations.

Some days after this subchapter was written, another link emerged in the chain of associations of the spiky shape, in connection with Susanne's past traumatization. This happened when the artist showed figures 5.2 and 5.3 to a friend and shared the interpretation concerning the thorny spike of True Blue. Near the end of the conversation, a very painful memory from Susanne's past flashed in her mind—the bullfight painting by R. Domingo y Fallola (which will be presented in detail in subchapters 6.3.4 and 8.3.3). The recollection of this image was accompanied by a sudden surge of horror, which made her cringe. Nevertheless, she fetched a photo of the painting (Figs. 6.10 and 8.51) and asked her friend to look closely at the details of the injured horse. Then, she suggested comparing them to the mountain's spiky cavity (Fig. 5.3 (2–4)) in *Hypocrisy* and the thorny spike in True Blue. Overcoming all her resistance to look at the horse and the belly area, Susanne recognized similarities between all three items resembling a thorny spike shape. The result of this comparison reactivated the feeling of abhorrence she has had toward the bullfight painting since childhood.

As it will be described in chapters 6 and 8 more fully, for many years Susanne's memory had displaced the location of the horse's injury in Domingo's painting from the animal's upper torso to the middle of the belly. This area is a highly sensitive spot for Susanne because of her omphalophobia. Here we can observe a smaller dark triangular form, which turned out to be the horse's left stirrup. In her childhood, Susanne did not recognize this object and mistook it for a part of the animal's body, until analysis clarified the matter. The spiky shape, the "wound" (displaced into the location of the belly's middle), the stirrup (in the same place), and the red shape between the horse's front legs—all have presumably woven their threads into a fabric of horror. The above associations could point to multiple neurotic fixations that trigger her sensitive reactions. Accordingly, if we are on the right track, the very root of her idiosyncratic perception of the wound in the middle of the horse's belly as a highly traumatizing experience could have reflected some prior repressed destructive and libidinal reveries linked to her navel (see chapter 8). Those fantasies could be the basis of her affective assessment of the details of the images we have discussed. This case shows the manifestation of the latent meaning and gives an impressive example of how particular shapes can be recognized as derivatives of unconscious symbolism.

5.2.4 The Flip-over Effect

During the analysis of True Blue, we discovered in the butterfly's imagery a twisted formation in each of the hind wings, which the artist named "the flip-over effect" (Fig. 5.1 (m) and a more detailed view in Fig. 5.13 C). By this term, Susanne refers to the presence of the half twist in each of the outer frame elements of the hind wings before they merge into a single outer element at the bottom. The twisted surface has the appearance akin to a Möbius strip, i.e., the topside and underside of each outer frame element are exposed to view simultaneously near the twist.

In Susanne's art, the flip-over effect can be traced back to numerous childhood drawings. The earliest she could find was drawn when she was age 11. In this design, the twist occurs as a play of crossing lines, where the two opposite surfaces are revealed by the flip-over effect, distinguished by two different colors (Figs. 5.5 and 5.6).[11] The idea of showing both sides of an object simultaneously is observed again a few years later in a drawing, *Grapes for the Table*, 1974 (Figs. 5.7 and 5.8), and it has continued ever since in her art.

Another of Susanne's works, *Sleeper* (1989) (Fig. 12.4), which we will analyze extensively in chapter 12, displays a clear flip-over effect in the forearm of the figure, depicted at the area approaching her wrist. Furthermore, the figure reveals a conspicuous twist in the undulating curvature from the right shoulder to the waist, then up to the buttocks and down the legs. This wave-like configuration of the body kindles a sensual flair. (We meet something analogous to this 14 years later in *Longing* (2003); see further below.)

In her *The Letter of the Law* (1995) (Figs. 4.7 and 4.8) and *The Takeover* (1997) (Fig. 4.14), the flip-over effect undergoes further development that we might associate with some aspects of her father's ambivalent personality. In the first work, the sharp turn of the judge's wrist and his pointing finger express his power to decide the defendant's fate. The magisterial finger of the judge in this painting was previously identified as analogous to the authoritarian finger gesture that her father used to make. In the second canvas, the flip-over effect appears in some of the arms of the octopus, which metaphorically hint at the ultimate control that creeps into every aspect of the governmental system which is symbolically represented by the appropriate buildings of the legislative, executive, and judiciary branches.

Painted three years before *Give Me Wings!*, another instance of the flip-over effect can be observed in the painting *Intermission* (2001) (Fig. 10.21, detail in Fig. 5.9, area in question red encircled), whose central figure is a development of a detail from an older work, *Monaco* (1989) (Fig. 5.10). In both paintings, a white fur stole embraces the shoulder and body of a lady in the foreground (*Monaco*) and the diva in the center (*Intermission*). The shawl runs on the back of each female figure in a serpentine manner. In *Intermission*, it displays its sides like a Möbius strip that entwines around the exposed back of the woman, heightening the sensual allurement of the body with its teasing, winding shape.

We meet another such writhing erotic curvature in Susanne's *Longing* (2003) (Fig. 7.18) in the shape of a small red nude, squirming at the bottom of the painting. This is revealed simultaneously, through the contortion of the torso, abdomen and

11 A pencil-and-marker drawing of a couple by the artist, 1967.

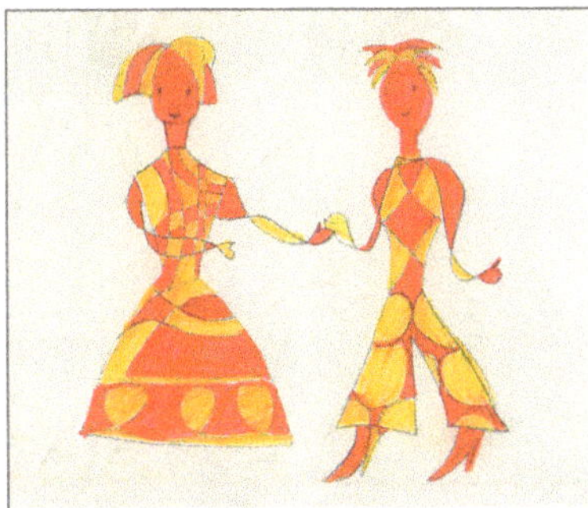

Fig. 5.5. Susanne Schuenke, a marker drawing of a couple, Sept.18 1967. Detail from a 6 x 4 in sheet (image size: approx 4 x 4 in (10 x 10 cm)). Collection of the artist.

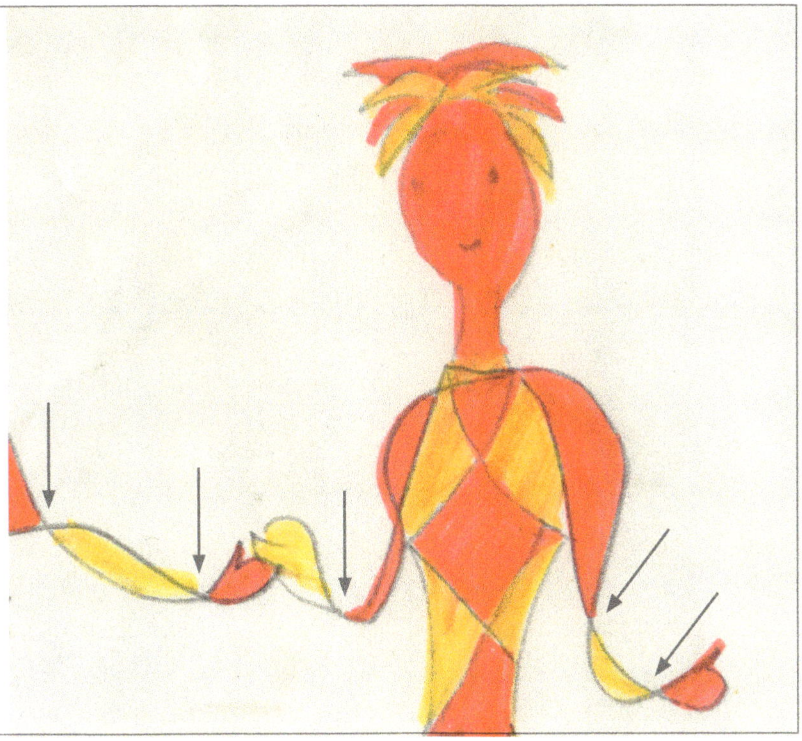

Fig. 5.6. Detail from Fig. 5.5. Arrows added, indicating the area of flip-over effect.

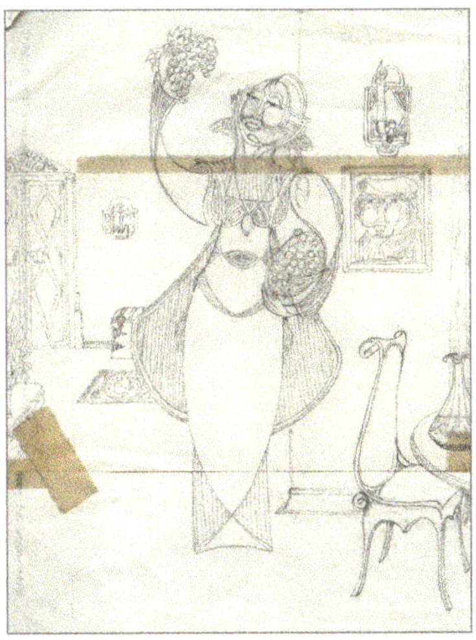

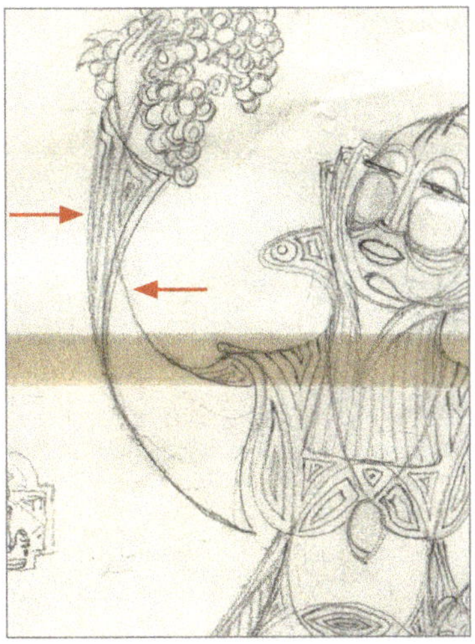

From left to right:

Fig. 5.7. Susanne Schuenke, *Grapes for the Table*, Aug. 29, 1974. Drawing on vellum paper, approx. 11 x 8 in (28 x 20 cm). Collection of the artist.

Fig. 5.8. Detail from Fig. 5.7: flip-over effect in the arm (arrows indicate the area).

buttocks. It underscores the seductive character of the image. The examples—*Sleeper, Intermission,* and *Longing*—show that the flip-over effect allows Susanne to present a shape or a situation in more than one view simultaneously, including sensual intimation. Doing so, she purposely invites the observer to leave rational reality and become immersed in the artist's sensual fantasies.

What is the source of these configurations in her art, which she designates as the flip-over effect? The artist's recollection of her childhood supplies several items of interest. First, her parents' collection of sea snail shells, with their spirals, twisted contours, and shining surfaces, had fascinated Susanne ever since her childhood. Secondly, she joyfully remembers her parents using a party decoration, which was made of twisted strips of colorful foil hanging from the ceiling. Air currents moved those ornamental objects, slowly alternating their elegant configurations in kaleidoscopic permutations revealing the ribbons' contrasting colors on their front and back.

The third association brings us to Susanne's scientific curiosity. In her youth, along with her avid interest in physics and cosmology, she read numerous books in the field of biology and

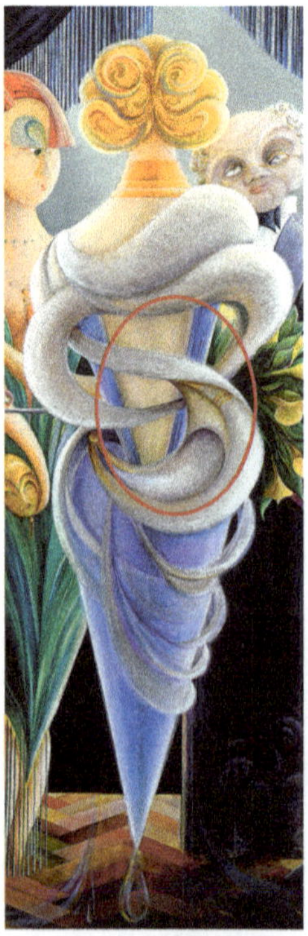

Fig. 5.9. Detail from Fig. 10.21: The diva from *Intermission*.

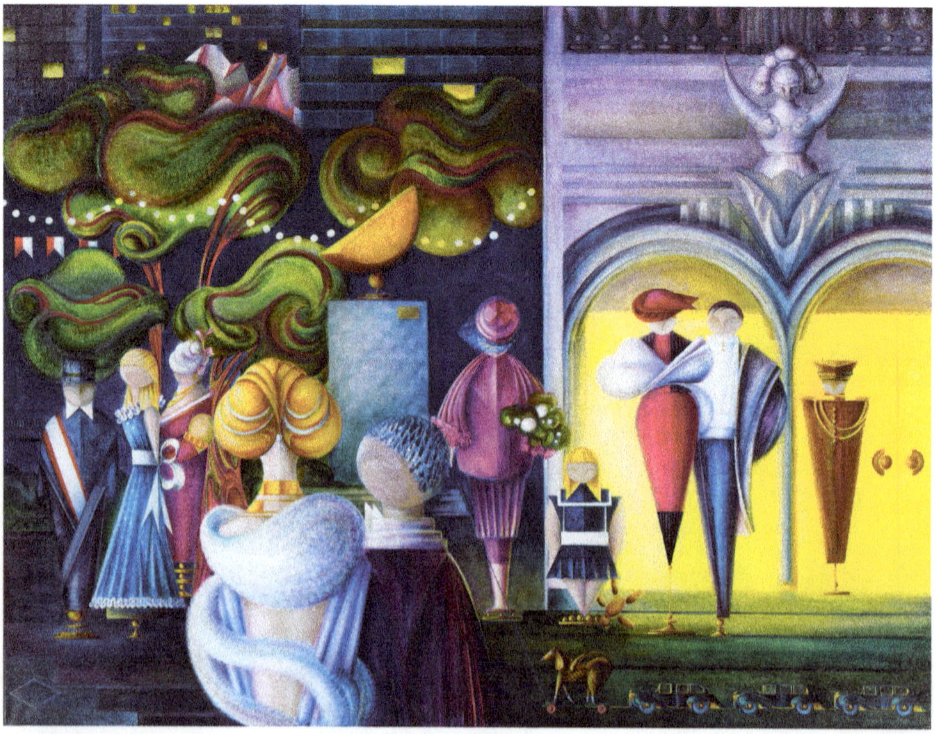

Fig. 5.10. Susanne Schuenke, *Monaco*, 1989. Oil on canvas, 48 x 60 in (120 x 150 cm). The Vignold Group corporate collection, Germany.

even seriously contemplated studying genetics at university after graduating from secondary school (high school). This desire grew stronger when she saw the model of DNA in *The Double Helix* by James D. Watson,[12] which she read in a German translation at the age of 15. From the book, she learned the story about the discovery of the structure of DNA. "Double helix" is the term used by its discoverers, James Watson and Francis Crick, to describe the configuration of the DNA molecule. By Susanne's estimation, the twist in the Möbius strip and her flip-over effect, recalls the essential characteristic of the spiral structure of the DNA as seen in scientific illustrations.

Another sample comes from her father's painting, where there are configurations that qualify for Susanne's criterion of the flip-over effect. For instance, a detail from the upper left corner of *The Weightlifter* by Heinz-Günter Schünke shows birds whose wings display shapes comparable to the configuration in True Blue's hind wings (indicated by the arrows in Fig. 5.11). Lastly, her parents' graphic design works were instrumental in stimulating her curiosity in the art of letter design and calligraphy. In her youth, being dissatisfied with the bland covers of her textbooks in high school, Susanne designed jackets for her own copies, illustrating them with a great variety of script styles, typefaces, fonts, and even foreign alphabets and writing systems.[13] On her own initiative, she devoted a considerable amount of time to calligraphy exercises with ink and nib in different copperplate writing styles, in German as well as in various foreign scripts,[14] among which Armenian was her favorite.

She finds great joy in the beauty of the abstract shapes of the letters, their lines floating, crossing over, alternating from thin to thick strokes, including numerous figurations reminiscent of her flip-over effect, which can be observed by those who are familiar with calligraphy brush

12 James D. Watson, *The Double Helix: A Personal Account of the Discovery of the Structure of DNA* (London: Weidenfeld and Nicolson, 1968).

13 These included Greek, Russian, Armenian, Kufi (Arabic script), Chinese, and Egyptian hieroglyphs.

14 Her script styles were modeled after the tables of various writing systems of the world found in Denis Diderot's 18th century Encyclopedia, *Encyclopédie, ou dictionnaire raisonné des sciences, des arts et des métiers.*

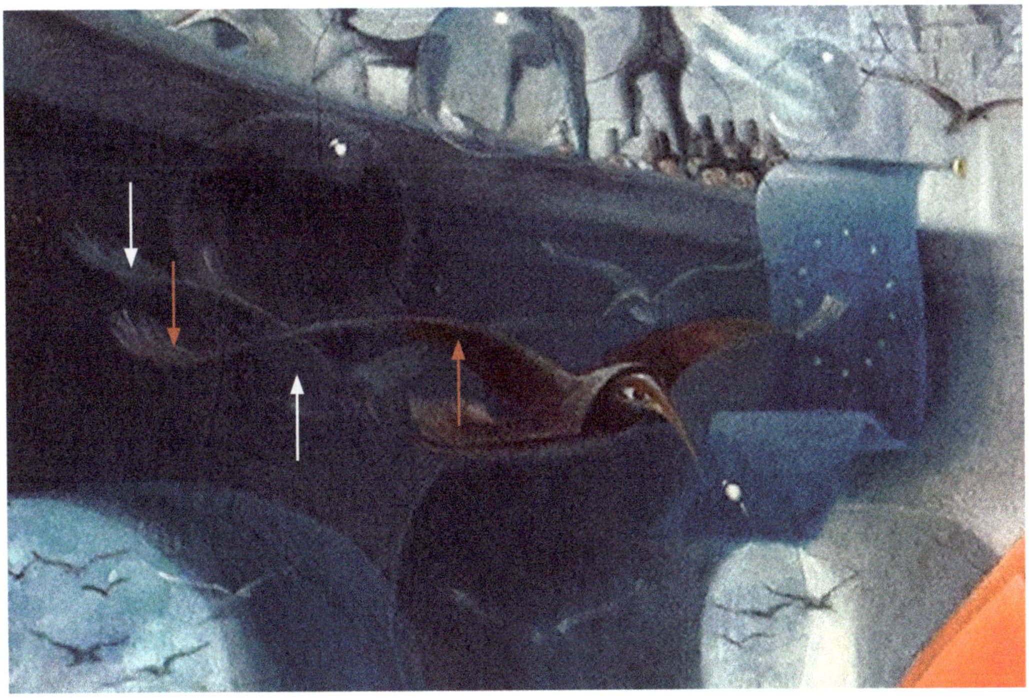

Fig. 5.11
Detail from Fig. 4.5: Heinz-Günter Schünke, *The Weightlifter*, 1978.

Arrows pointing to the occurrence of the flip-over effect in the birds' wings.

Red arrows indicate the top and underside of the front bird.

White arrows relate to a second bird further behind.

and nib strokes.[15] Furthermore, she learned to write in an old-fashioned German script called Sütterlin, widely used before World War II but it fell out of favor after 1945. Her mother used the script to write her shopping lists, notes, and letters. Naturally, Susanne wanted to be able to read and understand them. She adopted the script to sign her name, and it has been her official signature ever since. When she writes "Susanne" with a brush, there are multiple flip-over effects in the letters. Therefore, regarding the artist's recurrent application of the flip-over effect in her art, we assume Susanne's childhood experiences may have played a significant role in the use of this visual presentation to manifest different meanings.

Susanne was thrilled to recognize the pattern of the flip-over effect, when she observed the distinct hand movements that are used by Balinese and Spanish flamenco dancers. She was instantly attracted by the compelling dynamic motions of those dances, employing varying twisting turns of hands and arms resembling the flip-over effect, which triggered in her mind a strong sense of familiarity. While imitating a dancer's hand gesture, she had a spontaneous reminiscence of a comparable hand movement by her mother. When she was five and a half years old, she had to have a picture taken for a passport, and little Susanne was sitting in a photo booth looking around. Suddenly, she saw her mother's gloved hand touch Susanne's chin and, with a particular twist of her wrist, gently turn her head straight to face the camera.[16] In describing this episode, another memory came to mind. It was her father's photo shoot for a product advertisement, in which her mother's hand, clad in a long, golden leather glove, twisted gracefully in an arc (Fig. 5.12). The artist indicated that fond sentiments accompanied the recollection of these events. Susanne has an identical sentiment when she describes her fascination with dancers' rotating hand gestures.

15 Regarding Susanne's interest in the calligraphy and graphology of various languages, which was mostly self-initiated, we cannot exclude the possibility that her predisposition could have stemmed from phylogenetic memory. Her maternal grandfather (whom Susanne met only three times as a child) was a highly regarded and admired teacher at the Gymnasium in Berlin where he taught Hebrew, Greek, Latin, and French, and who in his later years, also learned Russian and English. His interest extended well beyond linguistics, as he was an avid student of archaeology, art history, geography, and other fields of intellectual endeavor. After retiring from teaching, he took up cross embroidery and carpet weaving as his pastimes. In addition, the artist's maternal great-grandfather was also a teacher, and among the school subjects he taught were calligraphy and dancing. The interest in language, calligraphy, and art is a common thread that had run for at least the last several generations in her family lineage.

16 The hand gesture could be described as identical to screwing a light bulb into an overhead socket.

The reactivation of the positive feelings stored in Susanne's memory could stem from the similar motions of her mother's hands.

She also had the same emotional state when she viewed, in a documentary film, slow-motion footage of a hummingbird's wing movements, which she considers being analogous (except for the rapidity of the motion) with the gesticulation of human dancers. The researcher asked the artist if butterflies also have such flip-over patterns in their wing motions while in flight. Susanne replied that to the best of her knowledge she did not think so. The analyst encouraged her to watch some slow-motion films of butterflies in flight to confirm her answer. After observing some appropriate footage, she acknowledged the existence of the twisting motion of the wings during the butterflies' flight. Although she had no detailed knowledge about the motion of butterflies' wings in flight, Susanne intuitively painted the comparable flip-over configuration in the wings of True Blue years before the present study.

Looking closely at the different stages of the design of *Give Me Wings!* (compare Fig. 5.13 (A–C)), it can be seen that the twisted surface of the hind wing's outer elements, which is the basis for the flip-over effect in this painting, does not exist in the first drawing (creative drawing II). In the compositional drawing, we can observe a "wobbling line" (as the artist describes the unintentional swerving of her ink line when she was tracing the pencil drawing), which was preserved in the next stage—the watercolor. At the beginning of the oil painting, the flip-over effect was not intended (Fig. 5.14), but it emerged during the painting process. It was incorporated into the final oil version, deriving as a new element from that wavering line in the watercolor.

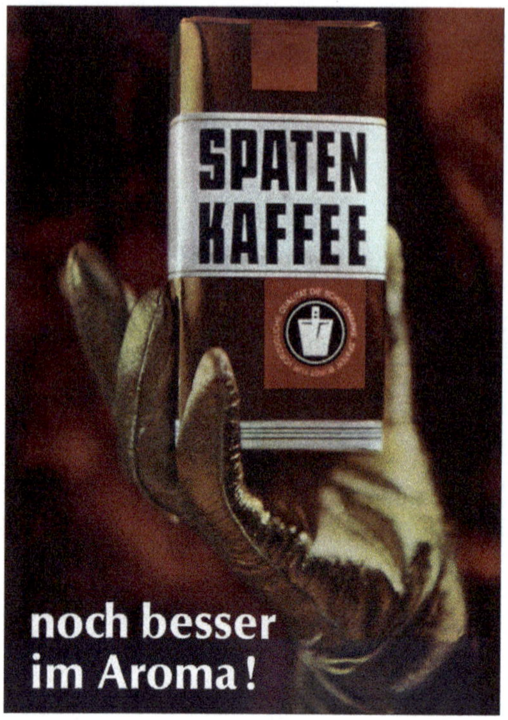

Fig. 5.12. Heinz-Günter Schünke. Photo for a coffee advertisement (mid- to late- 1960s).

The artist remembers that, while applying additional layers of colors, this figuration came spontaneously into existence under her brush. She depicted a certain section of the outer frame element of each hind wing and gave it the illusion of being turned over before merging together. Because this development might have been unconsciously determined, it supports our assumption that this specific formation signified different emotions from the past or psychic states and brought them into the open in the guise of a visual metaphor. There are several hypotheses to explain this assessment.

Paying closer attention to the serpentine outline that accompanies a twisted surface, so characteristic of Susanne's flip-over effect, we have found her attraction to this S-shaped curvature from her childhood drawings onward. Such configurations are widespread in the visual arts, and many years later, she learned from her art studies the aesthetic theory formulated by the English painter William Hogarth (1697–1764) about the serpentine line (S-shaped curve). Hogarth expounded on the use of the S-curved line in his book, *The Analysis of Beauty* (published 1753). In his self-portrait, *The Painter and his Pug,* (1745) (Tate Gallery, London), he painted the serpentine line along with its name ("The Line of Beauty") on a painting palette to commemorate the curved line's significance in his aesthetic theory. This concept interested Susanne due to its congruency with her preference for S-shaped curved lines in her art. Aside from the aesthetic considerations and emotive effects (as Hogarth proposed), the occurrence of the flip-over effect along with the S-curves by Susanne could metaphorically present a wide range of latent content.

We could interpret the flip-over effect as a metaphor for Susanne's changing attitude toward her father throughout her life. As a child, she was filled with admiration for him, but, as an adult, she became more and more critical of him. In

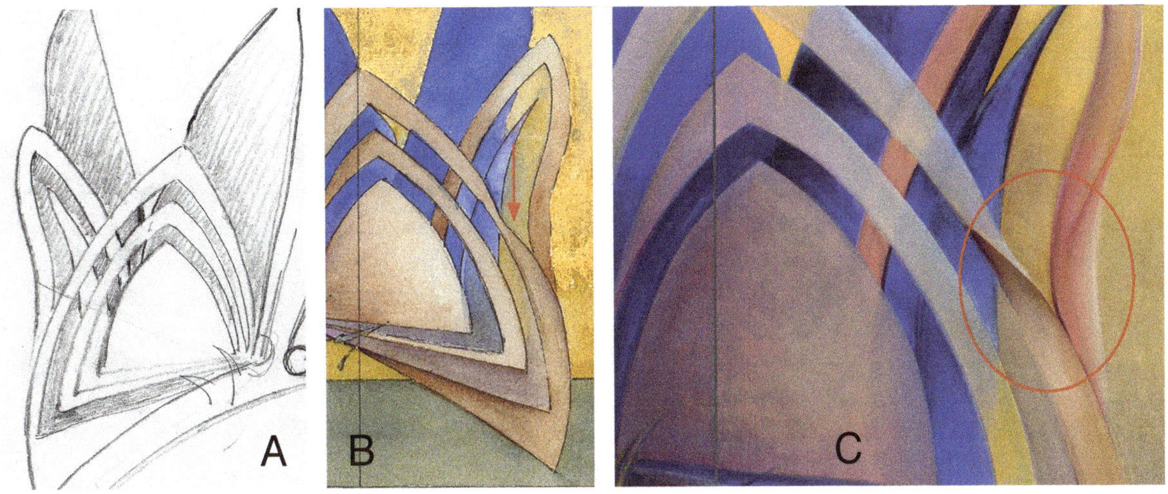

Fig. 5.13. Illustrating the flip-over effect in True Blue's hind wing (arrow and circle added).
(A) Detail from creative drawing II, Fig. 2.3: no irregularities.
(B) Detail from the watercolor, Fig. 2.10: a "wobbling" contour (arrow).
(C) Detail from the oil painting, Fig. 1.0: a flip-over effect (encircled in red).

her early 20s, when Susanne embarked on her university education, her relationship with her father started to evolve steadily in the opposite direction from its erstwhile harmony to parting from many of his ideas, attitudes, and values. She was particularly critical of his tendency for self-glorification. Although Susanne had achieved the academic accomplishment that her father was proud of (earning M.A. and Ph.D. degrees), in his angry moods, often prompted by her growing independence, he began to increasingly disparage her intellect, expressing his disregard for many of her perspectives. The daughter could no longer endure her father's despotic demeanor and choleric outbursts. This process of growing apart was very painful, with deep disappointment on both sides. The bond between the admiring child and loving parent turned into a series of confrontations and eventual rejection of each other—"a flip over" of what was once a loving relationship.

We detect some metaphorical representations of this aspect of the father–daughter relationship in the images of *Give Me Wings!*. The posture of True Blue in respect to the other butterflies on the podium could indicate that he is arrogantly turning his back to the center of the painting where two large butterflies are situated. He confronts Little Why who is intent on challenging True Blue by trying to land on the same podium level as his. However, he is ready to defend his place from any attempt at intrusion, by parading a mixture of aloofness and intimidation through his posture, accompanied by a warning flash of the eye. The antennae of Little Why and True Blue are held against each other like the fencers' epées before a duel. This reflects Susanne's perception of the unfolding scenario in her relationship with her father, and the imagery symbolically projects the family situation in visual metaphor. As remarked before, in her younger years she used to admire her father, particularly for his creative and intellectual prowess, but she also considered that he should

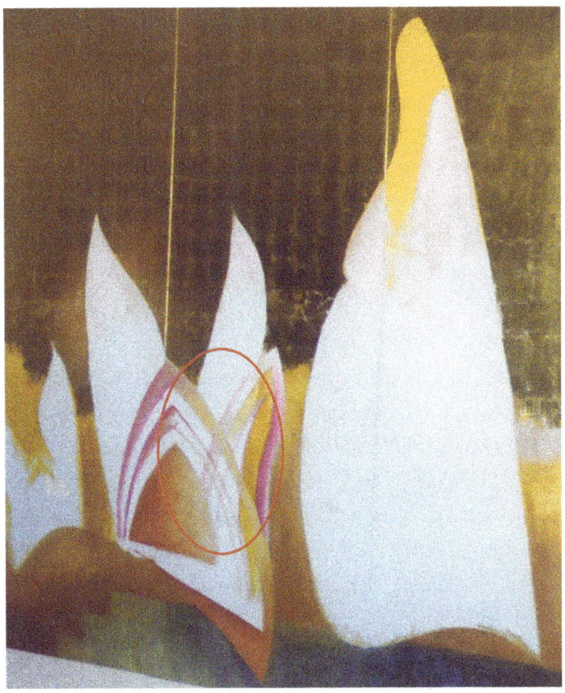

Fig. 5.14. A snapshot from the beginning stage of the oil painting showing no flip-over effect but with a slight thinness in the area in question.

respect basic dignity, freedom, and fairness for all the members of the family, of whom he was quite dismissive. Over the years, she came into conflict with her father because of his authoritarian, unjust efforts to control and subjugate his family. This could have been a significant source of the difficulties that arose in Susanne's relationship with her father, as the loving attitude between them gradually dissolved and painfully turned into one of estrangement. The protracted struggle with her father was stressful for her psyche, which later became involuntarily reflected metaphorically in the imagery of *Give Me Wings!* and, particularly, in the flip-over effect.

This interpretation of the flip-over effect as a metaphor could be found in the alternative characteristics in the image of True Blue. On initial impression based on posture and position, size and color, and even name, True Blue appears as a glorious creature. Yet the artist unintentionally embedded several subversive deconstructive elements in the butterfly's appearance, like the thorny spike and cut-out design. Additionally, Susanne designed the upper part of the butterfly's image and the lower one with contrasting qualities in shapes (complete versus fragmented) and colors (bright, pure, and strong versus dim, muted, and pale), which metaphorically reveal her perception of the positive and negative emotional experiences she had with her father.

The positive qualities shown in the butterfly's radiant front wings as "sapphire glow" (idealization) flip over into the negative qualities represented in the pale, dysfunctional hind wings (disappointment) The peculiarities of the imagery could metaphorically signify Susanne's ambivalent attitude toward her father—a mixture of her admiration for his talents and achievements, and of a deep resentment of his despotism.

This polarized perspective could reflect an integration of conscious contemplation, intuitive perception, and unconscious tendencies. The ambivalence could have been caused by her subjectivity, refracted by the prisms of the conscious and the unconscious. The spectrum of the anatomical peculiarities of the butterfly and his colors as visual metaphors manifest this process.

Not a single feature of True Blue's image can be understood in isolation, as each constitutes a part of complex interconnections. As such, the features must be interpreted in their combinations, in which we can recognize multifarious meanings, displayed through creative imagery in allegorical form, a good example of which is the flip-over metaphor.

Due to her mother's efforts to conceal their father's peculiar mental condition from the children, Susanne did not come to fully recognize the anomalies in her father's personality until she was well into her adulthood. The most evident of the father's neurotic issues was his denial of anything related to death. For example, he forbade his family members to wear or own any kind of black clothing, and he did not allow them to speak of death in general, nor of any specific person dying or even the possibility of it. He never pronounced the fatal word, *death*, in High German (*Hochdeutsch*, used throughout Germany for formal speech and writing), always referring to it only in the Low Saxon (*Niederdeutsch*) pronunciation (see subchapter 11.3.1 for more on this). Furthermore, he was under the spell of a range of superstitions, which caused him to become highly agitated whenever the children tried breaking certain taboos or probed into the rational reasons for their existence. It was forbidden to wash laundry between Christmas and New Years, walk under a ladder, and have an owl in the house, to name a few. He never disclosed his fear that violating those prohibitions would bring death to the person or the family, but the mother shared this discreet information with her daughters. The mother was generally indulgent and protective of her husband, and she never openly condemned him. Moreover, she excused his behavior as indicative of the peculiarities of his personality. This was particularly true with sicknesses and injuries, as he would become enraged at the children for becoming sick or being hurt. As noted, during the many operations Susanne underwent in her adolescence, her father rarely, if ever, visited her in the hospital. Whenever his reactions were disturbing to the children, the mother expected them to respect his vulnerability as the consequence of his war experiences. The most she would do to express her displeasure was to say something like, "You are out of your mind!" Susanne was hesitant to share this information, as it is still painful and guilt-inducing for her to speak negatively about these childhood situations with her parents. Therefore, the shadow side of her father's personality, which often emerged by a sudden "flipping" of his moods, might be unconsciously expressed by the artist's psyche in the guise of the flip-over effect.

Summarizing the above contemplations, we assume that the flip-over effect could symbolize a dialectical reality, presenting its different contrasting aspects like light and shadow, black and white, yin and yang, or plus and minus. On the one side, there are positive perceptions—good mother, good father, good others. On the other side, there are negative aspects of their behavior. These appropriate life experiences are coded unconsciously in the BrainMind[17] as symbolic images. In Susanne's iconography, this information, we assume, is ciphered by the flip-over effect.

Moreover, this peculiar shape-configuration could manifest even repressed instinctual tendencies—the topic to which we now turn. In the paintings *Sleeper, Intermission,* and *Longing*, introduced already in this subchapter, noticeable expressions of sensuality are present in various details of the artworks: the figures' twisted body movement, their erotic posture, nudity—all compositionally emphasized. In all three canvases, the artist depicted the flip-over effect which could be a sign of underlying libidinal longing and hidden wishes, indicating the existence of seductive fantasies coded in the particularities of the images.

Susanne's habit of frequently sleeping with her parents in their bed when she was a small child could have provided a fertile ground for the unconscious to symbolize this desirable experience in her creative expressions. The sensations of physical touch and body scent that she garnered from being close to her parents gave her psychological security and relief. They were also effective in alleviating her fear of being alone, of being in the dark, and of being abandoned. The actual contact reduced Susanne's anxiety.

The parents' bed was formed from two twin beds joined together, and Susanne normally slept on the mother's half of the bed, usually lying on her side but positioning her body in such a way as to establish close contact with both parents. As she remembers, she would stretch and twist her body so as to be reassured of the presence of her parents by simultaneously touching one of them with her toes while leaning her back against the other. When the artist looked again at the twisted red figure in the painting *Longing* and the turning posture in *Sleeper*, she saw some analogies to her current sleep positions, including the contortions that she had used to get maximum physical contact when she was sleeping with her parents. These postures essentially have never changed since her childhood. These sleeping poses, resembling S-shaped curves, led us to assume that they were condensed and converted unconsciously into the sexual symbolism of the flip-over effect.

The original feelings might have been forgotten, but we can conceivably find their secondary expressions. They are various remarkable details of the artist's metaphorical visualizations in her paintings, by which unconscious symbolism is manifested. The created symbols are signs that express different erotic impulses, desires, and sensory inputs by various unpredictable metaphorical forms. The process continues to be a puzzle for the rational way of thinking. It remains the exclusive domain of the unconscious. The various possible interpretations as presented above for the flip-over effect demonstrate the complex, multivalent nature of the symbolic manifestations of the unconscious in the figurations created by her imagination. From the perspective of the unconscious, this visual metaphor can be applied to the father, Susanne herself, and others. The findings in this study concerning the factors that determine the process of the formation of symbols can bring additional insight into how the latent content of the unconscious manifests in creativity.

5.3 The Coloration of True Blue

Having examined the possible unconscious meanings of the shapes, lines, structures, and composition, we now turn to the colors. Applying coloration for the watercolor version of *Give Me Wings!* (Fig. 2.12), the artist chose a strong, vibrant blue, announcing its bold presence like a percussional fortissimo passage at the beginning of a symphony. Selecting this color for the front wings of the butterfly, Susanne set a prime chromatic focus of the design (Fig. 2.13 (a)). From that moment onward, the blue of True Blue (personification of the father) has dominated the left half of the painting, which was later counterbalanced with the blazing orange of the butterfly Firebird (personification

17 For an explanation of this term, see chapter 13, footnote 30 (page 380).

of the father) (Fig. 2.13 (d)), who glares in striking tones as the center of attention on the right half of the canvas.

The information about the sequence of the color choices was received from the artist's memory. The analyst inquired as to how she was able to recollect the precise steps by which the colors were laid after five or more years from the time of the completion of the painting. It turned out that for most of her paintings Susanne was able to recall the dominant color, which she usually applies at the beginning. Engraved in the artist's memory, this account could indicate that choosing the first color could be similar to the first lines and shapes that are drawn spontaneously (automatic drawing) and are never really forgotten. Although the artist is convinced that she deliberately planned all the colors and evaluated the consequences of her choices for the composition, our research discovered she often acted under the influence of impulses in selecting a particular color.

Her choice of the vivid blue for butterfly No. 2 could have been swayed by the strong impression she received from observing the blue morpho in the butterfly conservatory in New York. However, her enchantment in the conservatory while observing the living butterflies was presumably the reactivation of significant emotional experiences that had remained dormant in her mind from earlier times, which might be traceable to the appropriate past events. Fourteen years earlier, she had bought a preserved blue morpho in a Plexiglas cube from an artsy boutique, which she came to value highly for its beauty. She portrayed it in her 1989 painting, *The Connoisseur,* in a naturalistic manner (Fig. 5.15).[18] Moreover, regarding an iridescent, shimmering surface similar to the blue morpho's wings, the following came to her mind. She went in her teens with her father to an exhibition of the works of the Swiss symbolist painter, Arnold Böcklin (1827–1901). The canvas, *Mermaids at Play* (Fig. 5.16),[19] caught their admiring eyes in the show. It depicted the masterfully painted scintillating fishtails of the mermaids and a laughing baby mermaid enjoying the splashing waves.

She still remembers her father commenting with great praise, how he was captivated by Böcklin's ability to depict this shimmering effect. Years later, he recreated his impression of such iridescence when he rendered a large nautilus shell in his own painting, *The Weightlifter* (Fig. 5.17). All these significant experiences might have set the stage for Susanne's strong emotional response to the blue morpho and its marvelous hue at the butterfly conservatory.

In contemplating the importance of previous experiences, we can add another memorable event relating to butterflies. When Susanne was about 26, she visited an antique show with her mother. A visit to this kind of event enabled her to experience and evaluate paintings and other beautiful art and craft objects with her parents, who had keen eyes for such things. As she was browsing through the exhibits, she saw a shimmering set of silver cutlery adorned with a butterfly motif at the end of each handle (Fig. 5.18).[20] Susanne immediately fell in love with the silver, which astonished her mother, because it usually took her daughter a long time to develop a liking for anything. She helped Susanne to acquire the set, and today she enjoys her butterfly cutlery as much as she did that day at the antique show.

As mentioned before, when Susanne encountered the live blue morpho for the first time in the butterfly conservatory decades later, her emotional perception of its enchanting, shimmering surface arose out of a fertile ground already predisposed by her previously favorable experiences with butterflies. The artist, perhaps subconsciously, associated the blue morpho's irresistible, ever-changing iridescent surface nuances with Böcklin's painting, her father's

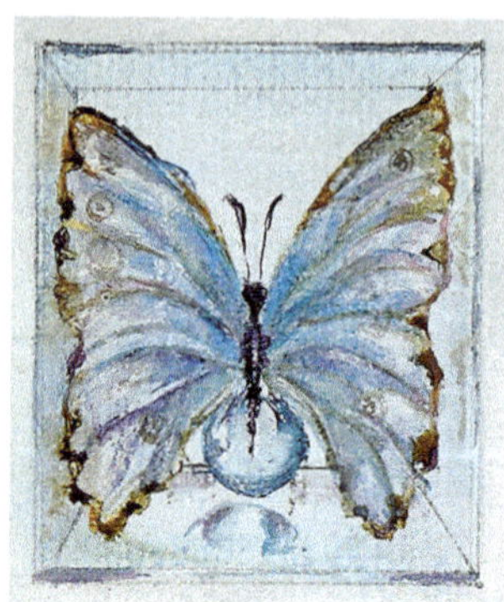

Fig. 5.15.
Detail from Fig. 6.6: "Blue Morpho" in a plastic cube.

18 See chapter 6 for our discussion of *The Connoisseur* (Fig. 6.6). All the butterflies in this painting were depicted in yellow or some variations thereof, except one, a blue morpho, singled out in a Plexiglas cube and placed above the others.

19 Arnold Böcklin, *Mermaids at Play* (1886), Kunstmuseum Basel, Basel, Switzerland.

20 The Art Deco butterfly silver flatware is known as *Sommerfugl* (English: butterfly). It was designed by Frigast and produced between 1927 and 1943 by different licensed jewelers in Copenhagen, Denmark.

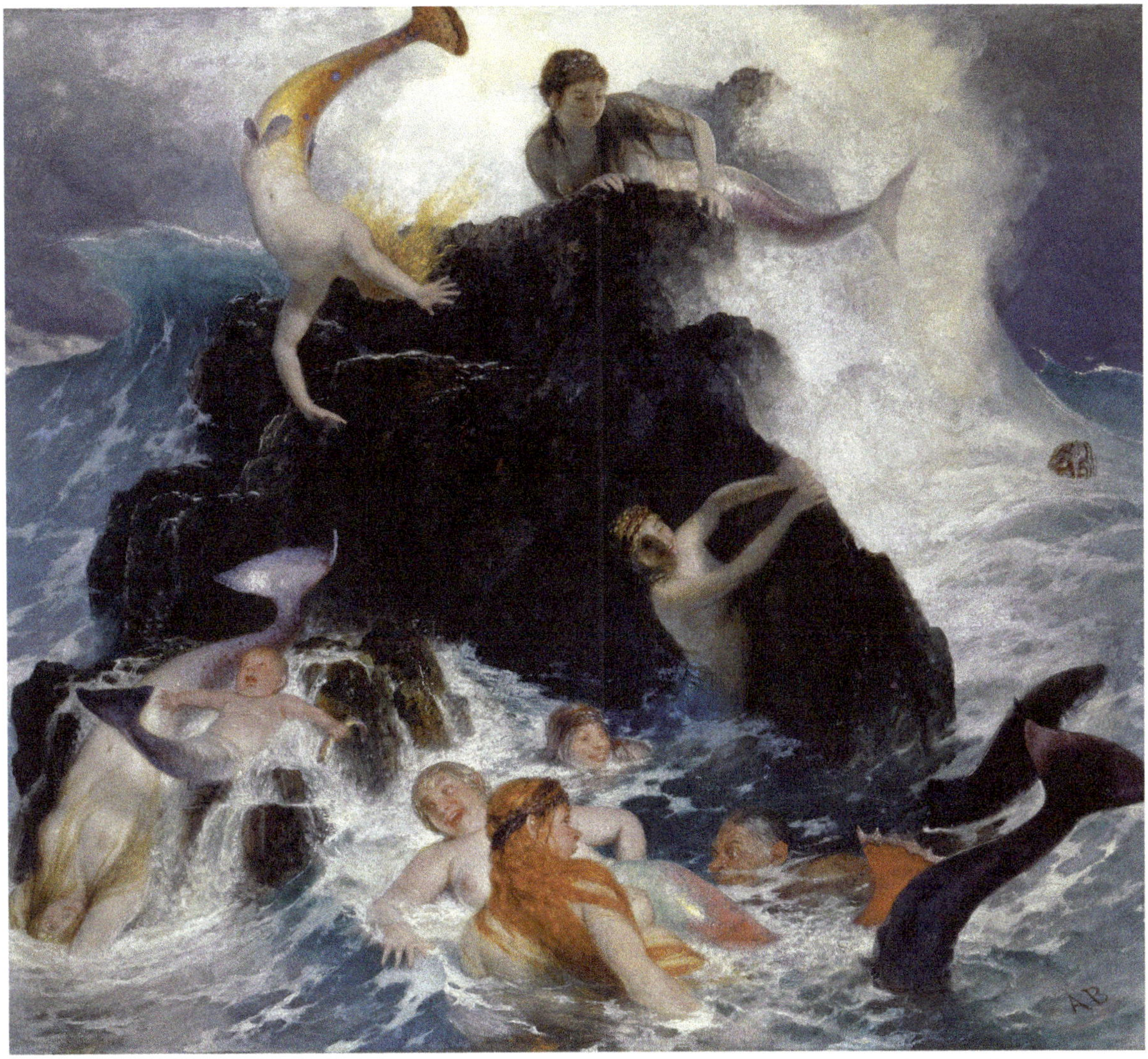

Fig. 5.16. Arnold Böcklin (1827-1901), *Mermaids at Play*, 1886. Oil on canvas, 59.5 x 69.5 in (151 x 176.5 cm). Kunstmuseum Basel (Switzerland).

praise of this work, and his own rendition of this specific appearance with the nautilus shell in his *Weightlifter*. Years before, Susanne had observed how her father had painted the effect of sheen. He had built up layers of translucent paints, and she followed his glaze painting technique.[21] She expressed the chroma of butterfly No. 2 by choosing ultramarine, the most vibrant blue available to her, which she combined with a red underpainting in the final oil painting to underscore the intensity of her coloration.

Before interpreting Susanne's choice of this color, we will examine the oil painting technique that the artist usually employs. Susanne

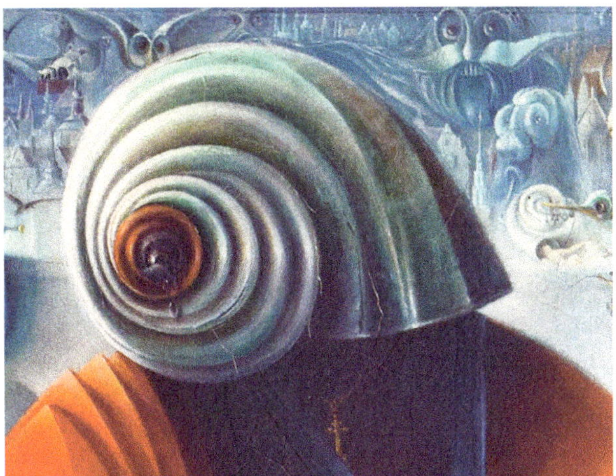

Fig. 5.17.
Detail from Fig. 4.5.
Heinz-Günter Schünke, *The Weightlifter*, 1978.

21 Susanne learned this oil paint technique from her father. Sometimes he would apply more than ten layers of glazing in certain areas of his paintings.

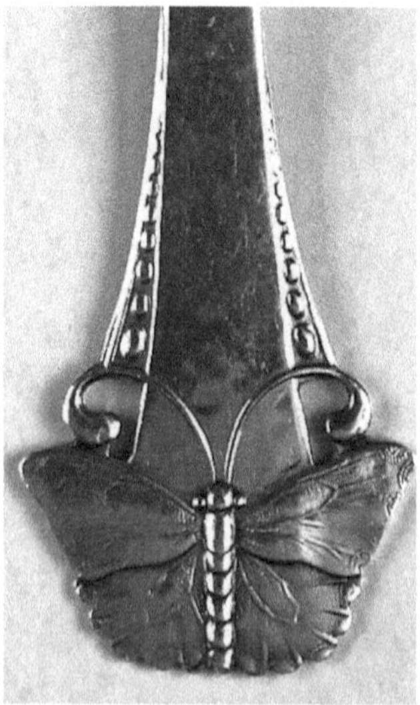

Fig. 5.18. An image of the handle of the Danish silverware *Sommerfugel* by Frigast.

paints her canvases in the age-old technique of *Lasurmalerei* (English: glazing or glaze painting), which allows the artist to develop the strength of a chroma, including its hue and variations, by building it up in layers of glaze. Therefore, she first applies a suitable underpainting, adds modulations, and finishes with transparent glaze, thereby achieving a specific color appearance that is strong and pure. Any nuances (i.e., shading and highlighting) achieved in the underpainting influence the final perception. Using the glazing technique, the painter can magnify the intrinsic intensity of a transparent color by using an appropriate hue for its underpainting.

As noted previously, for True Blue, Susanne had assigned a distinct hue—ultramarine blue, which is a fully transparent color; i.e., some of the incoming light is reflected back after passing through the transparent layer, producing the highly impressive luminosity of the color. However, there is a drawback: The intensity of the tone cannot be increased either through the physical thickness of the applied layers of ultramarine or by mixing with another color. Any admixture to ultramarine will cause significant losses in its brilliance. Darkening, for example with indigo or black, will dull the blue's liveliness. Lightening by mixing ultramarine with white will dilute the hue to a mediocre creaminess. The artist states that, after experiencing the brilliance of the ultramarine in the watercolor version of *Give Me Wings!*, she strove to equip the butterfly on the oil canvas with a singular, awe-inducing resplendence, which she later described as "sapphire glow" in the poetic commentary, whose vividness exceeds that of the aquarelle.

Facing this technical challenge of the oil painting medium, she built up layers, aiming to attain a final chroma of glorious blue. Susanne prepared the groundwork with a first coat of color—a striking, bold red underpainting, intentionally chosen as the foundation for the future "firework of ultramarine." A rare snapshot taken during the oil painting process (Fig. 5.19) proves that the front wings of butterfly No. 2 once were a fiery purplish red. Moreover, a close, scrutinizing look at the upper left contour of the right front wing still shows today a hairline-thin trace of the red underpainting.

As the next step, she added modulations in the center area of the butterfly by diluting the purplish red for a lighter appearance, and darkening the marginal areas of the front wing with additional violet. After a drying period, she applied glazes of ultramarine on top of the purplish red so as to present the front wings in a highly energetic blue (Fig. 5.20 (A–C)).

Through such a procedure, the artist received a splendid, shining blue coloration for this butterfly. The intensive red underpainting significantly influenced the final appearance. Red was an unusual choice to heighten the intensity of the blue. She considered it a mere technical ploy. However, True Blue was the only butterfly among the seven that she treated with such a peculiar, contrasting underpainting. The artist's deep emotional involvement and inspiration, combined with the magnificent blue and the unexpected choice of the purplish red, led us to suppose that underneath the synergy of these two colors lurked a specific latent content, forged by the artist's unconscious. Its coded metaphorical message remained hidden until further rigorous analysis brought it to light.

Accordingly, we probed further. Susanne considers blue to be a very calm, soothing color, and she suggests that symbolically it can indicate a state of placidity. But the "sapphire glow" of True Blue's front wing radiates remarkable inner energy, which does not correlate well with tranquility. The artist thought that she explicitly singled out this brilliant color to signify beauty and positive qualities, which she admired in the shimmering visage of the blue morpho. Nevertheless, it is notable that she exclusively chose butterfly No. 2 to

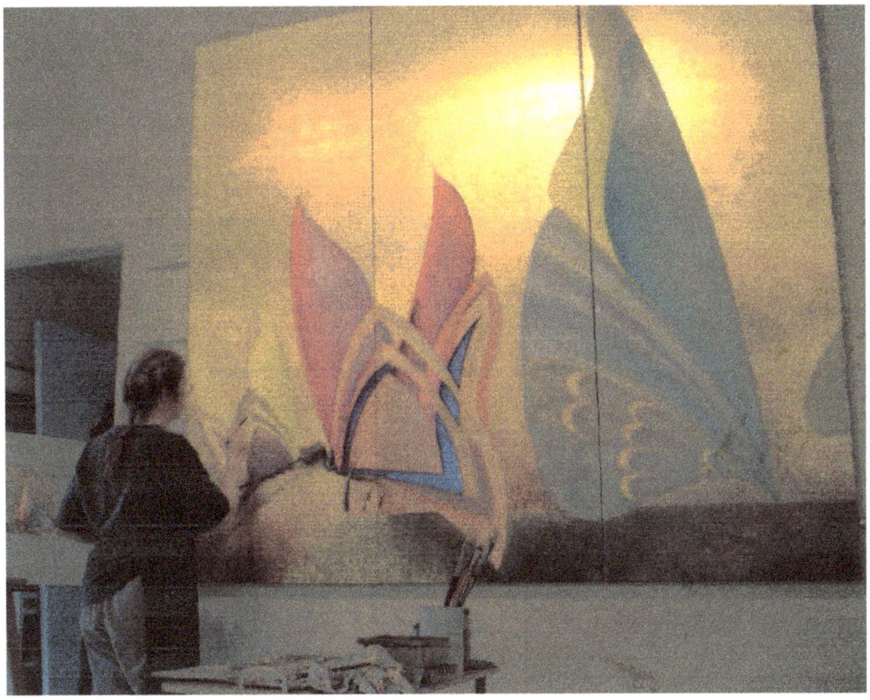

Fig. 5.19. Snapshot from the painting process, spring 2004: The front wings of butterfly No. 2. Purplish red underpainting prepared for layers of glazes.

be the fitting bearer of this distinction.[22] Although Susanne was convinced that the decision solely arose out of her conscious rational consideration, we assume the choice of color has been determined by the unconscious personification of the father by this butterfly. Young Susanne's doting attitude toward her father found its matching metaphorical expression when she implicitly used the dazzling appearance of the blue morpho's coloration, creating the image of butterfly No. 2 and later naming it True Blue. The image of this butterfly evinced Susanne's childhood veneration, respect, and love for her father, which were unconsciously personified in the butterfly.

As we recognized True Blue to be a personification of Susanne's father, the red undertone began to reveal further connotations associated with him. In hindsight, Susanne thinks that the use of this red could be an expression of the simmering emotions, desires, and other "red-hot" issues that dwelt beneath a deceptively calm surface. Accordingly, the purplish red can be an unconscious cue that not everything is stable or well under the magnificent blue façade, which raises questions concerning how "true" True Blue is. A clue to the reader is that the chapter heading for each butterfly is accompanied by a short subheading in italics. These cryptic comments came spontaneously to the artist's mind and reflect, like the sobriquets for the butterflies, specific meanings. The remark at the beginning of the chapter for True Blue—"But it is not true"—may signify that the butterfly's thrilling appearance conceals some negative meaning for her that undermines the beautiful surface.

Underpainting in purplish red.

Glaze layers in translucent ultramarine.

Layered: The centerfield C showing the final appearance—glowing ultramarine.

Fig. 5.20. Schematic view of the process of underpainting.

22 Additionally, she reasoned that the front wings of butterfly No. 2 offered the largest undivided surface to display this color.

While growing up, Susanne observed her father's demeanor outside the family. She witnessed that he behaved quite differently in public, especially in his relationships with his professional and social acquaintances, with whom the father never lost his temper. The calming and elegant blue presents an attractive façade, covering up a hot temperament symbolized by red. The color integration could be the chromatic metaphor of the artist's perception of the father, who promised and failed to fulfill, and who preached democracy to the children but ruled as a despot. He established and enforced strict rules of conduct in the family, with which everybody had to comply. For Susanne and her older sister on rare occasions in their early years, a failure to obey could mean an abrupt flogging with a bamboo rod. The father used the same rod to perform little magic tricks for the children, for example, to make chocolate candy "rain" on their beds from the ceiling. The reward and punishment might have conditioned Susanne to follow conformist behavior.[23]

Her father proclaimed that he was solicitous of others' opinions, and, during family discussions, he would ask for critiques of his viewpoints. However, when criticism was offered, he invariably responded with hostility and aggression, which often made the conversation collapse into a scene of yelling and verbal abuse. As Susanne grew older, her father's behavior became increasingly problematic and a source of awful confrontations between them. Accordingly, the "false blue" can stand for some facets of her father's personality and behavior, which can be traced not only to the peculiarities of the butterfly's coloration, but also to the other significant aspects of True Blue's metaphorical features that have already been discussed: the sharpness of the front wings, the cut-out design of the hind wings, the thorny spike, and the flip-over effect.

The striking blue on the surface of True Blue acquires its magnificent splendor from a purplish red underpainting, therefore, their inseparability becomes apparent. Their integration in the butterfly's image may reflect Susanne's ambivalent attitudes toward the father, expressed unconsciously by dual chromatic symbolism of red and blue. Accordingly, it will be beneficial for the analysis to acquire a more detailed view of the factors that motivated her to use the purplish red hue as an underpainting, which lets us obtain a more complete understanding of the creation of True Blue's coloration.

In Susanne's palette, a deeply saturated, transparent red, "alizarin madder lake deep" (formerly called "crimson"[24]), is her most prized color (see subchapter 8.3.3, Red Content). A drop of blood, like a shiny red pearl, comes to her mind to describe this hue. It is the sight she had seen on countless occasions as her father, who suffered from diabetes, had to check his blood sugar level several times a day during the last two decades of his life. The color also reminds Susanne of her father's ruby red Porsche, which he owned when she was a young child. Although this crimson color is Susanne's favorite and the preferred choice, it is moderately represented in her oeuvre as the hue to establish the center of attention in a work. (One of the rare exceptions is *The Takeover* in Fig. 4.14 with a blazing red octopus.) In view of her love for crimson, it would be reasonable to expect that Susanne's creative mind would choose this hue as the appropriate underpainting for butterfly No. 2, metaphorically representing her father. However, according to the artist, she would never consider crimson a fitting hue to boost the brilliance of ultramarine, because crimson also contains a certain amount of yellow, which as an underpainting would undesirably dull the beautiful ultramarine and deprive it of all its glorious shimmer. Instead, she spontaneously chose the purplish red as the underpainting for True Blue's front wings.

This specific color is important in her palette, where it has mostly served to intensify or modify other colors. It is rarely used as a major chroma by itself. Purplish red appears as the principal color only once before the creation of *Give Me Wings!*, in a painting called *The Choice of Entrée*, (1993) (Fig. 5.21), where the hue draws the attention to the affluent, middle-aged lady who dominates the scene. The purplish red flashes up as the color of a tight-fitting skirt that clothes her voluptuous

23 Writing down this passage reminded Susanne of the phrase "sugar bread and whip"—the German equivalent of the English phrase "carrot and stick." It also brought back the memories of her father sarcastically citing (on more than one occasion) one of his favorite sayings of Nietzsche: *Du gehst zu Frauen? Vergiss die Peitsche nicht!* (You go to women? Do not forget the whip!). Susanne always saw a great contradiction in her father's quote, in view of his professed stance for equal rights for women.

24 This specific hue, like nearly all of her oil paints, comes from the Mussini brand. Alizarin is a synthetic pigment that replaces the traditional pigment which was the main ingredient for "crimson."

curves. Susanne remembers selecting this hue, which in her view is an "unsettling color," to underscore the woman's questioning mind facing a young, modish looking waiter who offers her an array of delectable culinary choices on his tray.

In another painting, *Allegro, (*2008) (Fig. 5.22 (a)), we can observe a more explicit underlying sensual connotation than in *The Choice of Entrée.* The newer work focuses on a single pair of oversized,[25] curvaceous legs colored in the nuances of purplish red. Instead of being attached to a torso, they emerge from a bouquet of crimson roses, encircled by a series of multicolored rings. The artist remarked that, when she was in her teens, her father had a commission from a lingerie company to design a series of posters, which required him to utilize photographs of various undergarments exhibited on a torso mannequin in black velvet supplied by the client. Her father created a montage for each piece of lingerie and replaced the body with a multicolored flower bouquet. The similarity between her father's design and her own painting was striking and eye-opening to her, as she had no conscious recollection of the parallel while she was creating *Allegro.* Overall, the sensual nature of *Allegro* is easy to see, and here the purplish red was apparently used to accentuate it. Moreover, when this painting is turned upside down (Fig. 5.21 (b)), the upturned legs reveal an astonishing similarity with the formation of the front wings of True Blue (a personification of Susanne's father). In consequence, we are inclined to posit that the use of the purplish red color in both paintings establishes a visual signifier used by the artist unconsciously to represent the sensual aspect in her images.

The end of our Ariadne's thread that guided us to our understanding of the latent significance of the underpainting in True Blue appeared accidentally. Recalling the painting process, the artist consistently called the specific hue of the underpainting for True Blue "magenta." During our research, she had the urge to check her oil paint tubes for this color. To her dismay and confusion, she could not find a tube with the name "magenta." Instead, she had a paint labeled "ruby lake deep,"[26] a hue that is comparable with magenta. She realized that she had never had an oil paint designated with the name "magenta." How could she have been so mistaken?

The artist's misnaming of the hue for the underpainting immediately attracted the analyst's attention to this error, which could be the result of some unconscious determinations. From our foregoing experience analyzing the trace of the unconscious in Susanne's art, a far-reaching misidentification, error, or verbal miscue almost always has led to a latent meaning upon closer examination. Our analysis has repeatedly unfolded a classical pattern of development, in which the artist continues to open up new vistas and hidden passages in often unexpected ways while responding to the analyst's probing. Frequently, Susanne stumbled upon a long-forgotten detail or an astonishing free association that triggered a new insight, and which guided us to the right track.

In accordance with psychoanalytic practice, the researchers tried to discover the latent meaning behind this considerable mistake. The artist was astounded to have made such a blunder.[27] Then, in a flash, a scene from her childhood came up. She was visiting a commercial print shop with her father. It was a favorite treat for her to accompany him to this place, being able to see and experience all the fascinating machines, their rotating cylinders, the distinctive smell of inks, and piles of papers and printing proofs all around. Commercial printing is based on a color model called CMYK. It means the color separation of the full-color image into four standardized colors, which are known internationally in the printing industry by their initials (emphasis given by the

25 The gigantic scale of the legs is discretely contrasted with a miniature lute player sitting on the second step of the stairs.

26 The proper oil paint name for this hue which Susanne used in 2004 is Rubinlack dunkel (English: ruby lake deep), which comes from the Mussini brand of oil paints manufactured by the German art paint maker Schmincke. Traces of this red underpainting are still visible even in the finished painting. They are particularly noticeable on close examination, lurking around the upper contours of the wings toward the tips, revealing hair-thin strips of the ruby color.

27 The paint pigment magenta (originally called "fuchsia") was derived from a synthetically developed dye, called fuchsine, in 1860, and it is not a traditional color in fine art. Around 2000, the synthetic Quinacridone entered the selection of pigments available for artist's paints, facilitating many additional red hues, including paints named magenta or Quinacridone magenta, which are available from several established oil paint manufacturers. Schmincke, the German manufacturer of the oil paints Susanne uses, started to include this synthetic alternative among their traditional formulas soon after 2000. But magenta had not been in Susanne's palette at the time when *Give Me Wings!* was painted (2004).

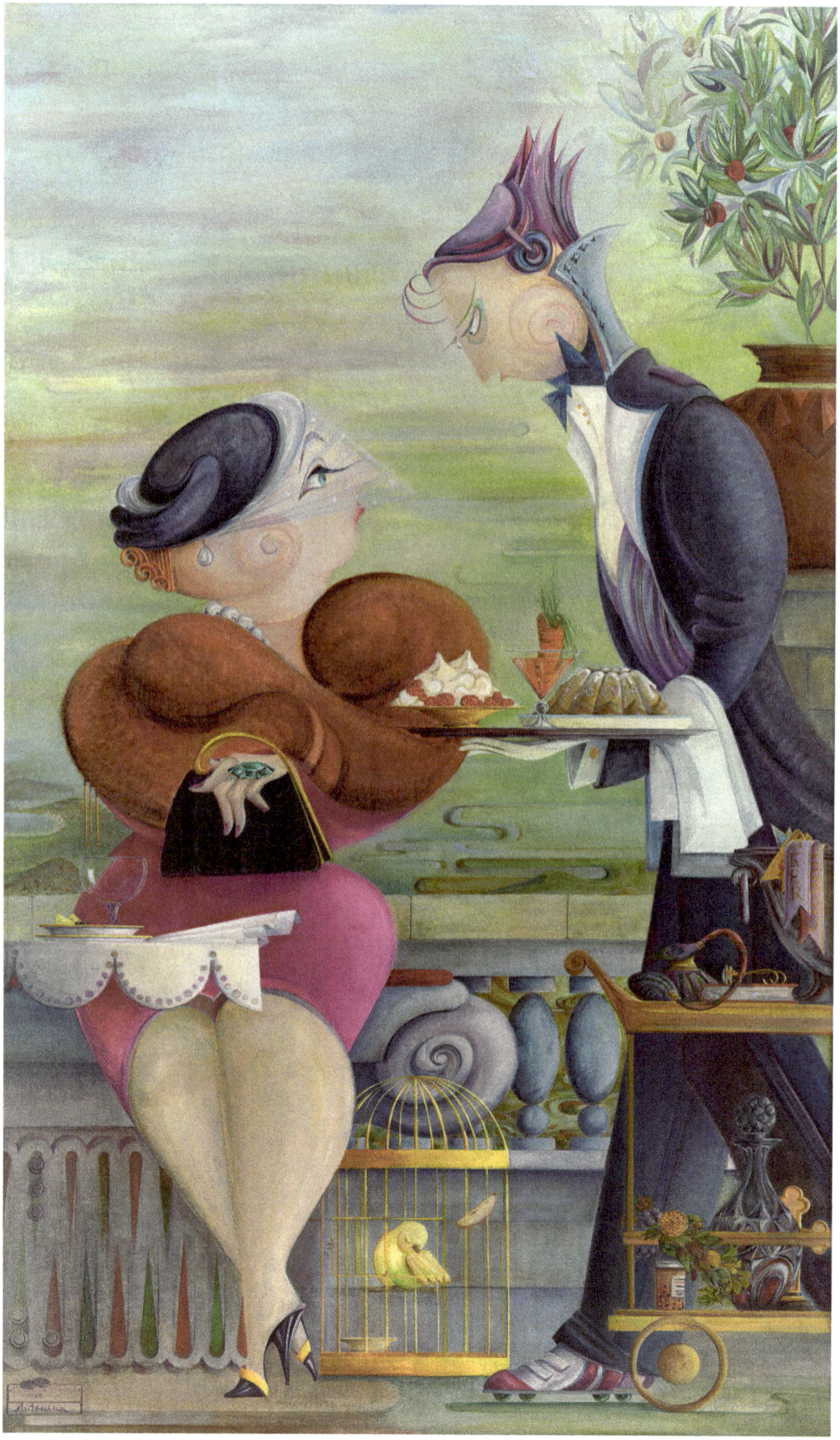

Fig. 5.21.
Susanne Schuenke,
The Choice of Entrée,
1993. Oil on canvas,
63 x 37 in (160 x 93
cm). Collection of
the artist.

authors): **C**yan (for blue), **M**agenta (for red), **Y**ellow, and **K** (so-called **k**ey-color for black). Susanne has been familiar with the nomenclature since her youth, as she was used to seeing print proofs separated into these four printing inks.

She recalled the print shop and its smell, the delightful experience of being admitted to her father's professional world, where she bathed in the superb respect that Herr Schünke received from the workmen, who also paid a courteous regard to her. Susanne immediately understood why she persisted all along in using the term "magenta" for the underpainting: The color brings back the feeling of this exclusive time she shared with her father. Thus, the artist had mistakenly called "magenta" the hue that she had used for the underpainting of True Blue (the personification of her father). The name came spontaneously to her mind, although she did not even possess such a hue among her paints. It is likely that the term became, in this context, a signifier of her positive emotional connection with her father. The erroneous repetition of this term in describing the underpaint color could have been caused by the unconscious desire to keep this experience alive. We consider that this mistake is analogous to a Freudian slip. In mistakenly calling the color of the underpainting, "magenta," Susanne revealed her passionate attitude toward her father.

In striking contrast to the brilliance of the front wings, the hind wings of butterfly No. 2 display a variety of color nuances that range from a dark muddy violet to a nearly white-gray, and from rose to a light flesh tone. Susanne openly states that she does not favor violet (see subchapters 6.3.2 and 6.3.4 for more details). Using this color (especially in dull nuances) in her works is usually an indicator, explicit as well as implicit, of a metaphorical expression for some negative meaning. We assume the peculiarities of the hind wings and their changing violet nuances may represent the unattractive features of the father's personality. Susanne began to experience the crumbling of her idealization of him in her adult years, as the rift between father and daughter developed into a messy, unpredictable, and painful conflict.

Regarding the chromatic appearance of the butterfly True Blue, we have made a few discoveries concerning the possible origin of the artist's color choices and their personal unconscious symbolism. These findings will be repeatedly revisited throughout this text and further reinforced with examples from the analysis of other images in the painting.

5.4 Possible Additional Personifications in the Image of True Blue

We presume that various features of this butterfly's imagery metaphorically represent the personification of the artist's father. However, objectivity required the research to touch on other viable possibilities, even if we were able to find only a few signs and clues to offer an alternative to our interpretation. Principally, we can assume that more than one individual could have been incorporated into the personification of this butterfly. According to the experience of dream analysis and our research, a person, an issue, or a traumatic situation can manifest in various unconsciously coded metaphors with multiple meanings, which are condensed and presented in visual images. Furthermore, this proclivity of the unconscious for condensation can involve more than one person or occurrence, so long as they share, from an individual perception, certain common characteristics.

As this study demonstrates, Susanne's father had the strongest impact on her development. We have remarked that from her childhood into her early twenties, she worshipped him with uncritical, youthful fervor. Later, her adoration slowly declined into a very tense and confrontational relationship during her adulthood. As we have shown, all these aspects are present in the imagery of True Blue as visual metaphors, articulated in the butterfly's structure, coloration, and compositional placement. We still ponder: Are there other important persons in Susanne's life who can provide our study with as good a match as her father? Is there evidence that can be established through the correspondence between the visual metaphors found in True Blue and her significant emotional experiences?

The obvious starting point for this exploration would be her former spouse, 20 years her senior, with whom she lived for almost 17 years. It is noteworthy that Susanne does not like to use the term "my husband" when talking about her former partner, which demonstrates her detachment from the traditional institution of marriage and its assumed roles for each gender. She did not wish her wedlock to be cast in the

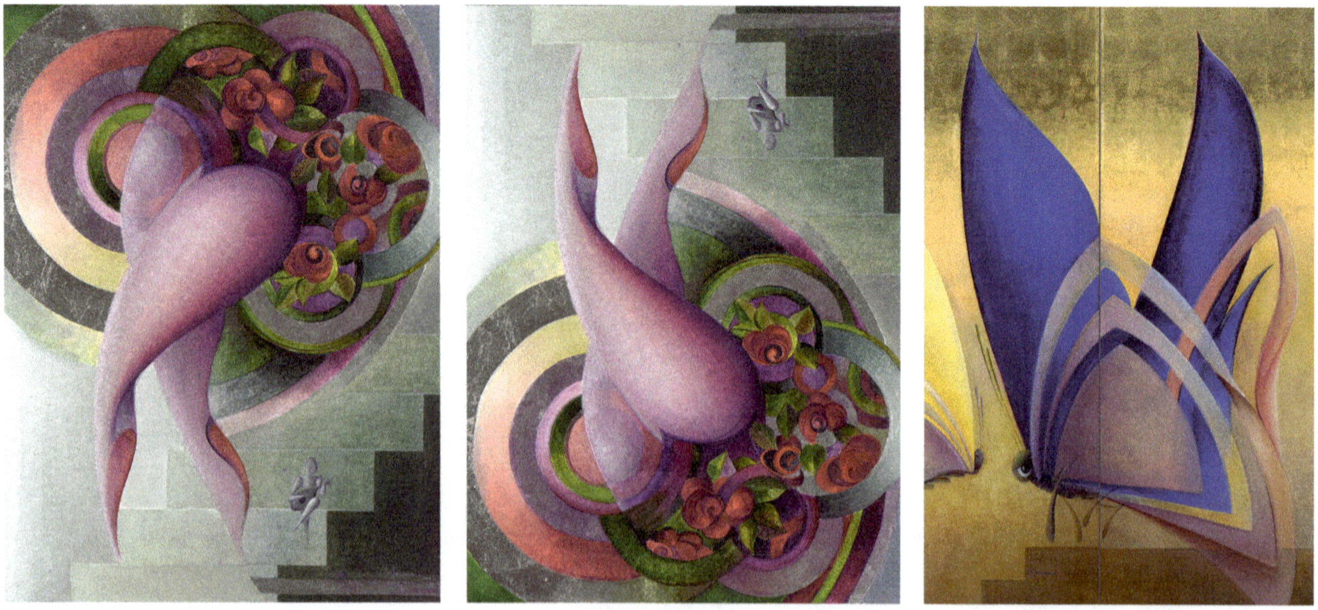

(a) *Allegro* (b) *Allegro* upside down and reversed (c) True Blue for comparison

Fig. 5.22.
(a) Susanne Schuenke, *Allegro*, 2008. Oil and palladium leaf on canvas, 24 x 18 in (61 x 45.5 cm). Corporate collection, Jacksonville, Florida.
(b) and (c) The comparison of *Allegro* and a detail from *Give Me Wings!*.

light of the romanticized bond between two sexes. Susanne very reluctantly entered this legal union, which was to be valid for a period of five years and then to be renewed by mutual consent for another five years. During her marriage, she kept her maiden name and continued to make her own decisions concerning her business, health, and friendships independent of her spouse. It was one great advantage of their marriage that they could move freely between Europe and the U.S. (her spouse was a U.S. citizen) beyond the usual visa restrictions. Susanne's partner gave his full support to her efforts in creating and exhibiting her paintings, and he took care of the practical aspects of their lives. As a benefit of her marriage, Susanne became quite independent. Living in the United States far away from her parents gave her the personal freedom that she valued so highly. However, the marital relationship did not grow into a trustworthy and devoted partnership. After a few years, it became clear that the marriage had to end, but getting out of it turned out to be a long drawn-out process. Whether her partner's actions, characteristics, or her attitude toward him were also incorporated into corresponding metaphorical expressions in the imagery of True Blue remains an unresolved question.

The little passion and emotional engagement that Susanne felt for her former spouse is far less than the close rapport that she had had with her father. On this basis, we could not establish a sufficient foundation for the possible unconscious impact of her former spouse on the creation of the image of True Blue. The glorified aspect of the butterfly's front wings is especially not in accordance with Susanne's feelings toward her former husband. Susanne disclosed certain facts about him: His gambling addiction, four marriages and divorces, shattered relationships with all his children, financial mismanagement, and loss of friendships. She considers that the failure in the emotional, social, and economic aspects of his life was caused by his reckless and impulsive behavior without appropriate assessment of its consequences. This negative evaluation of his personality could possibly find its match in certain unfavorable characteristics of her father, whose metaphorical manifestations we found in the peculiarities of True Blue's hind wings, such as cut-out design, thorny spike, flip-over effect, and an unfavorable coloration.

Toward the end of this lengthy, detached, and disappointing relationship, Susanne met a new male friend who was, again, significantly older than she. The essential qualities of this friend overlap with many of the characteristics of her father. These include a creative mind with a great appreciation for the arts and nature, a highly developed intellect with exceptional knowledge in a surprising range of fields, and a high social status. The similarities also include traumatic life and war experiences that left physical and emotional scars. There are some comparable aspects of temperament and serious health problems. In hindsight, she understands now that the friendship was developed by her desire to replace the ideal father figure that she had lost, and this platonic relationship offers such a possibility. It is essentially based on freely sharing many aspects of their Weltanschauungen, resulting in deep mutual trust and admiration. Inspiring her to grow her self-esteem and self-confidence, the new friend has begun to play a leading role in the artist's life.

At the time of the creation of *Give Me Wings!,* this friendship was flawless, and it gave her many positive outlooks that enriched her creativity. With such close parallels to her father's personality, the butterfly True Blue could possibly partly also incorporate a personification of this new friend. Accordingly, we could contemplate the idea of a double personification, in which the details of True Blue could reflect metaphorically both her father and this highly valued friend.

Finding the conflation of the similar characteristics of Susanne's friend with those of her father in the metaphoric images of True Blue gives indirect confirmation of the presence in Susanne's psyche of the "father complex." The latter determined her propensity for the chain of transferences from the primary libidinal object (father) to the secondary objects (husband, male friend).

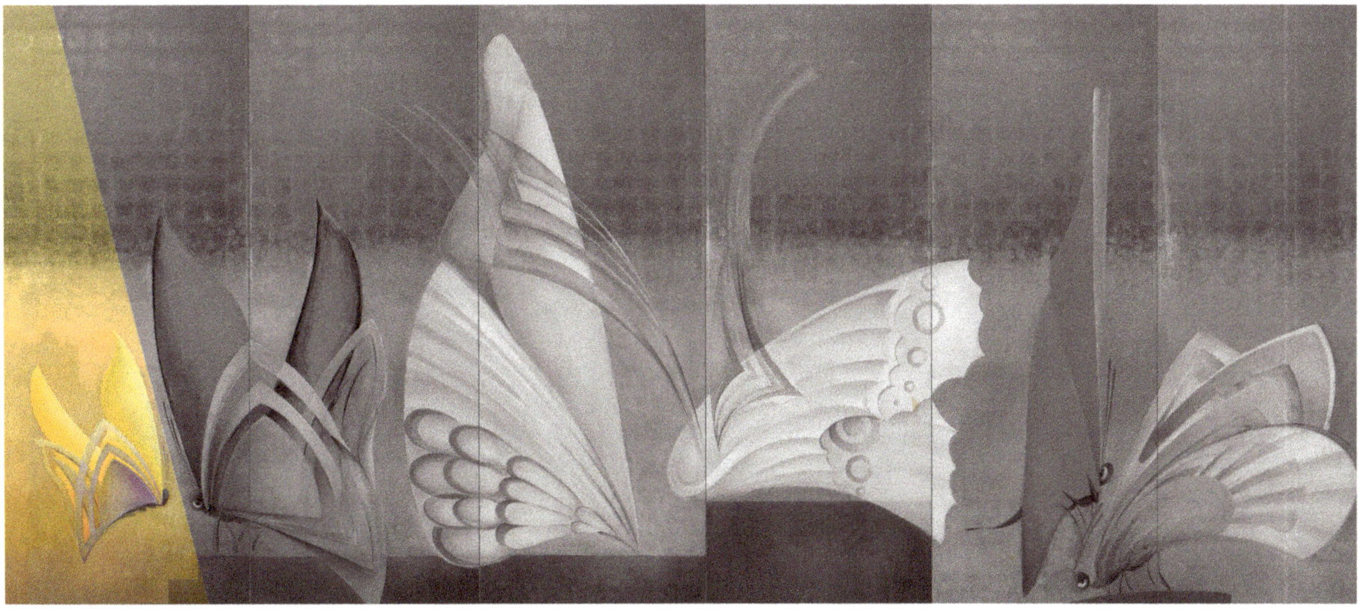

Fig 6.0. *Give Me Wings*! with butterfly No.1, Little Why, highlighted.

Little Why lives her nature to the fullest—questioning endlessly her minority role and significance—copying big True Blue in despair to reach one day his adapted Aloofness and Royalty. Little Why is torn between her admiration of the sapphire glow and the recollection of the values in her own lemony clarity. Little Why jumps up whenever she thinks someone will threaten her painfully fought success to approach the podium—but she herself is the only one who really anchors this position.

—From the artist's poetic commentary, 2004

Chapter 6.

The Small **Butterfly No. 1 — Little Why**
The yellow question mark

6.1 The Name

Throughout the painting process, this comparatively small butterfly floating above the ground was "the little yellow butterfly" in the artist's thoughts. For the sake of simplicity, it soon became "Little Y." This abbreviation sounded to Susanne's ears as a homophonous phrase, "Little Why." The artist spontaneously adopted this as the nickname befitting an inquisitive child, as alluded to in the poetic commentary and expressed in the image of this butterfly. Susanne felt attracted to something positive and familiar in this sobriquet due to the persistent interrogative quality encapsulated in the word "why" in the name. For her, this expression condenses the experience of the young individual, who searches, learns, and adjusts while assimilating into the world of adults. During the analysis, the artist linked the name with her incessant question, "Why?" which she has been asking ever since she could speak, indicating one of her typical personality traits at an early age.

The temperament of little Susanne was marked by impatience and persistent demands for instant gratification so typical of many young children who are intolerant of delays in having their desires fulfilled. Her "I want!" would normally be followed by the repetitive "Why?" if the request was not promptly met. In Susanne's early years, "why" was her favorite byword, which severely tested the patience of her mother, who used to say to her daughter, "You were born with 'why' on your lips." In those years, questions like, "Why am I small? Why do I have to wait? I want it now!" were Susanne's dominant concerns. Most of what Susanne asked for was denied because, in the parents' eyes, the child was too young and inexperienced. They told her that many things had to wait until she was more mature. Apparently this parental judgment carried over well into her teen years and later, as they thought their daughter was not sensible enough even in her early adulthood. As a consequence, this pattern of request and denial continued in obstinate fashion well into her 20s and early 30s, which had become a cause of immense frustration, particularly on account of her notorious impatience. Her father's pronouncement, "You have to wait!" became a significant source of her resentment and distress, often bringing her to annoyance. Susanne's comments and questions frequently broke into her father's protracted monologues during family discussions. He considered her interruptions to be insolent and one of Susanne's worst traits. In her adulthood, such behavior triggered fierce fights between them, accompanied by outbreaks of his choleric temper tantrums, as he felt his authority was being disrespectfully challenged. He responded to his daughter's audacity with verbal chastisement.

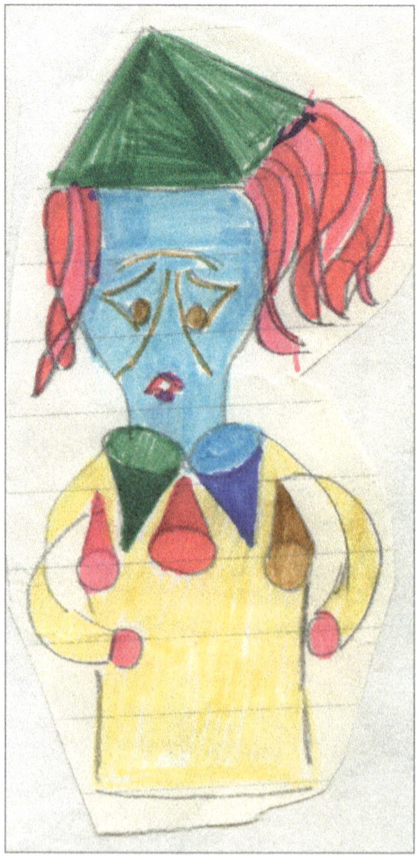

Fig. 6.1. Susanne Schuenke, *Angry Susanne*, Sept. 16, 1967 (date from the archive time stamp). Drawing with color markers, image size: 4 x 3 in (10 x 8 cm). Collection of the artist.

Susanne felt constrained by the many conditions imposed on her life because she had to postpone the fulfillment of her desires until some indefinite future time. Her parents tried to inculcate this approach to life in her psyche. However, she had a low tolerance for any limitation to which she could not agree or was made to feel coerced into accepting. The above narration finds a fitting illustration in a portrait, which Susanne drew of herself when she was 11 years old, called by her mother *Angry Susanne* (Fig. 6.1). In this picture, the girl colored her hair red as if on fire and her face blue, and added gestures and facial expressions that visualized her frustration. This image lets us intuit the inner stress that has resided in her psyche since her childhood. Over the decades, Susanne has learned to deal with her impatience in a more refined manner. Nevertheless, her hallmark utterance, "Why?" continues to dominate her mind, not only as the pithiest remark to question the validity of any statement concerning life's fundamental issues, in which she is deeply interested, but also as a mark of her defiance and independence.

The depiction of Little Why in the painting shows the butterfly frenetically jumping to get up on the pedestal. That, along with her portrayal from the poetic commentary pointing to the infantile nature of the small creature, reflects a childlike behavior that the adult Susanne still sometimes displays. The little butterfly's eager and ambitious ascent toward the podium symbolizes Susanne's desire to win acceptance, to succeed in the outside world, to master the obstacles presented by reality, and to overcome insecurities. Such are the dominant aspects that can be garnered from closely observing Susanne's personality and life. The image of butterfly Little Why offers a metaphorical representation of the state of isolation and alienation that the fledging artist once experienced by being excluded and kept from finding a spot in the established order in her profession. In this context, the square steps at the left side of the podium, which appear like a row of saw teeth in stark contrast to the butterfly's smooth, dynamically curved underside (Fig. 6.2), could be interpreted as an allegorical expression of those painful circumstances.[1]

The butterfly's aspiring jump to land on the podium illustrates Susanne's dream of sharing the same pedestal with the "others,"[2] which would mean in real life that Susanne "has arrived." The imagery implies that she, as Little Why "questioning ... her minority role" (from the poetic commentary), still hopes to be included, embraced, and loved. Her assignment of the female gender to Little Why in the poetic commentary could provide us with an additional indication for the artist's unconscious self-identification with this butterfly.

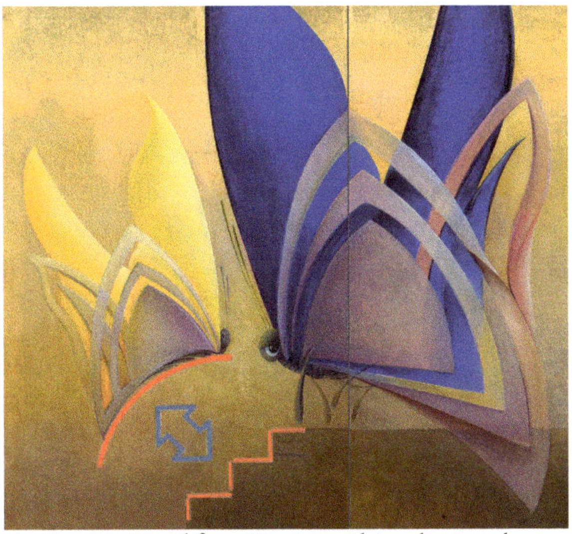

Fig. 6.2. Detail from Fig. 1.0 with overlay in red: podium steps (shaped like "saw-teeth") and Little Why's curved baseline (blue arrow for clarification).

The foregoing analysis gave us sufficient ground to assume that the image of butterfly Little Why constitutes a personification of Susanne, and the forthcoming discussions will add validity to this statement. The image's posture of eagerly jumping, the position of being excluded from the podium, and the unfavorable coloration reinforce each other and metaphorically underscore the artist's desire to be accepted and included.

6.2 Shape and Place

6.2.1 Little Why as a Copy of True Blue

Butterfly No. 1, Little Why, jumps into the scene from the left with flapping wings, heading toward butterfly No. 2, True Blue, who guards the podium and blocks the newcomer's path to a spot on the platform. This pair of butterflies is connected in several aspects, including the genesis of Little Why. As mentioned in chapter 2, the artist selected, from the creative drawings, most of the butterflies and modified them to build a coherent composition. Little Why was born from butterfly No. 2. The artist reproduced the latter one's configuration, turned it around, and reduced its size to nearly half of the original. Through this transformation, the new butterfly appears as a mirror image of butterfly No. 2 (Fig. 2.10), except for its size and orientation, making it an offspring of True Blue. The matching images of this couple contain significant metaphorical meaning that unconsciously manifests the relationship of daughter and father in accordance with their personifications in the guises of Little Why and True Blue. From her childhood on, Susanne had always placed her father on a lofty pedestal and idealized him as the highest authority. She strove to be like him and achieve his personal qualities and intellectual strength, including his artistic accomplishments.

In her youth, Susanne wanted to be a boy, wear trousers, ride a motorbike, and drive her father's car. Desiring to imitate the father's behavior and inclinations, she undertook to operate his electric model trains and toy race cars or play with his collection of die-cast matchbox cars and antique tin soldiers. Moreover, the young Susanne decided one day to dismantle a large broken alarm clock that belonged to the children in order to emulate her father, who had a hobby of disassembling antique grandfather clocks for cleaning or repair. This episode captures Susanne's sedulous mimicking of his hobbies and activities, aiming for his approval. Because, from the onset, she was quicker in learning and noticeably superior in her artistic talent and activities to her older sister, she

1 Later in subchapter 6.3.1, we will introduce the artist's painting, *The Connoisseur* (1989, Fig. 6.6), in which she consciously coded the distasteful experiences that artists often go through with dealers, agents, principals, critics, or directors.

2 A condensed expression incorporating the parents, siblings, friends, and contemporary artists.

received much more paternal praise. Usually, when her mother bought a selection of clothes for her daughters, young Susanne was often displeased with the items and refused to wear any of them. With her father's encouragement, she would change her mind and accept the outfits. She clearly valued her father's opinion above her mother's. These and similar instances from Susanne's childhood exhibit her strong desire to identify with her father by assimilating his judgments and preferences.

The artist admits that creating Little Why by copying True Blue so closely could have reprised her desire as a child to be equal to her idol, her father. Furthermore, positioning Little Why's head a notch higher than that of True Blue in the painting might symbolize her ultimate ambition in confronting her father, to the point of even to triumph over him. We assume the elevated position of Susanne's head (personified by Little Why) could signify that she was hoping to surpass her father despite his towering stance (represented by True Blue).

In the previous chapter (subchapter 5.2), we enumerated and analyzed the details of True Blue's image and found support for our assertion that they were metaphorically encoded by the unconscious, reflecting the artist's father in various aspects. This includes such matters as his personality with its certain deficiencies and his biography, which was riddled with various traumatic situations. The image of Little Why, depicted with comparable metaphorical expressions, might share a similar meaning of some insufficiencies that relate to Susanne herself.

The recurring medical problem with her ears since age four eventually resulted in a severe loss of hearing. This condition seriously affected her physically and psychologically. Susanne also characterizes issues that pertain to her self-esteem and body image as "shortcomings." For many years, young Susanne was the smallest among her peers. She felt discouraged, as she had always desired to be tall. She suffered an inferiority complex regarding her height. Furthermore, she was preoccupied with her appearance (facial dysmorphophobia) which focused on the shape of her chin. It became a decades-long obsession that she finally solved in her mid-forties through a surgical procedure, which she secretly underwent without her family's knowledge. Since then, she has grown accustomed to looking at herself in a mirror without shying away from the image. She was still recovering from the operation when she rendered creative drawings I–III in December 2003 which led to the creation of *Give Me Wings!*.

Previously, the lacerated wings in the image of True Blue were interpreted as a reflection of Susanne's father's traumatic war experiences. Similarly, we can look at Little Why's related cutout wing structure and perceive it as a metaphor to signify her deficiencies and inferiority.

What made it worse were her father's critical opinions of her, which were loaded with stinging putdowns, and her emotionally fraught reactions to them. The confrontations with her father, that began in her late teens and continued into adulthood, inflicted emotional "battle scars" on Susanne. She regretted her failure to develop the appropriate psychological attitude so as to come to terms with him and live in peace. Therefore, Susanne visited home, caring for him for a time, when he was already bedbound, and she tried to overcome his mental anguish.

Another deficiency, according to Susanne, was connected with her gender conflict. She thought it could be more valuable to be a boy. (See chapter 8, footnote 48, and subchapter 9.3.3.) From this perspective, the lacerated pair of hind wings of Little Why, particularly the spiky shape at the center of the left hind wing (Fig. 6.4 (c)), might be considered as unconscious symbolism underscoring this "gender defect." This specific feature of Little Why was derived through the transformation of a certain detail in the image of True Blue.

By examining the development of these two butterflies' images from the compositional drawing to the watercolor and finally to the oil painting, a notable difference is observed between the spiky shapes in the right hind wing of True Blue and the left wing of Little Why. In the compositional

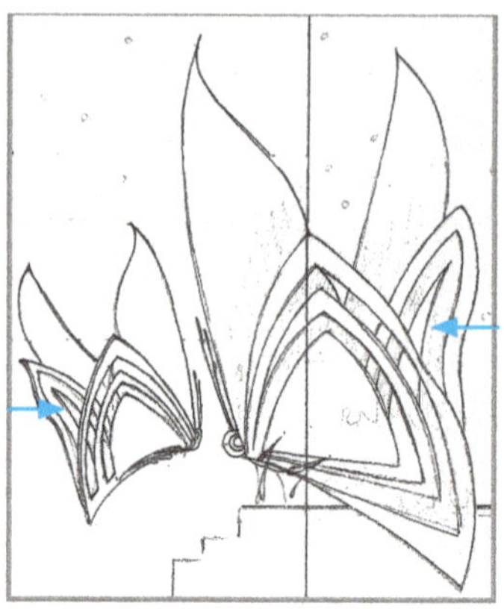

Fig. 6.3.
Detail from Fig. 2.0.
Arrows pointing to the spiky shape in butterflies Nos. 1 and 2.

drawing (Fig. 6.3), the spiky shapes in both butterflies are nearly identical except for the size, but during the watercolor painting process, the artist reshaped this thorny figuration in True Blue to incorporate it as part of his right front wing. As a result his right hind wing was drastically hollowed out and only a narrow, ribbon-like "outer frame" remained to form the entire wing (Fig. 5.1(j)). However, the spiky configuration that Susanne adopted from True Blue for Little Why in the compositional drawing remained unchanged in the watercolor and oil versions. This narrow, pointed shape continued to serve as a principal central element in this little butterfly's left hind wing, surrounded by the outer frame element and separated by a "see-through" area (i.e., empty space) (Fig. 6.4 (c, b, and d).

In view of the fact that True Blue's spiky configuration went through further development after the compositional drawing, this thorny configuration in Little Why corresponds more closely to the design of butterfly D (predecessor of True Blue) found in creative drawing II. The preservation of this original shape in Little Why could carry an unconscious determination, and we hypothesize that it might convey a possible phallic implication, which was tucked away in the last "piece" of the composition.[3] The presence of phallic symbolism in the artist's works has already been briefly touched upon in chapter 4, and we will present further examples of it in our analysis of other butterflies (Nos. 3, 4, 5, and 6).

6.2.2 Differences in Some Details Between Little Why and True Blue

The butterfly Little Why, a mirror image of True Blue, shares with him the overall design of the wings, but she differs in specific details. The endings of the front wings are not so sharp. Her left hind wing is less lacerated, with the spiky shape being part of her hind wing (compare Fig. 6.4 (a, d, and c) and Fig. 5.1 (a, l, and k)). Furthermore, True Blue's idiosyncratic flip-over effect and dissolving areas in the hind wing's middle element (Fig. 5.1 (i))

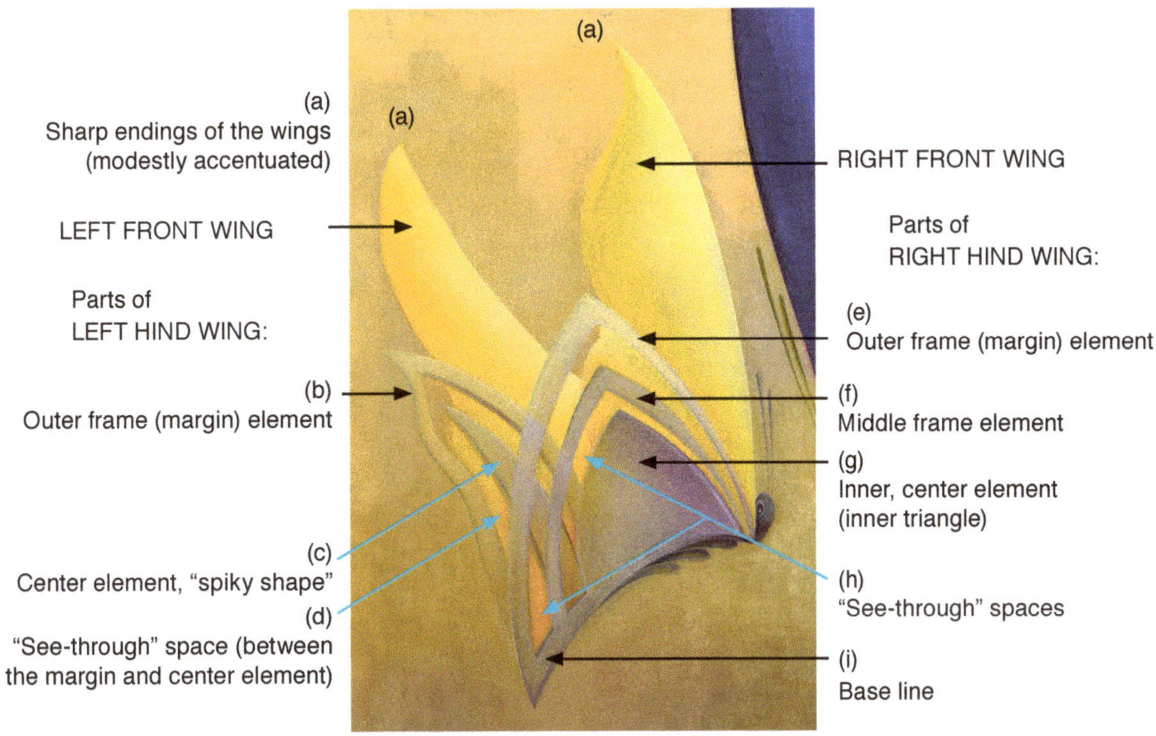

Fig. 6.4. The structural details of butterfly No. 1, Little Why.

---

3 We remind the reader that Little Why was the last butterfly to be added to the assembly of the butterflies, and it was created to complete the composition only after the artist overcame her hesitation to duplicate the image of butterfly No. 2 (True Blue).

are not repeated in Little Why. These deviations can point to weighty consequences, as they offer further insight into the metaphorical meanings behind those details in both butterflies which refer to differences between the father and the daughter.

The explicit sharpness of the tips in True Blue's front wings underwent a modification toward a softer appearance in Little Why. Additionally, the light yellow coloration of her front wings made them nearly fade into the background (Fig. 6.4 (a)). The distinction could metaphorically reflect the behavioral differences between the daughter and her father, with Susanne having a better command of her temperament and conduct than him, although her personality is not precisely even-tempered, either.

Juxtaposed with the imposing appearance of True Blue, the virtues of Little Why could be overlooked in this "David and Goliath" pairing. The little butterfly, aside from her diminutive size and unremarkable color, lacks, as listed above, such intricate features as the flip-over effect and dissolving areas. As mentioned previously (see chapter 5.2.4), Susanne judges the flip-over effect as a very elegant and attractive twining of lines. By creating this visual effect intentionally in the oil painting, the artist elaborated the image of True Blue. Accepting the recurrence of Susanne's flip-over effect in her art, as a stylistic characteristic, we focus on its iconographic representations which convey specific metaphorical meanings. The dissolving areas are less frequent but clearly evident in a few of her works,[4] appearing always in the context of alluding to (according to Susanne) "something higher, which our human brain cannot conceive."

Why did the artist not copy the flip-over effect and dissolving areas from True Blue and use them in Little Why during the oil painting process? The omission could just be due to her general tendency to avoid monotony and repetition by intentionally making similar images asymmetrical and nonuniform in some aspects. That could have resulted in some differences we observed in two otherwise basically homogenous designs. Yet, our analysis indicates that virtually all the image details in *Give Me Wings!,* as well as those of the other paintings we have analyzed, have shown the influence of the unconscious in their formation to various degrees. We suppose that behind the exclusion of these two specific details from the image of Little Why lies an unconscious message. We posit the assumption that the absence of these extraordinary features could reflect unconscious intent to differentiate herself from her father, with whom she shared personality characteristics. Furthermore, it could also symbolize her rebellious struggle against some of his dogmas. It is also a possibility that Susanne refrained from openly expressing some of her most intimate and dearly held thoughts, ideas, and convictions, particularly regarding transcendental realities. She guarded herself by camouflaging them from her parents and acquaintances.

We judge those unusual features, the flip-over effect and dissolving areas, in True Blue (a personification of Susanne's father) as manifestations of certain latent meanings. This statement finds illustration in the following fantasy of Susanne's. One of her childhood reveries spontaneously came to light during the analysis of the topic concerning her early teen fantasies, which prompted us to consider the subject of the flip-over effect from an additional angle and hypothesize its metaphorical meaning. In this early teen fantasy, she imagined herself to be the leader of a tribe, of which she was the only female member in a group that included approximately ten boys, all of whom slept in a large room (with the beds arranged as in a dormitory). As the head of the tribe, she chose to sleep each night with a different boy in his bed without sexual activity,[5] so that she gave everyone her attention without favoritism. We assume, under the purview of the universal unconscious, this imaginary story might be rooted in humanity's matriarchal past. Her fantasy could be considered to stem from evolutionarily determined tendencies for polygamous relationships. However, it could also be an expression of the development of Susanne's personal unconscious in accordance with the incestuous drive, uncovered during analysis, and her experience of sleeping until age eight in the bed with her parents, which might be reflected in the bed-sharing motif in the fantasy.

4 For example, *The Four Elements.* (See Fig. 9.26 and its detail, Fig. 9.27: the dissolving areas in the multiple layered platform, on which the hand rests.)

5 Asked about nudity in this fantasy, Susanne recalls that everybody was properly dressed in their pajamas. The concept of sleeping without sleepwear was unknown to Susanne until her late 20s.

In this context, the fantasy points to a possible new interpretation of the flip-over effect and dissolving areas in the image of True Blue and their absence in Little Why. Namely, young Susanne could have wished that her parents' firm moral stance, molded into a stiff iron frame, especially her father's, might somehow "dissolve" and pave a way for the possibility of sharing with her mother the father as a libidinal object,[6] which would be equivalent to flipping over. The absence of the two features removes a source of Susanne's embarrassment due to the possibility of bringing the private, sensual content in the image of Little Why into the open, since the butterfly is her personification. From the psychoanalytic point of view, the superego's censorship repressed both formations in the imagery of butterfly No. 1 to veil the crucial meaning of the flip-over and dissolving effects from disclosure.

This way, the image of Little Why might demonstrate the phenomenon of repression, selective censorship, and camouflage. We assume that these two effects are expressed differently in the unconscious visual representations of Susanne (Little Why) and her father (True Blue), due to a presumed selective filter in the artist's mind. It enforces a tighter control over the revelation of the latent content specific to Little Why than over that of True Blue. Other similarly concealed messages have been unmasked throughout this study in the numerous details of her paintings. These comparable manifestations of the unconscious were also disclosed through an analysis of the artist's biographical information and associations related to the specific particularities of the images. These findings, we believe, support our assumption above.

The above discussion indicates that unconscious signs and metaphors can be polysemous, even contradictory. The variegated inferences derived from a set of associations pertaining to the flip-over effect and dissolving areas are a good example of the complexity of unconscious symbolism. We refrain from excluding certain interpretations in preference to a particular one, because each could well be valid once its context or nexus is taken into account. We must keep in mind that, from the perspective of the unconscious, the same metaphor or sign can be used to represent multiple aspects that are polar opposites depending on the context. In the realm of the unconscious and its limitless variety of expressions, the mentioned contradictory signs and metaphors could exist simultaneously, representing the conflicting tendencies among the interrelationships of id, ego, and superego.

6.2.3 Fringe Figures

One of the compositional peculiarities of *Give Me Wings!*, important for our interpretation, is the position of butterfly No. 1, Little Why, at the far left of the painting, and No. 6, Fanning Everything, at the far right. These two butterflies are confined to the fringe areas of the painting. The artist's explanation for this placement is that it was necessitated by compositional considerations. Notwithstanding her conscious deliberations, we assume that there are also unconscious determinations that influenced the choice of these specific positions among the butterflies. Another significant aspect to observe is that the directions toward which these two butterflies want to move are blocked by True Blue and Firebird (both being personifications of Susanne's father), each with a confrontational stance. It has been argued that Little Why can be construed as a personification of Susanne. Furthermore, in chapter 7, we will make the case that butterfly No. 6, Fanning Everything, stands for her mother. Accordingly, the placement of the butterflies could reflect the reality of the hierarchical order that revolved around the father. He governs (as butterflies No. 2 and No. 5) the two peripheries of the painting, where Little Why (Susanne as a child) and Fanning Everything (her mother) reside. This is mirroring the leading role the father played in Susanne's family, symbolically indicating the secondary roles of his daughter and wife. Thus, the spatial arrangement, in which the individual butterflies take their ranks, could be interpreted as a reflection of the actual hierarchy in the family. The artist characterizes these butterflies at the margins as "fringe figures," which metaphorically encapsulates the real family situation.

The term "fringe figures" was probably inspired by Susanne's experience of London's theater scene. Some of the city's best known theaters are found on Shaftesbury Avenue in the West End

6 This probability was mentioned by M. Klein (1975), part II subchapter 11: "The Effects of Early Anxiety-Situations on the Sexual Development of the Girl."

(comparable to New York's Broadway). There are also what Londoners call the Off West End "fringe theaters." Many of the latter ones are minor stages located in the surrounding neighborhoods or even in local pubs. There, young (and some not-so-young) performers and experimental playwrights present their acts at lunchtime shows, lasting 20 to 30 minutes. If they are sufficiently good, there is a chance to be picked up for mainstream stage productions in the theatre district. Therefore, for Susanne, "fringe" means someone who is delegated to play a peripheral role in a particular social relationship.

The butterflies Little Why and Fanning Everything became "fringe figures" in correspondence with their positions, according to their unconscious personifications. This association ("fringe") revealed Susanne's recognition of her mother's and her own childhood status in the family as "supporting actors" to the father, who was the only star in the spotlight on the "family stage." The "drama" that is unfolding at the two edges of the painting is as follows: The personification of Susanne's mother, Fanning Everything, has taken on a submissive posture at the far right. Little Why, a personification of the artist at the opposite end, is hovering in front of the paternal butterfly, True Blue. Susanne hopes to be accepted and gain the same foothold as her father, but she feels still rejected and marginalized. Compositionally, as "fringe figures" butterflies No. 1 and No. 6 function as mediating components between the edges of the painting and butterflies No. 2 and No. 5.

The artist sensed that because these two butterflies were acting as the focal points of the composition by their striking color properties, they needed sufficient room and non-competitive images to separate them from the border areas of the painting. She reasoned further, however, that this could balance the intense chromatic energy emanating from True Blue and Firebird. As a consequence, the area had to be cushioned with counterbalancing "fringe" butterflies, whose primarily purpose was to enhance the striking appearance of butterflies No. 2 and No. 5. This arrangement can be interpreted to signify that the mother and daughter are subordinate to the father as the patriarch of the family. This was in spite of his declarations that acknowledged the equal rights of his wife and daughters. His attempt to maintain his masculine authority resulted in curbing the rights and dignity of the other family members. He considered that the women had to follow his guidance, and the mother and the daughters were subjected to his directives. Further analysis in the following section will reveal an additional unconscious determinant, which probably had led to the arrangement of the two butterflies at the margins of the compositional drawing.

6.2.4 Buffers

As explained in chapter 2, the artist built the compositional drawing (Fig. 2.11) starting with the trio of butterflies as the central components (Fig. 2.5). By flanking them with the addition of two butterflies (No. 2 and No. 5) facing toward the margins, the central group received an additional emphasis (Fig. 2.8). However, placing these figures toward the edges of the composition gave the artist an uncomfortable feeling of incompleteness. To release the tension, Susanne felt that she had to extend the composition and supply something in the spaces adjoining the periphery of the painting. She did this by populating the left margin with butterfly No. 1 and the right with butterfly No. 6, making these two images play the role of the supporting cast. Having done so, the artist felt satisfied in completing the compositional drawing, which she thought was wholly based on aesthetic considerations.

After observing this specific arrangement and taking into account the artist's explanation, we were led to ask: Did an unconscious motivation exist behind this compositional development? The search for the answer to this query did not bear any fruit for some time. Then, a breakthrough came. When the artist tried to describe the process of creating the composition and her concept of grouping these butterflies, she spontaneously used the words "buffer zone." This triggered the idea of imagining the painting as a ring-shape configuration, forming a closed continuous scene. Therefore, we can read the design not only in a linear way (from left to right) but also in a circular arrangement (Fig. 6.5).

This is not the only example of this approach in Susanne's oeuvre. She has created more than one artwork on multiple panels with a linear sequence of the individual parts that could also be viewed in a circular presentation, which gives an additional dimension and meaning to the composition.[7] When the painting *Give Me Wings!* is viewed in this circular configuration, Little Why and Fanning Everything, back to back, come together and form a barrier against the butterflies No. 2 and No. 5 (Fig. 6.5). Each butterfly (Nos. 1 and 6) is a buffer to one another and against one of the two personifications of Susanne's father, True Blue and Firebird. This situation offers a key to understanding the unconscious determination of this composition. It signifies various aspects of the relationships and interactions that existed in the family, which are encoded in the butterflies' images and their placement.

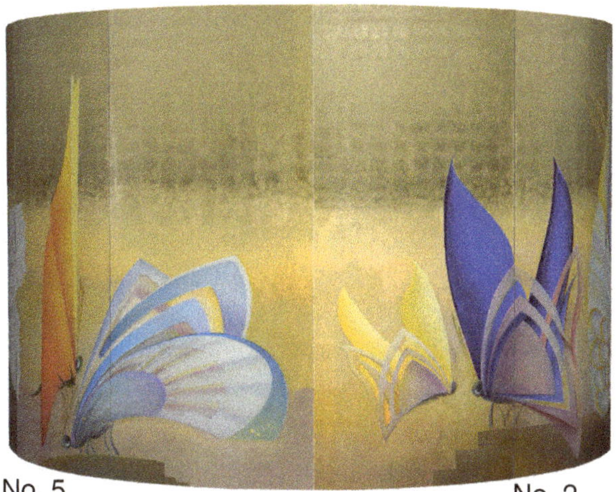

Fig. 6.5. Circular arrangement of the linear composition, demonstrated on a lampshade: No. 6 (the mother) and No. 1 (Susanne, as a child) become "buffers" between No. 5 and No. 2 (both, the father).

We assume this "buffer" metaphor was processed from the real-life situations that existed in her childhood. Until the age of eight, she often slept in the parents' bed, achieving physical contact with her father and mother while lying between them.[8] In her teens, Susanne also acted as a "buffer" by defending her father against her mother in family arguments and conflicts. She was always in "his camp" until her early 20s (more about this below). Therefore, when seen in the circular view of the painting, the latent metaphorical meaning of "buffer" represents one of the unconsciously coded aspects of the butterflies' arrangement that signifies the child-parent relationship.

In interpreting the unconscious message in the placement of the butterflies from the "circular canvas" perspective, we see the mother (Fanning Everything) protecting the child Susanne (Little Why) from the "bad" father (Firebird) by placing herself between Firebird and Little Why. Susanne (Little Why) is situated in front of the mother (Fanning Everything) to separate her from the "good" father (True Blue) (Fig. 6.5). In this view, we recognize a metaphorically apt representation of Susanne's unconscious attitude toward father and mother, which was coded in the images of these four butterflies, reflecting the symbolic visual narrative of the Elektra complex. Susanne's spontaneous verbal expression, "buffer," was the key to deciphering the visual metaphors that were encoded by the unconscious in the arrangement of the butterflies' positions.

6.3 The Coloration of Butterfly No. 1, Little Why

The color of the front wings of Little Why is a monochromatic lemon-yellow. The hind wings echo the nuances of violet from the hind wings of True Blue with some deviations, which turned out to be important for our interpretation. Asked why she chose those hues for the little butterfly, the artist, instead of giving a straight answer, remarked that she does not like either yellow or violet. Then, she went on to explain that both tints combined in the same context become very unfavorable according to her personal hierarchy of colors. She added further that she had intentionally used this combination in some of her works to express negative meanings. This came as a surprise to the analyst because butterfly No. 1 was recognized to be an unconscious personification of Susanne. He wondered why she chose an inauspicious coloring to depict this image. Since the artist did not remember having the intention to use the unsympathetic colors for Little Why, her decision presumably had come spontaneously, which motivated us to delve further into investigating Susanne's chromatic choices.

7 Among several examples, we name two which are represented among the illustrations in this book: *The Land of Iro-Ha* (Fig. 12.9) and *The Elements of the World* (Fig. 10.6).

8 Her mother, reflecting on this situation, remarked to her adult daughter, "Why do you think your younger sister was born so many years later?" She was obliquely implying that Susanne's presence was affecting the parents' intimate relationship.

6.3.1 The Color Yellow—Connecting Butterfly No. 1, Little Why, and Butterfly No. 5, Firebird

In chapter 2, we have already described the sequential process by which the artist assigned the hues of each butterfly in the watercolor design (Fig. 2.12) that she accomplished in a single, uninterrupted session. According to the account, the artist chose yellow for Little Why's front wings after four other butterflies (including True Blue and Firebird) had already received their specific colors. Firebird's striking orange coloration dominated the right half of the composition, and the artist felt that it was important to repeat some of his color values somewhere else in the painting to prevent this orange from becoming an isolated and unbalanced occurrence. The choice of yellow for Little Why was a conscious decision made primarily to replicate some of Firebird's hues. Susanne accomplished this by echoing the yellow tones (including the saffron yellow) of butterfly No. 5 with the light yellow in No. 1 (including whitish areas). By this "echoing," Susanne means the repetition of some nuances relating to color or shape or both in other images of a composition. As such, she reproduced the nuances from Firebird's front wings in the ones of Little Why, as a metaphorical connection between father and daughter, personified by these images.

When the artist directly picked up the light yellow from Firebird, she considered this color as embodying an indirect reference to the orange and saffron yellow of said butterfly. Through the chromatic quality, Susanne connected the two images, although completely unaware of the unconscious symbolism that linked her personification with that of her father's. Analogously, by endowing Little Why with the basic design of True Blue and with the violet hue of his hind wing, the artist unconsciously embedded the same message, metaphorically expressing the favorable emotions the daughter had toward the father.

In this context, it should be noted that Susanne's conscious decision to give Little Why's front wings a pale yellow hue (which she calls a "weak yellow") was based also on her desire to avoid any strong, competing color that would take attention away from True Blue's glorious ultramarine. Again, there is an unconscious element in this decision, as the choice of color reflected Susanne's transferential attitude toward her father, which she was not aware of being metaphorically represented by the images of True Blue and Little Why at the time of the creation of *Give Me Wings!*.

While making reference to the ideas echoing the orange of Firebird with yellow, repeating the violet of True Blue, and avoiding competition by subduing the color of Little Why, Susanne had the following associations concerning how she gave support to her father. As mentioned previously, throughout her childhood and adolescence she always sided with him against the mother in family discussions. Those discourses played a very important role in the family's life, sometimes lasting for hours, which were "splendidly performed" by the father and endured by his wife, who vented her frustration by inhaling an endless number of cigarettes. For the mother, the usual pattern was to protect the oldest daughter, whereas Susanne typically joined and defended the father's points of view, which strengthened their tie. We can surmise that the chroma of Little Why was used to equipoise the coloration of True Blue and Firebird, metaphorically reflecting the factious family situation where Susanne held her father's stance.

Contemplating the origin of the coloration of Little Why further, it is of interest to look at *The Connoisseur*, (1989) (Fig. 6.6), which the artist created 14 years prior to *Give Me Wings!*. In this work, Susanne consciously used numerous yellow butterflies[9] to symbolically represent the visual artists who are the objects of the collector's rapacious appetite. This perception could have unconsciously influenced the choice of color for Little Why. Before delving into other associations, Susanne's experience with yellow butterflies in her childhood should be mentioned.

When she was growing up, the all-yellow "common brimstone" butterflies used to make their seasonal visit to the parents' garden. It is significant to note the German name for this species is *Zitronenfalter*, meaning "lemon butterfly"

9 The depicted butterflies are mostly of the species Common sulphur, a yellow butterfly with some black markings. One is a single common yellow swallowtail. The painting also features one isolated blue morpho, the species that was, as mentioned in chapter 5, a model for True Blue.

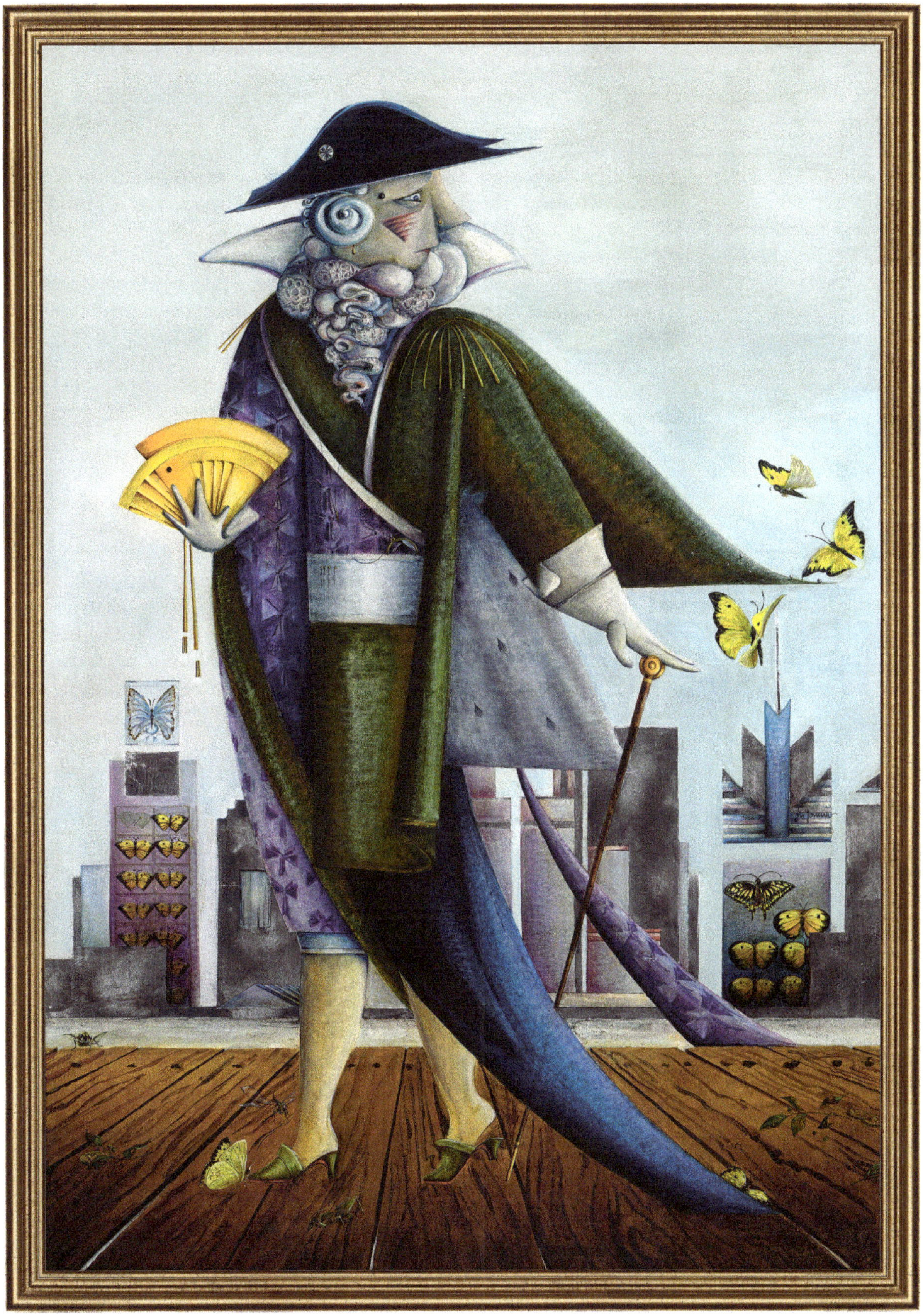

Fig. 6.6. Susanne Schuenke, *The Connoisseur,* 1989. Oil and silver leaf on canvas, 48 x 33 in (122 x 83 cm). Collection of the artist.

in English, which makes its connection with Little Why's coloration direct and evidential. We find the same sense in her poetic commentary for Little Why (Susanne's personification), which contains the following phrase: "recollection of the values in her own lemony clarity," that is contrasted with the glorified "sapphire glow" of True Blue (the father's personification). The "lemony clarity" in this context evokes a slightly "sour" association as a symbol expressing a negative connotation with the word "lemon,"[10] and it could also be understood as a metaphorical expression of Susanne's inferiority complex.

Exploring the topic of her self-image further, all her life Susanne judged herself neither tall enough nor at all beautiful, and she thought this evaluation was shared by others. Moreover, the artist considers that she has not yet fulfilled the ambitions and expectations of her parents, because she is, like the butterfly Little Why, still striving "to approach the podium." Placement on this platform would indicate wide recognition and appreciation of her works. This scenario found its expression in *The Connoisseur,* where the Manhattan skyline metaphorically alludes to prestigious exhibitions and internationally acclaimed collections. The hierarchical podium in *Give Me Wings!* could be an anticipation of the realization of these dreams.

Up to her mid-twenties, Susanne's life had been ruled by a profound sense of obligation and guilt toward her parents, which in turn caused her to undervalue her own achievements and potentials. That significantly defined her inferiority complex. In those years, the world appeared senseless, and she was troubled to the point where the thought of death had become attractive as a way out of her existential dilemma. The perceived inadequacy of her existence, both physical and psychological, in those younger years could be unconsciously reflected in the image and the name of Little Why, metaphorically visualizing Susanne's low self-esteem. The butterfly is small, pale in her chromatic appearance, and unable to join the "big guys" on the podium.

6.3.2 The Color Violet in Connection with Butterfly No. 2, True Blue

In the oil painting process, the artist chose, for the hind wings of True Blue, the nuances of light violet changing into rose and, for the hind wings of Little Why, the violet merging into yellow. This coloring pattern made the hind wings of Little Why resemble, not only in shape but also in coloration, True Blue's hind wing (Fig. 6.7 (B)). Butterfly No. 1 is an echo of butterfly No. 2. Thus, the artist represents the little butterfly emulating the kingly[11] True Blue, and this metaphorically reflects Susanne's youthful attitude of idolizing and imitating her father. The choice of violet was guided not only by conscious considerations but also influenced by the unconscious roots of her psyche, as was the case for yellow.

In the watercolor, there is a clear definition between the yellow area of Little Why's front wings and the violet area of the hind ones. However, during the oil painting process, Susanne modified the hind wings of both Little Why and True Blue with small but noticeable changes (compare Figs. 6.7 (A) and (B)), which included an increase of yellow for Little Why and a stronger nuance of violet for True Blue. At this stage, the two hues (yellow and violet) in the hind wings of butterfly No. 1 merge gradually from one to the other—with light yellow flooding into her hind wings, reducing the area of pale violet and softening the former contrast between the two colors. The artist's conscious intention was to develop subtle differences to give Little Why a bit more individuality and to distract from the similarities that exist with True Blue. Nevertheless, in spite of these explicit artistic considerations for the color variations that Susanne employed, the influence of the unconscious is more than likely at work. In the oil painting, we can observe the changes in Little Why's hind wings as the result of the decrease in violet caused by the increase in yellow, while True Blue's hind wings became conspicuously violet and reddish. These color modifications may have some unconscious meaning. They could signify

10 For example, the word is used informally to describe a person or thing to be flawed, imperfect, or a failure, and Susanne has been familiar with this secondary meaning of the word. The awards that are given for incompetence are often called "lemon awards," as in the annual Harlan Page Hubbard Lemon Award given for the worst advertisement.

11 In the preceding chapter, we mentioned that Susanne vacillated between two names, "Royal Blue" and "True Blue," to choose as soubriquet for butterfly No. 2 to be used in her poetic commentary. She eventually settled on the latter, but the idea of this butterfly being kingly or royal remained implicit in her mind.

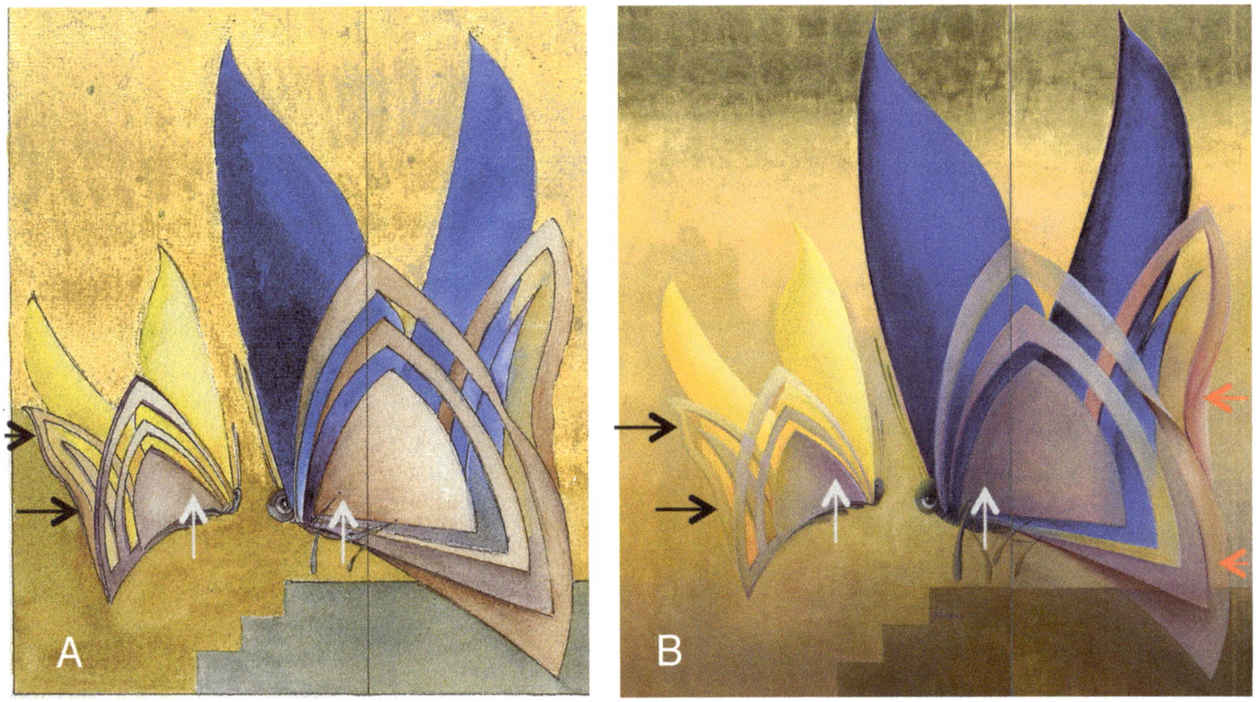

Fig. 6.7.
Comparison of the hind wing colorations of butterfly No. 1 between the watercolor and oil painting:
(A) Detail from Fig. 2.12, the watercolor.
(B) Detail from Fig. 1.0, the oil painting.
White arrows refer to nuances of violet;
black arrows refer to yellow; red arrows refer to rose areas.

the increasing differences that emerged between the father and daughter as Susanne grew into her adulthood and began to distance herself from her idolized model (the father). Namely, the object of her adoration in childhood had turned out to be a constant source of conflict and attempted intervention in her life. In her 20s, a growing rift developed between her and the father, reflected in progressively diverging opinions about many topics dear to Susanne. She struggled for many years to step out of his shadow and find her own identity, but claiming individuality came with a high price. The paternal rejection increased, along with growing criticism from the former idol. Susanne felt humiliated, as if she were permanently consigned to the role of a child and deprived of her self-worth. Yellow is the individual color for the unconscious personification of little Susanne in this assembly of metaphorical images of seven butterflies. Accordingly, the increased amount of yellow in butterfly Little Why could also underscore Susanne's inferiority complex, manifested metaphorically as lemon-yellow, where the word "lemon," as previously argued, might imply a sense of insufficiency.

These considerations show that multiple tendencies can be condensed and coded by the unconscious in the expansion of yellow observed in the hind wings of butterfly No. 1. This is not difficult to conceive, since Little Why personifies Susanne in her younger years, when she began to recognize, in early adulthood, the contradictory traits of her father. The transformation of the colors may metaphorically indicate Susanne's growing dissension, which eventually resulted in a break away from her previous dependency, claiming her own individuality. Therefore, the small but significant variations in color and shape in the hind wings of Little Why, in comparison to True Blue in the final oil version of *Give Me Wings!*, metaphorically denote this process of estrangement. The artist's conscious declaration of color assignment due to compositional balance is overridden by unconscious influences.

6.3.3 Coloration of Butterfly No. 1, Little Why, Under the Aspect of Color Theory

The following discussion is derived from a comparison of the colors of Little Why, True Blue, and Firebird under some aspects of color theory.[12] Butterfly No. 1 is painted in the hues of yellow (a primary color) and violet (a secondary color, resulting from red and blue). These two hues establish a complementary contrast. Therefore, according to color theory, they interact in a harmonious way. In comparison, the overall tints of butterfly No. 2 are the primary color blue in the front wings and the secondary color violet in the hind wings. In this case, the two tints do not achieve complementary contrast, because the third of the primary colors, yellow, is missing in these hues. For this reason, they are considered to be analogous colors. For butterfly No. 5, Firebird, the same observation is valid. His wide range of shades contains two primary colors, yellow and red, the combination of which produces the secondary color orange. But the third primary, blue, is absent in Firebird. Thus, the chroma in butterfly No. 5 stands only in analogous relation.

We were able to arrive at some thought-provoking statements by following Susanne's knowledge of the general color theory with its categorization of primary and secondary colors and the complementary contrasts presented in the butterflies, along with Susanne's individual attitude toward colors and their combinations, and her distinct iconography of colors. The examination of the above factors, especially her personal preferences, gave us the basis to expect that any of the color choices by Susanne is meaningful on both the conscious and unconscious levels. Bearing this in mind, a hypothesis can be derived from the comparison of the color combinations found in Little Why, True Blue, and Firebird.

The butterfly Little Why has all three primary colors, while True Blue and Firebird possess only two of the primary colors in their makeup. This specific aspect of their coloration (complete or incomplete presence of the primary colors) might reflect the influence of the unconscious processes on the choice of hues for the butterflies. The presence of all three primary colors in butterfly No. 1 (Susanne) could imply richness, whereas having only two primary colors in each of butterflies Nos. 2 and 5 (both representing personifications of the father) could mean deficit. The color scheme could symbolically express Susanne's unconscious tendency to counteract and to obtain compensation for the father's domination over her. Although True Blue and Firebird each lacks one prime color, they dominate the painting by their striking chromatic appearances, reflecting Susanne's childhood perception of the father's authority.

We could assume that Susanne (as personified by Little Why) is engaged in a competitive relationship with her father (personified by True Blue and Firebird). In this context, there might be an unconscious disposition in her psyche to elevate herself above her competitor, which could have been the source for assigning to her pictorial

12 A short summary of the basic aspects of the generally accepted color theory, well known to artists (regarding subtractive colors, i.e., paints) follows below. In a very simplified understanding, any hue of paint commonly employed by artists can principally be achieved by using one or more of the three primary colors (red, blue, and yellow). Mixing two of the primary colors results in a new hue, called secondary color. There are three secondary colors: violet (resulting from mixing red and blue), orange (mixing red and yellow), and green (mixing yellow and blue). When one of the primary colors is kept unchanged and the other two mixed into a secondary color, applying these two hues (one pure and the other mixed) side by side creates a complementary contrast. In this way, according to color theory, all primary colors are present either pure or in the form of a secondary color, which is considered one of the ways to achieve color harmony. Such pairs of complementary hues are yellow with violet, red with green, and blue with orange. Each of them is also called complementary contrast. Several other color schemes are commonly used with the aim of producing an appealing color combination, and they also refer to the positions of the hues on the color wheel. One of these color schemes is the analogous one, which employs two to four neighboring colors on the wheel. According to the traditional association of colors with temperatures, yellow and red are associated with the sun and fire; ergo, they are considered to be "warm." On the other hand, blue and green are related to ice and shading leaves; therefore, they are "cool." For color theories, especially the complementary color scheme, consult the following books listed in the bibliography section: *The New Encyclopaedia Britannica*, vol.3, page 470 (1987); Jean Robertson 2000, and Becky Koenig 2009.

personification (Little Why) the maximum attributes (i.e., all three primary colors), while depriving the same for the father's personifications (i.e., each receiving only two primary colors). This conceivably mirrors the childhood scenario, in which Susanne desired dominance, even over her father.

Our earlier observation that Little Why's head is portrayed at a slightly higher position than True Blue's supports the above assumption (see subchapter 6.2.1). The analysis of the metaphorical meaning of the specific nuances of Little Why's coloration, which the artist calls "pale yellow and pale violet," further augments the premise. Those colors possess a lower saturation (intensity) and a lighter value (a higher content of white). True Blue with his dark, saturated sapphire glow and Firebird in blazing orange are in striking contrast to the light appearance and the decreased chromatic intensity of Little Why. The butterfly's coloration could be interpreted as a metaphorical expression for a weak, immature child who is pale and sickly,[13] and has to keep on growing and developing to attain the level of vigor displayed by her father (as seen in True Blue and Firebird). Had Little Why's yellow and violet been painted to full intensity and depth, they would have definitely challenged the chromatic dominance of True Blue and Firebird, but to provoke her father would not have been permissible for Susanne as a young child. In spite of her desire for flamboyant colors, she had to be inconspicuous. In this regard, Little Why's subdued hues can be interpreted as a camouflage for her aspiration to claim dominance. She tries to hide her "completeness" (three primary colors) through the less intensive tinges in comparison with the butterflies, True Blue and Firebird, which have "incomplete" chromaticity (each having only two primary colors), not withstanding their brilliant coloration. The deficiency that Susanne unconsciously assigned to the visual personifications of the father can therefore be considered as a metaphorical signifier of her father's controversial character, which Susanne came to perceive as an adult.

6.3.4 Possible Unconscious Roots for the Artist's Personal Attitude Toward Yellow and Violet

Susanne, as an art historian and artist, has accumulated extensive knowledge about traditional color symbolism. However, an individual iconography has developed in her art over the years, which diverges, sometimes essentially, from generally associated meanings.

Regarding her personal attitude toward yellow, she does not follow the common positive perception of the color as representing luminosity and sunshine. She judges the color by its various chromatic nuances, many of which she does not like (e.g., lemon yellow), while a few (e.g., saffron yellow), she does. This overly selective attitude toward the color prompted the analyst to question if there were some unconscious bases that spurred the formation of the artist's bias concerning yellow and its variations, of which she explicitly and implicitly uses, some as negatives and others as positives, in her art. We have identified many isolated associations of yellow (as well as other colors) going back to her childhood, from which we have singled out a few pertinent cases. We will present several associations and interpretations that might shed light on how yellow, violet, and other colors could be correlated to significant emotional experiences in the artist's past.

While viewing the paintings that belonged to her parents in Susanne's childhood home, we pay close attention to two canvases that had been distressing to the young Susanne in which the colors violet and yellow are prominently displayed. The first work, *Das Springen nach Allensbach* (English: *The Jumping Procession to Allensbach*),[14] (1965) (Fig. 6.8), was created by her father, and it presents a parade of very stylized, robot-like beings with cylindrical torsos and metallic surfaces marching across a landscape. Each of the six figures in the foreground is given a unique hue, with the first three being male and the last three, female. The males are equipped with pairs of arms attached to the torso with metal hinges. All of them are moving by hopping over jump ropes, which they

13 In chapter 8, Pale Moonlight, the word "pale" will be discussed in detail in connection with the weak and sick child that Susanne was.

14 "Allensbach" is an abbreviated reference to the leading public opinion research institute in Germany ("*Das Institut für Demoskopie Allensbach*") founded in 1947, which played an influential role in German political campaigns and public policy debates, particularly in the Federal Republic period.

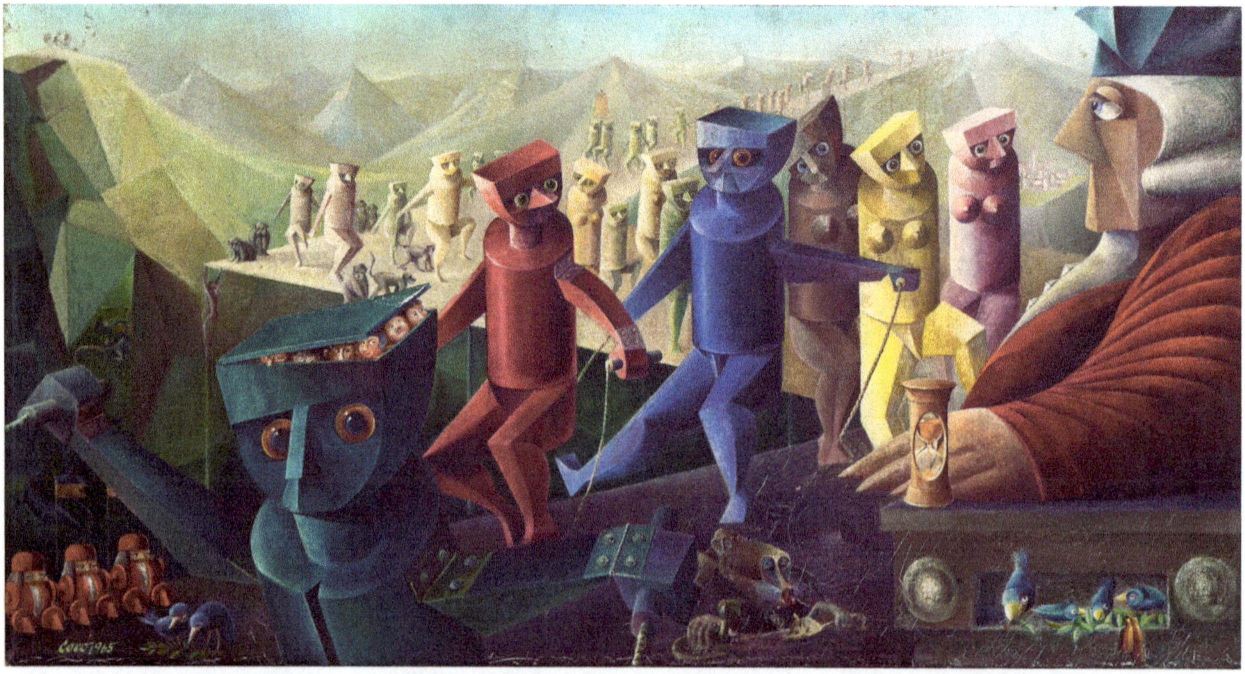

Fig. 6.8. Heinz-Günter Schünke, *Das Springen nach Allensbach* (The Jumping Procession to Allensbach), 1965. Oil on canvas, 19.6 x 38 in (50 x 97 cm). Collection of the artist's family, Germany.

hold in their hands. The gender of the three female figures following the males is identified by a pair of cone-shaped breasts for each figure, which is tipped with nipples. Curiously, the female figures are all missing their arms, which prevents them from holding jump ropes (Fig. 6.9).

The father explained to the family members that the lack of arms symbolized the powerless state of women in society, where only men are allowed to "jump" (that is, to climb the social ladder). The images of the women and the father's accompanying explanation about their deprivation of rights were highly disturbing to Susanne, and that experience could have created her related worries. Being forbidden to jump became for Susanne a symbol of various societal biases and restrictions that deprive women of their human liberties. At the time this painting was executed, the eight-year-old Susanne was unaware of such limits that women were generally subjected to in society. She was used to having the freedom to enjoy all kinds of desirable activities, including games played with a jump rope, which she did alone or with friends in the neighborhood.

It is important to note that her father painted the female trio in *Jumping to Allensbach* in shades of yellow, violet, and violet-purple. It could be assumed that Susanne's mind associated these hues with the distressing image of the

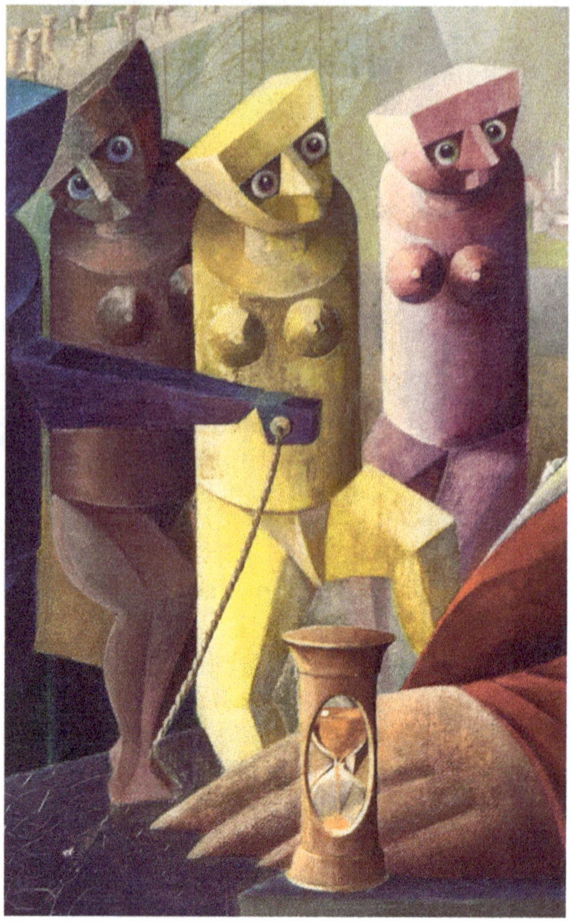

Fig. 6.9. Detail from Fig. 6.8: Group of three females.

powerless women. Therefore, these colors and their combination might have been planted in Susanne's mind as a symbol of inferiority. Since her youth, Susanne has never tolerated discrimination and exclusion by reason of gender. Whenever she encounters such a situation, she reacts with outrage. The colors associated with the women in the painting could have become the hues of depreciated human worth.

The second artwork, *Bullfight Scene* by Roberto Domingo y Fallola[15] (Fig. 6.10), may deliver additional clues to interpreting the symbolic significance of the color combination for Susanne. We will analyze this painting's influence on Susanne extensively in subchapter 8.3.3. At this juncture, the following discussion focuses only on the appearance of violet and yellow in Domingo's work. The painting depicts two bullfighters, a black bull, and a seriously wounded white horse, emphasized by a large yellowish spotlight. The costume of the matador contains muted yellow, and that of the torero, pale violet. Both bullfighters hold capes (red and gold, respectively) that are lined in violet (Fig. 6.11).

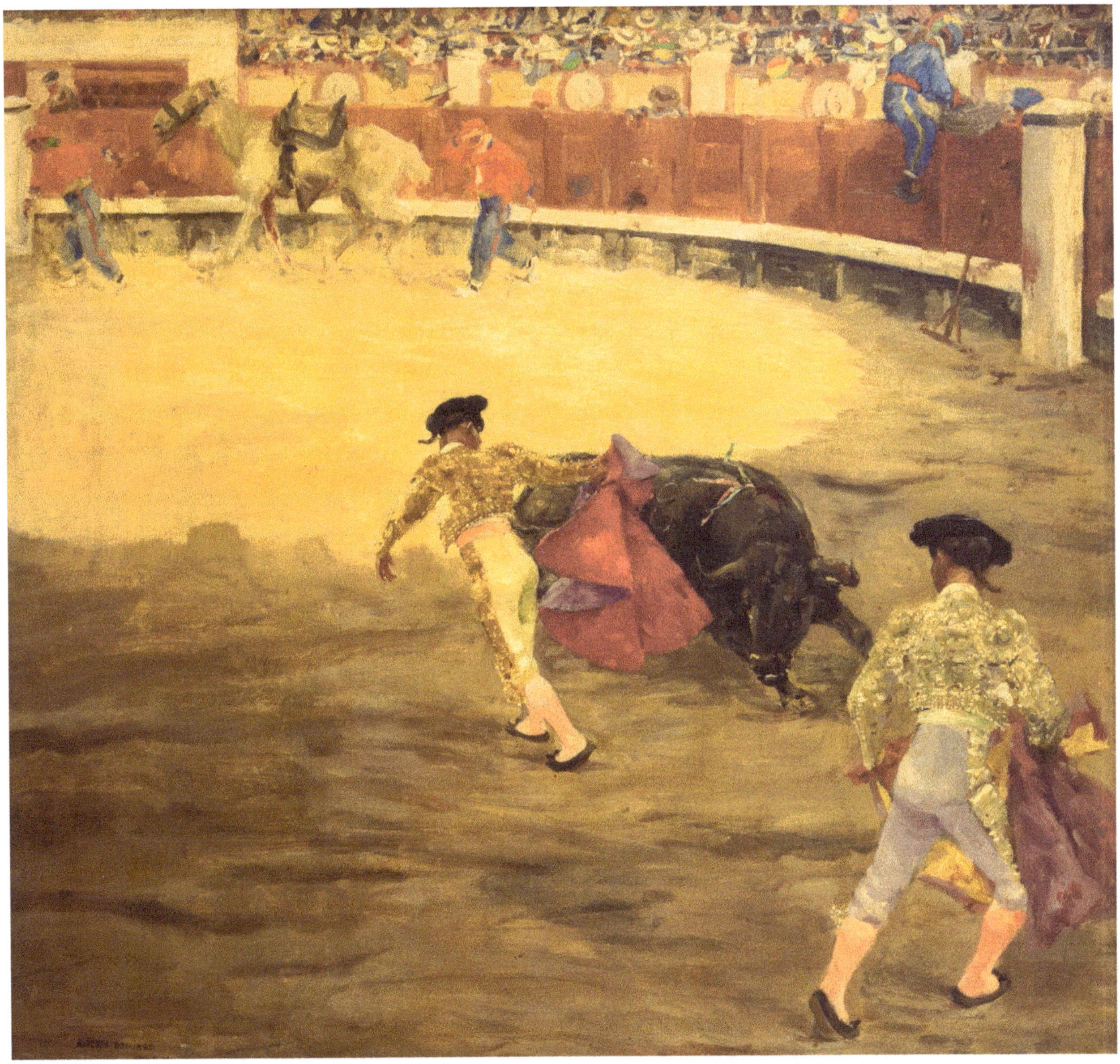

Fig.6.10. Roberto Domingo y Fallola, *Bullfight Scene*, circa early to mid-20th century. Oil on canvas, 25 x 26.7 in (64 x 68 cm). Collection of the artist's family, Germany

15 Roberto Domingo y Fallola (Paris, 1883–Madrid, 1956), Spanish impressionist.

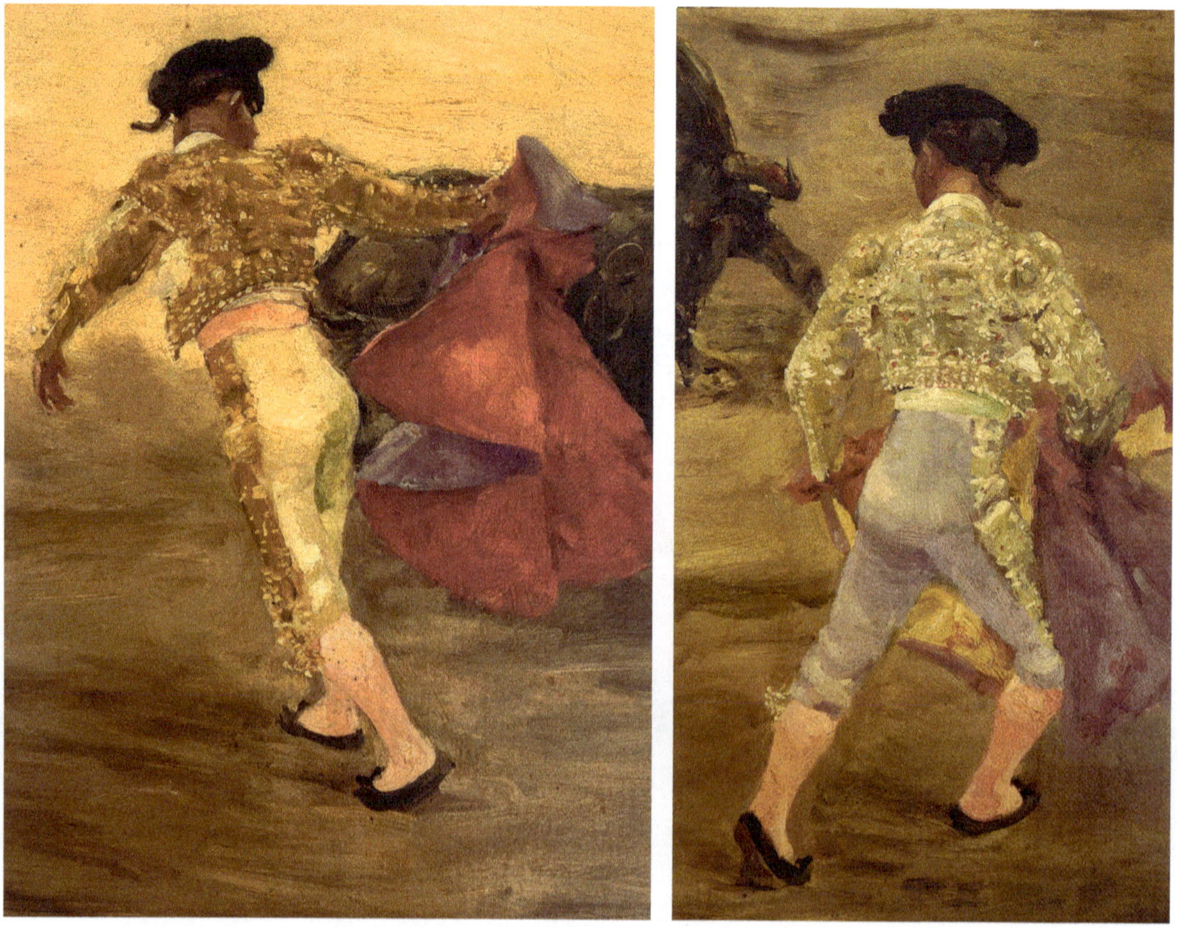

Fig. 6.11. Two details from Fig. 6.10, showing the colors yellow and violet in the costumes of the matador (left) and torero (right). Note the violet lining of the capes.

Susanne has despised this picture and averted her eyes from it all her life because of the injured horse,[16] which she understood in a specific way. She always thought that the horse was gored by the bull in the belly, which is significant in connection with her omphalophobia. It is still traumatic for her today to look at certain details of the painting, and she always becomes emotionally perturbed, unable to distance herself from the work's impact. Susanne hated the painting very much, and when the family moved in her early teens, the artwork was not displayed anymore. She did not see it again until our study was undertaken. A glimpse of the horse (Fig. 6.10 and its detail Fig. 8.51) causes acute, palpable horror, and she immediately diverts her glance from the injured animal, trying to avoid the specific area that for her signifies cruelty, aggression, and suffering. Instead, she tries to focus her attention on the bullfighters, who are dressed in yellow and violet (Fig. 6.11). This negative emotional perception possibly could have been integrated into her unconscious with the colors in question, which caused the hues to be associated with feelings of disgust and horror. The analysis of this painting brought to light a concrete traumatic emotional experience, from which the researchers were able to deduce the possible origin of Susanne's attitude toward the combination of yellow and violet.

Susanne has frequently used yellow and violet to express negative content. Examples can be found in the artist's paintings such as *The Connoisseur*, 1989 (Fig. 6.6), *Change in the Weather*, 1988–91 (Fig. 6.12), *Born To Starve*,

16 She continues to hate the painting and still suffers from horror today by looking at, or even thinking of or imagining it. When she was preparing the illustration of the painting for this study, she placed a blank square over the offending area to avoid seeing the gruesome details. She wonders how her parents, as adults concerned about their children's education, could have had such a painting hung in a prominent place to be seen by their young children.

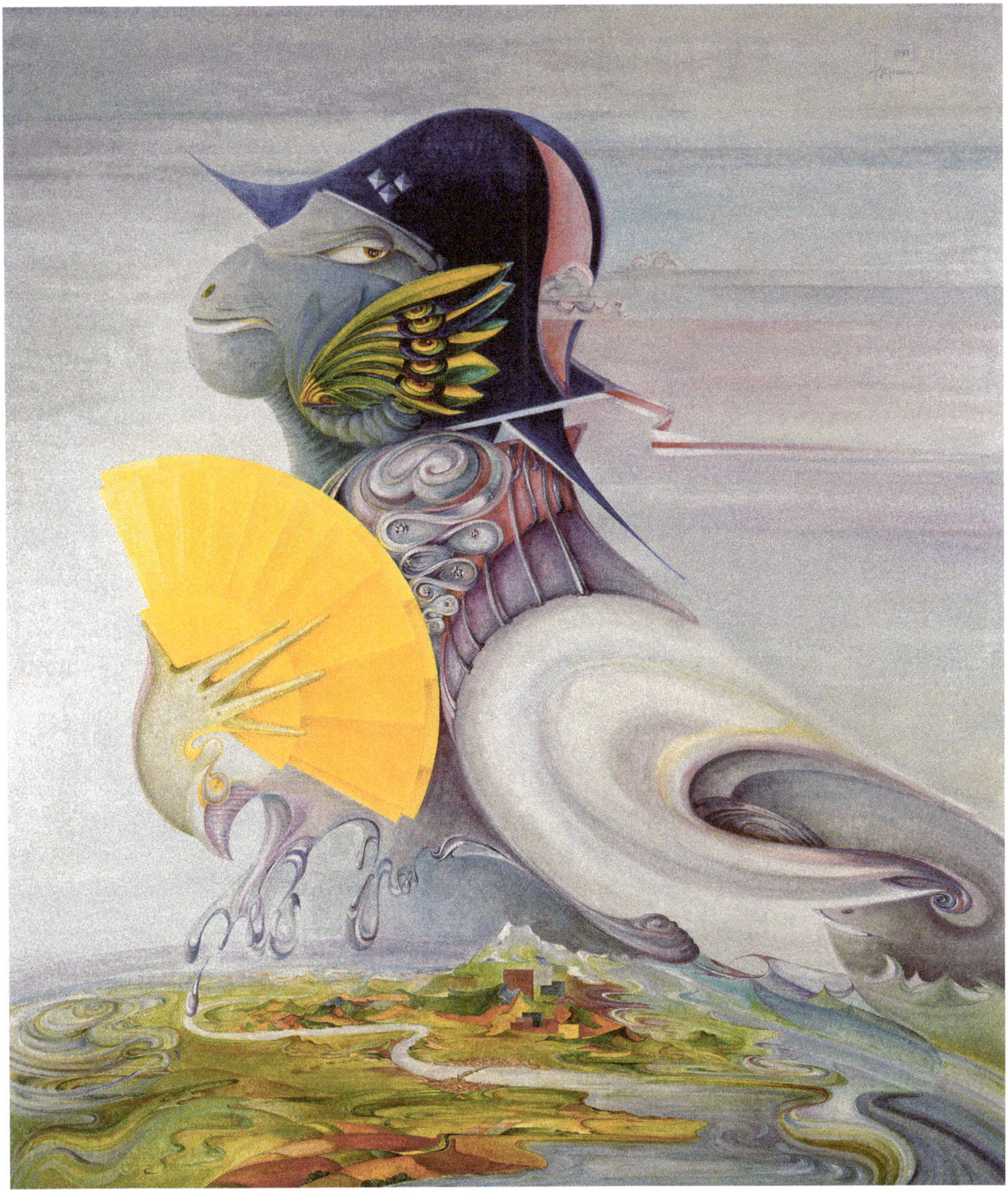

Fig. 6.12. Susanne Schuenke, *Change in the Weather*, 1991.
Oil on canvas, 55 x 48 in (140 x 122 cm). Collection of the artist.

1985 (Fig. 6.13), and *Greed*, 1985–89 (Fig. 6.14). In *Born to Starve*, she intentionally combined the disliked yellow and violet to dress the two standing figures, who are at the forefront of an endless queue of impoverished women. All of them are supposed to hold infants in their arms, whose future is symbolically foretold by the equally immeasurable file of crouching skeletal adolescent figures below. Susanne remembers that she intentionally chose those colors as the "most disliked ones" to underscore her heartfelt grievance against the situation so prevalent in some parts of the world.

If in the artist's mind a strong correlation was established between the two colors in question in the sense of diminished worth, we might assume the following. Susanne, personifying herself as a child in the guise of Little Why, signifies unconsciously her sense of inferiority, especially in comparison with her father. In this context, the posture of

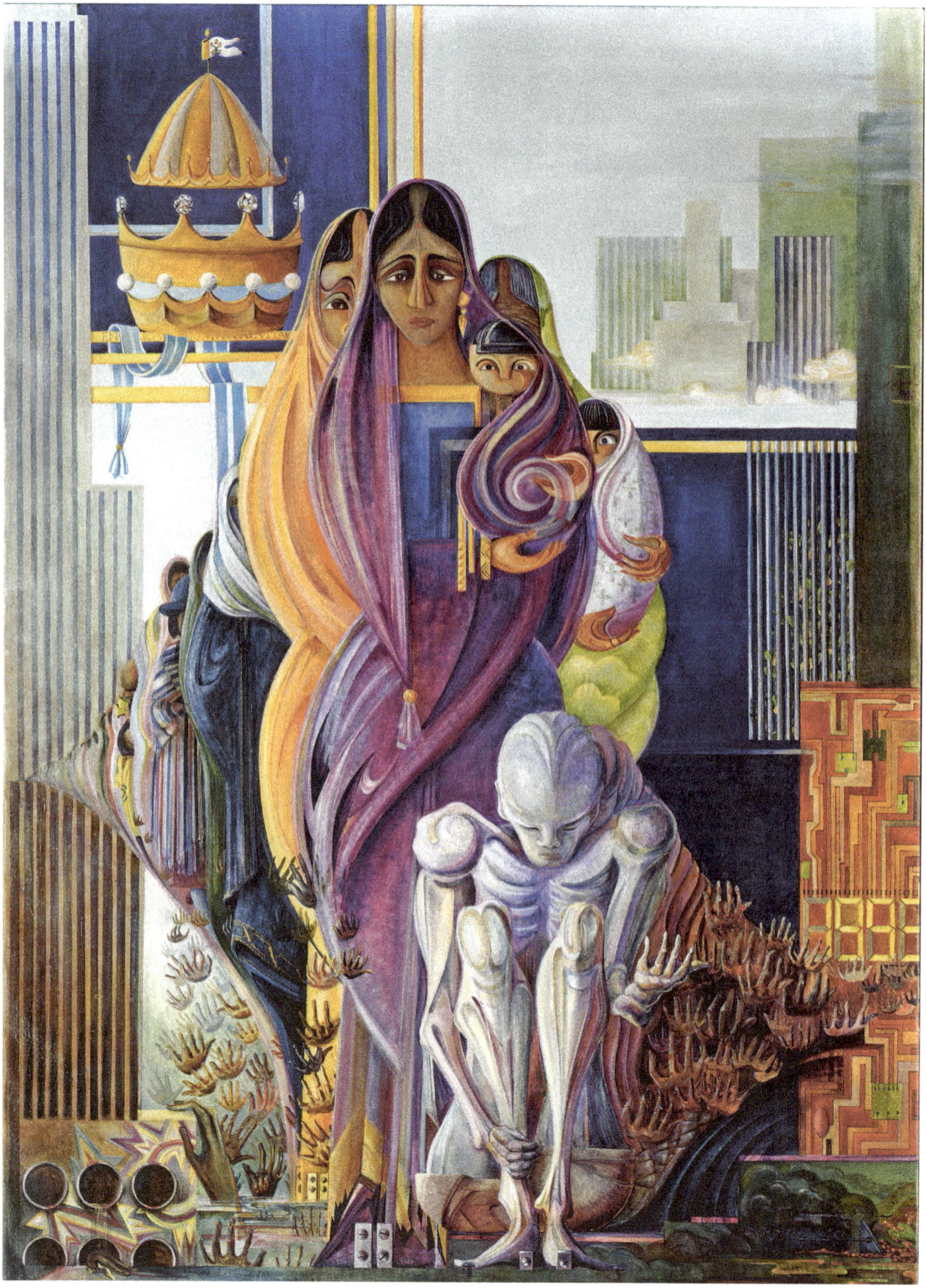

Fig. 6.13. Susanne Schuenke, *Born To Starve*, 1992. Oil on canvas, 54 x 40 in (137 x 102 cm). Collection of the artist.

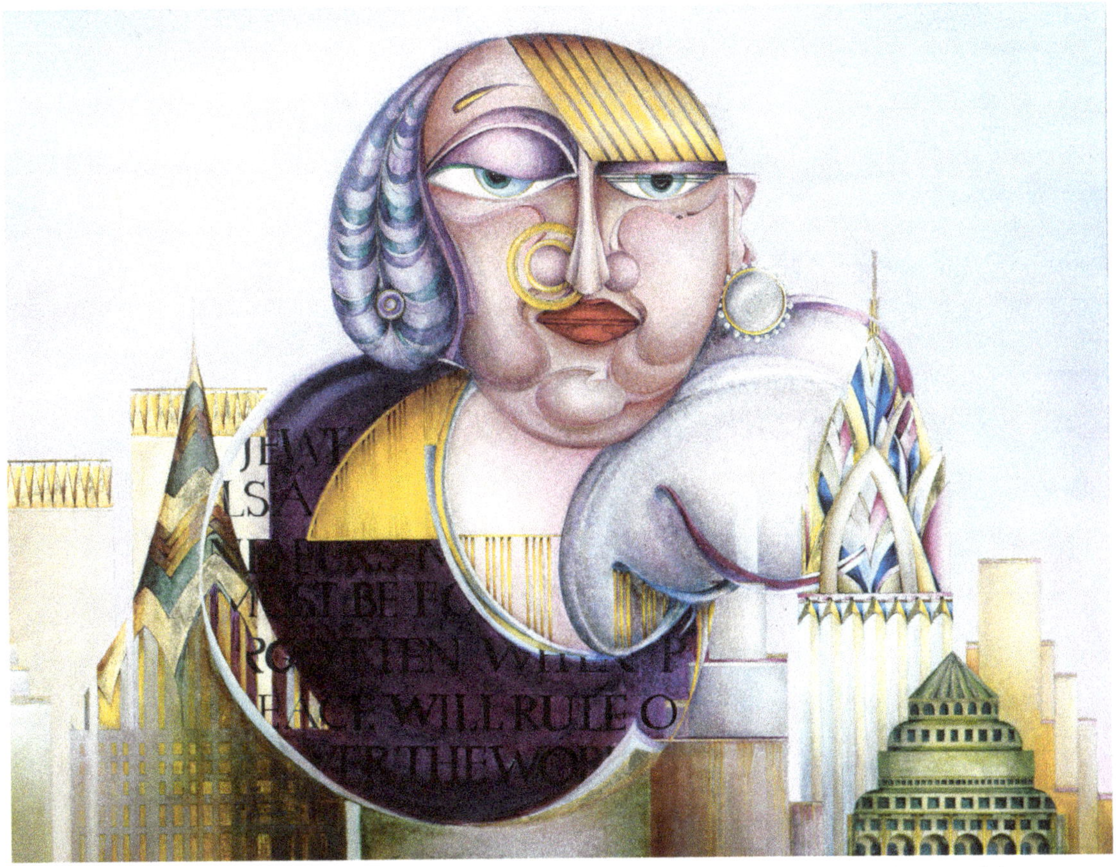

Fig. 6.14. Susanne Schuenke, *Greed*, 1989. Oil on canvas, 30 x 40 in (76 x 100 cm). Collection of the artist.

Little Why metaphorically indicates Susanne's eagerness to "jump" on the powerful station (here represented by the podium) where True Blue (her father) is situated.

A further reinforcement of Susanne's dislike for the color combination of yellow and violet occurred in her teens. She was preparing a gift for her mother, which involved a piece of deep ultramarine-violet silk. As she was working with the present, her mother unexpectedly walked into the room, saw the beautiful fabric, and asked the daughter what she was doing with it. In order to conceal the true purpose, Susanne had to come up with an impromptu excuse, and she said that she was sewing something for herself in the combination of violet and yellow. This was a diversion, since she had not considered using yellow with this gift at all. Susanne's mind had spontaneously invoked the most distasteful color combination that she could imagine to mislead the mother and hide her real intention. The stratagem worked only too well, as her mother replied that the color pairing was quite tasteless. Afterward, for many years her family mocked her for choosing this specific color combination, which they judged as the epitome of bad taste. This experience strengthened Susanne's preexisting aversion for the two hues. In regard to Little Why's colorations, we consider the pale violet of her hind wings combined with yellow reinforced the negative meaning.

With the above discussion in mind, we now delve into how the artist applied the tints that she consciously disliked, for butterfly Little Why, who personifies herself.

6.3.5 Positive Perception for the Colors Yellow and Violet

First, we will see if all the instances of the use of these two colors in question are negative in Susanne's paintings. We will also inquire as to whether those colors have always been unfavorable to her. One of her early works, a watercolor from 1979, shows Buddha's head in shades of yellow and green (Fig. 6.15), which can be considered as indicating positive content. This image was created by Susanne after she saw an antique, gray stone bust of Buddha in an exhibition. The artist already had a sympathetic attitude toward Buddhism in

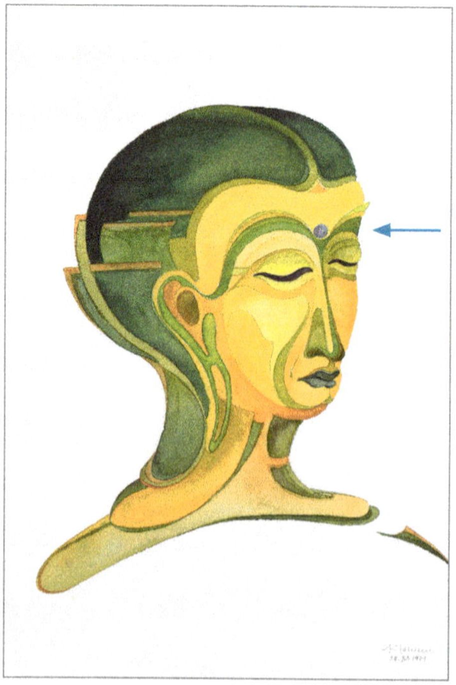

Fig. 6.15. Susanne Schuenke, *Buddha*, 1979. Watercolor, 15¾ x 11¾ in (40 x 30 cm). Collection of the artist. (Arrow added to point to "third eye.")

her adolescence, and she transformed the favorable impression into her own language of lines and coloration. She applied yellow in her portrait of the Buddha to express his spirituality, which is usually represented by gold. It is a common practice in world art to use yellow in the appropriate context in lieu of the precious metal.

Another example in which Susanne substituted yellow for gold is found in *Intermission*, (2001) (Fig. 10.21). The diva's necklace and the paraphernalia of the military uniform of an officer were painted with the same nuances of yellow as the blonde head of the central figure and the bouquet of flowers being presented to her. The yellow coloration in *Intermission* indicates the elevated status of both the diva and her admirers.

More than two decades after her first Buddha image in watercolor, Susanne painted his portrait in oil (*Buddha II*, 2005). The face was depicted on gold leaf, which then was accented with a few brushstrokes of translucent hues of yellow and ochre (Fig. 6.16).

In Susanne's youth, her father experimented with gold leaf on a few occasions, incorporating it into his oil paintings, and he suggested to his daughter to try it out herself. With this encouragement, she discovered the compelling qualities of precious metals as an amazing extension of the painter's palette, especially for emphasizing specific symbolic meanings in her artworks. Gold became for her a transcending hue, like a "super color," reserved mostly for contents with a spiritual implication. In adopting this medium, the artist joined the millennial-old, worldwide tradition. Susanne has been freely employing this additional chromatic choice of gold leaf to underscore certain positive messages.[17]

In some paintings, Susanne applies both yellow paints and gold, as in *Give Me Wings!*. The pale, lemony yellow of Little Why metaphorically expresses a complex of inferiority (negative message). The background surrounds the butterfly in a sea of gold (positive message). In the metaphorical language of the artist, the

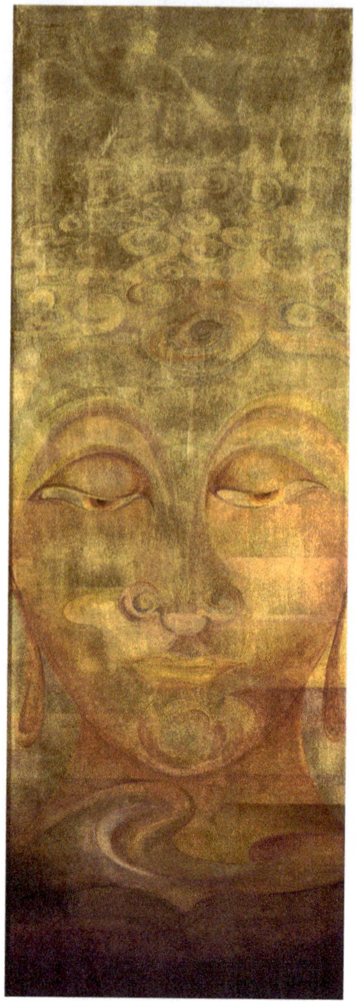

Fig. 6.16. Susanne Schuenke, *Buddha II*, 2005.

Oil and gold leaf on canvas, 53 x 20 in (140 x 50 cm).

Private collection, Florida.

17 Examples of the use of gold leaf are numerous in her paintings, and they will be discussed in the section analyzing the Golden Background (see chapter 12).

all-pervasive golden background around the butterflies represents an abstract depiction of hope for spiritual fulfillment (see chapters 10–12). In this environment, Little Why, as personification of Susanne, manifests her aspiration in the ongoing realization of this perspective.

With the above analysis of yellow, it is apparent that the symbolic use of this color is twofold for Susanne. On the one hand, the "ordinary yellow" from the oil palette is often used in a negative context. On the other hand, the artist uses gold leaf for the positive messages that she wishes to convey. Hence, the presence of two different appearances of yellow (oil paint and gold leaf) in the same painting implies contrasting messages. The negative and positive influences experienced in the artist's life are interwoven into the imagery that she creates as a coherent narrative.

In accordance with the positive meaning of violet for the artist, we will mention several associations that can correlate this color with certain emotionally positive experiences in her childhood. Susanne's mother was born in the month of May, and her birthday was always a family celebration, in which branches of blossoming lilac were a permanent feature for the anniversary decoration. At age six or seven, Susanne used her pocket money and proudly bought a bottle of perfume for her mother as a birthday present because it was in a box with a design of lilac blossom in pale violet. The gift was received with appreciation, and Susanne still takes much pleasure in retelling the story with her face beaming. With such a memorable event in her life, vividly remembered, it is possible that her mind was conditioned to associate violet with positive memories of her mother.

This positive association, retained and reinforced over many years, eventually influenced the coloration of a painting, which Susanne created while still in high school, for her parents' silver anniversary, titled *Silberhochzeit* (English: Silver Anniversary), (1976) (Fig. 6.17). The painting portrays her parents embracing and kissing each other, with the father holding a pair of paintbrushes in his hand, and the mother, a cigarette in hers. The white cuff of her mother's sleeve is rendered unmistakably in violet nuances—an unintentional color choice by the artist, who discovered this detail 40 years later during our analysis.

Other pleasant associations with violet and yellow could have formed over many years in connection with two German brands of chocolate favored by Susanne. One, named Milka, for decades has been well known for its pale violet or lilac wrapping paper. Another, Feodora, came in a pale yellow or cream-colored wrapper. She ate these bars of chocolate in significant amounts during her teens, consuming one and even two bars (each bar 100 grams or 3.5 ounces) per day. Subsequently, she developed

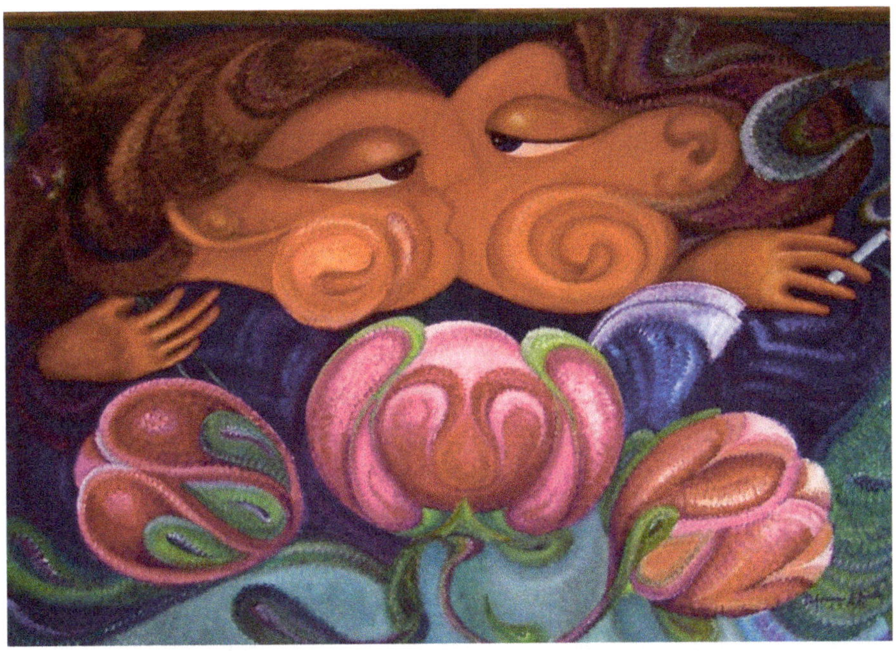

Fig. 6.17. Susanne Schuenke, *Silberhochzeit*, 1976. Acrylic on canvas, 47¼ x 59 in (120 x 150 cm). Collection of the artist's family.

a dependency on chocolate that never left her, although she had to curb the consumption drastically in her adulthood. Uncovered in our analysis, the serendipitous combination of the colors arising out of her confectionary pleasure from the past, made Susanne exclaim: "Did I paint myself in the colors of my favorite chocolate brands' packaging?" Her spontaneous remark might not be far from the truth. After all, the two hues, yellow and violet, were used to form the image of Little Why, who is the personification of Susanne in her youth.

Another example of the combination of yellow and violet, which seems to represent a positive association, is found in one of the countless color drawings that Susanne made in her childhood. In this particular piece, (*Fashionable Couple*) (1967), which was created when she was 11 years old, a couple is shown with bright green skin and hair, but with violet faces that share the same hue with their footwear. The woman wears a golden necklace and bracelet (colored in yellow and ochre). The man is featured with a light blue suit and a yellow shirt, which is visible through its collar and cuffs (Fig. 6.18). Both figures are depicted in similar body postures, making nearly identical arm and finger gestures. The man holds a cigarette (both parents once were chain smokers), and the woman makes a hand gesture, which looks like a typical expression of Susanne's father (see chapter 5, hand gesture "Spitze"), making the drawing's connection to her parents evident.

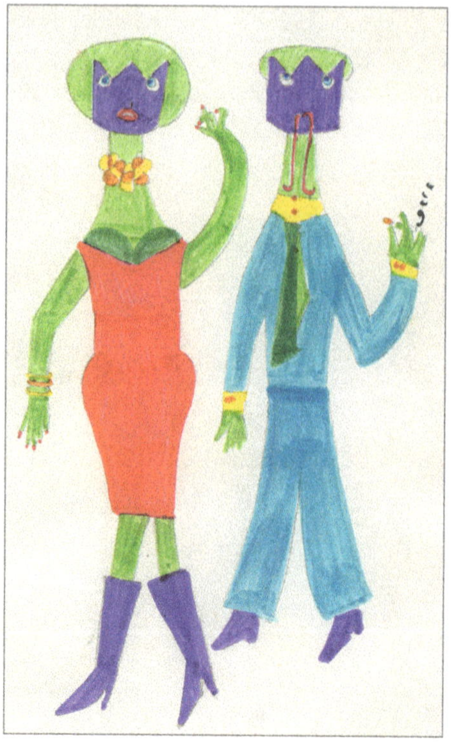

Fig. 6.18. Susanne Schuenke, *Fashionable Couple*, Sept. 25, 1967. Color marker drawing, 8 x 6 in (20 x 15 cm). Collection of the artist. Note the strong violet faces and boots/shoes, yellow collar and cuffs, and yellow and ochre for gold jewelry.

The final association on our list is a stuffed toy, one of three identical mice in violet a hue that were given by the mother to each of her adult daughters as a Christmas gift. The parent could not have foreseen the long-lasting impact of her whimsical present, which became an emotionally charged object of great importance to each daughter—a token of their mother's affection. Over the years, the mice became a symbol of the strong tie that still exists among the sisters (Fig. 6.19).

Both violet and yellow have been ambiguous hues for Susanne. The use of these colors in her art reflects this ambivalence, since both negative and positive contents are metaphorically represented by them in the imagery. Their latent meanings are connected with the artist's significant past emotional experiences, particularly in her early years.

6.3.6 Color Temperature

Concerning the so-called temperature of a color, Susanne does not always follow the generally accepted associations of "warm" and "cold." For example, she perceives most of the blue hues as being "warm" colors, whereas yellow, especially lemon-yellow, she views as "cold." That is contrary to the established stereotypes on the matter. One must wonder on what ground the artist's idiosyncratic color and temperature correlation came about. Her peculiar perception of blue as "warm" might be because navy blue was the dominant color of her warm clothing (woolen sweaters, cardigans, and overcoats) throughout her childhood. Moreover, the artist recalls that among the significant emotional experiences of her childhood are feelings that her mother called "freezing Susanne." The term was used by her to describe the sensation of cold that her daughter often experienced as a response to emotional events, especially when she felt that she lacked sufficient attention from her parents. The best treatment for this was immediate and sympathetic parental care, which involved cuddling and rubbing to warm her, and being wrapped in the warm clothes mentioned above. Over the

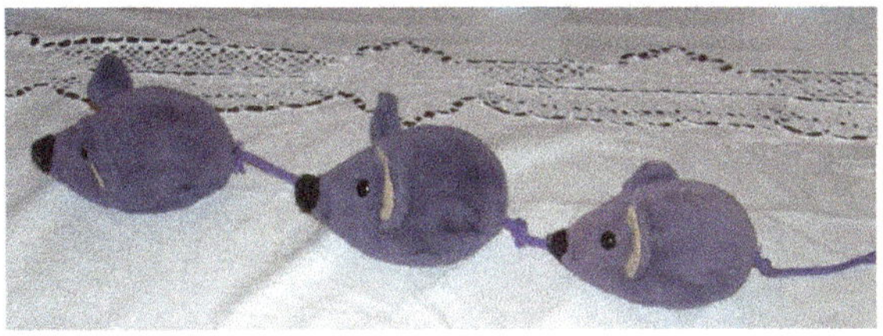

Fig. 6.19. The three mice, a gift from the artist's mother to her daughters. This photograph was taken in 2010 when the three daughters were together after the funeral of their father. The playful arrangement expresses the strong bond among the sisters.

years, this loving care might have had a strong influence on the formulation of her concept of blue as "warm."

Regarding the origin of Susanne's evaluation of yellow as a "cold" color, the following subtle influences from her younger years might have established this perceptual connection in her mind.[18] Starting in her early youth, Susanne was familiar with bright yellow daffodils as the traditional flowers symbolizing early spring and the Easter season.[19] Among the many other yellow blossoms were crocus and forsythia, which would appear as the first blooms in March, while the weather was still cold in Germany, even occasionally freezing. The shades of yellow she observed in those flowers blossoming even in snow could have formed the correlation between the color and its perception as being cold. This happenstance could illustrate Susanne's idiosyncratic way of linking the color of the object with a specific circumstances (e.g., temperatures).

In her 20s, Susanne drew for her friends a painting of the emperor penguin that lives in one of the coldest places on earth—the Antarctic region. Watching those majestic birds at the zoo, she admired their graceful black and white plumage—complemented by the pale-yellow breast area and the striking yellow ear patches above the neck—and enjoyed their diving skills and waddling walk. She came to know the mercilessly cold living conditions of the emperor penguins in their natural habitat through a television documentary, which gave her a renewed respect for the flightless birds. Again, following the artist's pattern of color association noted above, the patches of yellow seen in the emperor penguins could have been unconsciously associated in Susanne's mind with the cold of the environment in which they live. Hence, her encounter with the cold climate birds with a yellow ruff could have been an additional source, perhaps reinforcing her earlier experience, contributing to her association of the color yellow with cold.

Before closing this chapter, let us present some cultural considerations relating to Susanne's generally unfavorable perception of the color yellow. Growing up in postwar Germany, inevitably she learned about the catastrophic war and the abominable persecution of the Jewish population under the Nazi regime. Among the images of cruelty and bloodshed that she saw in photos and movie footage was the badge of the yellow Star of David. Jewish people were forced to wear this mark of identity, and it was often accompanied by the word *Jude* (Jew) written on it. Although Susanne did not personally encounter any overt anti-Semitism in her family or in West Germany as she was growing up, she became aware through study of the persistent historical roots of this bias. She was and is still astonished about the intolerance of people based on their ethnic attitude. Susanne shares the widespread, heavy sense of guilt and shame about the horrible events of the recent past.

Another connection to the "bad color yellow" comes from a lecture on art history that Susanne attended at the university, in which she was informed that a yellow veil or a part of garment could be used to signify sin and shame in the portraitures of courtesans, especially during the Italian Renaissance. It is probable that her father knew about this iconographic meaning when he painted *The Street* (Fig. 8.38), which portrayed one of the prostitutes in a yellow dress. Susanne incorporated those negative meanings of yellow intentionally in the painting *Tango for G-7* (Fig. 6.20), where each of the female participants on the dance floor wears a yellow veil. In the context of this painting, the innuendo refers to the political prostitution of representatives who forsake ethical principles in favor of specific calculations and gains.

We have included the last two associations above in our research in accordance to the artist's personal evaluation of yellow as conveying

18 There is no connection between the color yellow and warm clothes in Susanne's mind. She cannot remember seeing any pieces of clothing owned by family members when she was young that were colored yellow.

19 In Germany, daffodils are named "Osterglocken," literally "Bells of Easter."

negative content. Susanne's personal iconography of colors became an important characteristic of her artistic imagery, reflecting different psychological influences. We consider that additional discoveries of emotionally significant experiences, which have been repressed, are necessary to arrive at explanations in which we can invest our full confidence. Therefore, our data do not yet allow us to draw more definitive conclusions about the artist's individualistic color perceptions and their use in her art from a more over-encompassing perspective.

However, over the course of this study, it has become increasingly clear to us that like a drop of water can reflect the essence of the whole universe, so every small detail (in reference to shape, color, composition, content) of an image that Susanne creates can carry evidence for the whole range of the artist's conscious and unconscious processes. This includes the influences of her family and environment; her thoughts, attitudes and perceptions; her fantasies, complexes, dreams, traumas, and so forth.

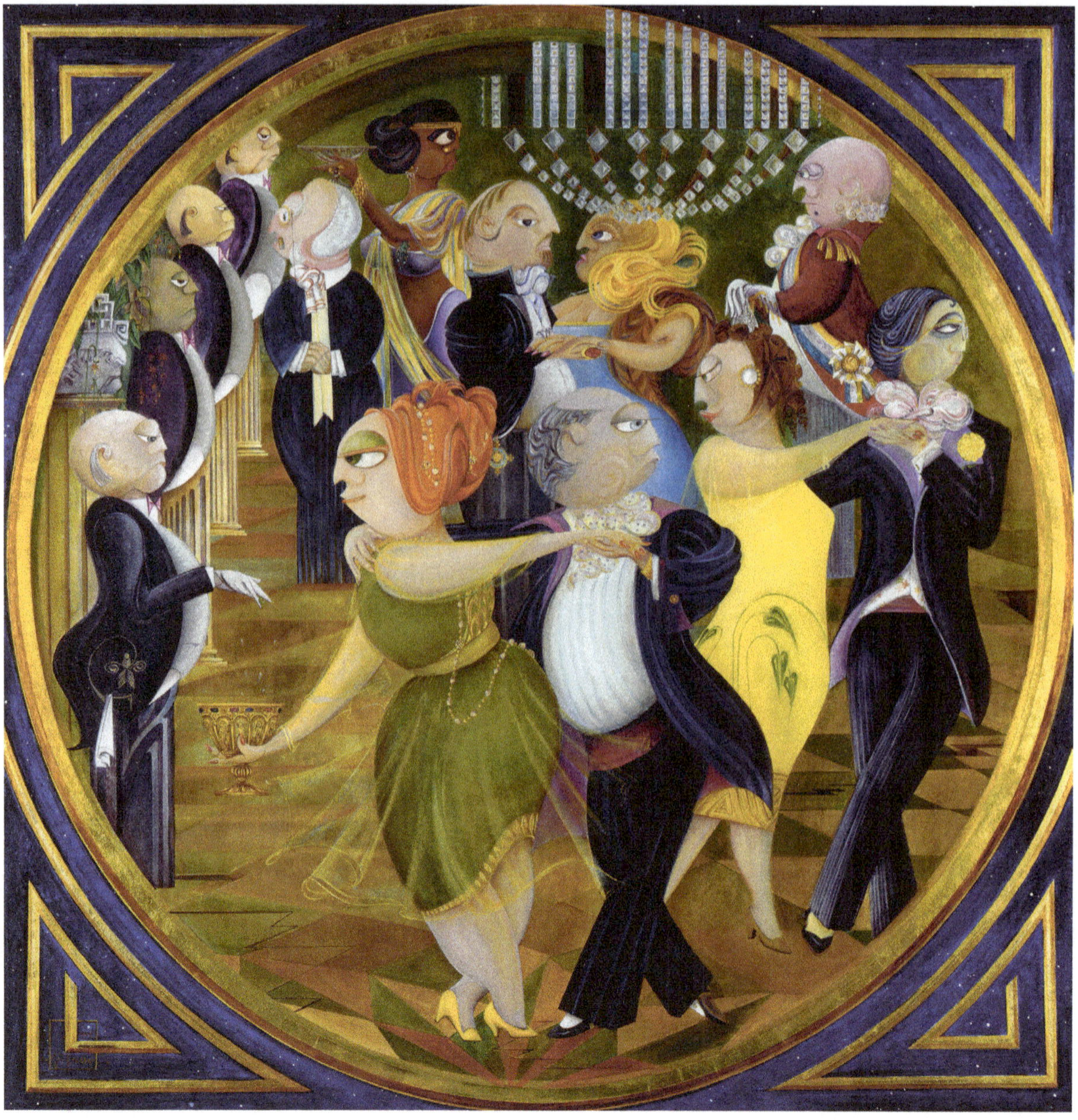

Fig. 6.20. Susanne Schuenke, *Tango for G-7*, 1992. Oil and gold leaf on canvas, 30 x 30 in (127 x 127 cm). Private collection, Florida.

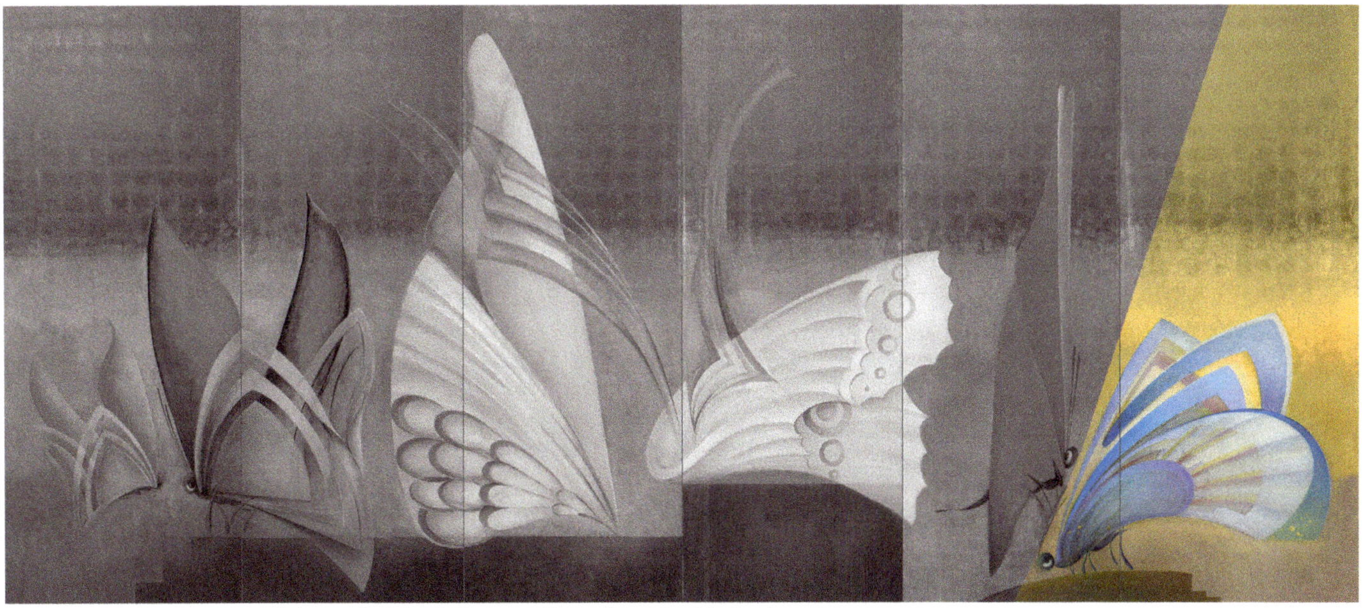

Fig. 7.0. *Give Me Wings!* with butterfly No. 6, Fanning Everything, highlighted

Fanning Everything seeks approval under all circumstances, gracefully twisting diplomacy into a charade of shallow loveliness to cover high-quality opportunism. Dancing at every wedding, Fanning Everything is nowhere home. In the display of countless alternatives, she thins down her integrity to tasteless chatter.

—From the artist's poetic commentary, 2004.

Chapter 7

Submissive **Butterfly No. 6 — Fanning Everything**
Lost in details

7.1 The Name

Compared to the other butterflies in *Give Me Wings!*, butterfly No. 6, Fanning Everything, is the most complicated one in terms of shape, lines, and colors. When Susanne invented the name for this butterfly, the expression "Fanning Everything" did not come as easily as most of the others did. The basic motivation for the first part of the name could be traced to the artist's observation that butterflies' wings themselves could spread out like a fan,[1] which was noticeable as early as in the three sketches done in the butterfly conservatory (Figs. 7.1 and 7.2).

Such a shape was later developed further in the hind wing of butterfly No. 6 and modified in the two butterflies Nos. 3 and 4. The artist thought that butterflies regulated their body temperature on summer days by sitting in the shade and slowly moving their wings up and down like humans cooling themselves with a fan. Susanne's mother occasionally used a fan during hot days to create an impromptu breeze to refresh herself. She had a rigid fan made from peacock feathers and some other folding fans made of various materials in her collection. Using those artfully crafted, handheld fans would have been rather old-fashioned in Germany after World War II, but Susanne's mother

1 The word "fan" already appeared in a first, short description of the painting by Susanne, jotted down during the late summer of 2004. This earlier text states (explanations and emphasis in brackets added here for clarification): *"Next to him,* [i.e., Firebird] *the wings* [of the following butterfly] *fan out in segments and subcategories of segments…"* The poetic commentary was written in October 2004, in which all butterflies spontaneously received their specific names.

took a certain pride in continuing to use them as her upper-middle-class parents had done in the era of the German Empire before World War I. The fan was a reminder of her wellborn pedigree and its prestige.

Susanne used the gerundial form of the verb "fan" ("fanning") and believed she covered several meanings of the word with this choice. For her, "fanning" meant spreading out from one point in different directions. She incorrectly thought that "fanning" signified acting in a servile manner. Her misunderstanding derived from listening to people in conversation using the word "fawning" to describe flattering behavior. Without seeing the word, she guessed it was spelled "fanning." When the artist created the name in 2004, she was still actively building her English vocabulary. She does not remember if she knew some of this word's specific nuances[2] at that time.

We now recognize that the word "fanning" has several connotations for Susanne. The term indicates not only the practical function of a fan providing comfort to someone and relieving the person from uncomfortable feelings of high temperature, but it can also be understood as referring to a person's attitude toward helping others. Following the trail of this term's metaphorical meanings, another association arose in the context of wooing, when the artist recalled the peacock in her parents' garden. He was parading around his peahen during mating season with his upraised, spectacularly vibrant tail, aiming for the female's favorable response. Susanne called this servile manner of mating ritual "fanning," by which she actually meant "fawning." This memory, associated with her mother's beautiful peacock feather fan, perhaps established a metaphorical connection between the bird's ingratiating courtship behavior and the mother's fan.

This figurative comparison might have determined Susanne's understanding of the meaning of "fanning" as an ongoing servile and flattering attitude designed to achieve the desired results for the flatterer, which is to Susanne a quintessential example of opportunistic behavior. Her mother always behaved dutifully and was sometimes even submissive to her father to avoid frictions and conflicts. Accordingly, it would have

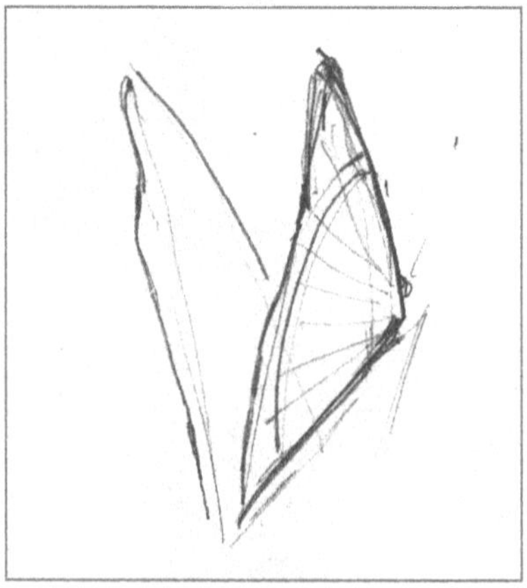

Fig. 7.1. Detail from Fig. 2.1f. Sketch.

Fig. 7.2. Detail from Fig. 2.1f. Sketch.

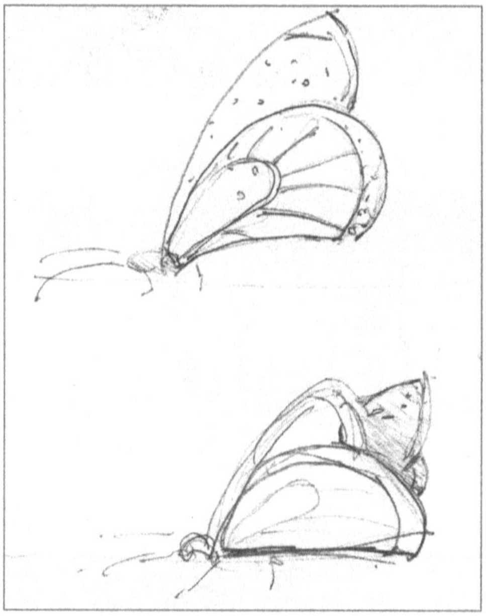

been more appropriate had butterfly No. 6 been named "Fawning Everything" instead. However, we had noted already that the meaning of the word "fawning" had become conflated mistakenly in the artist's mind with "fanning" by her auditory perception. Therefore, the fawning attitude of her parent was implied in the moniker "fanning," which she associated with her mother in naming this butterfly, Fanning Everything.

The striking variety of details in the image of butterfly No. 6 incorporates several features possessed individually by the other members of the butterfly assembly. While all those butterflies have their discrete peculiarities, butterfly No. 6

2 The understanding of "fanning" in accordance with the expression "fan a fire," to increase its strength, might have been known to her, but it was not her immediate association. We could assume that unconsciously this meaning might have played more into the naming process than the artist was aware, because of the metaphorically specific contents of butterfly No. 5, situated next to No. 6, who was already named "Firebird" (see chapter 4).

appears as a hybrid creation. The front wings of Fanning Everything principally imitate the distinct angular wing contours and cutout design of the hind wings of Little Why and True Blue (butterflies Nos. 1 and 2, Fig. 1.0). The fan-like structure of butterfly No. 6 can also be recognized in Pale Moonlight's multi-colored lines radially fanning out from a point and in Touchless Misty's pleat-like ridges radiating from the "head." The coloration of Fanning Everything contains hues of light blue that are reminiscent of Pale Moonlight, and it also reproduces some whites from Touchless Misty. Furthermore, it faintly echoes the orange nuances from Firebird in pinkish hues. The artist had played with the various characteristics of other butterflies that are incorporated in butterfly No. 6 as an agglomeration. She struggled to find a fitting word to express the image's plethora of features, and finally came up with the solution of adding the word "everything" to "fanning" to form the nickname "Fanning Everything," which turned out to possess far richer metaphorical implications than what the artist had originally thought.

Susanne recalls feeling annoyed by the name "Fanning Everything" because it evoked certain negative undertones This is expressed in her acerbic description of butterfly No. 6 in the poetic commentary: "Fanning Everything seeks approval under all circumstances, gracefully twisting diplomacy into a charade of shallow loveliness to cover high-quality opportunism." Following the first three identifications of the butterflies (Firebird and True Blue as personifications of Susanne's father and Little Why as herself), the question arose: who might this butterfly represent that is isolated at the right margin alone with Firebird on a secluded hill? After considerable hesitation, the artist finally had the answer: "Mother." With this pronouncement, we began to probe if butterfly No. 6 might be an unconscious personification of Susanne's mother. Besides the submissiveness, the assertion could find further support in other details of this butterfly: her placement at the peripheral and lowest position on the podium, the image's resemblance to a fan (an important attribute of her mother) as well as that of the sun (the humanized sun in Mother's last painting; see subchapter 7.2.2), and the presence of yellow globules (hints of eggs/reproduction).

Susanne, in evaluating her parent's submissiveness, comments that her mother always wanted peace in the family. Thus, the mother had to accept the dominance of her husband. She tried diligently to find compromises and excuses to protect the children from paternal ire when their school performance failed to live up to his expectations. Looking back, Susanne thinks of her mother as the bending reed in the saying: "A reed before the wind lives on, while mighty oaks do fall."[3] She further remarks that her mother, with incredible patience, gave in often to the "storm-maker" to pacify him, yet she managed to preserve her own inner values and composure to the end. The mother, in her wisdom, accepted her situation and leaned to adapt to the flow of circumstances without being drowned by them, in order to benefit her family while avoiding conflicts. Aside from being a housewife and mother, she was involved in the family's business by managing its bookkeeping and administration. In addition to being her husband's main assistant, she contributed significantly to his work, which kept her buried in demands.

For many years, the mother carried much of the family's emotional strains due to Susanne's medical odyssey. Nevertheless, as a teenager, Susanne used to criticize her mother because she was unwilling to stand her ground against her father's domineering demeanor. It took the daughter many years to appreciate her parent's sacrifice and respect her endurance and courage. Over a decade later, Susanne's gratitude became more compassionate when her mother suffered the devastating consequences of a stroke. Recognizing the personal toll that her mother had to pay for taking on such a sacrificial role, Susanne had decided in her late teens on a different life course to keep from falling into the same trap. She resolved not to follow the duties that her mother accepted: the biological (being a mother and caring for children), behavioral (submission to a husband), and social (confined to being a housewife) roles. She could not imagine those expectations for her own life.

Susanne was asked to what extent her mother might fit the description of the butterfly's character in the poetic commentary. She answered with great wavering that there might be some parallels.

---

3 This version of the wisdom of Aesop's fable from the 5th century BCE appeared as early as in Geoffrey Chaucer's *Troilus and Criseyde* (II.1387–9).

However, she stated that this did not make the verbal characterization of butterfly No. 6 a truthful portrayal of her mother. She insists that the critical remarks about Fanning Everything would grossly misrepresent her mother. The statements about opportunism ("a charade of shallow loveliness," "tasteless chatter," and "nowhere home") are in Susanne's view fundamentally inappropriate for describing the mother's character. She felt guilty about throwing such an unjust accusation as "high quality opportunism" at her mother, as the word "opportunism" is, for Susanne, harshly negative. During televised parliamentary debates, she observed her father loudly and angrily accusing various politicians for their cowardice in not standing on their principles and capitulating to opportunism and profit. For him, opportunism was closely connected with fawning—the outright flattery of the more powerful, by which the sycophants aimed to garner certain favors with no thought of personal integrity.

Having adopted her father's view of opportunism, equating it with servile parasitism, Susanne expressed this in verbal characterization of the image of Fanning Everything. The butterfly's apparent submissiveness and the pastiche of diverse details in the design are the visual and metaphorical equivalent of this concept. Fanning Everything's body posture shows a distinctively lowered head,[4] an eye looking upward in unease, and bowed legs that seem about to give under an invisible weight.[5] The imagery could also indicate her willingness to yield for the sake of solidarity and support, which in turn, would be symbolic of her perseverance and inner strength in keeping the family together. Such expediency made her relationship with her husband sustainable and her peacekeeping efforts successful. Therefore, the posture of butterfly No. 6 (as personification of Mother) is readily intelligible when the domineering stance of butterfly No. 5 (personification of Father) is taken into consideration. Firebird tramples over Fanning Everything, with the result that even her antennae must yield to this pressure. Firebird's hind wing looms over the head of Fanning Everything, and she bows before his towering presence. This scene would also aptly describe the submissive attitude of Susanne's mother toward her dominant husband during their long years of marriage.[6]

Susanne witnessed all this with increasing dismay and despair. Her critical observations resurfaced unconsciously in the visual image of submissiveness displayed by butterfly No. 6. Throughout the painting process, the artist intuitively disliked Fanning Everything and that underlying feeling may have lead to her uncompromising criticism of the butterfly in the poetic commentary. Although these negative judgments could symbolize shadowy facets of the artist's attitude toward her mother, we wondered if Susanne's dislike might have additional sources apart from her mother. The analysis would have to probe further into the roots of her perception in search of such credible alternative explanations.

Butterfly No. 6 displays an "overdose" of visual variety in shapes, lines, and colors, including configurations reminiscent of a fan, the sun, and fractals, which are themselves all positive. This assemblage of features, combined with the outspokenly negative verbal characterization of Fanning Everything, led us to suspect that there was more than one person embedded in the metaphorizing of this butterfly by Susanne. Her description of Fanning Everything in such biting terms could be due to unconscious references to various subjects (multiple personifications of this butterfly). When asked whom she would correlate with that disapproving criticism in the poetic commentary about Fanning Everything, the answer came immediately: "Aunt Hella!" Here, the artist felt no remorse in expressing her contempt for the blatant opportunism of her relative. Susanne endlessly heard from her parents their harsh evaluation of the mother's sister, who was unabashed to "dance at all weddings" and whom they characterized as being "as opportunistic as a weathervane." The artist's association with Aunt Hella opens up a Pandora's box of emotional events, a reservoir of tainted memories and painful episodes that has remained vivid in Susanne's mind.

---

4 The head of butterfly No. 6 is lower than all the other butterflies' heads.

5 "Weight" can be understood as synonymous with the emotional pressure from which the mother and daughters all suffered.

6 Susanne states: "My mother sold her soul. She did not really stand up for herself or fight to stop my father from running over her and destroying her. Sometimes she even used alcohol to escape. My mother wanted peace under all circumstances, and she was ready to abide by any restrictions to that end. She let my father rule over her completely."

This aunt was the mother's older sister. She was tolerated by Susanne's parents, but always criticized in the worst way, especially by the father. Even today, Susanne has not forgiven her aunt for some of the things she did when Susanne was between 10 and 12 years old. For example, when Aunt Hella found out that Susanne's younger sister was about to receive an anatomically correct life-size male baby doll for a gift, she thought it indecent and pressured Susanne's mother into "castrating" the doll, which resulted in the plastic member being melted away by a hot iron—all this witnessed by Susanne. The neutered doll had a gaping hole in the groin which was then promptly covered up with a bandage.

There are more haunting memories in connection with the aunt. On one occasion, Aunt Hella took Susanne to a movie, and they watched a cinematic version of the *Nibelungenlied* (*The Song of the Nibelungs*), a famous epic poem of Germanic mythology, which was beyond the interest and comprehension of an eleven-year-old Susanne. It had repercussions: A specific shot from the movie left lasting, traumatic consequences on her. In the scene in question (here we follow Susanne's recollection—not quite the actual storyline), a castle is conquered and the leading, victorious soldier throws a crying baby boy, the son of the defeated hero, over the castle's battlements. This scene was accompanied by the horrid screams of the mother, and Susanne wept after seeing the movie. Aunt Hella, immediately realizing the trouble on the horizon, ordered Susanne not to tell her parents about what she had seen.[7] Additionally, on another occasion, Aunt Hella had come back from a movie and described an incredibly bloody scene of cutting eyes with razor blades in vivid detail. The visualization of this image has haunted Susanne to this day as one of her most distressing and nightmarish visions, which in all likelihood became one of the triggering elements of her phobia of sharp blades and knives.

These experiences were highly charged with negative emotions for Susanne, who continues to react strongly with voice and body language indicative of revulsion and self-protection when recalling these incidents. Her unwillingness to forgive Aunt Hella for the emotional suffering that she caused might also extend to her mother's complicity in allowing the aunt to behave so callously. From this perspective, the devastating judgment in the poetic commentary could well have been aimed unconsciously at both her mother and Aunt Hella, since the strong sense of resentment could still be stirred whenever those deplorable events with her aunt came into focus in her mind. These feelings indicate the persistence of dreadful memories still painful within Susanne's psyche. The recollection of the castration of the doll triggers such a strong emotional response in Susanne that she cannot forget either her mother's behavior or forgive her aunt, the real instigator, who was cheering her sister on from the sidelines.

While analyzing and writing about these events, Susanne's aichmophobia and omphalophobia were rekindled. She gestured like someone preparing for self-defense, followed by a sudden sense of being cold, which forced her to reach for a blanket. The outbreak of her phobias after analyzing the memory of maiming the doll, which resulted in a hole in the toy's belly, may substantiate the hypothesis of the existence of Susanne's castration complex. In this perspective, the phallic symbolism of the center element in Little Why's left hind wing (Fig. 6.4 (c)), which was additionally emphasized by the cutout design of the wing, could carry an appropriate latent meaning. This is in line with the result from our chapter 9 discussion, where we debate the phallic frontal shape of butterfly No. 4, Touchless Misty, being intersected by the dividing line between the canvas panels, as if to slice the shape in question. The figuration could be connected unconsciously to the castration complex. Furthermore, if we were to take the same point of view and interpret the blue kidney shape ("womb") in Fanning Everything also as a phallic form, we would see a comparable crossing of the shape by the dividing panel line. This reading would mean that a phallic shape had been inserted unconsciously into the image of Fanning Everything (representation of mother/Aunt/Susanne), reflecting young Susanne's past fantasies. Keeping those observations and hypotheses in mind, we ponder whether the artist may have unconsciously merged the above-mentioned associations and condensed them into the noted assumption above.

7 The movie Susanne is thinking of is almost certainly *Die Nibelungen–Teil II: Kriemhilds Rache* (1967), (The Nibelungs–Part 2: Kriemhilde's Revenge), in which a child (3–4 years old) is indeed killed by Hagen in a banquet hall, but the only thing the audience sees on the screen is Hagen swinging his sword toward the viewer, who is supposed to guess that the child was killed by that sword blow.

Returning to the negative characterizations that we encountered in the poetic commentary, we doubt whether they fit the artist's mother according to Susanne's perception of her personality traits as she had experienced them. Regarding especially "opportunism," Susanne emphasized that she was not putting her mother in this corner. After all, she is grateful that her parent made compromises and sacrifices for the sake of family unity and the children's benefit. In contrast, the "high-quality opportunism," as written in the poetic commentary, captures Aunt Hella's prevailing personality most fittingly, whose words and actions were continuously driven by the motivation for self-promotion and personal gains. The striking diversity and controversial facets of butterfly No. 6 signify the possibility of a complex mixture representing multiple individuals in one image (the phenomenon of condensation), and they could even allude to some aspects of the artist as well.

Susanne admits that life has forced her to make many compromises to adjust to difficult situations, to "gracefully twist," and to acquiesce to others. She may have crossed the boundary of her personal integrity so that she could get along better in life. In such a context, one may be obliged in extraordinary circumstances to behave with the show of hollow charm and shallow smile, dancing at all weddings. This kind of prospect might have annoyed the artist, forcing her into "a charade of lovely shallowness," prompting her to condemn herself for displaying the very thing that she had been critical of in others: "high-quality opportunism." Although Susanne vehemently fights against the suspicion of being an opportunist, she thinks that the majority of people have some opportunistic tendencies. She is self-critical of the extent to which she has been forced to make accommodations and compromises in order to find her footing in life.

In the course of the analysis, the painted image of butterfly No. 6 will reveal some metaphorically coded tendencies, which are not in congruency with Susanne's caustic words found in her commentary on Fanning Everything. Those are the pleasant spread of a fan, the structure of the omnipotent sun, and the metaphors of fractals, all of which are Susanne's favorite topics. It may be that these two contrary sets of metaphors (visual versus verbal) accurately reflect the ambivalent views of her mother in Susanne's psyche. From this perspective, her assignment of Aunt Hella to the negative personality profile of Fanning Everything could be a subterfuge to avoid recognition of her presumably critical view of her mother. The totally negative characterization of Fanning Everything in the poetic commentary could be an important outlet for the unconscious. In writing the commentary, the artist implicitly phrased her hostile feelings against Aunt Hella.

7.2 The Features of the Fan, Sun, and Fractals in the Hind Wing and Their Symbolic Meaning

The hind wing of butterfly No. 6 can be seen as subdivided into three areas. A blue kidney-shaped inner segment, a whitish middle element with a complex subdivision by itself, and a slim, blue outer one (Fig. 7.3 (k), (j), (i)). The inner and outer parts will be the topics of subchapter 7.4. For now, we will focus on the analysis of the details of the middle element with its radial-line structure, which led Susanne to three different associations: a fan, a sun, and a fractal arrangement.

7.2.1 The Configuration of the "Fan"

As mentioned previously, the fan configuration was the artist's primary association of the butterflies in the butterfly conservatory, as one can see in her sketches. She developed this design through all stages of the painting, and we can observe the spread-out structure clearly in the middle segment of the hind wing of butterfly No. 6. This part of the wing is dominated by a radial subdivision with long, faintly gray lines that echo the sticks of a semi-opened fan (Fig. 7.3 (j)). Susanne felt that this analogy was so compelling that she encapsulated her impression in the naming of the butterfly. The image of a fan appears repeatedly in the artist's oeuvre, carrying various important symbolic meanings. Historically, fans made of expensive materials with elaborate decorations have been a luxury item, serving as a signifier of wealth and high status. In addition to its practical uses, this modish accessory has been utilized to convey symbolic self-expression, such as fanning oneself in self-praise, closing it suddenly to express one's displeasure, and hiding facial expressions, often of contempt and derision. In her designs, Susanne metaphorically expresses various meanings by this time-honored fashionable accessory.

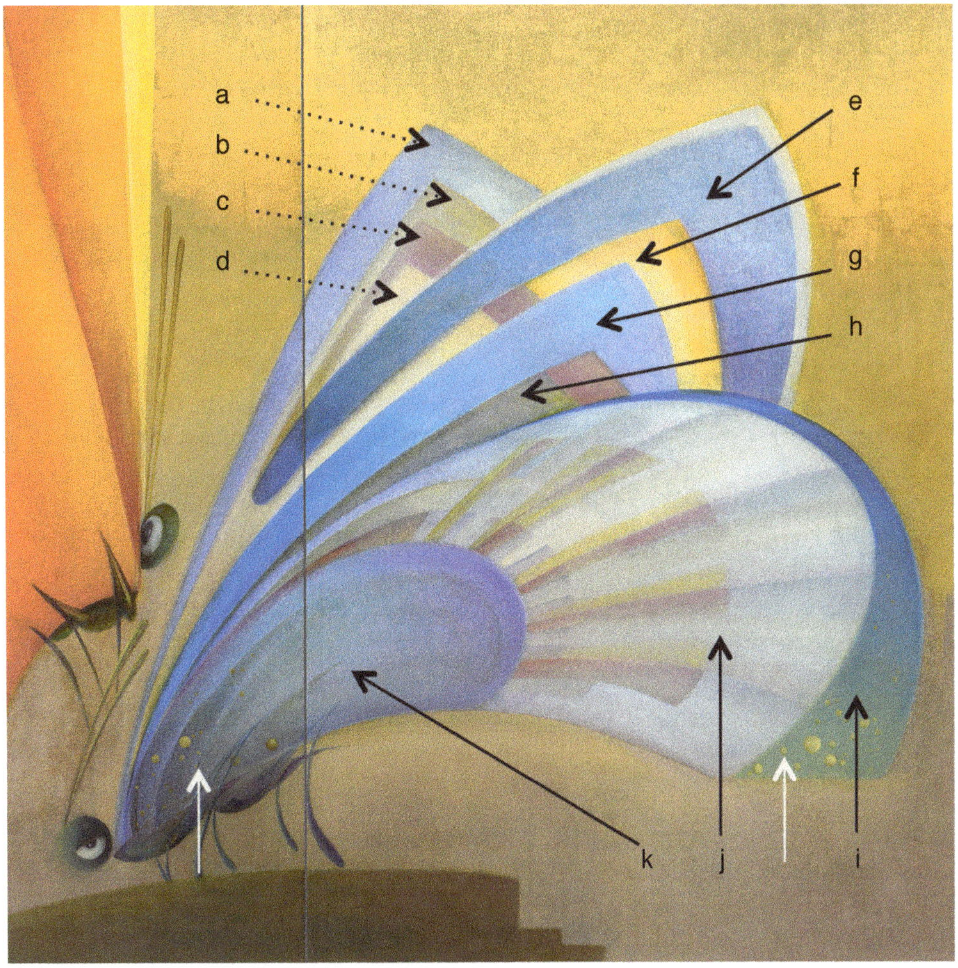

FRONT WINGS:
Right Front Wing:
(a) Outer frame element of the front wings
(b) Cut-through space between the outer and middle frame elements
(c) Middle frame element
(d) Cut-through space between the middle frame element and center part. (Center part not visible)

Left Front Wing:
(e) Outer frame element
(f) Cut-through space between the outer and middle frame elements
(g) Middle frame element
(h) Cut-through space between the middle frame element and center part. (Center part not visible)

HIND WING:
(i) Outer segment
(j) Middle element
(k) Inner segment (kidney shaped)

Fig. 7.3. Detail from Fig. 1.1. Butterfly No. 6, Fanning Everything.
White arrows point to yellow globules in the inner and outer segments.

One of the earliest paintings, in which Susanne includes the fan as a symbolic sign, is *The Connoisseur*, (1989) (Fig. 6.6). It was analyzed in subchapter 6.3.1 in regard to the metaphorical meaning of the color yellow. She depicts an avid collector as an arrogant person,[8] who fans himself, turning away from some butterflies, which Susanne intentionally represents as artists[9] that are following in his wake, hoping to gain his attention. A black beauty spot is placed distinctively on his temple, and a similar one embellishes his yellow fan, matching the natural wing marks of the Sulphur butterflies swarming around his trail. With a haughty attitude, the connoisseur cools himself with a fan that looks like a stylized imitation of the natural butterflies, which are displayed in his showcases in the background. In this painting, the themes of butterfly and fan are tied together. The butterflies are employed as metaphorical representations of the artists and the fan as a symbol of pride and arrogance.

Two years later, Susanne repeats a yellow fan analogously in the painting *Change in the Weather* (Fig. 6.12). In this canvas, a sly-looking, chimerical ram-headed militarist is brandishing a fan in hubris, flaunting the unchallenged greatness of his martial exploits. In this portrayal, his fan resembles a radiating sun with its awe-inspiring symbolic undertones. Through such dual imagery (fan/sun), Susanne emphasizes the ram's illusion about his grandeur, exhibiting his intoxication with power, distinction, and vainglory, metaphorically equating himself with the sun.

8 The connoisseur is deliberately dressed in a manner that belongs to the 18th century, including the red-sole, high-heeled shoes as part of fashionable décor. The costume stresses an effeminate flair.

9 The connoisseur is actually the person in power, who makes or breaks the career of the fine artist. The use of the butterflies here to signify visual artists is a good example of personification.

The diptych, *Dusk and Dawn*, (1994) (Fig. 7.4), features two figures, personifying the end of a day and the beginning of a new one. The fan in the hand of Dusk (Fig. 7.4, left panel), with its wide range of hues from yellow to red, mirrors the chroma of the setting sun. The allegorical figure Dusk will fold his fan in the immediate future. The expected closure of the fan could indicate the "setting of the sun." The sunset is sure to be followed by the dawn. The order of the canvases and their title symbolically express this, in which *Dawn* comes after *Dusk*, emphasizing the artist's optimistic vision of the process of life.

In the butterfly conservatory, she perceived that butterfly wings had some natural similarities with an opened folding fan. In the painting *Give Me Wings!*, three butterflies (Nos. 3, 4, and 6) have wings that evoke this fan configuration. The lines in the middle element of the hind wing of Fanning Everything strongly resemble this structure, but they clearly lack any traces of three-dimensionality. Similarly, one would be hard-pressed to find distinctly defined depth in the middle element of Pale Moonlight's hind wing, where the radial line arrangement alludes to a fan structure. By contrast, Touchless Misty clearly is painted as having three-dimensional structures in both of his wings, and with the use of lighter and darker nuances in the coloration, the artist "sculpted" the pleat-like forms to achieve depth perception. Some of the shaded contours further support this illusion of three-dimensionality.

Dimensions have a meaningful role in Susanne's art. From an artist's point of view, whether to paint an image with the appearance of two- or three-dimensionality is a meaningful choice for the painter. Susanne is quite familiar with the traditional techniques of perspective, light, and shade to render the illusion of depth. Painting "dimensionality" holds a special meaning for her,[10] since the expression of dimensions opens the door to the presence of significant inner messages, which metaphorically unfold in the peculiarities of the images.

"Having more dimensions" means for Susanne that the figure or object in question holds higher importance and, correspondingly, a lack can hint at a lesser valuation. In many of her paintings,

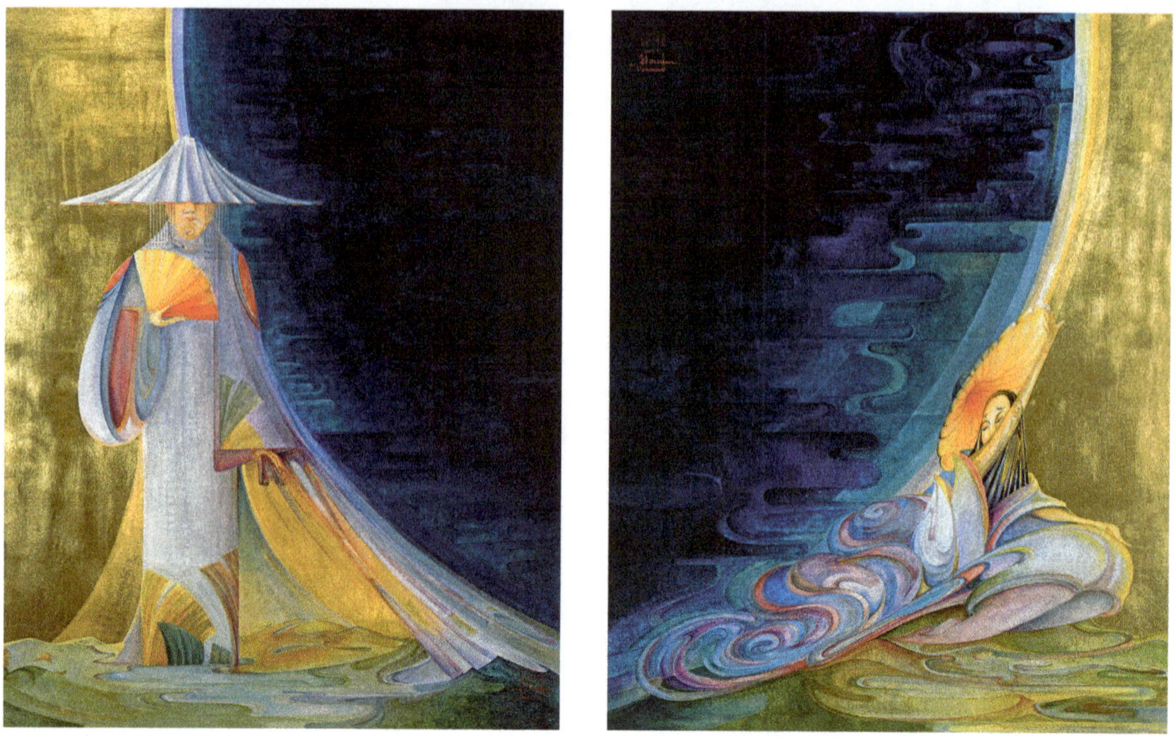

Fig. 7.4. Susanne Schuenke, *Dusk and Dawn,* 1994. Diptych, oil with gold leaf on canvas, 34 x 28 in (85 x 71 cm) each. Private collection, Aachen, Germany.

10 Dimensions became a fascinating topic for Susanne in early adolescence when her curiosity was piqued by the apparent possibility of extra dimensions beyond the three that were familiar to the world of classical physics and our everyday experience. Accordingly, she read up on the various ways mathematicians and physicists dealt with the idea of dimensionality in relativity theory, quantum mechanics, fractal geometry, and string theory.

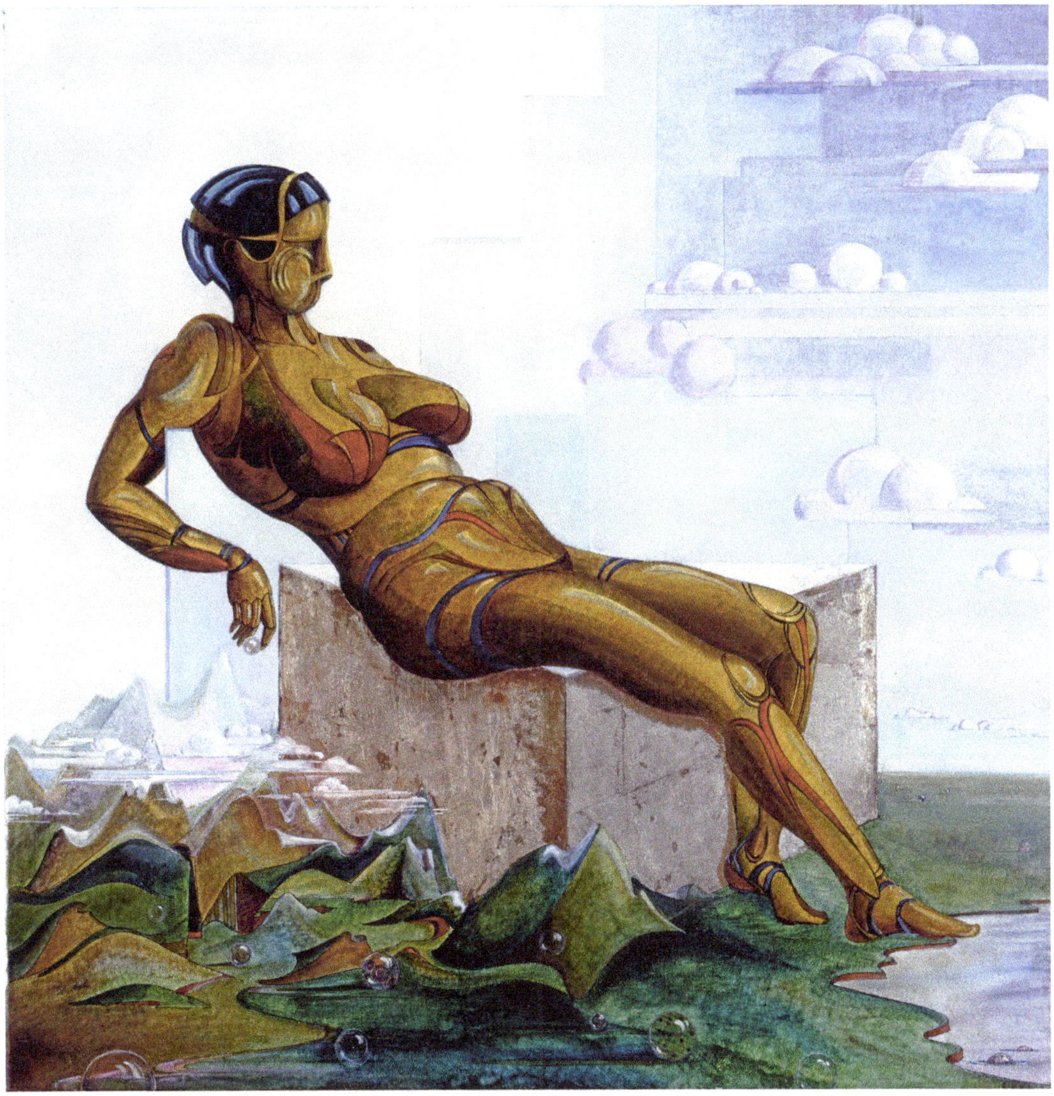

Fig. 7.5. Susanne Schuenke, *Epochs of Mankind*, 1989. Oil with silver leaf on canvas, 32 x 32 in (80 x 60 cm). Collection of the artist.

she has brought out the illusion of multiple dimensions to indicate immaterial value. For example, in *Epochs of Mankind, (*1989) (Fig. 7.5; for more details, see Fig. 7.28) or in *Watching Us*, (1995) (Fig. 7.6), the artist assigns the appearance of three-dimensionality to each of the heavenly figures who lean on a two-dimensional, vertically positioned plane, which represents the restricted nature of earthly existence. By endowing the figures with three-dimensionality, she expresses the "higher, supernal value or status of the divine entity." The absence of a third dimension in the fan structure (i.e., its "flat" surface appearance) in the hind wing of butterfly No. 6 could imply that this butterfly was relegated to a minor rank by Susanne's unconscious mind. In comparison, Touchless Misty with the sculptured features of his wings garners much higher appraisal. The "dimensional difference" between Fanning Everything (as the supposed representation of the mother) and Touchless Misty (as Susanne herself) could indicate metaphorically a competitive situation, in which the mother comes in "second."

7.2.2 The Theme of the "Sun"

Radial lines emanate from the rounded kidney-shaped area of the inner segment of Fanning Everything's hind wings. This radiating structure (Fig. 7.3 (j)) could also be perceived as an archetypal representation of the sun. The figuration of the yellowish and reddish strips on both sides of the grayish "ribs of the fan" enhances the impression of those diverging shapes as the

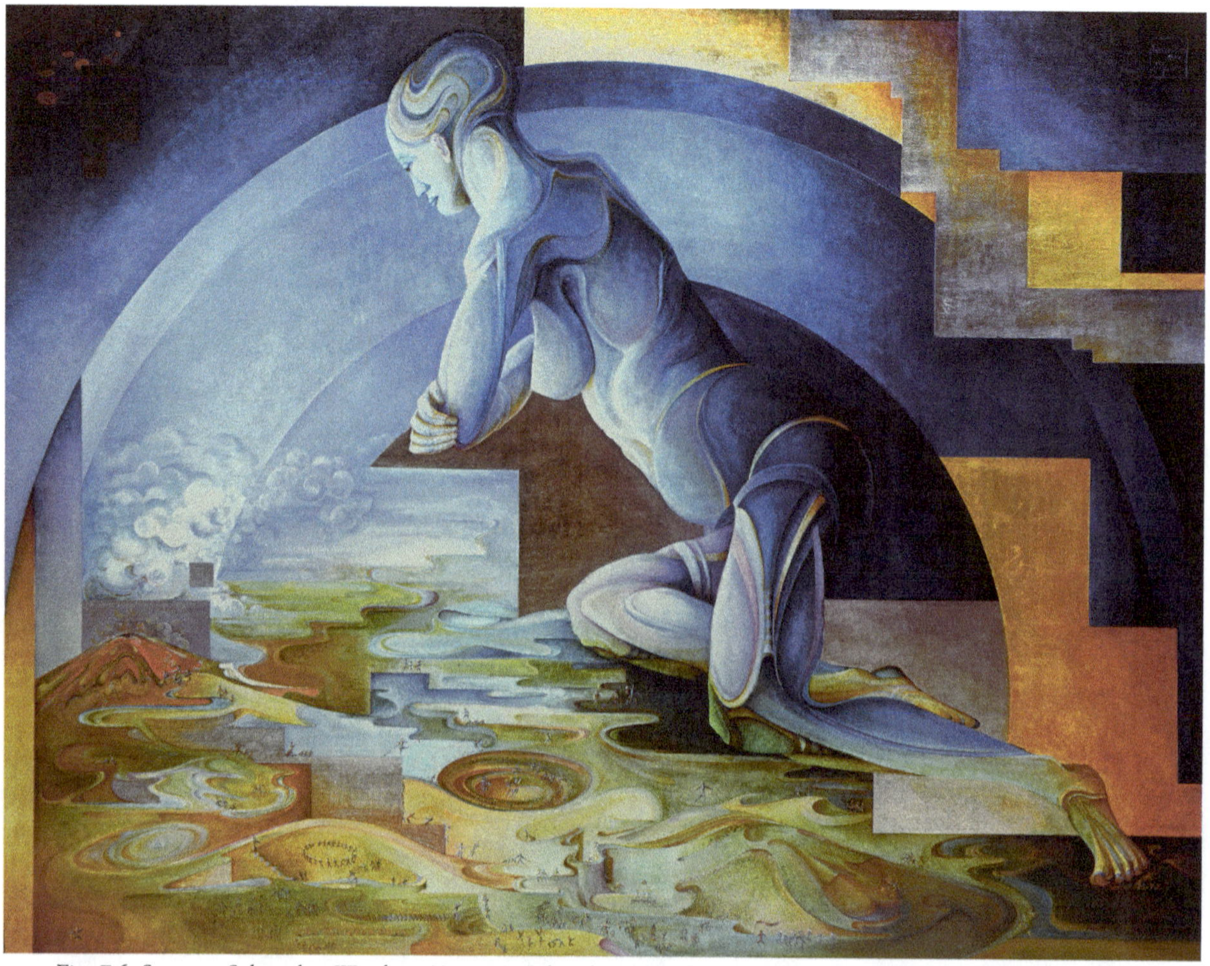

Fig. 7.6. Susanne Schuenke, *Watching Us*, 1995. Oil with gold leaf on canvas, 59 x 78½ in (150 x 200 cm). Collection, of the artist.

stylized image of the radiating rays of the sun, which Susanne associates strongly with the Art Deco sunburst motif (Fig. 7.7).[11] This specific arrangement reactivates her positive emotional memories of the past. Those were the family's daily engagement in the arts, the father's high regard for this art style, and the discussions with the parents and their friends about the Art Deco pieces that they collected.[12] Susanne rendered the image of the sun with human facial features in several of her illustrative designs (see Figs. 7.8 and 7.9). The topic of the anthropomorphized sun reminds Susanne of her mother's paintings—particularly her last one, entitled *Happy Morning* (Ruth-Eva Schünke-Fietze,[13] (1996) (Fig. 7.10)).

In *Happy Morning*, a small child is depicted frolicking in a garden-like landscape that is idyllic and paradisiacal. This is a metaphoric visualization of what her mother always dreamed—a life of peace and happiness for the whole family. The toddler's head is adorned with yellow horns and tiny round bells that form a crown of light, which could be associated with the rays of a rising sun (Fig. 7.10). Susanne remembers her mother calling the image, "the little sunshine." In the upper right of the painting, a tilted, humanized face of the

11 The stylized sunburst is a motif frequently used in the decorative arts during the early 20th century in Europe and America. The apex of the Chrysler Building (New York, 1929) imitating a sunburst is one of the best known examples of this popular sun symbolism from the Art Deco period.

12 Among the family's art and antique collection were objets d'art from the Art Deco period, which her father was particularly fond of. The family library even had a book dedicated to the application of the sunburst motif in various designs, which Susanne became thoroughly familiar with. In her art, we can relate the image of sunburst also to configurations such as in *The Portal of Surprise* (Fig. 10.15).

13 Ruth-Eva Schünke-Fietze (née Fietze, Berlin 1926–Düsseldorf 2002).

sun, with some identifiable features, such as an eye, eyebrow, lips, and hair, peeks through a gap in the clouds. Susanne's father and his daughters saw in the allegorically drawn humanized sun a certain likeness to the face of the mother. They interpreted the painting as the child basking happily in "the mother's attentive sunshine." A romantically woven wreath with pink roses frames the scene, whose four corners depict the faces that personify the four winds, the Anemoi, which are often found in illustrations accompanying fairy tale and Greek mythology books. A pair of classical columns, one at each side, and lattice-work complete the dreamy stage set for a peaceful and beauteous world. The title of the work, *Happy Morning*, is actually taken from the writing (in English) on the ribbon that the toddler waves joyfully in his hand. The child's cheerful face and gait in the idyllic scenery could be the projection of Susanne's mother's lifelong dream of happiness, love, and joy in the family.[14] Therefore, when the mother died, the family chose this particular painting to accompany the obituary letter.[15] As the symbolic expression of Mother's longing for happiness *Happy Morning* is a significant and enduring link which connects Susanne to the "lost paradise" of her childhood. This watercolor is the mother's last painting, and the family greatly treasures it as an embodiment of her abiding love.

It is worth noting that *Mami*[16] often referred to her daughter as "freezing Susanne," and once she even painted her shivering child in a small sketch. During family vacations at the North Sea, when Susanne stayed in the cold sea too long and came out of the water shaking, her mother would immediately try to soothe her by drying Susanne with towels, rubbing her body, and clothing her in warm garments. On numerous occasions, her mother remedied Susanne's complaints and frailty with a hot water bottle and woolen underwear.

In her adult life, "freezing" became one of Susanne's conditioned responses to emotionally stressful situations. When she feels sad, isolated, or misunderstood, she begins to freeze, which might be as brief as ten minutes until her mood changes. When such an incident occurs, Susanne often wants a blanket or a cardigan, even if the room is reasonably warm. She has come to recognize that "going cold" has become synonymous with the acute need for attention and care in difficult circumstances. Furthermore, she has come to

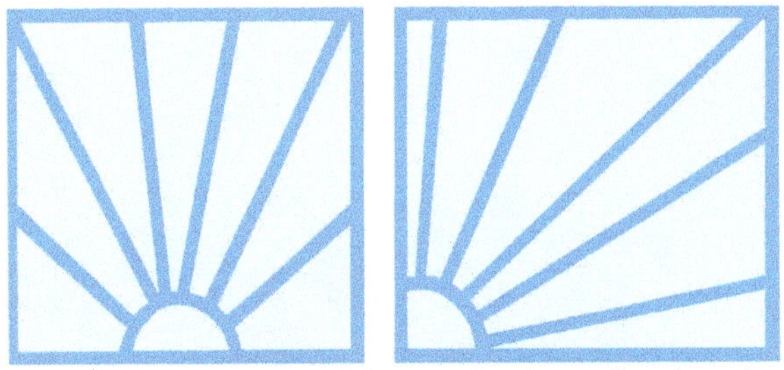

Fig. 7.7. Two versions of the popular design "Sunburst" from the Art Deco period.

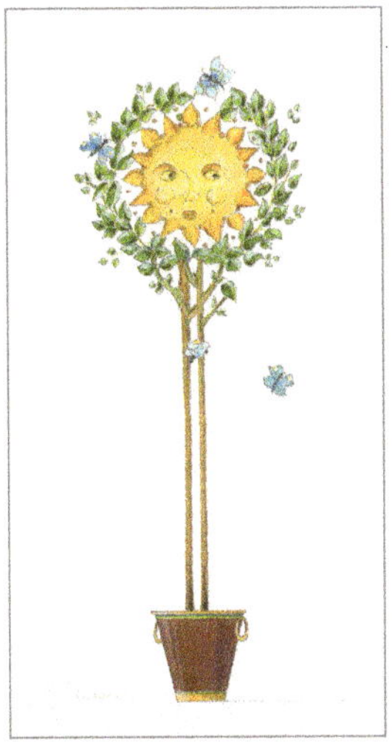

Fig. 7.8. Susanne Schuenke, *Suntree* (book illustration of the unpublished work Chess for Children), (1991). Watercolor, 9½ x 4 in (24 x 10 cm). Collection of the artist. An example of the artist's storybook style sun.

Fig. 7.9. (below) Susanne Schuenke, *Miss Sunshine* (I), 2000. 5 x 7 in (12.5 x 18 cm). Private collection, Virginia. The artist's version of a benevolent, partly humanized sun.

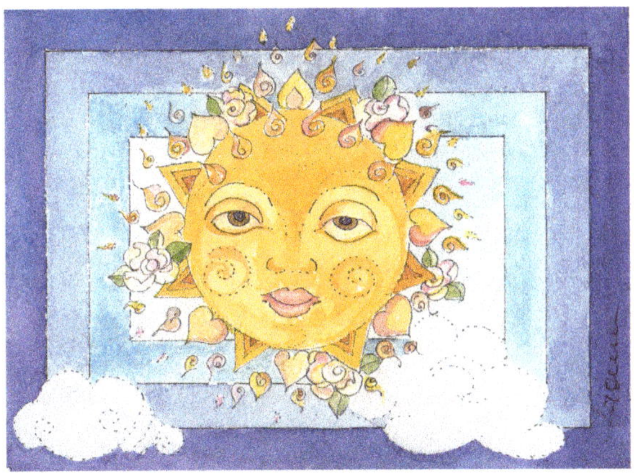

14 The mother once said that she was an unwanted child and had not received much attention from her own mother (who already had three children before her), as she was brought up mostly by a nanny.

15 Susanne owns the watercolor study drawing for *Happy Morning* and cherishes it as a dear memento of her mother.

16 While editing the text of this book, Susanne noticed that she had accidentally typed "Mami" (the German equivalent of "Mommy") instead of the intended English word "mother." Since this "mistake" further underscores the intense emotional attachment she still feels for her mother, we have decided to leave this specific expression in the text.

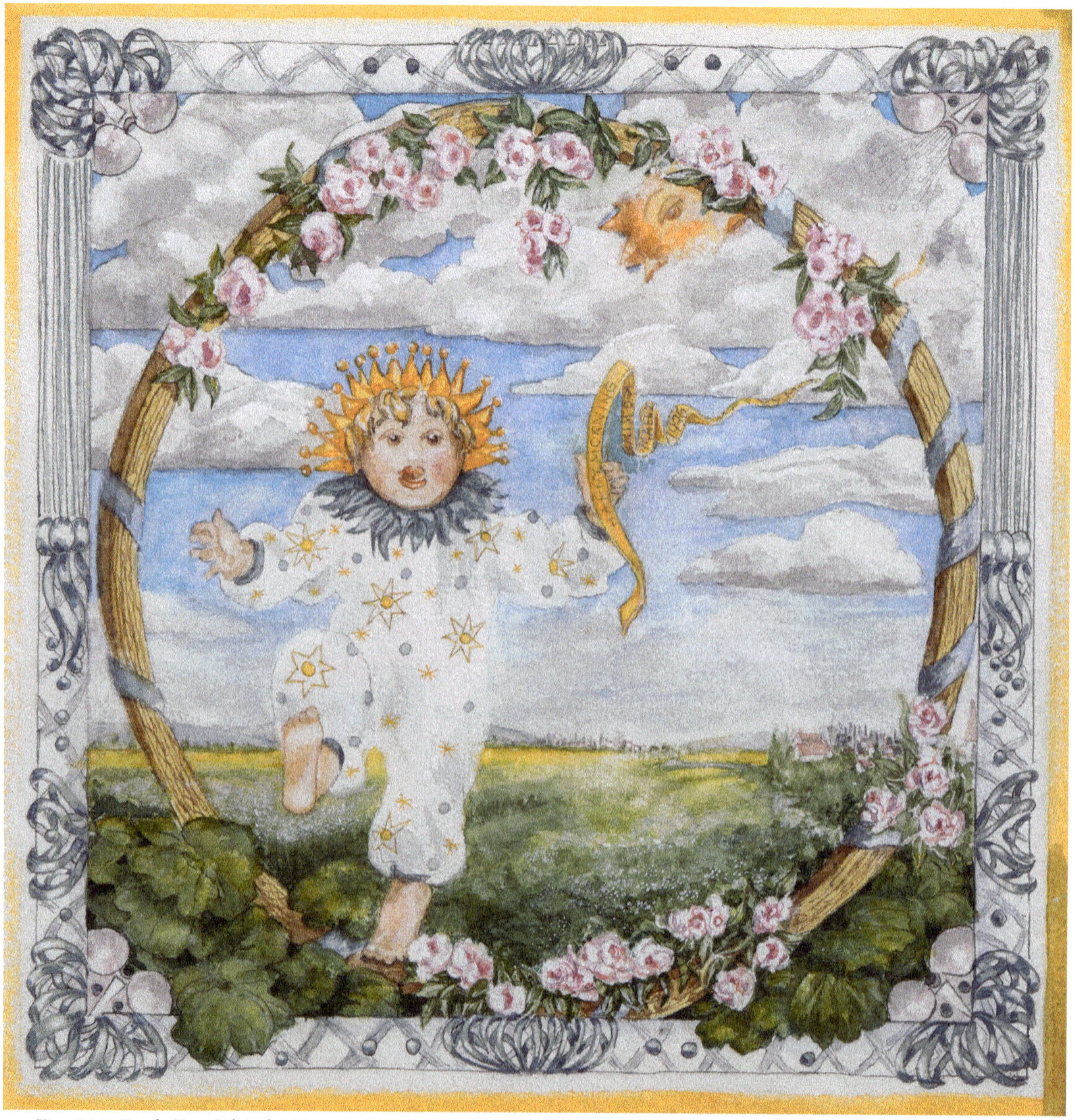

Fig. 7.10. Ruth-Eva Schünke-Fietze, *Happy Morning*, 1996. Watercolor, 7 x 7 in (18 x 18 cm). Collection of the artist's family, Germany.

associate everything that gives warmth with her mother, and, consequently, sunshine has become one of the symbolic representations of her mother.

A decorative brass relief with a humanized sun, cherished as a good luck charm, was a loving souvenir in the family. When Susanne was in her early teens, her mother bought this metal relief and hung it on the front door to the home, where it was welcomed by all. Susanne follows the mother's custom and keeps a similar sun symbol on the entry door to her studio (see Fig. 7.11).

In her works, she frequently adds sun symbolism to indicate the greatness and prestige of the person being portrayed. In *Where to Go?*

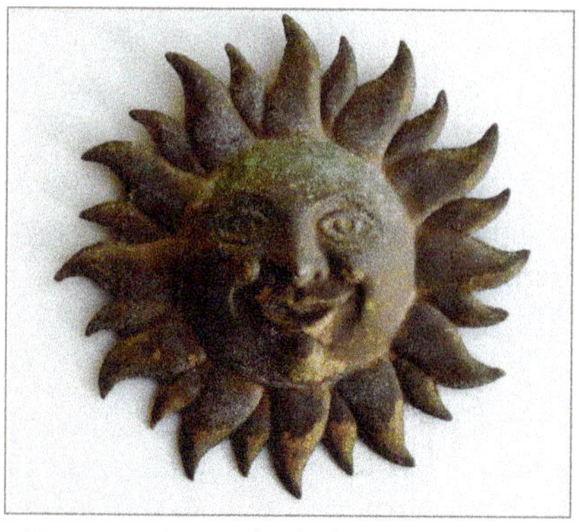

Fig. 7.11. A metal relief with a sun face (a snapshot of the front door of the artist's studio). Diameter 3½ in (9 cm).

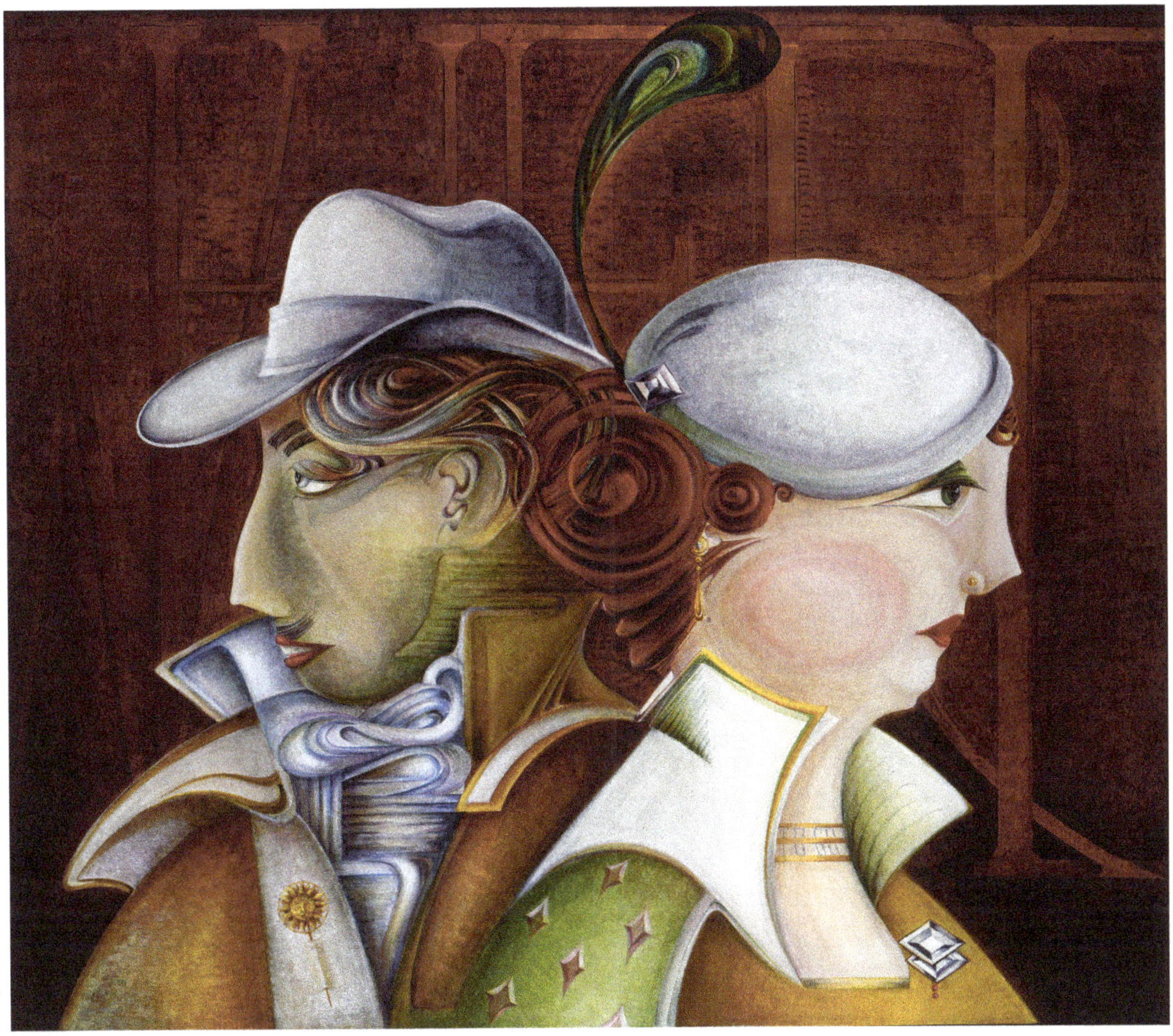

Fig. 7.12. (above) Susanne Schuenke, *Where to Go*, 1990. Oil with silver leaf on canvas, 37 x 44 in (94 x 110 cm). Collection of the artist.

(Figs. 7.12 and 7.13), Susanne chose the sun emblem for the pin on the man's lapel with the allusion to Louis XIV of France, the Sun King, to stress the elitist membership of the subject depicted. The artist remembers that she actually modeled this badge after the relief on her door, as shown in figure 7.11.

By rendering the "radiating sun" in the center part of the hind wing in Fanning Everything (personification of the mother), Susanne symbolically bestowed "high status" with this proud display on the mother. Also, the artist might have unconsciously substantiated her parent's inner pride in her upper-middle-class origin. Thus, with the positive symbolic attributes of the sun, the artist expressed a metaphorical connection with her mother. This supports our assumption that Susanne's mother is being unconsciously represented in the figure of butterfly No. 6. From the above consideration, we suggest that in Susanne's mind the sun has become a personal iconographic symbol for her mother.

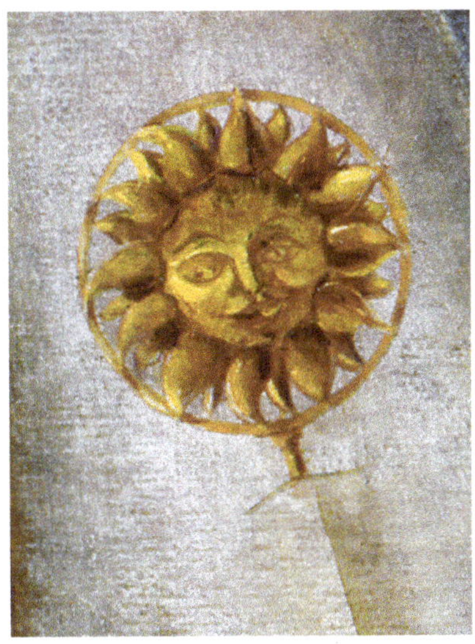

Fig. 7.13.
Detail from Fig. 7.12 : Lapel pin.

7.2.3 The Topics of Fractals and Self-Similar Repetitions

In the middle part of the hind wing, the painter intentionally created an appearance of a fractal-like structure.[17] This aspect in the design becomes clear in creative drawing II (Fig. 2.3), where this area is subdivided by five double lines. On both sides of these lines, she placed shapes similar to each other, with decreasing lengths and widths (Figs. 7.14 and 7.15). With this, Susanne represented her interpretation of the idea of fractals by creating an arrangement with three iterative reductions in size to envision the recursive aspect of fractals in her art.

In the watercolor and oil painting (for detail, see Fig. 7.16; for a schematic diagram, Fig. 7.17), the third iteration was abandoned due to the limitation in space, but one can still easily imagine this iterative reduction to go on indefinitely, presumably progressing toward the infinitesimal. The artist employed this visual arrangement to introduce her allusion to the phenomenon of fractals, which widened her repertoire of visually representing "other" dimensions in her art, using it as a metaphor in her personal iconography. *Give Me Wings!* is not the first painting where she intentionally used the idea of fractals. For example, *Longing* (2003, Fig. 7.18) has an explicitly fractal-like structure (details are shown in Figs. 7.19 and 7.20).[18]

An important feature of fractals is already captured in their name. The Latin origin of the word is "*frangere*," meaning "to break." Benoit Mandelbrot, who coined the term "fractals" for these abstract geometric figures, stresses the usefulness of fractals in describing objects that exhibit a high degree of irregularity, as is the case with most objects in nature.[19] Irregularity is also an important element in Susanne's drawings and paintings, and as such, she feels attracted to fractal geometry and its different kind of organizing principles. The structure of some butterflies in *Give Me Wings!*, especially Fanning Everything, with her rather asymmetrical shape and wide range of forms, is a clear instance of Susanne's conscious (and unconscious) preference for avoiding monotonous uniformity. She often chooses not to adhere to

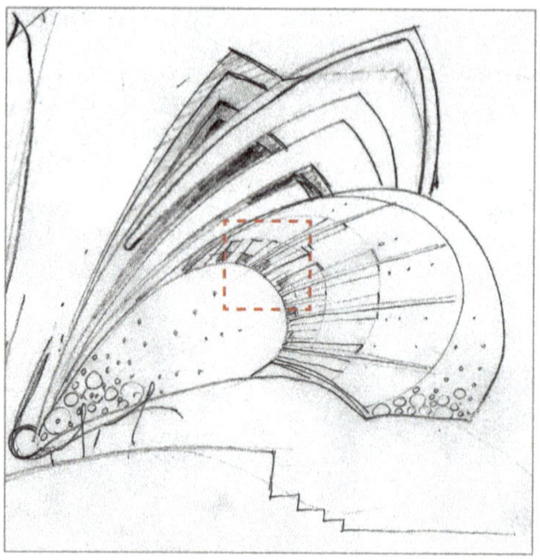

Fig. 7.14. Detail from Fig. 2.3 (creative drawing II), with a selected section marked in red; note the four subdivisions after three scaling iterations.

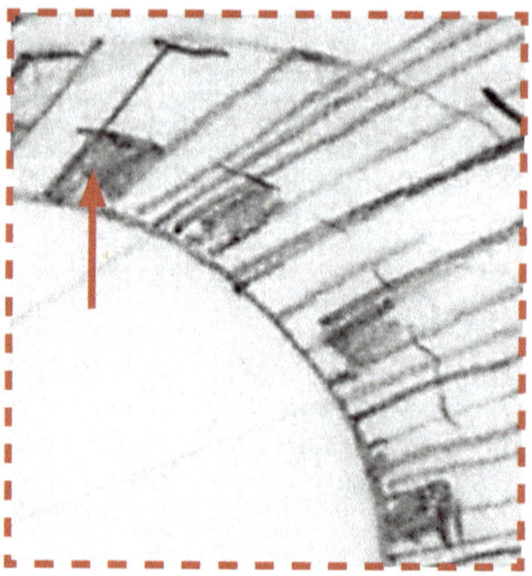

Fig. 7.15. Detail from Fig. 7.14: the selected section enlarged. Arrow points to the third iteration.

17 Fractal geometry is a new branch of mathematics that had its nascent origin in the late 19th century but saw its most explosive development with the advent of computer technology in the late 20th century. Benoit Mandelbrot played the leading role, particularly after the publication of his book, *The Fractal Geometry of Nature* in 1982, in the popularization of the idea of fractals and spurred the extensive use of appropriate computer programs.

18 In the specific configuration of this painting, Susanne represents fractals using a definite mathematical iteration rule (dividing each previous fractal in half on each iteration). The application of the iteration rule results in self-similar objects in different scales (five scales to be exact).

19 As he wrote (Mandelbrot 1983, page 4), "The corresponding Latin verb *frangere* means 'to break:' to create irregular fragment. ... that, in addition to 'fragmented' (as in *fraction* or *refraction*), *fractus* should also mean 'irregular,' both meanings being preserved in *fragment*." His examples from nature include the highly irregular fragmented coastline of Britain (Mandelbrot, 1983: chapter 5), mountains, growth of trees, shape of clouds, etc.

the symmetrical forms of the classical aesthetics, which dominated Europe for centuries.[20] Irregular forms dominate the universe, and for the artist, they constitute the essence of the "art" of nature, where we can discover surprisingly simple patterns underlying apparently complex forms with their awe-inspiring intricacies.[21]

For Susanne, fractals represent a philosophical perspective that rejects a world as defined solely by its rational parameters. By using fractals in the wing design of butterfly No. 6 under the guise of a mathematical phenomenon, Susanne metaphorically rebels against the common way of thinking. The discovery of fractals unlocks structures in nature that had been beyond traditional human knowledge, and she perceives this as an enlightening experience. She sees a mystery behind the fractals' infinitely varying manifestations; this phenomenon can only be met with awe and wonder. Thus, for the artist, fractals can liberate her from an overdependence on conventional thinking and adherence to the rational conscious. Moreover, they spur her intuition and inspire the unpredictable expressions in her creativity.

The automatic unconscious processes resemble the fractal matrix as a structure of limitless iterations. The dynamism of the unconscious transgresses the borders of formal logic and rationality. The irregular patterns of transformation of biological drives, affective systems, and socio-cultural influences through a huge network of associations and metaphors find expression in various formations. The reader can grasp these patterns, to some extent, through the discoveries of unconscious symbolism. The recognition of the metaphorical meanings of all the created images in *Give Me Wings!* support our assumption.

Susanne decorated Fanning Everything with her favorite icon, a fractal pattern, which presumably carries a message of primary importance, and the presence of this feature is singular among

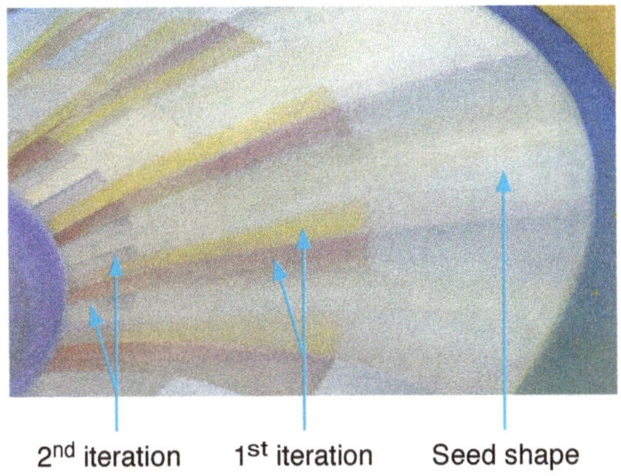

Fig. 7.16. Detail from Fig. 1.0.

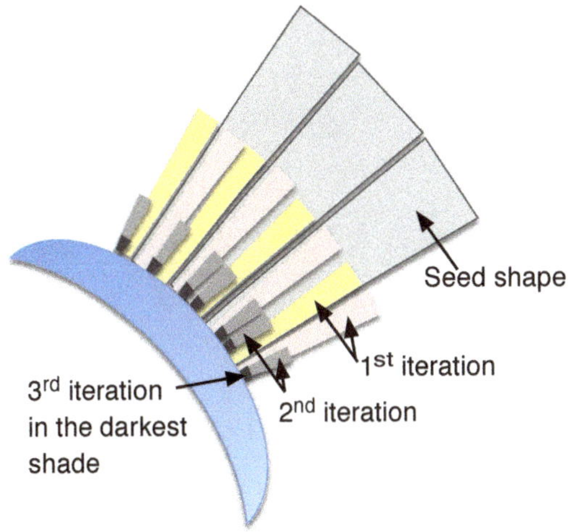

Fig. 7.17. Diagram for the fractals as self-similar repetition of butterfly No. 6 (the third iteration appears only in creative drawing II; see Fig. 7.15).

the ensemble of the seven butterflies. This aspect of Fanning Everything resonates with Susanne's original way of thinking, her peculiar complexes, multiple facets of personality, and interests and habits. This might point toward a partial personification of the artist herself in butterfly No. 6 which is metaphorically coded in the fractal-like features of this butterfly. The application of fractals, a concept very dear to the artist, in

20 Irregularity, asymmetrical harmony, and all manifestations of chaos and disorder were traditionally ignored by Euclidian geometry, judged as less valuable and most often viewed as negative or even "foreign" in European cultural history. Renaissance art, with its celebration of "classical" harmony and symmetry, was followed by the "Baroque" style (named in a derivation from the Portuguese term for an irregularly-shaped pearl), which was characterized by explicitly irregular forms. This was, in turn, superseded by a triumphant style of classicism that emulated the stylistic formalism found in classical antiquity.

21 The shell of the nautilus is one of the many clear and convincing examples from nature. The chambers of this shell, lined along a spiral, are in their pattern surprisingly proportional to the golden ratio, which might be approximated by using the Fibonacci sequence (0, 1, 1, 2, 3, 5, 8, 13, 21, 34, etc.). For more on the Golden Ratio, see Mario Livio, *The Golden Ratio*, 2002. The nautilus combines irregularity and asymmetry to form a complex recursive pattern, and it is a exquisite example of a fractal.

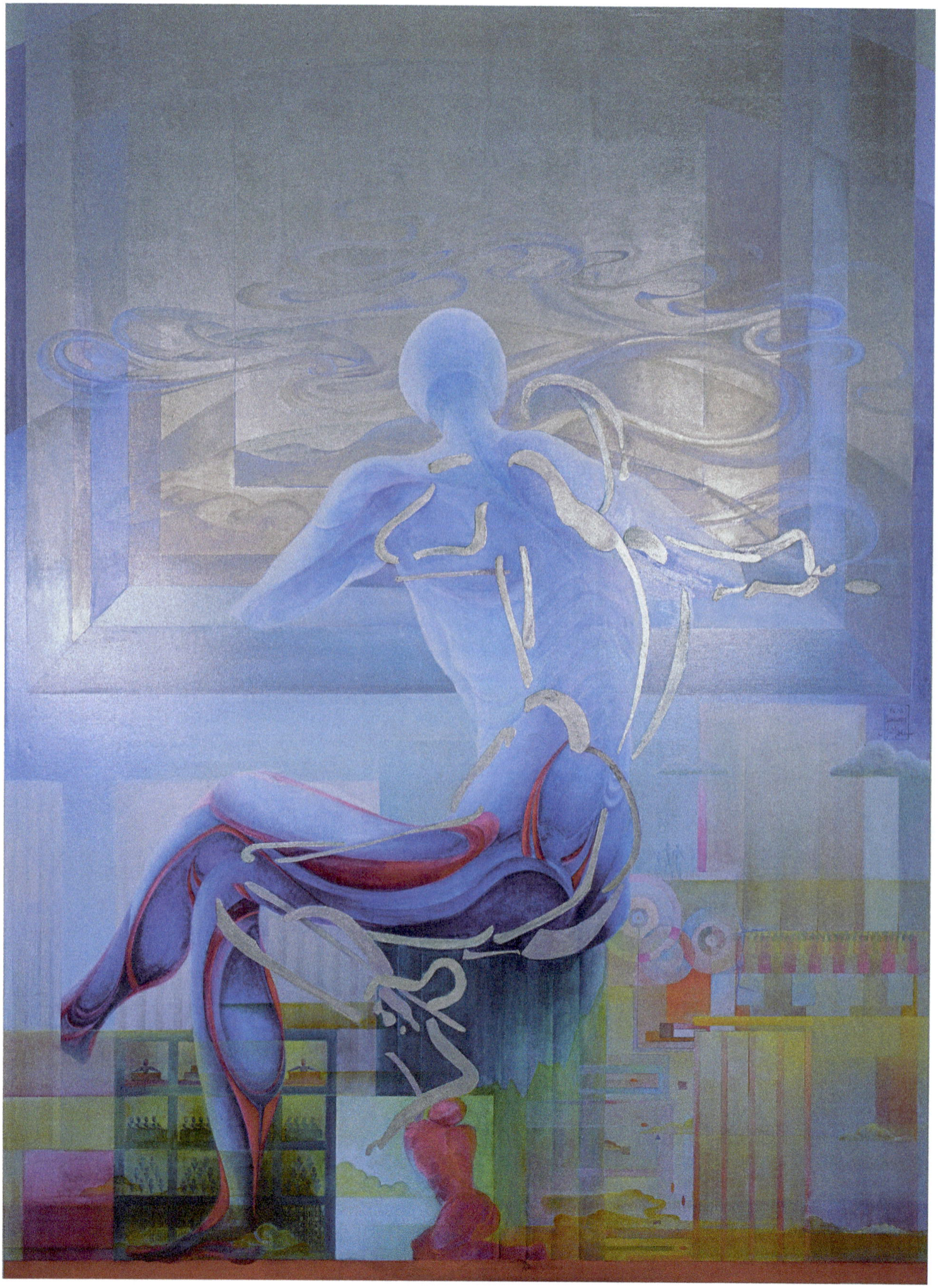

Fig. 7.18. Susanne Schuenke, *Longing,* 2003. Oil with palladium leaf on canvas, 79 x 59 in (200 x 150 cm). Collection of the artist. (Note the fractal structure near the bottom by the figure's hip.

Fanning Everything could support Susanne's personification, but it certainly came as a surprise to her, since she likes this butterfly least of all. This attitude might require further explication. All her life, Susanne tried not to be like her mother, who was placed in a secondary role and ruled by an authoritarian male partner. Susanne had no intention to follow the pattern of behavior set by her mother. She judges that the potential of her parent was never fully realized. Figuratively, her mother was a "fractured being"—in the literal sense as related to the etymological root of the word "fractal."

The incorporation of fractals into the image was based, according to the artist's recollection, on her intended aesthetic design considerations. She just thought that it was a great idea when she did it. However, the utilization of fractals in Fanning Everything's image could also be assumed to signify the existence of unconscious influences, as we have indicated, confirming our assertion of the artist's partial personification in this butterfly.

At first, Susanne resisted acknowledging this hypothesis. But, she agreed that fractals, as an important feature of Fanning Everything, are directly correlated with her. Eventually, she told the analyst that she was willing to grant 17% as her maximum share in the image of this butterfly.[22] She was asked: why the number 17? Susanne replied that, on the positive side, 17 belongs to the prime numbers, which is a class of integers she likes. Therefore, it could express her partial acceptance of her personification in Fanning Everything. On the negative side, 17 is a strange and ugly number for her, which she thought reflected her refusal to fully accept the assumption of her somehow being metaphorically incorporated into this butterfly's image. Then Susanne had a sudden insight that 17, under the aspect of the digit sum (a method of calculation she uses often), is calculated as 1+7 = 8, which is a number she cherishes highly. She also points out that a figure eight laid on its side would form the symbol for infinity with compelling symmetry, which she equates with eternity. Furthermore, Susanne associates the perception of the number eight with her favorite color red, which could have become established through a specific dream[23] with an obvious connection to her father (see chapter 8.3.3: "Red Content").

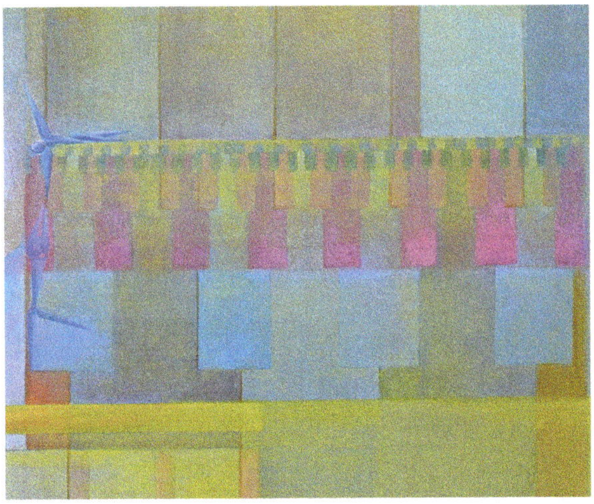

Fig. 7.19. Detail from Fig. 7.18: fractal structure.

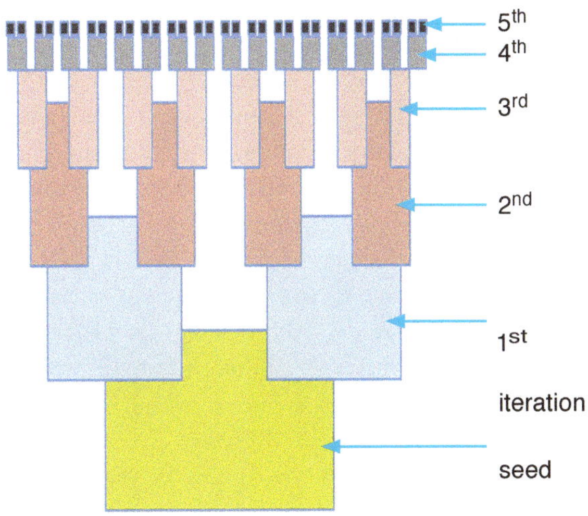

Fig. 7.20. Stylized fractal structure as it appears in Longing (Fig. 7.19). Drawn for this publication.

22 Susanne sometimes likes to associate abstract concepts with numbers, which come spontaneously into her head. In general, she has an idiosyncratic attitude toward numbers and judges some numbers as unfavorable and others as attractive or even "beautiful."

23 Susanne has always thought that the connection between the number 8 and the color red originated from a dream she had when she was in her teens. In the dream, there was a group of friendly German Shepherd dogs, each wearing a collar with a rectangular plastic tag hanging down lengthwise with rounded corners. Each tag had a different color with an incised number, which appeared white against the colored background of the label. One particular marker caught Susanne's attention: a red tag with the number 8 inscribed on it. That is about all she could remember, but since then "8" and "red" have been engraved in her mind as a favorable combination. She could associate the German Shepherd with an important professional colleague and friend of her father, whom she knew throughout her childhood and whose house she

Since Susanne cherished fractals, her psyche might have manifested this feature as a sign of her partial identification with the butterfly's image. Moreover, the chain of spontaneous associations has allowed us to uncover the hidden unconscious identification of Susanne with her mother, confirming our initial conjecture. In this context, fractals could be analogous to a specific meaning of the sun, which Susanne incorporated into the image of this butterfly as a personification of her mother, expressing the daughter's reverence for her. Additionally, given that the unconscious significations may be polysemous, fractals as a symbol might also represent the negative influence of her father's autocratic reign, under which the other family members suffered (figuratively "got broken"). Thus, fractals could be a metaphor for the adverse psychological consequences for members of the family. Therefore, multiple personifications in Fanning Everything become plausible.

We will briefly mention other self-similar repetitions in the design of butterfly No. 6, and refer the reader to Fig. 7.21 for clarification. Recursive patterns can be observed in the hind wing. It is subdivided into four semioval bands (marked with red lines), each of them bound by two parabolic lines. Those shapes actually follow the outer contour of the innermost ovoid shape in increasing radii, resembling the adjoining part of the kidney. Akin to widening ripples, they self-repeat the parabolic contour to the edge of the hind wing. Another set of repetitive, "self-similar" patterns appears in the front wings of the butterfly, where we counted ten such recurrences of curved line configurations, each of which is formed by a pair of convex curvilinear lines meeting at a vertex and defining the basic wing shape (marked with orange dotted lines in the figure). It should also be remarked that Fanning Everything's two front wings, formed from these recursive patterns, are analogous to the configurations in the hind wings of butterflies Nos. 1 and 2.

The artist's attraction to the idea of endlessly self-repeating configurations may have had its inception in her childhood, when little Susanne loved to delight herself in watching her image

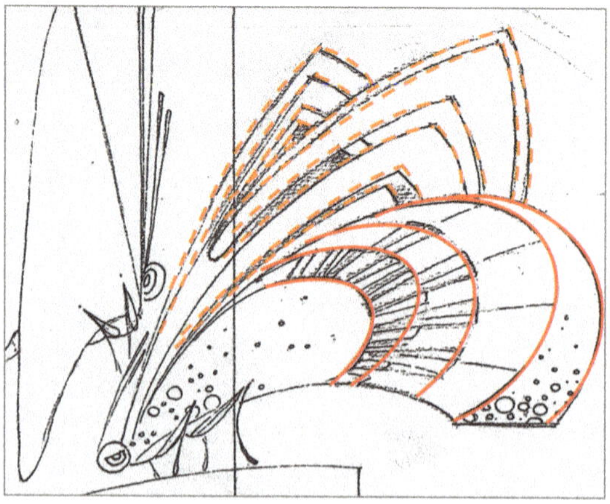

Fig. 7.21. Detail from Fig. 2.11 (the compositional drawing) illustrating the self-similar recurring shapes in butterfly No. 6, red lines highlighting the curved forms, and the orange dotted lines the spherical triangular forms.

be literally "repeated." She accomplished this visual illusion by standing in the center of a large three-sided (trifold) mirror, and the effect of her reflections being replicated endlessly and vanishing into infinity fascinated her greatly. Many years later, a comparable repetition of images appeared in her paintings, the dominant shapes reinforced by smaller replicas. The most striking application of such self-similar repetition in her art can be seen in *Born to Starve* (1992). There are two queues of destitute people, one made up of impoverished mothers with their infants, and another, the starving adolescents with their open palms begging for help (Fig. 6.13). In the painting *The Long Journey* (1995), reiteration can be observed in a file of numerous tortoises following the one at the forefront (Fig 7.22).

Susanne's penchant for repeating self-similar patterns is amply noticeable, for example, in *Le Week-End* (1998) (Fig. 7.23). There are sets of repeated patterns manifest as the vertical stripes in the distant mountains, the leather strips wound around the horn of the car, the reflections on the bell of the horn, on the headscarf of the passenger. Also recurrent in this painting are curvilinear shapes in pairs, such as the brass horn and its rubber ball; the man's round leather cap and his shoulder; the top and the open parts of the front wheel housing; and the eyes of the driver and the passenger. Our observation finds corresponding attestation

visited frequently with her parents. In addition, the shape of the tags reminded Susanne of colorful PVC plastic card samples, which came bundled together with a fastening ring. Susanne once received such a bundle as a gift from a master carpenter whose workshop she visited with her father. For the young child, it was a treasured item.

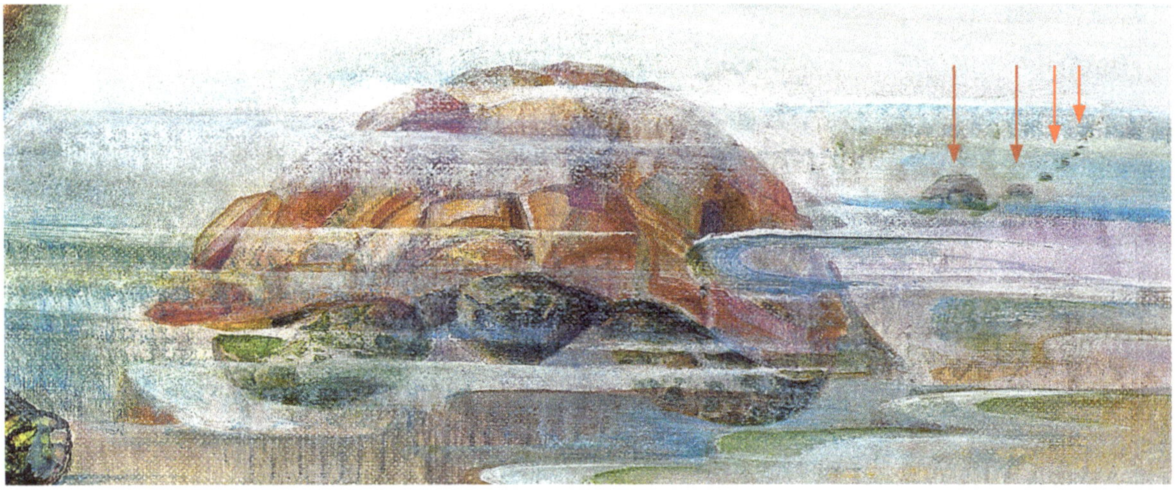

Fig. 7.22. Detail from *The Long Journey* (see Fig. 8.9 for a full image).
Arrows point to the endless row of tortoises, continuously decreasing in size and vanishing into the horizon.

with Briggs and Peat,[24] who extend the concept of fractals and self-repetitions to creative art and describe them in terms of "reflectaphoric shapes"[25] in such works as the Japanese painter Katsushika Hokusai's *The Great Wave off Kanawaga*, 1830–33, and the Flemish painter Hans Memling's *Portrait of Maria Portinari*, 1470–72.

The manifestation of the phenomena of fractal structures and self-similar repetitions in Susanne's art mirrors her sui generis creative style. They are quintessential examples by which we can analyze the artist's singular use of analogies, allegories, metaphors, and symbols, which reflect the modus operandi of the unconscious.

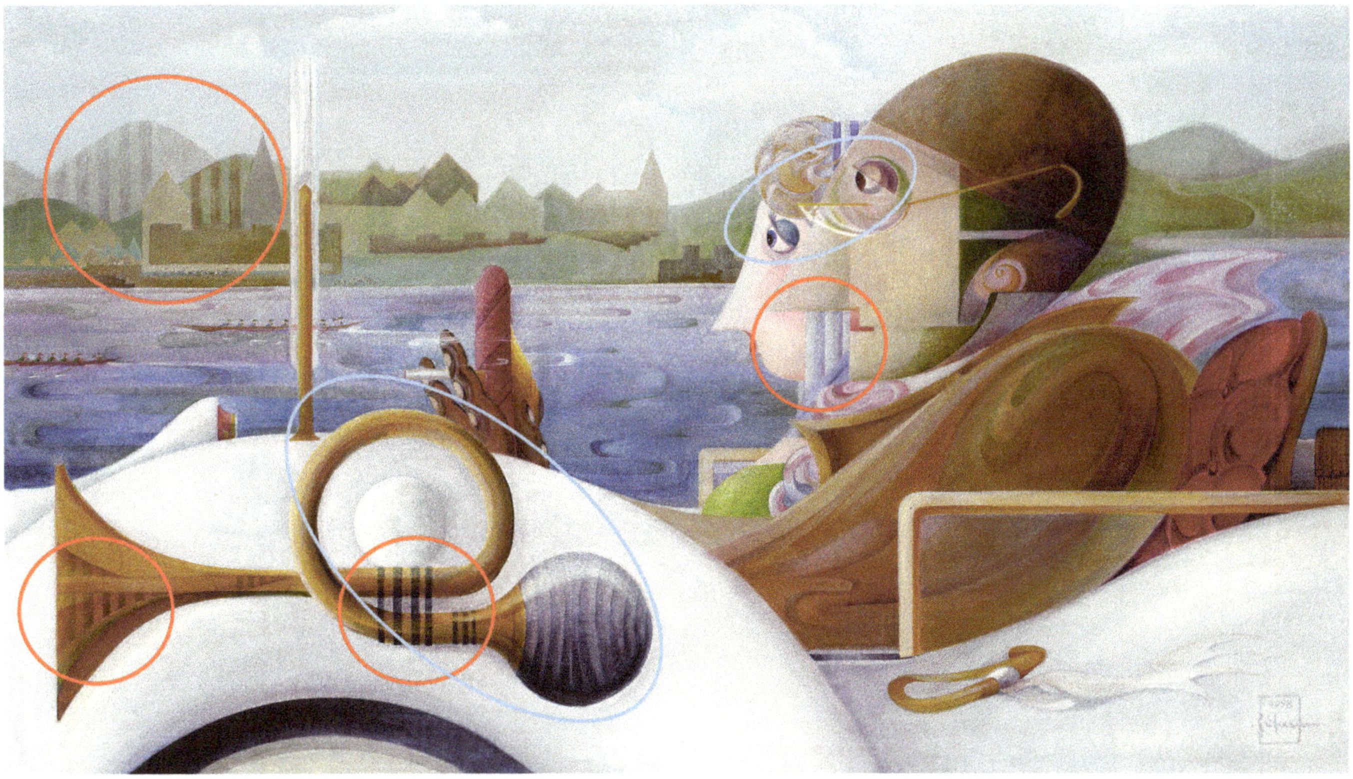

Fig. 7. 23. Susanne Schuenke, *Le Week-End*, 1998. Oil on canvas, 23 x 43 in (64 x 110 cm). Private collection, Chicago, Illinois. Recursive vertical line shapes are marked with red circles; circular and semi-circular shapes are marked with blue ovals.

24 Briggs and Peat 1989

25 Ibid, page 199.

The unconscious may have the same roots and governing principles as those of fractal algorithms. The automatic unconscious processes resemble the fractal matrix as a structure of limitless iterations. The dynamism of the unconscious transgresses the borders of formal logic and rationality. The irregular transformative patterns of biological drives, affective systems, and socio-cultural influences find expression through a huge network of associations and metaphors in various created images in the artist's work. Some contemporary scientific articles postulate that the brain, as one of the most remarkable results of the evolution of life, could have a "fractal organization"[26] and that there are possible similarities between fractal patterns and perception.[27] Fractals might play far greater roles than previously suspected in the shaping of our world, in the functioning of the BrainMind, and in the determination of the multiple peculiarities of the personality and patterns of behavior, as well as complexes, mental disorders, neuroses, dreams, and amazingly diverse expressions of imagery. The unconscious metaphorically expresses the universal and personal experiences in the created images using various modifications.

In the above context, the repressed destructive and libidinal tendencies of the unconscious could find their "iterations" in the process of bifurcating (branching out) transformations, developing from simplicity in the beginning (the Primary processes—Id) to the state of individuated and increasing complexity in their exteriorization (Secondary processes—Ego).[28] In accordance with above hypothesis, it may turn out that the constitution of the above processes is analogous to the matrix of fractal geometry.

7.3 Bubbles and Spheres in Susanne's Life and Paintings

Bubbles only exist for a moment: While one is still admiring their short-lived beauty, they will unavoidably burst and disappear. Accordingly, bubbles, taken as a metaphor, became one of the symbols for the brevity of life in the concept of "vanitas"[29] in European iconography. The metaphor of bubbles for ephemerality will be discussed in Susanne's works where she extended the figurative meanings of these spheres with a wider range of representations.

The pervasive presence of spherical forms in Susanne's art even spills into her daily life. She deliberately uses colorful, opaque, and translucent marbles to embellish her personal environment.[30] Tracing the artist's attachment to marbles and bubbles brought back many fond memories of her childhood. Around age 13, Susanne received a memorable gift from her parents: a game set of 28 marbles, each of them either of blue or clear glass approximately one inch in diameter. Before this gift, Susanne only knew of toy marbles of small size that were made of clay in dull colors, and she had no interest in playing with them. However, those new, unusual marbles kindled her fantasy to create imaginary games with them[31] which determined her love for them and started her ever-growing collection of glass spheres.

During Susanne's adolescence, when the family moved to a house in the countryside, her mother introduced a tradition from her own childhood, decorating the garden with clusters of colorful glass globes (gazing balls) mounted on poles and planted in the flowerbeds. They resembled oversized Christmas balls. The Christmas tree itself was decorated every

---

26 Kitzbichler 2009

27 Pincus 2009

28 Panksepp and Biven 2012; Carhart-Harris and Friston 2010

29 In the early 17th century, the concept of "vanitas" became popular as a moral warning of the transient nature of life, success, power, and wealth. It reminded the people of the time to refocus their lives on cultivating their spirituality and ensuring their souls' safe arrival in the eternal hereafter (Schneider 1999, p. 77). The German expression, "*Sein Traum zerplatzte wie eine Seifenblase*" (His dream burst like a bubble), describing the failure of an endeavor, offers a particularly vivid illustration of this concept.

30 Susanne's marble collection is composed of a rich variety of spheres made of glass or stones, including semi-precious stones. However, she has never incorporated beads into her collection, because they have not been perfect spheres due to their holes, and she considers them "damaged" and having "two navels." Consequently, she has a very negative perception of beads in accordance with her omphalophobia. This topic will be discussed at a greater length in chapter 9, subsection 9.3.5.

31 Besides the 28 marbles, the game set included a three-tiere structured made of three plates of Plexiglas that were supported by four metal rods, and each board was perforated with a set of holes in which to fit the spheres. Susanne ignored the game instructions that came with the set, made up her own fantasy "rules," and positioned the marbles at her whim.

December with many shiny glass spheres. Whenever Susanne painted a Christmas tree from early childhood on, she drew the ornaments as simple circles, as children tend to do. Her earliest memories of circles, bubbles, and marbles are intertwined with emotionally positive experiences as mentioned above, and they are ultimately associated with motherly love. As a student, Susanne moved out of her parents' home. Since then, she has begun to use the blue marbles as a table décor and has added over the decades many more sizes and colors for the same purpose.

Another memory of emotional significance pertaining to circular objects or shapes comes from her father's profession. In his creative photography, large, clear, and colorful spherical shapes in a non-descriptive setting were an important element. Often he practiced change of focus in his photographs for artistic effect—turning reflections into oversized circular or hexagonal shining "spots." These dots became even more prominent when the images were printed in an exhibition-size format (18" x 18" or 40 x 40 cm), and they dominated the enlargements, giving them a surreal appearance. In hindsight, Susanne thinks they could be seen as bright bubbles. She was accustomed to those pictures from the age of six or seven onward.

As mentioned previously, every detail of forms and colors and their interactions has a special significance for Susanne. The artist intentionally uses spheres (marbles, bubbles, and circles) in her paintings to convey ideas and attitudes that transcend the limitations of conventional perception. Still, the unconscious' message comes on board with them as a stowaway. Uncovering these messages might shed some light on how they have been coded through metaphors, symbols, and analogies in visual images. Artistic imagery results from the visual transfigurations of significant emotional experiences that have coalesced with coincidental attributes present at the time of their happenings. The discovery of these circumstances allowed us to make understandable her idiosyncratic sensitivities which are otherwise inexplicable. The received data helped to explain the formation of the symbolism of her favored circular shapes.

The following artworks will show how the metaphorical meanings of spheres and bubbles evolved in Susanne's paintings before the creation of *Give Me Wings!*. The watercolor *Buddha*, (1979) (Fig. 6.15), depicts a head in three-quarter view in hues of green and yellow with a light blue sphere on its forehead. With this shape, the artist marks the spot where the "third eye" is traditionally located, indicating the state of enlightenment that the Buddha achieved.

In *The Sea of Time*, (1981–82) (Fig. 9.1), Susanne intentionally represents water as an analogy for time. An immense being rises from the sea,[32] holding in his hand a huge transparent teardrop, which could symbolically stand for a single moment or a lifetime. For our topic in question, we

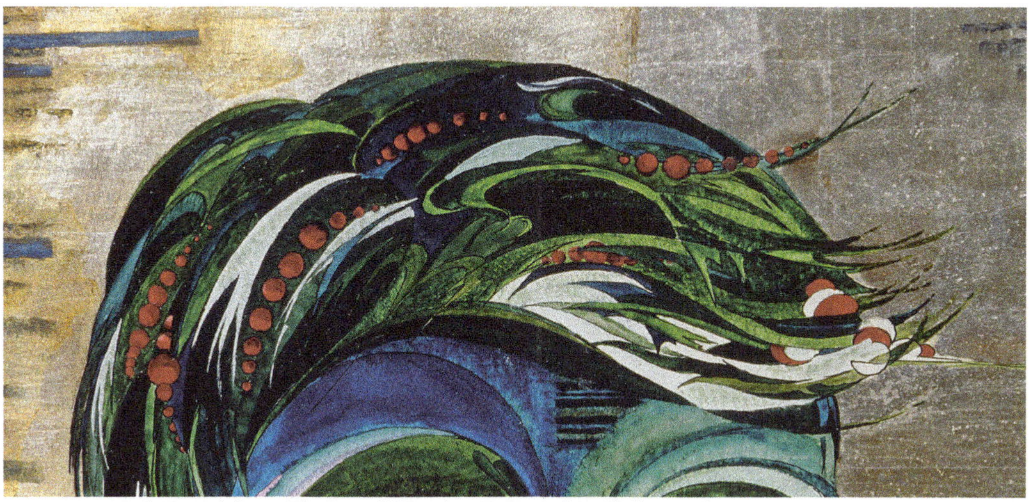

Fig. 7.24. Detail from *The Sea of Time* (see Fig. 9.1 for a full image).

32 We will return to this painting and the artist's unconscious identification with the created portraiture in chapter 9. With a small number of exceptions, all her portraits are her imaginative creations, not based on any human model. One of the exceptions is *Intelligence,* discussed in this subchapter in the main text. This face is actually drawn from the artist's image in the mirror because she "did not have a model" to study certain details in the facial physiognomy.

focus on several strands of solid red spheres flowing from the hair, some of them streaming away into space. With this, the painter intended to show the mental energy of thoughts, fantasies, and desires, which are sometimes so overpowering that they figuratively (as Susanne phrases it) "go out from the head" (Fig. 7.24). The artist's characterization indicates that these scarlet, energetic spheres could be considered as the visualized messengers of Susanne's obsessive preoccupation with various harmful tendencies and their persistently recurring appearance in her mind.

London Tube, (1988) (from a watercolor version of 1981) is the artist's first and most overwhelming impression of London and its subway (Fig. 7.25). The themes in this painting are the noise in the subway tunnel, the immense crowd of passengers, and Susanne's feelings of loneliness and isolation. Instead of realistically depicting people, she painted diverse clusters of opaque white, blue, and green marbles, which substitute for human beings and their interactions on the subway platform.

Intelligence, (1985) (Fig. 7.26), is an early painting where, in two of the side scenes, she endows bubbles with a metaphysical significance. As the artist explains, a being that personifies "Intelligence" rises out of the waters of creation. In his right shoulder, an oval-shaped window opens upon a space filled with man-made chains, barbed wire fences, walls, and natural obstacles like mountains and night's darkness (Fig. 7.27). All of them are meant as signs of restrictions. Out of these hindrances, bubbles ascend into the heights of freedom, unfettered by material restraints. Here, for Susanne, the bubbles symbolize the mental energy of thoughts, hopes, dreams, and imagination that are able to travel nimbly and far to overcome any limitations.[33] Translucent spheres also appear in the right

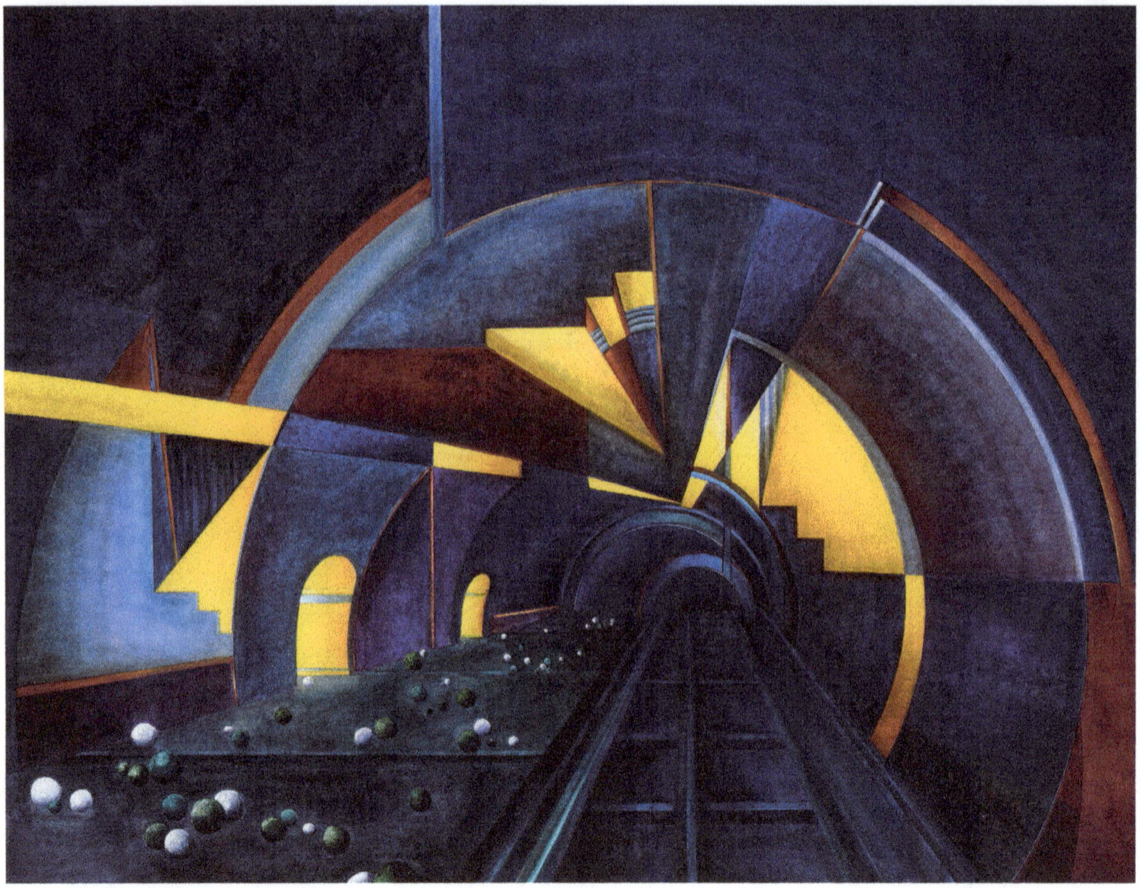

Fig. 7.25. Susanne Schuenke, *London Tube*, 1988. Oil on canvas, 23½ x 31½ in (60 x 80 cm). Private Collection, North Carolina

33 This reminds Susanne of a centuries-old German saying that became popular in the revolutionary upheavals of 1848: "Die Gedanken sind frei" (English: "The Thoughts are free."), meaning that they cannot be extinguished by any measure of censorship or imprisonment. The saying was adopted by Joseph von Eichendorff (1788–1857) in his poem, *Verschwiegene Liebe*, and was reiterated by Achim von Arnim and Clemens von Brentano in their collection of German folk songs, *Des Knaben Wunderhorn* (1806–1808).

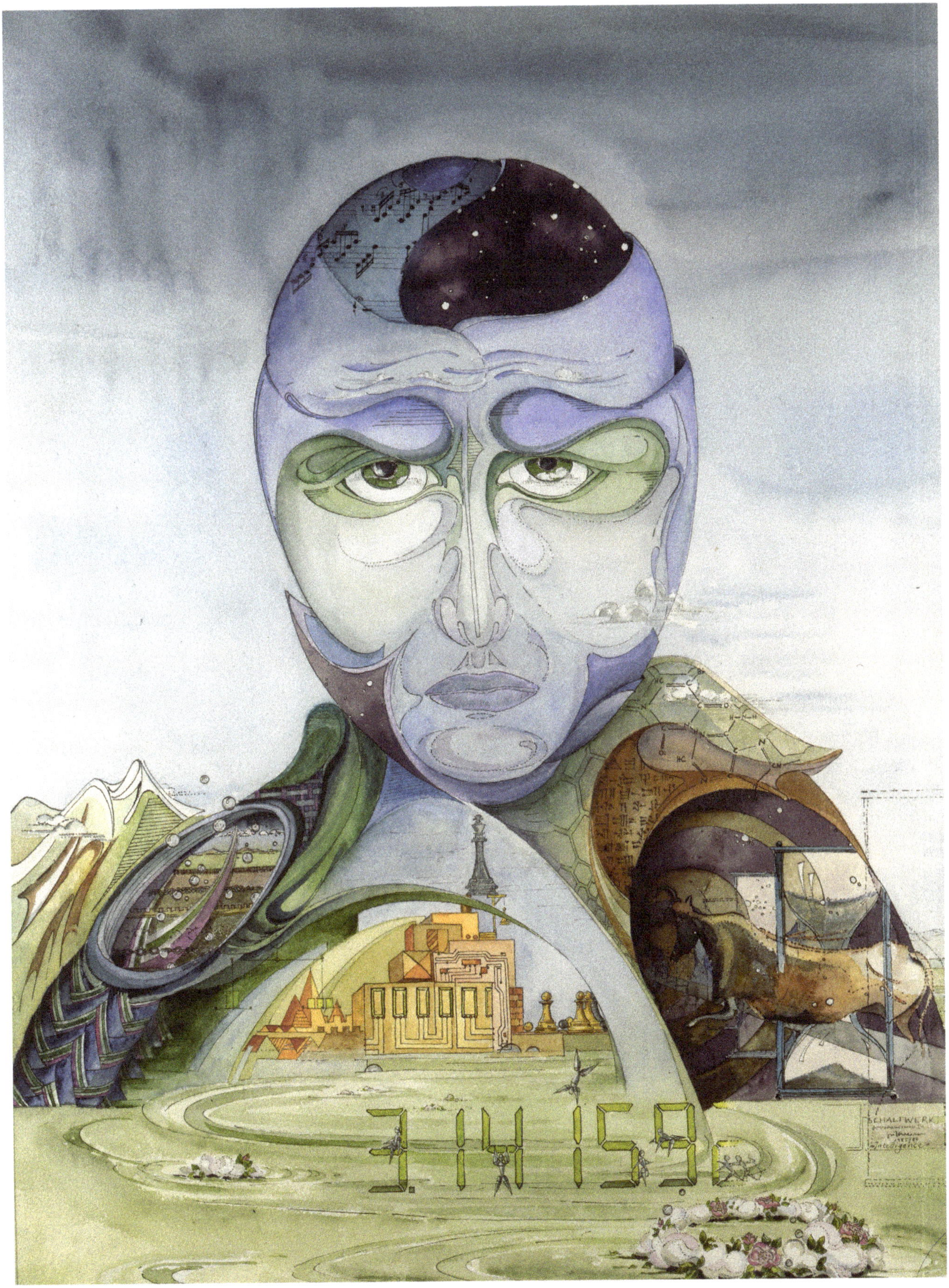

Fig. 7.26. Susanne Schuenke, *Intelligence*, 1985. Watercolor, 25 x 20 in (64 x 50 cm). Private Collection, Ohio.

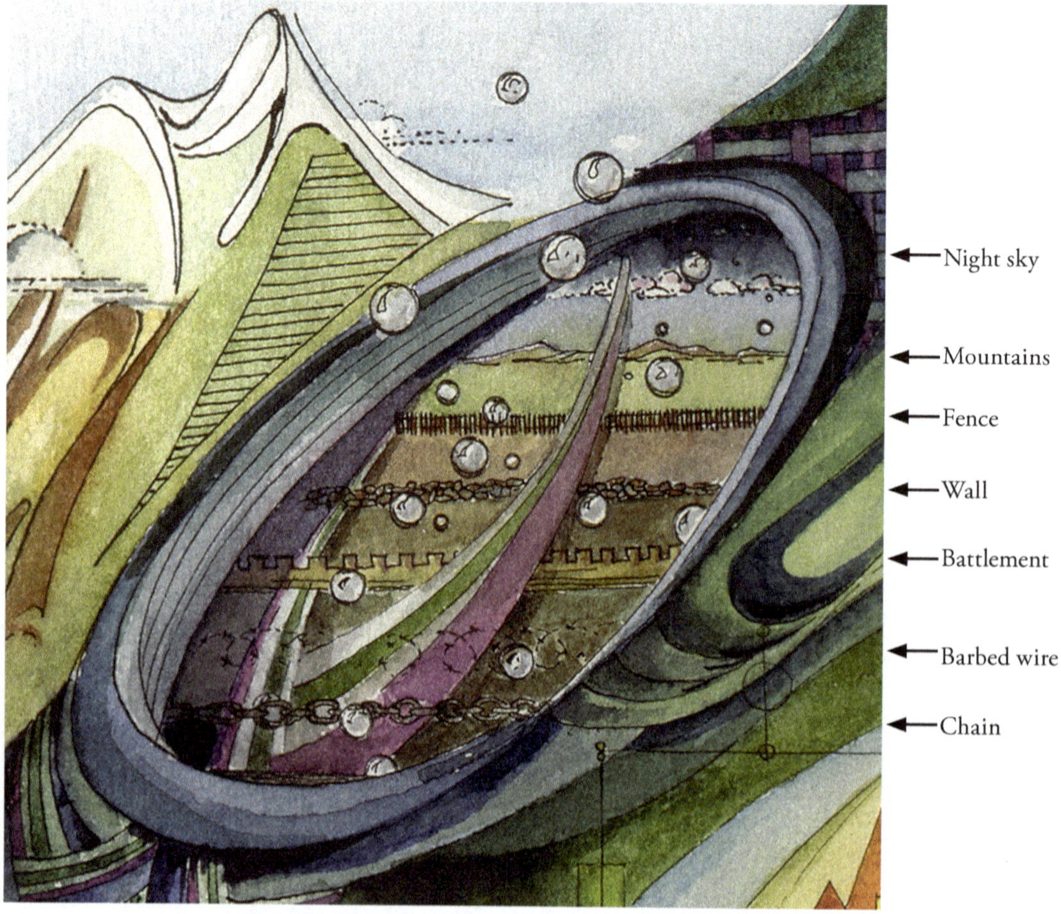

Fig. 7.27. Detail from Fig. 7.26: Natural obstacles and man-made borders.

foreground of the painting, ascending from a wreath that floats on the waters at the base of the painting. The chaplet is fantastically woven from white clouds and pink rose blossoms with their leaves.[34] Susanne blended such unlikely items to metaphorically represent ethereal dreams (symbolized by clouds), and tangible beauty (represented by flowers). Bubbles emerge from the garland and drift upwards like the scent of flowers, by which the artist intended to represent radiating vitality.

In *Epochs of Mankind*, (1989) (Fig. 7.5), the goddess of time is depicted as a seated deity releasing translucent spheres (bubbles) from her hand into the world. Susanne meant the bubbles to stand for different spans of time, from centuries to millennia. Each of the bubbles symbolically points to a selected epoch (three examples in Fig. 7.28). One contains the cuneiform script of the ancient Mesopotamian civilizations. Another shows the wheel with wooden spokes invented thousands of years ago, while a third bubble with a gothic trefoil tracery evokes the Middle Ages. A fourth one harbors the gears of a machine alluding to the mechanical inventions and their use from the 16th century onward. The bubble directly below the goddess's hand encloses microchip patterns, hinting at our present "era of electronics." Finally, the future is represented by the sphere in the goddess's hand. All these bubbles illustrate the paradox of time, and how our awareness of it over the many human epochs is subject to mankind's myopia, which prevents us from seeing what is outside of our "time bubble." In the artist's thought, a century is as ephemeral as a bubble from the perspective of the cosmic scale of time. Thus, our life of "threescore and ten" [35] may count less than "a blink of an eye," while for the immortal gods, eons become a game of blowing bubbles.

In the painting, *Past, Present, and Future*, (1994) (Fig. 7.29), Susanne again depicts her vision

34 This wreath on the water also evokes associations in Susanne's mind with the sort of beautiful offerings one would make to a deity.

35 The Biblical expression for 70 years, presented as the average human lifespan.

of the structure of time, the three aspects of time as personified by a trio of anthropomorphic figures, representing from left to right: Past (in blue), Present (in green), and Future (in yellow). Past and Future, shown from behind, each display a stylized sand clock integrated into the back of each head (Fig. 7.30). To indicate the flow of time, the lower part of the hourglass in the head of Past appears as a double bulb filled with opaque globules, intended by the artist to illustrate past experiences, including unresolved, burdensome occurrences that exercise their influence on the Present. Also, a big blue hair lock of Past overshadows the right eye of Present, influencing "its" perception. Susanne explains this may determine Present's subjectivity. The artist developed the face of Present intentionally from the figure in *The Sea of Time*, (1982) (Fig. 9.1), and our analysis recognized these images as unconscious personifications of Susanne contemplating the meaning of existence. Both faces bear a thoughtful, pessimistic expression, which aptly describes the artist's general attitude in her quest for life's meaning. The personified Present, placed between Past and Future, holds a single red sphere[36] between her lips, which symbolizes the time "now." She gazes toward Future, questioning the present moment, wondering what it might bring about in the ensuing course of her destiny. In the image of Future, the upper chamber of the hourglass is filled with translucent bubbles streaming in increasing concentration down toward the narrow neck (Fig. 7.30). These bubbles metaphorically represent ideas, plans, intentions, and fantasies, which are expected to be fulfilled. However, perhaps they will only exist in their imaginative states because numerous obstacles prevent their realization according to the reality principle. The latter, as a barrier to the pleasure principle, could be unconsciously

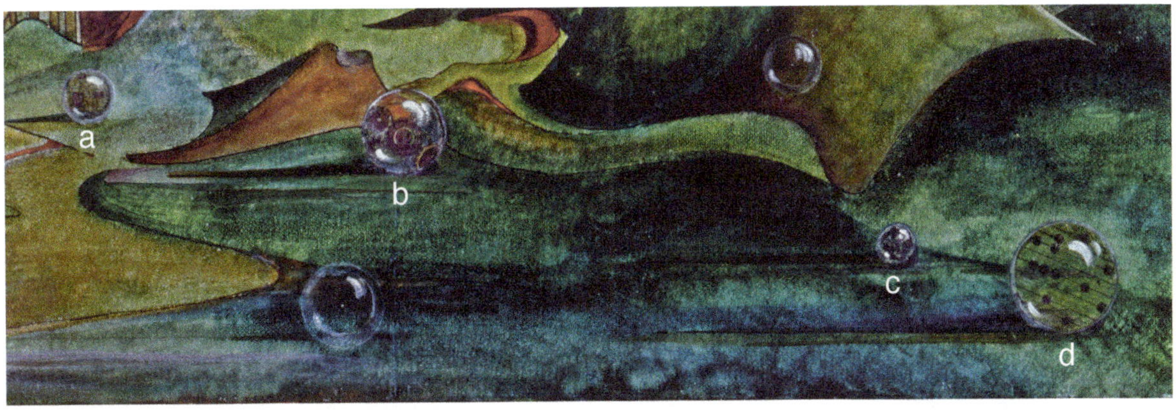

Fig. 7.28.
Detail from Fig. 7.5: a selection of bubbles representing historical epochs with specific details (letters added for identification).
(a) Computer chip. (b) Cogs and gears. (c) Trifold (gothic tracery). (d) Abacus.
See below for the enlarged view of three bubbles.

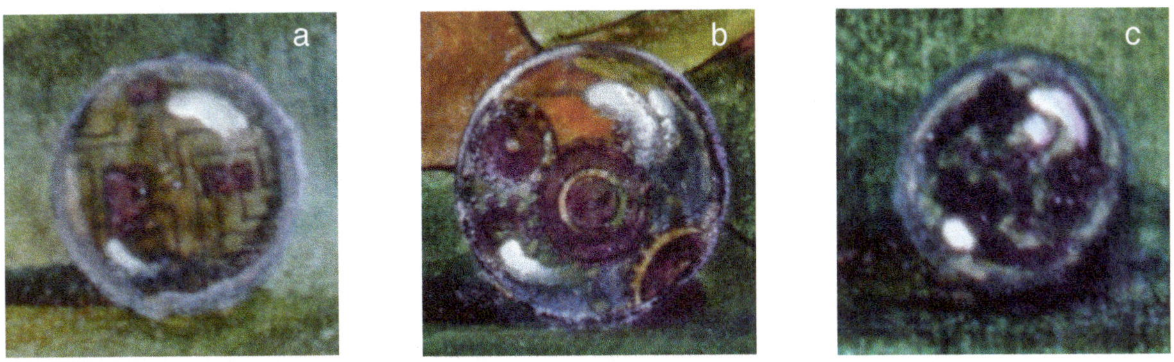

36 The artist intended the red sphere on the lips to be an abstraction representing an utterance made in the present moment.

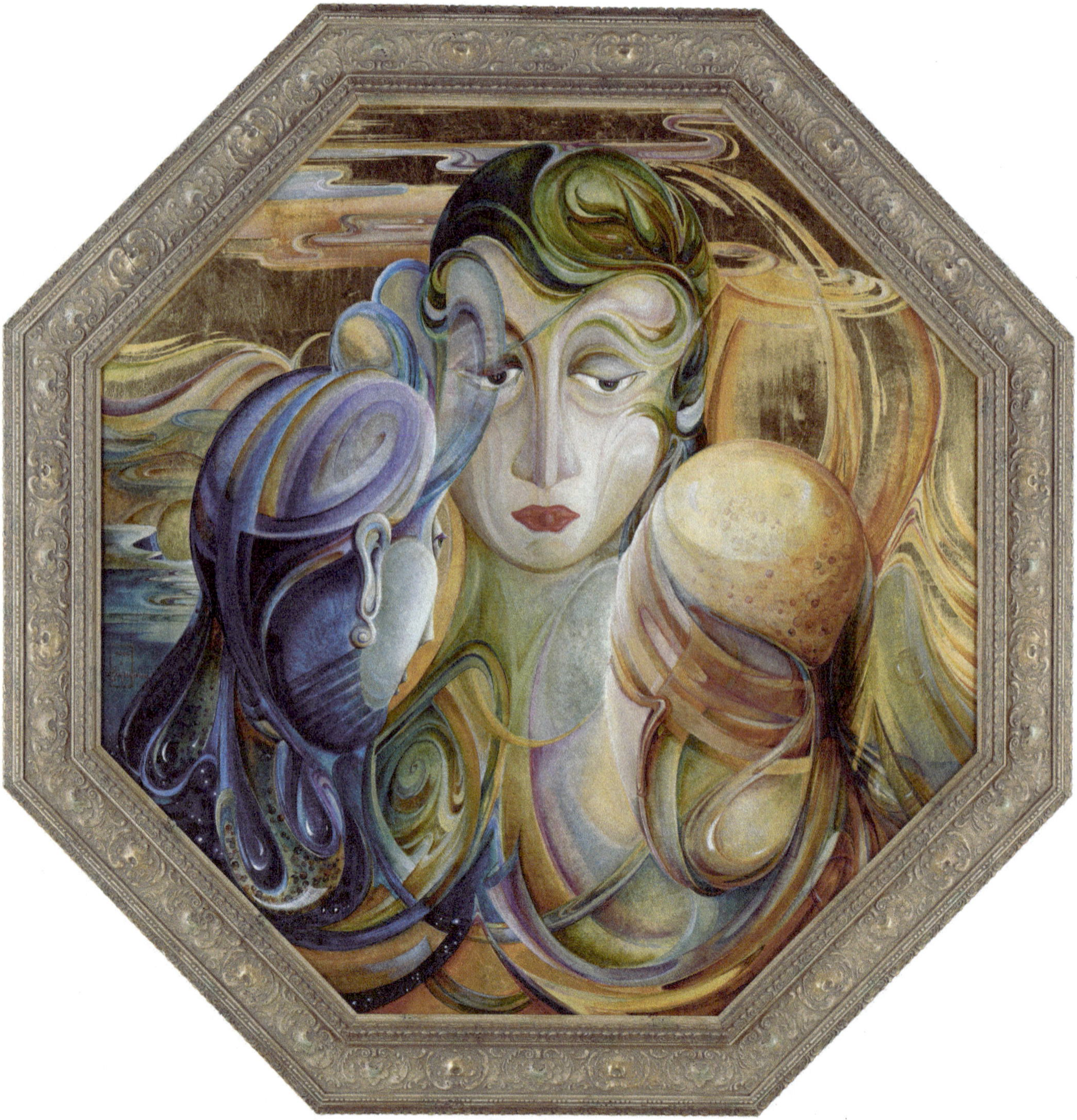

Fig. 7.29. Susanne Schuenke, *Past, Present, Future*, 1994. Oil with gold leaf on canvas, 36 x 36 in (90 x 90 cm). Collection of the artist.

represented in the ribbon-like shapes encircling the middle of the ovoid head of Future. Imaginations, represented by bubbles, are blocked from passing through the neck of the hourglass of Future due to the repression of their actualization.

In Susanne's art, another symbolic meaning of the bubble emerged with *The Portal of Surprise,* (1994) (Fig. 10.15), and in *The Rise of Karma,* (2000) (Fig. 10.26). In both canvases, these translucent spheres express the human soul. We will give a detailed interpretation of these paintings in subchapter 10.4.4 ("Images of Soul in Some of Susanne's Paintings") in conjunction with the analysis of butterfly No. 7, Air, as a personification of spirituality.

The above overview of the paintings reveals an abundance of spheres and bubbles that contain polysemous metaphorical meanings. Over several decades, the artist has used these circular shapes to intentionally represent such subjects as: enlightenment (*Buddha),* temporal paradigms (*Epochs of Mankind*), mental energy (*Sea of Time*), people caught up in their day-to-day existence (*London Tube*), hopes and dreams (*Intelligence*), and the passage of time and future potentials (*Past, Present and Future*). Additionally over the years, the spheres came to express the eternal core of our beings, the soul (*Portal of Surprise, Rise of Karma*).[37] Susanne has an idiosyncratic emotional attitude toward bubbles, marbles, and circles. She sees them as beautiful, complete, ideal, and possessing an inviolable perfection. By contrast, most people would see bubbles as embodying the brevity of existence, since they are highly unstable, and thus symbolize illusions. Furthermore, according to the artist, spheres represent our four-dimensional space-time reality in its clearest, most compressed form. She imagines them as miniature representations of stars and galaxies or an extremely magnified rendering of elementary particles. She envisions them as metaphorically mirroring "everything in the universe," representing material, psychological, and spiritual essences. In the following discussion, we will see that Susanne unconsciously endowed the bubbles with further specific symbolism in *Give Me Wings!.*

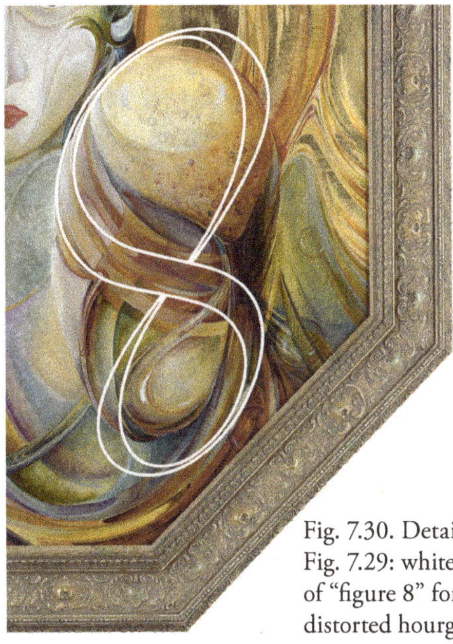

Fig. 7.30. Detail from Fig. 7.29: white overlay of "figure 8" for the distorted hourglass shape.

7.4 Globules in the Hind Wing and Their Meaning

We return to the inner and the outer segments of the hind wing and their specific features that are important for the interpretation. Distributed in clusters near the head, numerous tiny yellow spheres rise up in the blue kidney-shaped segment (Fig. 7.3 (k)), and similar spheres, more concentrated at the bottom area, appear in the outer frame segment (Fig. 7.3 (i)). The tiny globules in the wing of Fanning Everything are portrayed as floating up, suggesting they are free of gravity. The artist prefers to call them bubbles, in spite of their opacity. These globules, resembling fish eggs, are unique to Fanning Everything and are absent in the other butterflies. The diminutive size of these spheres could function as camouflage, keeping their possible meaning under the radar. This calls for our special attention, because the spheres are loaded with symbolic meaning for Susanne, playing a significant role in the metaphorical expressions found in her oeuvre.

The preceding review of the role of spheres (such as bubbles and marbles) in Susanne's life and art, their personal importance, and their metaphoric significance in her paintings was our starting point for the analysis of the symbolism of

37 The selected paintings demonstrate the different symbolism of spheres for Susanne. Her oeuvre contains many more comparable examples.

the globules in the hind wing of butterfly No. 6. In this section, we will focus our attention on some new aspects concerning the metaphorical meaning of these spheres.

We will follow these features from the first sketches in the butterfly conservatory through the designs of the creative drawings I–III, the compositional drawing, the watercolor, to the final version in the oil painting (see also chapter 2).

Among the sketches the artist made from her observation in the conservatory, there are two butterflies (Fig. 7.2) whose sprinkled dots and irregular spots serve as allusions to the circular marks on the natural butterflies' wings. These details were the first appearance of what would later become the globules in Fanning Everything. In reference to the spots in creative drawing II, we note that the artist equipped the image of butterfly E, the predecessor of Fanning Everything (Fig. 7.14), with a number of distinctively larger circles next to the butterfly's head, which were repeated toward the bottom of the outermost segment of the hind wing. The smaller circles, which appear to stream away like bubbles in a champagne glass, follow the direction of the radial lines. In the watercolor and the oil painting, these spheres still appear freely floating, but their overall presence is reduced in number, size, and density of concentration. They do not appear in the middle segment anymore. Furthermore, the artist has abandoned their translucent character by depicting them in opaque yellow.

In regard to Susanne's oeuvre, she often uses spherical forms to represent human beings or their souls metaphorically (*London Tube*, *The Rise of Karma*). In her creative drawing I (Fig. 2.2), the artist sketched miniature stick figures symbolizing people, whose presence made the butterflies in the drawing gain a gigantic proportion (see chapter 2). She designed creative drawing II without such figures, but with another prominent detail. There are numerous circles of different sizes, four tiny ones outside and many inside butterfly E. Two of those circle shapes are nearly the size of the creature's head. We may wonder if the artist unconsciously replaced the stick figures with the circles as metaphorical substitutes for people and placed them mostly inside this monumental butterfly, which eventually became Fanning Everything.

In the compositional drawing for the watercolor, butterfly No. 6 continues to feature those globules, but for the first time circles also appear in the area around each butterfly, with the sole exception of Fanning Everything (Fig. 2.11). The artist's initial reason for filling the space between the butterflies with spheres was to connect and bind the members of the assembly together compositionally. Susanne imagined the bubbles as tiny drops of spray from a perfume aerosol, with the butterflies inhaling this fragrance that filled the air around them. We assume that the artist's avoidance of placing the spheres outside of Fanning Everything and keeping them only inside this butterfly could have been determined by some unconscious imperatives.

After all the butterflies had received their coloration (including yellow globules for butterfly No. 6) in the watercolor painting, Susanne decided to use gold leaf for the background. She felt that this might add something extraordinary, perhaps even a higher dimension in accordance with her established iconography to represent superior values.[38] For the hue of the bubbles, which filled the space between the butterflies, she selected a light blue that she considered also as a spiritual color,[39] and, in this way, she reinforced the metaphorical message already laid down with the golden background (Figs. 2.12 and 7.31). With this gold and blue color combination, perhaps the artist unconsciously wanted to surround the butterflies with a spiritual aura.

In the final oil painting (Fig. 1.0), there are no longer any spheres in the space around the seven butterflies. As she began the oil painting process, the artist still planned to add bubbles to the background, but then she realized that the shining gold with its meaning of spiritual essence[40] amply substituted for the small spheres, and their specific appearance was no longer needed for the message.

38 See subchapter 12.3: "Golden Background."

39 We have indicated previously that Susanne considered gold and blue as spiritual colors, and they were used as such in her *Buddha* from 1979, where yellow, as a representation of gold, was used for the head and blue for the Bindu ("third eye") and lips.

40 In the paintings *Destiny* (1988, Fig. 9.21), *The Portal of Surprise* (1994, Fig. 10.15), and *Past-Present-Future* (1994, Fig. 7.29), Susanne also used a golden background to symbolize a sacred dimension.

This brings us to the question: why did she place globules inside the hind wing of butterfly No. 6, and what might be their meaning? When the analyst inquired about this placement, the artist answered that she perceived the inner and outer blue segments of the hind wing as receptacles, capable of containing the spheres. Susanne's instant association with those globules was that they would come outside in due time after maturation.

Asked for specific examples that relate to the globules, the artist suggested such items could represent ideas, hopes, dreams, and even eggs. They might stand for the realization of the human individual's potential, which may or may not be fulfilled. At last she admitted that eggs could signify the theme of reproduction. In this somewhat circuitous way, Susanne accepted the association that globules might well stand for offspring, whether children, brainchildren, or even artworks. Finally, this opened a discussion about the possible meanings of Fanning Everything's kidney shape and the "eggs" inside it, and whether this combination of images can be interpreted as an allusion to pregnancy. The kidney-shaped part of the wing could represent a stylized womb with gestating eggs or, alternatively, testes producing sperms. Susanne offered the last alternative interpretation (testes/sperm) to draw attention away from what she felt was a repellent function, i.e., to identify the kidney-like shape and globules as a womb with eggs. However, both womb and testes lead to the same concrete association of procreation. Nevertheless, Susanne continued to be persistent in her diversion from this topic, interpreting Fanning Everything's "vessel" only as a metaphorical, conceptual possibility. She even stressed that this reservoir of potential could also exemplify a brain with all the ideas bubbling up inside. Susanne fiercely resisted any attempt to maneuver the discussion toward a subject that is very sensitive for her, i.e., reproduction.

Despite her antipathy toward reproduction, she could not completely deny the similarity between the kidney shape in the hind wing and a womb, whose potential, she admits, consists of conceiving, gestating, and then releasing offspring[41] out into the world. After surmounting her powerful resistance, the artist confessed that she had already associated the kidney-like shape (which she has never liked) with a reservoir containing eggs—possibly as early

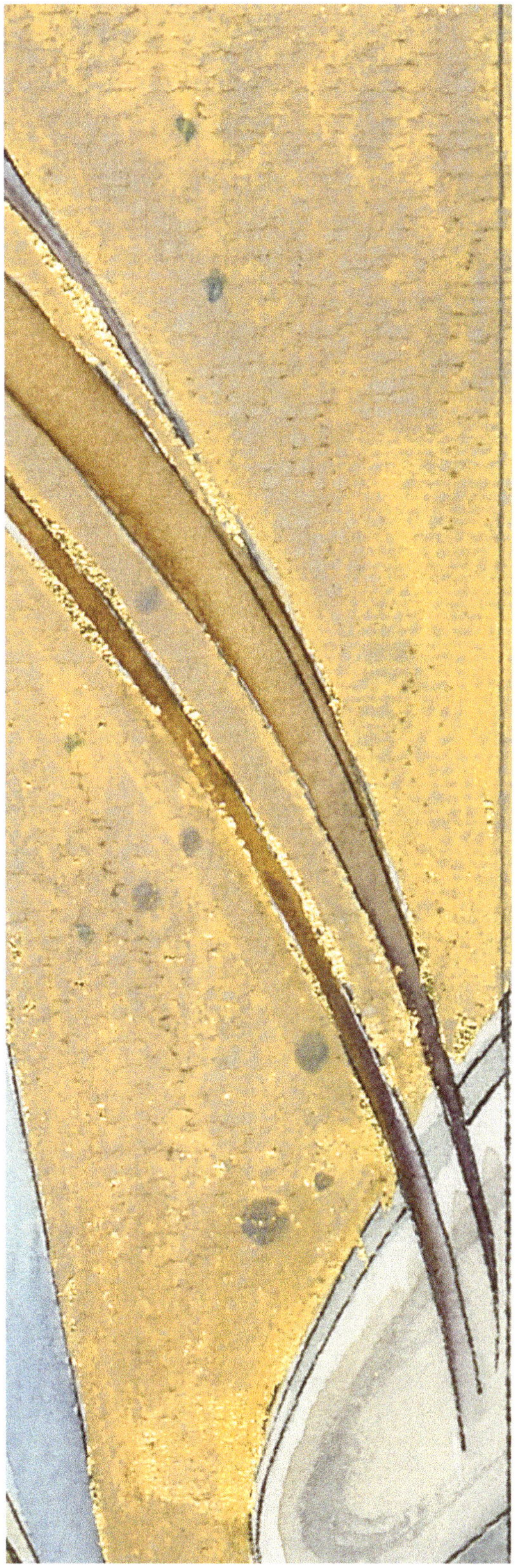

Fig. 7.31. Detail from Fig. 2.12, Before the Flight, the watercolor for *Give Me Wings!*
Detail shows the area between butterflies Nos. 3 and 4 with part of the left wing from butterfly No. 7 showing light blue bubbles rising.

41 Susanne prefers to use the word "offspring" instead of "children."

as when she worked with creative drawing II. She remembers thinking of it during the watercolor stage. Susanne's body language clearly expressed her abhorrence of reproduction. For example, she made disapproving sounds, tried to distract attention from the subject with her movements (such as scratching her arms), and rejected the topic of reproduction out of hand with a resounding "No!" When it was suggested that the yellow of the spheres inside Fanning Everything might be an unconscious reference to the yolk of an egg, and therefore an allusion to reproduction, the artist brought down her fist hard on a tabletop to reinforce her rejection of the thought.

Susanne's annoyed reactions can be interpreted in more than one way. Her anger could be due to her perception of being pushed to accept certain ideas with which she has no sympathy. There is a high probability that she was avoiding the subject because it is a taboo topic for her. For a detailed description of the development of Susanne's denial of parenthood for herself, see subchapter 8.2.4: "The Scales and 'Missing' Scale."

We suppose her idiosyncratic responses to this issue rest upon some conscious and unconscious foundation. As mentioned, Susanne consciously views these spherical shapes as metaphors for thoughts, hopes, and plans, which may or may not become realized. Furthermore, Susanne's conscious assessment was that her mother's artistic creative potential was essentially undermined by her subservient role in her marriage. Thus, those spheres could be assumed to stand implicitly for her mother's unrealized potential.

This metaphor could also imply her mother's reproductive fecundity, which the daughter chose not to emulate, but she could hypothetically harbor an unconscious, envious attitude about it. Being confronted with the last statement, Susanne answered laconically: "This thought is for me further away than Pluto." The suspicion of her holding such a strong biological imperative in the unconscious caused strong protest, even though the analysis indicated that it was based on her own association. Susanne tried to recover from this "accusation," using intellectualization as her defense mechanism, by pointing out over and over again that she could metaphorically see other things in the globules. These could be anger, plans, anxiety, ideas, desires, aggressive thoughts, traumatic fears, phobias, problems, and emotional conflicts. Sometimes they go out and disappear like bubbles, but often they remain trapped in her mind, tormenting and forcing her to struggle with them. She says that her brain is still "full of these opposing mental energies," which she experienced more often in the past.

The above account prompts us to ask, in what sense is the topic of reproduction such a troubling one for Susanne. Each time, when the subject was brought up, she has been overcome with a sudden feeling of extreme fatigue as an indicator of her distress. She was seized by a strong desire to lie on the floor. Her manner was as if she were fighting someone trying to forcefully pull her down, against which she had to make a real effort to avoid giving in. Therefore, the intensity of her evasive reactions, avoiding the discussion of this specific symbolic meaning of globules relating to pregnancy, deserves special attention.

Globules might possess symbolic significance of a highly sensitive nature in connection with her father complex, pointing toward the existence of a veiled, unconscious meaning. This idiosyncratic topic for Susanne is probably connected with her fantasies involving reproductive themes, which might be concealed in the symbol of the globules.

Reveries and fantasies have always played an important role in her life. She says that sometimes she lives more in the world of the imagination than in the world of everyday reality. In her childhood, she was overwhelmed with fantasies, ideas, thoughts, and emotions with positive as well as negative undertones. Susanne's inclination to involve herself in fantasies, some of which are sexual and aggressive, and her resistance to the suggestion that the globules in Fanning Everything have a productive connotation lead us to assume that their symbolism could metaphorically express biological tendencies for procreation. That proclivity could have been substantiated in accordance with Susanne's incestuous fantasies (father complex) through the early stages of her sexual development. We cannot find direct evidence of this (especially, specific memories from early childhood) because of Susanne's amnesia, which could be due to the repression mechanism.[42]

42 In support of this statement see a reverie described in subchapter 6.2.2, page 92 and a fantasy in chapter 8, footnote 73.

Moreover, our above assumption could be supported by some of Susanne's contemporaneous fantasies. With great hesitation, she began to share one fantasy, stating first, "I like bubbles very much." Then she continued, after a lengthy pause, "A few days ago, I had a fantasy, a mental image of my navel and a small marble laid in it. I did not like that!" She mentioned that, in this context, marbles, globules, and bubbles are, for her, interchangeable. The researcher then asked a rather risky[43] question: "What do you think could be the connection between the bubbles and the navel?" This elicited the following association: "Connection to a womb? The navel is the hole through which something can come out[44] and because this poses a danger, it has to be closed, protected, barred, and locked." Soon after the disclosure of the reverie and the comment on it, Susanne blocked any further discussion on the topic, which could possibly be connected with the primary fantasies of her childhood, in which thoughts on the theme of reproduction were of significant importance. As confirmation of this, we recall when 7½-year-old Susanne was informed that her mother would have a baby in half a year, which would grow in the mother's belly. After the daughter asked how the baby got in her body, the mother answered: "When two people sleep in one bed." The girl continued to periodically sleep with the parents in their bed until the baby sister was born. Susanne, to her dismay, was promptly dethroned from the prestigious sleeping place.

Susanne's sensitivity to the topic of procreation could have an unconscious connection with her repressed early childhood fantasies about the realization of her biological drive for reproduction. In this context, the instinctual urge found a visual expression in the globules inside the butterfly Fanning Everything, which is a personification of her mother and a partial one of the artist herself.

The metamorphosis of the sexual instinct, especially its incestuous aspect, resulted in ambivalent emotional conflicts which could be the basis of her rejection of reproduction. The artist's outspoken antipathy toward having children is in accordance with Freud's statement that "every prohibition must conceal a desire."[45] The contemplation of various aspects mentioned above (family, society, history, overpopulation, education, child abuse, and biological factors) provided a fertile ground on which various influences contributed to form her personal taboo concerning the topic of reproduction (antinatalism, see subchapter 10.4.5).

7.5 The Front Wings

To better understand the metaphorical meaning behind the structure of Fanning Everything's front wings, we will consider their details as they appear in creative drawings I, II, and III (see chapter 2). After executing the initial sketches in the butterfly conservatory, eleven days later, Susanne drew three creative drawings successively (Figs. 2.2, 2.3, and 2.4). The very first butterfly in the creative drawing I was a design that later became the butterfly Air (Fig. 2.2, A). The artist also utilized its peculiar see-through wing structure as a blueprint and developed it further in the creative drawing II as the hind wings of the butterfly D, which later became the butterfly True Blue (Fig. 2.3, D). A similar design process was applied to create butterfly E which was to become the butterfly Fanning Everything (Fig. 2.3, E). In this drawing, two butterflies D and E are facing each other as if locked in battle, the tension of which is nearly palpable. The curved incline indicates the butterflies' respective hierarchical advantages, with butterfly E holding the higher ground against the challenge from butterfly D.

Among the three butterflies in creative drawing III (Fig. 2.4), we observe butterfly H (later Firebird; see Fig. 2.4, H), posing over what appears to be a prone butterfly F, underneath.[46]

43 Risky, because one of Susanne's untamed phobias has revolved around the navel (*omphalophobia*). The mere mention of the word still results in a strong emotional and physical reaction, as do any images of a navel or a finger gesture pointing to it.

44 At the moment this conversation was going on, she suddenly experienced a sharp pain ("like a lightning bolt") in her lower vertebra shooting toward the navel. This sensation brought her into an acute state of suffering from horror, resulting in her cringing body movement and contorted facial expression of distress which were apparent to the analyst. It should be also noted that when this incident occurred (a shooting pain running up to her navel), Susanne was already under treatment for ongoing lower back pain for several weeks.

45 Sigmund Freud, *Totem and Taboo*, from *The Basic Writing of Sigmund Freud* (1995, page 861).

46 Butterfly H was drawn last, which is confirmed by the hatched pencil lines of H's hind wing laid over the traces of G. Butterfly F was depicted before butterfly H in this creative drawing, which is verified by the contours of butterfly H's

The domineering stance and towering form reflect the essence of butterfly H. Only butterfly H is used from creative drawing III in the compositional drawing, as the artist did not adopt the other two butterflies (F and G) in the future development of the painting. Susanne erased butterfly G during the creative drawing process immediately after its depiction, as evidenced by the still visible traces of butterfly G. Days later, regarding butterfly F, she intuitively felt that this butterfly in its prostrate, sprawling posture was unsuitable for the compositional drawing. The artist remembers that after creating butterfly H, she experienced feelings of emotional discomfort and, therefore, stopped further drawing. The unconscious personifications of Susanne and her parents were already embedded in the design of the three creative drawings. In all likelihood, her family experiences, in which Susanne observed her mother repeatedly domineered by her husband, could have found its symbolic expression in the scene of creative drawing III and been the root of the daughter's distress.

Because creative drawings I, II, and III were drawn spontaneously without a given topic, interruption, or major corrections, we apply the term "automatic drawing" to them. These drawings, interconnected by a single plotline, restage the artist's past in a condensed narrative with complex visual metaphors. In creative drawing I, we observe a trio of butterflies assembled in resting harmony. However, in the creative drawing II, we find a scene of confrontation, and in the creative drawing III, the arena shows a clear distinction between the winner and loser.

Susanne's significant past emotional experiences were transmuted into a cohesive visual narrative, unconsciously personifying the butterflies as the members of her family during each stage of the "story building." Looking at the drawings from this perspective, her father appears as the butterflies D and H, while the mother as E and F. In the compositional drawing, the watercolor, and finally the oil painting, (Figs. 2.11, 2.12, and 1.0), butterfly E from creative drawing II was paired with butterfly H of creative drawing III. In the process, E's superior position in the second drawing was lost, as butterfly H was given the dominant posture over E. By pairing E and H, the artist retained the humiliating situation from creative drawing III, but the visible "defeat" of butterfly F was replaced with a subtle subjugation of butterfly E. Aggression was clearly depicted in the second and third creative drawings, where butterflies E and H were in a superior position respectively. By the time all the butterflies were combined and arranged in the compositional drawing (Fig. 2.11), butterfly H had assumed a dominant position and butterfly E was reduced to the status of having been subdued. These hierarchical shifts reveal a remarkable scene in which a family struggle for power had taken place (see more details in chapters 4 and 5). As a final outcome, we observe on the left side that True Blue (father) keeps Little Why (Susanne as a child) in check, while on the right, Firebird suppresses Fanning Everything (mother, Susanne). However, the similarities that can be found in the hind-wing structure of the butterfly True Blue and the front wings of Fanning Everything, could infer that the latter was, figuratively speaking, also endowed with ruling power. In accordance with real-life situations, the mother, personified in butterfly Fanning Everything, held autonomous responsibilities in household management, child-rearing (school, healthcare, clothing), and the family business's finances and bookkeeping.

Moreover, based on the correlation that exists between the front wing structures of Fanning Everything/mother and hind wings of Little Why/Susanne, we can assume a metaphoric presence of Susanne in the imagery of Fanning Everything. This assertion supplements our prior assumption of her partial identification with Fanning Everything that we had already made on the basis of the fractal structure in butterfly No. 6's hind wing, a configuration highly valued by the artist.

Furthermore, the similarities between the structure (spherical triangular shape and cut-out design) of True Blue's hind wings (father), Fanning Everything's front wing (mother), and Little Why's hind wings (Susanne) could signify the father's influence over them, metaphorically presenting the psychological mechanism of introjection. The same process determined the creation of Little Why as a virtual replica of True Blue (father).

In chapters 4 and 5, we described in detail Susanne's identification with her father, and her childhood desire to emulate him and reach his level

lower hind wings that are purposely not crossing over the lines of butterfly F.

of mental resources and personal power. Susanne openly admits that she strove to copy and even hoped to exceed her father in success and prestige: "I copied my father so much. As a teenager and young adult, I was under the illusion that this imitation would bring me comparable status and power." Her father often exercised rigid authority over Susanne, which she resented and wished to oppose with a matching counteraction. Susanne's persistent ambition for status and dominance might have prompted her unconsciously to signify her fantasized desire to reach supremacy over her father and even exert her authority over him, as her mother had in different life situations. This statement found its expression through the imagery of *Give Me Wings!*.

The structure of the hind wings of Little Why (Susanne), analogical to the hind wings of True Blue (father) and front wing of Fanning Everything (mother, Susanne), could metaphorically express the double identification of Susanne with both her parents. Concerning the father, the daughter has the desire to possess his authority and have, like her mother, some dominance over him. The image of Fanning Everything which also partially personifies Susanne, and encapsulates the similar structure existing in the images of True Blue and Little Why (father/Susanne) could confirm our above hypothesis.

To sum up, butterfly No. 6 is a complex mixture of ambivalent and contrasting signs. We face a significant discrepancy between the positive metaphorical meaning in the details (fan, sun, fractals) of the butterfly's imagery and the negative assessment of Fanning Everything in the poetic commentary. The evaluation reflects the artist's clear antipathy toward this butterfly, arising from certain issues pertaining to Susanne's attitude, especially to her aunt (see pages 116-118), same as the topic of reproduction which repels Susanne, the latter represented metaphorically by the globules in the inner and outer segment of this butterfly.

Initially, we assumed that butterfly No. 6 is the unconscious personification of the artist's mother. This presupposition was based on the clearly submissive posture of Fanning Everything toward Firebird coupled with such features as a fan and the sun which were associated with the mother. Another strong indicator for an unconscious personification of the mother was the blue shape with yellow globules that was decoded as a womblike vessel containing eggs as an allusion to her fecundity.

However, the insertion of a fractal structure into the fan/sun arrangement (in the hind wing) and the specific configuration (the related angular contours and cut-out design of True Blue's and Little Why's hind wings) in Fanning Everything's front wing lead us to assume that butterfly No. 6 also metaphorically and partially represents Susanne.

As mentioned, the painted image with positive attributes (fan, sun, fractals) stands in stark contrast to the relentless condemnation heaped on this butterfly in the poetic commentary by the artist. Those judgments could be connected with Aunt Hella, who casts her shadow on this image. She enters into the scene through a backdoor in Susanne's comment on the butterfly Fanning Everything. In the family, this aunt was defined as an unreliable persona, and a prototype of a guileful opportunist who moved like a weathervane. Susanne succinctly qualified the memory of her in her statement, "... dancing at every wedding ... display[ing] countless alternatives ..." Recalling her mother's remark about the aunt's chameleonic skills, the artist assumes that the striking variety of colors she took from each of the other members of the group can be tied to the mostly negative memories about her aunt, which are still painful for Susanne. Fanning Everything's multicolor might be the metaphoric equivalent of her aunt's chameleon-like ability to change her "colors" according to the circumstances. Alongside the characterization which could be a perfect match for Aunt Hella in the poetic commentary, we consider the possibility of displacement. Susanne unconsciously might have substituted her mother with the family's black sheep. This way Susanne might disguise her ambivalent thoughts and feelings about her parent, which were caused by the various complexes that were formed in her childhood. Subsequently, the complicated structure that interweaves the diverse details of Fanning Everything and their metaphorical meanings, together with the poetic commentary, could well be the result of amalgamating the representations of several members of the family in this one butterfly. This overview can thus make the artist's inexplicably negative attitude toward this butterfly more understandable.

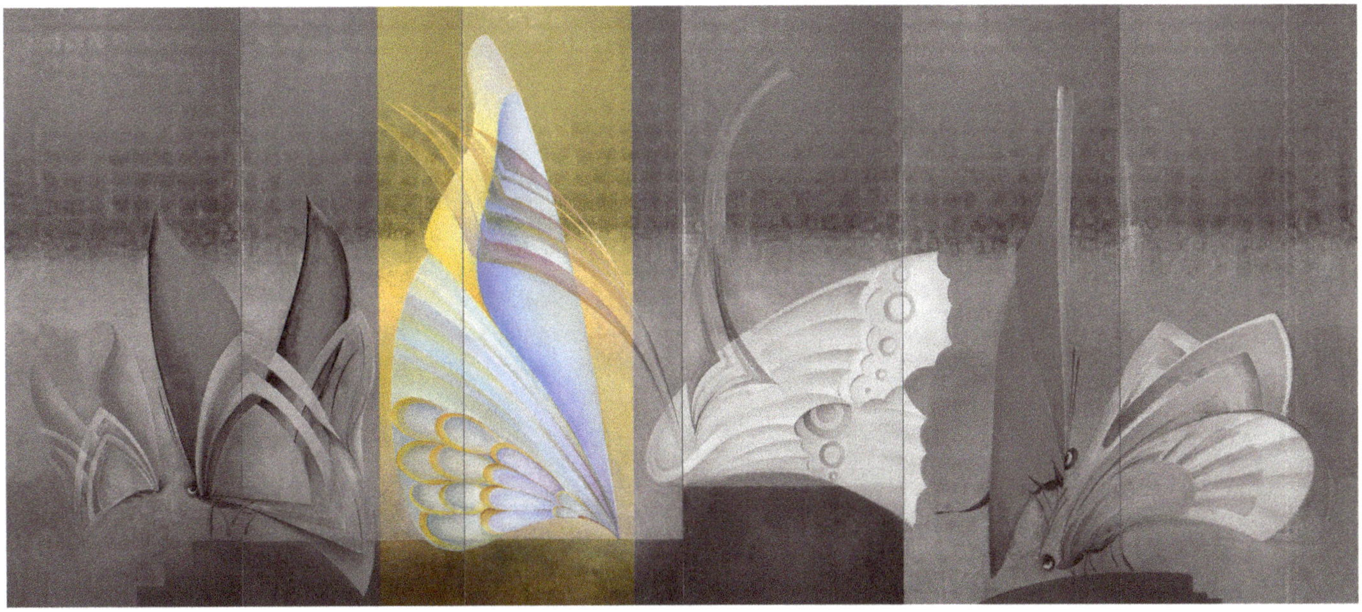

Fig. 8.0. *Give Me Wings!* with butterfly No. 3, Pale Moonlight, highlighted.

Pale Moonlight is much larger than her vaguely defined talents: her sketchy acknowledged qualities and her barely illuminated brilliance. Her essence is concentrated at the core from which all her strength, beauty, endurance, and courage stream out, [*and*] *radiate in spiraling loops or in graceful bends, sharply marking the division between "here" and "there." A glimpse of orange within the innate, energetic nucleus lets you wonder what* [it] *could be when uncapped and let loose.*

—From the artist's poetic commentary, 2004.

Chapter 8

The Majestic **Butterfly No. 3 — Pale Moonlight**

Silent and gentle

8.1 The Name

Butterfly No. 3, Pale Moonlight, was named, like most of the other butterflies, during the writing of the poetic commentary,[1] where Susanne expresses her perception of this creature's essence. The artist's christening of the butterflies shortly after she completed the painting was fortunate, because her choice of words gave us an important key to the interpretation of the painting's imagery. It was discovered that the nickname for each butterfly brought forward traces of the artist's unconscious and touched the core of its latent content deeper than the initial impression might suggest. The associations relating to the names connected the researchers with implicit messages which manifested in the artist's imagery. Analyzing Susanne's creation of the sobriquet "Pale Moonlight," we uncovered multiple sources that might have determined this choice. We comprehended it after we had scrutinized possible meaningful connections among the components "moon," "moonlight," and "pale," before considering their interplay.

1 Reading the poetic commentary, it is not easy to identify which butterfly in the painting is Pale Moonlight and which is Touchless Misty. The butterflies No. 3 and No. 4 possess characteristics, which could find their match in both descriptions. However, the decisive clue is revealed in the phrase "the elegant polished white surface" (see chapter 9 for analysis of this expression) which is the feature belonging only to butterfly No. 4 (Touchless Misty); therefore, Pale Moonlight is butterfly No. 3.

8.1.1 Moon and Moonlight

Susanne has various associations relating to the "moon" and "moonlight" in her personal, educational, and cultural contexts. The uncovered information can explain how her significant experiences were processed by the unconscious and found their transmuted expressions in the image of Pale Moonlight.

The common folklore expression, "The man in the moon" refers more correctly to "a face of the man in the moon"[2] which children growing up in a Western culture learn to discern in this lunar optical illusion. Little Susanne loved to hear about the humanlike moon, when her mother often read to her the children's book, *Der kleine Häwelmann.*[3] According to the artist's fragmented memory of the story and pictures in the book, a little boy named Häwel will not go to sleep and impatiently rocks his crib until it starts to float away, passing through the window and traveling up in the sky to the moon, where he rolls it over the face of the kind and jovial moon. The moon, depicted as a human face in pale yellow colors and with a big round nose, expresses annoyance with the boy's disrespectful behavior, but tolerates his impertinence.[4]

As far as Susanne can remember, the boy Häwel naggingly repeated: "More, good old moon, more!" and her mother, whenever repeating the story to Susanne, declaimed this phrase with special emphasis. Susanne would smile with joy when hearing about the little Häwel rocking his crib beyond any measure, getting on every adult's nerve, wanting "more, good moon, more … ," and traveling through the window into the moonlit sky beyond. As a teenager, Susanne used to read this favorite bedtime tale to her younger sister, reliving her pleasurable emotions. Recalling the story still evokes those worry-free early years in her life. To this day, she retains a strong affection toward the daring boy and wishes to possess his freedom and adventurous spirit and make it her own so as to explore the world and reach beyond the ordinary.

Asked about the earliest memory of her perception of moonlight, she answered that it might have been during the family vacation on the North Sea coast, watching the moon shining over the sea. For the child, that reflection on the water was surely a cause for excitement, because while growing up in a metropolitan area, she had no chance to experience a moonrise over the unobstructed horizon. At home, the moon was clearly visible for her in certain phases but only in an unimpressive size and mostly in the daytime; even at night, the pale light of the moon was drowned by the urban light pollution. In her youth, she learned to recognize the moon phases with a mnemonic device. Her mother taught her to name the phases according to the configuration of the first letters of the words *abnehmend* (German for *waning*) and *zunehmend* (German for *waxing*) as written in the old fashioned *Sütterlinschrift*[5] (Fig. 8.1)

Fig. 8.1. An old-fashioned German mnemonic for identifying the moon phases based on the first letters for "waning" and "waxing" (in German, A and Z, respectively when written in the traditional Sütterlin script).

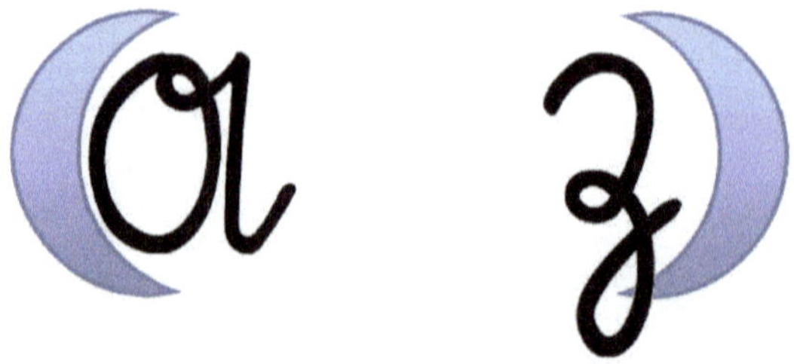

Left: "Waning" in German: "abnehmend"; A in Sütterlin.

Right: "Waxing" in German: "zunehmend"; Z in Sütterlin.

2 This is the association that the people in Western cultures usually see in the light and dark areas visible on the disc of the full moon. An East Asian observer perceives a different pattern—the rabbit in the moon. In other regions of the Earth, the perceptions are even more diverse.

3 *Little Man Häwel*—this is still a popular German children's book written by the German poet Theodor Storm (1817–1888) and illustrated by Elsa Wenz-Vietor, published in 1926. This edition from 1926 is established as the classic version and remains in print today.

4 In the actual story, the situation does not turn out to be so pleasant, at least for a while. The moon, finally exasperated with the child's impudent behavior, goes behind the clouds and leaves the child forlorn in the darkness until at last the sun comes up. Of course it has a happy ending; it is noteworthy that the unpleasant part of the story was suppressed from Susanne's memory.

5 Sütterlin script: A handwriting script that was created by the German graphic artist Ludwig Sütterlin, who was commissioned by the Prussian Ministry of Science in 1911 to replace older German handwriting styles. The script was taught widely in German schools before the end of World War II, but it is no longer in use as the standard contemporary handwriting script. (We had already mentioned the script in chapter 5, page 71.)

The moon remained a fascinating topic for Susanne. In 1968, when she was age 12, NASA's Apollo Program made the latest world news headlines as Apollo 8 and its three astronauts journeyed to the moon, entered its orbit, and observed the far side of the moon which had never been seen before by the human eye. In July 1969, two astronauts landed on the moon for the first time. Susanne followed this story very closely with great enthusiasm. She became so enthralled by the space program that she collected every news report, magazine article, and any other printed material that she could find. She dreamed of becoming an astronaut, but at the same time accepted the improbability of that happening because of her poor health and unfamiliarity with English. In this context, the moon might have signified the unattainable for her. Nevertheless, in her optimistic moments, she once made a promise to her little sister that "one day we will fly to the moon," perhaps thinking that the continuing advancement in technology would one day allow ordinary people to travel to the moon at an affordable cost. Thus, the earth's satellite could also be interpreted as an allegory for Susanne's hope that what seems impossible may become realizable in the future.

Inspired by the Apollo program, from 1968 onward throughout her teen years, she learned more about the moon from popular science books[6] about astronomy, physics, and cosmic and biological evolution, along with some science fiction reading. Certain well-known facts about the moon appear in her artworks as symbols and metaphors. For example, the moon is the natural satellite of planet Earth, and its radiance comes from reflected sunlight. The earth's gravity holds the moon in its orbit, and the moon's presence has gradually been slowing down the earth's rotational period to the present length of 24 hours. Furthermore, the moon has no atmosphere, and without it, there is no shield against the impact of countless asteroids which make craters and organic structures untenable. The potential metaphorical meaning of some of these facts has influenced the artist's iconography, and they may even account for her self-identification with this scarred satellite of the earth.

Susanne began observing the moon in the night sky at age 13 when her family moved from the densely populated city into the countryside with a better view of the open sky. She had access to her father's Zeiss binoculars, which enabled her to look at the moon up close in its different phases. She could discern the details of the craters, seas, and other surface features, especially the "Mare Tranquillitatis" (the Sea of Tranquility), whose soothing poetic name encapsulated the feeling of peace she experienced watching the moon. Her enthusiasm for astronomy and space exploration was such that she built scale models of the Saturn V rocket and Apollo Lunar Module from model kits with many minute details, including the detachable ascent module.[7]

For many years, she had a large wall map of the earth's satellite in her bedroom. In 1993, living at the beach on the Atlantic Ocean, she used a powerful telescope to observe the moon. She experienced the rotation of the earth firsthand, as the moon's image would move out of the telescope's field of vision within a short span of time due to the earth's motion.

In her adolescent years, Susanne eagerly learned about the moon from popular science books. She also loved to read classical literary works by such authors as Johann Wolfgang von Goethe, William Shakespeare, East Asian poets, and others who described their perceptions of the moon. For example, in the context of moon and moonlight, we quote an excerpt from the poem "*Dämmerung senkte sich von oben*" (English: *Twilight Descended from Above*)[8] by Johann Wolfgang von Goethe (1749–1832), which impressed Susanne by its aesthetic language. She studied this text in high school and came to learn it by heart. (The text in italics is Susanne's translation.)

---

6 Nothing of this was connected with the school curriculum, as it was her own personal choice, which was supported by her parents who believed very strongly in education and learning. They were more than happy to provide Susanne with what she wanted for that purpose.

7 More than 25 years later (around 1993), Susanne had the opportunity to visit the Kennedy Space Center on Cape Canaveral and saw life-size models of the lunar module, rockets, and other artifacts of the Apollo program, which brought back fond memories of her youthful zeal.

8 Jeismann 1973, page 206.

Nun am östlichen Bereiche
Ahn' ich Mondenglanz und –glut,
Schlanker Weiden Haargezweige
Scherzen auf der nächsten Flut.

Durch bewegter Schatten Spiele
Zittert Lunas Zauberschein
Und durchs Auge schleicht die Kühle
Sänftigend ins Herz hinein.

Now, in the eastern realms,
I guess the shine and glowing fire of the moon
Slender willows' fibrous branches
Chatting with the nearby flow.

Through the moving play of shadows
Trembles the magical glow of Luna
And through the eye creeps in the coolness
Soothing into the heart.

Through her great interest in classic Chinese and Japanese poetry and art,[9] she became familiar with the important role the moon played in those far Eastern cultures. Her admiration for Asian art had a discernible influence on her own design.[10] For example, in her watercolor, *Vom Lärm und Frieden dieser Welt* (*About the Noise and Peace in this World*, 1981; see Fig. 8.2), she depicts a person en face who is distressed by the contemporary urban conditions of polluted air, contaminated water, and pervasive noise. In contrast with the noxious environment in the right side of the painting, the artist presents an entirely different landscape: A world of nature unadulterated by human hands. There we can see a rear view of a translucent head, rendered in outline, permeated by the moonlight. With this image, Susanne visualizes the power of

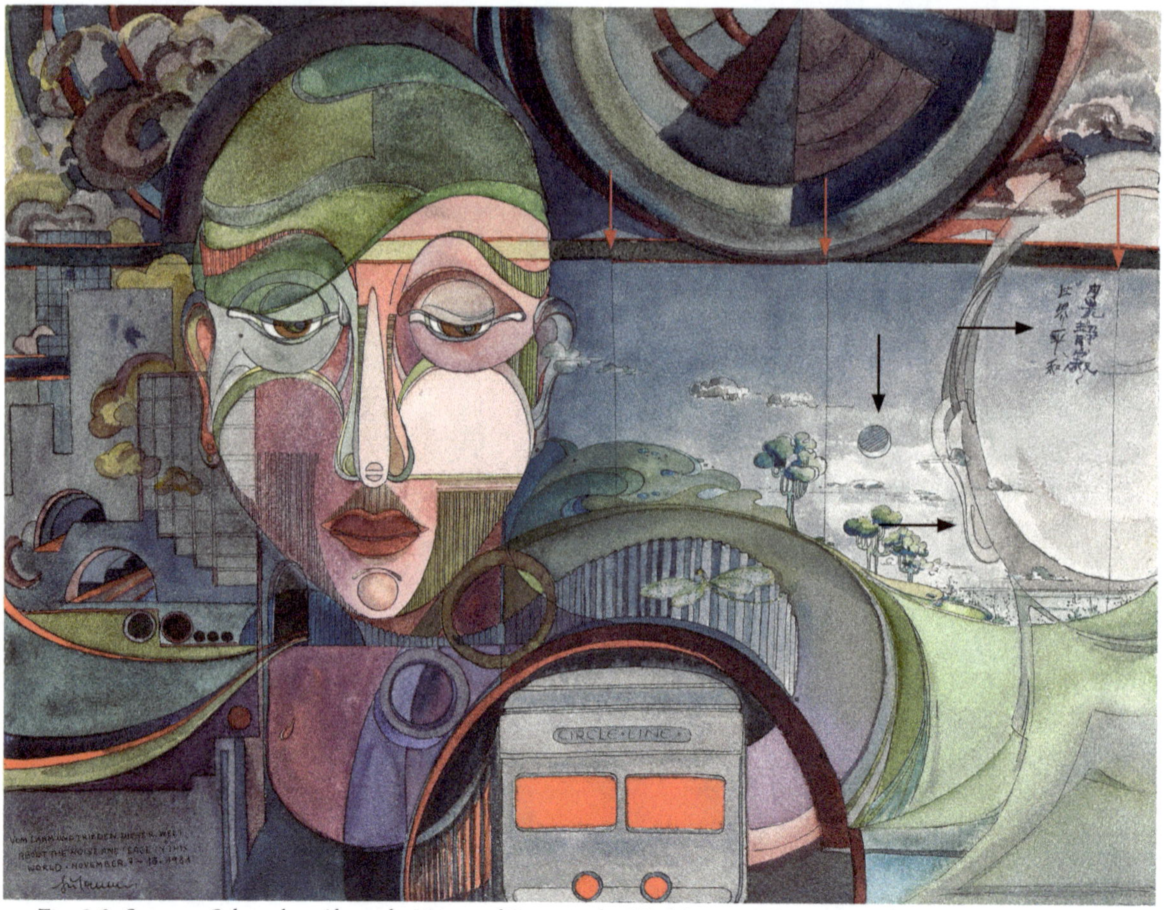

Fig. 8.2. Susanne Schuenke, *About the Noise and Peace in this World*, 1981. Watercolor, 14 x 18½ in (36 x 48 cm). Collection of the artist.
Red arrows are added to indicate the corners of the folding screen; black arrows point to the following: the moon, the projection of the head on the right side, and the imitated Chinese characters of a poem inside the head.

9 For example, painting, lacquerware, porcelain, calligraphy, textile, and theater masks.

10 Japanese folding screens might possibly have influenced the artist's choice of the six panels and the dominant golden background in *Give Me Wings!* (see chapter 12).

imagination and meditation to attain peaceful stillness in the midst of the noisy world. She even adds an imitation of Chinese characters, scribbled inside this diaphanous head. It reflects her reverence for Li Bai's[11] famous poem, *Moonlit Night,* which she read in English:

Over my bed the moonlight streams,
making it look like frost-covered
ground; lifting my head I see
the brightness, then dropping it,
and I'm filled with thoughts of home.[12]

Susanne remembers a Japanese poet's remark that sorrows can be soothed by looking at the moon. This accorded well with her own perception of the cherished celestial object which evokes a feeling of tranquility and promotes awareness of the fleeting nature of human existence. She feels adoration, awe, and wonder for the moon as these feelings have been expressed in Western and Eastern cultures in various symbolic figurations. For instance, the theme of "Musashi Plain"[13] in Japanese poetry and painting often combines the plants and mountain from this famous landscape with a lunar rise, exemplifying the Japanese appreciation of the moon (Fig. 8.3).

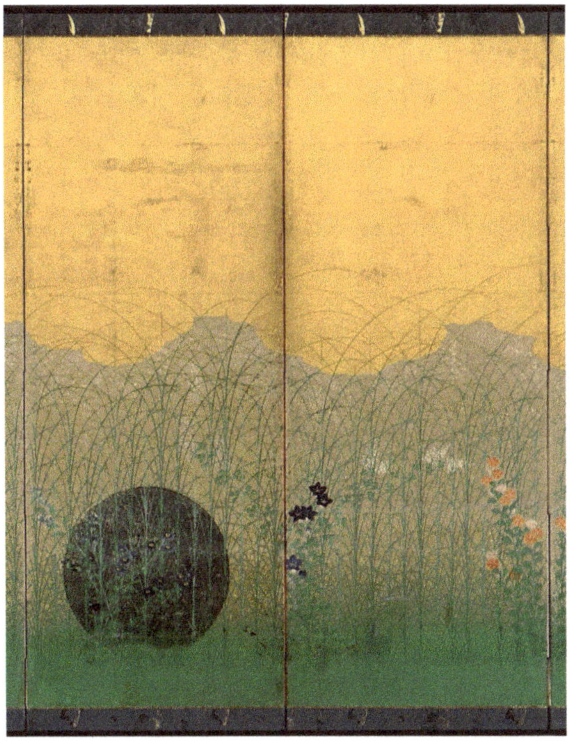

Fig. 8.3. Detail from a Japanese screen, *The Plain of Musashi, Mount Fuji and the Moon*, Anonymous, circa 1760. Art Gallery of South Australia, Adelaide, Australia (for the full image, see Fig. 12.7). Note the full moon over the horizon.

On the Musashi Plain
There is no mountain
For the moon to enter.
From grasses it rises,
And into grasses it sets.[14]

As emphasized in the two poems quoted above, the moon serves as an icon reactivating certain deep emotions of the past and longing for their recurrence. Susanne has a certain affinity for these East Asian aesthetic sensibilities. As a result, her response to the moon is more sentimental than to the sun. Her attitude concurs with such traditional appreciation of the moon in the arts of both the West and the East. She remarks that her preference for the moon is quite likely due to its visibility in the night sky, where the presence of the earth's satellite is inseparable from stars and galaxies.

Moonlight is the night's counterpart to sunlight, and there are noticeable perceptual differences between the two in spite of the fact that the light of the moon reflects the sun's illumination. In its color temperatures, moonlight is approximately 1,500 kelvins lower than sunlight, and it is always associated with "cool" and "silver" (or "white") hues, whereas "hot" and "gold" (or "yellow") attributes belong to the sun. Although moonlight is bright enough at or near the full moon phase, there is no comparison with the intensity of sunlight. The prolonged viewing of the moon does not cause any physical harm to the observer, but the sun does, for example, due to sunburn and damage to the eyes.[15]

The artist utilizes these typical characteristics of the sun and the moon to express her own specific

11 Li Bai (also spelled Li Po, Li Bo, Li Pai, and Li Tai-Peh), 701–762 CE: A Chinese poet of great fame who lived during the Tang dynasty.

12 This English translation quoted from Alley (1981, page 18).

13 See Munroe (1983, especially cat. numbers 2, 7, 27).

14 A poem originally by Minamoto no Michikata (1189–1238 CE); quoted in Munroe (1983, page 34).

15 Susanne's mother suffered frequently from a sun allergy during family vacations at the beach. Due to this experience, she always applied ample sunscreen on the children.

symbolic meanings. Sometimes she weaves them together with their generally known iconography with its traditional allegorical and metaphorical interpretations. For example, the symbolism of the sun is known to Susanne to be connected with Louis XIV of France ("the Sun King"). The monarch adopted the sun as his personal emblem—whereupon the king's courtiers took the cue and called him by that title ("le Roi-Soleil" in French). Her mother, when provoked or exasperated by her husband's autocratic behavior, sometimes would exclaim to him with the riposte, "You are the king."[16] In such a context, the daughter thought of herself as just a moon in the light of the sun and wondered how much she merely reflected the qualities of her parent. This metaphorical comparison of the moon as a celestial entity that is always condemned to play a subsidiary role to a greater entity, the sun, matches the hierarchy in the family.

The artist's self-identification with the moon could indicate a low level of self-esteem. This arose out of the daughter-father relationship in which her father was perceived by the family as the "sun king" whose esteem Susanne had to honor and accommodate. However, in spite of the moon's secondary role, she immerses herself in the nostalgic longing for the idyllic feelings from her childhood that the moon evokes. Aside from summoning the feelings of a happier time, she also associates moonlight with elegance, calmness, timelessness, and all-pervading peace.

It is worth noting that the allure of the moon for Susanne extends to her fascination with the moonstone, a semiprecious gemstone, found in a few of her jewelry pieces. The light scattering in many directions by the stone's adularescence creates a comparable psychological and spiritual feeling to what she would experience with the natural light of the moon. One can imagine the silvery celestial illumination and the gentle, milky-blue sheen typical of this kind of semiprecious stone. The connection between "moon" and "moonstone" led Susanne to buy moonstones. When she holds one in her hand, enjoying the play of its light, she imagines having a piece of the moon.

Another aspect of the similarity between the light from the moon and the moonstone is the reddish-yellow color of the rising moon at night and the opalescence of the transmitted light through a fine quality moonstone (due to Rayleigh scattering: see Fig. 8.42). It is remarkable that for a long time in our analysis, Susanne did not associate the moonstone with moonlight. Only during the analyst's discussion with the artist (see subsection 8.3.2) concerning the orange sheen in opalescent glass objects did she suddenly recognize the analogy between the light from an opalescent gemstone and the color of the rising or setting moon. The glimpses of orange color could have metaphorically united both moon and moonstone and, in the artist's mind, turned them into a symbol with overlapping unconscious meanings. This topic brought us to the analysis of another important item in the parents' art and antique collection—the Sabino Butterfly, which will be discussed in subchapter 9.2.

We may assume that all the impressions discussed above merged in Susanne's psyche and evoked a network of associations, fleeting manifold fantasies, and a kaleidoscope of feelings. Some of them are connected with emotionally significant experiences involving her parents, inspiring her creativity. Before we turn to the analysis of a selection of those artworks, we provide a short excursion into the artist's choice of the adjective "pale" modifying the noun "moonlight."

8.1.2 Aspects of the Term "Pale" in Pale Moonlight

Susanne recalls her mother using a German word "blass" (*pale* in English) to describe her daughter's face turning sickly as a child. When this happened, her mother would immediately check Susanne's temperature and look at her tongue for any indication of illness. Similarly, the parent was quick to notice the girl's tiredness when she had worked on her drawing or a painting for a while, and her mother would habitually say: "Susanne has exhausted herself—she looks peaky and pale around the nose."[17] Such an expression conveyed her tender, caring attitude toward her daughter and her readiness to protect her.

16 The idea of domineering like a king might have affected Susanne's father's sense of self-importance, and he incorporated the lion as his zodiacal sign (Leo) with his signature on some of his oil paintings (Fig. 4.5, bottom left corner).

17 In German: "*sie sieht spitz aus und ist blass um die Nase*," meaning literally: "she looks spiky and is pale around her nose."

Traditionally, the word pale ("aristocratic pallor") is also used to describe the appearance of the lighter complexion of the upper social class in Europe, in contrast to the more vibrant skin color of the peasants, who worked in the fields, with their skin sunburned to a darker hue.

Once, when Susanne's mind was occupied with the thought of and desire for death, she felt attracted to several paintings whose subject was the postmortem view of the dead. One of these was *The Death of Chatterton* by the English Pre-Raphaelite painter Henry Wallis,[18] depicting an impoverished, young aspiring poet who committed suicide. In the painting, the diffused daylight streams through a window illuminating the ashen, pale skin of his lifeless body, as if to hint at the poet's aristocratic dignity in his eternal repose. In this context, there was another painting, *A Dead Soldier* (Italian school, 17th century, NG741, National Gallery, London), which impressed Susanne deeply by its haunting beauty when she saw it in 1982. The waxy, grayish-white pallor of the corpse's face and hands demonstrates paleness with its deadliest implication. The same hue is also used sometimes to describe the sheen of the moon.

Some other artworks that romanticize death have been highly attractive for Susanne. Among them, John Everett Millais' *The Vale of Rest*, 1858 (Tate Gallery, London), is one of her most favorite paintings, since she first saw it in 1981. She feels strongly drawn to the somber and dignified mood of the scene, and its soothing and meaningful silence is nearly palpable for her. She perceives it "like a bridge between here and there." (See subchapter 8.2.7.)

Consequently, for Susanne the word "pale" often carries a negative connotation—a sickly complexion that causes the mother's concern. On the other hand, the extraordinarily light skin-tone ("aristocratic pallor") can signify elevated status and elegance. Moreover, although death is for most people a repellent subject, for the artist it might be an inviting fantasy, possibly reflecting unconscious destructive complexes revealed through the analysis of her art (see especially the analysis of butterfly No. 4, Touchless Misty).

8.1.3 Paintings with the Topic of the Moon in Susanne's Art

All of the previously touched memories, associations, and factual knowledge concerning the moon and its light metaphorically recur in her painted imagery. They have become interwoven in her mind and are transfigured unconsciously into symbolic images. We will discuss a group of paintings where the artist has employed the moon as the symbol for various meanings. While most people associate moonlight with romance and sentimentality, for Susanne it symbolizes a wider range of implications and emotions. The first two canvases to be discussed present the moon as the central focus. Then, we will examine some works which reveal additional symbolic meanings of the earth's satellite for an understanding of the unconscious determination of the peculiarities of the image of the butterfly Pale Moonlight.

In the painting, *Between Yesterday and Tomorrow*, (1989) (Fig. 8.4),[19] the artist depicted an anthropomorphic face that resembles the cratered surface of the moon. It is placed in a cosmic setting surrounded by a wide, silver framing border indicating vast space. The artist explains that she consciously designed the right half of the face illuminated in cold, whitish light, metaphorically assigning it to represent the past that is known. The left half she shaded in hues of dark bluish-gray, intended to indicate the future that is yet unknown. The glance of the "moon face" is directed away from the starry night of the past toward the bright, dawning future as a metaphorical expression of hope. The present is visualized by a plumb bob defining the momentous point "now" on the imaginary time line that divides past and future. Time is denoted beneath the face by a drum clock (Fig. 8.5), which continuously marks the passing moments, while the face appears to stand still in the present. The fluted side of the clock, inscribed with Roman numerals, moves clockwise with its markings illuminated by the light emanating from the head. This indicates the artist's experience of the cyclic process of "light" and "dark" phases in her life, alternating between hope and despair. This impression reflects the artist's biographical situation when she designed this painting.[20] At

18 Henry Wallis (1830–1916), *The Death of Chatterton*, (1856) Tate Gallery, London.

19 The small initial sketch for this painting goes back to 1985–86, and the final oil painting is rather large (4' x 5').

20 The original oil sketch is dated July 1986. The artist felt "stuck" in the third year of her doctoral program without a

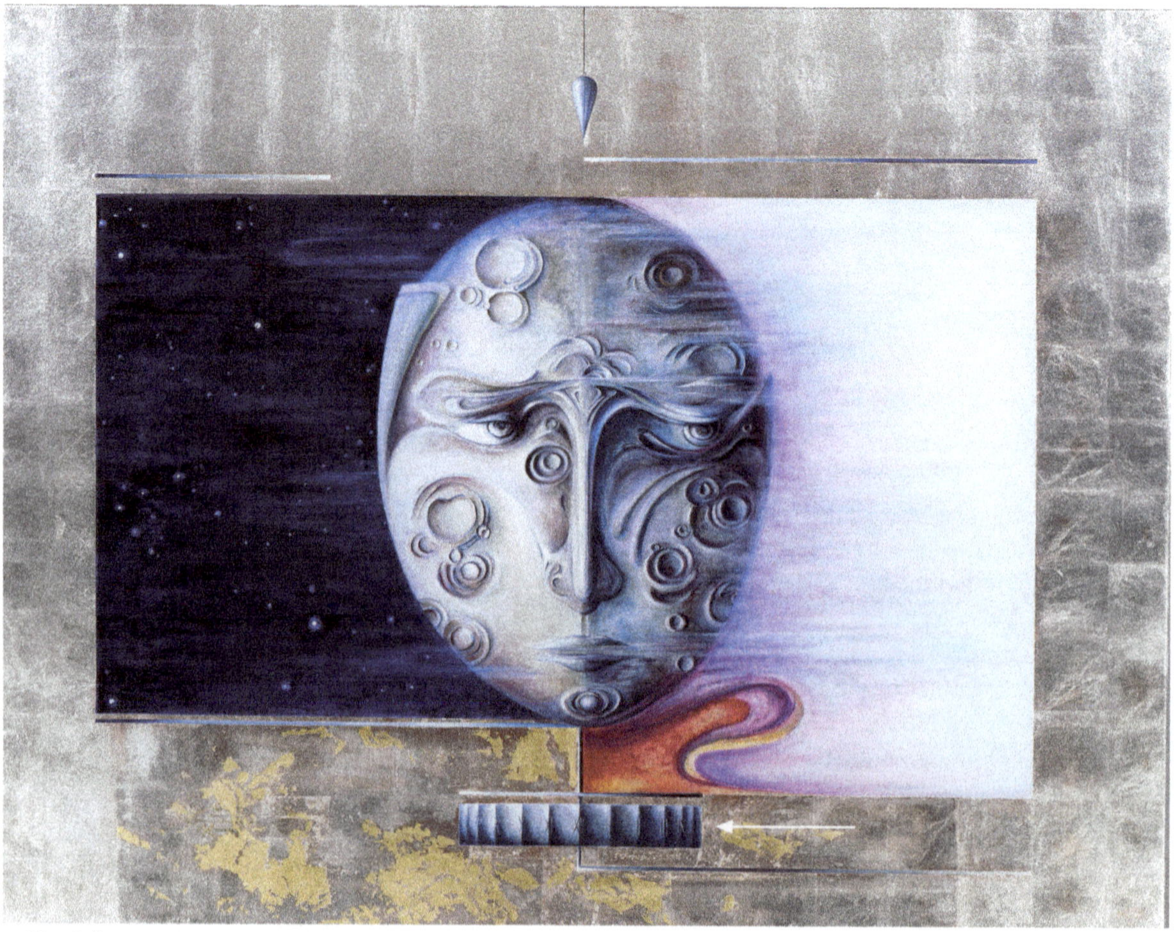

Fig. 8.4.
Susanne Schuenke, *Between Yesterday and Tomorrow*, 1989. Oil, gold and silver leaf on canvas, 48 x 60 in (120 x 150 cm). Corporate collection, Germany. The arrow points to the drum clock.

that time, Susanne was convinced that she had to work toward the desired achievements, which were to be beneficial to her "later" in a distant future, as her parents indoctrinated her to believe. As a consequence, it took her four decades to understand that waiting for "later" should not mean missing out on living in the present.

With a distinctive reference to the lunar surface that is battered and scarred by dangerous encounters with its surrounding world, Susanne symbolized the predicament of human existence, whose history is filled with sorrow and suffering. All of her perceptions of the moon and moonlight, which were outlined earlier, find multiple visual representations in this painting. The pockmarked "moon face" is an unconscious projection of Susanne's own self, her thoughts, emotions, and experiences condensed into this visual metaphor.

We recognized a further detail that could confirm the self-identification of the artist with this face. It is a shape on the right side of the head (left side from the perspective of the viewer) resembling a bandage, reminding the artist of the covering[21] she wore after each ear surgery in the hospital. Susanne had had problems with her right ear since she was four years old, which then developed into various life-threatening conditions during her adolescence, demanding extensive surgeries. The ear still remains a delicate spot in her life. Her mother, looking at the daughter face to face, always referred to the troublesome ear as "your left ear," because that was the side the mother saw from her perspective, but in doing so, she wrongly identified the right ear. As a consequence, the artist always thought that it was her left ear which was problematic until her 20s, when she finally realized the mistake. She attributes

clear outlook for the future.

21 "*Ohrklappenverband*" (English: earflap bandage.)

her lifelong difficulty in telling instantly right from left as rooted in this childhood confusion. It is interesting to note from an analytic perspective that Susanne unconsciously placed what we interpreted as a bandage in the location of the right ear in the image, and she alluded to it correctly as the "ill one," while there was no such object painted on the left side of the moon face.

The second painting focusing on the earth's satellite is *The First Hour of Full Moon*, (1996) (Fig. 8.6). There also exists a poetic description that Susanne wrote after the completion of the work. The text mirrors the artist's dream about a sublime state of peace which was expressed in the painting. Every sentence holds clues to the interpretation of the expression of her unconscious, as manifested in verbal and visual signs. The italics are added to emphasize the metaphorical cues for interpretation.

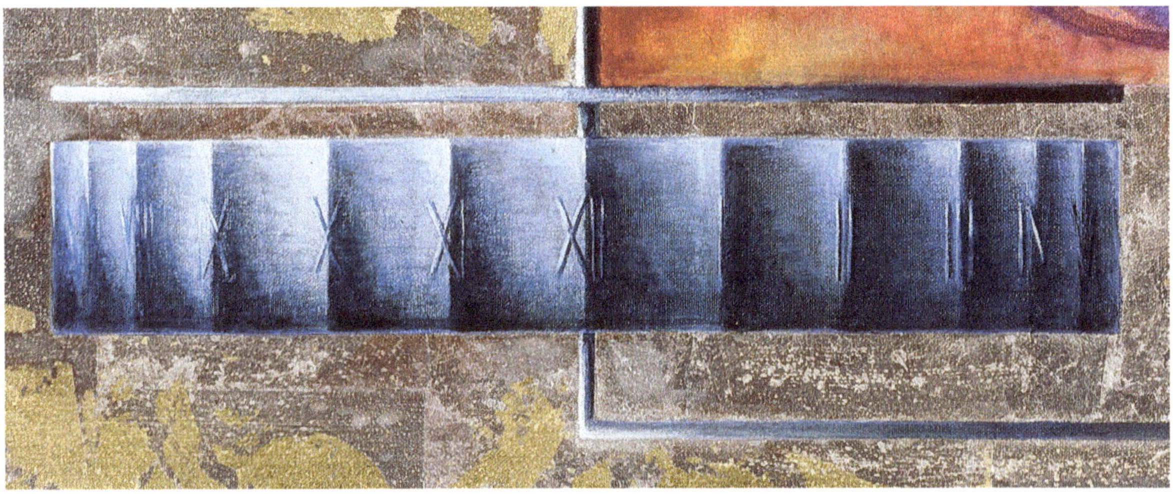

Fig. 8.5. Detail from Fig. 8.4. Drum clock with Roman numerals showing the segment from 6 p.m. to 6 a.m.

(Susanne's text:) "*Untouchable, radiant white, perfectly round and perfectly still,* the Full Moon rises to the apex of the sky, pouring her *magical atmosphere* over the resting world. But before she reaches her *state of tranquility*, a dramatic color change occurs. The sky *echoes the memories* of the sunset with hues of mauve and purple, and a tiny, bright *orange*-vermillion *point* heralds the *Grand Entrance* of the Full Moon.

"Meanwhile, within moments, the point grows to a line, a bow, and a segment, in which the *red transforms into* a softer, creamy *orange.* You think to hold your breath, wishing to fix that fraction of time when the perfect circle detaches from the earth's horizon. *Free like a sailing boat* severed from its pier-cables, the disc of the moon *floats in a gracious arc upwards.*

"*Swirling clouds* reflect the dramatic contrast, which comes with the change of characters on the sky's celestial stage. The dark, impenetrable indigo clashes with an opalescent quality of white that outlines the shapes and clusters surrounding the central figure.

"As the color gets lighter, the moonrise continues at a sedate pace. Still she brightens continually to a staggering white quality, which seems to be unsurpassed in the night sky, reaching the center stage, controlling the *eternal walk of time.*

"The formations of the clouds mirror the paradox of movement and change during this period when we wish that time stands still. They replay the *mystic fantasy* of man, *imagining the disc of the moon* being held by *Selene's invisible hand guiding it through its orbit*, while the *other hand removes the veil of darkness* from the sleeping landscape, pouring silver over the earth.

"And if you are awake to *witness the rise and glory of the Full Moon*—live with it, share its glory, and fill your heart and memory—until the next time." (End of Susanne's description.)

Correlating text with image, we observe the vast range of the creativity of the unconscious and its ability to express itself in new and prodigious ways. If we make a comparison to music, we can describe the unconscious as playing life's symphony on different instruments, solo, in trio, or with the full orchestra, while managing different melodic lines along with the main theme.

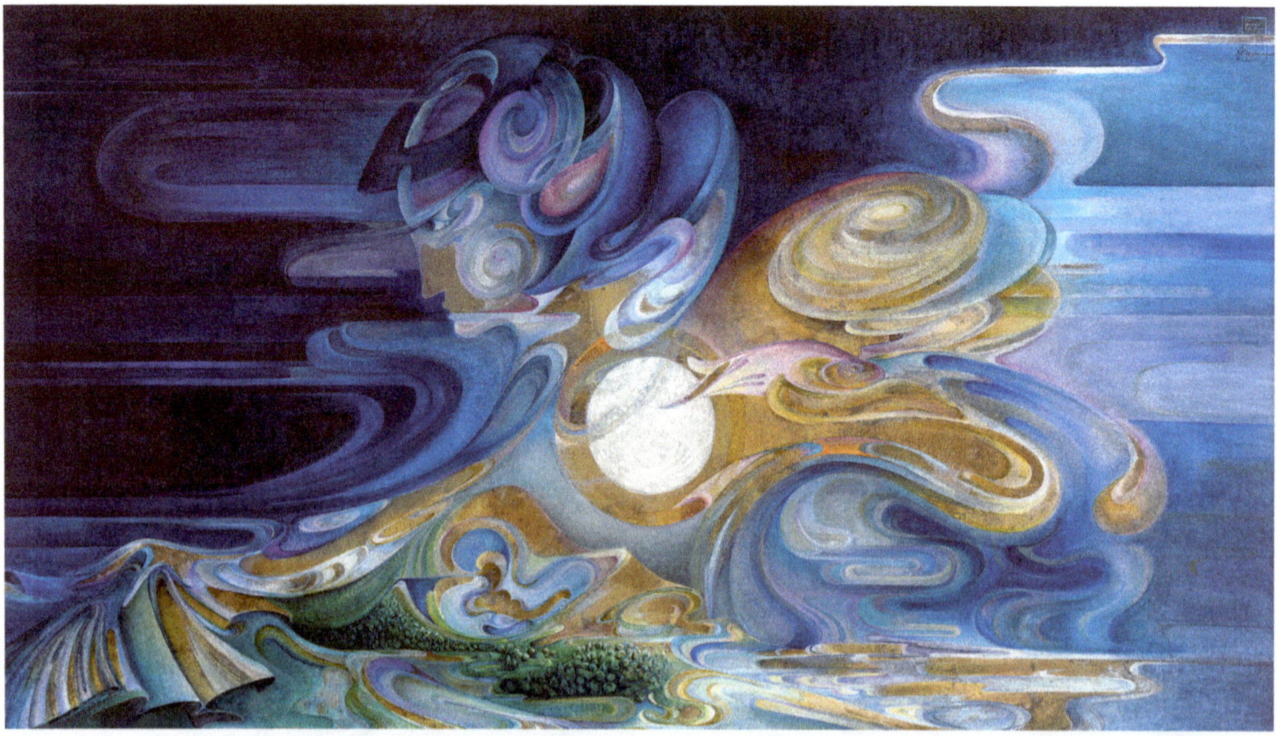

Fig. 8.6. Susanne Schuenke, *First Hour of Full Moon*, 1996. Oil and silver leaf on canvas, 44 x 79 in (90 x 160 cm). Private collection, Florida.

Here, we have two readings to account for the unconscious, allegorical messages in this painting. Firstly, the moonrise is analogous to the artist's life from childhood to adulthood, signifying the realization of her parents' intent and guidance for her, as well as the necessary adjustment in her life in becoming an independent person. The lunar disk represents the personification of Susanne and a symbol of her ascending destiny, *"floating in a graceful arc upwards."* In addition, it echoes memories of a paradisiacal early childhood, which she would have liked to recapture in her life. In this context, the world of her idyllic childhood could be reflected in the landscape with toy-like, small trees, in whimsical waves swirl effortlessly. Out of the curly clouds, an elegant hand gently pulls the blanket of darkness away from the miniature world beneath. The female profile in the sky—Selene, the ancient Goddess of the moon—acts like her parents, who were tightly guiding her existence for many years. Upon looking at Selene's left hand, Susanne suddenly had a free association with the judge's hand in her painting titled, *The Letter of the Law* (Fig. 8.7). Our comparison of the two hands reveals a close kinship in their configurations (Figs. 8.7 and 8.8). As we have analyzed earlier, the judge's hand in this watercolor is for Susanne a signifier of authority, in general, and of her father, in particular (see, subchapter 4.2). Therefore, the same symbolic meaning was imaginatively expressed in a new variation directed by her creative unconscious. She only became aware of that similarity during our analysis.[22]

Another interpretation posits that Selene personifies Susanne herself, conjuring her own destiny like a goddess, taking matters into her own

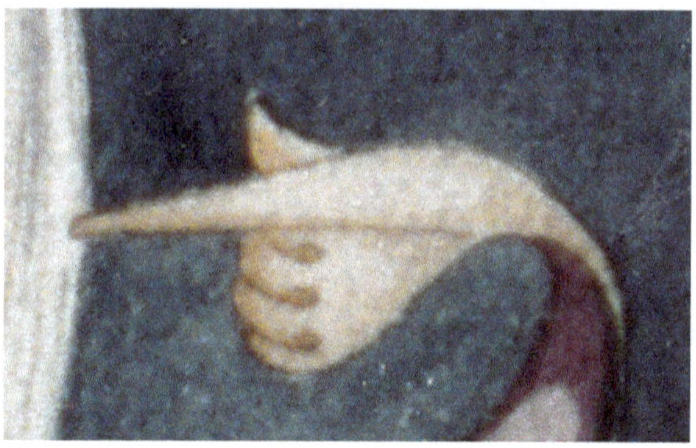

Fig. 8.7. Detail of the hand (turned by 90° to the left and flipped vertically) from *The Letter of the Law*. (For the full image, see Fig. 4.9.)

22 Another example of such an authoritarian hand can be seen in *Ideology* (Fig. 4.11).

hands. The figure of the moon goddess dominates the painting, and the artist in this role would be guiding herself through the darkness to the light ahead. This offers another correlation to Susanne's process of adjustment and transformation whenever she overcame inner obstacles and, as a consequence, many difficult circumstances and "dark parts" of her life. Literally "taking matters into her own hands" echoes a traditional Sufi saying that everything is in our hands, the wisdom of which Susanne began to practice over the years.

On the one side, Susanne, in the metaphorically passive role, is personified with the disk of the moon, guided by her parents. On the other side, the artist takes on the active role as the Goddess herself. Both identifications are expressed unconsciously.

For many years, the painting's wordy title, *The First Hour of Full Moon*, was shortened by Susanne in her private oeuvre listing as "Moonlight," which entities, the Goddess Selene and the butterfly Pale Moonlight, possess the same symbolic meaning: Personal power and majesty—the qualities that Susanne has always desired in her life.

The Moon Goddess' left hand holds another surprise—an unintended optical illusion. Many observers of *The First Hour of Full Moon* have noted that there is a figure of a fish in the light purple hues next to the upper right part of the moon's disc. The body and tail of the fish appear to be embedded within the shape of Selene's hand, whereas the fish's head, in a darker tone, faces to the right, away from the disc (Fig. 8.8). The artist did not perceive any of this. She could only identify the hand that she had explicitly designed from the swirling pattern of clouds. During the analysis, however, she finally recognized the shape of the fish, particularly its "head," and even had some specific association to comprehend the roots

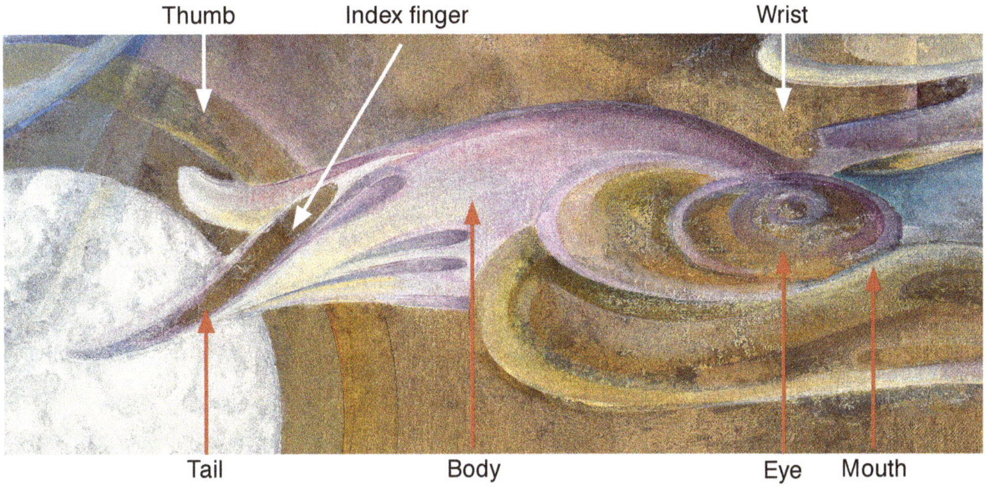

Fig. 8.8.Detail from Fig. 8.6.
White arrows point to the elements of the goddess' left hand.
Red arrows point to the same elements now seen as parts of a "fish."

may have been the source for the spontaneous naming of butterfly No. 3 as "Pale Moonlight." It could mean that the artist unconsciously identified the potent attributes of the deity, Selene, with this dominating butterfly in *Give Me Wings!*, reflecting her dream to be in control of her own destiny. The name of butterfly No. 3 was born while writing the poetic commentary, which was done nearly eight years after her commentary on *The First Hour of Full Moon* with its reference to the Moon Goddess Selene. It is probable that the passage of time was irrelevant in reviving her self-identification with the moon. It may be reasonably assumed that these two of this cognitive inhibition of her perception, to which we now turn for a possible interpretation.

The design of Selene's left hand is almost identical with the judge's hand in *The Letter of the Law* which we had recognized (see chapter 4) as a signifier of authoritative power. In *The First Hour of Full Moon* (created several months after *The Letter of the Law*), the artist implicitly used the same hand-configuration that may also be interpreted as a marker of authority. Moreover, it turned out that Selene's wrist resembles a fish head. Thus, the artist unconsciously created a double image as an ambiguous illusion of hand/fish. The image of an entire fish is perceived by most people, but not by Susanne. This may reflect deep complexes relating to some unconscious symbolic significance of fish based on cultural and archetypal precepts.[23] We have remarked in chapter 7 on her strong aversion to the topic of sexual reproduction. Therefore, it is plausible that her conscious mind may have exercised censorship so as not to identify this optical illusion so obvious to others.

This hand/fish image and its complex psychological undertone is another example of the rich reservoir of unconscious symbolism out of which Susanne's paintings manifest. These strata of implications include not only sexually-explicit references, such as phallic symbolism and reproduction, but also figuratively refer to any power, prestige, and authority which are traditionally associated with patriarchal dominance. Many of these aspects were already partially discussed in different chapters (chapters 4, 5, and 7). We will revisit them again in chapter 9, but the artist's designs are so rich in multifaceted metaphors and symbols that we are by no means able to make the claim that our study has exhausted their interpretations nor explored all the avenues whereby they can be uncovered.

The moon also features in the watercolor *About the Noise and Silence in this World* (Fig. 8.2). We recapitulate and expand its interpretation. After residing for a month in London, Susanne depicts her impressions of her new environment and the psychological aspects of her adjustment to it. She presents a portrait of a person, with whom she can easily identify, whose head is caught figuratively between the wheels of a subway train, alluding to his[24] life being entrapped by the head-splitting, mechanical noises. Through the figure's shoulder, which is hollowed out into a subway tunnel, a train speeds out with its windows and headlights all lit up in an alarming red color. The face in mauve and muddy olive hues, in combination with the heavy eyelids, expresses great sadness. The cityscape with towering high-rises is cloaked in smog and bleached out into paleness. With this scenery of polluted urban life and the central figure's melancholic mood, one can sense the state of mind in which Susanne found herself living in this major metropolis—mentally drained and depressed. At the right of the painting, the artist rendered a soothing, dreamlike landscape, illuminated by a gentle, white waning moon. Soft moonlight flows through a ghostly head seen in outline. The idyllic scene unfolds as a setting for meditation and imagination, to which a person can escape from the noisy, polluted world and transit to a higher, desirable state of existence of peace and harmony.

In summary, in this painting, the moonlight is suggested as a remedy for the dispiriting circumstances of hectic, modern urban life by promoting a positive mental condition. Through submergence into the beauty and tranquility of nature and meditative states, one can transcend to realms of a higher existence. Twenty-two years later, in a new context, a comparable aim can be discovered in the artist's image of Pale Moonlight, whose verbal and visual characterization indicates the artist's idea of "*here*" and "*there.*"(More about this, see chapter 10 and subchapter 12.4.)

A depiction of a full moon appears as a small detail in another painting, *The Long Journey*, (1995) (Fig. 8.9), where the artist presents a large tortoise with images representing numerous significant achievements of mankind which are illustrated on various segments of the creature's carapace. In one of them, the topic of "emotions" is metaphorically expressed: a white lunar disc is embedded in a mystic haze and surrounded by a few bars of musical notes taken from Beethoven's *Moonlight Sonata* (Fig. 8.10).[25] In this manner, Susanne paid homage to the great maestro and to one of his most famous compositions. His potent notes are capable of evoking some of the most refined and sublime emotions that the human mind can ever experience. Her heightened sensibility, elicited by moonlight, resembled the emotional response that she experienced with Beethoven's composition. It is on this basis the artist was inspired to juxtapose two elements of the imagery (moonlight

23 Fish is foremost a symbol of fertility in many world myths, both East and West. It should also be noted that different cultural implications point to an association with the male sexual organ (fish as phallic symbol).

24 The artist declares this person is a male and refers to the facial hair (beard) as sufficient identification. On the other hand, undoubtedly there are feminine characteristics, for example, the strikingly red lips.

25 Ludwig van Beethoven (1770–1827), Piano Sonata No. 14 in C-sharp minor *Quasi una fantasia*, Op. 27, No. 2, (1801), popularly known as the *Moonlight Sonata* (this romanticized title was given by the German music critic Ludwig Rellstab five years after the great composer's death.)

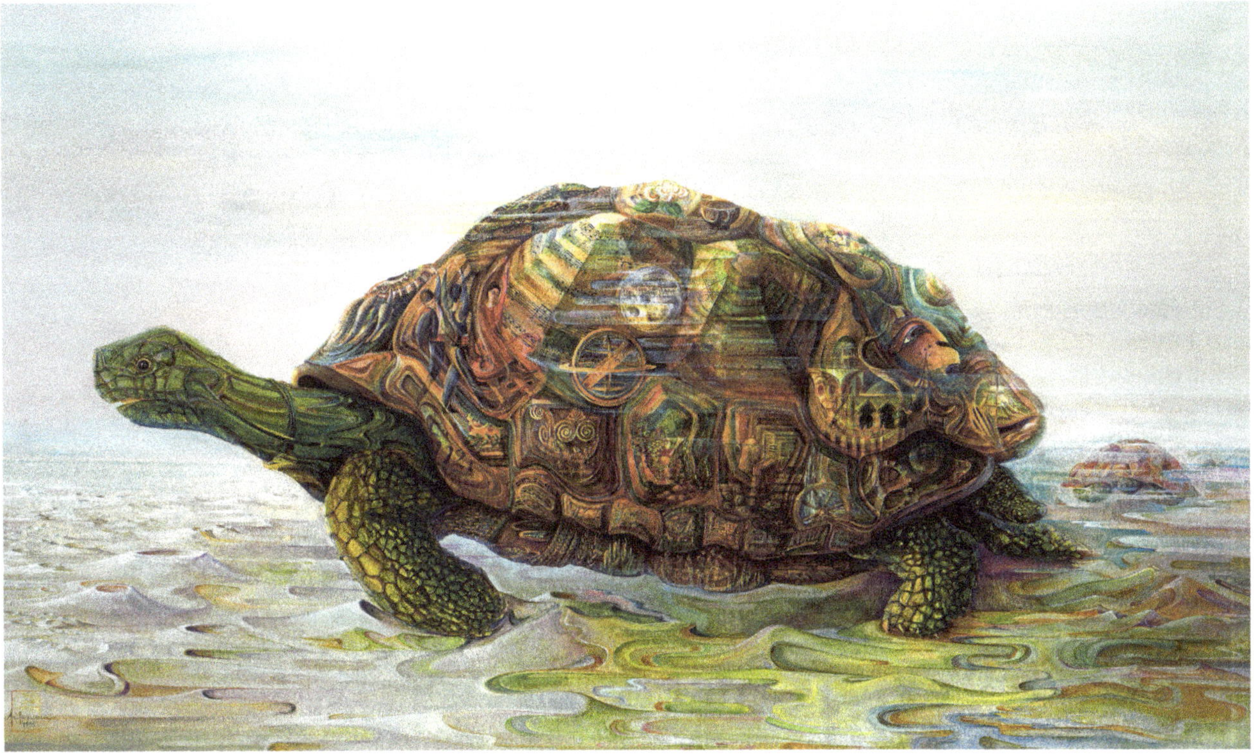

Fig. 8.9. Susanne Schuenke, *The Long Journey*, 1995. Oil and gold leaf on canvas, 19 x 57 in (85 x 145 cm). Corporate collection, Florida.

and music). Both of these subjects are capable of deeply affecting the inner life of human beings. The artist's metaphorical pairing of the two aspects in *The Long Journey* is an invitation to the viewer's mind to contemplate the nature of beauty and harmony. In this painting, Susanne expresses her hope for the advanced development of civilization; appropriately, she uses the metaphor of a tortoise traversing a vast expanse of barren landscape, covered with dusty gray craters. Her expectation is that this journey will gradually lead humankind to fertile ground, and the earth will bountifully blossom.

Susanne also incorporates the moonscape as a metaphor in the next two works: *Michael* (2002) and *The Flight of Wisdom* (2005). The artist was asked to illustrate the novella by Leo Tolstoy, *What Men Live By,*[26] and she presents her imaginative interpretation of the archangel Michael, the leading character in this short novel, in the painting titled *Michael,* 2002 (Fig. 8.11). She portrayed the left half[27] of the archangel's face, which is radiating supernal light, as a hint

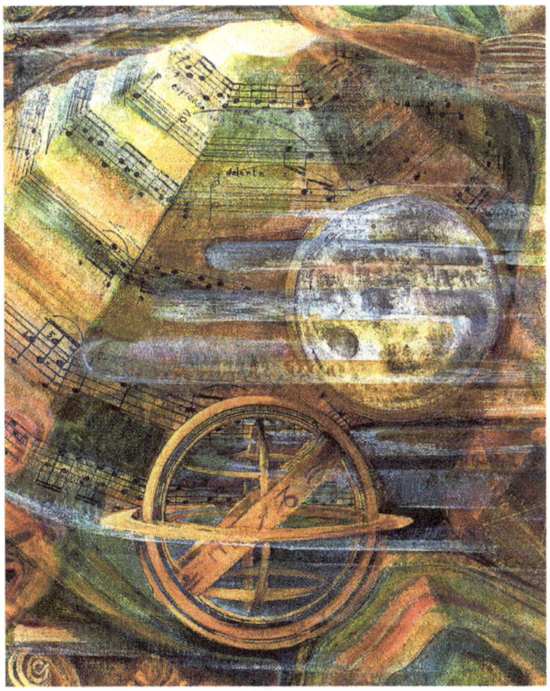

Fig. 8.10. Detail from 8.9: Segment with full moon and quotes from Beethoven's *Moonlight Sonata*.

26 Leo Tolstoy (1828–1910) *What Men Live By*, 1881.

27 As a reminder: Right and left side of a face are named from the painted subject's point of view. For the following description, it might be helpful to cover one half of Michael's face to experience the contrasting expressions between the left side being luminous and the right one, gloomy.

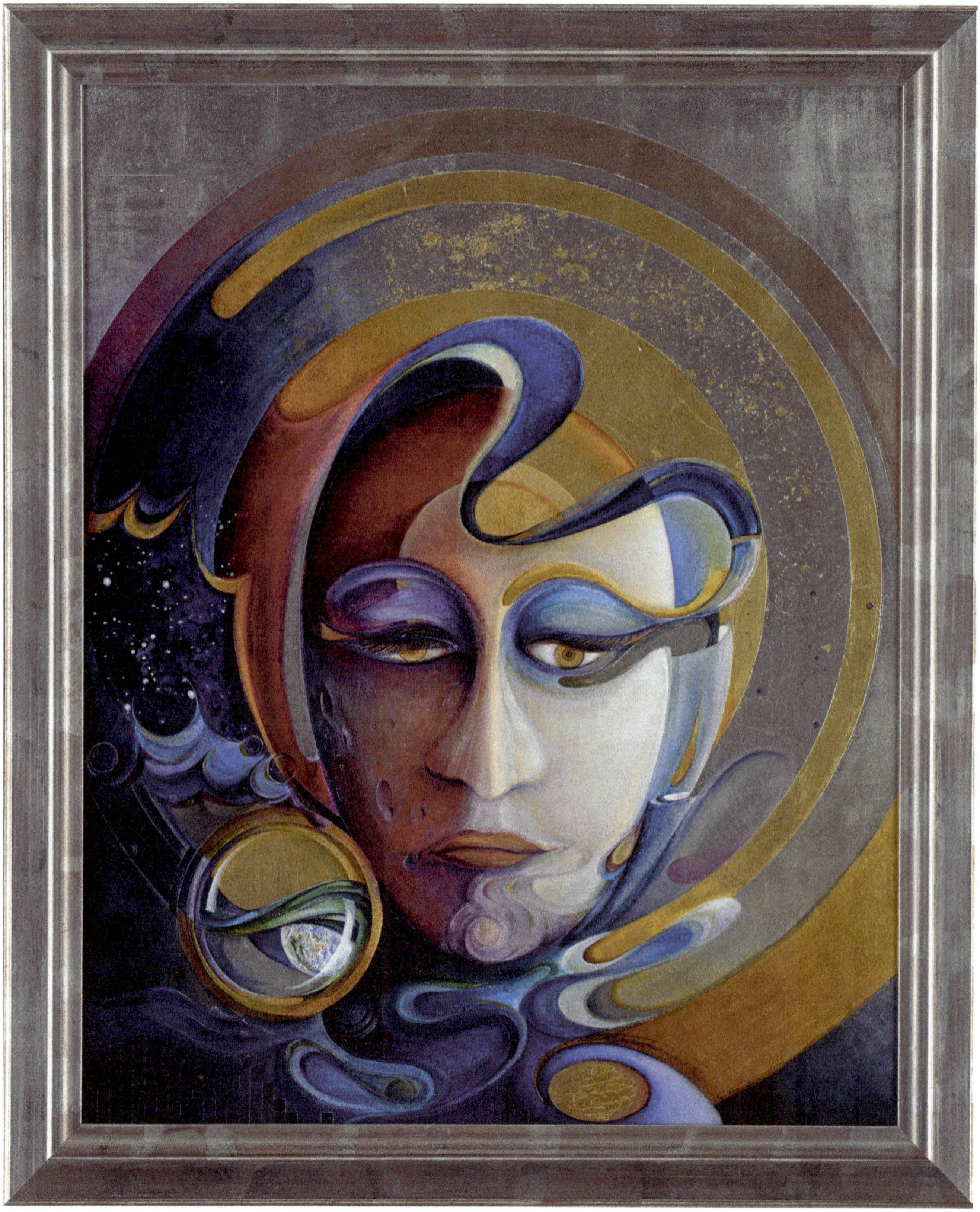

Fig. 8.11. Susanne Schuenke, *Michael*, 2002. Oil, gold and palladium leaf on canvas, 34 x 28 in (85 x 71 cm). Private collection, North Carolina.

of his true heavenly origin. The right half of his face is depicted as a cratered, dark moon (Fig. 8.12) to indicate the predicament that the angel experienced in a human body during his earthly sojourn to which God had sentenced him for his disobedience.

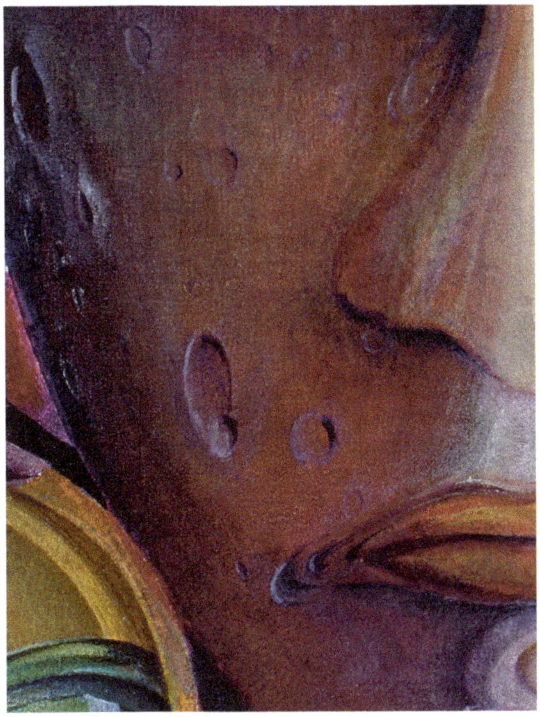

Fig. 8.12. Detail from Fig. 8.11:
Craters as the signs of wounds or scars.

In this image, Susanne portrays the scarred, moon-like surface as a symbolic indication of suffering, signifying her self-identification with the pockmarked satellite. Those "wounds" result from asteroid bombardment, a fitting metaphor for the afflictions caused by the "blows of fate," which life delivers, as her father repeatedly prophesied.[28] The crater scars set in the gloomy right half of the face allegorically capture the father's grim prognostication, "Life will punish you," which Susanne projected on Michael's portrait as the punishment of God.[29] In juxtaposition, the left half of the archangel's face shines with the ethereal, "whitest of white" illumination, manifesting the Divine glory, conveying the artist's vision of the highest spiritual value. Susanne considers only the dark side of the face as a corporeal structure, which is subject to physical harms as indicated by the cratered surface. In contrast, she regards the luminous side as made of heavenly light, which is a metaphor for transcending the painful problems of bodily existence through the attainment of spiritual illumination—enlightenment. In this painting, Susanne splits the "cratered moon" and "moonlight" into diametrical aspects, and considers the first as worldly, negative, and pessimistic, and the second as spiritual, positive, and optimistic.

In *The Flight of Wisdom*, (2005) (Fig. 8.13), a grieving figure leans on an untidy heap of colorful books, a few even gilded, which hints at their precious knowledge amidst a hostile desert environment that resembling the dim cratered moonscape. Some books appear to be flying away from the pile. Susanne rendered this flight of books as a visual metaphor for the decline of spiritual wisdom in the contemporary world that threatens to bring the population of the earth to the brink of self-destruction. If humanity loses its spiritual beacon, it will ruin its home planet, a rare oasis of higher life amongst billions of stars.

Without the guidance of wisdom, environmental, biological, or nuclear disasters will turn the blue planet into a lifeless rock. This expresses her apprehension for the survival of human civilization's hard-won achievements. With this prospect in mind, Susanne again uses the image of the dark moonscape (Fig. 8.14). She imagines that if humanity loses its wisdom, the progress in knowledge and material achievement would come to an end, and the world would become dusty, gray,

28 As described in chapter 4, Firebird.

29 As an afterthought, Susanne has a surprising association with the "shallow" scars (i.e., without the crater walls) on Michael's face. It reminded her of the scars that were made when her infant sister scratched herself on the face with her fingernails. Those scars did not disappear, and they are still there, although only detectable by the knowing eye. In this context, the scars on Michael's face might also metaphorically represent Susanne's silent grievance against her parents. They figuratively inflicted a permanent "wound" on her younger sister by devaluing her potential, such as postponing her higher education. In Susanne's eyes, her sister was "wounded by these circumstances."
Also, her older sister reminded Susanne of an incident involving a doll, which was afterward nicknamed "Scarred Henni," (German: Narben Henni) as the little Susanne had taken an ink pen and drawn marks all over the face of her doll named Henni. No cleaning agent could remove the ink, and her mother, desperate to conceal the damage from her husband, turned to drastic measures. Her mother scraped the offensive "tattoos" from the doll's face with a pair of nail scissors, but that resulted in a scarred face, which strongly reminded Susanne of the smaller "craters" on Michael's cheek.

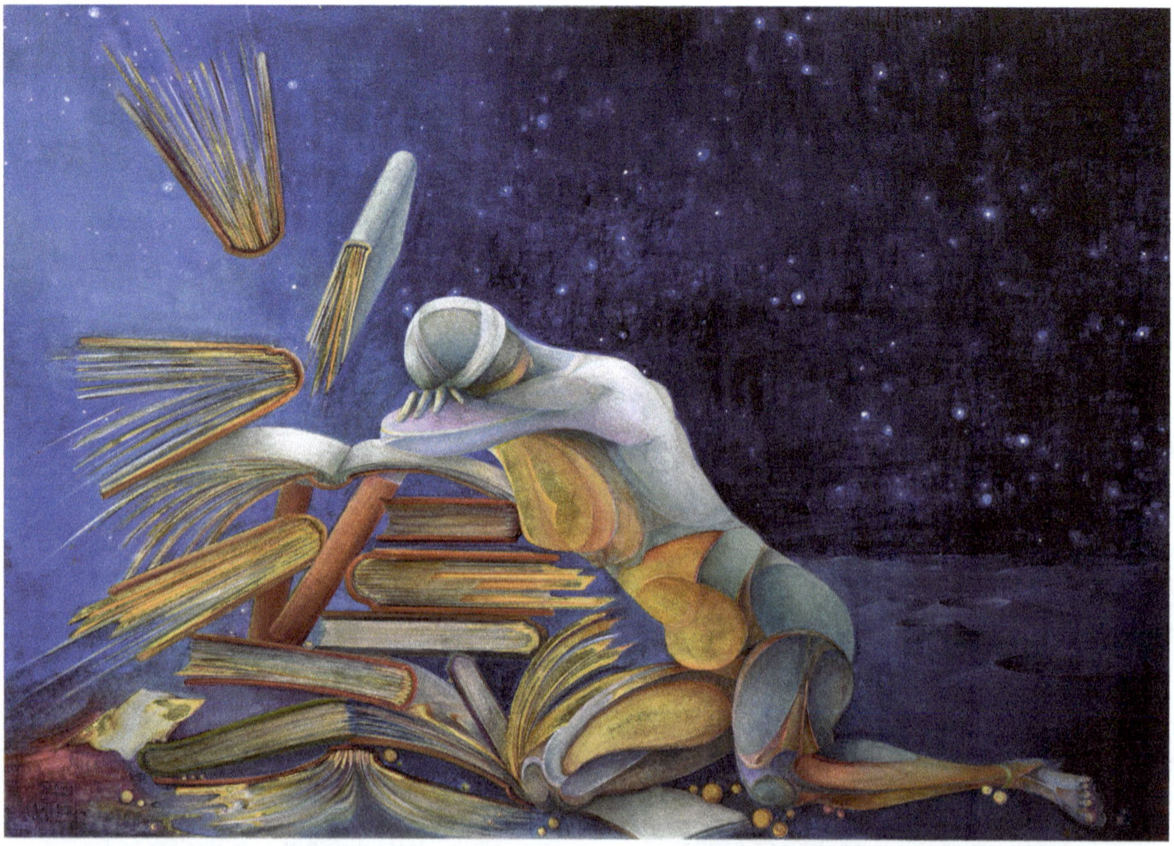

Fig. 8.13. Susanne Schuenke, *The Flight of Wisdom*, 2005. Oil and gold leaf on canvas, 35 x 51 in (90 x 130 cm). Private collection, Florida.

silent, and dead. In this work, Susanne identifies herself with the painting's grieving, dejected figure, signaling her anxiety and fear for the direction of the contemporary world, which threatens to be on the verge of a new "Dark Age." She dreads that the blindness of pure materialism and ideological extremism will detach humanity from spiritual development.

Susanne shares the sympathetic traditional perception of the moon that is held by most people. In her iconographic use of the image of the moon, two messages can be ascertained. On the negative side, it is employed as the signifier of past victimization through its scarred and pockmarked surface. On the positive side, the artist portrays the moon and its soothing light as a benevolent and inspiring image which conveys uplifting, optimistic messages. In *Give Me Wings!*, the butterfly, Pale Moonlight, has a mostly favorable representation in the artist's mind, although it has traces of distressing topics that are subtly interwoven into the imagery. Had she named butterfly No. 3 "Pale Moon," the negative undertone could have led to different consequences for the interpretation. With the choice of the word "moonlight," the artist unconsciously avoided the associations with the moon being scarred, cratered, and lifeless. Instead, she implicitly emphasized the unearthly, ephemeral illumination of the moonlit night when she had experienced occasions of profound silence, emotional calm, and the sense of spiritual freedom. That granted her, albeit temporarily, a relief from her overwhelming pessimistic perception of the world and inspired her imagination and creativity. The image of the butterfly Pale Moonlight and its characterization in the poetic commentary will find further clarification in the interpretation of the details of its lines, forms, and colors.

8.2 Peculiar Details in Shape, Line, and Color and Their Significance for the Interpretation

After presenting different associations for the two words forming the compound name "Pale Moonlight" and their connection to past experiences recalled by Susanne, we now turn to the image itself. We examine specific features

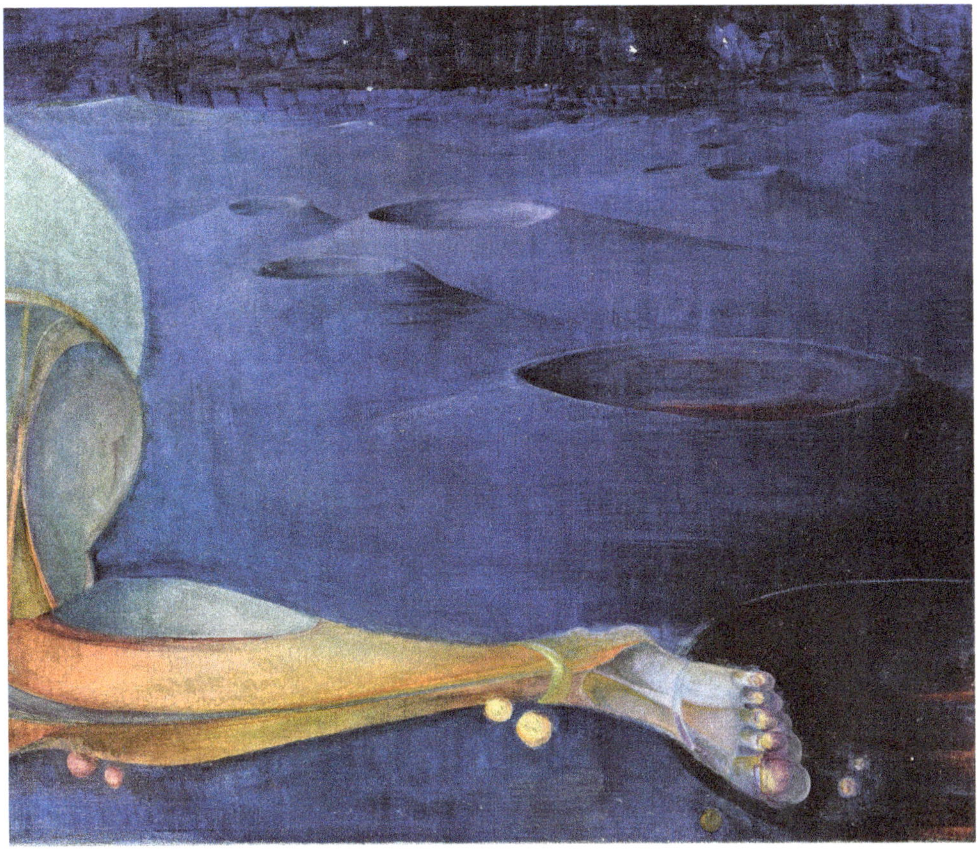

Fig. 8.14.
Detail from Fig. 8.13. Moonscape with craters.

of this butterfly, aiming to understand the unconscious determinations in the creation of these characteristics in accordance with their underlying meanings. First, we point to a small area at the bottom of the hind wing through which the contour of the podium is visible (Fig. 8.15 (f)). This telltale detail by its translucency contradicts the overall impression of opaqueness of the butterfly's wings. Each peculiarity of the image becomes valuable in our understanding of latent contents that we will try to verify.

8.2.1 Closed Wings

Among the seven butterflies, Firebird, Touchless Misty, and Pale Moonlight have their wings firmly closed. Pale Moonlight's wings appear to be so tightly pressed together that, at first, it is difficult to distinguish the butterfly's front and hind wings. In chapter 5, it was suggested that the closeness of the wings of Firebird symbolized some specific facets of father's personality and behavior, which he successfully had hidden and kept under lock and key from the world all of his life. Analogously, Pale Moonlight blocks any view into the topside of her wings which could be, like Firebird, interpreted as a metaphor for strictly guarded secrecy.

Susanne has her own taboo topics, such as fleeting "inappropriate" thoughts and fantasies connected with sexuality and aggression. As far as she is concerned, due to cultural and parental disapproval of those risqué issues, they must remain unspoken. Therefore, the tightly shut wings can be correlated with the intention of the conscious to suppress and of the unconscious processes to conceal the repressed content by coding and transforming it into symbolic formations. The locked wings can metaphorically allude to the existence of psychological complexes and tendencies and other unfulfilled personal ambitions prohibited by family and society.

In contrast to the closed wings of Pale Moonlight, we see the open wings of Air, a butterfly in flight, floating effortlessly above the podium, free from its earthly gravity and restrictions. In short, "closed" signifies repression and restriction, while "open" symbolizes the realization of potential and aspirations. The nature of the butterfly Air will be discussed in detail in chapter 10.

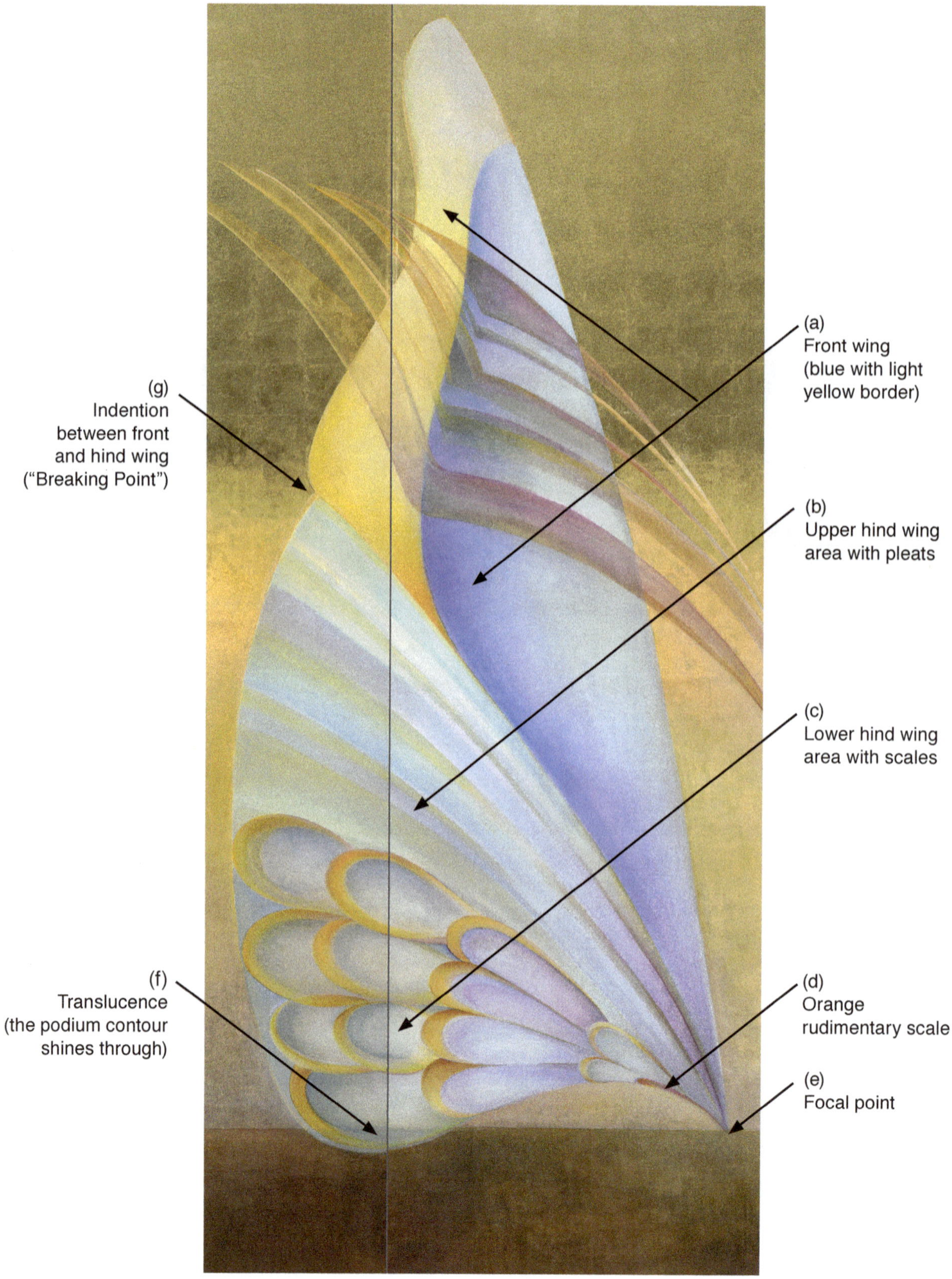

Fig. 8.15. Details from Fig. 1.1. Butterfly No. 3, Pale Moonlight.

8.2.2 Majestic

Towering above the others, Pale Moonlight is factually the tallest and largest of the seven butterflies. During the analysis, Susanne spontaneously characterized this dominant member of the assembly as "majestic" and "soaring up in undisturbed grandeur." With these terms, she metaphorically conveyed a paramount status that glorifies Pale Moonlight. Susanne usually uses the word "majestic" as a laudable word, expressing her admiration for a person's character, his/her wisdom, heedfulness to others, and appropriate action. In her eyes, true personal majesty obligates one to certain kinds of behavior, especially a prudent and compassionate exercise of one's authority and the accompanying personal power. Such a wise attitude, free of abuse, is what she defines as greatness, and only on this basis does she accept authorities and others' personal prerogatives.

Susanne's concept of "majesty" encapsulates her longing for a human standard by which individuals strive for harmony and mutual respect among all members of humanity. However, in reality such a desirable state of affairs was never to her satisfaction correctly practiced even among her family members. The image of Pale Moonlight pictorially captured the dreams of achieving human majesty. The word "majestic" to describe Pale Moonlight is laden with much symbolic significance.

Susanne's self-identification with this towering butterfly could have some roots in her childhood, when she had admired outstanding height in people. She was the smallest in her class, and she wanted to be tall. Although in her later teens she finally reached the height of 5'7" (170 cm), for many years she still wished to grow a little more because somehow she associated "being tall" with becoming "important and recognized" and connected tallness with her concept of beauty.[30]

Speaking of height, the painting *Give Me Wings!* measures 79" (200 cm) vertically and Pale Moonlight reaches 69.7" (5' 9½"; 177 cm) in height. The butterfly surpasses Susanne's current height by approximately two and a half inches. Insofar as this butterfly is a personification of the artist, it can be construed that through the actualization of its superior height in the oil painting, she could have unconsciously realized her childhood wish of being tall.[31] This might well have been an additional source of her spontaneous praise for butterfly No. 3—"soaring up in undisturbed grandiosity."

The parents acknowledged Susanne's intellect, her dedication to learning, her curiosity, discipline, outstanding artistic gifts, and her strong focus on the task, especially in creativity. They tried to provide her with the resources and opportunities needed to enrich and advance her education and art.

Susanne thinks that her parents paid too much attention to pointing out her shortcomings instead of balancing their attitude with encouraging praise. For example, she has the proclivity for decisive action, for which she received repeated criticism as being impulsive and reckless. She was especially chastised for her impatience and notorious interruptions during her father's speeches, which led to his sudden outbursts of anger and tirades against what he felt was Susanne's insolence and disrespect. All this was far from the desired parental acknowledgement that she craved, and the teenager was in dire need of the loving approval of her beloved parents in order to develop a well-grounded self-confidence in her capacities to deal with others and the world.[32] Moreover, as an adult Susanne received a biting remark from her father that alluded to her efforts in life being "lecherous for applause, only"[33] which further eroded the ability to place confidence in her own self.

Susanne was raised under the unchallenged authority of her parents, dominated by the father. This went along with the traditional autocratic family structure in Germany at that time, under which her father and mother also grew up, being born in 1924 and 1926 respectively. Due to a certain aloofness in her parents' social life and the tenuous connection they kept with the outside world, some of the social changes, which were beginning to affect the traditional autocratic and patriarchal

30 Susanne developed low self-esteem based on her negative self-assessment of her physical attributes. This topic will be covered more extensively in the next chapter.

31 In reality, Susanne's height overreached both her sisters and her father in her adulthood. Only her mother was slightly taller.

32 Her art was accepted by her father, but after reaching her adulthood, he began to put her down in many other aspects: behavior, aims, friendships, ideas, philosophy, and spiritual contemplations.

33 Her father's expression in German was "*lobesgeil*," a term Susanne always found insulting. "*Lob*" means "praise" in English but of the word "*geil*" (English: lascivious), carries a connotation of being carnal, horny, or libertine.

family structure in industrialized societies after World War II, did not reach Susanne's family. As a consequence, her parents continued to uphold an ingrained traditional family hierarchy and used firm practices in the upbringing of their daughters. The prolonged situation of such a constrained domestic environment, where the parents acted not only as guardians but also as wardens, led Susanne, during her teen years, to develop a growing sense of low self-esteem and depressive reactions. Specific individual circumstances worsened the situation. The child was weak, had health problems, and was not satisfied with her appearance, which obviously contributed to her growing sense of inferiority and alienation. On the other hand, such a family situation fostered the development of autocratic tendencies in her.[34] It is confirmed by her demeanor, her tendency to dominate in relationships and discussions, and in the conduct of her personal life which exhibits a strong "will to power."[35] Susanne herself considers such a tendency as necessary for independence and freedom. She does not deny this behavior pattern, which has been observed and reported by her relatives, friends, and counselors. Painting the butterfly Pale Moonlight with such a lofty height and attractive appearance could confirm the presence of her lifelong personal desire to be dominant and admired, as we have recounted above. In creating the imagery of this butterfly with such a visage, Susanne might well have unconsciously actualized her longing from childhood to be recognized and praised for her worthiness and abilities which, in turn, could have found expression in the artist's poetic commentary: "Pale Moonlight is much larger than her vaguely defined talents, her sketchy acknowledged qualities, her barely illuminated brilliance."

The glorification of Pale Moonlight may compensate for the disappointment the artist suffered in life, where her desire to earn sufficient parental approval and recognition never came true. The choice of the words "majestic" and "soaring up in undisturbed grandiosity" might metaphorically reflect the appropriate tendencies in the artist's psyche. Susanne has the propensity to create forceful images in many of her works; the image of Pale Moonlight is a fitting example.

Among the numerous large paintings[36] in Susanne's oeuvre, there is a portrait of *The Warrior* (9' high, Fig. 8.16). His weather-beaten face (nine times larger than life-size) expresses pain and regret for past experiences which have replaced the former glory of power. The portrait of *Tanja* (6½' high) (Fig. 10.28) pays homage to humane beauty, the power of love, and spirituality, hailing these values of her friend as "larger than life." *Grand Canyon* (9' high, Fig. 8.17) is dominated by a precipitous landscape scorched in red, which plays out an emotional response to the majesty and power of untamed nature. *Seventeen Legs* (9' high, Fig. 10.9) features a pair of gigantic female legs that dwarfs the observer to insignificance. With this imagery, Susanne symbolizes the rule of a gigantic colonial power.

The creation of powerful images is typical of Susanne's oeuvre, reflecting some facets of her personality. We have said in our description of Fanning Everything that Susanne can display certain patterns of submissive behavior, which she identifies with femininity. This conduct coexists openly or latently with her tendency to command, a blueprint of her father's demeanor, which dominates her behavior. She considers this attribute as mostly a masculine model. She does recognize the virtue of being diplomatic and willing to compromise, but her keynote disposition in most instances is to remain firm and convinced of her ideas and opinions. She equates this with personal confidence, regardless of the topic, be it a trifle in her everyday life or a fundamental philosophical issue. In this context, it is difficult to argue against her convictions based on purely rational, evidential, and practical discourse. Her rigid resistance is not easy to overcome. We identify here a replication of the model of her father's authority, as an intrinsic part of his personality. In her adult life, her decisiveness and desire for personal sovereignty, as well as her tenacity in striving toward an independent life, have

34 In this context, the works of Alice Miller in developmental psychology show that children subjected to totalitarian or abusive environment display the proclivity to create a similar behavioral environment as adults (Miller 1980).

35 The phrase is of Nietzschean origin, but here is used as Alfred Adler adopted it in his individual psychology, as referenced in his 1929 American publication, *The Science of Living*, chapter 3: Inferiority and Superiority Complexes (German edition: *Lebenskenntnis*, 1978).

36 More about these paintings will be discussed in the appropriate chapters: *Warrior* in subchapter 13.2, *Tanja* in subchapter 10.4.5, and *Seventeen Legs* in subchapter 10.2.

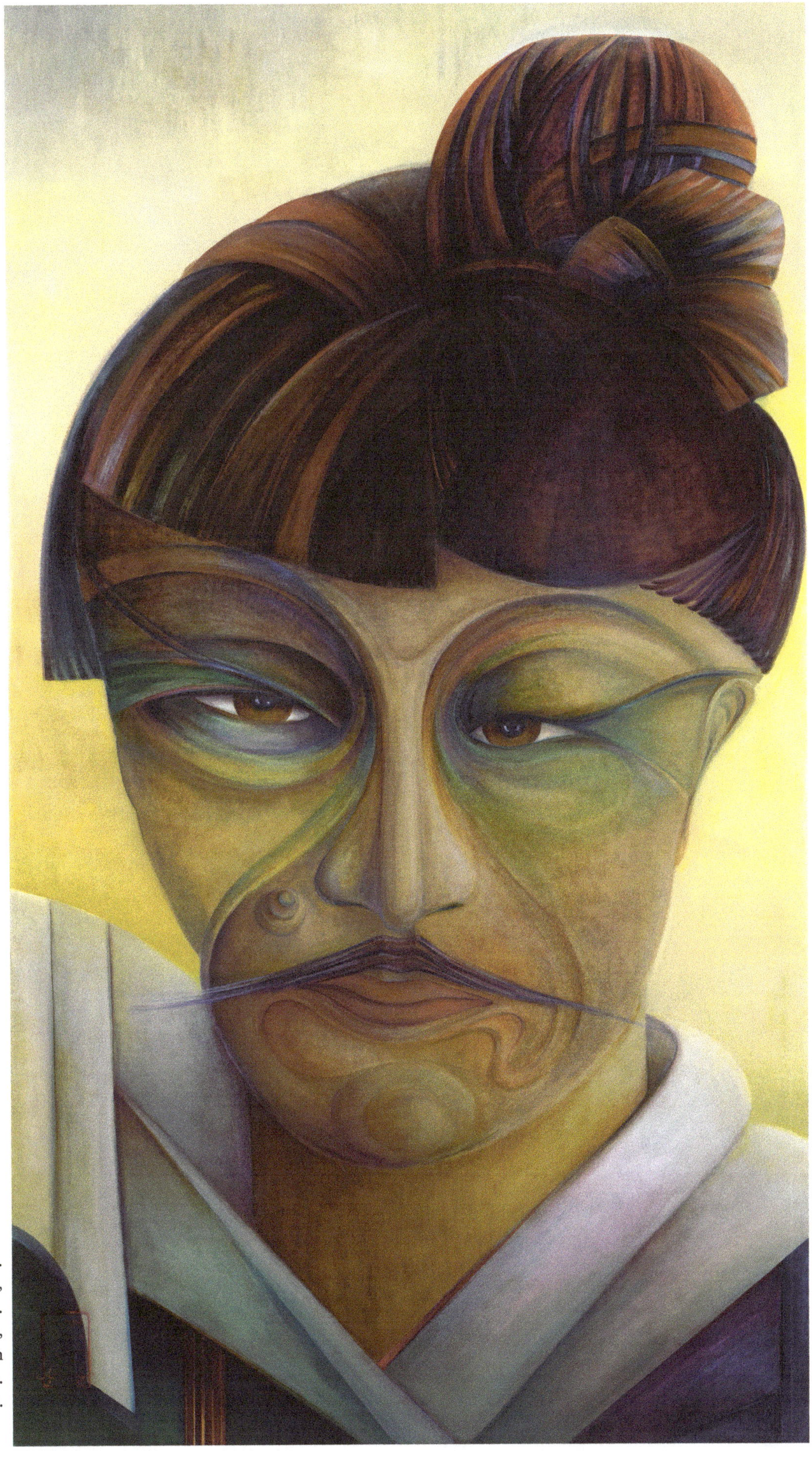

Fig. 8.16.
Susanne Schuenke,
The Warrior, 2005.
Oil on canvas,
108 x 62 in
(274 x 157 cm).
Collection of the artist.

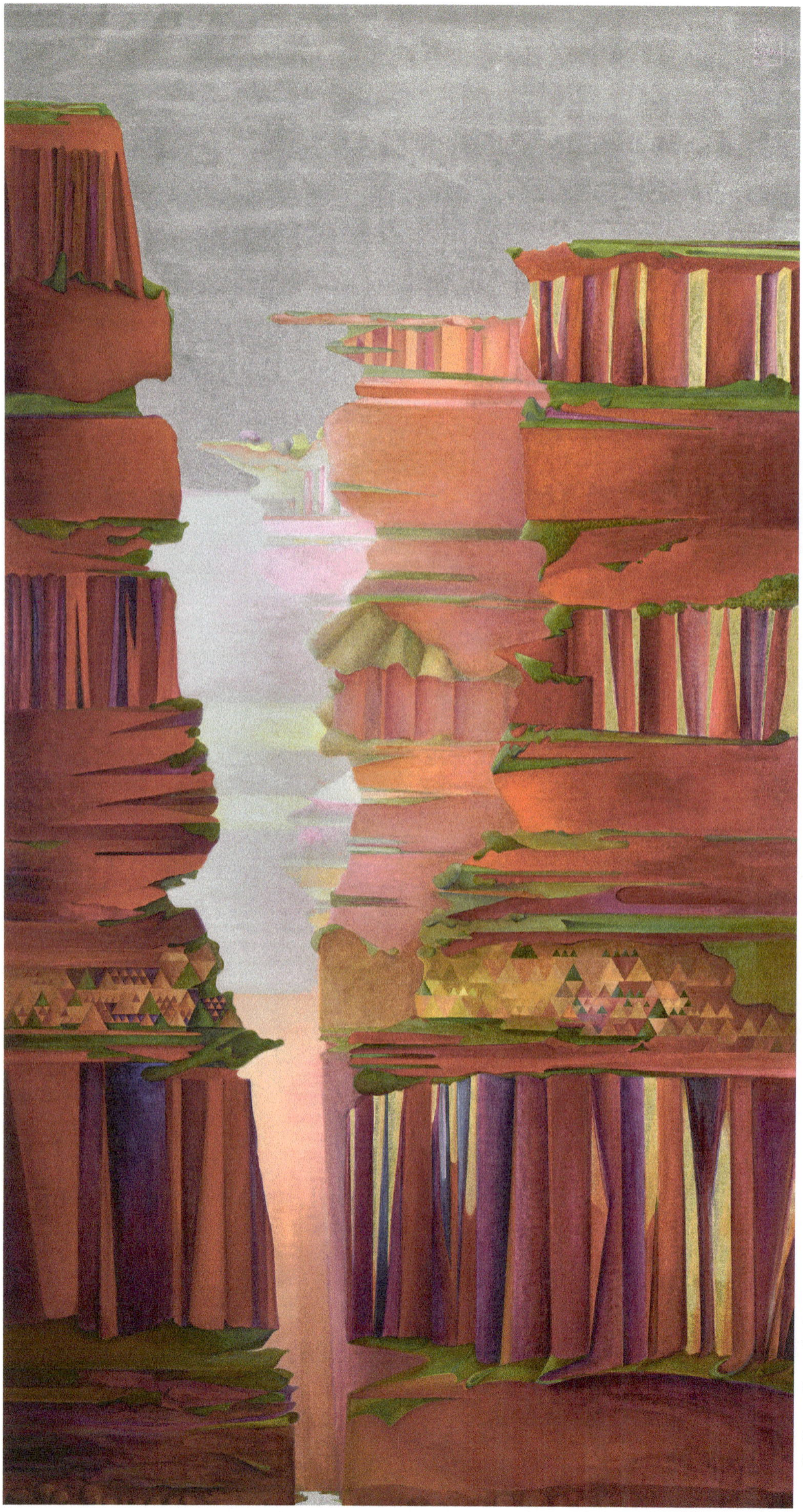

Fig. 8.17
Susanne Schuenke,
Grand Canyon, 2006.
Oil gold leaf on canvas,
108 x 59 in
(275 x 150 cm).
Collection of the artist.

been the hallmarks of her individuality. Susanne's propensity for the realization of such behavior patterns could find further confirmation in another important emblematic feature of this butterfly—the single point at the location of the head.

8.2.3 A Focal Point in the Location of the Head

The multitude of lines, which construct the shape and subdivisions of the image of Pale Moonlight, originates from a single point. We refer to this in the following discussion as the "focal point" (Fig. 8.15 (e)). This specific location, in reference to the butterfly, is usually associated with the head. The focal point appears as a feature on which everything else pivots. A comparable configuration was identified by the researchers in the artist's earlier watercolor, *The Letter of the Law* (Fig. 4.8). The judge's uncompromising finger tapers to a point, symbolizing justice's dictatorial power. We correlated this shape (see the collage in Fig. 4.6) with the spiky end of Firebird's lower hind wing, which resembles the pointed finger of her father and was recognized as Susanne's metaphor of his power. Being focused on a single point could be seen as an allegory for the primacy of a life dedicated to a worthy task on which one's entire attention and effort must be expended.[37] This statement was repeated innumerable times by Susanne's father as encouragement and also as a warning. He insisted that Susanne follow his "commandments" closely, claiming that they were protective rules against adverse repercussions for her benefit. Had she failed to comply with them, so he prophesied, there would be due punishments from life for the disobedience.[38]

We suggest that the artist could have unconsciously transferred this metaphor of authority (*The Letter of the Law* and Father's finger) in Pale Moonlight's focal point, representing Susanne's sovereignty. The upper part of Pale Moonlight's front wing could also be compared with an upward-pointing finger directed toward the golden background (Fig. 8.15 (a)), which we contemplate as a signifier for a new and hopeful outlook in her life (see more on this in subchapter 8.2.6). In this context, the upward pointing "finger" can be construed as a positive aspect of her father's guidance which did help Susanne in strengthening her personal integrity and achieving her professional goals. This stands in contrast to the threatening finger of the father embedded in the image of Firebird, where the "finger" pointing downward symbolizes authority and suppression.

Relating to the symbolism of the authoritarian pointing finger, we return to the artist's phobia of sharp objects, already touched upon in earlier chapters. As mentioned, most sharp points, be it the end of a knife, a scissors tip, syringe needle, fragments of glass, or the tip of the raised index finger, could have become a symbol of threatening power over her. The potential for harm, associated with those items, actualized the fear that points to unconscious complexes. Among sharp objects, Susanne most feared the syringe needle, the use of which was all too frequent. The painful invasions into her body by the act of injecting occurred when she was hospitalized in her late childhood and adolescence. This could have been the external trauma which fueled her phobia, causing it to grow in magnitude over the years. A symbolic sexual meaning of these objects also could be surmised, with all the consequences for that angle of interpretation.

Under another possible interpretation, one can perceive the focal point as a pivoting, equilibrist act. "Standing on one point" could be a metaphor for the enormous energy and capacity Susanne must mobilize to cope with the various challenges and demands of her life, both internal and external. Dealing with life's issues, Susanne carries out many balancing acts: between Europe and America, between the emotional connection to the family in Germany[39] and her own independent life in the New World, between her inner and outer realities, and so on. This requires great flexibility and internal resilience, much like keeping balance on a tightrope. In this interpretation, Pale Moonlight's focal point is also a metaphor for this complicated process of ongoing adjustment.

---

37 One of the father's constantly repeated reproaches and admonitions to Susanne was "Concentrate, 100% concentrate! You are not Julius Caesar, who could do three things simultaneously..."Another of his sayings was, "You could even become a street cleaner, but you must be the best street cleaner!"

38 The father's "commandments" were mostly sound pieces of advice as to how to succeed in life, but they were issued in the tone of a non-negotiable command: "Do as we do!" or "My way or the highway!"

39 Susanne's parents disapproved of her husband, whom they refused to meet all their lives, and were opposed to her move to America.

There is an impressive polarity between the large mass of the butterfly's wings and the single point on which it all rests. The butterfly's precarious position on the pedestal could be a metaphorical expression for the force of circumstances that demand balancing acts in Susanne's life. It is necessary to keep her inner equilibrium and hold down a fluctuation between the extremes, especially her tendency for falling into deep pessimism and despair. There is a plethora of problems, including medical issues, professional situations, family relationships, and marriage and its dissolution. Moreover, the continuous challenge to find the meaning of life has darkened Susanne's mood in different phases of her life. She often considers herself to be an equilibrist, but she chooses "not to look down" anymore as she walks the "rope" of her life, overcoming its challenges.

On the one hand, the tapering design of the focal point in Pale Moonlight can symbolize the idea of corralling various personal resources into a singular focus and aim. On the other hand, everything radiates from this locus: power, variety, beauty, strength, and the ability to branch out in many directions. In the poetic commentary, this is expressed as, "Her essence is concentrated at the core from which all her strength, ... beauty, endurance and courage streams out ... "

As we complete the discussion on the varying aspects of the focal point of Pale Moonlight's image, it should be mentioned that its sharpness could be compared with the features on the tips of True Blue's front wings and in the hind wing of Firebird, whose hostile dispositions were described in chapters 4 and 5. This observation supports the premise that Pale Moonlight, like these two butterflies, harbors aggressive tendencies in her image. This should not come as a surprise since "aggressiveness" is an integrated part of Susanne's unconscious, and, as such, it is inevitably represented in all the instances of the artist's personification. Regarding the aspects of aggression, we will have more to say in the next chapter when we analyze the wings of the butterfly Touchless Misty.

8.2.4 The Scales and "Missing Scale"

The surface of butterflies' wings is covered by microscopic scales. The artist depicted them in Pale Moonlight as monumentalized loops. Susanne so disproportionately magnified them that a mere thirteen "scales" cover nearly half the surface area of the hind wing. With such an enlarged size, they have become a visual analogy to the term "heroic scale."[40] With this extraordinary magnification, Susanne added another element of grandeur to the "majestic" butterfly No. 3.

In regards to Pale Moonlight's scales, the artist associated them with iconographic characteristics of the cult statue of *Ephesian Artemis.* Susanne reluctantly admitted that, in the past, she already had thoughts about a resemblance of the stacked rows of elliptical scales of the butterfly and the legendary multiple large ovoid configurations adorning the chest of the ancient Greek goddess (Fig. 8.18). Through her studies in archaeology, Susanne is familiar with drawings and model reconstructions of the statue of the goddess Artemis, which stood in her temple in Ephesus in Asia Minor and was worshipped throughout classical antiquity. The legendary sculpture was equipped with several rows of multiple oblong objects, commonly interpreted as "breasts,"[41] symbolizing her important role as a fertility goddess. The image of the Artemis of Ephesus with rows of breasts, which Susanne had often met in archaeological references, had probably remained essential in her creative mind, influencing her imagination.

In view of Susanne's free association linking the scales in butterfly No. 3 with the peculiar attributes of the Ephesian Artemis image, and taking into consideration Susanne's perception of their similarities, we assume that these shapes in their size, configuration, number, and arrangement were unconsciously created in accordance to the symbolism of the fertility goddess.

Our analysis has revealed that the topic of reproduction has been an upsetting, even traumatic subject matter for Susanne. Her initial reaction to the association with the rows of breasts of the *Ephesian Artemis* evoked a feeling of distress

40 This term is used in the history of art to characterize some oversized or exaggerated proportions employed in painting, sculpture, and architecture in the various epochs of human history, including the present time, for example, in religious art, and in communist and fascist propaganda arts. (Bammes 1973, page 32, Fig. 26)

41 Recent studies indicate that these ovoid objects could be gourds that were often considered as fertility symbols in Asia. Regardless of their nature, most scholars on these ellipsoidal objects agree that they are used as a symbol of sexual fecundity.

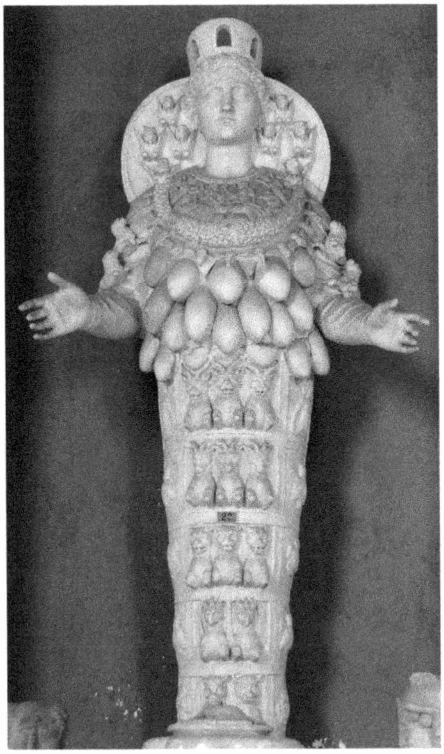

Fig. 8.18. *Ephesian Artemis.*
A statue from the *Villa Adriana* near Tivoli.
2nd century AD, marble. Vatican Museum, Rome, Italy.

accompanied by a body language commensurable with rejection. The artist was aware of Artemis' fertility symbolism. As previously noted (see chapter 7), she developed an outspoken negative attitude to the issues of reproduction and motherhood, in which she had refused being involved. The unconscious integration of the round shapes into the imagery may symbolize a lingering conflict with regard to reproduction. Her persistent position on this matter could reflect some ambivalent, latent thoughts about procreation in connection with incestuous tendencies in her early childhood.

Breasts are a sensitive topic for Susanne. There is an oscillation between the experiences of pleasure in touching them (autoerotism) or being touched by someone else, and the fear of getting them hurt, possibly as punishment for self-satisfaction which has resulted in oppressive guilt that she has suffered since childhood. This assumption could be substantiated by a specific fantasy which started at the age of six or earlier and continued throughout her growth into adulthood.[42] Susanne fastidiously avoids being present when mothers are about to breastfeed their infants. In museums or during her art research, she has steered clear of artworks which could cause her strong negative reactions, especially to seeing injured breasts.[43]

The shape of the scales in Pale Moonlight's wing resembles the kidney shape in Fanning Everything, which contains yellow globules as allusions to ova in a womb (see chapter 7). The yellow crescent configurations that outline the bluish part of the scales can be compared with the pastel-colored, inner semielliptical formation which surrounds the kidney shape in Fanning Everything. (See Fig. 8.24 (a) and (c).) The observed similarity and the thematic correspondence support that the topic of reproduction is manifested symbolically in the scales of butterfly No. 3. Accordingly, we assume that behind their exaggerated size is an implicit and powerful force which is thrusting out for its expression. The remarkable amplification of the scales underscores the significance of the unconscious message about the topic of reproduction.

As stated repeatedly, the issue of reproduction is a hypersensitive one for Susanne in thought, speech, and imagery. If a conversation happens to touch on the matter, Susanne will vacillate between a blanket refusal to deal with it or attempt to try her best to disengage from it by a sudden emotional outburst, animated by anger, painful gestures, or tears. Susanne has neither the experience of pregnancy nor the desire to actively seek it, as she abhors getting involved in any such specific situation.[44] Reproduction is an essential aspect of life, and its necessity has been supported by many social, ideological, and religious views which prompt human beings to fulfill their biological and social exigencies. Therefore, in the family and in society, Susanne encounters many problems when she announces her attitude toward the functions and processes pertaining to reproduction.

42 For details of this fantasy, see footnote 73 in this chapter.

43 For example, images of the martyr St. Agatha (Murray, 1996, page 5).

44 Some years ago, for the first time in her life, she went with great hesitation to visit a friend's daughter who had just given birth two hours before in a hospital; Susanne expected to see the baby in a maternity ward. However, imagining the horrid event of birth that had just transpired a few hours ago, the idea of seeing the baby so soon was a rather uncomfortable prospect for Susanne. Thus, she was afraid to look at the newborn, but fortunately the baby was wrapped up in cloth, which made it easier for her to cope with the experience.

We now examine how and where the reproductive drives are re-channeled in Susanne's psyche and resurface in her creativity. The observation that the multiple breasts of the Ephesian goddess and the scales of the butterfly Pale Moonlight share notable similarities, leads to the conjecture that the imagery of the oval prolonged scales seen on the butterfly's wing is the embodiment of the artist's reproductive drive. In spite of her explicit repugnance toward reproduction, the oval and other symbolic images suggestive of the procreative aim erupt through all the layers of her "iron-clad" suppression. This signifies the powerful presence of a biological drive underlying the images of her paintings.

Susanne's attitude toward reproduction was formed under the influence of multiple factors. Starting from childhood, despite playing with dolls and teddy bears, she does not remember if she ever fantasized being a biological parent. Previously we have pointed out that her parents had followed many of the traditional, authoritarian patterns of family hierarchy. Curiously, this did not extend to the way they raised their daughters. They made no concerted effort to prepare the girls to fall in love with the right man, settle down, and have families of their own, thus fulfilling the traditional goals of marriage and motherhood.[45] The artist's recollection of her family life indicates no sign on her parents' part of coaching the children in this context. None of the daughters can remember ever having heard their parents speak about possible grandchildren. Up to their early teens, Susanne and her sisters had only tenuous and rare contacts with their grandparents; after that, those stopped completely. In this respect, her parents acted as consummate nonconformists, breaking the traditional bond between the generations, the bond that was still held as the ideal virtue in the postwar Germany of the 1950s and later. The parents' isolation from their own parents and siblings, with little or no contact with them after their marriages kept Susanne and her sisters from establishing close and affectionate relationships with their grandparents.

Susanne's mother and father stressed that their daughters focus exclusively on higher education as the only way to avoid depending on a man for economic support. According to this principle, Susanne strived for many years, trying to live up to their stipulation: Learning was everything. After high school, she dedicated another ten years of her life solely to getting her university degrees, (M.A. and Ph.D.). Academic demands dominated, so she created only a few artworks during the decade.

This one-sided existence, entirely consecrated to her intellectual development and the accumulation of knowledge, was empty of any other facets of life and contacts outside the family, except for a few friendships with her fellow students. The parents tried to indoctrinate an aversion in their daughters toward the carnal aspects of human existence and enforced it at every turn. Possibilities of courtship, sexual liaisons, marriage, and parenthood, or even just plain, close friendships were discouraged and repudiated by the parents. This might have substantiated Susanne's negative attitude toward parenthood.

As we mentioned previously, since the age of 11 or 12, she had reasoned that it would be wrong to add more offspring in such a dismal environment. She considered the world to be overcrowded and highly manipulated due to heedless exploitation and extreme inequality. Children would innocently be made to suffer from these conditions. Over the course of many years, she had observed how badly children were twisted, abused, impaired, and damned by negative surroundings, actions, behavior, restrictions, and bias of the people and groups around them. Following that train of thought, Susanne decided to avoid the guilt of having inflicted these wrongs on children of her own at all costs.

From the above considerations, it can be reasonably asserted that they must have played critical roles in the suppression of her innate drives for procreation throughout her life. Susanne found a successful outlet (sublimation) in her academic and artistic achievements, through which she could fulfill much of her creative potential. As an artist, she has concentrated all her energies on painting, embedding her works with ideas, observations, emotions, visual metaphors, and spiritual insights. Through her creativity, she invites the observer to experience aesthetic and intellectual pleasure combined with a philosophical contemplation of our existence.

45 Susanne's sisters unanimously voiced the opinion that their mother and father completely failed to provide or promote any chance of their daughters being favorably disposed socially to meet with potential partners.

Susanne knows that her paintings have touched countless people, and she hopes their perceptions will positively influence their lives. At the present time, she can look back proudly on her achievement spanning the last 30 years, creating more than 200 oil paintings and possibly double that number in watercolors. *Give Me Wings!*, the painting central to this study, has been seen by more than five million people passing through the main lobby of the internationally-renowned health clinic in Jacksonville, Florida, since the autumn of 2004. On numerous occasions, people have commented to Susanne that "her paintings were her children," and in this sense, she might have figuratively fulfilled her duty to create new life on this planet.

Beyond her expressed concerns regarding the general topic of reproduction, let us inquire into the other specific causes for its downright rejection hidden by her intellectualization. In the following, we present some additional, plausible explications on this topic. According to a psychoanalytic understanding of the situation, we assume that the instinctual forces and their suppression have led to an ongoing battle in Susanne's mind. The signs and metaphors in her paintings are circumstantial evidence of a reproductive drive which is constantly repressed, rechanneled, and sublimated. We have already noted that the depiction of the set of oversized scales on Pale Moonlight and their metaphorical meaning reflects biological drives. In spite of suppression, the reproductive drive has succeeded in breaking through all the layers of resistance and has expressed its existence by various outlets. The artist argues that her gender choice for all the butterflies in the poetic commentary was decided by her desire to have an equal numbers of males and females (three each, with No. 7 being genderless) in the ensemble. Therefore, we assume that the decision for Pale Moonlight to be female was not so accidental, and it was determined unconsciously by the creation of the oval loops in the butterfly's hind wing with their gender-specific implication.

In the context of the repressed reproductive instinct, closer attention must be paid to Susanne's omphalophobia (the fear connected with the navel), from which she has suffered since her youth. The navel is the obvious remnant of the birthing process and the reminder of the umbilical cord; the thought of this causes Susanne to cringe. Pregnancy, childbirth, and the navel are all very sensitive topics for her, and they cause a great deal of discomfort, even panic reactions, especially when she is confronted with images or suggestive words pertaining to the topic of reproduction.

Susanne remembers the biology class in sixth grade when the anatomy of birds and eggs were taught in detail, and she instantly associated the spiral bands of tissue in an egg with the human umbilical cord, pregnancy, and birthing. After that, she immediately found eggs disgusting and, consequently for a long time, would neither handle them in preparation of food nor eat them. Some years later, when Susanne saw published photographs showing the human embryo developing in the womb, she experienced panic and horror. Susanne's abhorrence of the umbilicus literally turns "paradise into hell" as, instead of appreciating the body and its sensual nature, the navel becomes a symbol of the most dreadful aspect of the physical existence which triggers one of her phobic reactions—a heavy burden that she has been carrying for decades.

The artist tried to organize the regular arrangement of Pale Moonlight's oversized scales in overlapping layers of "spiraling loops." In the oil painting, a careful counting of the well-ordered cluster reveals that one loop (scale) is missing at the bottom of layer 2, resulting in nonuniformity (Fig. 8, 19). The artist explains what happened: When she was equipping each scale with a yellow

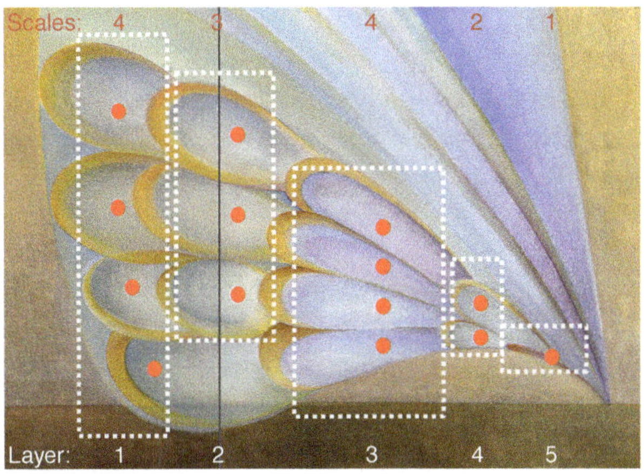

Fig. 8.19.
The "scales" in the butterfly Pale Moonlight.
Counting "layers of scales": numbered and encircled in white.
Counting the scales per layer: marked with red dots.
Layer "5" has one scale: rudimentary scale in dark orange.
Blue arrow points to the area of the "missing scale."

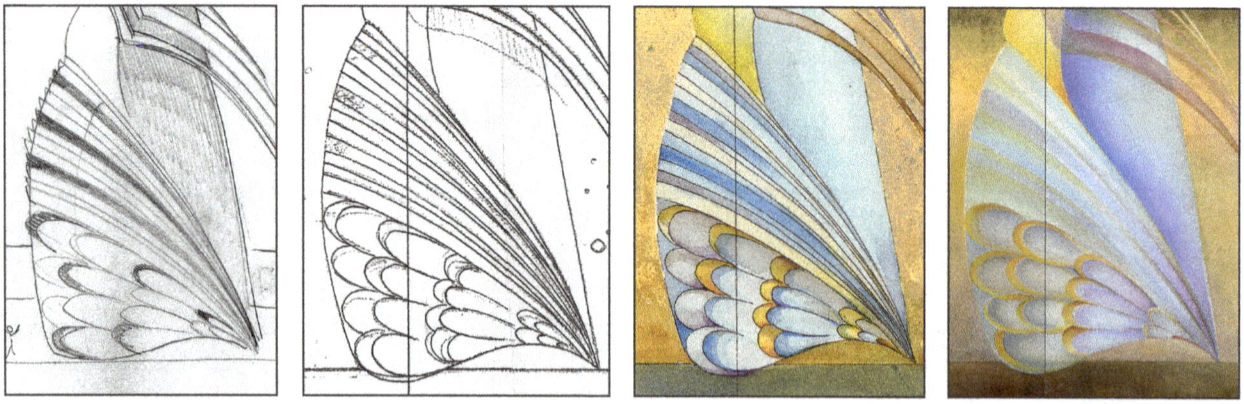

(a) Creative drawing I (side reverse for comparison). (b) Compositional drawing. (c) Watercolor. (d) Oil painting.

Fig. 8.20. Development of the scale section in the hind wing of Pale Moonlight (details from Figs. 2.2, 2.11, 2.10, and 1.0).

oval margin area, there was not enough space for another scale at the bottom of the hind wing. Instead of squeezing an additional scale into the second layer (that would fill layers 1, 2, and 3 each with four scales), she decided to leave one loop (scale) missing in the second layer. She reasoned to herself that this would also break up the monotony of the scales being arranged too orderly, that is in accordance with her penchant for uniqueness and avoiding the repetition of a uniform pattern. This tendency, we can already trace in subtle irregularities in the preparatory drawings and watercolor (Fig. 8.20).

Being different and above the ordinary is a recurring theme in Susanne's designs, and we can illustrate the manifestation of this attitude in the peculiarities of the images of her painting *Persian Summer*, (1988) (Fig. 8.21). Of the five densely arranged chrysanthemums (Fig. 8.22), three are presented as open blossoms (Fig. 8.22: (1), (2), and (3)) and two as closed (Fig. 8.22: (4) and (5)). In their configuration and pattern, these specific differences became understandable only during the analysis by the discovery of the metaphorical meaning behind the design. The five flowers could hint at a possible representation of the members of Susanne's family: two parents and three daughters. Two of the three wide-open chrysanthemums could represent the mother and father (Fig. 8.22: (1) and (2)).[46]

They show a regular, unexciting arrangement and color design, which entirely lacks pollen or seeds, possibly indicating that they are beyond their reproductive years. The artist describes the third open blossom as "enigmatic, irregular," because its image displays all kinds of unexpected deviations from the pattern of the other flowers in regard to color and the arrangement of the petals. In addition, those petals in the central area are noticeably larger. From the psychoanalytic perspective, the third open flower (Fig. 8.22: (3)), positioned at the top-most area of the painting, is identified with Susanne, metaphorically expressing her educational achievements and the "blossoming" of her artistic talent.

When designing this flower, Susanne remembers that she was thinking of "breaking away" from a standardized pattern. "Being different," the mantra of individualism, was of high value in her family, and she developed an ideological precept of not following well-trodden, commonplace paths. She assumes the specific kind of distinction manifested in the five chrysanthemums could be an unconscious "commentary" which allows us to identify the individual family members. Her two sisters could allegorically be represented by the

46 The modulation of light and shadow identifies the individual petals as open or closed. Flower No. 1 is the largest in size, having a narrower rim for its petal, and each petal itself has a color contrast (yellow-purplish), whereas flower No.2 has a wider white rim, and a regular pattern in the arrangement of the petals, which are either white or ochre. We assume that the first flower could metaphorically represent the father (featuring the largest size) and the second, the mother. It is noteworthy that flower No. 1 (father) overlaps with flower No. 3, which we identify as Susanne. Furthermore, flower No. 2 (mother) partly covers the smaller of the closed flowers, No. 4 (presumably the younger sister). The older sister (flower No. 5) had already moved from home, which could reflect the family situation at the time of the painting.

pair of closed buds that might mirror the artist's perception (in 1988) that they "had not developed their potentials yet." To confirm this metaphorical representation and its corresponding meaning, we can point to the peculiarity of the petals of the three chrysanthemums that represent Susanne and her sisters. The petals are sprinkled with minute spheres, which might stand for pollen globules or seed-like grains, unconsciously hinting at their reproductive viability.

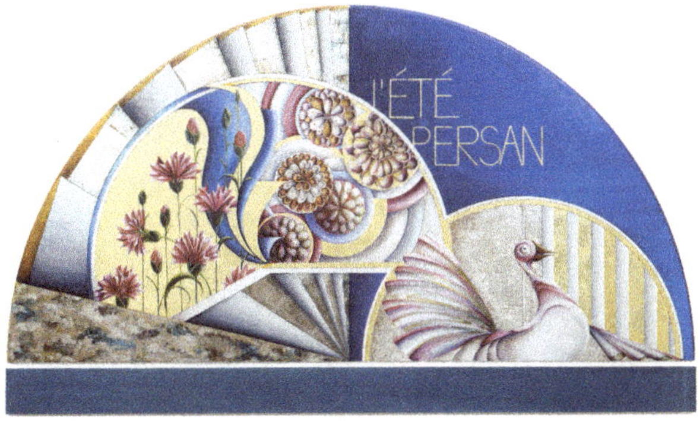

Fig. 8.21. Susanne Schuenke, *L'Eté Persan* (*Persian Summer*), 1988. Oil, gold and silver leaf on wood, 43 x 79 in (110 x 200 cm). Collection of the artist

The shapes of the petals of the blossoms in *Persian Summer* resemble the wing scales in butterfly No. 3 (Fig. 8.23), which are specific to this butterfly. The obvious similarity between the petals and the scales could indicate that they have an associative meaning of reproduction. In *Persian Summer*, the third blossom stands out by its explicit irregularity, which we interpreted above as the implicit representation of the artist. We noted a deviation (a missing scale) in the otherwise well-organized arrangement of scales in Pale Moonlight. As we have remarked previously, Susanne recognized this during the painting process and consciously accepted the break in the monotony of the orderly design. However, taking a cue from the blossoms in *Persian Summer*, we shall now explore the arrangement of the scales for the possible presence of an implicit message. Such latent content could be associated with the missing scale.

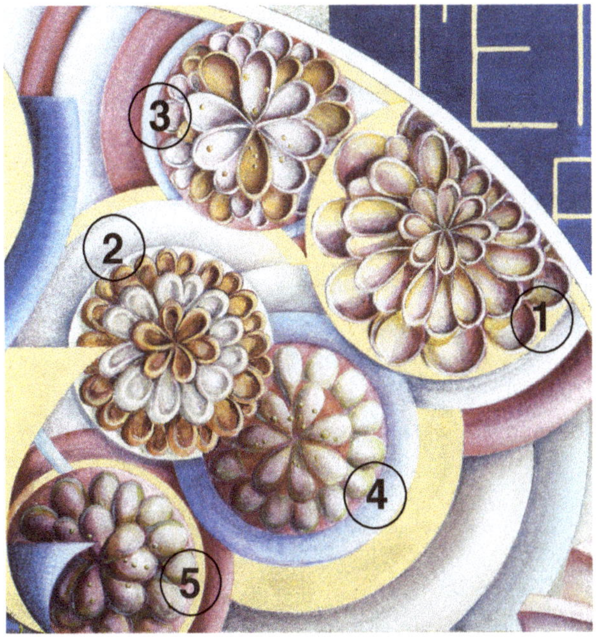

Fig. 8.22. Detail from Fig. 8.21 showing five chrysanthemums (overlaid numbers were added for identification purposes).

The shape in each of Pale Moonlight's scales could also be detected in the analogical, rounded and elongated formations in the front of butterfly No. 4, Touchless Misty, and the kidney shape of butterfly No. 6, Fanning Everything (Fig. 8.24). We have assumed (see chapters 7 and 9) that those latter configurations represent unconscious phallic symbolism. It might be suggested that in the scale of Pale Moonlight a comparable symbolic meaning could also be recognized.

The round shapes and their patterns of arrangement on the goddess Artemis's torso and Pale Moonlight's scales share visible similarities. The imagery of these ellipsoidal configurations is an embodiment of the prominent feminine physical attribute—the breast. Nevertheless, the loops of Pale Moonlight are notably prolonged, and therefore could possibly also intimate a phallic shape. It might be questioned as to how a symbol that stands for the breast could relate to the phallus, but the manifestation of dual or even multiple meanings in one image (condensation[47]) is typical for a peculiar unconscious symbolism. This assessment has found continual support in our analysis. The missing scale in Pale Moonlight could signify a sense of incompleteness stemming from a feminine castration complex and that could be a basis for the development of an inferiority complex, subjects which will be covered in detail in chapter 9.[48] This peculiarity of Susanne's psyche, especially in view

47 Freud describes in detail this mechanism of dreamwork in his *The Interpretation of Dreams* (Freud/Brill 1995).

48 As was mentioned previously, Susanne wanted for many years to be a boy and had some appropriate desires for adventures befitting a teenage boy (riding a motorbike, working on a ship, etc.), which her parents straight out denied to

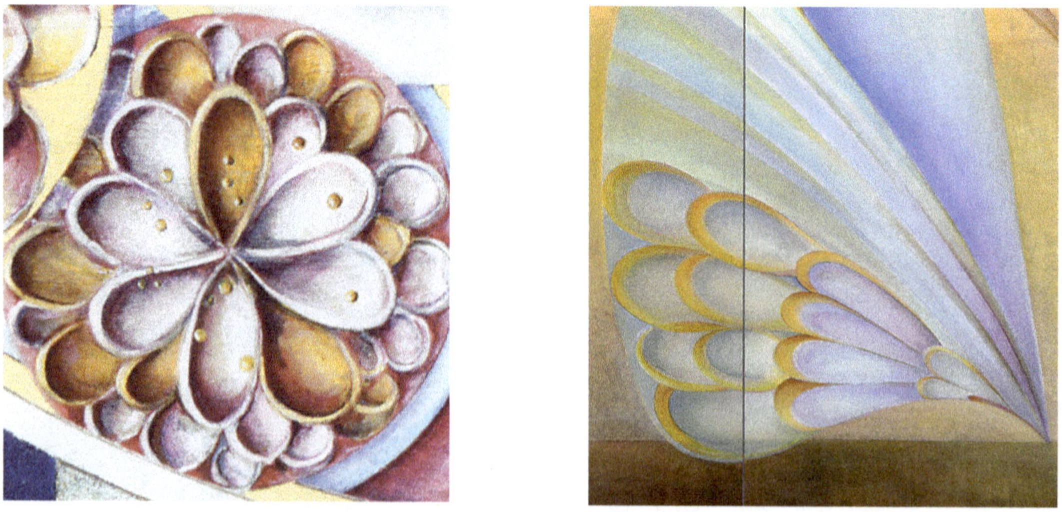

Fig. 8.23.
Collage for comparison.
Open blossom (detail from Fig. 8.22 "3" turned 180 degrees to highlight the edges) in comparison with the loops of Pale Moonlight.

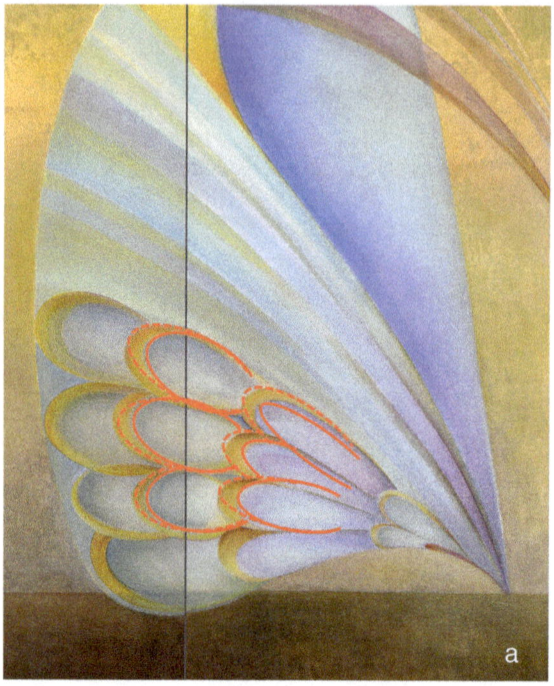

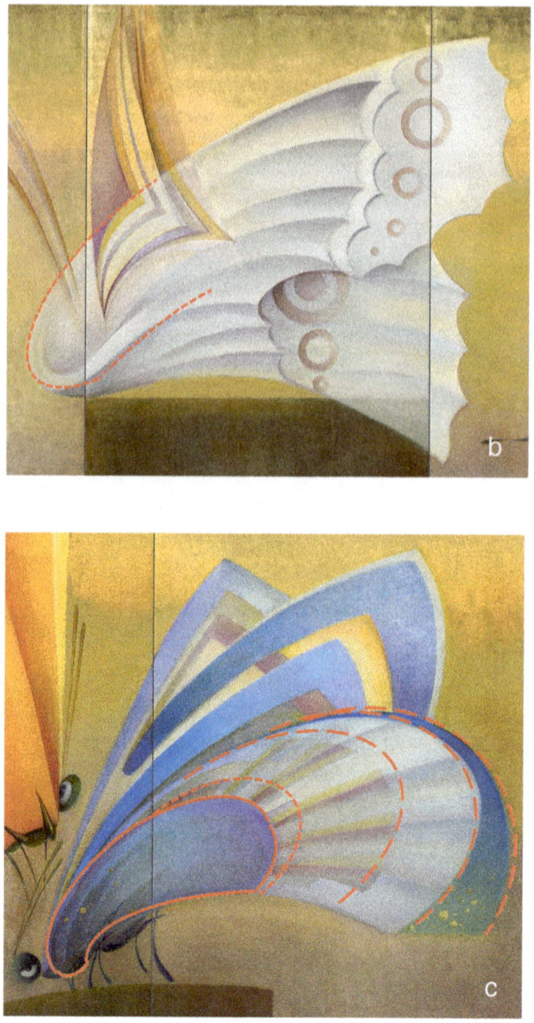

Fig. 8.24.
Shapes of possible phallic symbolism, outlined in solid and dotted red:
(a) Pale Moonlight (multiple instances in the loops, only some are outlined).
(b) Touchless Misty (in the rounded front).
(c) Fanning Everything (in the kidney shape).
Solid line: blue kidney shape.
Dotted line: conjectured "bigger kidney shape."

of her masculine patterns of behavior from her childhood onward, could be a foundational constituent for her inner gender conflict. In accordance with the characteristics of Susanne's personality, her biological predisposition to the masculine model of behavior was modified by other factors imposed by family and social circumstances.

The artist's psychic disposition could well be a source for some peculiarities in her imagination which constructively contributed to her artistic creativity. This statement finds confirmation in the multiple appearance of phallic symbolism in the images of butterflies Nos. 1, 3, 4, 5, and 6, reflecting her aforementioned pattern of masculine behavior. Her generative, psychic energy[49] of this predisposition could have been transmuted into appropriate imagery in her art.

In this context, there is another important association with an item from Susanne's childhood. She recalls that when she and her older sister were around the ages of seven and ten respectively, each of them received a piece of jewelry from the parents—a fish-shaped pendant made from brass (Fig. 8.25). It was composed of numerous little metallic plates, which represented the fish's scales nested in overlapping layers. This small, flexible item had a special appeal for Susanne as a play object.[50] Comparing the loop shapes on the hind wing of butterfly No. 3 and the scales from the fish jewelry, we find the resemblance between them to be persuasive. We assume that the scales of the fish pendant also influenced the design of Pale Moonlight's loops. As mentioned before, the fish is often considered as a fertility or a phallic symbol (see footnote 23). With this understanding, the scales, as a significant feature of fish, could substitute for the fish itself, representing appropriate unconscious symbolism of it. This phenomenon of replacement is well known from dreamwork as described by Freud.

8.2.5. Allusion of Multiple Pleats

Above the scales, in the upper half of the hind wing of Pale Moonlight, there are numerous narrow stripes which originate from the focal point and spread out in white and pastel hues of blue and yellow. In the predecessor of this butterfly (butterfly B in creative drawing I), these specific lines stream out from the same point but end in a typical zigzag pattern (Fig. 8.20 (a)) hinting at three-dimensional, multiple pleats similar to a folding fan, which was the artist's conscious intention. In the compositional drawing (Fig. 8.20 (b)), the artist abandoned that serrated contour because the predecessor of Fanning Everything, butterfly E, had a pronounced fan structure already, and she did not wish to repeat it. However, in both the watercolor and the oil painting, the upper

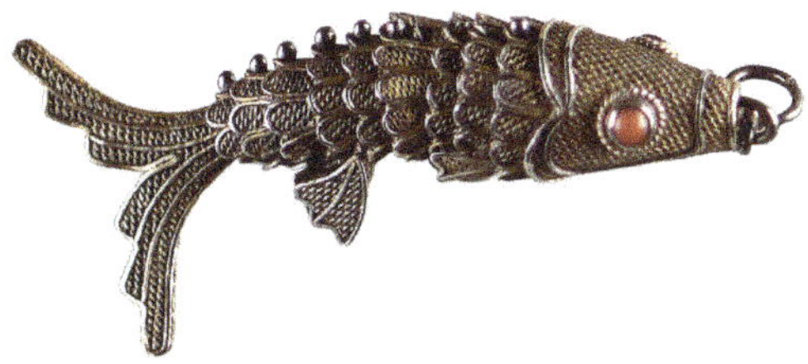

Fig. 8.25. A fish pendant, brass and coral, approximately 2 inches (5 cm) long.
Below: a close-up showing nested scales.

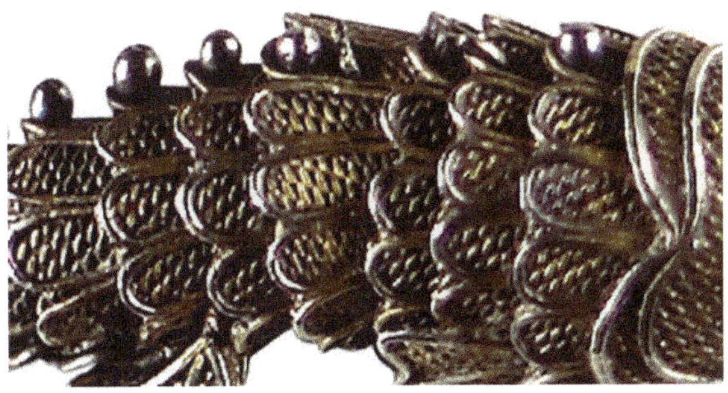

her. In this context, a family friend remarked once that she was the true "son of her father." Regarding Susanne's tomboy behavior, in one of her very private conversations with her mother, she asked Susanne, being despaired of her daughter's refusal to behave properly like "a woman," if she was interested in gender change surgery. The mother's question came as a surprise to Susanne since the idea never crossed her mind—possibly because of her phobia of medical procedures.

49 In accordance with the point of view of C. G. Jung, who wrote: "But primitive people, who, like the ancients, make the freest use of phallic symbols, would never dream of confusing the phallus, as a ritualistic symbol, with the penis. The phallus always means the creative mana, the power of healing and fertility, the 'extraordinarily potent,' to use Lehmann's expression ... " (Jung 1974, page 105). This understanding is based on Jung's mythological conceptualization of the meaning of phallic symbols as metaphoric expressions for fecund, creative energy.

50 The description of the fish jewelry was done out of Susanne's memory, and she was not sure about the details because she had not seen the piece for many years. She was encouraged to look for it, and after the piece was found, it overwhelmingly confirmed the similarity of its scales with the loops in Pale Moonlight.

part of Pale Moonlight's hind wing still follows that original "pleated" pattern and is accordingly designed with stripes that alternate in bright and darker tones, with their gentle light-and-shadow contrast alluding to a slightly folded surface (Fig. 8.20 (c-d)). Close to the focal point, there appears a stronger modulation in darker color nuances that includes traces of burnt orange (we discuss this hue and its far-reaching implications extensively in the subchapter 8.3.2).

In this manner, Susanne created an illusion of a three-dimensional surface reminiscent of a slightly open folding fan. Presumably, by embedding in the butterfly image one of her mother's favorite objects—a folding fan, with which she was symbolically associated—the artist reveals her unconscious identification with the mother. The fan configuration and its metaphorical meaning were analyzed previously in the context of the personification of the mother in the image of Fanning Everything, and the pleats in Pale Moonlight could be commensurate with a similar interpretation.

8.2.6 The Front Wing

Pale Moonlight's front wing is a large, monochrome area of light blue with a wide, yellow edge on the top left side (Fig. 8.15 (a)). Both colors have zones of higher intensity hues; the blue is remarkably deeper toward the left margin of the area, and the yellow edge is more intense toward the top edge of the hind wing. The structure of the front wing with its vertical orientation soars high up, culminating in a gently rounded, whitish tip which strongly contrasts with the golden background. This configuration leads us to a repeated association with a pointing finger. It is directed upwards to the golden background which might be seen as a literal hint, shedding light on the hidden unconscious message embedded in Pale Moonlight's front wing. Such an interpretation could find confirmation in the artist's personal life exactly during the time when *Give Me Wings!* was designed and painted.

During a period of nine months, from the initial drawings to the finished oil painting, a significant change in her life was building up. Being trapped in a legal partnership,[51] Susanne was mentally and emotionally depleted and burdened with increasingly heavy economic obligations. She felt suffocated and drained, until she happened to find a friendship with a new confidant. He opened her mind and gave her new perspectives on many different aspects of life, the world, and spiritual matters. Furthermore, with him, she was able to enjoy discussing daily affairs, philosophical ideas, societal and world issues, as well as intimate and confidential personal problems without any hesitation. Designing and painting the butterflies in a time of growing trust and friendship gave her a new hope for a different course for her life in the future, with renewed confidence that life could take many positive turns. Susanne had dreamed for many years for such a perspective, and her desires seemed to have come true. As a result, her new optimism and point of reference were metaphorically coded into the configuration and coloration of the front wing, signifying a hope for positive fulfillment and development in the future. In this regard, the large area of the front wing can be perceived as a cloudless blue sky—calm, without competition, compelling events or issues—with only peace and harmony.

In this context, the allusion to the pointing index finger, mentioned in reference to Pale Moonlight's wing tip, could be construed as being directed toward this hopeful and fulfilling vision of the future, reflecting the idealized friendship which she saw solely in spiritual terms at that time. In accordance with this, the absence of any traces of the color burnt orange in the upper part of Pale Moonlight is noticeable. We will discuss this specific hue in the upcoming subchapter 8.3.2. Burnt orange might indicate symbolic representation of sexual drives in the unconscious iconography of Susanne.[52] The confirmation for the above assumption can be found in another painting. A year after the completion of *Give Me*

---

51 This phrase summarizes Susanne's attitude toward the topic of marriage. Keeping her maiden name, she never referred to her married spouse as "my husband" but as "the one I am married to." She always considered her marriage as a form of contract that was subject to review and renegotiation after a five-year period. In reality, the force of habit made it difficult to implement the rule while the situation continually became less and less favorable to the renewal of the contract. However, about four months after the completion of *Give Me Wings!*, she asked her spouse for a divorce.

52 The color burnt orange can convey other iconographic meanings asides from its symbolic use for sexual drives in Susanne's creativity; for example, in indicating danger in *The Terminator* (see chapter 4 and Fig. 4.16).

Wings!, the platonic friendship had transformed into an intimate relationship, and the burnt orange color found a remarkably strong expression in the painting *Tree Flame* (Fig. 8.26). The new life situation was coded in a painting of a young maple tree in autumn foliage, depicted as one large flame soaring up in several tongues. The red dominates and the orange wraps all around and reaches the hue of burnt orange in some areas, whereas the green, witness to the season before, is only minimally represented. Therefore, in this context, the flame, in such intense coloration, symbolizes the sudden flare-up of sensuality that Susanne had not really experienced before. This interpretation of *Tree Flame* further clarifies the symbolism of the burnt orange color (for more on this, see subchapter 8.3.2) which was clandestine[53] in the image of Pale Moonlight and enigmatic ("a glimpse of orange") in the accompanying verbal commentary quoted at the beginning of this chapter.

8.2.7 Indentation and Analogous Contour

Pale Moonlight's left contour bends gracefully in a sequence of convex and concave curves from top to bottom, which is divided by a small indentation where the front and hind wing overlap. This happens to be on the border between the disappearing fog below and the rising golden background above. Susanne named this spot "breaking point" (Fig. 8.15 (g)), characterizing with this term the sharp and uncompromising interruption of the otherwise seamless flow of the butterfly's contour. The breaking point in Pale Moonlight is meaningful for our interpretation, and the deeper insight into its metaphorical meaning comes from the cryptic description of this butterfly in the poetic commentary: "Her essence is concentrated at the core from which all her strength, beauty, endurance, and courage stream out, [and] radiate in spiraling loops or in graceful bends, sharply marking the division between 'here' and 'there'" (emphasis added).

The quote identifies the realms of "here" and "there," terms which play a significant role in Susanne's personal Weltanschauung. In subchapter 12.4, we will introduce in detail the philosophical perspective behind these terms that will embrace the essence of Susanne's anticipations, consciously and unconsciously presented in her concept. For now, we merely mention that her ideas about "here" and "there" find metaphorical expression in the peculiarities of Pale Moonlight's front and hind wings. Therefore, a short recapitulation of the unconscious symbolism embedded in the wings follows below.

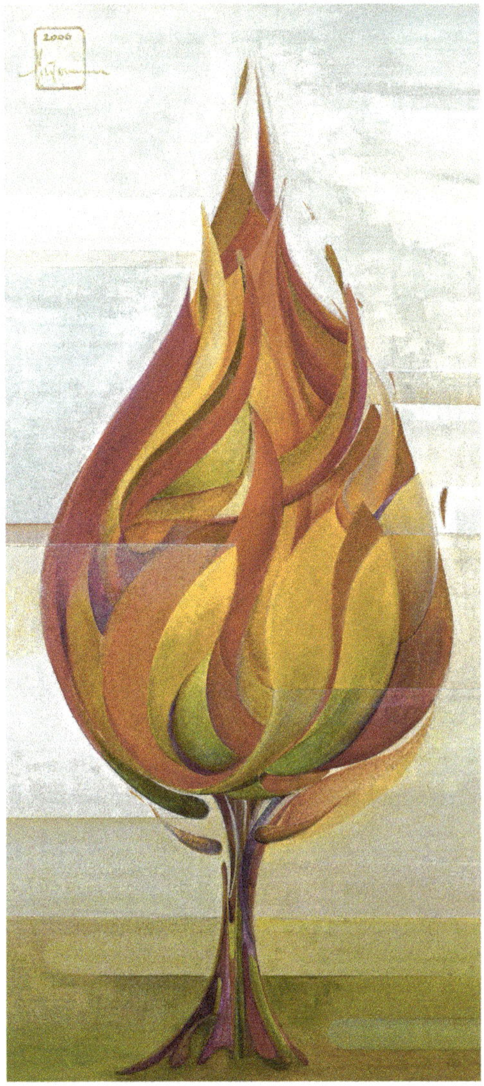

Fig. 8.26. Susanne Schuenke, Tree Flame, 2005. Oil and gold leaf on canvas, 29 x 13 in (73 x 34 cm). Private collection.

The hind wing represents the realm of "here." The focal point is the origin from which her individuality sprang, grew, and evolved. The pleats metaphorically echo the structure of an opened folding fan, illustrating different aspects of Susanne's potentiality. The scales bear strong

53 The areas of this burnt orange are very small and situated in obscure locations, so that they can be easily overlooked.

references to the topics of unfulfilled fertility and sexuality, and the glimpses of burnt orange symbolize instinctual sexual and aggressive drives.

The image of the front wing connects with the realm of "there." The upper part of the configuration of this wing is associated with an unconsciously designed finger, pointing into the golden background; this could be compared metaphorically with a beacon pointing to a brighter future, in which she hopes to achieve harmony, peace, and higher spiritual state.

We find confirmation of this assumption in the metaphorical expression contained in the artist's color choice. By cladding the majority of the front wing in blue, Susanne unconsciously incorporated many different influences and associations she had come to acquire in connection with the cultural and universal symbolic meanings of this coloration. She has her own personal symbolism for blue, which partially overlaps with the widely accepted meaning of this color. She shares the traditional view of the color blue to be a noble, "spiritual color,"[54] a calm color of relaxation and contemplation,[55] the color of the cloudless sky, air itself, the peaceful sea, and, in general, a symbol of endlessness and tranquility. The use of blue in combination with the topic of moonlight, triggers in the artist the memory and emotions she experienced during those nights when she was bathed in such otherworldly radiance. The reader might recall the interpretation of the watercolor, *About the Noise and Peace in this World*, which we presented at the beginning of this chapter. In this artwork, Susanne imagined that moonlight had the power to assist in achieving enlightenment, to evoke exalted emotional reactions, and to let the mind travel in another dimension.

With the moonlight association in the butterfly's name, the artist refers to the lunar illumination that has enchanted humanity for ages. We find an additional source of interest in the broad, yellow border of Pale Moonlight's blue front wing (Fig. 8.15 (a)). The artist associates this pastel yellow with sunlight, gold, the Divine light, and, last but not least, the color of the robes of Buddhist monks. Using the combined symbolic value of light blue and yellow heightens the elucidation of the metaphorical message embedded in the finger-shaped front wing "pointing at the golden background" and at the realm of "there."

A similar breaking point also exists at the comparable spot in the design of Firebird, where it doubtlessly marks the separation between the front and the hind wing (Fig. 8.27). The overall left contour of Pale Moonlight is, in most aspects, analogous to the one of Firebird. Both contours, running down from their rounded top, form a concave curve and then make a sudden turn to the right until they reach the breaking point, from which they emerge running downward in a convex curve. The curvature is more pronounced for Pale Moonlight than for Firebird, and as each contour reaches the bottom of the wing, the shapes diverge considerably. The repetition of the contours could unconsciously indicate an inner tendency on Susanne's part to imitate the idealized object (father). A clear example for this mimicry are the identical shapes of butterflies No. 1 and No. 2, already discussed in chapter 6, where we discovered that Susanne's personification (Little Why) was literally mirroring her father's personification (True Blue). The analogy between the left contours of butterflies No. 3 and No. 5, which the artist did not come to realize until the

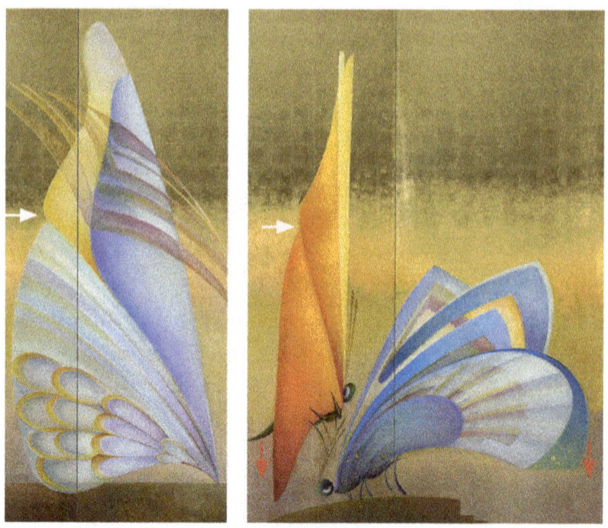

Fig. 8.27. Comparison of shape and contour in the wings of Pale Moonlight and Firebird.
Left: Pale Moonlight.
Right: Firebird and Fanning Everything
White arrows point to the breaking point.
Red arrows point to the reddishness in the background.

54 Blue as the color of heaven is also traditionally associated with the Virgin Mary (Murray 1998, page 59), and in Hinduism, blue color is linked with many deities such as Shiva, Vishnu, and Krishna.

55 Birren 1997

analysis, could be a significant indicator of a reciprocal relationship between these two butterflies expressed metaphorically. Keeping in mind that Firebird represents the father and Pale Moonlight Susanne, the resemblance between their contours could be considered as a manifestation of the phenomenon of identification. However, the similarity is not total. Pale Moonlight's wings trace smooth and pronounced convex/concave contours, while Firebird's wing silhouette is less accentuated. Furthermore, the contours differ significantly at the top and the bottom wing tips. In Firebird, they are sharp, whereas in Pale Moonlight, rounded. The similarities and differences are perhaps indicative of Susanne's unconscious perception of her father and herself which takes into account their shared and their contrasting characteristics.

8.3 Colors

8.3.1 The Specific Role of the Colors Blue and Yellow

The symbolic significance of the colors blue and yellow in Pale Moonlight has been partially discussed above. As mentioned, these two hues were interpreted as a specific metaphorical expression in connection with the painter's concept of "there." We now explore an additional, peculiar role that these two colors play and the unconscious basis behind their selection.

In her youth, the artist did not care much for blue and found this tint boring,[56] because the parents' preferred choice for the girls' clothing was navy blue and white. In the 1980s, during her studies in London, the National Gallery became a favorite place to visit regularly, and in the exhibition rooms showing Italian Renaissance paintings,[57] she discovered the beauty of paintings done in "light blue with soft yellow and/or gold." She soon applied this stunning revelation to several of her early watercolors and paintings (a good example is *Waiting for Tomorrow,* (1988) (Fig. 8.28)), and in her oeuvre descriptions she gave them the evaluation "elegant." A wide range of nuances in blue hues has entered her palette since then, although blue has never dominated her artwork. The artist recalls that, possibly for the first time, she intentionally applied the full power of blue, mostly ultramarine, to *First Hour of Full Moon*, (1996) (Fig. 8.6), and, to her surprise, she liked it.

As stated in chapter 2, the blue morpho butterfly was among the artist's most memorable impressions from the butterfly conservatory in New York that she visited by chance in December 2003. The species fascinated her with its compelling, oscillating range of icy, light blue hues, which morphs the butterfly from an intense blue-violet into a nearly silver-white hue, depending on the angle of the light reflecting from the butterfly's wings (Fig. 8.29). We can assume that her emotional response to the blue butterfly was possibly due to latent affects based on her perception of its iridescence, a reactivation of positive experience from her late childhood (see chapter 5, True Blue, concerning her visit to an Arnold Böcklin exhibition with her father). We will revisit the significance of iridescence for the artist in chapter 10, butterfly Air.

Two weeks after visiting the butterfly conservatory, she drew creative drawings I–III, and she spontaneously scribbled on the first drawing at the margin, "gold, blue, white/beige" (Fig. 8.30). This was a personal reminder for a future work involving butterflies as subjects, even though she had no specific plan for a composition. This coloration plan was written spontaneously, and we assume it was determined by Susanne's awe of the unearthly iridescence of the blue morpho's color, as well as her remembrance of her experience in London with the color combination inspired by the Italian Renaissance masters. "Blue" and "white" from the annotation on the drawing are references to the changing colors of the living butterfly, whereas the "beige" came as an afterthought for the rather unremarkable brownish marks on the insect's underside.

Although a gold hue is not present in the actual butterfly, it is mentioned at the head of the list of colors, possibly reflecting her impression from the

56 Susanne's mother always dressed the children in proper outfits—with the dominance of "marine blue" (dark blue) combined with "fresh" white. Susanne caustically recollects: "I was always dressed in blue, blue, blue—even my hair ribbons were blue for 10 years or longer."

57 To name a few examples: Alesso Baldovinetti (circa 1465), *Portrait of a Lady in Yellow*; Giovanni Bellini, *The Doge Leonardo Loredan* (1501/02); Masaccio, *Virgin with Child and Angels* (1426), and a French diptych from 1395, the famous *Wilton Diptych* (all: National Gallery, London).

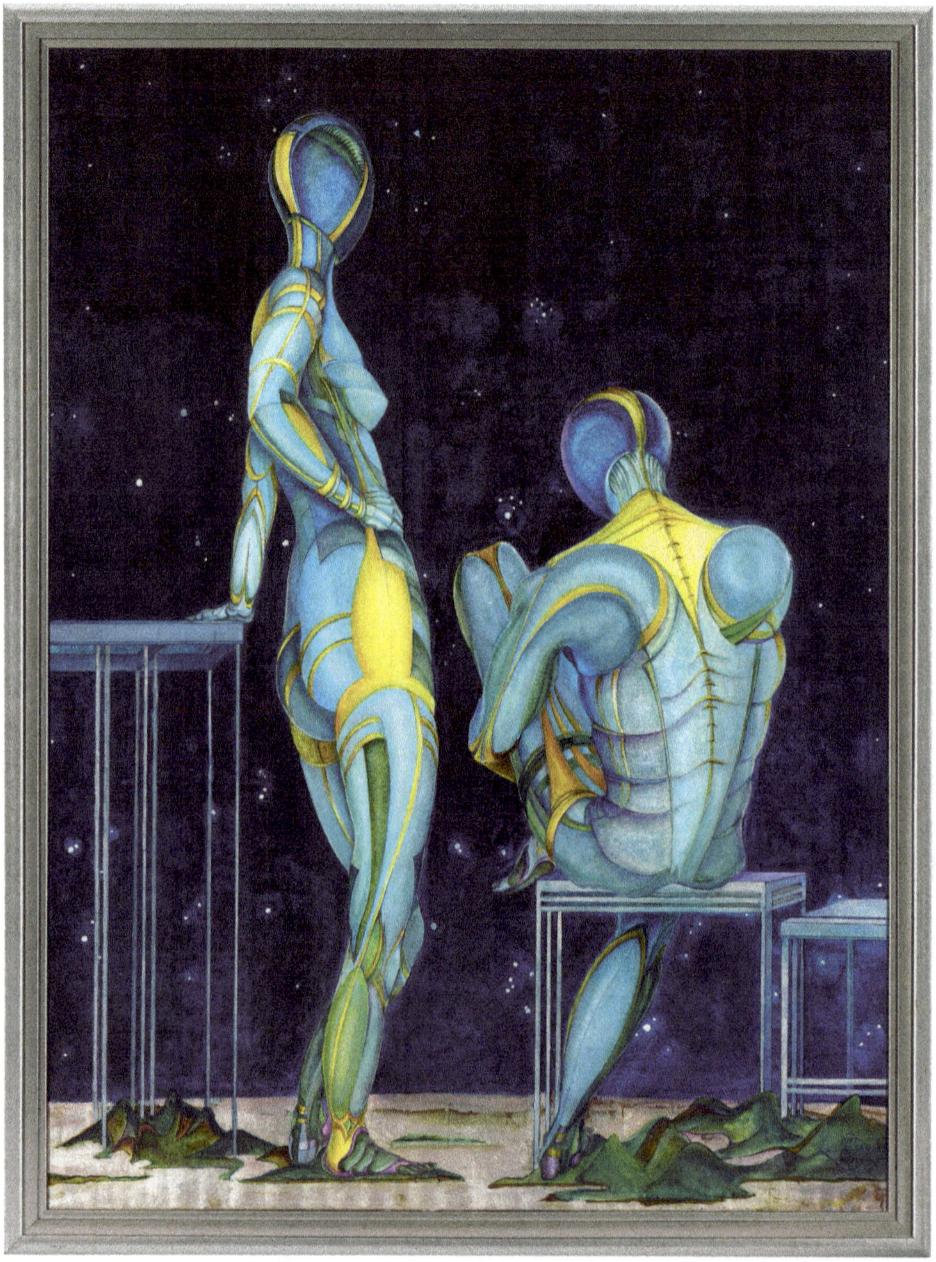

Fig. 8.28. Susanne Schuenke, *Waiting For Tomorrow*, 1988. Oil and silver leaf on canvas, 48 x 36 in (121 x 91 cm). Private collection, Florida.

beauty of the mentioned Renaissance paintings, many of which utilized gold. At the time Susanne began to work on *Give Me Wings!*, she was well experienced in using gold leaf as part of her palette to convey a connotation of spirituality and otherworldliness in her paintings (see chapter 12 on this topic).

However, the very first color which was applied to the watercolor was not gold but a strong blue for the front wings of butterfly No. 2, True Blue, in an attempt to imitate the color of the blue morpho she admired. In the process, she experienced again the excitement of the incomparably brilliant, ultramarine blue of this butterfly that she saw in the New York conservatory. From the color plan, the artist also selected and developed the whitish coloration of butterfly No. 4. Next, still continuing to follow her remembrance of the blue morpho, she modified the dominant monochromatic color of True Blue to pastel blue, combined it with a creamy yellow border, and applied this color duo to the large front wing of Pale Moonlight.

For the hind wing, she assigned multiple bands of alternating pastel hues of blue, yellow, and white for its complex coloration. In this way, Susanne began to balance the dominant, radiant

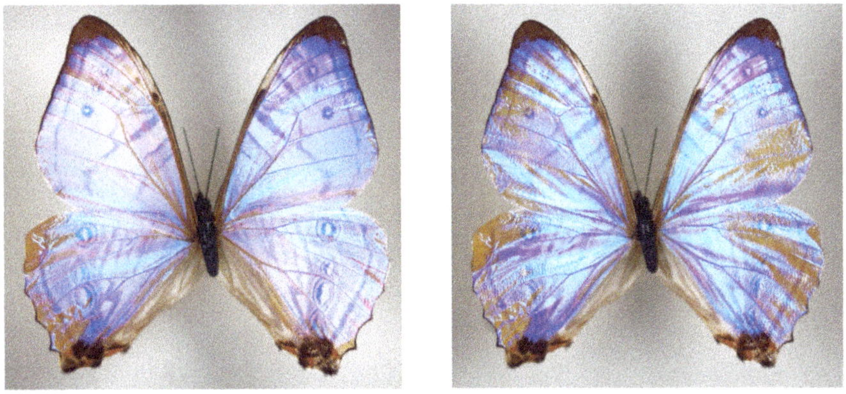

Fig. 8.29.
Two photos of the same Blue Morpho butterfly (Species: *Morpho Morpho sulkowskyi*) from two slightly different angles, demonstrating how the changing angle of reflection alters the iridescent pattern on the wings.

ultramarine of True Blue's front wings, which would have otherwise monopolized the viewer's attention. The artist met this challenge with the idea of "sophistication versus flamboyance."[58] It is probable that she was aiming to surpass her father, and the exquisite colors of Pale Moonlight were sending a metaphorical message to the effect that "I have now become more refined than you." Confirmation of this intention came later, when she completed True Blue and tinted his hind wings a weak, muddy shade of mauve, which significantly dampened his spectacular appearance in comparison with his neighbors.

8.3.2 A Rudimentary Scale and the Color of Burnt Orange

Pale Moonlight's lines stream from a singular focal point, and even the scales' arrangement on the wing is no exception. A sliver of burnt orange, which the artist calls "rudimentary scale" (Fig. 8.31 (c) and (d)), originates from the focal point on the underbelly[59] of the butterfly.

This "scale" already emerges in creative drawing I, and is fully developed in the compositional drawing. In the watercolor, this minute shape is painted in burnt orange hue, in contradistinction to the other scales that received blue and yellow tints. This single, dark orange scale was modified further in the oil painting, where it became extremely elongated and clavate. We have paid special attention to the rudimentary scale because of its likely correlation with the meaningful reference in the poetic commentary: "A glimpse of orange within the innate, energetic nucleus lets you wonder what [it] could be when uncapped and let loose."

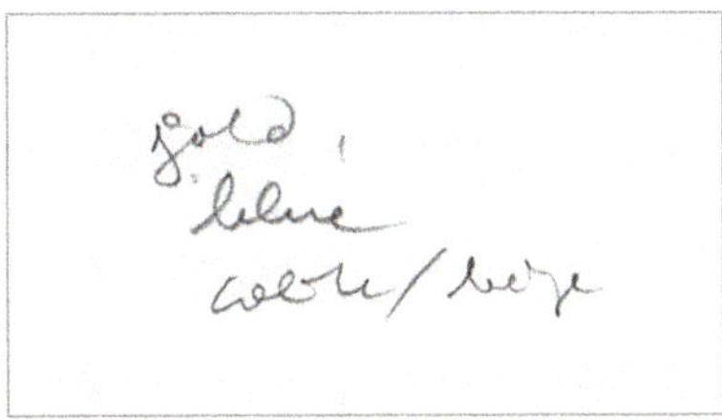

Fig. 8.30.
The artist's note about colors (detail from Fig. 2.2).

Small traces of burnt orange reappear in the yellow margins of the other scales of butterfly No. 3 in assorted modulations (Fig. 8.32), and similar occurrences of the hue are also found in various locations of five more butterflies. The artist claims that they are not accidental byproducts of the painting process, and she admits they might be her inclination to emphasize the three-dimensional nature of the scales. The repeated appearance of traces of burnt orange, where the neighboring hues are different (details to be found in the appropriate chapters), could mean that the color must have been applied to specific locations based on some determinations. This is likely the result of certain latent motives, possibly reflecting unconscious processes that could be analyzed comparably with dreamwork.[60] As stated before, Susanne does not like most shades of orange. For her, this paint is "ugly, not nice," and even speaking about it causes her body language and facial expressions to convey disgust, as if some sensitive nerves or open sores have been touched. She intuitively associates these colors with some threatening energy, but she has no rational

58 This phrase could reflect her father's comments in which he stressed the inconspicuous elegance as a higher value than ostentatious exhibition (see chapter 12).

59 The location "underbelly" for this explicitly slim orange scale could hold some unconscious meaning, since this is a physical area usual connected with sexual organs, although the artist never consciously realized it.

60 Freud 1913, *The Interpretation of Dreams.*

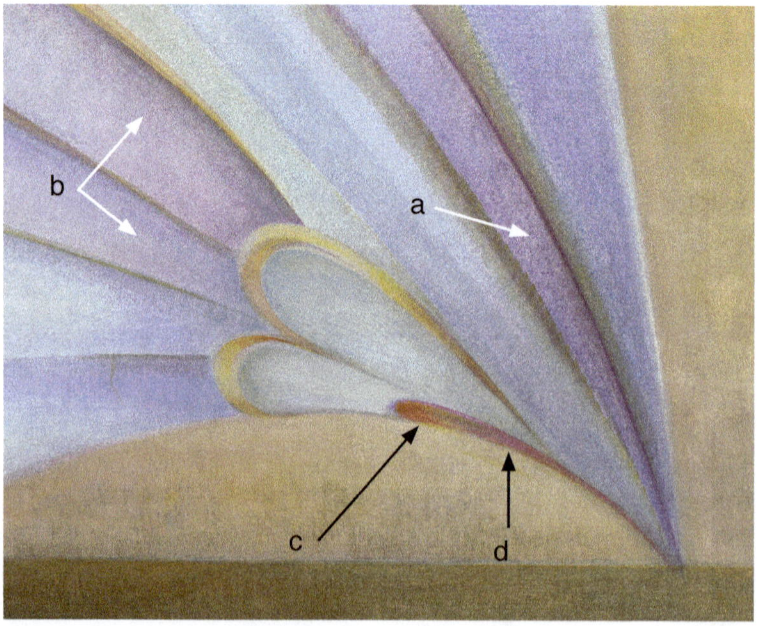

Fig. 8.31.
Detail from the butterfly No. 3:

White arrows point to red content that shifts in the blue coloration to violet (a and b).

Black arrows point to the rudimental scale. (c: top in burnt orange; d: reddish area).

explanation. In order to trace why this aversion to orange hue might have been imprinted on Susanne's mind, and how her unconscious attached a specific symbolic meaning to it, we take a closer look at some significant facts connected with this color.

First of all, there is the artist's image of Firebird with his irrepressible flood of orange. She characterized this in the poetic commentary as "burning orange." In chapter 4, we established a correlation between the butterfly's coloration and that of the book cover, *Born in Fire—Steel*. The initial interpretation of the details and coloration of Firebird, the first butterfly to be analyzed in our study, was limited, because the artist was at an early stage of revealing the manifestations of the latent content. As a consequence, the data available were insufficient to deliver a more consistent and integrated view of her unconscious symbolism.

After five years of research, we have gained many additional pieces of information that led us to revisit the analysis of coloration of Firebird in conjunction with Pale Moonlight's hues of burnt orange that

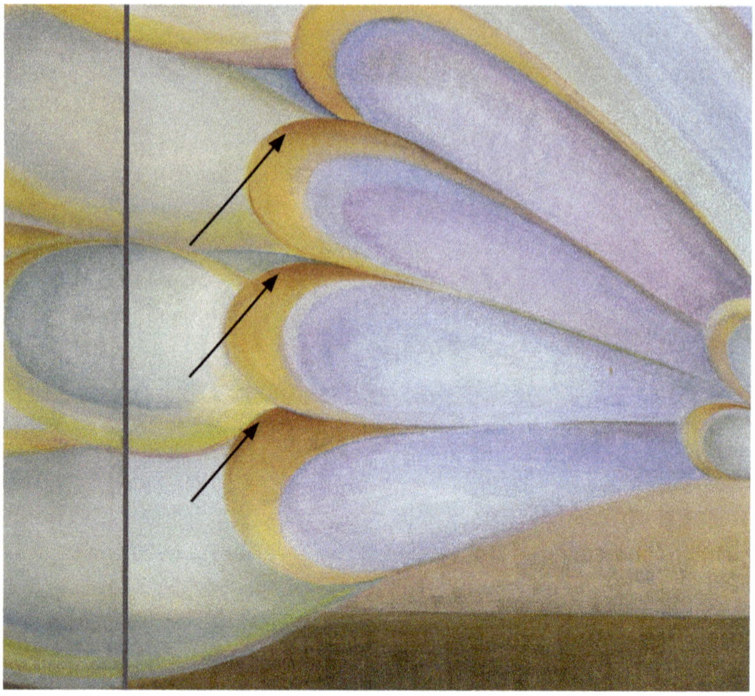

Fig. 8.32.
Detail of Pale Moonlight with arrows pointing to additional areas of "burnt orange."

the artist had found so noteworthy in her wording "glimpses of orange." Our attention was directed again to the cover photograph of the book *Born in Fire*, where the colors, ranging in a broad spectrum from yellow and orange to burnt orange, surround the white-hot center of the molten metal in a blast furnace, signaling the incredible heat and danger of fire (Fig. 4.3). This picture could epitomize the immense energy of fire, whose vigorous heat is able to melt iron ore. The butterfly Firebird simulates those colors with an intense inner glow, just as we can see them on the book's dust jacket. This butterfly represents the artist's father as she perceived him: His wide spectrum of vigorous emotions, his unquestionable dominance and authority, his outpouring of creative energy, and his explosive temper and verbal aggression. Aptly, Firebird presents a visual metaphor, originating from an analogy between the extreme emotional expressions of her father's character and the image of glowing steel.

Furthermore, the palpable eroticism visible in her father's artwork, in contrast to his attempts to censor topics relating to sexuality from family conversations,[61] was unconsciously integrated into the image of Firebird. At the time of the analysis of Firebird, the disclosure of this specific interpretation would have been premature. Only in the continuing process of research did it become possible to make an assumption about the metaphorical expressions of instinctual tendencies as they were encoded in different butterflies including, for example, Pale Moonlight, through the presence of the burnt orange hue in their particular details.

Another link in the chain of interpretations can be added from the linguistic perspective. With the book, *Born in Fire*, Susanne learned some specific vocabularies, which did not belong to the average elementary school curriculum. One of them was the German word *Kokille* (English: casting mold), and the child mistakenly thought that this was the name for the elongated slab of steel, the ingot, produced in the casting process that she saw in one of the pictures in *Born in Fire*, where several of them were shown still glowing in burnt orange (Fig. 8.33).[62] Susanne likes the word "Kokille,"[63] particularly its sound. It is worth noting that the nicknames for her parents both adopted by their close friends and by themselves, which were also used for signing their artworks, were "Coco" for her father and "Cocine" for her mother. The name "Cocine," with the second *c* being pronounced as *k*, is nearly homophonous to "Kokille."

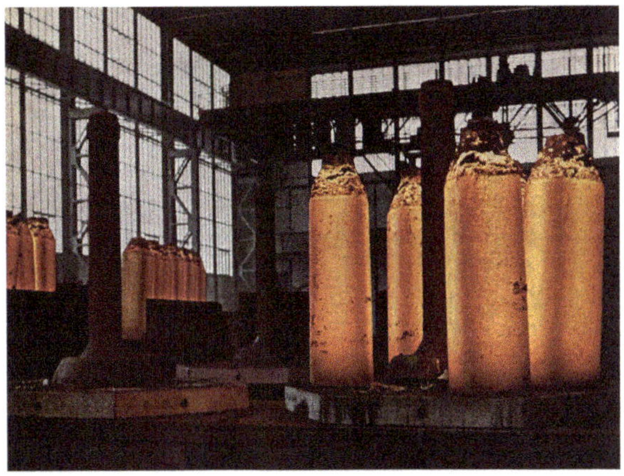

Fig. 8.33. Picture from *Born in Fire*—Steel, plate 40, showing the ingots, still glowing hot out of their molds.

Continuing our inquiry into Susanne's past for the origin of her perception of burnt orange as a signifier for some specific meaning, the research finds plausible sources in several artworks in her family's possession. In her parents' bedroom, right above the headboard hung a pair of amorous 18th century French hand-colored copperplate prints after Louis Leopold Boilly. In the first print, *La Douce Résistance* (Fig. 8.34), a couple standing by a half-closed door is engaged in foreplay in a darkened room with a view of a bed right behind them, symbolically insinuating the future course of

61 Sexuality was a taboo topic in her family. If the subject ever came up, the parents gave only terse and antagonistic remarks, discouraging any further discussion on the matter. The father judged sexuality as an "animalistic drive," and the mother categorized it as "unappetizing," which was as far as they would comment. Only when Susanne was in her early twenties, her mother once remarked that her husband was always "full of vigor," which Susanne interpreted to mean that her mother was alluding to her husband's strong sexual drive.

62 In reality, Kokille is the technical term for the mold into which the molten steel is poured to form the ingot. These ingots seem to ooze potential danger even in the book's illustrations, and Susanne associated them with her father's hot temper. In conjunction with Susanne's symbolic way of thinking and father complex, it is conceivable to find phallic symbolism in the ingot. Consequently, in the process of unconscious transformation, the hues of dark and burnt orange could have become a visual sign for wild sexual drives, reflecting the danger of incestuous tendencies.

63 A possible connection to this might be the German word "*killekille*"—an interjection, the English equivalent of which is the baby talk expression, "tickle, tickle."

the action. Of particular interest here is the color of the gentleman's frock coat, which is dark red-orange or salmon red,[64] while the lady's gown is white. The second print, *L'Amant Favorisé* (Fig. 8.35), depicts what appears to be a scene of post-coital bedlam during which the man escapes in a hasty and surreptitious retreat through the backdoor in a dark corner with his outer clothes under his arm, while his lover buys him time by the door latch.[65] In the left foreground, an orange piece of clothing prominently hangs over a chair.

These images were in Susanne's environment for as long as she can remember. She was frequently exposed to them, as she used to sleep with her parents until around the age of eight as we have repeatedly mentioned; they are precisely the sort of mysterious pictures that engage the curious young mind to no end until one day everything falls into place. Susanne does not remember her mother ever making comments about the prints or the nature of their subject matter, which would have been obvious to the experienced adults. The significant attributes of Susanne's perception of these two scenes are thus: the love affair in dark surroundings; the color orange, as a dominating tint of the clothes worn by the male suitors. Therefore, these shades of the color orange could have become an important signifier for a sexually-charged situation in the artworks that were displayed in her parents' bedroom.

When Susanne was between the ages of eight and eleven, her father created the following two paintings. First, in a nightclub scene (Heinz-Günter Schünke, *Bar Scene,* 1964), her father

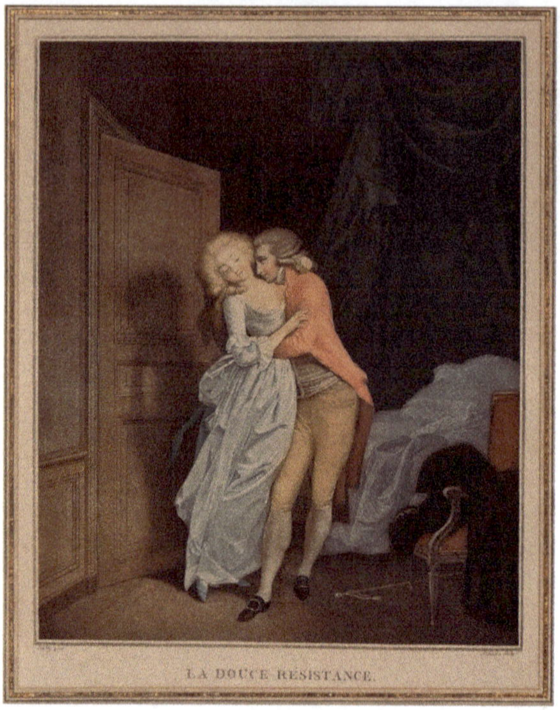

Fig. 8.34. Salvatore Tresca (1750?-1815), after the work by Louis Leopold Boilly (1765-1845), *La Douce Resistance,* circa 1800. Colored copperplate print, 24.8 x 20.8 in (63 x 53 cm). Collection of the artist's family, Germany.

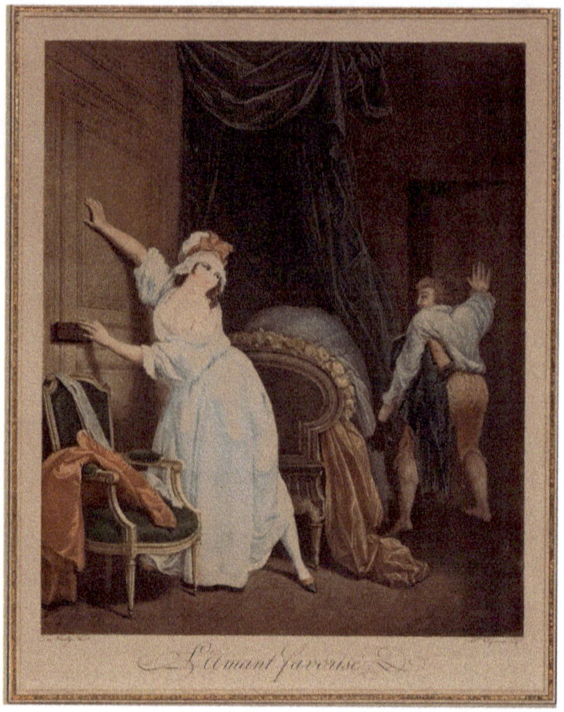

Fig. 8.35. Alexandre Chaponnier (1753-1806), after the work by Louis Leopold Boilly (1765-1845), *L'Amant Favorisé,* 1791. Colored copperplate print, 24.8 x 20.8 in (63 x 53 cm). Collection of the artist's family, Germany.

64 The description of the color is done in accordance with the artwork in Susanne's family collection. The color itself can be characterized as hues from dark orange to salmon-red. Before she had the opportunity to see the actual artworks again, Susanne had described—relying on her memory—those jackets as being in the spectrum of dark orange.

65 Scrutinizing the copperplates during our analysis, we discovered that "the couples" are not identical in the two scenes, i.e. the women's hair color is different, but Susanne perceived them all her life as the same people involved in a secret affair. The depiction of the scene in *L'Amant Favorisé* leaves open whether the lovers had consummated their love or had been interrupted before the climatic act; this is left to the imagination of the viewer (as it might have been for young Susanne's inquisitive mind).The given illustrations (Figs. 8.34 and 8.35) were taken from the artworks that were in the bedroom of Susanne's parents for over five decades; hence their less-than-ideal appearance due to exposure to light, cigarette smoke, etc.

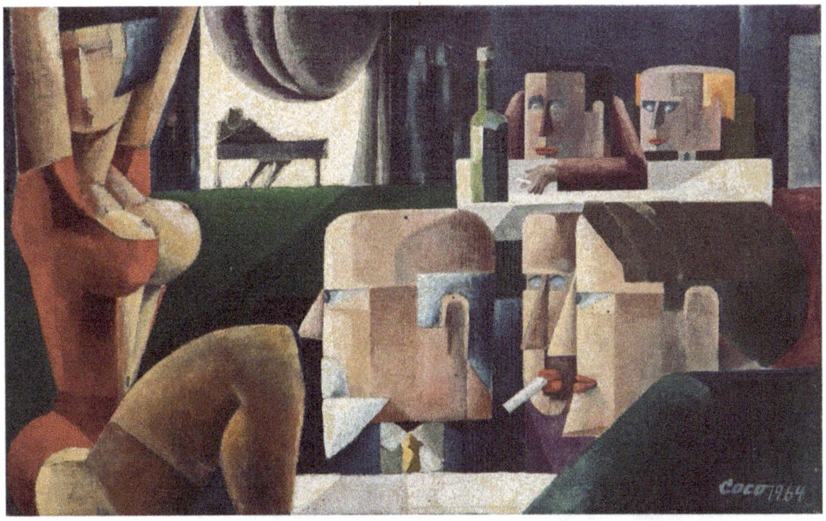

Fig. 8.36.
Heinz-Günter Schünke,
Bar Scene, 1964.
Oil on canvas, 12.5 x 20.8 in
(32 x 53 cm). Collection of the
artist's family, Germany.

depicts a strip-tease act that is drawing all the attention to the scantily dressed woman in fiery red lingerie (Fig. 8.36). The feminine bounty is eagerly appreciated by the rapt eyes of the male patrons. They are spellbound by the alluring sight, especially the two men in the upper right corner of the painting. The head of one of them features a distinctive detail—striking orange hair that flares up like an alarm light to signal the erotic tension in the person (Fig. 8.37, detail).

The second painting by Heinz-Günter Schünke with explicit sexual content is *Die Strasse* (English: *The Street*), 1965–68 (Fig. 8.38), where one of the six sauntering prostitutes sports a hairdo in burnt orange (Fig. 8.39, detail). Her father's two paintings certainly must have kindled the child's curiosity and even enchanted her imagination.[66] Then, those canvases were associated with other such images (for example, the two copperplate prints) where Susanne's psyche picked up the similar orange coloration in some coincidental details (clothes and hair) which became essential in those sensually charged scenes. This could be one of the crucial pathways to the gradual formation of her uniquely personal chromatic iconography, in which the orange hue, particularly its darker tints, became a marker for sexuality.

In both works, her father applied orange for the hair and bright red hues to spotlight breasts and abdomen. With this striking coloration, he symbolized sensual thoughts and lusting desires. The paintings feature areas of burnt orange in small but distinctive places, and they contain topics revolving around the flaunting of sexuality in an uninhibited manner, including strip-tease. Such a spectacle was usually confined to the red-light district in conservative post-war German society. Susanne's father openly discussed this subject matter in his art with a small private circle—his family members, friends, and guests.

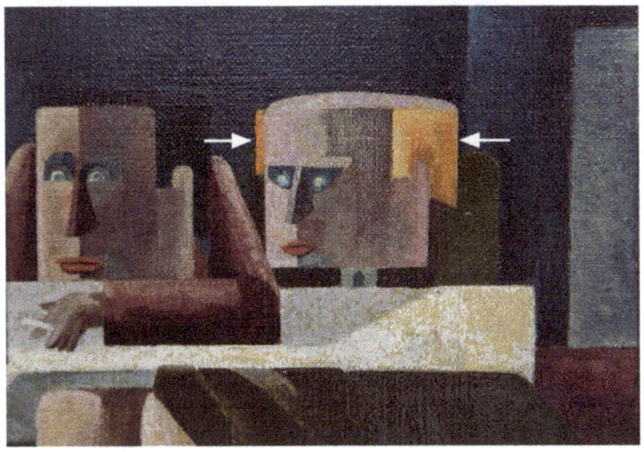

Fig. 8.37. Detail from Fig. 8.36 with added arrows pointing to dark orange.

With these paintings, we show how, in her youth, Susanne was exposed to the topic of sexuality by colorful images in her home environment contradictory to her parents' censure of sexual matter in family conversations. The colors red and orange in these paintings might have unconsciously shaped the formation of her color symbolism at an early age, and, consequently, her father's influence on this might be significant.

66 Susanne clearly remembers her father's explanation of the topic of the painting, *The Street*, to family members as well as to visitors, stating the social need for prostitution on the account that some men were unable to find a suitable sexual partner, and, as a consequence, prostitutes fulfilled their sexual needs, which otherwise might result in violent sexual crimes. From his point of view, the prostitutes provided an important (and necessary) service to society.

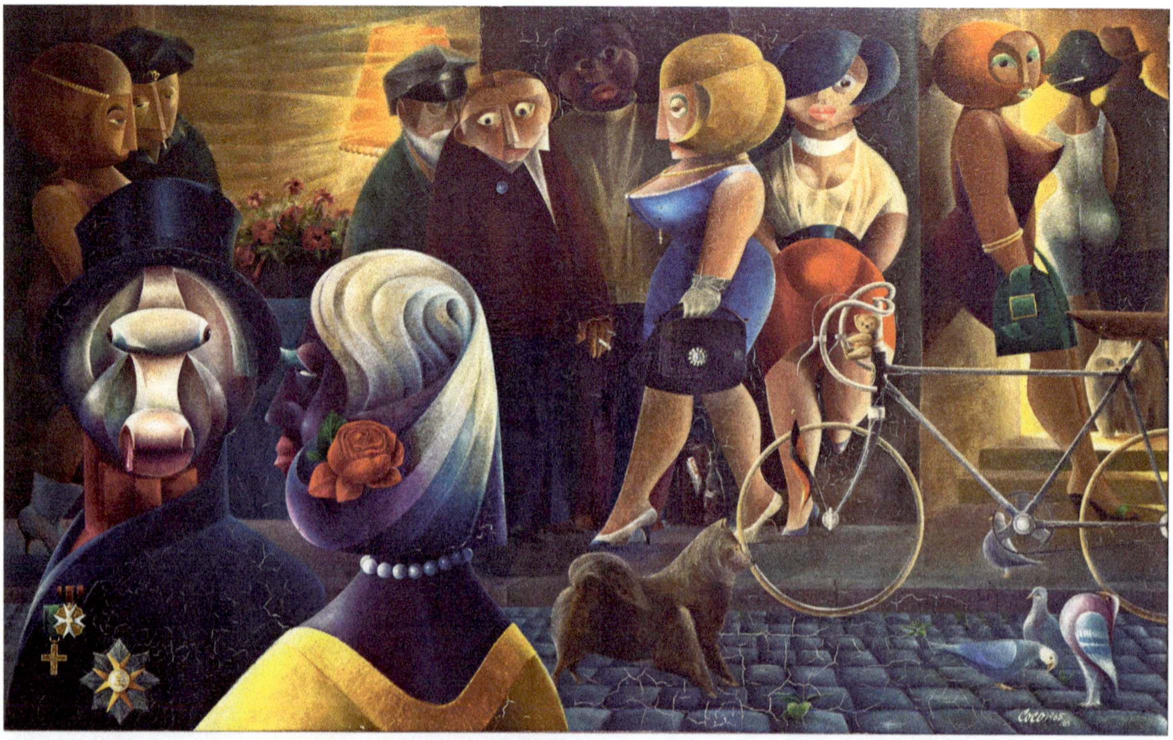

Fig. 8.38. Heinz-Günter Schünke, *The Street* (*Die Strasse*), 1964. Oil on wood, 25½ x 46½ in (70 x 118 cm). Collection of the artist's family, Germany.

Also, it is worth mentioning the parents' gift of the fish-jewelry, mentioned previously in conjunction with the possible sources of Pale Moonlight's scales (Fig. 8.25). The artist could not remember if the fish's eyes were made from turquoise or coral, but after fetching the actual piece, it turned out that the eyes of her fish were made from orange-red coral and its color was similar to the orange-hued clothes, including the darker nuances, in the copperplate prints above the parents' bed. Moreover, the coral is also close in hue to some parts of the rudimental scale in Pale Moonlight, a detail that we correlated with the unconscious symbolism of the sexual drive. These observations could give additional support to our assumption of the specific meaning of the burnt orange color in Susanne's artwork.

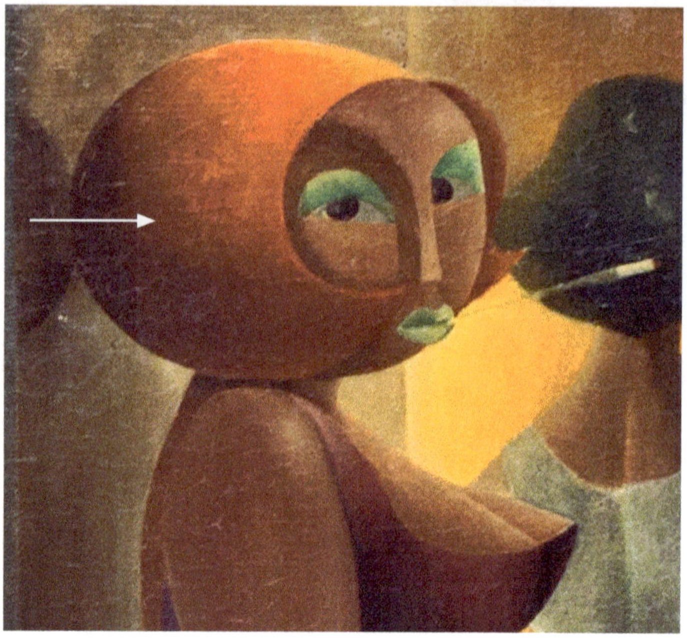

Fig. 8.39. Detail from Fig. 8.38. Woman with orange hairdo; added arrow points to "burnt orange."

A further association brings the spectrum of orange hues, especially dark orange and burnt orange, to Susanne's memory. Once, her parents had to design an advertisement for a set of dishes made from a translucent plastic, a novelty at that time. Among the pieces were a pitcher and a ladle, both in a translucent dark orange color. Susanne remembers clearly her parents making remarks about such "bad taste," wondering how someone could want that "ugly color for dishes."

Another childhood memory in context with dark orange brings us to the large strips of translucent, dark orange photographic negatives, which were in Susanne's family but handled solely by her father in his capacity as a professional photographer (Fig. 8.40). These films themselves have no negative implications for Susanne, although their dark orange color had an unattractive connotation for her. The selection of signifiers with negative or positive meanings is a very specific mechanism of the unconscious processes, and sometimes even ordinarily insignificant items could become important indicators of highly emotionally charged attitudes. There is the possibility that Susanne's enhanced sensibility to homophonic and homonymic words comes into play in this case. There is no direct conceptual connection between the noun "negative" in the phrase, "photographic negative," denoting the reversed shades and color values of photographic images and the adjective "negative" implying something unfavorable or antagonistic. However, it could be construed that, in Susanne's mind, both denotations became fused to express transferential attitude to her father with the color burnt orange. According to the network of associations presented above, dark orange film negative and the coloration of burnt orange in itself became integrated into the formation of the appropriate unconscious symbolism with its related meaning.

As we proceed with the research to find the source behind her attitude toward the hues of orange, it should be recalled that Firebird is totally clad in this tint. The coloration escalates into burnt orange in the sharp, narrow wedge just above his head, in the lower front wing and, to a greater intensity, down in the lower tip of the butterfly's hind wing (Fig. 4.2 (8) and (9)). The latter shape

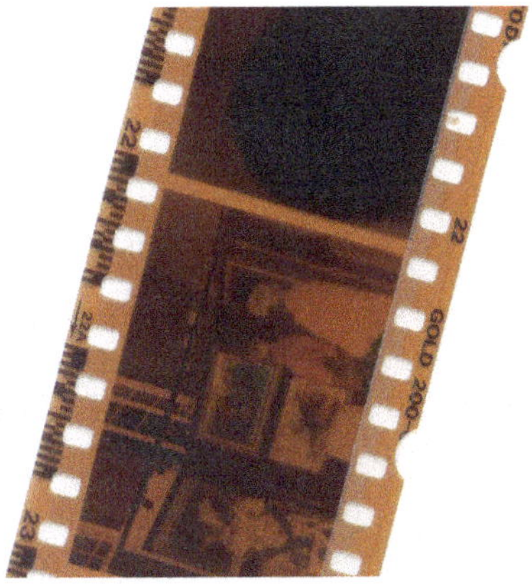

Fig. 8.40. A typical photographic negative (in its dark orange color).

was recognized as a metaphor for the downward pointing "authoritarian" finger of her father. With this gesture, the artist unconsciously signifies the presence of strong tendencies, reflecting masculine power and dominance. Susanne speculates that, with this patriarchal digit,[67] she had also metaphorically depicted her father's dogmatic judgments and denunciation of sexuality, when he labeled and devalued it as an "animalistic drive." The parents persistently expressed the opinion that sexuality outside of artistic expressions was repellent. Their abhorrent attitude toward "animal" forces was incorporated into her own value system. This impelled her to further suppress her sexual and aggressive drives associated with these bestial life forces. They were, as surmised above, unconsciously signified with the colors orange and burnt orange in her art works, the hues which became the metaphorical representation of her instinctual impulses.

From this unconscious symbolism, her antipathy toward the color orange could be manifested, and her statement in the poetic commentary might indicate her intuitive expectations of the power of biological forces: "A glimpse of orange within the innate energetic nucleus lets you wonder what could [it] be when uncapped and let loose."

In order to further our understanding of Susanne's use of dark orange in Pale Moonlight, we revisit Fanning Everything, the personification of Susanne's mother. This butterfly displays traces of burnt orange in her hind wing. One color strip

67 Susanne explains that in her personal experience, the finger pointing down is an expression of censure. Beginning with the historical knowledge of "thumb down" (referring to the Roman gladiatorial games in which the Emperor's thumb decided the fate of the defeated gladiators), any finger pointing downward signals, for her, the coercive power of orders and decrees, authority, and the demand for strict obedience.

runs in a slim curve above the left part of the blue kidney-shaped "womb" and four other shorter ones are arranged in the second iteration of the fractal structure (Fig. 8.41: arrows). These elements together create an intimation that burnt orange is surrounding the "blue womb." This formation allows us to consider the blue womb as an enlarged analogy of the individual scales of Pale Moonlight with their yellow borders. In accordance with our discovery of the underlying meaning of the kidney shape ("womb"), connected to reproduction and phallic symbolism, and also revealing the same symbolic meaning of the scale formation, we assume the identity of both shapes as carriers of the same latent unconscious message. With the revelation that the color burnt orange could be a signifier of sexuality, we have gathered additional support for the two foregoing assumptions. The reduction and fragmentation of areas with burnt orange in both butterflies (Nos. 3 and 6) could hint at the suppression of sexual tendencies expressed by assorted hues of this color. In this light, Fanning Everything's fragmented shape in burnt orange, might metaphorically illustrate the artist's mother's attitude toward sexuality, which was memorably expressed in the mother's pronouncement: "An unappetizing aspect of life." Insofar as Susanne was influenced by her parents and incorporated some of their thoughts and opinions about issues of sexuality, we suppose that the drastic reduction of one of the scales is illustration of their imperatives in this matter and could be interpreted as suppression in accordance with parental indoctrination (secondary processes). Moreover, the top narrow slice of burnt orange in Fanning Everything (white arrow in Fig. 8.41) is comparable in shape and color with Pale Moonlight's rudimentary scale. We suppose that the sexual symbolism of the latter in burnt orange is carried over in a more shrunken version (no rounded ending) in the butterfly which personifies the mother.

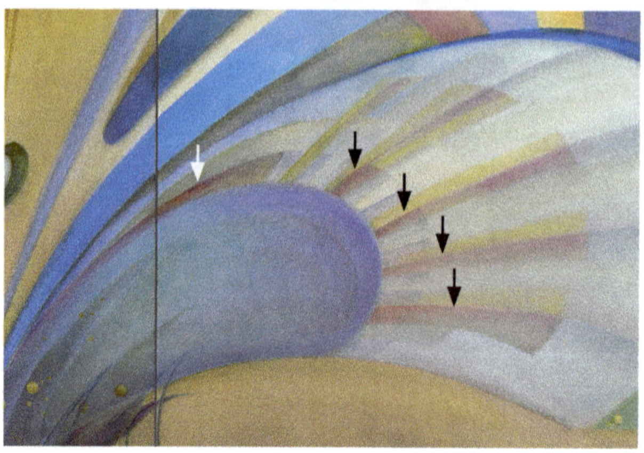

Fig. 8.41. Detail of Fanning Everything with arrows pointing to the areas in burnt orange.

The "sea of orange" flooding in the image of Firebird could be a metaphorical confirmation of her mother's commentary about her husband's sensuality (see footnote 61). The tiny orange traces (including the discussed reduced formation) around the kidney "womb" (Fig. 8.41) in Fanning Everything (the personification of the mother and partially of Susanne) could metaphorically indicate the unconscious perspective in which, in contrast to the father's virility, both the mother's and daughter's sexuality was seen as downright suppressed.[68] In Susanne's case, this may be due to her parents' demeaning attitudes toward sexuality and her fixation on the autoerotic stages of sexual development. The minute presence of burnt orange in Pale Moonlight, the personification of Susanne, may designate the diminished importance that the artist allots to this topic according to the above consideration.

The minuscule rudimentary scale in burnt orange can be evaluated as the result of the unconscious distortion of some latent content associated with strong instinctual tendencies. This could be considered as a diversion of the instinctual forces through minimization of their footprint, i.e., distraction by reduction. In spite of this camouflage, we recognize that the imperatives of instinctual tendencies are so powerful that they are broadly expressed in Susanne's imagery. She is afraid of their full emergence and has always held them in check—keeping the realization of those forces at a distance out of fear of being unable to master their unforeseeable potential repercussions. Her anxiety about the consequences is expressed in the poetic commentary as quoted before: "lets you wonder what could [it] be when uncapped and let loose," which is symptomatic of her fear of all the negative possibilities of losing control.

As mentioned before, Susanne has a fondness for moonstones[69] and opalescent glass because movement causes the light rays to be refracted inside the stone

68 It should be pointed that Susanne's two sisters independently confirmed this observation about their mother.

69 A pearly white semiprecious stone, consisting of alkali feldspar.

to produce a glow, ranging from pale orange to burnt orange hues in their white-bluish coloration (Fig. 8.42). She demonstrated the fleeting appearance of a fiery "glimpse of orange" in her necklace made of amethyst and moonstone, shifting them at various angles. With this, she suddenly remembered the opalescent glass art pieces, which her family owned. They always fascinated her as she attempted to find the "orange fire" reflected in them. One such object is a six-inch-tall glass sculpture of a butterfly with closed wings[70] in her parents' art collection. The artist distinctly remembers that when light shone through the pale, whitish crystal with traces of blue and green, it would trigger a striking orange glow from inside the glass, dependent on the light (Fig. 8.43). Susanne counts this small sculpture as one of her favorite pieces in her parents' house. She was stunned to find that for the longest time in the discussion about "orange glimpses" of Pale Moonlight, this opalescent butterfly never came to her mind. It is tempting to see how the unconscious, being so present yet so hidden, only comes into the awareness through the analytic "light" that is shone into its dark recesses.

Even the central butterfly, named Air, contains some glimpses of orange hue. This butterfly will be discussed further in chapter 10. The traces of orange in this "spiritual" creature could initially be seen as the presence of a foreign, carnal element in an otherwise sacred essence. However, body and spirit cannot exist isolated from one another, and always interact and interchange within the unity of the whole. Placed within the domain of the sacred to which the butterfly Air belongs, the faint orange in its configuration, symbolizing instinctual sexual drives, might be interpreted as flaws and impurities. The taint of orange could cause strong disgust in the artist's mind because she idealizes this image as "pure spirit." But the orange glimpses testify that her idealization is only an illusion. From this perspective, the almost elusive presence of orange

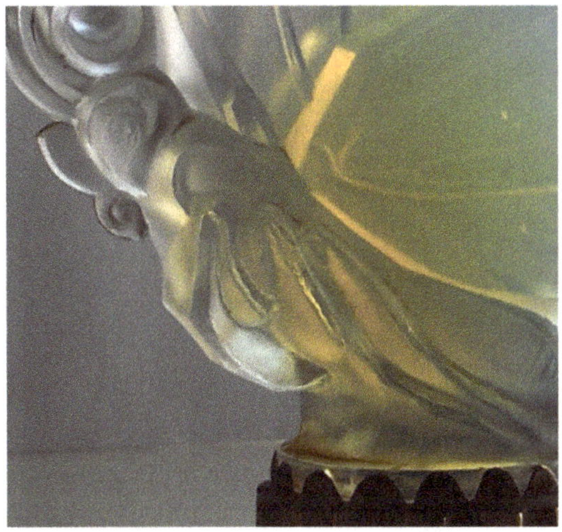

Fig. 8.43. Detail of Sabino butterfly from Fig. 9.5. An objet d'art made from opalescent glass; enlarged to show the orange flashes of light inside the material, observed in the original.

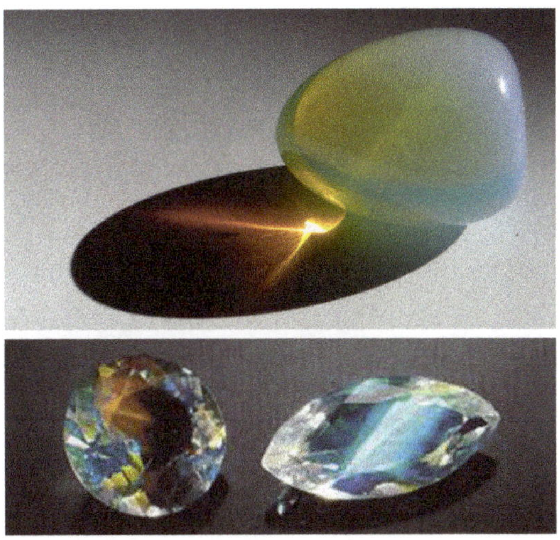

Fig. 8.42. Orange flashes caused by sunlight passing through an egg-shaped opalescent glass object (top) and orange reflexes in rainbow moonstone (bottom). (Rainbow Moonstone: source Internet).

traces can symbolize the integration of body and spirit. Acceptance of this dialectical truth is a significant step for Susanne toward recognizing the ambivalence of her inner realm.

The chain of above associations delivers sufficient indications that allow us to consider how the color burnt orange came to possess certain relevant meanings that have been imprinted in Susanne's mind throughout her life. Although the traces of this hue are slight, they point to a meaningful unconscious message. The components of her sexual and aggressive drives are coded accordingly by the symbolism of orange, embedded into the imagery.

Earlier, we discussed the fertility symbolism of the scales, as well as their association with possible phallic symbolism (subchapter 8.2.4). From this perspective, the skinny, club-shaped burnt orange

70 Designed and manufactured by the Art Deco glass designer and manufacturer Ernest Sabino (1878–1961), France, circa 1930s. This glass butterfly figurine will be discussed further in reference to Touchless Misty in subchapter 9.2.

scale at the bottom of Pale Moonlight's hind wing can be the sign for this significant function. The scale's important latent content is linked to sexuality, reproduction, and aggression.

Beyond *Give Me Wings!*, the manifestation of this hue with its equivalent meanings should be traceable in some of her other paintings. We found that the unconscious symbolism of this specific color already manifested in the painting, *Life Forces*, (1998) (Fig. 8.44), six years prior to the creation of *Give Me Wings!* In this work, Susanne depicted an abstract mountainscape with the intention of symbolically expressing four major aspects of human life. While honoring spirituality in this painting with the silver appearance of palladium leaf, the artist celebrates intellect with vibrant crimson red and acknowledges emotions with a wide range of blue.[71] Physical existence is represented on the canvas' bottom in pale greens, inside of which a few lines and hexagonal "cells" appear in a burnt orange which attracts our attention (Figs. 8.45 and 8.46).

Years before the creation of Pale Moonlight, in *Life Forces* the artist intentionally put the bodily existence down,[72] assigning it to a reduced rank. This indicates her attitude toward all biological phenomena.

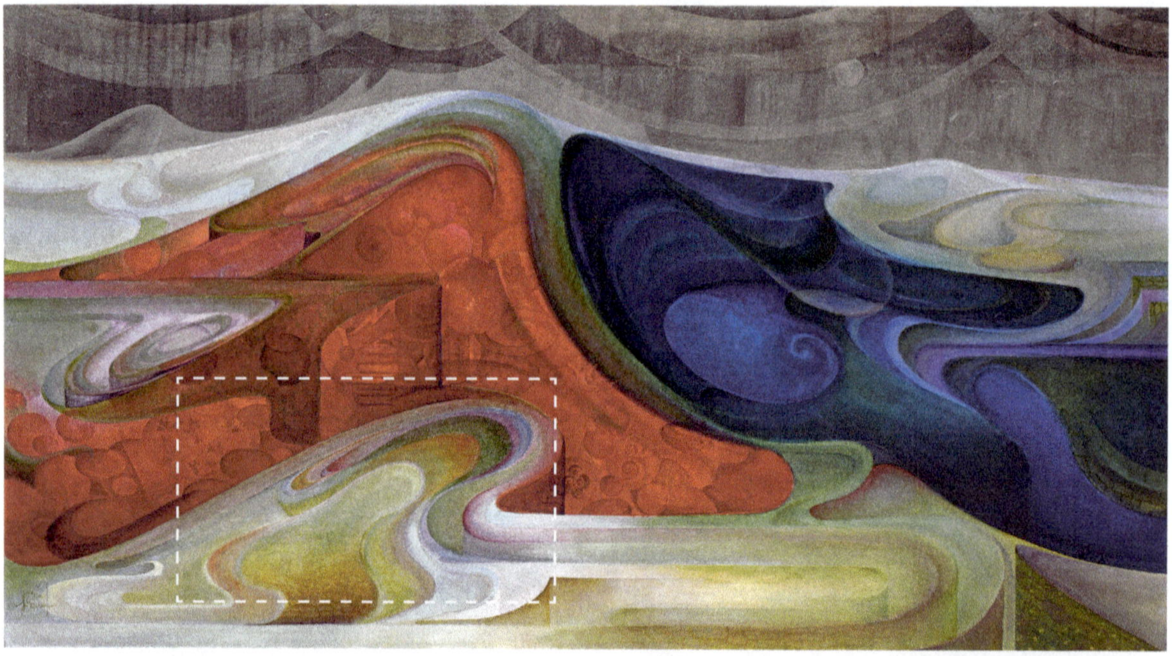

Fig. 8.44. Susanne Schuenke, *Life Forces*, 1996-98. Oil and palladium leaf on canvas, 30 x 55 in (75 x 138 cm). Collection of the artist. White overlay refers to the area shown in Figs. 8.45 and 8.46 as close-up views.

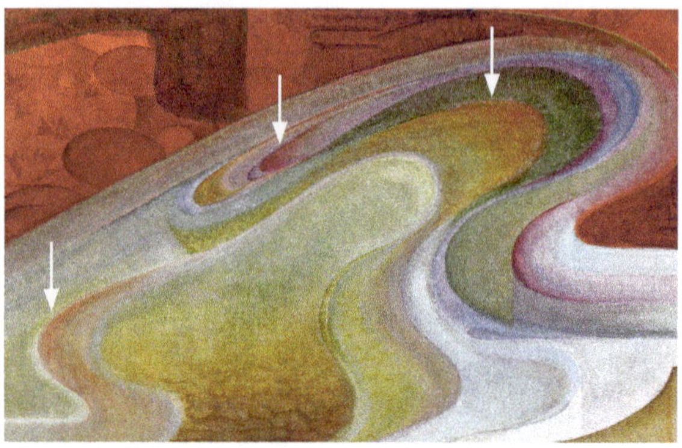

Fig. 8.45. Detail from Fig.8.44. Arrows point to the traces of burnt orange.

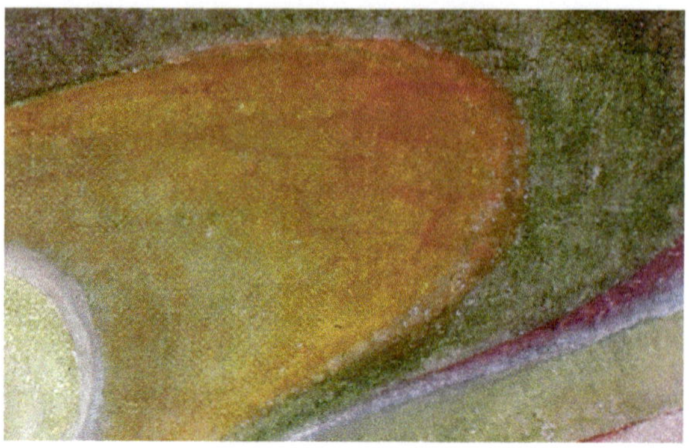

Fig. 8.46. Detail from Fig. 8.45. Burnt orange lines depicting hexagonal cell structures.

71 This color scheme is the opposite of traditional perceptions.

72 This is not only Susanne's individual attitude but also dominant social and cultural tendencies expressed often in art and literature of the past.

On the one hand, the extreme reduction in size of the orange lines could be markers of the low level Susanne gives to the matter of sexuality and reproduction in her hierarchy of values. On the other hand, their manifestation in visual metaphors, expressing the appropriate meaning in her painting, gives proof that they are powerful unconscious forces. The unconscious symbolism of burnt orange as a matrix for sexuality was gradually formed in Susanne's mind through significant emotional experiences, which we recognize in the discussed peculiarities of the painting. This understanding has brought us closer to the roots of her attitude to the color of burnt orange. Our comprehension was made possible by synthesizing and evaluating the nexus of Susanne's associations, memories, and imagery. In hindsight, it might be cogent that the artist applied the unconscious symbolism of burnt orange, representing sexuality and reproduction, also to the color of the organic hexagonal cell structures in *Life Forces*. These cells are with a membrane but lacking mitochondria and a nucleus; therefore, they could be considered as prokaryote. Susanne had this knowledge from high school, where she received extensive teaching in biology due to her keen interest in evolution and the origin of life. We assume that the artist painted the mentioned cell structure, unconsciously referring to simple organisms, which could be associated with primordial feelings. Therefore, the cell structures, outlined in burnt orange, could be considered as forerunners to the comparable appearance of the same hue in Pale Moonlight's scales. Through our analysis, we have recognized that both share an analogous metaphoric meaning in reference to the instinctual forces in the painter's developing iconography.

Burnt orange was assigned in *Golden Nectar* and *Tree Flame* (the latter one having been analyzed already at the end of subchapter 8.2.6), which were designed a year after the completion of *Give Me Wings!*. In both works, we pay particular attention to the artist's personal experience in light of the previous perceptions of orange glimpses in connection with different aspects of sexuality that were transmuted in the context of these paintings.

With the design of *Golden Nectar*, (2005) (Fig. 8.47), the artist followed a friend's suggestion to visualize her understanding of a positive sexual experience. As a consequence, it is a very private work for Susanne because she portrayed her intimate sensations and feelings, which she connected with a fantasy[73] she had frequently in her younger years. In a clandestine way, using intentionally metaphorical expressions, the artist hides the topic of sexuality

73 In a fantasy that Susanne had since her childhood (at the age between five and six) for many years, a woman (we shall call her C) was confined and forced to provide sexual comfort to a powerful man (B), who expected total obedience to his sexual whim from C. There was another man (A), who was in service of B and whose task was to "prepare" the woman sexually for B, which he accomplished by stimulating her breasts with his fingers. After the woman was aroused, B had a brief intercourse with her. In this arrangement, the woman's will and desire were completely ignored, and she was imagined as a helpless victim who was the object of A's manipulation, which she had no power to resist. After B was satisfied, C's role was finished and, like a discarded object, she would be sent back to her confined quarters. In this process, there was no cruelty from A or B and no physical pain for C—only the feeling of powerlessness toward the men who had all the power over her. The powerful B was a thoroughly unattractive man, who had no facial features, spoke no words, and did not make any gestures. In contrast, the facilitator A had some features: black hair, longer than average length; tall and dressed in dark clothes. A had no resemblance or association with anyone Susanne had known or read about, and in spite of his notable individual characteristics, she had great hesitation to consider him as attractive. Usually this fantasy climaxed with an act of masturbation, which gave her a moderate feeling of satisfaction. While fantasizing the scene of the breast stimulation by A, Susanne's fingers were on her breasts simulating the action of A. Being asked by the analyst who A could be, Susanne came up with the association that "this imagined person might be myself as a male identification." Assuming B to be a representation of her father, the analyst asked Susanne if the woman C was actually Susanne. Although she rejected the full identification with the fantasized woman, she admitted the possibility that she was impersonating the sexually enslaved C. We assume that the three participants in her fantasy were assigned their letters by Susanne's unconscious in accordance with their hierarchical importance. A was assigned the role of the facilitator that was necessitated by Susanne's moral integrity which prohibited her to offer herself to B on her own volition. Thus she had to be compelled to engage in sexual acts by someone else (the facilitator A)—who could be Susanne's alter ego in male disguise that somehow provided her with the excuse to absolve her from the damning judgment of the high-minded superego. B presumably represented her father as a reflection of her existing incestuous tendencies, while C was given a demeaned, passive status, who ostensibly participated in the sexual activity as the result of force and coercion by the domineering male participants. In fabricating such a role-playing fantasy, Susanne cast C as an innocent victim, forced to comply with the sexual desire of A and B. In this way, she dismissed any personal culpability for self-indulgence in the imagined fulfillment of her unacceptable desires. Interestingly, when we came to analyze the watercolor, *Mass Destruction*, (1984) (later re-named *Ten O'Clock News*; Fig. 8.50), the artist recognized, in the supine position of a victim on top of the pile of corpses (lower left of the design), the

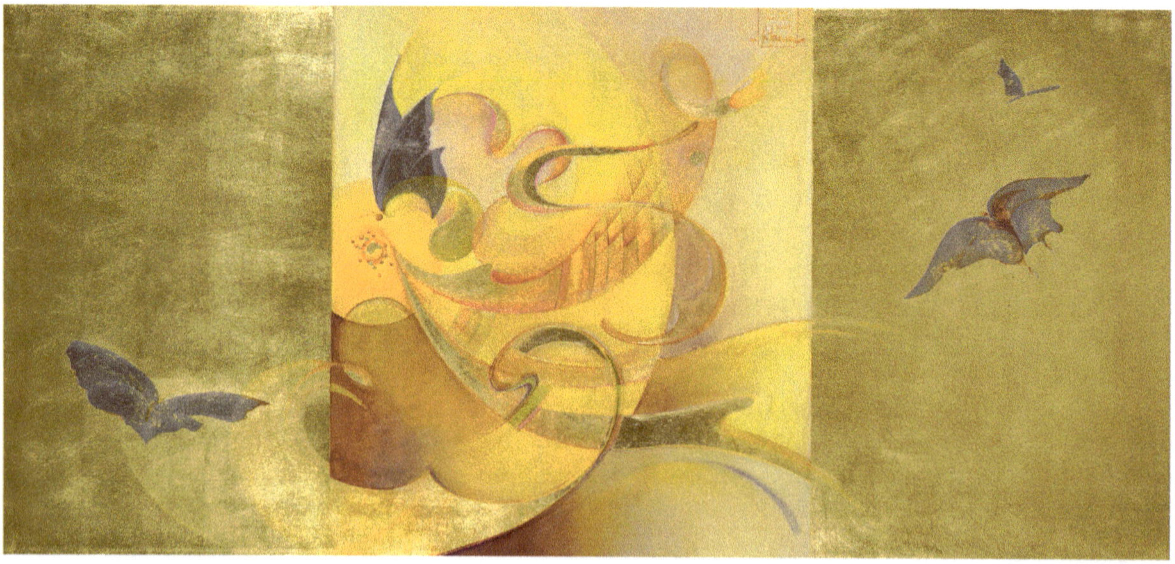

Fig. 8.47. Susanne Schuenke, *Golden Nectar*, 2005. Oil, gold and palladium leaf on canvas, 27 x 58 in (68 x 148 cm). Private collection, Florida

behind the painting's ambiguous title. Illustrating the subject, Susanne creates in abstract forms the design of a pair of golden curtains that are drawn aside to partially reveal a hidden secret. The scene discloses a partial view of an open yellow blossom rendered as a simple circular shape that is consciously chosen to camouflage the depiction of the breast, which is for the artist the most sensitive erotic area of her body. A rich repertoire of curvatures streams from the circle's central point like a whimsical dancing plume of smoke from a cigarette. By this design, Susanne aimed to indicate the irresistible scent of the blossom that is metaphorically equivalent to the highly pleasant sensation that would course through her body when caressing the nipple. Three silver butterflies are circling in the air, while the fourth sits and feeds from the nectar globules that surround the nipple-like, innermost circle. It can be observed that there is a certain resemblance between the wings of this fourth butterfly with the wings of the butterfly True Blue in *Give Me Wings!*, which is the unconscious representation of Susanne's father.

The blossom and the nectar spheres are the intentional, figurative analogs (replacements) for the breast, the hypersensitive nipple, and its surrounding circular area, areola, respectively.[74] A similar metaphoric comparison can be made between "weightless butterflies" and a caressing touch of fondling fingers.[75] The abstract, vapor-like curves and loops in the scene symbolize the realization of the artist's desires for pleasurable sensation. In the margins of those curvatures, several orange glimpses appear (Fig. 8.48 (a)), and one specific trace has a thin, very elongated clavate formation in burnt orange (Fig. 8.48 (a and b)) which is similar to the scale in Pale Moonlight (Fig. 8.49).

What is the message behind this shape in burnt orange which was placed automatically into the sea of yellow and gold in the image of *Golden Nectar*?

Intentionally, she chose yellow as a distracting color (as non-natural for the human skin) for camouflage of the breast. The artist applied a darker hue to the dominant coloration because, with color, she wanted to accentuate certain curvatures to visualize sensual experiences. She thought she

---

posture of C in her fantasy.

74 We should mention that flowers and blossoms could represent female genitalia (Sigmund Freud, *A General Introduction to Psychology* (1920), Part Two: The Dream X. Symbolism in the Dream). One can speculate that the wide open blossom in *Golden Nectar* expresses such appropriate unconscious symbolism. However there is the fact that Susanne's breast sensitivity far outweighs that of vaginal and/or clitoral sensitivity. For her, while caressing of the breast can deliver pleasurable experience, the genital area has been always neutral and any stimulation of it triggers a panic or fear reaction. We assume that the artist's sensual pleasure connected with breast, which was visually expressed in the painting, is a reflection of her fixation on non-genital stages of sexual development (autoerotism).

75 Susanne remembers well the experience of wonder when a butterfly landed on her arm and walked on her skin without exerting any sensation of weight.

was following the suggested topic of the painting by this action. However, we recognized that her unconscious influenced her choice by letting burnt orange flow into the darker shades. "Darker" in this context is equivalent of the strength of sexual feelings. We assume that she intuitively made this specific color choice under the influence of the unconscious symbolism of the color burnt orange already ingrained in her mind. Through the analysis of Pale Moonlight, this specific hue of orange was recognized as an unconscious signifier for sexuality. This color's reappearance in *Golden Nectar*—a work with an intentional sensual topic, concealed in visual metaphors—confirms our assumption. The elongated shape in burnt orange mentioned above brought to the surface, like the tip of an iceberg, the conglomerate of repressed sexual and aggressive tendencies. In the analysis of the painting *Tree Flame* (see subchapter 8.2.6), we came to the same assumption according to the significant personal circumstances which existed at the time, and were reflected in the visual image.

The color burnt orange could also be a signifier of the aggressive drive and, as such, surfaces in her art to convey the horrific suffering caused by violence and inhumanity. A prime example is the painting *Terminator* (Fig. 4.16), created in 1985, nearly 20 years before *Give Me Wings!,* which was briefly mentioned in chapter 4 in connection with Agent Orange. The colors orange and burnt orange run through the design of this painting denoting menace and aggression.

The artist clarifies the painting as follows. The soldier's helmet is shaped like the dome of a nuclear power station. His right shoulder is transformed into a retort, from which toxic chemicals drip, poisoning the air. Next to it, triggered by an electronic command, is a nuclear explosion with its mushroom cloud. The soldier stares threateningly at the viewer with a pair of inhuman orange eyes. His thumb is ready to press the button (also featuring traces of burnt orange) to launch further attacks from his arsenal. Two extremely sharp and imposing triangles, reminiscent of the jaws of a caliper in dark violet, rise from the bottom edge of the painting. They pierce the helmet and extend high into the sky. With this instrument, the artist meant to represent merciless modern weaponry capable of bringing about the utter destruction of civilization. *Terminator* offers an apt example of the artist's intentional use of orange and some other colors (for example emerald green)[76] that she considers to possess a negative implication with which she underscores despicable content.

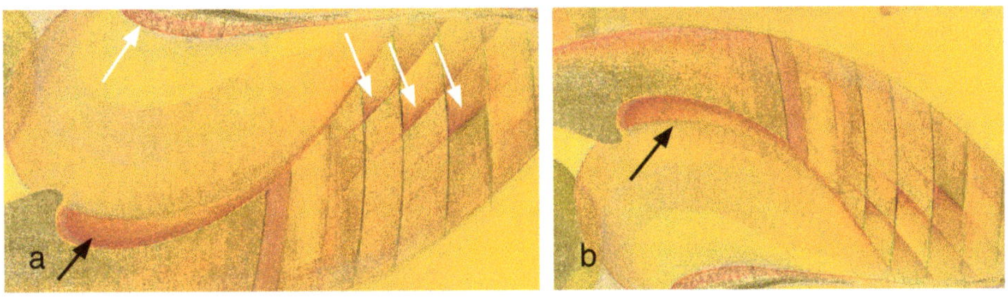

Fig. 8.48.
a: Detail from 8.47. Arrows point to burnt orange.
Black arrow points to a specific formation in burnt orange.
b: The same formation shown flipped horizontally and upside down for comparison.

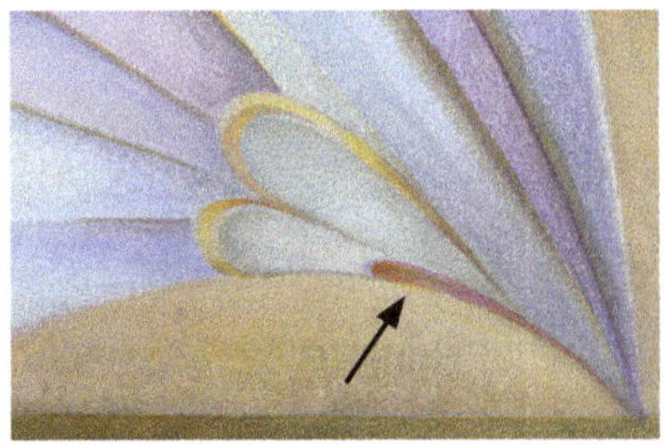

Fig. 8.49.
The rudimentary scale from Pale Moonlight (detail from Fig. 8.15). Arrow points to the area to be compared.

---

76 Susanne associates the tone Phthalo Green (Emerald Green) with decadence, degeneration, decline, and even evil. Her first reaction to this color was the thought of "poison," which led her to the memory of the parents' warning from her childhood to never let the toxic bluish-green areas of oxidized copper or silver vessels touch the mouth. Similarly, "Schweinfurter Grün" (German for Paris Green or verdigris) was one of her father's praised hues among his oil paints, but its production was abandoned a decade or more ago due to its high toxicity (due to copper acetoarsenite). Consequently, Susanne's mind designated poison or toxin as a metaphoric signifier to represent certain events or trends that are in her mind decadent and destructive for humanity's future. The "poisonous" phthalo green appears in *Terminator,* coloring the killer's face, eyes, and the skin of his hand (seen through the knuckle holes of his glove). His thumb, with traces of the same green, presses down on the button that triggers the extermination machinery, the wheels of which are also in shades of phthalo green. The original German title, written on this painting, is "*Walzwerk*" (English: rolling mill)—reflecting a conceptual metaphor of the organized and automated system of merciless mass destruction. The unconscious source for choosing this title, *Das Walzwerk,* probably came from her childhood favorite book, *Born in Fire,* where the topic (rolling mill) was covered as an important part of manufacturing steel products from hot ingots.

This aspect of symbolic coloration receives another confirmation through a second, similar painting, *Mass Destruction*, (1984), later renamed *Ten O'Clock News* (Fig. 8.50). In this watercolor, the artist depicted a warrior in a harlequin costume with an ammunition belt studded with test tubes as an allusion to various chemical weapons. He pours the fatal content of one tube over a heap of victims. The soldier's feet are made of wheels that roll on a track. Between the warrior's spread legs, a creepy octopus callously films the scene of the carnage. The octopus, painted in Susanne's highly disliked phthalo green, operates a typical newsreel camera from the 1960s. With this imagery, she metaphorically criticizes the obscene sensationalism of the mass media in covering the tragedy of war and spotlights its mercantile side, in which profits are derived from bloodshed and destruction. This perception made her change the initial title. The tripartite background illustrates a peaceful country life in fertile green on the right, the darkened, polluted cityscape in the center, and, finally, civilization's apocalypse on the left. In the latter part, the coloration ranges from pale yellow to dark orange, as everything alive is burnt up by the chemical and biological weapons of mass destruction. This coloration illuminates the doomsday scene and engulfs the topmost corpse.

8.3.3 Red Content

The artist perceives each of the butterflies in *Give Me Wings!* as having an "individual color character."[77] Colors are, for Susanne, often the carriers of beauty, but they are also suffused with meanings, some negative, and some positive. For the artist, Pale Moonlight is a "light blue butterfly." Nevertheless, in the lower part of one of the blue pleats in her hind wing, close to the focal point, the color shows a strong reddish content with a tendency to shift to violet (Fig. 8.31 (a)). Comparable color variants, although lighter, are found at the top two scales in the third scale layer located in the hind wing (Fig. 8.31(b)). Another reddish hue appears in the middle of the rudimentary scale, this time changing the coloration from burnt orange to red (Fig. 8.31 (c and d, respectively)). This specific, obscure appearance of red has a more far-reaching interpretation than a cursory impression might reveal.

The previous discussion of the burnt orange hue has pointed out a correlation, for Susanne, between this color and its symbolic, unconscious meaning, which connects with sexuality and aggression. The color burnt orange contains a predominant proportion of red in its hue. Could this have some consequences for the symbolic meaning of burnt orange in correlation with the symbolism of red?

Red, especially crimson, has been the artist's favorite color for as long as she can remember. In search of significant items or circumstances in her childhood connected with red, we find several clues in her home environment. The artist still holds dear in memory her favorite toy, a "railway conductor kit," equipped with all-red articles including a cap, a purse with a shoulder strap, a whistle, and a signaling paddle.

Susanne always chose red over blue. When her older sister and she received nearly identical gifts, the colors of red and blue being the only distinguishing differences, she would immediately claim the red one for herself without any compromise. The color red and its variations were quite common in the house. In the living room, one of the large armchairs was upholstered in deep red. The curtains in the sitting room had the same coloration. Her father painted some decorative designs on shutters, and the garage door had red triangles. The carpet on the stairs running up to the second floor, where the children often played, was crimson. Outside, a large hawthorn was covered with red-and-white blossoms in springtime. It served the tomboy Susanne as the perfect stage for all kinds of climbing games and flights of her childish fantasies. Also, the house, where the family lived until Susanne was 13, had a small garden in the back with trees, numerous shrubs, and a climbing rose that did not bloom for many years. How excited the family was when the deep red rose finally began to bloom. After that, the flowers blossomed every season. Until Susanne was nearly age ten, her father drove a fire-engine red Porsche. She loved that car very

77 Susanne uses the expression "individual color character" as corresponding to the particular traits of a person. The coloration can stand for various characteristics of individual distinct behavior, reflecting its specific inner meaning. The artist explains that for her colors are the carriers of emotions to complement thoughts and perceptions. They allow her to complete her evaluation of each butterfly, which she considers to have already been accomplished to a great extent through the use of the lines, shapes, and composition.

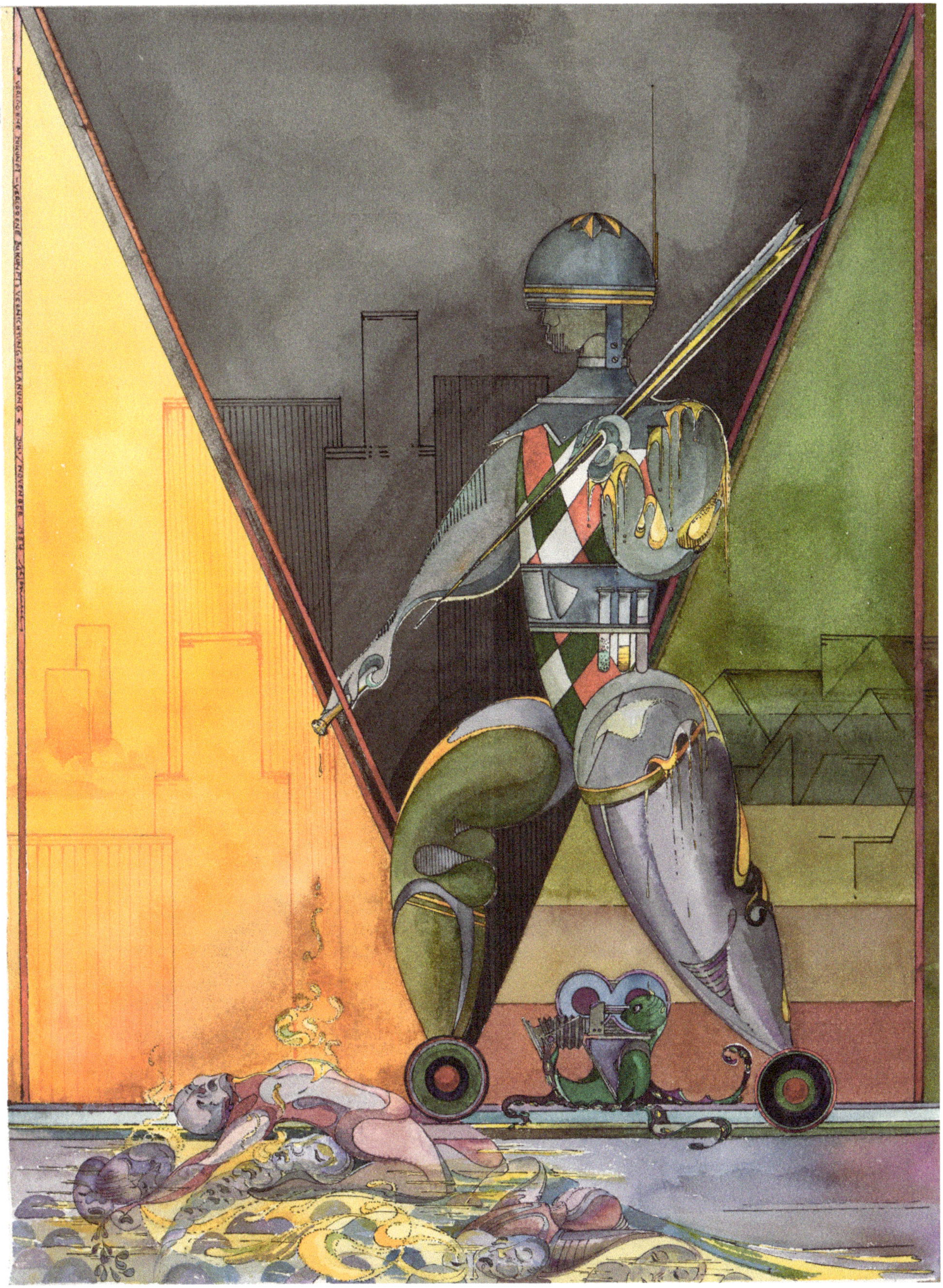

Fig. 8.50. Susanne Schuenke, *Ten O'Clock News* (*Mass Destruction*), 1984. Watercolor, 19 x 14¼ in (36 x 48 cm). Collection of the artist.

much and still fondly holds today the memories of the leather seats' scent and the parents' cigarette smoke wafting through the car. Red as a color for clothes was a different matter, and for the longest time, it was discouraged in her family, because the parents considered it too "loud" and inappropriate for a respectable outfit. Even today, this parental judgment dwells in Susanne who, in spite of all her love for red, has only a few really red clothing items. She still restricts this hue in her present living environment, with the exception of her collection of glass marble balls.

Art always had an important role in the household. Pictures covering the walls became a steady visual stimulus to the child's observing mind. Among them, there were some specific works, which had a significant influence on her. When Susanne was eight years old, her father started to paint in oil again after a long hiatus. His paintings were permanently on display in the house, some of which had prominent details in red whose significance will be discussed below. The plentifulness of red might have incited her to adopt this color as a part of the creation of her unconscious symbolism. The above fond memories of her childhood emotions, fantasies, and imaginations may give a glimpse of the many and diverse influences which contributed to her creativity.

Susanne's favorite color crimson is represented in her palette as "madder lake." Besides other references, she also strongly associates this hue with "a beautiful drop of blood on a fingertip—a fascinating shiny crimson pearl." Since her late 20s, her father's diabetes required constant blood checks, which included a drop from his finger being transferred to a special test strip. This image fascinated her, but before her father injected insulin, she always left the room hastily to avoid the anticipated horror.

Over the decades, many different aspects and circumstances have reinforced Susanne's fascination with the color red, and they contribute to her multifaceted, symbolic personal meaning for this hue. Besides her upbringing, she has continued to acquire additional knowledge about this color. For example, in her studies, she has accumulated more details about human perception of the color red, which individuals and groups in different historical periods, societies, and physical environments have associated with specific meanings. They established their own unique cultural iconography of red.[78]

8.3.4. Artist's Symbolism of Red—Genesis, Development, and Camouflage

We found that the paintings collected and displayed by her parents in her family home held important clues to discovering the hidden symbolic meaning that was built up in her unconscious concerning the color red. To stay in the chronological order of Susanne's exposure to these artworks, the first would be the pair of colored etchings from the parent's bedroom, which we mentioned previously. In both of these prints, the salmon-red[79] jackets belonging to the male lovers give the dominant color accents in an environment of a secret adulterous affair. (See subchapter 8.3.2.)

Next, there is an impressive oil painting, around 2 x 2 feet in size by Roberto Domingo (introduced in chapter 6) that hung in the family's living room throughout Susanne's childhood. It shows a bullfighting scene with a partial view into the arena (Fig. 6.10). In the foreground, a charging bull is surrounded by a matador, in a yellow-gold outfit with a black hat and red cape, and a torero in a silver-lavender outfit with a violet cape, who are teasing the beast. Infuriated by the lances in his back which cause blood to run over his black skin, the bull expresses its highly charged rage. The main light of the scene illumines the middle distance, where one of the assistants climbs over the red wall to escape from the danger. Left of this

78 The symbolism of the color red for humans could be traced to the raw, primal, and universal experiences, representing blood as the source of life. Another important context concerning the symbolic meaning of the color red is determined by the biological processes of the female body, in which menstruation, first intercourse, and birthing are unavoidably accompanied with limited hemorrhage. With this bodily connection, red is bound with the topics of sexuality and reproduction. Also, on cultural and social levels, numerous conventions, customs, objects, verbal and visual expressions call for red as the preferred symbolic color for sexuality. For example, flowers—especially roses—and other Valentine's Day gifts are all in this hue, and they are considered popular symbols to express the feeling of love, which find their metaphoric pinnacle in the form of the red heart. At the other end of the scale of social evaluation, specific red lights can indicate a sexually charged environment, a setting that coined the term red-light district as the synonym for the part of town frequented by prostitutes.

79 See footnote 64 in this chapter for more details.

tableau, two other assistants in red jackets try to lead away a wounded white horse, now riderless. This panoramic scene of cruelty, especially the sight of the stricken horse, causes pain, leading to Susanne's insurmountable aversion to ever focusing her eyes on the painting again. To this day, she abhors even the thought of this painting. This perception of the bullfight painting has not abated, and it has been a relentlessly stressful task for her to try to analyze her peculiar sensitivity to the image of the injured horse. We try to determine when Susanne's disgust for this painting began to emerge. She just could not remember from what time onward the painting was hung on the wall. For her, it had "always" been there. However, she recalled writing the letters of her name incorrectly while seated at a small table in front of the bullfighting painting without it distracting her. Thus the time must have been before she was six years and four months old.[80] Susanne became very sensitive to this painting later, before age nine, presumably some time after the birth of her younger sister and a specific dream (see below), when she began to pay attention to the depiction of the wounded horse which triggered her fearful thoughts.

Looking at the injured horse, with its flesh hanging down and blood gushing out, perhaps mortally wounded, Susanne curls in pain and struggles over the sight of the pierced "belly" that haunts her mind. She forces herself to talk about it and mentions an association, for the first time, of a link between spilled blood and the navel. This tie-in has brought to her a recollection of an unforgettable dream that Susanne had, presumably, between the ages of seven and nine.

In the dream, Susanne lies on her belly on a sled while sliding downhill in the snow, but soon her navel is caught by a nail, which pulls the navel and umbilical cord out of her belly. These details of the dream could be interpreted as the possible unconscious symbolic visualization of the fear of intercourse (nail)[81] and pregnancy (umbilical cord). The dream has been so horrible that Susanne has confided it to someone only twice in her life, and in spite of the passage of time, as she was writing it down for this study, she was promptly engulfed by feelings of heightened anxiety and fear that spurred her to try to protect her belly, tongue, and eyes, and made her wish "to run away into the darkness, into security, to crawl into Mami's lap."[82]

She has always thought that her fear of the navel (omphalophobia) began with this dream. Susanne's statement could find confirmation from a linguistic perspective. Through our analysis, she noticed that three German words, *Nabel* (navel), *Nagel* (nail), and *Nadel* (needle, as in a syringe) are homophonic. They all trigger a panic reaction in her.

We return to the bullfight painting, and Susanne's initial impression of the image formed in her young mind many decades ago. The peculiarities of the painting's subject let us construct a possible scenario for the formation of her idiosyncratic aversion to the content of this artwork, due to her omphalophobia. During the analysis, she was urged to take a closer look at the artwork, which she had persistently avoided doing for more than 40 years. She was highly astonished to discover the following: The horse's blood is streaming from a spot between its front legs (Fig. 8.51). For all those years, Susanne had mistakenly believed that the location of the gaping wound was in the middle of the horse's belly. Checking this specific area, we found a dark triangular shape, a Spanish-style stirrup with an extended toe cover. Overlooking this item could have been caused by the influence of some latent affect that had upset her sensitive mind and led to an incorrect perception.

---

80 The time references that we suggest in this subchapter are validated from known dates: Susanne's birthday in December 1955, and she entered school in April 1962 (age 6 years 4 months). Furthermore, the birth of her younger sister in March 1964 (Susanne is age 8 years and 3 months), and her mother's time of pregnancy until the birth (Susanne is age 7 ½ years onward). Susanne remembers rendering her name with "reversed letter S," before she entered school. Once in school, she learned quickly the proper script, and from then on wrote the "S" correctly. These details help us to reconstruct a plausible time frame. Consequently, her memory of the "wrong letter" must fall in the time before entering school.

81 During one of the editing sessions in which Susanne was tasked to type the manuscript, the word "intercourse" (before the word "nail" in parenthesis) disappeared from the typed text. Upon rereading the manuscript, the omission was discovered, and the relevant word was restored. Undoubtedly, words do get accidentally lost routinely in retyping of manuscripts. However, this particular mistake calls for special attention because of the "explosive" nature of the combination of the two words (intercourse and nail) in Susanne's mind. We consider it a Freudian slip, revealing Susanne's resistance to this interpretation, based on the unconscious sexual symbolism and her desire to escape from its implication.

82 This was quoted directly from Susanne's words which illustrate her regression to an infantile state in this panic-riddled situation.

From a psychoanalytic perspective, it could be cogent that Susanne's misperception displaced the location of the horse's wound to the animal's mid-belly, an area analogous to the position of the human navel. Thus, she failed to see the actual location of the horse's injury; Susanne is hyper-reaction strongly suggests that she unconsciously identified herself with the white horse as a victim. In accordance with the above information and Susanne's perception of her father, it is conceivable that the image of the bull might unconsciously have merged in Susanne's mind with her father. If so, the root cause of her omphalophobia can be traced to the combination of repressed libidinal and aggressive wishes, fantasies, and fears of their fulfillment which were buried in the depth of Susanne's unconscious from early childhood and are continuing to resonate. Confirmation of this assumption could be her incestuous desires, realized in her fantasy (see footnote 73), or her expectation of being injured as expressed in the dream of a damaged navel. The foregoing assumptions are in agreement with the Freudian approach as developed by Melanie Klein in her psychoanalytic research of young children.[83]

Susanne's strong dislike of Domingo's painting can be due to her abhorrence of the sight of cruelty in line with her own unconscious tendencies. Even now, seeing this scene causes her unabated distress. Her extremely idiosyncratic reaction to the picture we understand as a reflection of her own destructive complexes. Her expectations of threatening content find their symbolic equivalents in the danger-filled scenario reinforced by red attractors (blood, cape, arena wall) signifying aggression. Susanne's vulnerability lets us assume the mechanism of projection in her perception of the painting by the Spanish artist. It could be a reflection of unconscious symbolism, personal and universal.

During the discussion of the above episodes, signs of denial and self-protection were obvious in Susanne's body language, sometimes accompanied by a slight counterclockwise rotation of her head. Somehow she became self-aware of this peculiar reflexive movement and tried to reverse its direction to a clockwise motion. Asked why she moved her head in different directions, she said that she did it automatically to soothe her mind when she sensed that "she was under stress" while being confronted especially with scenes of violence and cruelty. This reflexive head movement in opposite directions might be considered as a defensive reaction to the analysis of the emotionally significant experience.

As was shown before, she has a hypersensitive reaction to any exposure of the navel, including any topic or image pertaining to this anatomical feature, and she assiduously avoids any such phobia-inducing situation. Her idiosyncratic perception of Domingo's painting is an appropriate example for this. At this point, we will recapitulate some facts which can support our hypothesis regarding the origin and development of her omphalophobia

First, we consider her dream of the injury to her navel, which was mentioned briefly above. Second, there is her distinctive reaction to the bandage placed on her infant sister's belly (enforcing the impression of a "wound"; see chapter 7). Third, we pay attention to a specific fantasy that occurred during a discussion regarding Fanning Everything, when the artist visualized a marble placed in the navel and imagined that the navel was a cavity somehow connected to the womb (see at the end of subchapter 7.3.3). On this matter, we may recall that Susanne, at the age of seven and a half, asked her pregnant mother how the baby got in the belly and was told, "when two people sleep together in one bed" (see end of subchapter 7.3.3). For young Susanne, that must have been a provocative statement, as she often slept with her parents in their bed until the age of eight. The answer could have generated a regressive reactivation of the possible early childhood incestuous fantasy even of being impregnated through the navel (displacement). The fear of such a possibility might have translated into her dream, in which her navel was torn and the umbilical cord forcefully pulled out of the wound.

We wondered if Susanne was exposed to a story of caesarean section early in her youth which could have added fuel to her anxiety, since in a C-section operation the abdomen is indeed cut open to bring the baby out. Asked about this hypothesis, Susanne unexpectedly had the spontaneous association with the Empress of Persia, Farah Pahlavi, who finally had given birth to a long-awaited crown prince. She recalled that her parents talked about this event, which was reported as a sensation

83 Klein 1975.

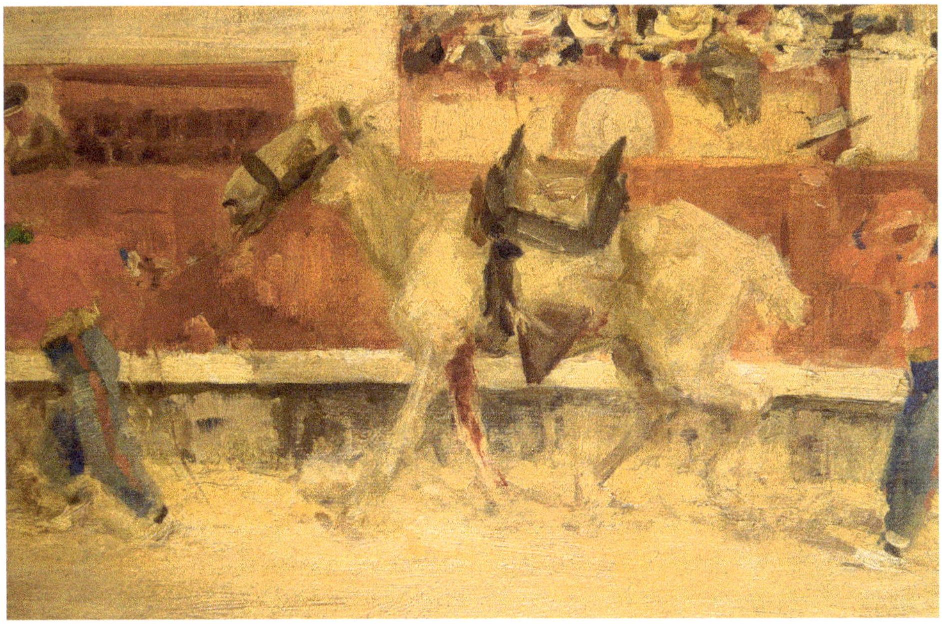

Fig. 8.51.
Detail from Fig. 6.10:
The wounded horse
from Domingo's
bullfight scene.

in the newspapers. According to these stories, the empress had delivered her son by C-section. However, checking historical records, we found no confirmation of this specific kind of birth for the prince. However, while it is important that Susanne knew about the possibility of babies being born through a surgical opening of the abdomen, she wrongly connected this with the birth of the crown prince that took place on October 31, 1960, when she was one month shy of her fifth birthday. Susanne's inaccurate recollection must have mixed and merged this information with some other remarks about C-section birth, reflecting her concern in context with her father complex, with appropriate incestuous and reproductive tendencies.[84]

Further seeking the roots of the artist's color iconography as it relates to red, we return to her father's previously mentioned paintings, *Bar Scene* and *The Street.* Those artworks were created around the time Susanne was eight years old. They apparently significantly influenced her by their sexually charged topics. The two paintings were permanently displayed on the wall of the family home, each of which depicts a woman dressed in crimson red in a strongly exhibitionistic posture surrounded by male clients who are expressing their lust (Figs. 8.36 and 8.38). The attractiveness of the "objects of desire" is enhanced by their accessories, such as lingerie, a skirt, and a rose, which are painted in eye-catching bright red. The influence of her father's painting can be observed in Susanne's unconscious iconographic use of the color red as the symbol of sexuality. Examples for this can be found in the red skirts which were depicted in her works *Choice of Entrée*, (1993) (Fig. 5.21) and *Room Full of Guests*, (2012) (Fig. 8.52).

We have already pointed out that red is associated with sexuality in both Eastern and Western cultures, either implicitly or explicitly. Her father's use of this color in his paintings is a good example of its association with a sexually charged situation. Susanne, however, has great difficulty accepting that her favorite color can be, and has been, used as a visual metaphor for a sexual topic she consciously wants to avoid.[85]

Her father's paintings and his comments about them indicate that he regarded the striving for

84 A C-section is *Kaiserschnitt* in German (literally: Emperor's cut) and the title of the Empress of Persia, Farah Pahlavi is *Kaiserin von Persien, Farah Pahlavi* in German. The connection *Kaiserschnitt* and *Kaiserin* is plausible.

85 For example, this specific modus operandi can be observed in *A Room Full of Guests* (Figs. 8.52 and 8.53). On the left side of the canvas, a leading social queen, dressed quite seductively, offers a surprisingly gray "apple of knowledge," which would normally be rendered in red. In the Western tradition, the red apple, particularly when it is held in a woman's hand, usually signifies sexual temptation; However this allusion has already been sufficiently expressed in the socialite's revealing clothing, and Susanne intentionally avoids employing this overused symbolic cliché. With the apple in lifeless gray, the artist refers to the lack of moral and spiritual foundations that underlie the socialite's lifestyle and its artificial values, which she seems to be attempting to promote to her naive female admirer, who is captivated by the diva's flashy,

sexual fulfillment as one of the fundamental needs of human existence (see footnote 64). However, this view was contrary to his indoctrination of the daughters on the subject of sexuality as an animalistic drive.

Susanne consciously blocks her feelings and thoughts pertaining to the topic of sexuality, and she does not involve herself on the subject matter willingly in her speech, action, or paintings. Regardless of her conscious dislike, the subject of sexuality reveals itself unconsciously in her paintings through symbolic manifestations. During our analysis, we discovered that the burnt orange color symbolizes sexuality and destructive tendencies in Susanne's iconography. At the beginning of our research, Susanne insisted her symbolic meaning of burnt orange was not correlated with red. Moreover, she asserted that her favorite color was antithetical to it, leaving her "pure crimson" free of any adulterating sexual contagion—so she thought. However, factually, burnt orange consists mostly of red.

Pure red is suppressed in the artist's design of *Give Me Wings!,* yet, faint red nuances are still inserted into different colors when they shift their hues toward red, for example, blue changing toward violet, or yellow toward orange. This shift can be a covert presence of red under the veil of other colors. It is tempting to assert that, in Susanne's chromatic iconography, the hues from violet to orange-yellow on a color wheel could be considered as "clandestine red," and, on that basis, the sexual symbolism of red can be applied to all these tints, but that would be an overly broad generalization. In this regard, it might be worthwhile to refer to an anecdotal saying attributed to Freud concerning a question posed by his pupil in regard to a cigar and its symbolic

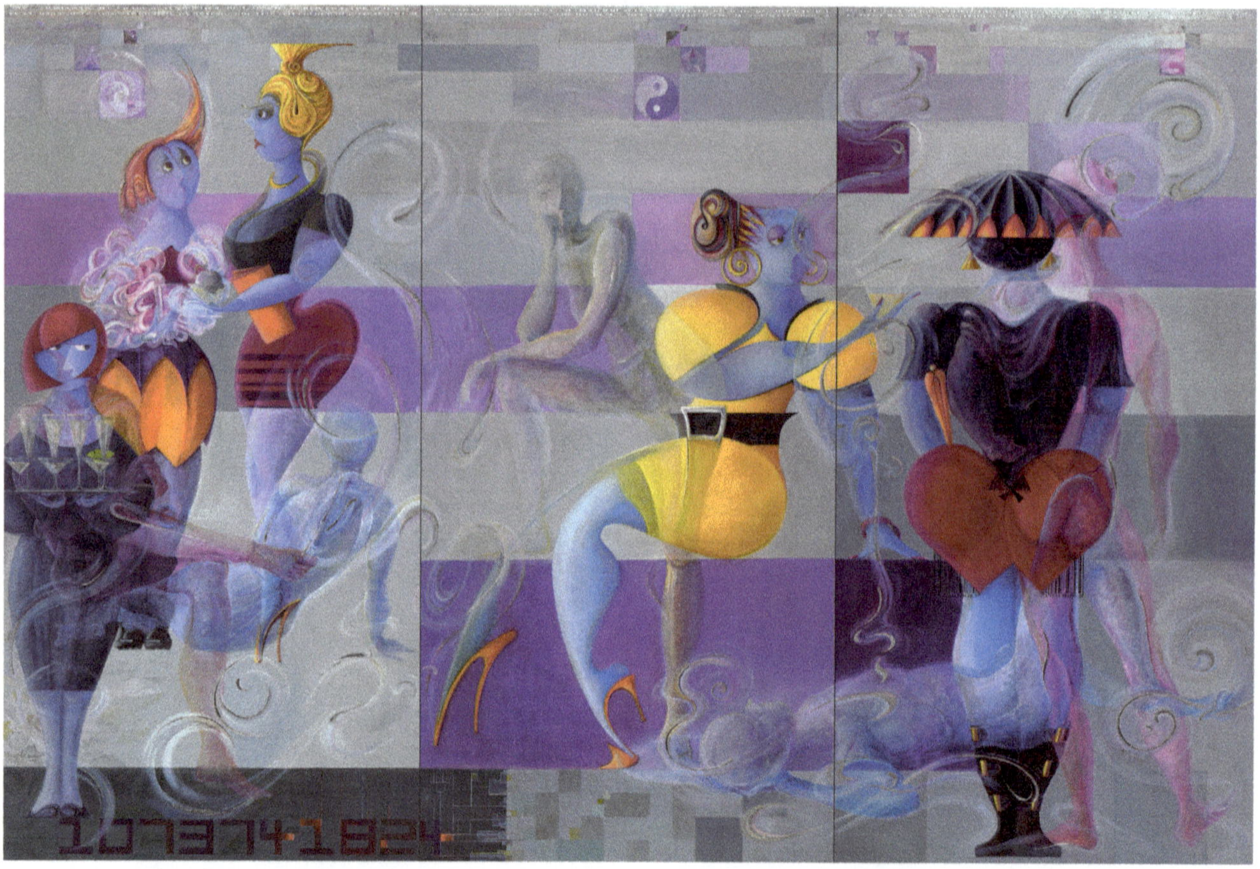

Fig. 8.52. Susanne Schuenke, *A Room Full of Guests*, 2012. Oil and palladium leaf on canvas, 77 x 116 in (195 x 295 cm). Collection of the artist.

glamorous life. The "queen bee" is offering the symbolical gray fruit in a drink of doubtful coloration in a martini glass, by which the artist explicitly and metaphorically indicates the dangerous mélange of "double intoxications" from drinking alcoholic beverages and making erroneous moral choices which could lead to the glorification of false values of life.

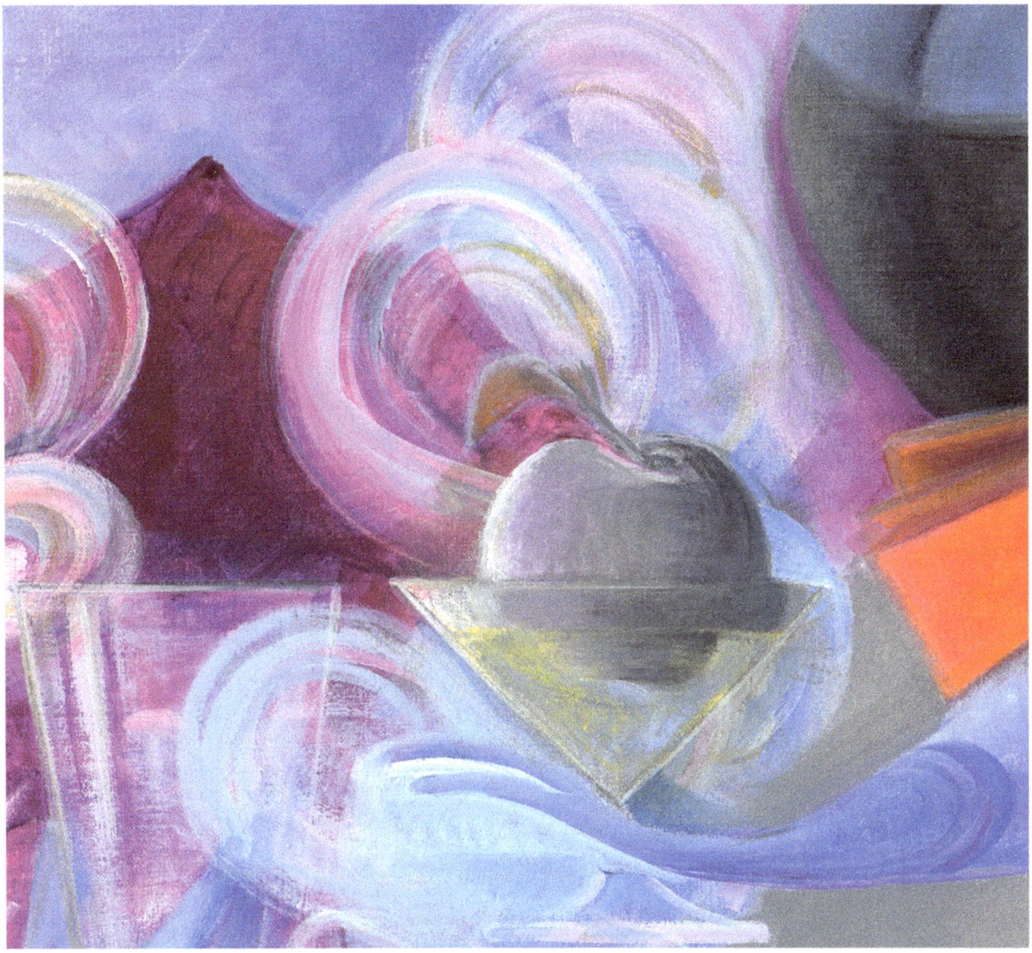

Fig. 8.53. Detail from Fig. 8.52: The apple of knowledge. Note the gray color and the double refraction caused by the glass and liquid.

meaning. Freud, instead of acknowledging the cigar's possible phallic symbolism, is said to have simply remarked, "Sometimes a cigar is just a cigar."

Each case of Susanne's use of red and its variations has to be viewed individually. The hues under consideration are direct neighbors of red on the color wheel and, because of this proximity, there is a possibility that the unconscious could substitute them for each other. With this in mind, we pay particular attention to the usage of different shades of red as a component of other tint.

Moreover, in the context of Pale Moonlight's hind wing coloration, we look at the presence of red as a hue added afterward to light blue (in the pleats and scales), yellow (in the borders of the scales), and burnt orange (in the rudimental scale). The application of thin translucent nuances of red on top of those colors changes them to light violet, orange-yellow, and a reddish area in the middle of the burnt orange scale, respectively. The added red casts a reddish nuance on the original color.

Knowing that red is Susanne's favorite color and that it appears repeatedly in her other paintings, the absence of pure red in *Give Me Wings!* is truly remarkable. Her own explanation, "that it did not fit into the composition" is not sufficient to understand the complexity of the total lack of pure red. Because every butterfly unconsciously represents either particular aspects of Susanne's psyche and/or some of her perception of the parents, leaving out true red could be interpreted as the consequence of her repressed instinctual drives, sexual and destructive, reflecting taboo principles. Confirmation of this, apart from *Give Me Wings!*, can be found, for example, in the images of her divine nude figures which she always painted in nonnatural colors, mostly in blue and green (see Figs. 10.15 and 8.28); she consciously intended to portray these figures as superior to humans, free of instinctual encumbrances. Thus, with skin tones different from those of humans, she avoided any implication of sexuality.

In contrast, when Susanne wants to emphasize sexual allusion, presumably in a negative sense due to her internalized attitude toward sexuality, she purposely uses a strong, muddy red hue. For example, in the painting, *Longing* (Fig. 7.18 and detail in Fig. 8.54), at the bottom of the scene, a nude male demonstratively poses in a sensual posture, emphasized by curvaceous contours. The figure is presented by the artist in a thoroughly muddy red, as if to underscore his carnal nature. This muted red is distinctively different from the bright red base line of the painting, on which this figure is placed.

A further illustration can be given with Susanne's "Legs Series," a set of six paintings, in which she followed the suggestion by a friend to portray the sensual aspect of feminine legs. Five of the six pairs of legs are painted in non-natural colors, mostly purple and violet with strong red content. Moreover, in each painting, the artist has augmented the pair of legs by surrounding them with various pure red objects, such as flowers, circles, rectangles, etc. We discussed one of them, *Allegro*, (2008), which shows the legs in light purplish red surrounded with a bouquet of flowers (chapter 5, p. 81, Fig. 5.22).

From the foregoing discussion, we can see that, in Susanne's art, the color red and its chromatic relatives play a significant role symbolizing the presence of sexual drives which manifest through the images of her paintings.

After analyzing the artist's symbolism of red in the above paintings, we return to the interpretation of nuances of red in Pale Moonlight's hind wing, which was mentioned earlier, indicating that the artist added some red content to the burnt orange hue of the rudimentary scale as well as to the coloration of the light blue scales and pleats (Figs. 8.31 and 8.32). This indirect presence of red is a possible allusion to sexuality through the use of a chromatic metaphor, which is in accord with other metaphors for sexuality expressed unconsciously in various suggestive shapes by the artist.

As we have noted before in connection with the scales, the topic of reproduction was rejected and repressed by Susanne. The same can be said of her application of color. Although she repressed the pure red, it was surreptitiously reintroduced as a violet, purple, orange, or burnt orange. The study lets us presume that the artist consciously and unconsciously used specific hues, in addition to shapes, to signal preference or rejection of instinctual drives.

The analysis of unconscious messages embedded in the symbolism of red in the artist's palette incentivized the researchers to pay further attention to the orange areas in the butterfly Firebird from this new perspective.

In this stage of the analysis, some new clarification can be added, which would have been premature at the time of the writing of chapter 5, which was dedicated to the analysis of Firebird. Naturally, orange incorporates an appreciable amount of red. Therefore, we assume that the symbolism of red could be expressed implicitly in the design of the orange colored Firebird. The avoidance of pure red in the creation of this and all the other butterflies could be considered an act of camouflage, which we have unmasked repeatedly in the analysis of numerous details of their images. Had the artist used pure red in creating this butterfly, it would have appropriately revealed its sexual symbolism. Dressing Firebird in passionate hues of orange, she unconsciously covered up red as a powerful signifier of particular sexual meaning.

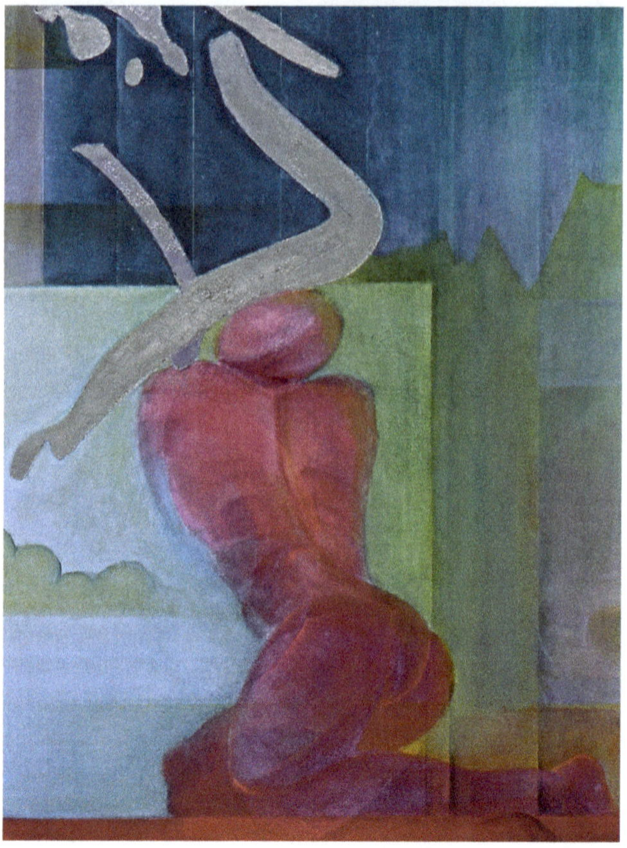

Fig. 8.54. Detail from Fig. 7.18: The red figure from the bottom of *Longing*.

With the name "Firebird," the artist literally and figuratively illustrated the blaze that reflects the burning desires that the young Susanne has harbored since her early childhood.

Susanne was fooling herself when she initially believed that Firebird expressed only the choleric temper tantrums of her father. However, with palpable presence, the glowing orange of Firebird, combined with his specific configurations, radiates unbridled libidinal forces. Also, in Little Why's hind wings there is a small area where the yellow of the inner core turns into an intensive orange, like a glow from a heat source (Fig. 8.55; see white arrows). This orange might well correlate to the hues in Firebird, signifying sexual drives. We additionally note an increase in the intensity of a faint red tint in the background below butterflies Nos. 1, 4, and 5, and to a lesser extent, No. 6 (personifications of the little and adult Susanne, father, and mother, respectively). In those areas, the air seems to be heated up by a slightly reddish light from inside the fog (Fig. 8.55; red arrows).[86]

This reddishness is due to the thin application of a red translucent paint during the last phase of the oil painting. The red is not part of the basic yellow-ochre mixture, but is a glaze laid on top of that base color. As far as Susanne can remember, she implemented this to "bring everything together." Involuntarily, the artist metaphorically represents her transferential attitudes.

In summary, the above analysis of the colors red, orange, burnt orange, a tinge of red in violet, and reddishness in some areas of Pale Moonlight further confirm the assumption about the unconscious meaning found in the details of this butterfly's appearance, which were made earlier from the interpretation of form. Through our investigation, we have come to recognize the

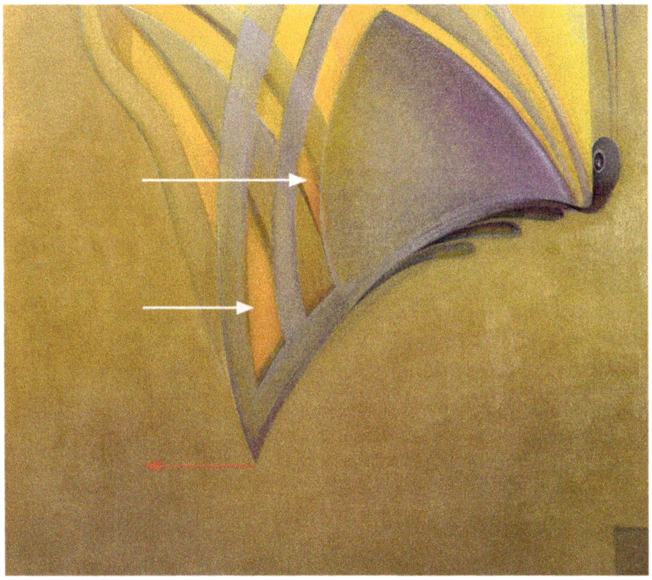

Fig. 8.55. Small areas in the hind wings of Little Why with shift toward intense orange (detail from 1.1).
White arrows point to the orange color inside the butterfly.
Red arrow points to the reddish surroundings of the butterfly.

artist's unrealized desires for dominance, and her repressed reproductive and instinctual drives in the appropriate metaphors of color and form. The unconscious symbolism of red was unintentionally slipped into the hues in some areas of Pale Moonlight. The same tendency can be observed with all the other butterflies.

The unconscious weaves its messages from emotionally charged events and also brings them to the surface through different channels. Utilizing the artist's free associations and reminiscences of the past, the combined results of the analysis of lines, shapes, composition, and colors allow us to calibrate the research's compass and aim the searchlight to discover the sources rooted deeply in the unconscious, which discloses its messages through various metaphoric manifestations.

86 The reddishness can be clearly noted in the original painting, but it is difficult to distinguish in the reproduction we have provided.

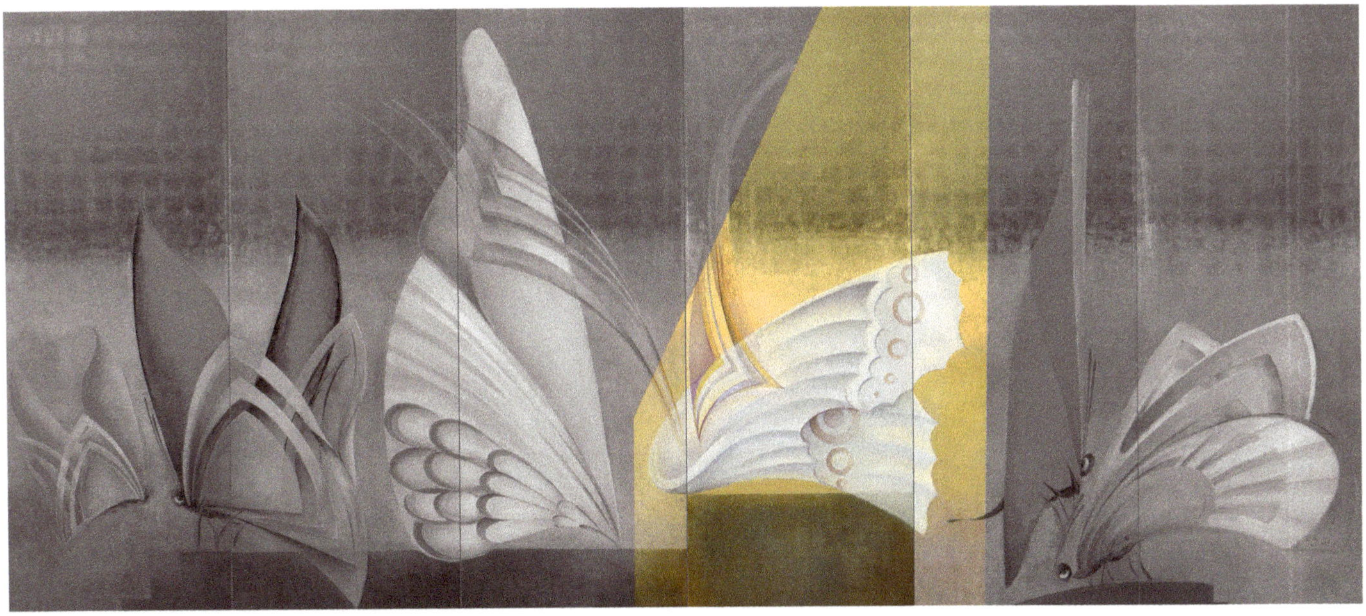

Fig. 9.0. *Give Me Wings!* with butterfly No. 4, Touchless Misty, highlighted.

Touchless Misty pretends fragile daintiness which hides his strict, structured strength underneath the elegant, polished white surface. Smoothly groomed rewards in academia and gliding weightlessly on the political parquet let him spread pleasant luster wherever his shadows dare to fall.

—From the artist's poetic commentary, 2004.

Chapter 9

Fragile Butterfly No. 4 — Touchless Misty

Undercover strength

9.1 The Name

To the right of the painting's center, the highest step of the podium is occupied by the white butterfly No. 4, Touchless Misty, which Susanne considers the most beautiful creature in the group. By presenting him[1] in a condition of polished cleanliness, seemingly free of blemish, she emphasized Touchless Misty's attractiveness by virtue of his elegance and purity. His whiteness can be perceived as forbidding any contamination. The veil-thin wings appear quite fragile, requiring protection from any harmful touch. However, beneath the gentle façade, a resolute, indefatigable strength exists that is manifested by his particular configuration of ridges and serrated contour and by his triumphal position on the podium. The artist created him with these contrary qualities, clad in a cold and unadulterated white, supposedly to underscore his rare nature as an extraordinary entity who could be a personification of her. Susanne's former husband was accustomed to mockingly calling her "alien" for many years, alluding to her "being so different," even facetiously playing on her "extraterrestrial origin." "Alien," with its connotation "to be not from this world," could reflect Susanne's recurring fantasies of "longing for the stars."

This concept of being an alien is well-illustrated in two of her paintings from her early student years, *The Sea of Time*, (1981–82) (Fig. 9.1) and *The End of a Long Day*, (1982) (Fig. 9.2), where analogous portraits dominate the scenes. Both images were identified by the artist during a discussion

1 In the poetic commentary, Touchless Misty is bestowed with a masculine gender.

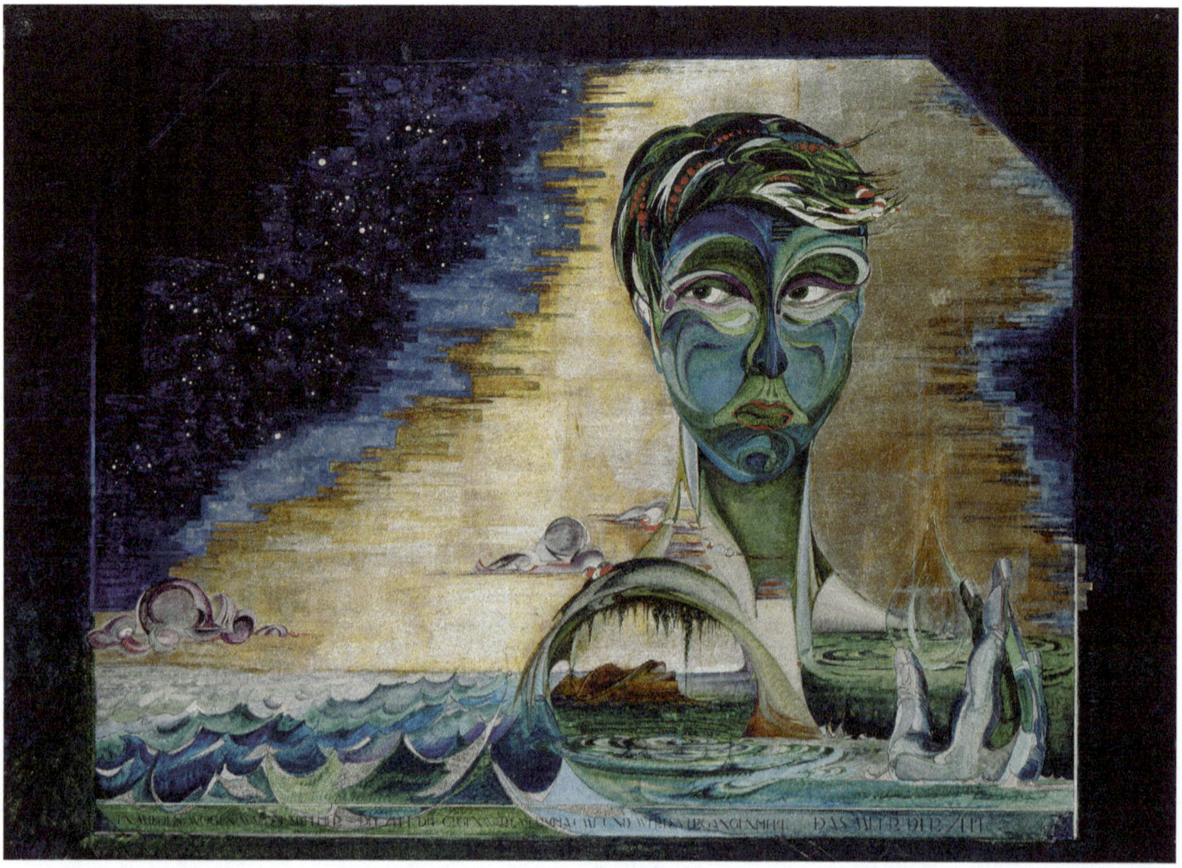

Fig. 9.1. Susanne Schuenke, *The Sea of Time*, 1982. Oil and silver leaf on board, 29 x 40 in (73 x 102 cm). Collection of the artist.

about these works as portraying herself, through which she represented her perception of the world. She projected herself as a detached observer, whose aloof facial expression conveys dismay and disillusionment about the affairs of mankind on this planet. By the bust portraits in these two paintings, the artist also revealed her own state of confusion and uncertainty about her existence. The observer can sense Susanne dreams that one day there will be a better world. Thirty years later, in *Give Me Wings!*, the white butterfly represents the same dream. This hope is metaphorically signified by Touchless Misty's immersion into the golden background and his closeness to and overlap with the butterfly Air that symbolizes spirituality (see chapter 10 and subchapter 12.3). Butterfly No. 4 remains anchored in harsh reality, represented by the podium (see subchapter 12.1), but Susanne has endowed him with superior placement and impressive presence.

Touchless Misty parades the unsoiled whiteness of his wings against such highly charged chromatic competitors as True Blue and Firebird. His sobriquet hints at a special attitude toward touch. It expresses the artist's perception of the mystery of this butterfly, and reflects a particular appearance that masks a complex blend of contrasting traits layered on one another. The name, consists of three elements—"touch," "less," and "misty."

9.1.1 "Touch"

The sense of touch evokes in Susanne's mind a kaleidoscope of associations and memories laden with contradicting meanings, feelings, and emotions. The artist has experienced that being touched could be a source of pleasure as well as pure horror. Since her childhood, Susanne has had a continual need for tactile human sensation, as it brings her an elation and contentment, which she has always craved. In those years, she was longing for such haptic experiences as being kissed and petted by her parents, sitting on their laps, and holding their hands. To be in attachment with her parents as much as possible, the toddler and little girl often desired to sleep with them. However, the child felt that she never received enough of these

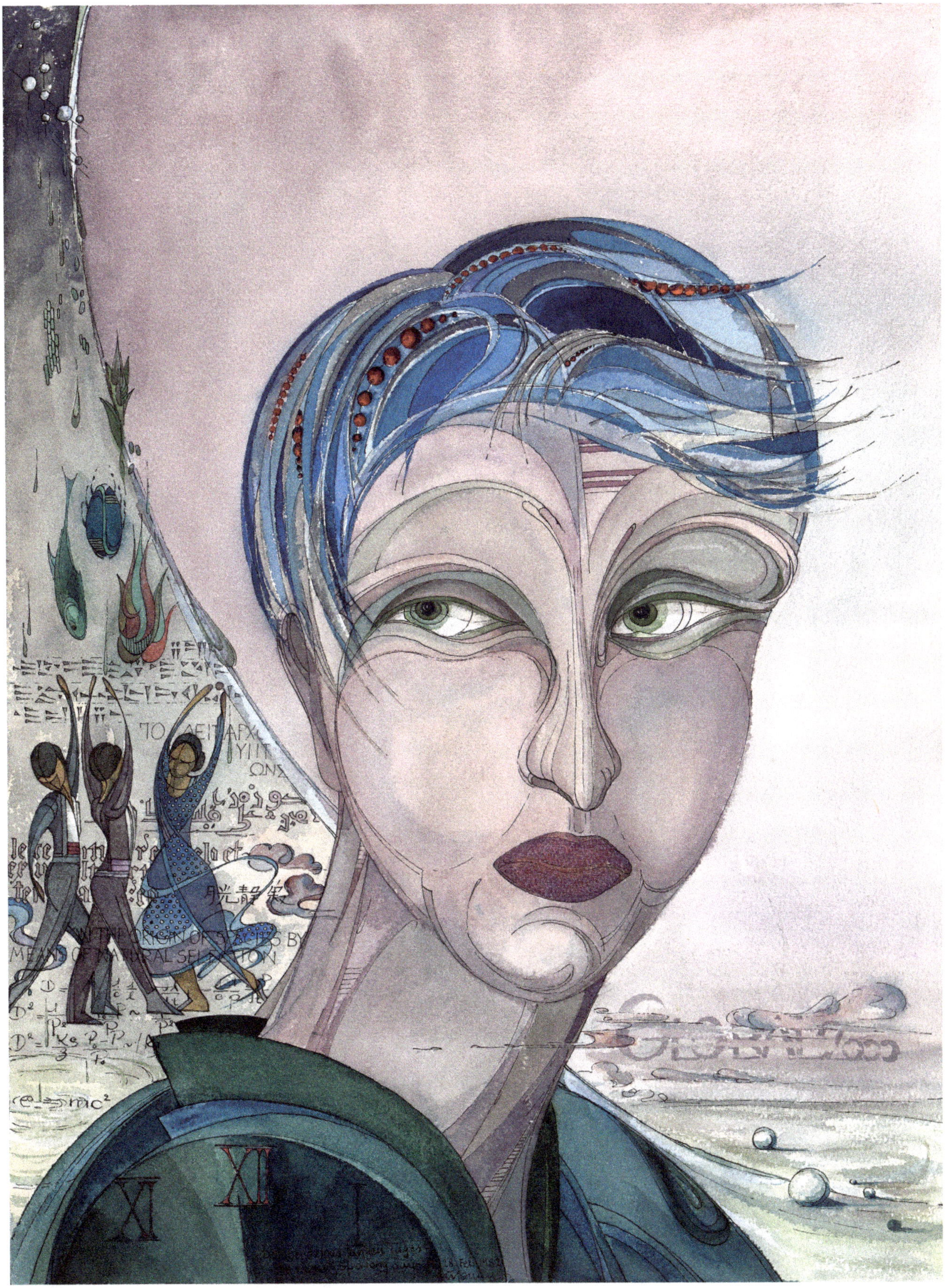

Fig. 9.2. Susanne Schuenke, *The End of a Long Day*, 1982. Watercolor, 25 x 20 in (64 x 50 cm). Collection of the artist.

intimate caresses because her parents began to limit their physical closeness as Susanne approached her preteen years.

Whatever pleasant touch she received was not enough for her. She invented a means of inducing pleasing tactile sensations on her own by rubbing the lip area under her nose against the corner of the bed linen and putting two fingers in her mouth. There are some small surface areas of skin on her body, such as the back of her fingers, below her nose, and under her eyes, which are especially sensitized. Gently stroking those places, Susanne can create a pleasant tingling that spreads to the rest of her body. For example, when she touches her knuckles, she can feel a sensation even in her legs. Susanne's craving for physical contact was so intense in her childhood that she would even cause mild self-injury by pinching her hands or picking at her lips. Doing so, she gained attention and a sympathetic response from her parents and siblings, who put their hands on hers to stop the quirks.

Even in her early adulthood, Susanne continued these habits, but the family eventually recognized the ploy. To stop this obsession, they verbally reprimanded her instead of touching her. Nevertheless, Susanne would still feel relieved due to the attention from her parents and sisters. Throughout her childhood, the daughter wanted eagerly to touch the skin of her mother's face and kiss her because it would bring her the sought-after sensation. She extended this desire to the soft cheeks of her aunt on her father's side, and she still remembers with sadness when her mother told her that she had to stop kissing the aunt. The parent reasoned that such intimacy was inappropriate for a child of her age (Susanne was probably around 11 or 12 at the time). As a consequence, she substituted the kisses of the mother and aunt with stroking and hugging her teddy bear. Even in her adulthood, she sometimes enjoys rubbing her face against a favorite stuffed animal, a purple mouse.[2]

Holding hands with someone dear to her gives her the assurance that she is not alone, and the physical contact allows her to be in communion with the person whose physical presence provides her with a sense of strength, security, and confidence. Susanne places a greater degree of trust in the emotional gratification derived from touch than in visual cues or assuring words, for in Susanne's experience either visual or auditory perception is more likely to be illusory. This is because sights and sounds can be artificially created (e.g., in recorded voices or reproduced images), whereas the sense of touch has proved for her to be more reliable in delivering a link to reality.[3]

Her trust in the reliability of tactile sensation could have begun in her early childhood. Until the age of eight, she often managed to be in the parents' bed, either alone or with them as she successfully revolted against being transferred to her own bed. She wonders how much that experience might have determined her ongoing yearning for touch.

In this context, Susanne recalled that her parents told her later in life of an event in her infancy, when contact with her mother as the primary caregiver was interrupted. The baby was just eight months old when the family took her and her three-year-old sister to the North Sea for their annual vacation. Foreseeing the difficulty of

2 The stuffed purple mouse (mentioned already in chapter 6 (Fig. 6.19)) was a Christmas gift from the mother to each of her three adult daughters many years ago. This hand-sized animal became a very significant emotional object, which Susanne personified as a living person, and later, her former husband named the mouse Rupert and began to speak on behalf of Rupert, creating humorous dialogues and playful gestures. Susanne treated the stuffed animal with much affection. He (i.e. Rupert) was her invaluable companion during countless stressful medical situations acting as a security blanket. As a talisman, he traveled with her through many countries. Over the years, his soft velvet fur faded and thinned out from countless kissing and hugging. He also became a "discussion partner" in this analysis because, through her written "dialogues with Rupert," she was able to discuss various topics, problems, and challenges from two perspectives: Hers and her confidant—Rupert's. In this way, she allowed the mouse as an imaginary friend to openly express different opinions and attitudes that referred to her past and present, thereby extracting valuable information for the research that she would not otherwise permit herself to voice. With Rupert as sounding board, she was able to partly circumvent the mechanism of her own censorship. This turned out to be a successful case of role-play, in which Susanne could effectively project her repressed childhood desires, and it enabled her to recollect numerous emotionally charged episodes.

3 Having been hard-of-hearing all her life, it is understandable that hearing is not a sense Susanne can rely on to provide an accurate reflection of reality. When it comes to the sense of seeing, it is somewhat astonishing that as a painter and obviously visual person, she considers sight also as "not sufficient to ensure true perception." She experiences the visual images of mass media and advertising, which are subjective representations that are often selected or edited for desired effects, as artificial. After all, the trustworthiness of visual representation has become increasingly diminished in the 21st century, when all sorts of digital manipulation, simulations, or fakes have become common.

caring for such a young baby either in a hotel or at the beach, they decided on the recommendation of the mother's older sister, Hella (a professional pediatric nurse), that it would be in the best interest of the infant to be cared for by the experienced staff at a local children's sanatorium. Although they visited their child every day, the separation must have had a traumatic effect on Susanne. Upon returning home from the vacation, the baby rejected maternal care after six weeks of detachment from her mother and only wanted contact with her father. Afterward, her parents voiced their regret about this episode, saying that had they known better, they would not have done it.

It is well known through studies that the disconnection of an infant from its caregivers has often adverse repercussions on the child's later development.[4] Susanne's obsession with touch also could well be rooted in this early experience of the temporary deprivation of her parents' care. The epithet "Touchless" could be a confirmation of the above interpretation. It is plausible that the constituent of the soubriquet "Touchless" is the expression of the unconscious desire "Touch me, be with me!" The wishes for pleasurable touch is traceable, for example, in her painting Golden Nectar (2005), where silver butterflies gently touch the petals and pollen of an open blossom (see chapter 8). This depiction symbolically and yet cryptically represents the sensitive areas of her body[5] (Fig. 8.47). This painting metaphorically reveals Susanne's yearnings for tactile sensations.

9.1.2 (Touch-) "Less"

In spite of her desire for tactile contact, Susanne developed an extraordinary fear of being touched by hands or objects on specific parts of her body (the navel and inside the wrist and the elbow), which also extends to the aversion of observing the same areas on others. When she sees someone else being touched on those places, she recoils in horror or reacts with abrupt body movements, indicating a flight response.

Suffering from various chronic diseases since around the age of four, Susanne was continuously under medical treatment, especially by ear doctors. Beginning at age 11 and lasting for over a decade, she experienced prolonged hospitalizations that subjected her to many incidents of medical personnel touching her in search of veins, and painfully piercing her skin with needles for injecting IVs. The experiences progressively made her fearful of touches to her hands, wrists, arms, and especially the crook of the arm (aichmophobia and haphephobia).

Those contacts were unforgettably distressing, and the painful memories of the hospital stays still linger in her mind, exercising a powerful sway over her and engendering a protective desire "not to be touched." She suffers from an overwhelmingly negative reaction when someone happens to touch these highly critical areas accidentally or during medical examinations. She defends her acute reaction as "rational," because she does not consider it unusual for people to react with anxiety and even with evasive body movements in anticipation of a painfully invasive procedure, whether it is real or imagined. However, the fear has become independent from the actual medical situation, which makes it an irrational one.

One of the most sensitive areas for her is the navel.[6] Susanne can not even touch her own navel, let alone anyone else's. Furthermore, her negative reaction extends to the auditory and visual realms. For example, the mere hearing of the word "navel"[7] or seeing of her own navel or any other person's, including in photographs, can still drive her to an agitated reaction, and it remains a source of extreme discomfort.

4 John Bowlby's Attachment Theory: Bowlby, 1982.

5 The inspiration for this painting was a friend's suggestion to illustrate how she experiences sensuality. The artist intentionally designed the blossom as a substitute for her skin. For more details, see the concluding part of the subchapter 8.3.2.

6 As was described in subchapter 8.3.4, Susanne has suffered from omphalophobia from childhood onward.

7 Susanne could not say (or read) the word "navel" in either German or English, without having a phobic reaction. She physically obliterated the word "navel" from her dictionaries by crossing it out beyond recognition. When she tried to explain to people that "she could not look at the middle of someone's body," she was not aware that the listener would inevitably conclude that "Susanne cannot look at the genital area." For her, the navel was the crucial body part in that region. The colloquial American expression for navel, "belly button," affected her in a particularly horrible way. She was visualizing it as a button that has holes through which a needle can be inserted. Those associations made the thinking of the belly button even more terrifying for Susanne.

In the context of the fear of touch (haphephobia), from the age of seven onward, Susanne had an irrational fear of being tickled. She would sleep in a defensive position, in a half-sitting posture with a blanket wrapped around her. She justified this as protection against imaginary tickling during the night. Susanne does not recall actually being tickled, and she cannot even speculate about what might have caused this fearful anticipation. This fear lasted until her teenage years, but eventually faded away.

"Touch" in Susanne's mind could be categorized as an essential aspect of sensuality. Her father typically used the word "touch" in the context of sexual behavior. For example, he would ask his daughters if a male in their company had behaved lubriciously, by saying, "Did he touch you? Did he want to get into your clothes?" Sexuality, as mentioned before, was a taboo topic in Susanne's family, and "touchless" would be a perfect epithet for the family's catechism, signifying the parents' disapproval of any expression or display of physical intimacy. According to the parents' values, it was mandatory that women must be "clean." Under this premise, the white, pristine butterfly Touchless Misty might metaphorically carry the artist's internalized parental directive—not to sully her purity. This doctrine from the past, which called for sexual abstinence outside marriage as the highest virtue for women, could have been a possible impetus for the artist's choice of the moniker "Touchless" for butterfly No. 4 to signify the suppression of sexuality. Touchless Misty, as a projection of the artist, carries the metaphorical meaning of being untouchable and unreachable which could function as a kind of camouflage needed to comply with parental and social expectations.

In a different context, "touchless" can also echo the parents' requirements with regard to the care of artworks. Ever since her childhood, Susanne heard their admonition "Touch it gently!" on innumerable occasions as she was about to handle one of the art objects, antique furniture, or china of the family's home environment. In this case, "touchless" could signify the need to protect the fragile, cherished items, many of which were valuable and rare.[8] Damaging or breaking any of them resulted in serious family distress, especially upsetting her father. To make matters worse, over the years Susanne did play with many of those objects and damaged a lot of them, and as a consequence, she frequently heard the warning: "Be careful. If you break it, it cannot be replaced."[9]

Decades later, enjoying her own collection of treasured antiques and fragile objects, she has come to a better understanding of her parents' concerns about the children's nonchalant attitude toward handling precious objets d'art that had managed to survive the ravages of time. As she began to hold the aesthetic beauty of art objects in high regard, Susanne found great pleasure not only in admiring their appearance, but also in experiencing them through touch, such as feeling a polished wooden surface, tracing the contour of a sunlight-warmed crystal, or gently stroking a silken textile, and so on. The one exception—the surface of drawings and paintings should never be touched. This is especially true for many of Susanne's paintings (including *Give Me Wings!*) as they involve delicate gold gilding, which is subject to degradation and damage if touched carelessly by bare hands. It is possible that for her "touchless" designates those things that are to be admired and enjoyed, but never touched, lest they become damaged or sullied.

From these associations, we find that the name "Touchless Misty" indicates ambivalence. The butterfly's beauty incites a desire to touch what is forbidden, and the name appropriately denotes this predicament. The dichotomous nature of "touchless" might be associated with fantasies from her childhood. Under this purview, "Touchless" could mean that touch, on the one hand, is unacceptable because it is a significant source of distress. On the other hand, as we have remarked, Susanne intensely craved the loving touch of her

8 Susanne's parents began to collect antique furniture and china immediately after they were married in 1951. Growing up in the family house, she was surrounded by objects that would ordinarily be found in museums. This taught her to share the parents' reverence for antiques and appreciate their beauty.

9 For decades, Susanne had a frightening daydream in which she would imagine the cupboard where the family stored the antique glassware, fell and suddenly all the crystal inside was shattered. In her fantasy, the event would happen just as she was replacing a glass back into the cupboard; and the dream would unfailingly end with her receiving the full blame and scolding for the catastrophe.

parents even in her adulthood. She remembers well longing for closeness, but too often being denied this desire. Thus, "Touchless" could also describe her perception that she was unfairly deprived of touch.

9.1.3 "Misty"

"Misty" is the second part of the compound sobriquet for butterfly No. 4. This word could hint at the butterfly's chromatic visual affinity with mist—the cool, white morning fog preceding sunshine. Susanne wrote another association in the poetic commentary, "Touchless Misty pretends fragile daintiness which hides his strict, structured strength underneath the elegant polished white surface." This implies that beneath the butterfly's clean and smooth façade lies a concealed, powerful essence, whose inner nature is yet unknown but eventually could be figured out. The two components of the name Touchless Misty coalesce as the appropriate epithet to express the quintessence of this butterfly. At first the white, partly translucent[10] exterior of Touchless Misty gives an illusion of fragility. Under deeper scrutiny, the ridges, sickle shapes, and serrated contours manifest an enigmatic backbone which will be examined further. The mentioned contradictions surround him with an air of mystery. Susanne made a connection between the words "mist" and "mystery" through wordplay, conflating the two words through homophonic association and their possible latent contents. Talking about this meaning, the artist recalls the surprising and powerful yearning she has felt since her adolescence, when looking into the night sky. As will be clarified in subchapter 10.4, living in this world makes the artist feel "like a guest on earth," and, having no problems with the concept of recurrent life-cycles, she likes to imagine that her true ancestry traces back to a world far away.

Susanne, in spite of having been born in the middle of December, has rejected the traditional zodiac sign of Sagittarius[11] and, instead, chose the unconventional Orion constellation to be "her personal zodiac sign"[12]—a close secret, which she shared only for this study. The constellation Orion, the largest in the northern winter sky, has exerted a strong attraction for her ever since she first mindfully looked at the night sky. The stars drew her toward them, and with great enthusiasm, she began to acquire knowledge of astronomy and cosmology from the age of 12 onward. She has perceived the universe as full of mystery, and her longing to gather knowledge about it has remained constant.

She especially recalls photographs of Orion's Horse Head Nebula, one of the constellation's most prominent features often reproduced in astronomy books. It is a dark, vividly contoured cloud of dust and gas that contrasts with its surroundings. The word *nebula* means mist, which for Susanne is synonymous with being perplexing and enchanting. As such, this obscuring medium would tend to hide something within or beyond its white envelope. Susanne's fascination with the dark, nebulous objects in the night sky, could be the possible source of the "Misty" portion of the butterfly's appellation.

The following consideration might shed further light on this "misty" connection. The artist studied Latin in high school, and she knows that the German word "*Nebel*" (fog, mist, or haze in English) was derived from this language. The word turned out to be highly problematic for Susanne, as the German word for navel is "*Nabel*," which is close enough in spelling and sound to "*Nebel*" to be highly threatening on the account of her omphalophobia. The topic of the navel, as we have discussed, has an extraordinary power over her mind. Her physical and mental discomfort with the word in her native language is carried over

10 The lowest part of his hind wing overlaps with the podium whose contour is clearly visible through the wings' texture due to its extraordinary thinness. Also, the golden background shines through the wings and is traceable as yellowish transparent areas amid the white.

11 Susanne never took a liking to the zodiac sign Sagittarius which is represented by a centaur (in Greek mythology, a chimera that is half man, half horse), who carries a bow loaded with an arrow, ready to shoot. She did not wish to be identified symbolically with a man-beast with the obvious inclination for aggression.

12 In Greek mythology, Orion is a heroic hunter whom Zeus placed among the stars, therefore, he became a constellation. Susanne's bias toward the name could have been reinforced by the science fiction story, Raumpatrouille—Die phantastischen Abenteuer des Raumschiffes Orion (English: Space Patrol—The Fantastic Adventures of the Spaceship Orion) which was a very successful German TV series broadcast in the later 1960s that her parents allowed her to watch. She had never known science fiction and the TV program fit well with her ongoing interest in astronomy.

to English just as strongly. When the offending word is spoken in either language, it determines her distress that manifests with anxiety (reading those words seems to have a less dramatic effect on her). Susanne's mind still responds to the sound of the word "nebula" with some degree of alarm, because it reminds her of the navel through the similarity of its sound to these German and English words. Omphalophobia, as mentioned before, has haunted Susanne for most of her life, and it remains a mystery to her, as she has yet to understand its meaning. The association with the word "nebula" is significant, as it is related to the German word for mist or fog (*Nebel*), and it could be construed as a possibly unconscious source for the artist spontaneously naming this butterfly with the word "misty."

When naming the various butterflies in the poetic commentary, Susanne associated the color of this butterfly with the light of the full moon as it is reflected in the clouds. She felt inclined to name butterfly No. 4 "Moonlight," but this sobriquet was already used for butterfly No. 3 (see chapter 8, footnote 1). Nevertheless, she incorporated her desire to link Touchless Misty with the moon, for example, shown in the following association. During analysis, Susanne stated that the moon evokes the same inexplicable longing and vision in the artist's mind as the Orion Nebula and "misty" could refer to the haze around the full moon that is comparable with images of a galactic nebula. With this juxtaposition of moon and nebula, Pale Moonlight and Touchless Misty could be considered as expressing related meanings, becoming complementary to each other as different sides of the same coin. In accordance with this metaphorical implementation, their reciprocal relationship is united by Air (personification of spirituality) at the core of this trio.

After contemplating a number of possible sources that inspired the creation of the name Touchless Misty, it may be assumed that this butterfly is another personification of the artist herself. Later, the interpretation of the details of Touchless Misty will show how different nuances of Susanne's experiences and facets of her personality are reflected in the butterfly's image.

9.2 The Sabino Butterfly

Susanne's multifold associations with butterfly No. 4, Touchless Misty, were collected over several years of research during numerous discussions with the artist concerning the peculiarities of this image. Among the butterfly sketches that were made in the conservatory, there is one (Fig. 9.7 (a)) with an accompanying note[13] scribbled next to it. We pay particular attention to the last line of the notation: "blue morpho," which points to the natural model whose characteristics (such as the serrated wing contour and eyespots) she incorporated in the sketch. The comparison of this sketch with the developmental steps toward Touchless Misty allows us to consider that this figure is the forerunner of butterfly C in creative drawing I (Fig. 2.2) and became butterfly No. 4 in the oil painting.

On closer inspection, the sketch reveals two layers of pencil strokes in the butterfly's wing contour. The first layer defines a "smooth" outline (Fig. 9.3, blue arrows), whereas the second pencil line is a "serrated" one (Fig. 9.3, red arrows).

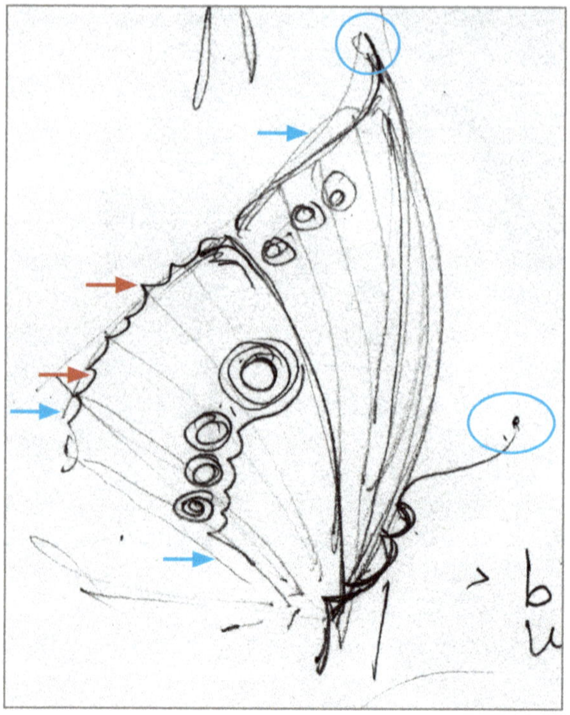

Fig. 9.3. A detail view of a butterfly from Fig. 2.1a, showing the initial wing contour as a "smooth line" (see blue arrows) and the overlaid second contour as a "serrated" line" in the hind wing (see red arrows). Encircled: details of the wing tip and antenna.

13 The accompanying note can be read as follows (from top to bottom); first line: *inside very iridescent light blue;* second line: *outside brown and eyes;* third line: *blue morpho.*

We can assume that the faint first outline could have been determined by her general perception of the wing contours of various butterfly species as can be seen in her sketches (Fig. 2.1). The second, "serrated line," drawn with emphasis, might have been inspired by individual species at the conservatory that were in front of her with moderate serrated wing contours (as some of the blue morphos possess).

There are some specific features in the image of Touchless Misty that we could not ascribe to the sketch: A sculptured wing surface, a significant cleavage between front wing and hind wing, a rounded front (head), and a pronounced serrated contour in both wings. We suppose that these differences could have come from the peculiarities of the artist's imagination and/or influence from another source.

An important angle serendipitously came to light during a discussion referring to Pale Moonlight while exploring the symbolism of "burnt orange" that was described in subchapter 8.3.2. As the discourse progressed, the artist referred to a flash of intense orange observable in the moonstone that she named "burnt orange," which led her to talk about opalescent glass and its fascinating color changes under natural light (Fig. 8.42). This, in turn, triggered a sudden reminiscence of an objet d'art by the Italian-French artist, M.E. Sabino, from her parents' art and antique collection (Fig. 9.4).[14]

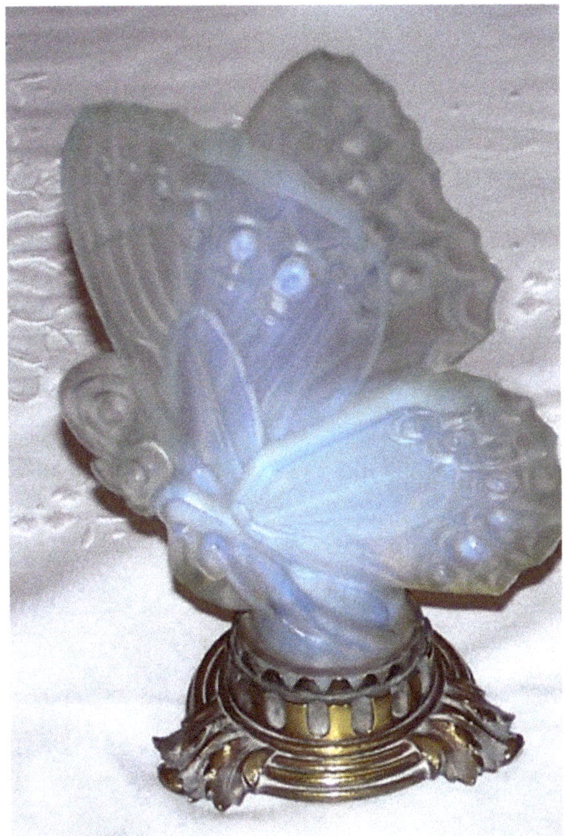

Fig. 9.4. A glass butterfly by M. E. Sabino in the artist's family collection. Opalescent glass sculpture mounted on a brass base, 6.3 inches (9 cm) tall, showing a strong bluish and milky white opalescence similar to a gem quality moonstone.

After that conversation, with her mind still engaged with Pale Moonlight and opalescent glass, Susanne searched for a photograph of this small sculpture, intending to explain the fascinating aspects of this glass material in different lights. When she found the photo, she was shocked to discover that Touchless Misty shared many similarities with this artful butterfly created by Sabino. As we compared Susanne's primary sketch of the blue morpho (Fig. 9.3) with a photograph of the Sabino butterfly illustrating its peculiar features (Fig. 9.4), we could readily see an intriguing correspondence between them, such as a series of round "eye" marks on the wings and a serrated wing contour. Up to that moment, the artist had not consciously connected her butterfly No. 4 with this sculpture, which was nevertheless latent in her mind. We consider that the prominent serration, accentuated through the three-dimensionality of the glass butterfly, significantly and unconsciously influenced Susanne's action to equip Touchless Misty with this characteristic. In redrawing the serrated wing contour and some other features of the Sabino butterfly in the image of Touchless Misty, the artist expressed a sense of significance attached to the glass sculpture, and she unconsciously relived a certain attraction she felt for this artwork. This appeal might have been triggered by her memory of the Sabino butterfly as objet d'art, the beauty of which she shared with her family. In the following, we list the comparable features between the Sabino butterfly (Fig. 9.5) and Touchless Misty (as seen in the oil painting, Fig. 9.6). In comparing the two images, the corresponding points of interest between the two figures are marked by the same letter in the illustrations:

14 Marius Ernest Sabino (1878–1961) was an Italian glass artist who established a well-known studio in France, where he became famous for his work in opalescent glass, especially in the 1920s and 30s.

a) The wing arrangement of Touchless Misty, with partially overlapping wings, closely mirrors the upper part of the Sabino butterfly.

b) The wings of Touchless Misty are painted in a way that indicates singularly pronounced three-dimensionality compared to all the other butterflies. This was accomplished through the use of shading and crease-like lines on the wings that gave the illusion of depth. The ridges of Touchless Misty are comparable with the ones on the Sabino butterfly's glass wings and their thick, solid appearance.

c) The "rings" on Touchless Misty's wings can also be recognized in the circular markings on the Sabino butterfly.

d) The overlapping wings create a very pronounced cleavage or "breaking point" in the contour of both butterflies.

e) The rounded front of Touchless Misty could be correlated with the smoothed outline, which embraces the details of a coiled proboscis in the Sabino butterfly (as highlighted with a dotted red line in Figs. 9.5. and 9.6, both marked "e").

f) The artist intended to display a delicate translucency in Touchless Misty. With the yellowish nuances in the wings, she created the illusion that the background was shimmering through. The effect is particularly apparent in the small brownish area where the hind wing overlaps with the podium. Translucency, especially in its opalescent effect, is one of the dominant properties of the Sabino glass butterfly.

g) The pale, reddish-brown color of the rings on Touchless Misty's wings could be compared with the changing play of light in some lower areas of the opalescent glass of the Sabino butterfly.

h) The serrated wing contour is conspicuous in both butterflies.

i) The base of both butterflies appears brownish.

These similarities between Touchless Misty and the Sabino butterfly sculpture were quite astonishing, but the artist had no awareness of them while she was working on *Give Me Wings!*. Only later in the analysis, as mentioned above, when Susanne was demonstrating the "orange glimpses" of an opalescent moonstone to the analyst, did she

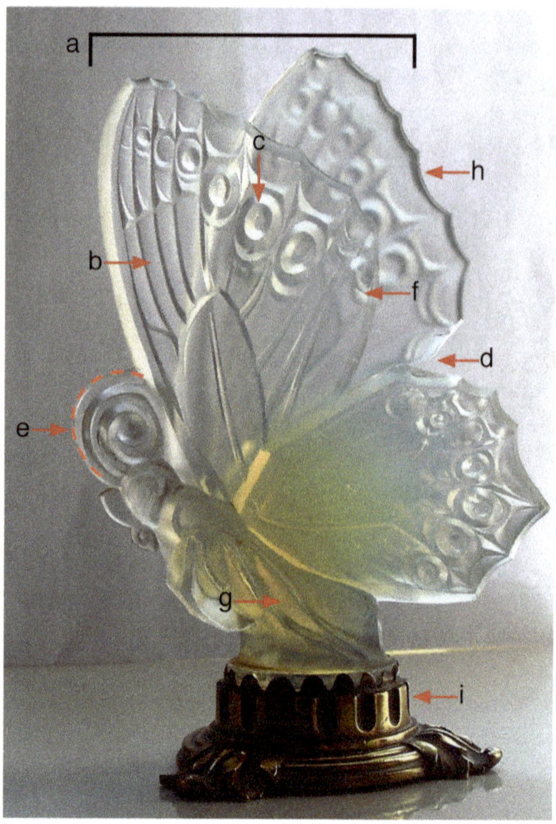

Fig. 9.5. A side view of the Sabino butterfly.

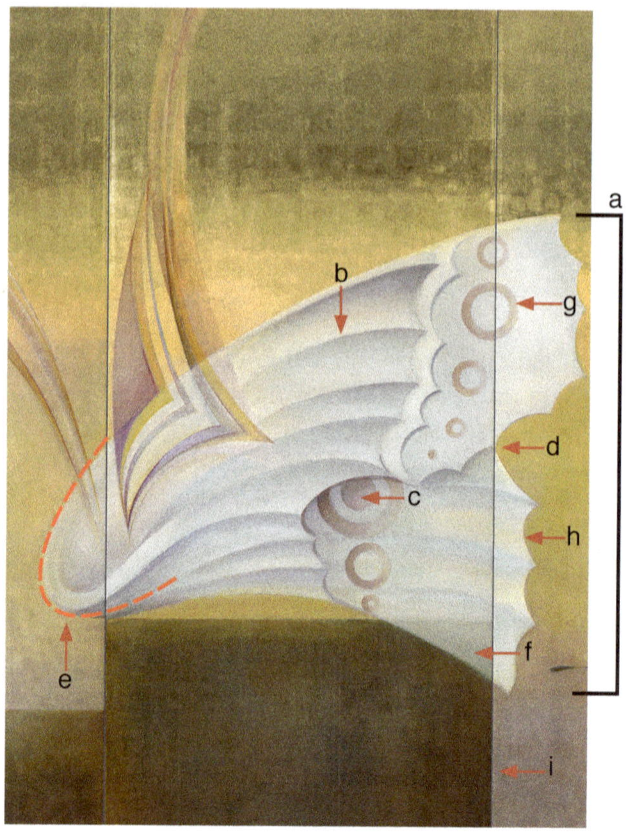

Fig. 9.6. Touchless Misty.

suddenly recall the opalescent glass of the Sabino butterfly and the positive emotions connected with this artwork. She clearly remembered that it was purchased from one of the fine-antique dealers during an annual art fair. For more than a decade, Susanne and her older sister were allowed to accompany their parents to the fair, an exciting event for the girls. They enjoyed listening to their parents' conversations with various art and antique dealers, who had become acquaintances of the family over the years. It was emotionally significant for her to be included in these expeditions, but it also trained her eyes to recognize the different styles, qualities, and other attributes of objects with which she was unfamiliar. When she recalled past visits with her family at the fair, her face beamed recalling the pleasures of those experiences.

The glass sculpture stood on the windowsill in a cozy winter garden, where the family enjoyed their afternoon tea and coffee. The Sabino butterfly was always admired, especially when the sunlight shone through the opalescent glass, giving it tinges of blue, green, and a mysterious orange glow inside the glass. The image had been imprinted in her mind as an outstanding representation of beauty, as well as a signifier of happy times in her childhood. Susanne considered this butterfly as one of her favorite objects from her parents' home, and she was surprised that she did not think of the Sabino butterfly much earlier. She recalled it only when the topic of the orange traces in Pale Moonlight came up for discussion. It is astonishing how strongly the memory of this much-loved object was suppressed. She suggested that maybe the painful development in her relationship with her father, which culminated in a major falling-out after her emigration to the USA, might be a reason for this. Even after he passed away, the tension of that period left her with continuing feelings of distress.

There is another possibility we should not overlook. The first name of the artist's elder sister is "Sabine," the feminine German version of the masculine Italian name "Sabino." This association might be coincidental, but we cannot exclude it as one of multiple factors, which determined the suppression of the Sabino butterfly from the artist's memory. This may have been due to the negative facets of the sibling competition that became part of the repressed emotional experiences of Susanne's childhood. Susanne's relationship with her older sister, three years her senior, was not very harmonious until both were in their thirties. Due to sibling rivalry and the girls' contrasting characters and interests, their relationship was full of tension. Susanne was highly gifted, especially in art, and a quick learner who was better with her school assignments. Her older sister was less successful in school. She often failed to fulfill her father's expectations, which was a source of vexation for him.

From the age of four onward, due to her frequent ailments, Susanne was a delicate child who demanded plenty of attention and care. Little Susanne managed to claim much of the parental time and support. With her more assertive temperament, she in effect replaced her elder sister, to become the premier child of the family. In later years, Susanne came to regret her impertinent behavior and childish cruelty toward her older sister. One particularly ignoble example of this was to repeatedly tease Sabine as stupid. She now realizes how deeply her sister was hurt by such tactless and unjust taunting. Susanne was often protected by the parents, who counseled Sabine to be "older and wiser" with regard to their conflicts. Unfortunately, this encouraged Susanne to continue her dominant behavior. Both girls played with the neighborhood children, but they did not have the same friends. The gap between the sisters widened during adolescence, and they shared only a few activities. Sabine left home in her early twenties, and Susanne only reconciled with her when both became independent from their parents. In subsequent years, she developed more tolerance and sympathy for her older sibling, and their relationship improved significantly.

Another possible cause for the suppression of the memory of the Sabino butterfly could be due to the presence of the clearly visible vein lines in the glass sculpture because this specific feature of the wings is apt to trigger tormenting associations[15] for the artist. The vascular patterns have never been faithfully reproduced in any of her butterfly images. Even in her otherwise realistically depicted butterflies in *The Connoisseur* (Fig. 6.6),

15 The specific vein structure, which every butterfly's wing displays more or less prominently, never appears in Susanne's paintings. Even when she is sketching from a natural model, she immediately changes the vascular lines into a fan structure. She has never drawn veins because she inevitably associates them with her phobia of the syringe, which was a source of many traumatic experiences, for her as a child at the hospital. Even typing the word "vein" in this text

Susanne painted the wing marks and subdivisions in her butterflies so that she would not consider them "vein lines." Upon remembering the Sabino butterfly and looking at its image, Susanne did not react to the vein lines in the glass statue with her typical manner. She perceived them more like "feather quills," although they were foreign features for a butterfly. This shows that if Susanne really likes the object, her mind may ignore a specific feature, to which she would otherwise have a phobic reaction. This attitude appears to be accomplished by substituting the threatening feature (i.e., veins) with something less so (i.e., feather rachides). This is indicative of an unconscious replacement to override a negative association and preserve positive emotions. The veins of the Sabino butterfly might have played a relatively minor role compared to other factors in her forgetting of the figurine.

From the above, it can be reasonably inferred that the Sabino butterfly could have significantly influenced the creation of Touchless Misty. The image of the glass sculpture has always existed as a source of emotional and aesthetic delight in her mind. Nevertheless, the similarities we found in certain features of the glass butterfly and Touchless Misty were neither consciously apparent to Susanne during the creation of *Give Me Wings!* nor in the many initial months that we spent analyzing Touchless Misty.

The Sabino butterfly was probably modeled after the blue morpho with a certain degree of artistic liberty exercised by Marius Sabino. Susanne also fashioned Touchless Misty partially after the blue morpho butterfly, but with the additional unconscious links to the Sabino butterfly. As a result, the image of Touchless Misty is a compound creation, partially embedding features of the natural blue morpho and those of the Sabino butterfly as well.

The thorough comparison of the peculiarities of the blue morpho, the Sabino butterfly, and Touchless Misty has been necessary in order to gauge the importance of their features so as to comprehend various influences on the artist's creative process. The similarities as well as differences between images and the sources of their design can demonstrate how the mind accumulates and records particulars of perception. The unconscious forges meaningful messages from the stored data and manifests them through visual metaphors and signs in a newly created artwork. In this transformative process, parts of perceptions, memories, impressions, and circumstances are processed, codified and transformed into certain singularities of shapes, lines, and colors in Susanne's imagination.

The image of Touchless Misty is a peculiar artistic creation, not merely a fanciful imitation of the original models. It is imbued with such imaginative attributes as an ambivalent structure consisting of fragility (daintiness) and strength (dragon wings). Its peculiar coloration is influenced by a specific perception of different prototypes. Furthermore, the butterfly holds an important hierarchical position in the composition and includes hidden optical illusions. The combination of those aspects could signify the unconscious interfering with the creative process and injecting its latent messages into the image.

We stated in subchapter 2.1 that even the artist's sketches of the butterflies at the conservatory contained some identifiable peculiar shapes, drawn presumably through "pure psychic automatism." As markers of the artist's significant emotional experiences, they are symptomatic of the modus operandi of the unconscious. The artist's unique perception of reality determined by the unconscious, and modified and integrated by experiences through transformative psychic processes, is channeled into the imagery. The following analysis of Touchless Misty's specific features allows us a deeper insight into the modus operandi of the unconscious.

9.3 Interpretation of the Details of Touchless Misty

9.3.1 The Significance of the Three-Dimensional Appearance and Its Evolution

Through the application of noticeable shading, Susanne gave the wings of Touchless Misty the illusion of a sculptured surface reminiscent of the Sabino butterfly. The lines that are fanning out toward the wing's right edges are painted to

causes Susanne visible discomfort. Seeing a vein structure triggers an immediate physical reaction from her, such as closing her eyes and hiding her hands (especially the back of the hands) in her clothes, as if to protect herself from the imminent approach of the needle anticipated by her imagination.

look like a series of raised ridges with soft, wavy valleys between them. Susanne, endowing this butterfly with depth, indicates a superior value[16] of Touchless Misty over the other butterflies. For this reason, we suppose that the position of this butterfly at the highest step on the podium was motivated by her favoritism. The artist originally thought that the placement was done for compositional considerations. We assume that the artist positioned this butterfly on the highest level unconsciously, signifying her desire to occupy the victor's spot. The elevation of Touchless Misty to this commanding position could well reveal Susanne's yearning to be the dominant personality. Furthermore, she has unconsciously located Touchless Misty (personification of Susanne) right next to the center of the composition in contrast to the fringe location of No. 6 (personification of the mother) and made her own personification considerably larger in size than butterfly No. 6. It should be noted that Touchless Misty's wings extend to three canvas panels of the painting. Only one other butterfly receives the same amount of panel spanning—butterfly No. 7, Air, as a representation of spirituality. The importance of Touchless Misty was not only represented by its central location in the painting, but it was further buttressed by an expansive size and three-dimensionality. The latter deserves a closer look into its development and meaning (see Figs. 9.7 and 9.9 for a schematic representation).

In the sketch from the natural models (Fig. 9.7a), we see that the butterfly which would become Touchless Misty was represented as a flat, two-dimensional entity. In creative drawing I (Fig. 9.7b), Susanne emphasized a certain area of its wings by shading lines (parallel hatching), hinting at three-dimensionality.

Further examining the sources of the three-dimensional appearance of Touchless Misty, we note that in drawing III, Susanne depicted (Fig. 2.4 and a close-up in Fig. 9.8) butterfly F with outspread wings, sketched as seen from above. In the same drawing, butterfly H, the forerunner of Firebird (a personification of Father), decisively dominates butterfly F, apparently forcing it into a prostrating posture. Moreover, the submissive butterfly appears damaged, as it lacks part of the wing membrane between the supporting "ribs."

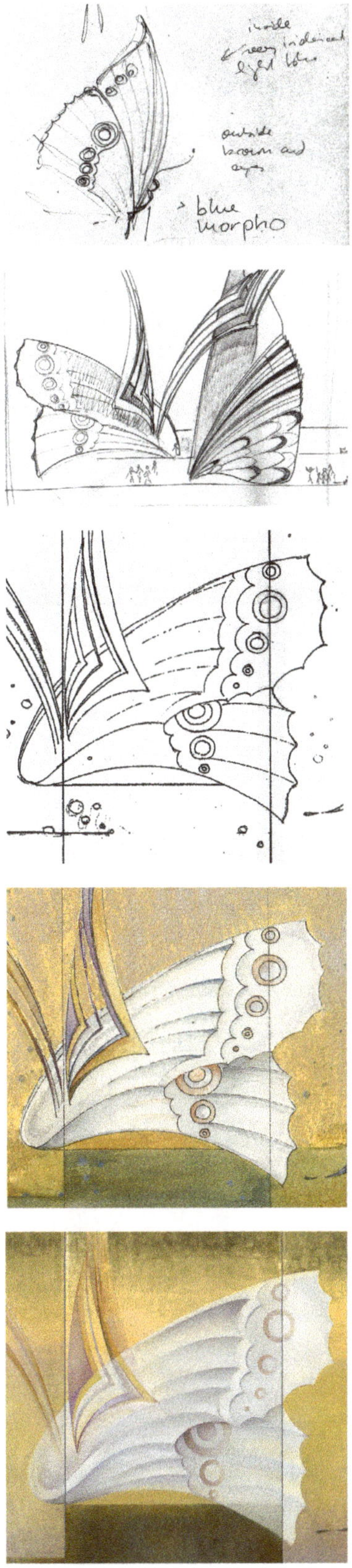

(a) Primary sketch from nature. Detail from Fig. 2.1a.

(b) Creative drawing I. Detail from Fig. 2.2.

(c) Compositional drawing for watercolor. Detail from Fig. 2.11.

(d) Watercolor. Detail from Fig. 2.12.

(e) Oil painting. Detail from Fig. 1.1.

Fig. 9.7a-e: Collage, tracing the developmental stages of Touchless Misty.

16 The correlation between dimensions and Susanne's hierarchy of values was explained in the preceding chapter 7 (see subchapter 7.2.1).

This image was not used beyond this stage of creative drawing III, but three aspects of abandoned butterfly F resurface in further development: a) the three-dimensional rib structure buttressing Touchless Misty (personification of Susanne); b) the "thickness" of a serrated contour, seen in the rear wing-profile; and c) the motif of the subjugated butterfly becoming a feature of butterfly No. 6, Fanning Everything (personification of Susanne's mother). It is very likely that the sculptured quality of butterfly F was unconsciously selected for the development of butterfly No. 4, leading to his modulated wing ridges in the final version, where the "ribs" have been replaced by ridges.

Touchless Misty definitively acquired its three-dimensional appearance in the watercolor stage of the painting (Fig. 9.7 d). Having retraced the origins of this image and the progression from the first drawings to the oil painting, we can clearly observe a gradual increase in the three-dimensional appearance of this butterfly. As shown earlier in Fig. 9.3, the initial sketch already contains "double lines" in the wing contour. In creative drawing I, the second pencil line is modified in a moderate serration, and it gives the illusion of thickness, furnishing the wing with a semblance of sturdiness. In order to facilitate an understanding of how Susanne imagined the layers comprising Touchless Misty's wings during the oil painting process, she drew a schematic diagram with a cross-sectional view of the wings (Fig. 9.9).

The illustration helps us perceive the conceptual guide that she employed in the shading to accentuate the three-dimensionality of the wing surfaces (layers 1 and 4 in Fig. 9.9) and demarcate the layers (indicated by the black arrows in Fig. 9.9). As mentioned in chapter 7, Susanne considers additional dimensionality in her images as a sign of a superior status.

The enhanced three-dimensional appearance of Touchless Misty[17] is of great importance to the artist. She felt the need, perhaps driven by the

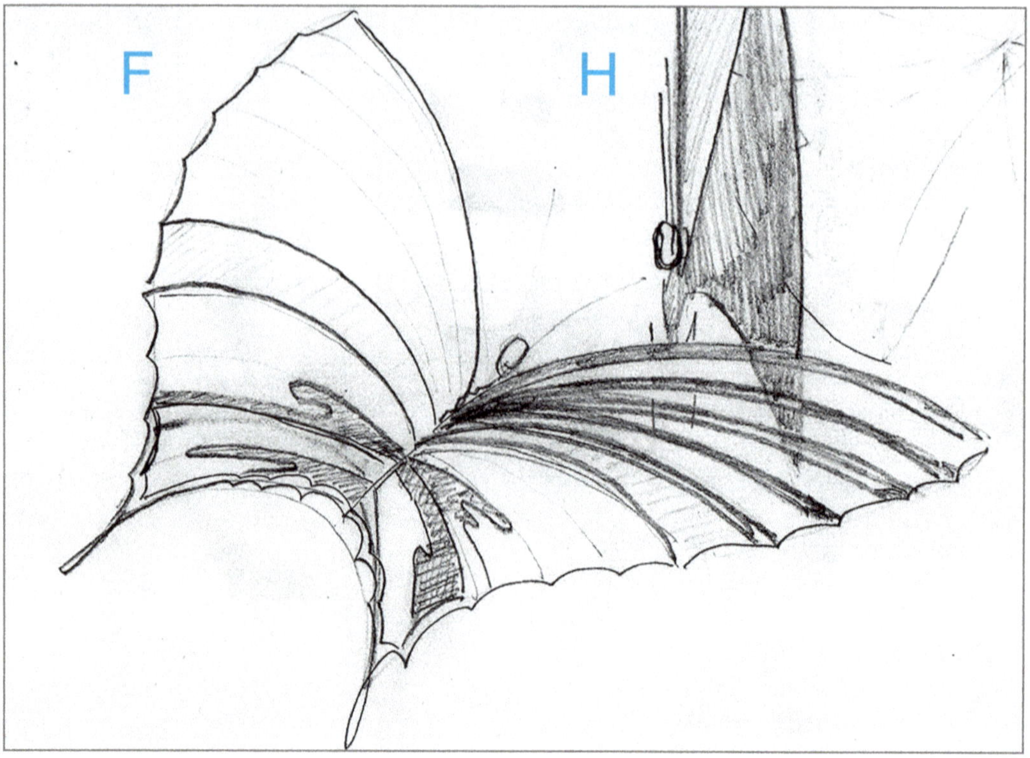

Fig. 9.8. The unnamed butterfly F. Detail from Fig. 2.4, creative drawing III.

17 It is worth mentioning that in the discussion about the possible presence of three-dimensionality in the other butterflies besides Touchless Misty, the artist insisted for a long time that Touchless Misty was the only one with those qualities, and all the others had flat wing surfaces. Gradually, however, Susanne overcame her subjectivity and acknowledged that this feature was not only found in butterfly Touchless Misty. Eventually, she came to admit that Pale Moonlight's stacked scales possessed a certain degree of three-dimensionality and that the shading in Fanning Everything's fan-like structure could hint at a three-dimensional wing surface. However the three-dimensional quality in Touchless Misty's dragon wings is clearly much more pronounced in comparison with the others.

Fig. 9.9. Schematic diagram visualizing, as the artist imagined, the three-dimensional aspect of the butterfly's overlapping wings in three layers:
Right: The dotted line in black indicates an imaginary cut through the front and hind wing.
Below: A cross-sectional view of the front and hind wings in pink and blue shades, respectively. The pink and blue arrows indicate the corresponding parts in the painted and cross-sectional views, while the black arrows point to the shaded areas that accentuate the layers.

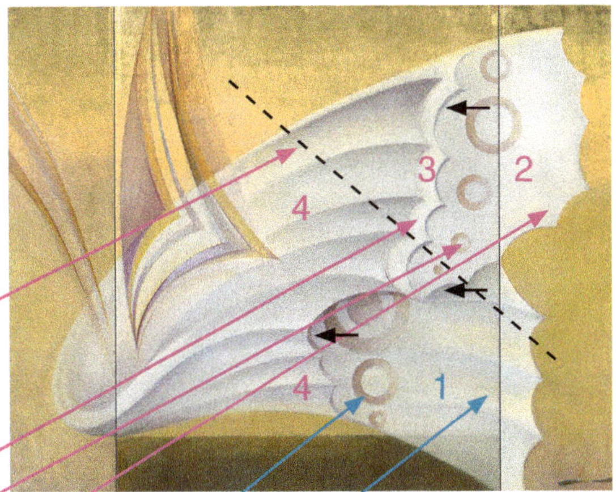

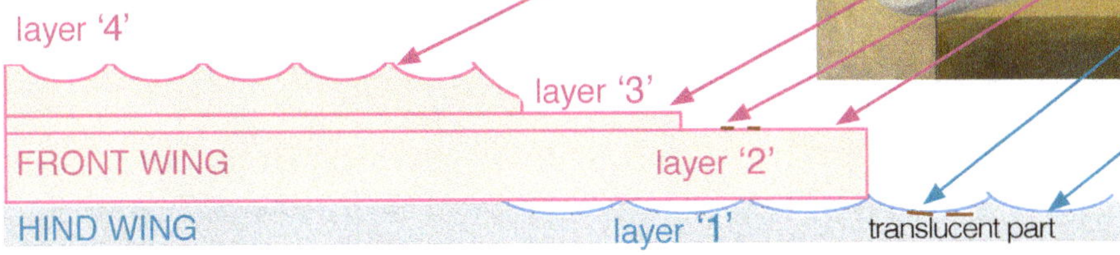

FRONT WING: Three layers shown in a cross-sectional view
Layer 2: flat with the circular pattern embedded in the same layer (circles indicated with brown lines)
Layer 3: flat like a plinth for the layer 4
Layer 4: pleated like a fan with well-defined ridges and rounded valleys

HIND WING: One layer
Layer 1: pleated (like the layer 4), with circular pattern embedded in the same layer (the circles indicated with brown lines)

unconscious, to assign to this butterfly the quality that is superior to the two-dimensionality of the others. This statement finds confirmation by the butterfly's location on the highest pedestal position involving three panels due to his breadth.

There is one more additional association of significance pertaining to the pronounced three-dimensional appearance of this image. According to the artist, the sculpted surface of this butterfly reminded her of the shell of a scallop, the creature's hardened crust, which is used to protect its soft body (Fig. 9.10).[18]

The shells of scallops, which Susanne has the opportunity to collect by the seashore, display a series of ridges on their surface. We found an analogy between their corrugated pattern and the appearance of Touchless Misty's wings. Just as the shell provides a protective exterior for the vulnerable mollusk, the comparable, three-dimensional surface of the butterfly could be understood as a defensive armor. By the phenomenon of personification, this could be interpreted as a shield for the artist's sensitivity. Here three-dimensionality takes on added importance, as it introduces the idea of depth, which in Susanne's mind implies additional security due to the thickness of the covering. In her childhood, Susanne had the habit of wrapping herself with an extra blanket in her bed at night. She was constantly searching for protection to keep her safe from possible or imagined attacks, not only from the outside world, but also from disturbing trends of her own inner world (latent impulses, forbidden thoughts, and inappropriate fantasies). Accordingly, Susanne unconsciously incorporated ridges into this butterfly's imagery, analogous to a protective scallop shell, which metaphorically signifies a defense from fearsome expectations.

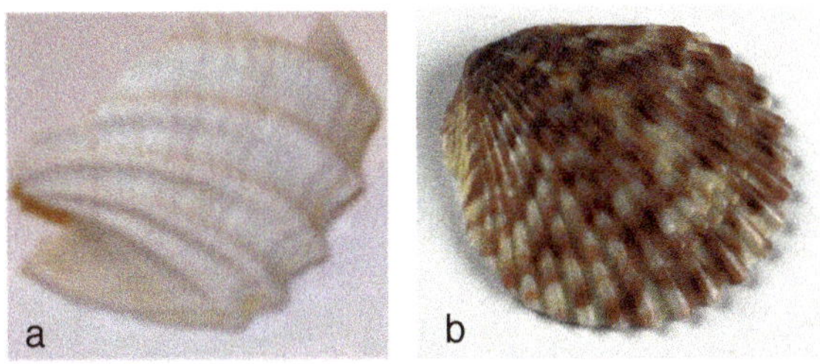

Fig. 9.10. Two sea shells from the artist's collection which she keeps for design reference:
(a) A scallop fragment.
(b) Atlantic calico scallop.

18 The topic of protection triggers a wide range of associations, including, for example, an analogy the artist saw between the pleated "fold/ridges" of Touchless Misty's wings with an elbow plate (couter) in medieval armor.

9.3.2 Translucency

In the oil painting, the artist created an illusion of translucency for Touchless Misty that is clearly seen where the wing overlaps the corner of the podium (Fig. 9.7 (e)). This feature neither exists in the compositional drawing nor in the watercolor. We note also traces of yellowish nuances in some areas of the front and hind wings, as the background is shining through the translucent white wings. The observer could even assume that the whole butterfly possesses such subtle diaphaneity. The artist painted certain parts of the wings to give the illusion that the shimmer of the golden background passes through the butterfly, and that could be perceived as an analogy to the stained glass windows of a Gothic cathedral.[19] The natural light shining through them is transformed into a play of chromatic splendor and ethereality, temporarily enchanting the believers' minds with a sense of the Divine presence. The yellowish glimmer on the wings, intended to signify the luminosity permeating them, links the butterfly with the realm of spirituality, symbolized by the golden background (see subchapter 12.3).

The intimation of otherworldliness is also underscored by Touchless Misty's partial overlapping with butterfly No. 7, Air, which represents spirituality (see chapter 10). As pointed out by Susanne, translucency indicates a certain fragility, suggesting that this delicate creature could be easily distressed or injured at the slightest interference. However, as the artist wrote in the poetic commentary, Touchless Misty "pretends fragile daintiness, which hides his strict, structured strength underneath an elegant, polished white surface." This implies that the gentle appearance of the wings could well be a disguise, and beneath the surface dwells steely toughness and resilience.

There are two aspects of Touchless Misty's strength. On the one hand, there is the golden background, the light of which[20] permeates the translucent white wings, signifying spirituality. On the other hand, there is his physical strength, symbolically expressed by the three-dimensional ridges and a serrated wing contour, which we came to dub as "dragon wings" (discussed in detail in subchapter 9.3.4).

These dragon wings features can be interpreted as a visual metaphor that reveals the aggressive drive as a powerful force that resides beneath the fragile facade of the image. The close correspondence between the visual and verbal metaphors (poetic commentary) indicates the related "strict, structured strength" of this butterfly through two different channels. It is in accordance with the discovered aggressive aspects of butterfly No. 4 and, as such, of an important part of Susanne's psyche.

9.3.3 Male Identity, Balancing Point, and Rounded Front

The initial impression of the gentle, translucent appearance of Touchless Misty, which the artist characterizes by such florid phrases as "fragile daintiness" and "elegant polished white surface," could lead to the perception that Touchless Misty is a female. Yet in describing this butterfly in the poetic commentary, Susanne clearly identifies the creature as a male through the use of masculine pronouns. Stressing "his strict, structured strength," the artist thereby unconsciously projects the strong animus aspect of her own psyche. Her behavioral tendencies and patterns throughout her life have exhibited a persistent desire to be a boy in her early and adolescent years, her preference to play a male-like role in relationships, and the abiding need to dominate in various circumstances.

Touchless Misty manifests an elevated hierarchical rank among the assembly of butterflies. This is substantiated by his three-dimensionality and the top position on the podium. We also have identified the animus-dominated traits of Touchless Misty's image by sickle shapes that form multiple serrated contours. These, taken together with the raised ridges, create a configuration which the artist associates with "dragon wings" (see next subchapter 9.3.4).

This image could mark the presence of aggressive tendencies lurking underneath the beautiful surface of Touchless Misty. The association with

19 Jantzen 1951

20 As it is explored in chapter 12 in the artist's iconography, the golden background symbolizes the realm of spirituality which lies, according to Susanne, at the core of human existence; as such, it is the foundation by which to overcome various challenging existential situations and "find the meaning of existence" (Victor Emil Frankl 1992) (More about this in chapters 10 and 12).

a dragon uncovers additional twists and turns that affirm Susanne's spontaneous preference for this butterfly's male identity. In this light, the artist's manifold recurring fantasies of horror and violence that had haunted her for many decades could be interpreted as the unconscious projection of her aggressive complexes.

The primarily horizontal arrangement of Touchless Misty's wings leads us to initially perceive that this butterfly is well-anchored at the highest level on the podium. However, a closer look at the image reveals that he is balanced precariously on a single point on the underside of his head, resting on the edge of the step. The butterfly's delicate position subverts the impression of his stability and discloses him as vulnerable to sudden shifts. Therefore, Touchless Misty, like Pale Moonlight, is an acrobat that mirrors Susanne's struggles in trying to adjust and counterbalance herself to the fickle and unpredictable circumstances of life.

The blunt shape of Touchless Misty's frontal part stands in noticeable contrast to the needle-sharp protrusion of Pale Moonlight's focal point. The artist, during a discussion, suddenly compared the rotund front of butterfly No. 4 with the obtuse point of a ballet shoe, on which a dancer balances. She marvels at the tremendous skill and strength such an effort requires. Susanne seems to identify her strains to keep an equilibrium in life with a ballerina's trembling stance. With the peculiar balancing posture of Touchless Misty (and Pale Moonlight as well), the artist signifies the unstable and transitory nature of her existence through her visual metaphor.

The rounded, jut-out shape of Touchless Misty's forepart is unmatched among the seven butterflies, which have otherwise angular shapes to their frontal contours. This specific rotund curvature might intimate a particular symbolic meaning. During her initial associations concerning this butterfly, the artist pointed out the affinity of Touchless Misty's rounded front (and its continuation into the ridges of the front wing) with the "kidney shape" in Fanning Everything (see chapter 7), as well as the round loops in the hind wing of Pale Moonlight (see chapter 8: Fig. 8.24 (a)-(c)). We have already hypothesized that the "kidney shape" and "loops" are symbolically related to the theme of sexuality and reproduction. In accord with this interpretation, we could also recognize Touchless Misty's frontal shape as a possible sexual signifier. In essence, this is comparable to the spiky end of Firebird's hind wing, which metaphorically represents her father's pointing index finger as phallic symbolism.[21] (see subchapter 4.4.2 and Fig. 4.6).

Another detail could confirm the validity of this assumption. The forefront of Touchless Misty extends into the space occupied by the left adjacent panel, whose vertical crevice dividing the panels adds emphasis to the separation of the protruding portion from the rest of this butterfly's body. In this context, the smooth and massively rounded front being narrowly separated from the rest of the body gives the impression that it has been "sliced off," a sign suggestive of a feminine castration complex. The same hypothesis was already discussed in the context of Pale Moonlight's "missing scale," which corresponds well with the above presupposition (subchapter 8.2.4).

9.3.4 The Raised Ridges and a Serrated Contour: Dragon Wings

The three-dimensional ridges, along with the multiple serrated contours found in the wings of Touchless Misty, are exclusive components of this butterfly. A series of concave indentations at the rear edge of the wings, which constitutes the serrated profile, is designated by the artist also as "sickle shapes,"[22] "reverse scallop shapes," and "spiky or thorny outline" (Fig. 9.11).

In the preceding chapters, we have identified the specific metaphoric meaning of spiky configurations for Susanne and the threatening associations they hold for her (see subchapters 4.4.1 and 5.2.3). Was this shape incorporated into the appearance of Touchless Misty to convey the same fearsome and malicious undertones? And,

---

21 In addition to the well-known significance of phallic symbolism (Freud, Jung, Lacan), an interesting observation from the article "Unconscious form-creation in art," by Anton Ehrenzweig (Ehrenzweig 1949) may be relevant in this context. Ehrenzweig emphasizes that two projection processes operate in perception: First, the innate tendency to perceive things as more analogous than they actually are; and second, a pan-genital urge to project sexual connotation onto any form perceived.

22 For Susanne, the sharp endings of a sickle shape signify this formation as danger, particularly when it is set in a series to form a serrated contour. The latter configuration represents the epitome of threat for the artist.

if so, what has been the underlying meaning of this imagery, concealed behind the façade of this innocuous white garb? In reference to the precisely defined ridges (with their concave slopes and serrated contour) of Touchless Misty, the analyst asked repeatedly what these formations might remind her of. Eventually, Susanne replied with a spontaneous association—dragon wings. This response led to an investigation of the possibility of a hidden message embedded in the imagery of Touchless Misty which could be deciphered through her perception of this ferocious and powerful mythical creature.

The artist was introduced to the Western myths of the dragon early in her childhood because of its frequent appearances in numerous folk legends and fairy tales,[23] many of which Susanne's mother used to read to her pre-school daughters at bedtime nearly every night. As she grew up and began to study Western and classical mythologies in school, her vision of dragons acquired from children's fairy tales was modified by such legends as the slaying of a dragon by St. George, and Siegfried killing a dragon in the German medieval epic poem, *Nibelungenlied* (Songs of Nibelungs).[24] In all those narrations, the dragons are depicted as aggressive beasts, spitting fire and presenting great danger to the populace, while keeping their lairs in caves or remote places and attacking anyone who dares to approach them. For warriors and heroes, the situation presented an opportunity to prove their bravery by slaying the dragons and appropriating the treasures that the beasts had hoarded or saving heroines from their captivity. Thus, in the fairy tales, the dragon was a monster to be feared for its destructive power.

The image of dragon is also metaphorically used to describe some specific personalities. For example, Susanne remembers that at around the age of 12, she read a modern tale to her younger sister about the adventures of a boy named Jim and his older friend Luke, a locomotive driver.[25] The two heroes had arrived at a village children's school, where the pupils were helplessly suffering under the tyranny of their fearsome teacher and principal, "Frau Mahlzahn" (German for "Mrs. Grinding Tooth"), who was a bad-tempered dragon with foul, noxious breath. Eventually, Jim and Luke tricked the dragon and liberated the children. For Susanne and her sister, the words "Frau Mahlzahn" became a humorous euphemism for bad breath in the morning just after awakening. We should also mention that "dragon" in German is a common colloquial expression for an overbearing or tyrannical woman,[26] especially when she is seen as domineering over her husband. In this train of thought, Susanne's younger sister sometimes would use the expression "*Hausdrache*" (literally "home dragon") to describe the family's female pediatrician.[27]

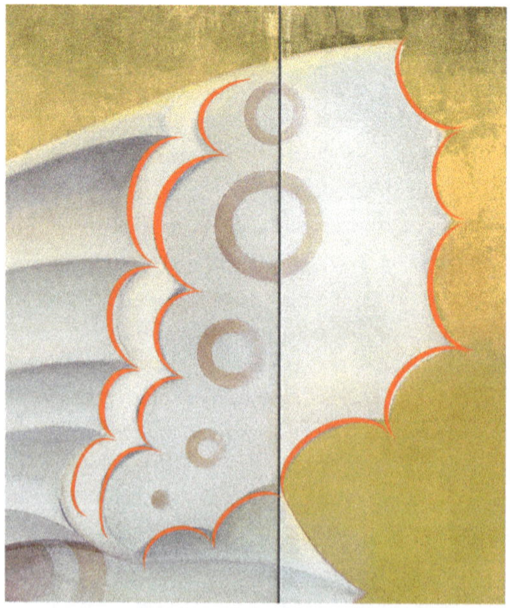

Fig. 9.11. Serrated contours accentuated with red overlays in Touchless Misty's front wing.

During her academic studies, the artist encountered many artistic depictions of legendary dragon-slayers from different centuries. The most famous subject was St. George who defeated a dragon to liberate a captive virgin. She remembers this Christian legend, and the corresponding painting by Paolo Uccello (1397–1475), titled

23 Those were from the collections by Johann Karl August Musäus (1735–1787); the Brothers Grimm (Jacob Grimm (1785–1863), and Wilhelm Grimm (1786–1859)); Hans Christian Andersen (1805–1875), and Ludwig Bechstein (1801–1860).

24 See chapter 7, note 7.

25 Michael Ende, *Knopf und Lukas der Lokomotivführer* (English translation: *Jim Button and Luke the Locomotive Driver*) (Stuttgart: Thienemann, 1960).

26 In German, "der Drache" (the dragon) is masculine. However it can be used to describe a female person (or a female dragon).

27 The younger sister in her early childhood had developed a great fear of the family's elderly pediatrician. She remembers the doctor, even decades later, as "a horrible dragon."

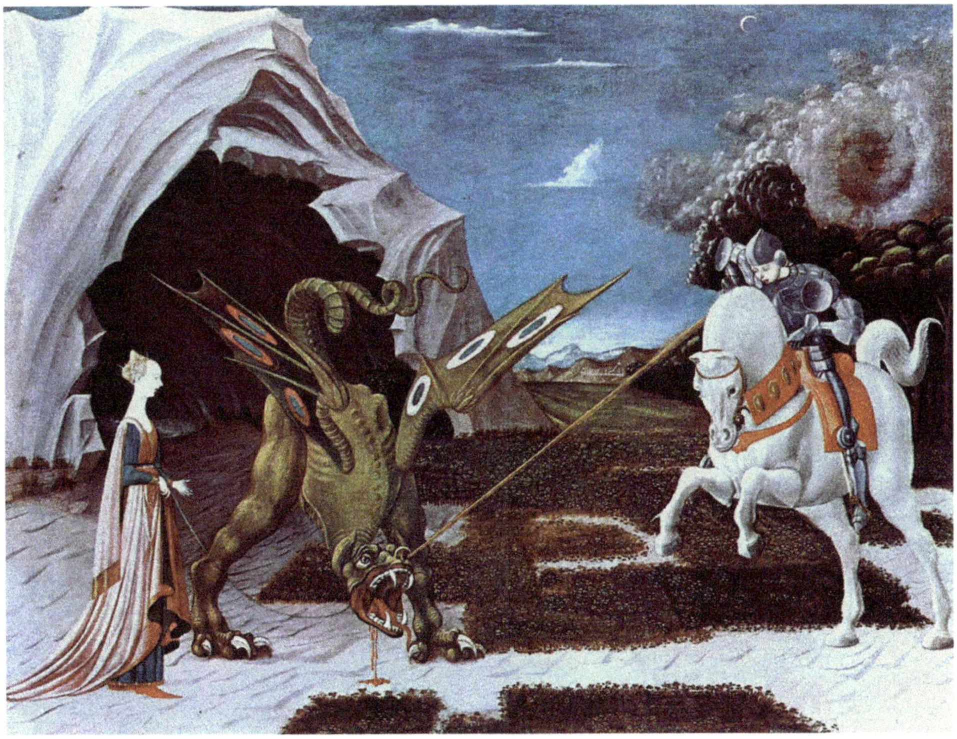

Fig. 9.12. Paolo Uccello, *St. George and the Dragon*, (circa 1455). Tempera on canvas, 22½ x 28¾ in (56 x 74 cm). National Gallery, London, UK.

St. George and the Dragon (about 1470, Fig. 9.12),[28] stands out in her mind even these days as a quintessential example of how an Occidental dragon might look.

The Italian Renaissance master depicted the dragon with a plump body, a pair of strong legs, and large, bat-like wings, accentuated with ridges, spiky contours, and decorated with a few ring shapes, red on the right wing, pinkish on the left one. Recalling Uccello's work, which she had not seen for many years, Susanne was astonished to discover the circular marks on the wings of the dragon, a distinctive feature, which had faded from her conscious memory. She favors circles as a very positive shape and red as a great color, but apparently she had completely forgotten about these features on the dragon, as well as another critical depiction: the actual lethal wound inflicted by St. George on the beast's eye. This last detail triggered an immediate reaction in Susanne, revealing the desire to protect her eyes from any imaginary attack by closing them firmly or covering them with her hands. We assume that the amnesia concerning this particularly harrowing feature of Uccello's painting was determined by the mechanism of suppression by censoring the artist's aggressive drive (more on this shortly).

Another dragon association that Susanne had are the sleek and fast "dragon ships" of the Vikings, known to the English and others who suffered the Norsemen's brutal raids in the early Middle Ages. The name of the vessels was an obvious reference to their prows being decorated with carved dragon heads. In this context, the "dragon" appellation given by the victims of the Norsemen's scourge evokes in Susanne's mind the vision of the overwhelming power, hostility, and extreme danger often associated with these ruthless seafarers.

Dragon wings as fancied by artists in the Occident are often modeled after the wings of bats, showing a wing contour with inverted curves, and edgy endings (for a typical example, see Fig. 9.13). The serrated outline is not limited to the mythical beasts or bats, but is also shared by some butterfly species (Figs. 9.14, 9.15, and 9.16), which Susanne recorded in a few of her first sketches (Figs. 9.17, 9.18, and 9.19).

28 The work now hangs in the National Gallery, London. Susanne had known this painting since she first saw it in the National Gallery in 1982. In a letter to her mother, she wrote humorously, "The dragon resembles a tame doggy on a lady's leash." (The artist's translation.)

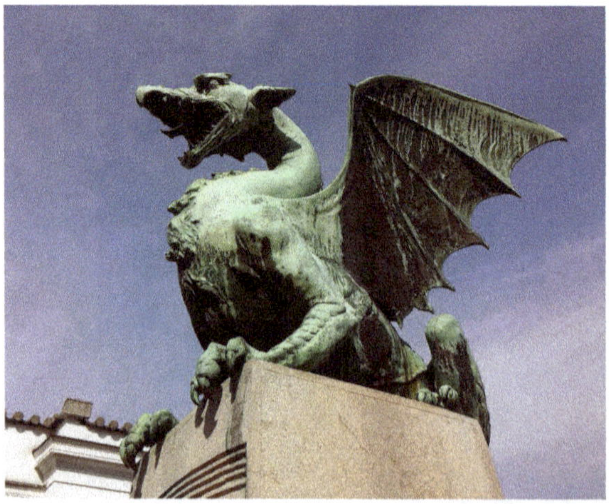

Fig. 9.13. Jurij Zaninović (1876-1946), Dragon, 1900-1901. Copper sculpture, from the Dragon Bridge in Ljubliana, Slovenia.

She is familiar with the imaginary anatomical features of dragon's wings in European art: their spiky scallop-like serrated wing contour; the ridges made by the underlying skeletal structure clearly visible on a thin, smooth surface; and even sometimes decorative elements such as circular spots or rings. We posit that this "dragon cliché" was highly influential in providing the foundation for the involuntary creation of the dragon-like features of Touchless Misty. In particular, the details of the sharp, raised ridges seen in this butterfly's wings make an excellent case for Susanne's association of Touchless Misty's wings with those of the dragon.

Anger and aggression rarely have been directly represented in Susanne's artworks, and any graphic depictions of brutal and lethal violence are mostly absent. However, over the years, she has alluded to those subjects in some paintings, disguising them in allegorical and metaphorical images. With that, observers might sense or recognize the presence of threatening scenarios through perceptions based on their own experiences and sensibilities. In the following discussion, we will examine a number of Susanne's paintings dealing with the theme of potential threat and violence, and we shall pay particular attention to the artist's choice of shapes, by which she tries to illustrate the subject.

In the painting, *The Sea of Time* (1981/82), introduced in chapter 7 (see Figs. 7.24 and 9.1), the central figure is depicted as encircled by the hostile sea. The threatening waves are characterized by numerous triangular shapes with curvilinear slopes that converge in needle-like crests. A number of serrated contours, formed in the stormy water and partially crowned with white foam (Fig. 9.20), are emblematic of Susanne's emotional state when she painted this work.

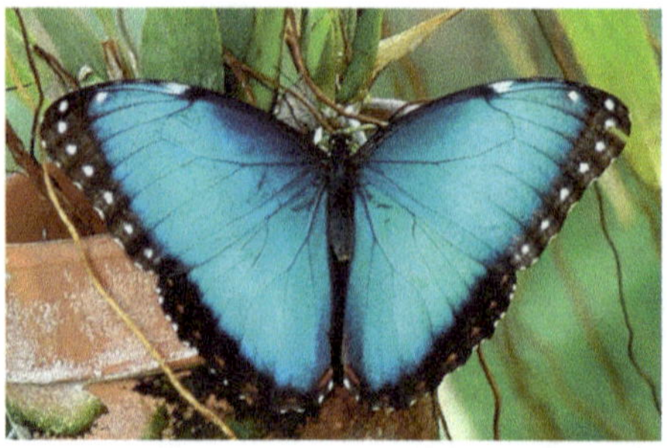

Fig. 9.14. Blue Morpho.

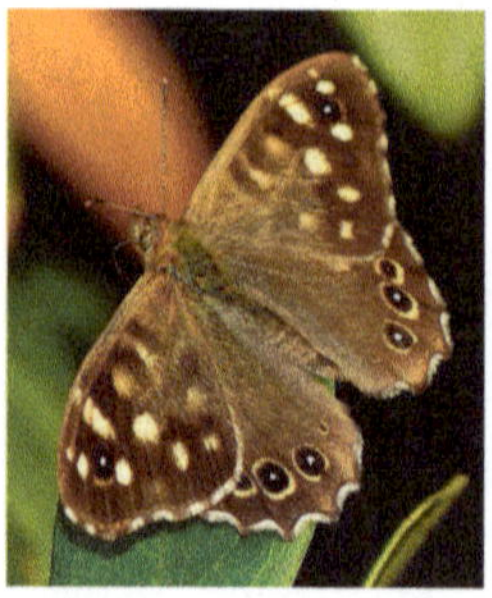

Fig. 9.15. Sharp endings and eyespots on a butterfly.

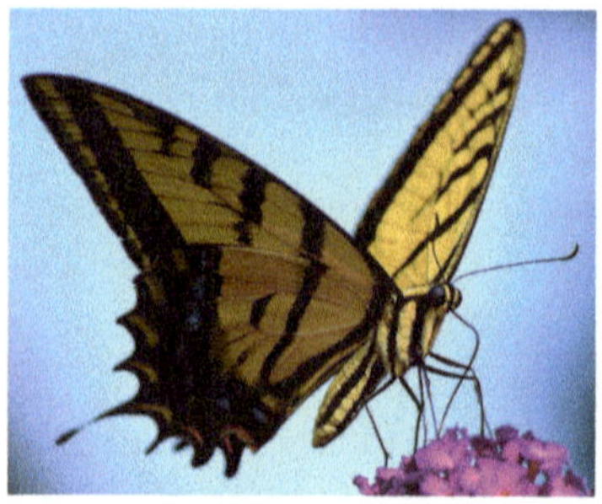

Fig. 9.16. Swallowtail butterfly.

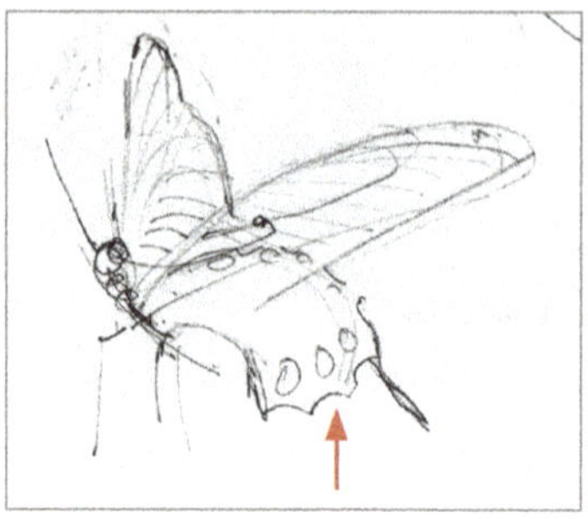

Fig. 9.17. Detail from Fig. 2.1b: Primary sketch from page "B Front.

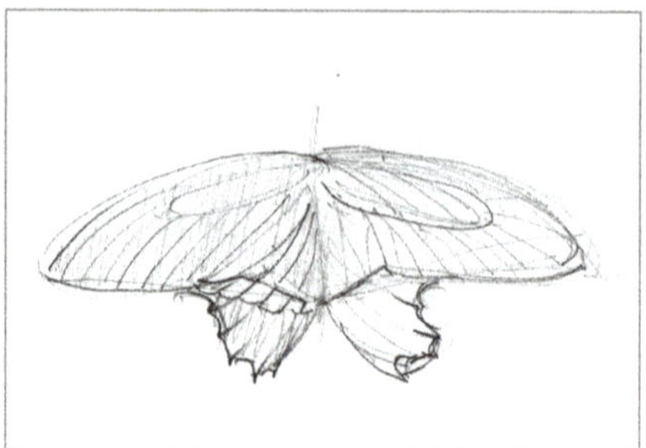

Fig. 9.18. Detail from Fig. 2.1e: Primary sketch from page "B Reverse.

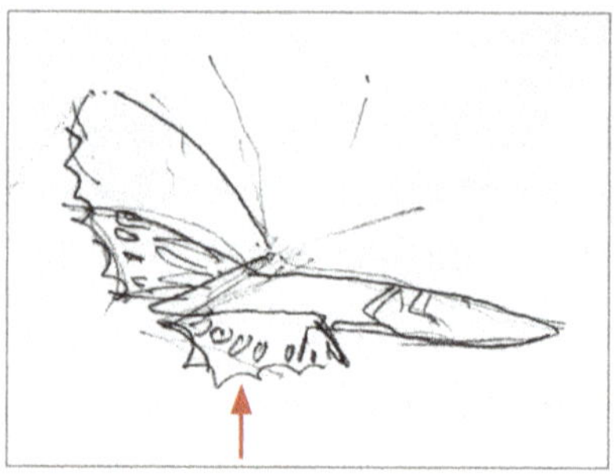

Fig. 9.19. Detail from Fig. 2.1d: Primary sketch from page "A Reverse."

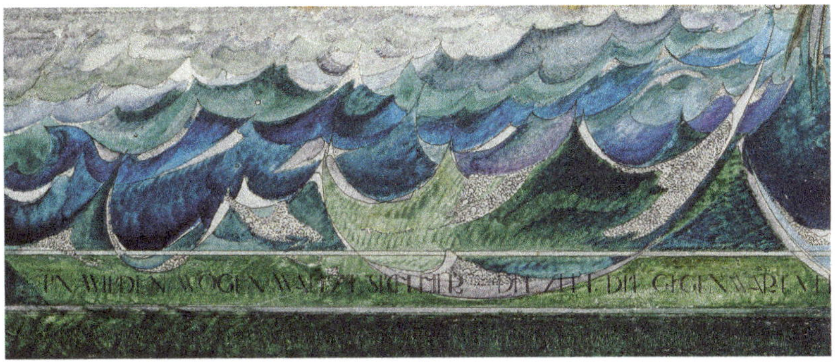

Fig. 9.20. Detail from Fig. 9.1: hostile waves from *The Sea of Time.*

The figure's head is embellished with strands of small, scarlet-colored spheres (Fig. 7.24). In our previous discussion, we considered these beads to be the metaphorical visualization of various notions and feelings that preoccupied the artist's mind, which she calls "thought energy." At the time this work was executed, Susanne was being overwhelmed with suicidal thoughts, and the red spheres could be the unconscious symbolic visualization of her desirable tendencies during these years toward liberation from life. Furthermore, spiky white strands streak the windblown hair, correlating with the turbulent clouds and tumultuous foaming waves,[29] painted also in whitish hues. All this is driven by a fierce wind, which could metaphorically signify the artist's troubled mind. We assume that her mood was transfigured into the visual metaphors of inanimate objects as the waves, wind, clouds, and hair, unconsciously representing the artist's inner turmoil.

In *Destiny* (1988, Fig. 9.21), Susanne metaphorically represents the perilous state of fragile human existence with a small puppet on a string dangling above the turbulent water, which

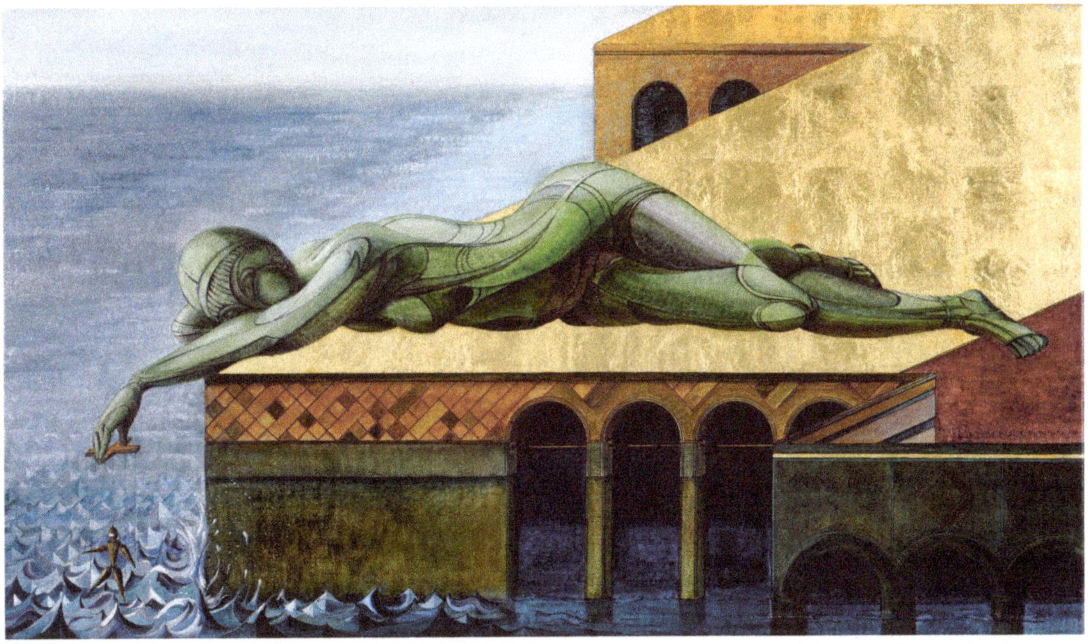

Fig. 9.21. Susanne Schuenke, *Destiny*, 1988. Oil and gold leaf on canvas, 24 x 42 in (61 x 106 cm). Corporate collection, Berlin, Germany.

29 The German expression, "*vor Wut schäumen*" (which could be translated in English as "foaming up in great anger"), Susanne illustrated literally with the foam of water. This expression might have been created by the analogy between the heated water, which bubbles with froth, and someone losing his temper during an intense argument or traumatic confrontation. When a person is arguing vociferously, saliva can result in foam. It should also be noted that the German verb for cooking, *kochen*, is related to *schäumen* (to foam), indicating heating and bubbling (or foaming) of water. Thus, the above saying was metaphorically expressed by the artist in the image of the foaming sea.

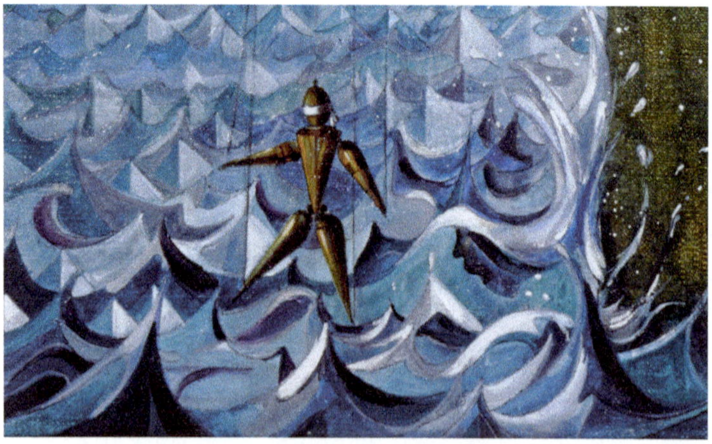

Fig. 9.22. Detail from *Destiny* Fig. 9.21: hostile waves.

symbolizes the "toils and snares"[30] of life. The hapless, blindfolded victim (Fig. 9.22) is surrounded by the stormy sea, which crashes against the wall, breaking into "angry" foam and spray. The waves in the foreground closely echo the sickle shapes in *The Sea of Time,* while in the further distance, they are arrayed like sawtoothed rows. The sharp tips of the waves and water droplets metaphorically emphasize the danger to which the marionette is exposed by Destiny's whims.

The painting *Michael* (2002), discussed in Chapter 8 (Fig. 8.11), contains comparable shapes. In the earthly left "half" of the scenery, the artist has painted some abstract figurations, whose contours consist of connected, irregular sickle shapes with sharp spikes (Fig. 9.23). Susanne remembers her intention to illustrate the human suffering caused by hatred as well as injurious circumstances which she metaphorically visualized in the image of said sickle-shaped forms, and has always experienced as threatening and painful.[31]

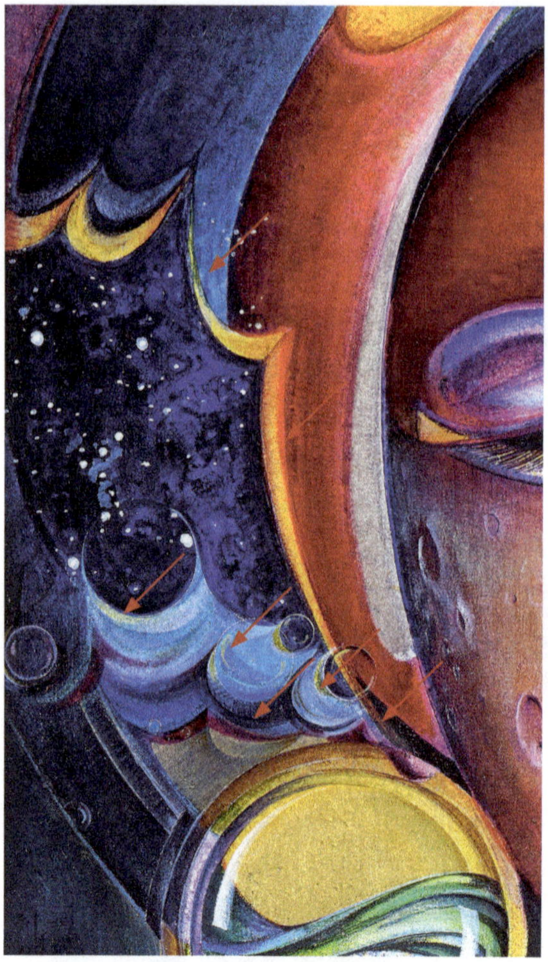

Fig. 9.23. Detail from *Michael*, Fig. 8.11: hostile waves from the left edge of the painting (arrows added).

The symbolism of aggression could be expressed in another variation of sharp-tipped shapes: An acute triangle that resembles an elongated, narrow spear, which we have identified in the following works. In chronological order, they are: *Ten O'Clock News* (1985, Fig. 8.50), *Terminator* (1985, Fig. 4.16), *Thunderstorm* (1989/90, Fig. 9.24), and *Change in the Weather* (1991, Fig. 6.12). In the first three works mentioned, these specific forms point to the topics of danger and destruction: in *Ten O'Clock News,* the lance of the warrior; in *Terminator,* the pair of elongated acute triangles, shaped like the jaws of a caliper; and in *Thunderstorm,* the path and pointed ends of the lightning flash and the craggy rock formation. All these configurations utilize the spear-like acute triangles, symbolically revealing the undercurrent of menace and aggression in the images.

Change in the Weather is another case in which acute triangular shapes are used to symbolically express aggression and militancy. The artist depicts a high ranking military officer with a face

30 A phrase quoted from the third stanza of "Amazing Grace" by John Newton (1725–1807).

31 In the imagery (Fig. 8.11) there are two white shapes below the proper left chin of Michael that could be mistakenly perceived as sickle shapes. However, the artist points out that the shapes are actually not isolated, independent figures, but, rather, they are two segments of a continuous curvilinear configuration that meanders and loops around Michael's head. This type of formation frequently appears in Susanne's paintings, and *Michael* is a good example of this. Thus, Susanne considers the two segments mentioned above to be benevolent in contrast to the hostile sickle shape with its pointed ends.

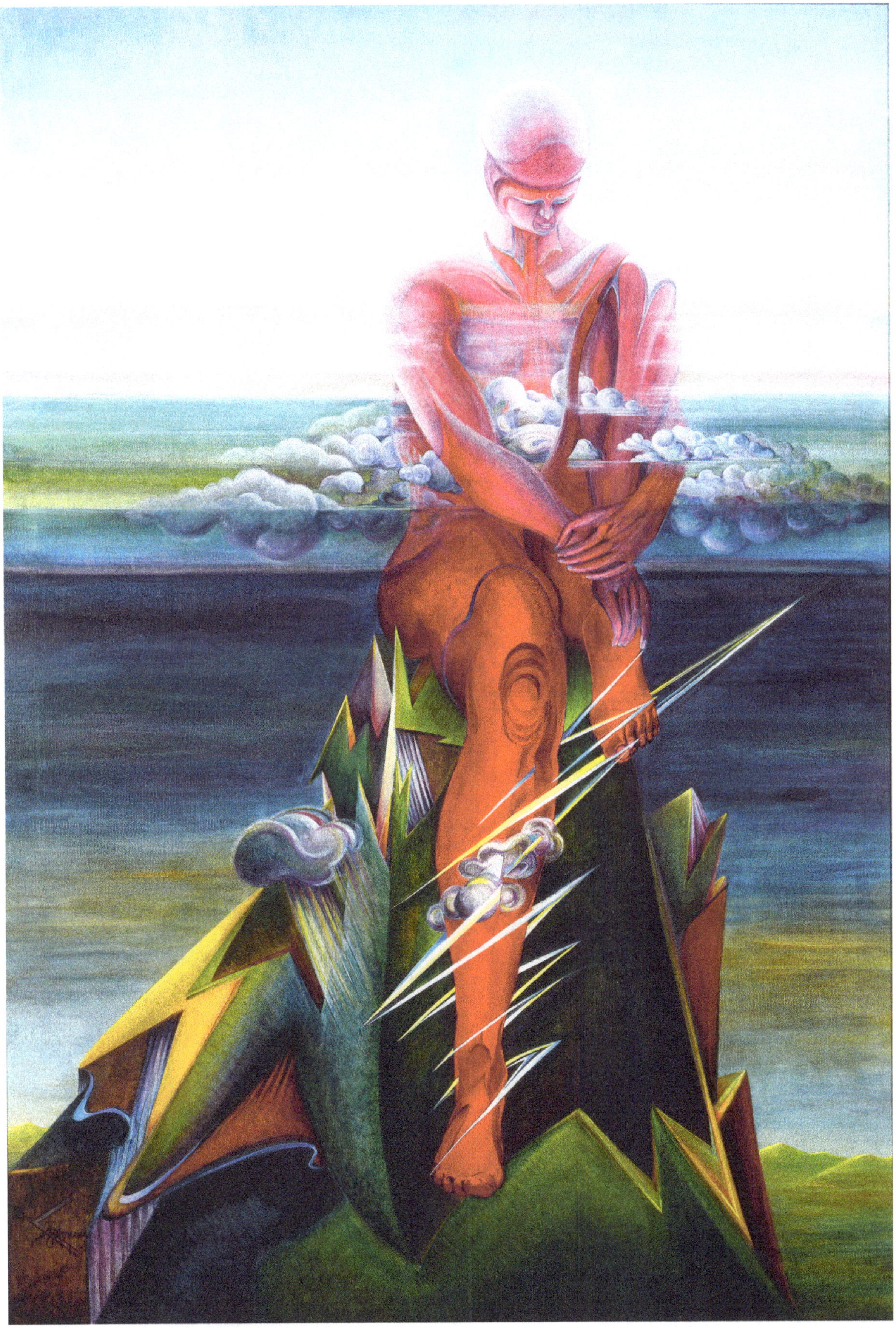

Fig. 9.24. Susanne Schuenke, *Thunderstorm*, 1989. Oil on canvas, 45 x 32 in (115 x 81 cm). Corporate collection, Ohio.

of a ram. The creature, fanning himself vainly with a large, sun-like fan, wears a bicorne military hat with tapered, needle-sharp ends, one of which terminates in a bayonet-like form. As the initial image began to take shape,[32] Susanne recognized a sheep's profile in it, which reminded her of the German expression *dummes Schaf* (English: stupid sheep). The idea was then used to portray the image as an allusion to a powerful person's lack of intellectual traits and his insidious nature. With this, the artist illustrates the well-known saying, "A wolf in sheep's clothing." In this painting, through visual metaphors, Susanne presents her conviction that the greatest threat to the world is the stupidity and heedlessness of those aggressive or arrogant political leaders who do not care about the adverse consequences of their malicious acts on humanity.

The militarist clutches the fan, his spike-like fingers seem to merge with its ribs, while the jaw area of his face is adorned by a number of divaricating stylized feathers with their distinct "eyes" resembling a peacock's tail (for a close-up, see Fig. 9.25(a)). This formation presents us with a further discovery: We can observe many parallels between Touchless Misty's wing configuration and the various shapes and formations in this "peacock feathers" region. These similarities include numerous convex and concave contours, the spiky ends of the feathers, and a blunt front to the left, from which the feathers originate. In addition, the "eyes" of the feathers could find their equivalents in the circular patterns on the wings of Touchless Misty. We also note that the "ridges" on the butterfly's wings are similar to the rachises (ridges) of the "peacock feathers" (see Fig 9.25a–b for a diagrammatical comparison of the parallels). All these details of the sheep-like creature from *Change in the Weather* find remarkable counterparts in the features of Touchless Misty. This leads us to suggest that in this painting, created more than a decade prior to *Give Me Wings!*, the artist's psyche already manifested the symbolic meaning of the militarist's aggression in sickle shapes,[33] which was concealed in the natural beauty of the peacock's feathers. Many of his plumage's configurations reappear in the dragon wings of Touchless Misty. The latter are, according to the artist, also camouflaged in "the most beautiful butterfly in the assembly."

In the design of Touchless Misty and the ram-militarist, latent aggression is manifested and cloaked behind charming façades. These are the splendid, decorative facial plumage of the officer and the peaceful white color of the butterfly. Until our analysis discovered the above correlations, the artist was totally unaware of these parallels.

In accordance with previous knowledge (see note 33) and comparing her use of sickle shapes in the ram and in the butterfly (Fig. 9.25 a-b) with the water in *Sea of Time* (Fig. 9.20) and *Destiny* (Fig. 9.22), we substantiate the artist's predisposition to transcribe aggressiveness into this specific crescent form, either singly or in a serrated contour. In effect, these shapes could be considered the artist's personal symbols of aggression. With this symbolism having been established in her mind, the artist also unconsciously applied the shape to the design of the butterfly Touchless Misty (Fig. 9.6 (h)), creating what we interpret as "dragon wings."

---

32 Even decades later, the artist clearly remembers the very beginning of her drawing. She was in the mood for "needing to draw," but without any idea of what it would be. In that state, the first few lines "simply came": There was first a plumb, curved configuration (later forming the face's profile), which she transformed to a sheepish mask on a stick. But that felt inadequate. An urge led her to add a strong straight line on top, which became the brim of the hat. Then she rendered a second curve as a counterbalance—a move that suddenly formed the top of the hat. Instantly she recognized the "Napoleonic hat," in the image which caused her to imagine the head as belonging to a person possessing immensely dangerous power, whose lack of character and wisdom could doom the world. The rest of the painting developed from that concept.

33 Concerning the influences of Susanne's past knowledge from her earlier years on the development of this particular symbol of aggression, a few episodes can shed light on the question why the sickle shape became such a cruel configuration for her. During analysis involving free association, she recalled the sickle-shaped Oriental weapons she saw in 1981 in the Imperial War Museum, located in the Tower of London. Then, she remembered that her parents constantly warned her to be careful with the sickle in the family garden, which she connected in her vivid imagination with the dreadful pain that might result from a wound caused by a tool of this shape. Since taking high school history, she knew about the sickle blades on the wheels of Persian chariots, mentioned in the context of the clash between Darius and Alexander the Great which could mow soldiers down inflicting horrible wounds.
In this context, we mention the scythe, the ancient farming tool used for cutting grain plants for harvest. The scythe has taken on a more grim aspect since the medieval period in the West as an instrument by which the Grim Reaper (the personification of death) cuts off people's lives. These factors—mostly rooted in the personal unconscious but possibly also in the universal—could have contributed to Susanne's idiosyncratic sensitivity toward the sickle.

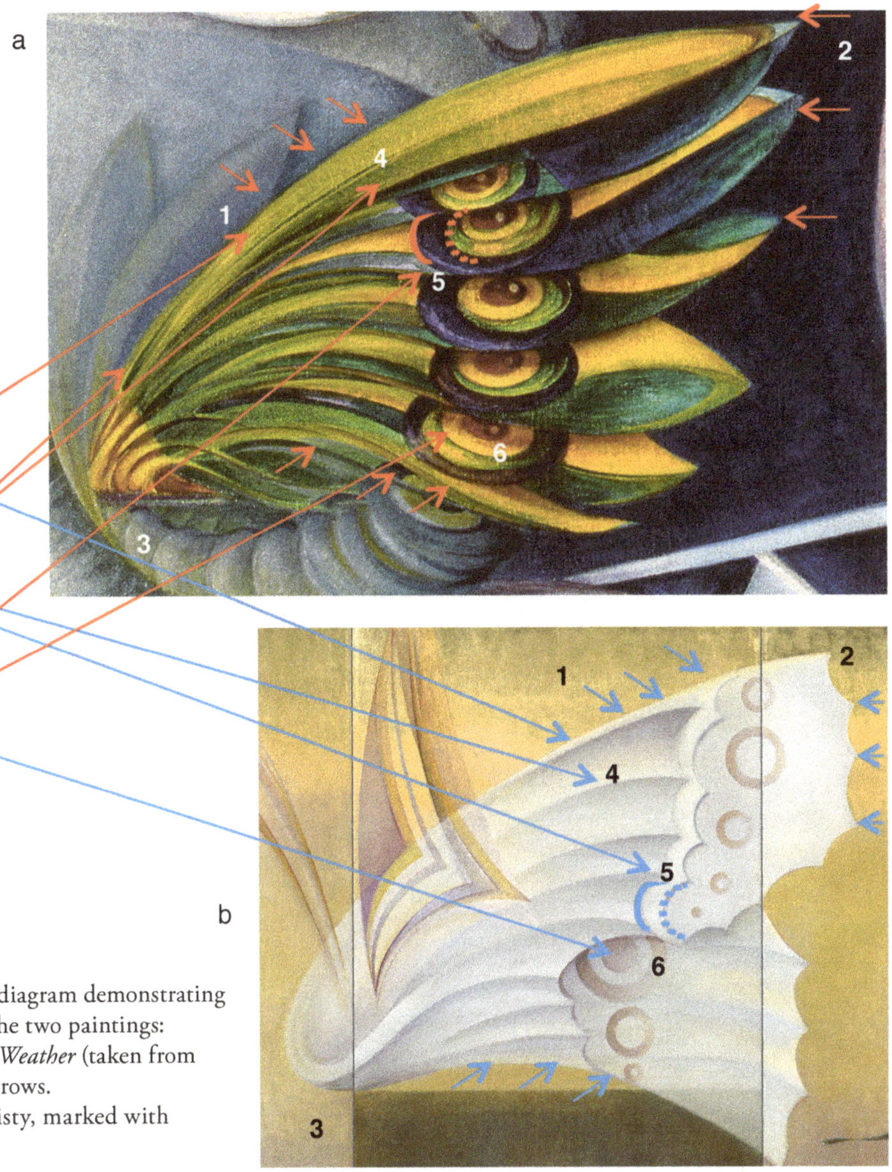

Fig. 9.25 a-b. A Comparative diagram demonstrating the similar features between the two paintings:
(a) Detail from *Change in the Weather* (taken from Fig. 6.12), marked with red arrows.
(b) Detail from Touchless Misty, marked with blue arrows.

Susanne unconsciously equipped this butterfly's image with certain attributes indicative of this mythological creature. Dragons are associated with supreme strength, supernatural power, and the potential for aggression in the imagination of both the Eastern and Western cultures. Certain features of the butterfly (ribbed wings, sickle-like shapes, serrated contour, and ring pattern as reminiscences of the dragon) are symbolic manifestations of unconscious processes connected to the complex of aggression, which was recognized by those observed peculiarities in the image of Touchless Misty. Uncovering these metaphorical meanings in the image of the butterfly's wings opened the analysis to the latent tendencies for aggression in the artist's psyche.

Susanne found it difficult to participate in the discovery of different expressions of this complex, and to consent to the vexing probing into her inner mind which could reveal some of the instinctual facets of her psyche. By overcoming her resistance, Susanne came to accept the existence of these aggressive tendencies, which this study unveiled in the "dragon wing" features of Touchless Misty. One of the constituents of the butterfly's sobriquet—"Misty"—already mirrors those veiled aspects. It alludes to something mysterious and uncanny (see subchapter 9.1.3), which drives our thoughts and behavior in an incomprehensible, mystifying way that does not consort easily with the superego's conscience and moral principles.

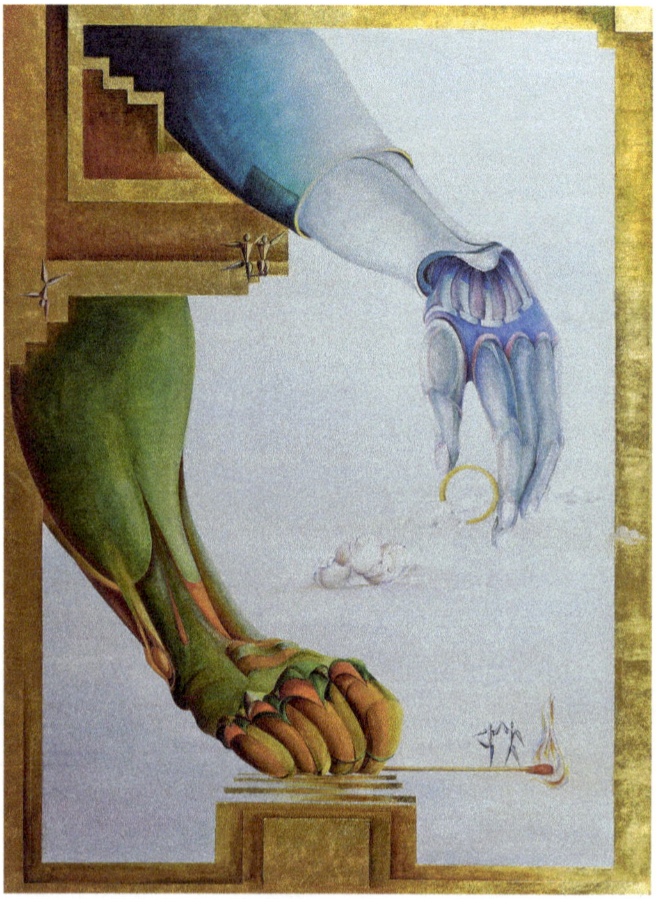

Fig. 9.26. Susanne Schuenke, *Air and Fire*, left panel from the diptych *The Four Elements* 1990. Oil and gold leaf on canvas, 48 x 36 in (90 x 60 cm).
Corporate collection, Germany.

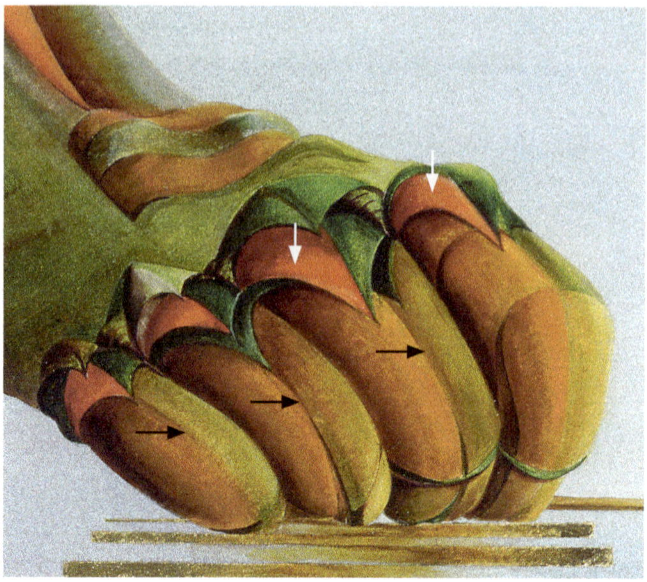

Fig. 9.27. Detail from Fig. 9.26.
Arrows point to sickle shapes (white arrows) and ridges (black arrows) in the hand.

While discussing this topic, Susanne spontaneously decided to search through the images of her earlier works. She found another image with a similar assembly of sickle shapes and ridges in the image of the "hand of fire" in the *Fire and Air* panel from her diptych *The Four Elements* (Figs. 9.26 and 9.27), which also conveys unconscious symbolism for threat and aggression.

Generally, Susanne does not display any signs of aggressive behavior. Throughout her life, she has never acted with real physical violence against another human being or even an animal (excluding pests) aside from two minor incidents at the age of seven, when she slapped a child and bit another. These events caused her parents to admonish her for the inappropriate acts. She will often relive accounts of brute force and cruelty she has read, heard, or seen on television and in the movies, as if they are real events that she has personally experienced, as the victim of aggression and violence. Her mind invents various scenarios of persecution and oppression, in which she identifies herself as the perpetrator of these acts. Furthermore, we can trace the existence of some haunting fantasies in her mind involving imagined cruelties committed against her that could be, as she speculates, punishment for aggressive intentions.

Susanne is highly sensitive to any information about violence—be it wars, social conflicts, crimes, or in interpersonal relationships. Consequently, she long ago decided to cut off the stream of distressing news by being highly selective in her access to its most obvious sources: newspaper, television, internet, and radio. She carefully selects movies and other visual material, such as documentaries and educational presentations. Susanne does not hesitate to leave a conversation in which the topic of violence accompanied by its grisly details is raised unexpectedly. She explains that the description and imagery of violence to which she was exposed would be permanently imprinted in her memory in vivid details, lying in wait until something triggered the memory to disturb her mind once more.

With such a predisposition, her mind is easily tormented by visions of horror and fantasies, especially of torture and mutilation involving the eyes, tongue, wrist, and navel, which are maimed by various implements, such as hammers, knives, needles, blades, and the like. In consequence, she is compelled to protect herself from potential threats by various means, some of which can be observed in her defensive gestures, such as wrapping her hands around her torso or covering her eyes or mouth to protect herself from the onslaught of imagined threats. These particularities of her behavior are well-known to her family and her inner circle of friends. However, she has managed to skillfully mask the explicit manifestation of her susceptibility to the fear of violence when she is in public spaces.

The expression of Susanne's latent aggression can be observed in her demeanor during a heated discussion, where she will fight tooth and nail to uphold her view. During such an exchange, she clenches her fists, furrows her brows, tenses her body (see Fig. 6.1 for how the young Susanne illustrated her angry state), and, occasionally, she may slam a table with her hand. Once, during a fierce argument, she somehow managed to divert her powerful desire to punch her spouse by bashing her fist into a nearby door instead, which nearly broke her wrist. Recognizing that her livelihood depended on her hands to paint, she swore never to use this outlet again. Over the years, she has also learned to disengage herself from conversations too sensitive for her.

When she was in workout sessions, she did an exercise where the arms alternately jab out to left and right in quick succession, and she was astonished at the quasi-automatic movement of her fisted hands. She imagined that a person standing in her "line of fire" would receive a powerful blow. Susanne describes herself like a detached observer viewing her hands moving of their "own will" without any guidance from her.

After discovering the metaphorical meaning of dragon wings, she accepted that violent impulses dwelt in her. Susanne revealed that in her occasional daydreams she experienced involuntary thoughts and fantasies with cruel content. Susanne rarely holds any actively violent thought against other people. Most of her latent aggressive tendency manifests in "what if" fantasies about various unlikely hypothetical chains of events which would somehow fulfill her desire for justice. These imaginary, speculative scenarios are one of her defense mechanisms for dealing with stressful situations. Moreover, for Susanne, the "solution" for threatening, violent impulses, instead of aiming the aggression against others, is to substitute herself as the target of this destructive energy, innumerable times imagining devastating consequences as a way out of the predicament.

Violent solutions lingering in her mind distressed her because of the moral judgment of her conscience, resulting in painful feelings of guilt and shame. Hence, the great waves of sadness inevitably came over her whenever she dwelt on those fantasies.

By delving into the latent content of her thoughts, Susanne helps us further validate our interpretation of the meaning behind the artist's painted image of Touchless Misty's "dragon wings." The analysis of their components has revealed the reverse side of this "peaceful" butterfly—aggressive features. In the artist's life experience, we find confirmation of the presence, development, and expression of substantive aggressive tendencies over many years (already touched on in prior chapters). We will list some more details regarding the aggressive drive in Susanne's psyche.[34]

In her early childhood, her wild anger and temper tantrums sometimes went untamed. When she could not get her will, she even resorted to using her teeth to express her fury. The unfortunate victims were her older sister on one occasion and a classmate on another at the elementary school, as mentioned. The parents, immediately and in no uncertain terms, prohibited her from behaving similarly ever again.

She tries to substitute her initial aggressive impulse with alternative action. To this day, when someone wants to put her down, even jokingly, it raises her hackles, and she will retaliate, although in a well-mannered and sophisticated way. In contrast to the above displays of latent aggression, during her regular physical workout with body and arm movements, Susanne feels an overwhelming urge to act out her aggression by throwing punches at an invisible opponent as strongly as she can.

These aggressive tendencies also manifested in rare marital situations in the past. We previously mentioned the incident when she nearly broke her wrist. Furthermore, by occasionally shouting at her partner, Susanne sadly emulated the example of her father who often yelled at his

34 When the discussion turned to aggression and fighting, Susanne immediately said: "I am hungry." She muses that consuming food, especially sweets, might be a defense mechanism for her violent impulses, and that this might be a hypothetical speculation why she eats so incredibly fast. About this, her mother used to say: "Susanne devours her food."

wife. In her adulthood, she began a long process of curbing aggressive tendencies, and over the years, Susanne slowly reached an appropriate level of self-regulation. Nevertheless, she continues to be vulnerable when she is confronted with reports or actual incidents of outright aggression, violence, and abuse. On those occasions, in fear of the haunting memories and associations that spontaneously spring up in her thoughts, she tries to escape such exposure.

Unfortunately, these traumatic events, suffered by others and coming to Susanne's attention, stay with her for decades. She invests an extraordinary amount of empathy toward the victims of cruelty, to the point that she identifies herself with them, imagining and feeling their fear, pain, horror, and despair. The above contemplation reveals the possible existence of unconscious double identification, in which the artist plays the roles either of the aggressor or the victim.

9.3.5 Rings, Circles, and Eyes

Ring and circle designs can be found in Susanne's artworks as recurring themes, appearing in various configurations, simple or complex, isolated or integrated, stacked or intertwined. They are an important part of her individual expression, and, as we analyzed in subchapter 7.3, have strong correlations with the latent content of the unconscious. The following examples show how the unconscious symbolism of rings and circles developed over time in the artist's oeuvre prior to *Give Me Wings!*

In a gift-wrapping paper design she did for a high school assignment in the 1970s (Fig. 9.28), we can observe numerous disks of varying sizes, painted with a number of colored annuli, and laid on top of each other. As she remembers, this design greatly delighted her aesthetic sensibility, and she came to employ the motif and its variations frequently in her future works.

In *L'Été Persan* (*Persian Summer*) (1988), (see chapter 8.2.4., Figs. 8.21 and 8.22), Susanne surrounded the blossoming chrysanthemums with concentric circular bands, which echoed and reinforced the flowers' colors. According to the artist, she intended the design to metaphorically hint at the blossoms' perfume radially spreading its attractive aroma. Susanne continued this idea in *Le Printemps Indien* (*Indian Spring*), (1989) (Fig. 9.29), where she provided, through concentric circles embracing each lotus blossom, an imaginative visualization of the scent wafting up from the midst of the petals. In her words, "the aroma of the flowers is spreading out in those circles like 'broadcasting waves'" (Fig. 9.30). In both paintings, the concentric circle shapes symbolize for her the strong, compelling nature of something delightful that the olfactory sense can perceive and appreciate, but which cannot be easily defined by words or visualized in images.

In many cultures, the circular shape that adorns the revered person in an artwork often takes on the symbolic role, signifying the exceptional importance of the personage, who is the object of worship. In the religious art of both East and West, this shape has been employed for millennia as the visual sign of the holiness that manifests as halos around such sacred figures as the Buddha and Christ. In her painting *Indian Spring*, Susanne rendered sets of concentric rings around the lotus blossoms making them analogous to aureolas. She painted them on the silver background above the water, designating the ethereal aspect of this natural scene.

Her fascination with the beauty of nature finds an interpretation in *The Land of Iro-Ha*, (1992), a six-panel Japanese-style folding screen (Figs. 12.9 and 9.31 (detail)). In this work, she depicts an imaginary mountainscape floating in a golden sea, enriched with clusters of white, pink, and lilac rings and spheres. These circular shapes

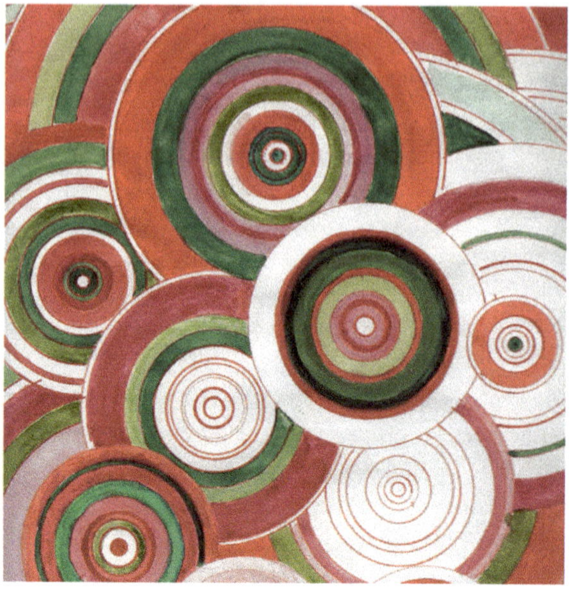

Fig. 9.28.
Susanne Schuenke, *Gift wrap paper*, 1976.
Watercolor and ink on paper.
Collection of the artist.

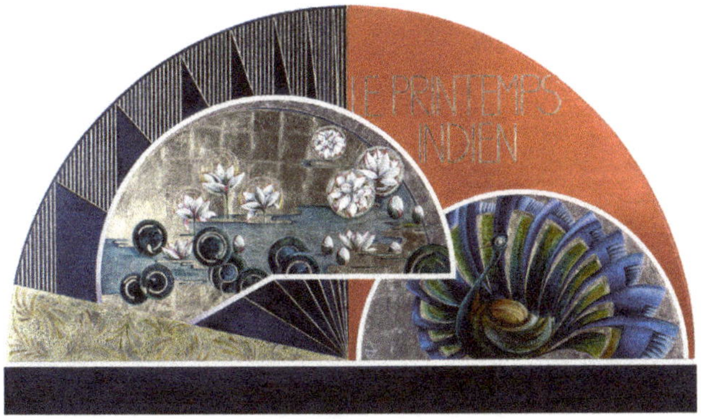

Fig. 9.29. Susanne Schuenke, *Le Printemps Indien* (*Indian Spring*),1989. Oil, gold and silver leaf on wood, 43 x 79 in (110 x 200 cm). Collection of the artist.

symbolize flowers and their ethereal, radiating allure. For this Japanese landscape, the artist chose a higher degree of stylization than employed in *Persian Summer*, reducing the image of flowers to multiple, concentric circles that reflect the beauty and harmony of nature. Through abstraction, she aims to symbolize the endless wealth of their shapes and colors and to stimulate the imagination of the viewer to reexperience the aesthetic joy in a fresh perspective.

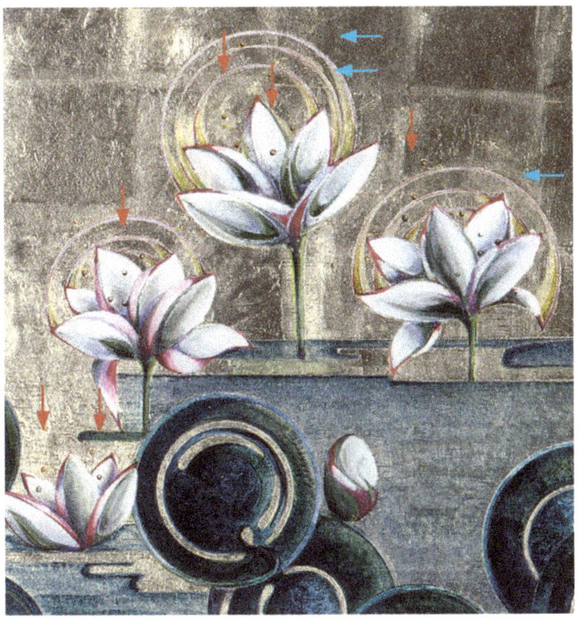

Fig. 9.30. Detail from Fig. 9.29 with overlaid arrows. Blue arrows show concentric circles around the blossoms, giving the appearance of "broadcasting waves". Red arrows point at rising tiny bubbles. The artist chose both visual elements to indicate the flowers' scent.

In the painting, the circles are conceived as flowers. The real objects and their abstract expression are interchangeable, i.e., the flowers' radial symmetry is mirrored by circles, and, reciprocally, the circles invoke the imagination of flowers. This observation leads us to the consideration of how the unconscious manifests its messages in forms that are compressed or condensed (symbolization). In the contemplative mountain scenery of *The Land of Iro-Ha,* (Fig. 9.31) Susanne chose to express the charm of flowers, their scent, and the interplay of colors through circular shapes as visual shorthand symbolizing timeless beauty and perfection. To complete her Asian-inspired design, the artist searched for a complementary literary comment (and its calligraphic representation) to be added to the folding screen, which she found in a traditional Japanese poem called *Iro-Ha* (or *Iroha*).[35]

For Susanne, a circle represents a paradox that embodies both infinity and finitude. This one-dimensional figure (a line) has a never-ending path without beginning or end. As a two-dimensional figure (a disk), it has a finite area limited by its circumference. This concept plays an important role in her design of the golden sky in *Heaven and Earth,* (1998) (Fig. 9.32), which is subdivided by an intricate play of concentric circles in the higher part of the canvas, only fragmentally shown, interwoven in asymmetrical patterns. They are associated with endless radiation. There is another circle (or sphere) in the lower region of the painting, which is bounded by a transparent cube. The artist has juxtaposed the extending circles in the upper half and the single, imprisoned sphere below, alluding to the endlessness of "Heaven" and the limitation of "Earth." Susanne rendered those circular forms in shades of gold, underscoring the spiritual values which are desirable to be realized on earth. As the artist considers the circle to be "the most perfect shape" and gold, "the most perfect color," she combines them together to metaphorically signify the advance toward an ideal existence. For her, the circle is synonymous with unabridged freedom and endless possibilities.

The metaphorical meaning of circles for Susanne even encompasses her favorite type of movement—twirling, which gives her the sensation of being encircled by the world rotating around her. As

35 "Iro-Ha" is one of the best-known poems in Japan, written by an anonymous author around 1000 AD. Susanne found it in a German compilation of Asian literature, and with the help of a Japanese friend, the poem is written in Japanese calligraphy on the front (see Fig. 12.9). We will revisit the artwork and the poem in chapter 12.

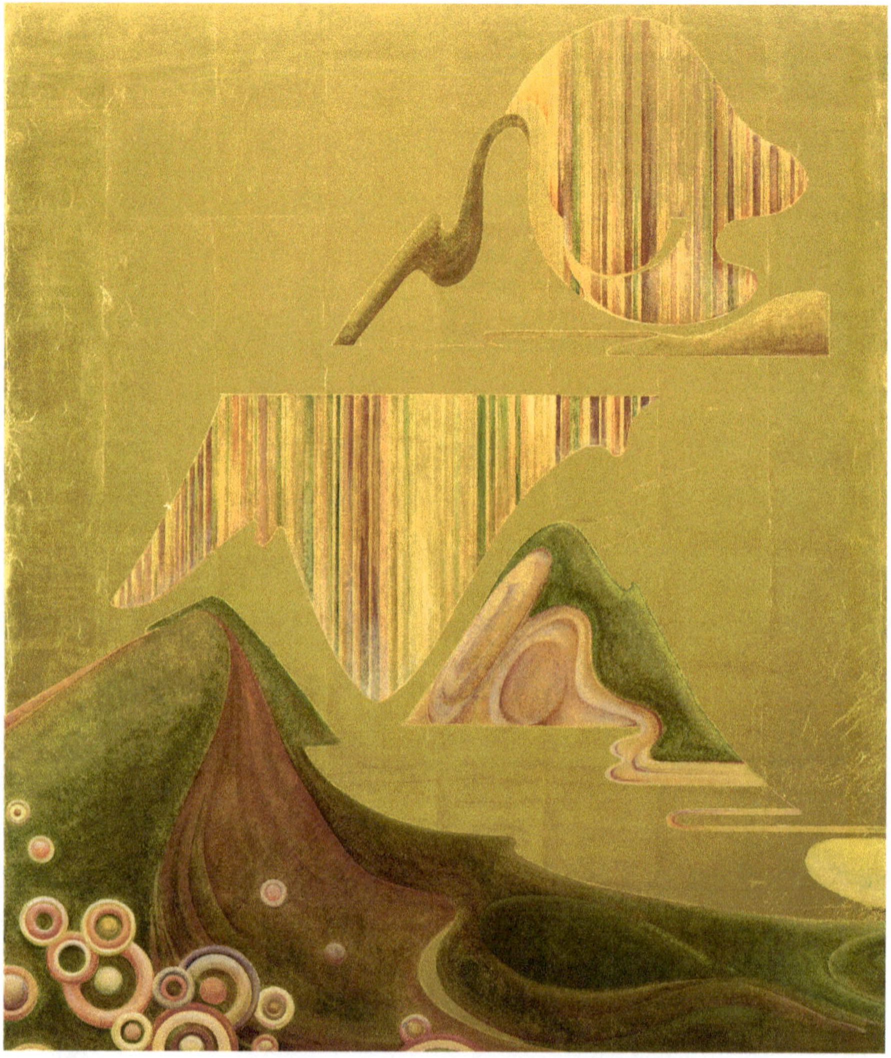

Fig. 9.31. Detail from one of the panels of *The Land of Iro-Ha* (Fig. 12.9): circles as abstract flowers.

she spins, her surroundings warp into streaks of colors, the perception of which she correlates with a certain artistic element in her paintings. Those are horizontal bars of color, energy traces that are trailing after a moving body, which she sometimes uses to express speed. Her painting, *The Big Race,* is a good illustration of this effect (see chapter 10, Fig. 10.12). Her predilection for this type of motion is not surprising, given her tendency to favor rapid movement. Her energy usually finds an outlet in fast actions, be it speaking, walking, reacting, or driving. Her friends jokingly describe her as moving "at the speed of light," not only in her imagination but also in her day-to-day activities.

Susanne's employment of the ring shapes for Touchless Misty (Fig. 9.33) might be based on a condensed perception of various models from nature and art that she has observed in her experience, for example, the blue morpho's underside (Figs. 9.34 and 9.35) or the Sabino butterfly (Fig. 9.5). Certain deviations from these models are a metaphorical expression of Susanne's individuality. We assume that the design was created mostly by her imagination in accordance with unconscious influences reflecting specific latent meaning. Is it possible that these shapes metaphorically carry different significations in her personal iconography? Might the unconscious symbolism of circular shapes in Touchless Misty be polysemous?

Conceptually, the artist perceives the circular shape as a strong and stable symbol of protection. The circle (or its variations) can appear as an image in her daydreams, where she pictures herself at the center of a circular column of energy that forms an impenetrable cylinder around her, invisible to all others. This protective visualization allows

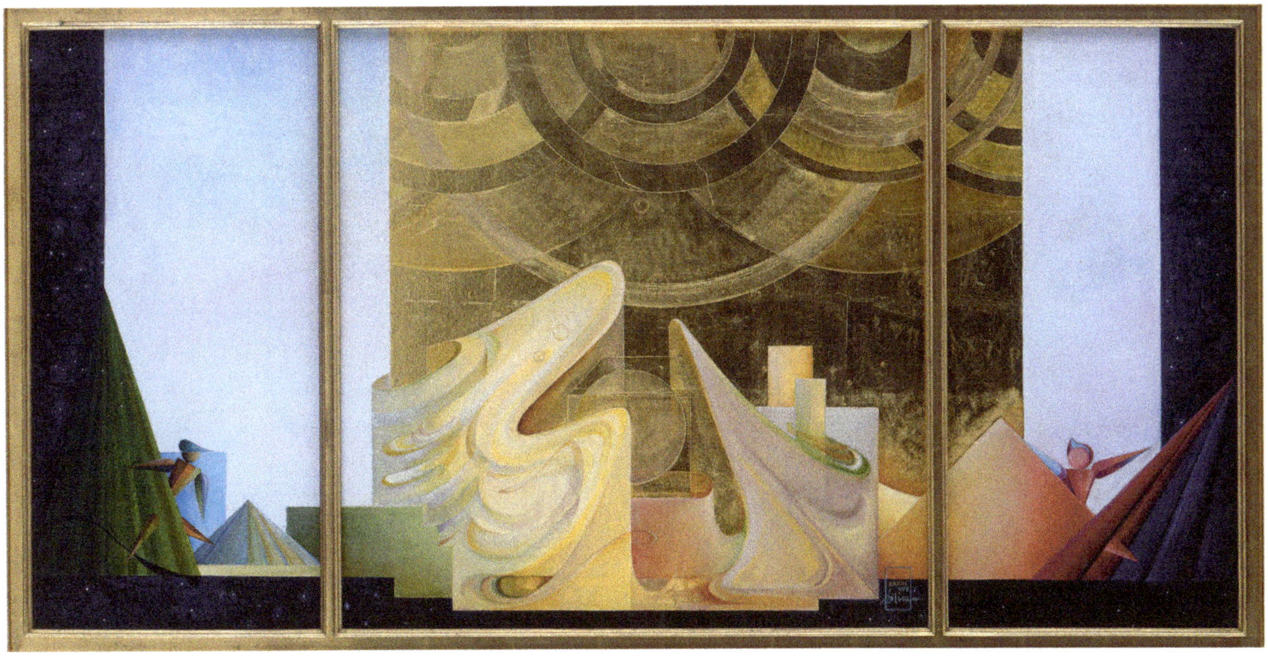

Fig. 9.32. Susanne Schuenke, *Heaven and Earth*, 1998. Oil and gold leaf on canvas, 21 x 45 in (55 x 115 cm). Private collection, USA. Note the concentric circle formations in the upper part.

her to meet dangerous challenges in her life and successfully overcome them. She can also project herself in fairy tales, wherein she has the power to cast a magic circle as a spell around a threatening adversary, thereby blocking the person's activity. The ring or circle can signify for her a defensive space that guards her against harmful impacts from outside and unseemly impulses from inside.

The wings of Touchless Misty display a number of pale, reddish-brown circular shapes—exclusive features among the assembly of the seven butterflies. These eight shapes share the same color with varying saturation and have different sizes: six annuli, one dot, and one target-like configuration whose upper part is partially obscured under a wing (Fig. 9.33). Their arrangement, flaunted like medals, signifies the wearer's importance and enhances this butterfly's prominent position in the painting. Touchless Misty is presented as the nonpareil among the group, unmatched by any of the other butterflies.

The artist remembers that she wanted to endow Touchless Misty with her favorite shape—the sphere, but aesthetically she felt it would destroy the butterfly's overall appearance. Instead, she compromised by settling on rings. The circular figurations (like the bubbles and marbles discussed in chapter 7) evoke positive emotions for Susanne because she sometimes fantasizes they keep her safely enclosed like the embracing arms of her parents, who gave her physical warmth and emotional shelter. Those forms provide her with a palpable sense of comfort in lieu of the intimate contact that Susanne longs for.

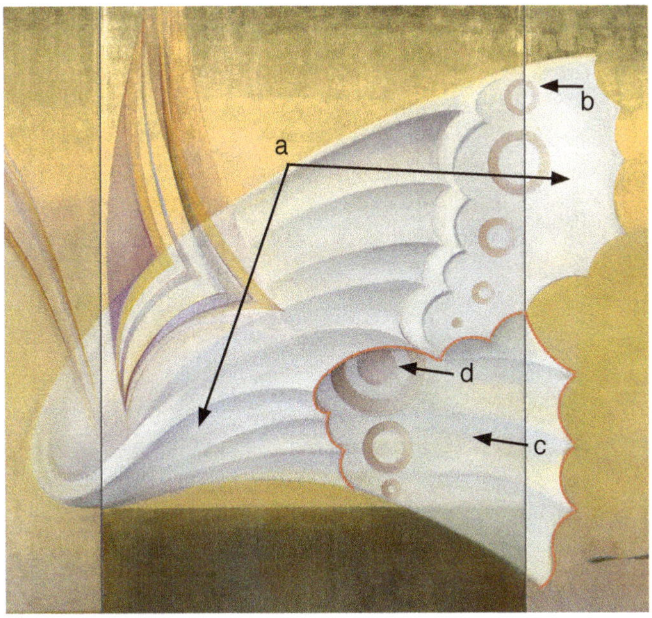

Fig. 9.33. Detail from Fig. 1.1. The ring formations on the front and hind wings:

(a) The arrows pointing to the extent of the front wing.
(b) Top ring.
(c) Hind wing (visible part encircled with the red line).
(d) Target-like formation in the hind wing.

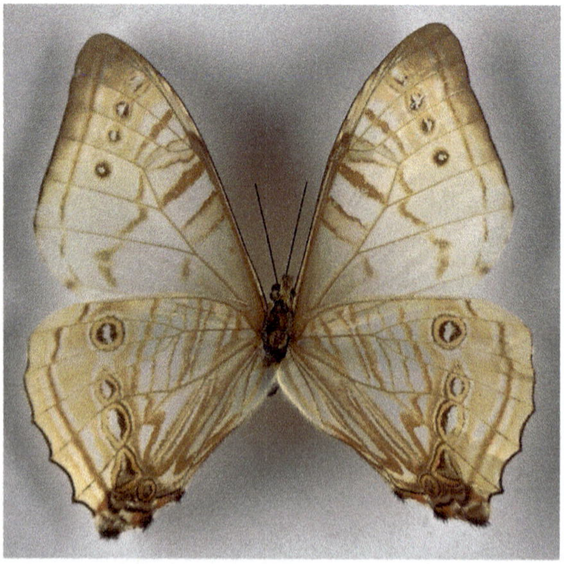

Fig. 9.34. (Also Fig. 8.29.) A blue morpho butterfly, showing the underside of the wings with their variations from off-white to brown and eyespots.

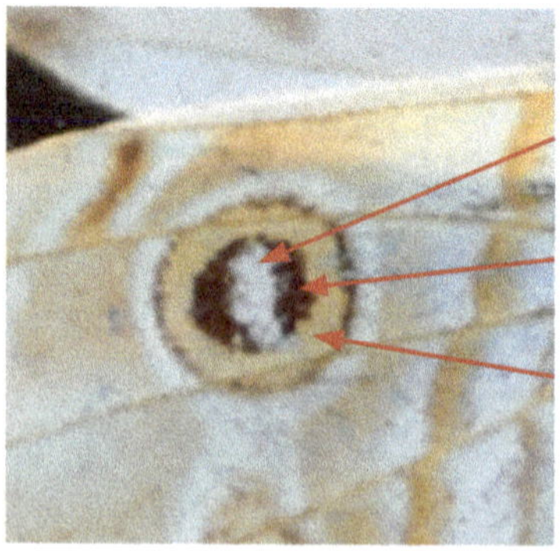

Fig. 9.35. Detail from Fig. 9.34 of an eyespot which appears to be a simulacrum of an eye of certain predatory animals.

On the conscious level, the rings on Touchless Misty serve to embellish the artist's design to heighten its attractiveness. Similar ring shapes appear in the design of the Sabino butterfly, which we have established as an admired objet d'art for Susanne and as one of the prototypes for butterfly No. 4.

Numerous examples from her oeuvre consistently deliver the proof that circle shapes are the artist's personal symbol for sublime qualities, such as beauty, harmony, and wholeness. The ring, as one of mankind's archetypal symbols, is considered in many cultures to be a sign of perfection, totality, timelessness, and perpetual recurrence.

Regarding the painting *Change in the Weather* (Fig. 6.12), we noted that Susanne employed the strikingly elliptical shapes of the peacock's tail feathers as the symbol of beauty and pride on purpose. The same tendency can be discerned in the comparable embellishment of Touchless Misty with an array of rings, as an unconscious recapitulation of what was intentionally expressed, for example, in *Change in the Weather*. Nevertheless, every specific individual element of the assembly of circle shapes might possess, aside from its shared role as decoration, other metaphoric guises of the unconscious that point to a multiplex of meanings. For example, the largest ring could simultaneously be, as we will see, an unconscious representation of an eye, target, breast, navel, and maybe other related meanings.

As mentioned, on Touchless Misty's wings, eight circular objects are spread out in prominent display, resembling marks of distinction that often adorn a person or a product.[36] In particular, Susanne associates this arrangement with medals, which again brings back memories connected with her father.

On several occasions during his career as a graphic artist, her father won awards from the German Association of Graphic Artists and the German Association of Photographers for his outstanding achievement in graphic and commercial art.[37] The tokens of recognition were presented as large medals, which were approximately 2 ½ inches in diameter. Her mother stored them in a round, antique china box which was a perfect fit for the medals, and occasionally Susanne and her sisters delighted in playing with these metallic discs. The circular shapes on Touchless Misty's wings could echo those accredited signs of acknowledgment that gave pride and admiration to the artist's family. This could be the underlying

36 Susanne also freely associated with the semi-circle arrangement of circular objects, relating to an array of medals displayed on some long-lasting commercial products that had won many medals and award ribbons over the years in various industrial fairs and exhibitions.

37 Bund Deutscher Gebrauchsgraphiker (BDG): renamed to the present name, Berufsverband der deutschen Kommunikationsdesigner; and Gesellschaft Deutscher Lichtbildner (GDL), renamed to Deutsche Fotografische Akademie in 1993.

meaning in the poetic commentary's remark about butterfly No. 4: "...rewarded in academia." Since this phrase does not accurately mirror her father's attainment, which was recognized by his professional societies, not by academia, Touchless Misty's "decoration" could relate more to Susanne's achievement than to her father's, particularly in view of her Ph.D. Therefore, the honorable acknowledgments could reflect Susanne's desire to equal his success and even to surpass him.

There is a noteworthy observation that the circular shapes decrease in size from top to bottom in both wings (with one exception of the small ring at the top of the front wing). This pattern may metaphorically hint at the existence of a hierarchical order. The gradual change in the size of the rings may reflect their relative value, since a greater size and higher placement generally imply that someone or something is proportionally more important. This fits with the placement of Touchless Misty on the highest step of the podium, which, as it will be shown in subchapter 12.1, is ranked as the most valuable position taken by the butterflies. Confirmation of this can also be found in the relative sizes of the butterfly's front and hind wings, where the front one occupies an area approximately three times the area of the hind one, which consequently assigns more visibility and attention to the front wing than to the hind wing (Fig. 9.33).

As with its universal connotation, the word "upper" has a superior symbolic importance for Susanne. This may explain the reduction in the size of the hind wing. The consequent prominence of the front wing, and its significance is supported by the optical illusion of the father's profile (discussed in subchapter 9.4, Fig. 9.54 (2)), where the contour of his forehead matches that of the front wing of Touchless Misty.

The small ring at the top is not in line with mentioned orderliness. This could be attributed to Susanne's conscious proclivity for breaking uniformity in design (Fig. 9.33 (b)). It could also be interpreted as an unconscious signifier of her resistance to some of her father's ideas and opinions, as a symbolic disruption of his orderly, patriarchal scheme.

Susanne follows her father's precept "to be on top"—the position held by the winner. She might be applying his notion by placing the image of Touchless Misty on the distinguished top step of the podium, reflecting desired social recognition. His credo has been ingrained in Susanne's mind since her younger years. This was exemplified by her father's favorite term for praise and approval, *Spitze* (German for *top*), which he often accompanied with a hand gesture of an open palm with his index finger and thumb forming a circle.

In her thinking and art, the words "upper" and "lower" have certain philosophical and symbolic significance. The idea of a superior status can be exemplified by such concepts as the "upper realm" which represents spirituality (see chapter 10, "Air" and subchapter 12.3, "Golden Background"), while the "lower realm" could stand for the biological level of existence (see subchapter 12.1, "Podium"). Susanne holds that what is earthly, biological, or instinctual must be regarded as of lower value. Therefore, the troubling desires, fantasies, and destructive tendencies arising from the affective system[38] must be suppressed and concealed as painful and unacceptable.

In looking at the arrangement of the circular objects, we notice that every ring is matched by a corresponding concave, sickle-like shape in front of it that forms the serrated edge. This is one of the peculiarities of the wing design of the butterfly, which constitutes a shadowy side of this "most beautiful" creature. As mentioned above, the artist failed to remember the large reddish circle marks on the dragon's wings while recalling the details of this creature in Uccello's painting (Fig. 9.12, and for an enlarged detail, see Fig. 9.36). We assume that unconsciously she was unwilling to associate her favorite circle shapes with this aggressive beast, and her aversion could reasonably be the cause for suppressing the memory of this highly significant detail in Uccello's dragon.

As jewelry, the ring had no value in Susanne's family, and the only rings she remembers were her parents' wedding bands, which they stopped wearing in their later years because of safety concerns.[39] For Susanne, the symbolism of the ring, especially in the context of matrimony, had no

38 Panksepp and Biven 2012

39 Susanne's mother had several painful experiences with her ring. In one incident, something caused her ring finger to swell up, but she did not pay attention to this until it was too late to remove the ring. As a consequence, she had to make an emergency visit to a jeweler to have the ring cut from her finger. Another time, her ring was caught in the pin of a door

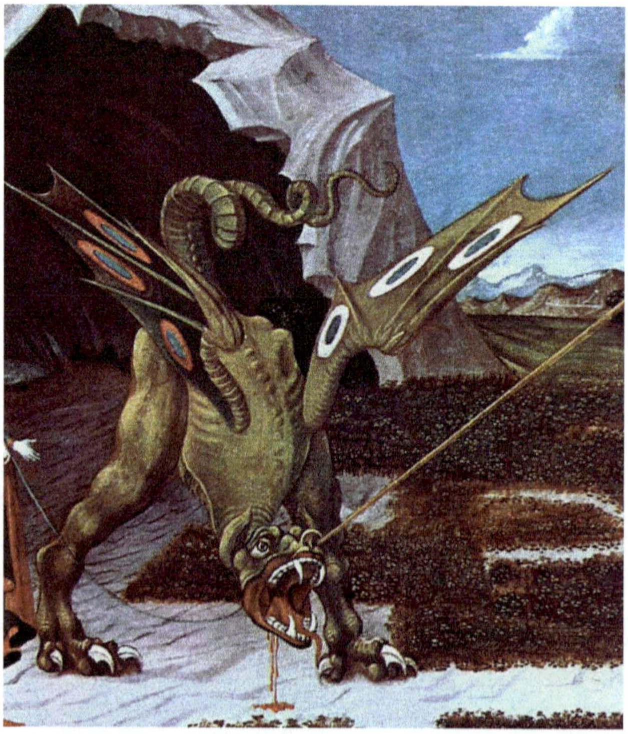

Fig. 9.36. Detail from Fig. 9.12.

significance, because she considered her marriage to be primarily a legal contract. Thus, the absence of conventional significance associated with the wedding ring might well have been determined by her parents' attitude, which she unreservedly accepted. Accordingly, based on the dismissive attitudes of Susanne and her parents toward the appropriate symbolism of the wedding ring, any romantic ideal as a potential source for the creation of the multiple rings in Touchless Misty's image appears to be lacking. Nevertheless, general cultural knowledge about the ring's metaphorical importance might have influenced the design of Touchless Misty's wings. Furthermore, we cannot exclude the possibility that transferential relationships and tendencies, having been formed in the framework of the Elektra complex, might have unconsciously employed this symbolism.

The unconscious may impress its messages through many different channels, condensing them into a single marker or symbol encoded with multiple meanings. For example, strangely enough for Susanne, the rings on the butterfly wings reminded her of valves on inflatable objects, in particular the old-fashioned floating air mattresses for swimming pools. The valves are little plastic tubes with covers pushed in after inflation and pulled out to deflate. The connection with valves was for her a direct reminder of the navel that was imagined to have been pulled out of her belly in the horrific childhood dream which we have previously discussed (see subchapter 8.3.4, page 199). Above all, the target-like configuration inside Touchless Misty's wing also bore a direct association with the navel for Susanne—a correlation she loathes.

Susanne remembers that when her newborn baby sister's diaper was changed for the first time she noticed a bandage on the infant's belly. As inquisitive as ever, Susanne asked her mother about it, and the mother explained that the bandage had to stay there for a few days, so the baby's navel could heal.[40] From that moment on, she never wanted to look at the baby's navel again, nor was she ever present at another diaper change, for what she had imagined happened to the baby at the hospital was too terrifying for her to be reminded of it again.[41]

She reacted in a similar manner about two years later when her mother, at the prompting

handle, which nearly broke her finger.

40 Susanne does not clearly remember her mother's exact wording.

41 Susanne in her imagination, cringes whenever she tries to envision the umbilical cord which came out of the mother's body being severed and knotted (knotting of the cord is the origin of the navel).

of her sister Hella, "castrated" a life-size male baby doll using a heated iron (see subchapter 7.1, page 117). It resulted in a hole in the groin area of the doll, which the mother covered with a bandage. Susanne's reaction to this mutilation must have been correlated with her traumatic perception of the bleeding navel of the infant sister and the haunting snow sledding dream, in which her navel was ripped apart. These three incidents could have coalesced into the formation of her omphalophobia. We assume that all three episodes are secondary situations, evolving into a network that points to the primary events of her incestuous fantasies, which very possibly became the major source for the development of Susanne's idiosyncratic sensitivity to the navel.

The "navel extraction in the dream," "damaged protruding navel of the infant," "hole (after the doll castration)," and, last but not least, the mother's "explanation of pregnancy, 'when two people sleep in the same bed'"—are roots of her omphalophobia. The latter one most likely originates in repressed early childhood attitudes and fantasies connected with the navel which became the signifier of former significant emotional experiences. Her omphalophobia has progressed to the point that whenever she sees African sculptures with bulging anatomical details in the abdominal area, she will quickly make an about-face in an attempt to avert conjuring up traumatic memories concerning the navel. Similarly, she cannot stand seeing photographic images and news broadcasts involving the sight of famine-stricken people, as among those, there are especially small naked children with bloated bellies showing their navels prominently, and such scenes would trigger a frantic reaction.

We cannot rule out the possibility that the target-like configuration in Touchless Misty's hind wing is somehow connected with the specific latent meaning of the navel in the artist's psyche. A review of butterfly No. 4's development from the earliest drawing stages will support the following conjecture. The formation is related to something so distasteful that Susanne unconsciously distances herself from this implication as far as possible, which leads to the process of suppression (hiding this mark from full view under the overlapping front wing, Fig. 9.33 (d)).

The reduction in the visibility of the hind wing and its topmost ring happened gradually, taking several steps from the initial sketch of the living models to the final oil version of Touchless Misty. In the sketch from nature, the hind wing and all the rings are fully visible (Fig. 9.7 a). However, in the creative drawing and watercolor (Fig. 9.7 b-e), the large ring is partially cropped, indicating that the hind wing is overlapped by the front wing in some areas. Eventually in the oil painting, the visibility of the hind wing is noticeably reduced.

We have previously noted that Susanne has the tendency to cover her eyes whenever she is confronted with highly stressful situations, which could trigger phobic reactions. The attempt to block her sight, we interpret to be emblematic of the artist's unwillingness to see certain aspects of her internal as well as external world. In this context, the particular ring in the image of Touchless Misty points to the same hidden issue: something that is not allowed or cannot be tolerated in its full view. The ring may be interpreted as a stylized partially covered "eye" as a metaphor of the "forbidden sight." It should be repeated that nudity was deemed a taboo in the artist's family. In their assessment, the nude body could trigger sexual interest or even arousal in the onlooker. Accordingly, the parents condemned any display of nakedness in the family home. This might have laid the foundation for Susanne's idiosyncratic attitude toward the publicly exposed naked body.

As remarked before,[42] the area of the navel holds the greatest sensitivity for Susanne. As a result, any viewing of it has always been a source of instant anxiety. However, it can be noted that sometimes Susanne will actually glance at the belly area (where the "ominous" navel is situated) of human bodies, whether in a photograph, a statue, or in actual people (such as at the beach, etc.). Upon this being pointed out, she claims that she does not do it, employing the defense mechanism of denial. When such a glance happens, her eyes are half closed while scanning the specific area of the image for a brief moment before her glimpse quickly moves away. Asked repeatedly why she looked away so hastily and what her thought was when she did it, her first reply was, "It is horrible." She later provided a more elaborate and revealing answer: "If I really

42 See chapter 8.3.4 and note 43 in chapter 9.

look, I have to come to a judgment, either it is good/positive/beautiful or bad/negative/ugly. And I do not want to be forced by my mind to make that judgment, so I avoid it."

These behavior patterns possibly reflect primary situations experienced by Susanne during her childhood. They might include the episodes of witnessing different parts of the parents' naked bodies, even their sexual activities, and the subsequent fantasies and imaginations arising out of those troubling incidents. These presumed original observations by the young Susanne must have been suppressed.

Among the circular shapes on Touchless Misty's wings, for the artist, the largest configuration constitutes the most striking mark (Fig. 9.33 (d)). In accordance with Susanne's free associations, this specific circular formation reminded her of an eye, then of a target (bullseye), and finally, of a breast.[43] In the course of this research, we have experienced more than once that Susanne delivers her free associations in the reverse order. She grades them according to her personal evaluation of upsetting feelings, naming the worst at the last. Therefore, we begin with the last on the list.

Susanne's association of the partially-covered, target-like formation on the wings of Touchless Misty with the breast could signify her avoidance of the topic of feminine physical characteristics. In view of her discomfort concerning the topic of reproduction (especially pregnancy), the half-concealed appearance of the "breast" might be indicative of her aversion in regard to reproduction.

As mentioned above, one of Susanne's defense mechanisms, when confronted with unbearable images, is to close her eyes, often shielding them with her hands. Similarly, the partially covered "breast" could be a signifier for the artist's troublesome perception of her femininity. Indeed, she remembers judging her mother's ample bust as unattractive and fearing that she would develop breasts like hers.

The interpretation of the artist's association of the largest of the ring shapes with a target might signify that Susanne, by her unconscious identification with Touchless Misty, feels herself to be under attack. This assumption is tenable if we take into account that Susanne often felt like a victim of biting remarks about her character and thoughts, especially from her father but also from some of her friends. Memories of those stinging criticisms may have metamorphosed into imaginary arrows aimed at Susanne. Looking to the topic of "attack" from a different angle, we can assume that one of her persistent nightmarish visions, in which sharp blades would assault her, might be a manifestation of punishment. These haunting fantasies are presumably connected with different aspects of the sexual and aggressive drives[44] that were censored and metaphorically attested to, for example, in the formation of a bullseye.

Finally, we return to the first item in the list of her free associations with the ring-circle configuration—the eye—which may be the most painful topic for her to unravel. Through her studies of world art, Susanne is quite aware of the most archetypal representation of the eye as the dark central circle (pupil and iris) surrounded by white color (eyeball). During the oil painting process for *Give Me Wings!*, the artist suddenly recognized an optical illusion of a face profile, formed from the wing contour which partially eclipses the largest of the circular patterns, strongly indicating "an eye" for her. She named it "Little Indian" because of its overall resemblance to what Susanne envisioned as a profile of a Native American warrior. We will return to this imagined face more thoroughly in subchapter 9.4 "Optical Illusions—Faces" (Fig. 9.54).

Recapitulating this subsection, we have found that layers of different coded meanings were condensed into the "mere decorative" rings of Touchless Misty. They belong to her personal symbols, which make up the unique iconography of her paintings. We have identified multiple meanings for the rings and suggested different interpretations. It remains an open question, whether it is ever possible to capture and recognize all the meanings held, processed, and created by her mind even for a single facet such as the ring shapes in question. Our approach here has been to analyze their aspects separately, considering that we should first learn as much as possible about the individual parts before attempting to understand the whole.

43 It turned out that in this set of associations, Susanne did not include the navel because she tried to evade discussing the topic by all means possible and keep it under lock and key.

44 See subchapter 5.2.1.

9.3.6 The Latent Meaning of the Eye

In the following, we will discuss how circularly shaped designs reflect latent unconscious meanings in the context of the artist's ommetaphobia.[45] In *Give Me Wings!*, we note that four of the butterflies (Nos. 1, 2, 5, and 6) are given humanoid eyes, identifiable mostly by the pupil, iris, white of the eye (sclera), and by eyelids, which the artist rendered in watercolor (see Fig. 2.12) and in the oil painting (see Fig. 9.37). Susanne is familiar with the anatomy of butterflies and knows that insects' compound eyes differ remarkably from those of vertebrates. Consequently, the presence of human-like eyes in these butterflies is an evident indication of the phenomenon of humanization. With these human attributes, she personifies the creatures.[46]

The artist explained that she affixed eyes on the thoraxes of the butterflies as a substitute for the head, and the dark green area surrounding the eye of each of them indicates they are part of an imagined head. By this representation, Susanne felt that she avoided making the eyes appear as if they were isolated eyeballs, an implication which she abhorred because of her obsessive fear of her (or others) eyes being cut out or pierced by sharp instruments.

Examining the sketches done from the live models (Fig. 2.1) and creative drawings II and III (Figs. 2.3 and 2.4), we note that the artist used simple circles or ovals to substitute for the insects' heads. In the subsequent drawing made for the watercolor study (Fig. 2.11), the precise outlines for humanoid eyes can be seen in four out of the seven butterflies, as mentioned above. This design, which she continued in the oil version, is exclusively found in *Give Me Wings!* among her paintings. It is very similar to a specific motif in the style of her father, who frequently painted a pair of spherical eyes on an egg-shaped object to represent a human being (Fig. 9.38).

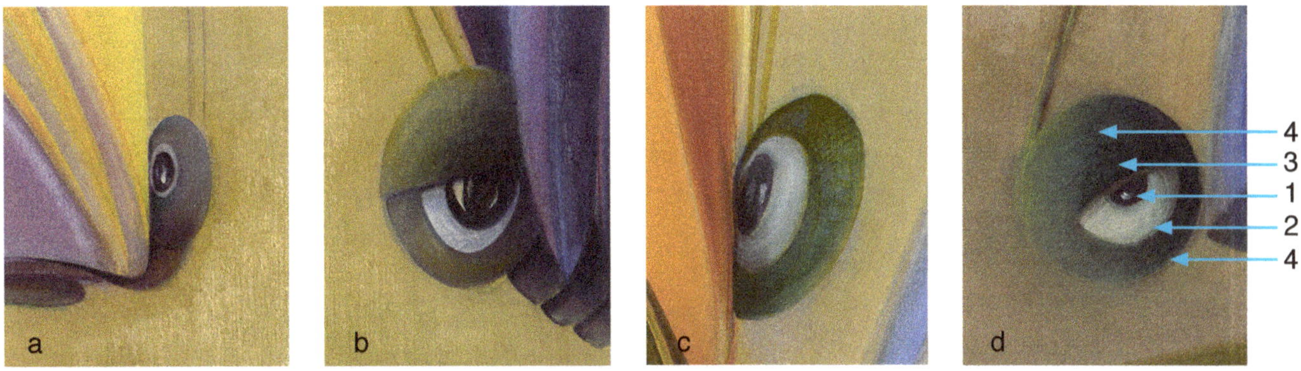

Fig. 9.37 a-d. Comparison of various eyes from *Give Me Wings!* (Fig. 1.0).
(a) Eye from butterfly No. 1. (b) Eye from butterfly No. 2.
(c) Eye from butterfly No. 5. (d) Eye from butterfly No. 6, with additional details:
(1) Pupil and iris, (2) whitish eyeball, (3) upper eyelid, and (4) reduced part of the head.

---

45 Ommetaphobia—the fear of injury of the eye.

46 The fact that the central three butterflies have neither a body nor head does not contradict the concept of personifying the butterflies for the artist. She argues that they were simply depicted in a higher degree of abstraction, in which the creatures were symbolically represented only by their wings. Furthermore, inquiring why butterflies Nos. 3 and 4 (personifications of Susanne) and butterfly No. 7 (a symbolic representation of spirituality) are not equipped with bodily parts (legs, eyes), we could assume that Susanne might have unconsciously avoided rendering anatomical features that might relate to their human equivalent due to her phobias (ommetaphobia, omphalophobia, venephobia, and arachnophobia). In creative drawing I, the artist added little stick figures (prototype of humans) to the winged creatures which immediately elevated these butterflies into monumental entities. This juxtaposition and the gigantic size of the creatures gave them a meaningful relation to the human beings and established an illusion that they might possess human-like qualities and personalities as well (see chapter 2, page 19). In creative drawings II and III, the phobia-sensitive parts were included, although in a rather clandestine way. The eyes and heads drawn are in such a high degree of stylization that they lack virtually all the anatomically recognizable details, making their appearance markedly abstract (reductionism; see Kandel, 2016). Thus, in spite of the depiction of the objectionable anatomical features in these two drawings, their highly condensed rendition can still support our assumption concerning the absence of the mentioned body features in creative drawing I, which is due to the artist's idiosyncratic reactions to them. This illustrates the dynamic nature of the modus operandi of unconscious processes.

As Susanne remembers, her father collected sets of mechanical doll-eyes that are used by toy manufacturers. Each set constituted two realistic-looking white eyeballs with pupils and colored irises, accompanied by the upper eyelids with lashes. The father's collection also included the brown, green, and blue glass eyes used to embellish stuffed toy animals like dogs and cats. These animal eyes were usually not spherical, but disc-shaped with only irises and pupils without the sclera, which were mounted on stiff wire. Nevertheless, their appearance was still remarkably realistic. All the eyes were kept in a drawer in the father's workshop. Sometimes Susanne would take them out of the drawer to play with them.

In his paintings, her father frequently depicted humanoid figures with ovoid heads whose eyes were modeled after the toy eyes of animal and human dolls (Figs. 9.38, 9.39, and 6.8), and were meant to convey multifaceted metaphoric significances.[47] Susanne makes it clear that he did not isolate the eyes from the head[48] but either placed them into a socket embedded in the head or on the surface of an egg, which substituted for a human head. As long as those eyes were still attached to a form resembling a head,[49] Susanne perceived that this representation signified human beings. These features of the eyes were typical of her father's art for depicting abstract human figures, and nearly 40 years later Susanne emulated his model (Fig. 9.37 (a)-(d)).

Before *Give Me Wings!*, Susanne had not represented a head comparable with her father's minimalism, but for the butterflies (and they still display the only example in her oeuvre) she chose a similar scheme. She uses the anthropoid eye to capture the essence of human characteristics. In doing so, the artist follows the well-known proverb: "The eyes are the windows of the soul," which can ascribe to them the peculiarities of someone's personality and its spiritual significance. Referring to this aspect of the eye expands the perspective for understanding the target-like formation as a highly stylized "eye"—a metaphor in Touchless Misty's hind wing.

For Susanne, eyes involve special sensitivity, and she continues to be horrified by dreadful visions involving them, against which she feels powerless to fight. Their meanings are still shrouded in darkness for her. Her phobia of

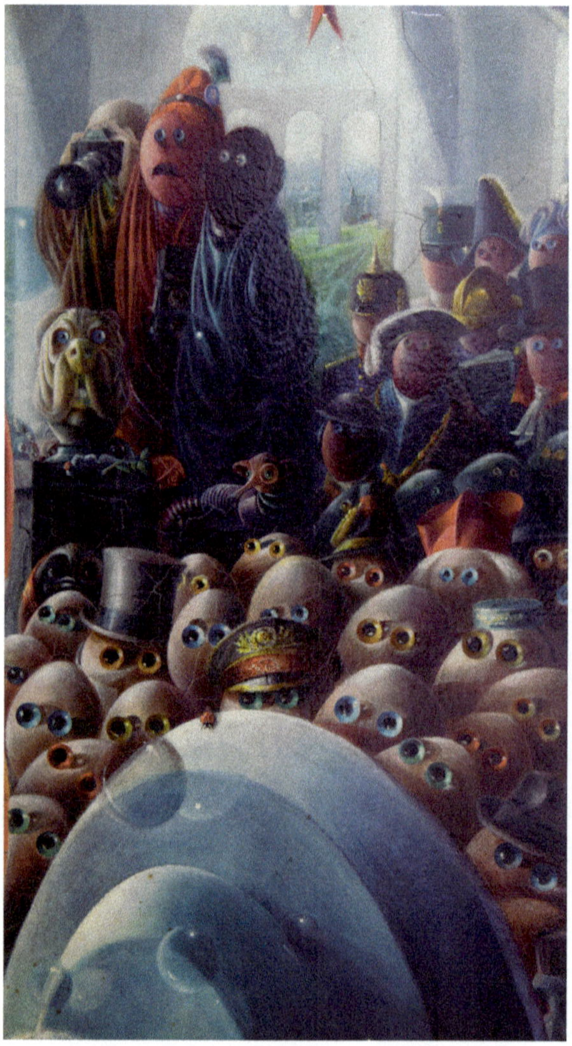

Fig. 9.38. Heinz-Günter Schünke, *The Weightlifter*, 1978 (detail from Fig. 4.5). A close-up of the crowd of spectators ("eggs with animal eyes").

47 For example, in the *Weightlifter*, the human spectators are equipped with toy animal eyes, whereas various creatures (chimera, hybrids, and fantasy animals) in the painting show humanoid eyes (with the sclera). We assume that Susanne's father metaphorically emphasized the bestial tendencies in humans and their corresponding behavior, represented by the animal eyes with such depictions.

48 Had he done so, it would have been unbearably cruel for Susanne. This unsolicited remark from her reveals again the particularity of her deep-seated phobia of being injured in the eyes.

49 Such a head could be in a cubistic style, as in *Future Shock* (see Fig. 9.39). Often her father painted a whole group of eggs to represent assembled human beings, each equipped with two eyes and sometimes furnished with accessories like hats to indicate their specific roles in society (see for example, in our discussion of her father's painting, *The Weightlifter,* later in this chapter).

blades haunts her mind, as she often fantasizes the sharp instruments attacking her eyes, and this frightening vision is so vivid that she shields her eyes with her hands whenever she senses the threat.

Susanne's fear of having her eyes cruelly damaged continues to be a puzzle in our research. External roots of this phobia could have come from mythological stories telling of the drastic punishments meted out to people (such as the blinding of King Oedipus) or from fairy tales, in which condemned individuals had their eyes mutilated with fire or sharp weapons. She knew these stories as early as age ten. These fearful mental scenarios were immensely exacerbated by Aunt Hella's tale, which she once narrated to Susanne while visiting the family. It was about a movie the aunt had seen, in which someone's eyeballs were cut with a razorblade. Susanne was probably around 15 when she heard this, and it horrified her so much that the recollection of it still perturbs her greatly to this day. We have asserted that the half-covered "eye" in Touchless Misty's hind wing could have been determined by the artist's troubled imagination, possibly connected to a traumatic, forgotten memory of destructive fantasies in her early childhood. We can only speculate about these lost memories, but her phobias regarding the cutting tools in her father's workshop or her mother's kitchen could be an associative bridge to the unconscious origin of her sufferings.

However, there is a recollection that could shed some light on her aichmophobia/ommetaphobia. A specific image from her father's creative photography brings some clues. In her attempt to remember this particular photo, she described it as an arrangement in which the father took a long, flexible helical spring (commonly known as a Slinky) to form a complete circle with an empty space at the center. Susanne associated this with a hole, likening it to an entrance to a cage (Fig. 9.40 a–b; in our reconstruction we used a half circle of the helical spring for demonstration).

During analysis, she remembered that this image also contained a doll's eye from her father's collection, which he placed in the previously mentioned empty space (Fig. 9.40 (b)). She continues to be under the impression that the long coiled spring was made of a thin spiral blade that threatened to cut the unprotected eyeball from

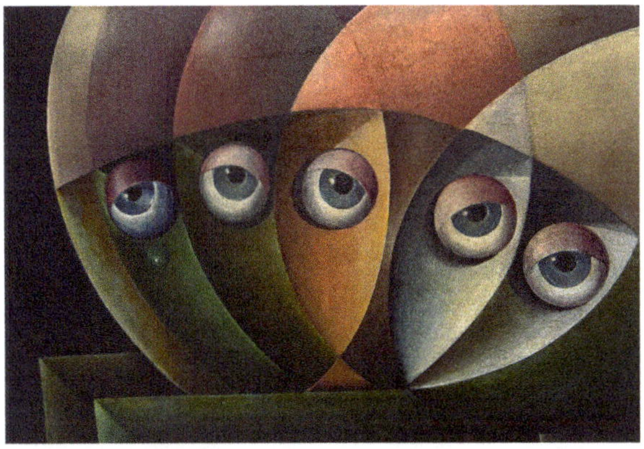

Fig. Fig. 9.39. Heinz-Günter Schünke, *The Future Shock*, 1965. Oil on wood. Detail of multiple heads with doll eyes. Note the upper eyelids.

all sides. This perception proceeds to trigger her phobia, which is vigorously expressed with intense emotional fervor and defensive body language.

Later, a search of her father's work records disclosed a printed copy of the photograph in question, which pictured a miniature china doll bust (with painted eyes) at the center of the circular coil spring, instead of the solitary eyeball that Susanne had wrongly recollected (Fig. 9.40 (c)). This mistaken remembrance, which substituted an isolated eyeball for a miniature doll bust, might be the significant clue that points to some possible roots of her fear of the eye being cut by a blade. We could assume that this replacement reflects the modus operandi of the unconscious, when the eye (i.e., the part) took the place of the doll (i.e., the whole entity).

Susanne represents the essence of living flowers in an abstract and symbolic way with circles, indicating that the real objects and their symbols are interchangeable. Analogously, the eye could substitute significant subjects (mother, father, sisters). Therefore, the tormenting horror visions concerning the eye might reflect repressed aggressive fantasies toward her parents and sisters since her early childhood. Secondary traumatic events (such as Aunt Hella's tale) may have later reinforced these early, primary traumatic situations. Such secondary traumas could have become the trigger for an outbreak of her ommetaphobia.

Susanne associates the steel helical coil spring with sharp edges with the threat of a razor blade, which, as we mentioned before, she perceives with horror and disgust. Any image or contemplation involving the eye could determine the expectation of attacks and imagination of damage to it. This would send Susanne into panic and revulsion. A further prompting by the analyst on this topic caused her to be highly agitated, due to instant visualization of a scene where razor blades cut someone's eyes. She reveals this condition with utter reluctance because it is unspeakable for her. When she was pressed to describe her thoughts on the matter, her neurotic reactions flared up, and it took a while for her to become calm enough to share her most terrible imagination: A detached eye that has been removed from a person's eye socket by gruesome violence which is too horrific and painful for her to think of. The horrible movie scene, which her aunt once described, is so engraved in her mind that any allusion immediately returns the visual imagination of it to her and constitutes an acute horror fantasy. This reactivates highly aggravated expectations of inflicted torture on her, which are easy to provoke and hard to suppress.

In her teenage years, these imagined scenes of mutilation were imprinted on her mind with an overwhelming emotion of unbearable terror. It kept returning endlessly, upon any circumstances. For example, the fear of a detached eyeball became so deeply embedded in her psyche that even a visit to an ophthalmologist's office could be stressful for her. To this day, an oversized plastic model of an eyeball, often displayed in an office, will make her scream in alarm inside, and it is quite a challenge for her not to panic.

Her dreaded reactions concerning eyeballs, navel, wrists, veins, etc. can even be triggered by subliminal stimuli, as her heightened sensitivity is rather extraordinary. Her aunt's tale of mutilation likely supplied the pivotal context that opened a Pandora's box full of suppressed tendencies and fantasies by their reactivation, pointing out their existence in the past.

This became an endless loop of reliving and fighting horrors that were to haunt and torment Susanne for many decades to come. This acute reactivity could have originated from Susanne's still undisclosed, significant emotional experiences from the past, especially from her early childhood.[50] We assume that latent affects could determine her fear involving injury to her eye to a frightening magnification. We might compare this analogically to the powerful lens of a magnifying glass, which can focus a multitude of the sun's rays into a single point of intense heat capable of starting a fire. As we have seen, there are numerous supersensitive stimuli (blades and sharp or pointed objects, to name a few) that can easily trigger immense inner reactions in the artist that are quite probably rooted in the primary situations from her childhood. Other possible subliminal sources from the realm of phylogenetic factors might be operative as well, but they are beyond the scope of our current study.

Coming back to the formation in Touchless Misty, which Susanne named "Little Indian," we can hypothesize that this image could bring some light concerning the artist's fantasies and phobias about eyes being wounded by sharp instruments such as blades. Later, in this chapter (see subchapter 9.4), we analyze the possible meaning behind this in accordance with Native American ritual

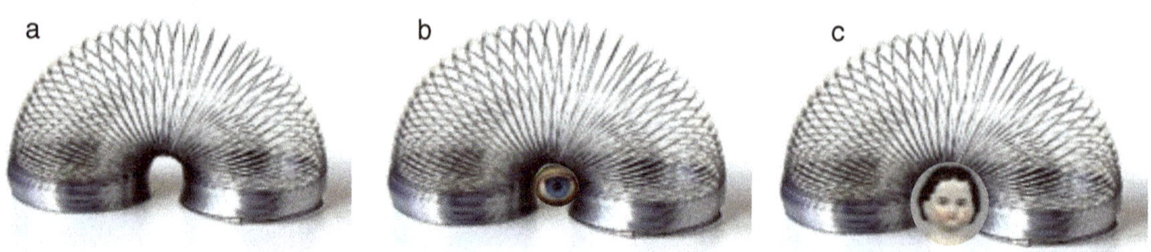

Fig. 9.40 (a-c).
(a) The helical spring.
(b) Reconstruction of the image as Susanne believed to be accurate (that is, how she thought her father constructed the assemblage) using the helical spring and a typical doll's eyeball.
(c) Reconstruction of the image of the actual assemblage according to the photograph in the family archive using the helical spring and a small porcelain doll's bust.

50 Klein 1975

cruelties. We recognize her self-identification with "Little Indian." We deduce that this image is a symbolical manifestation of Susanne's imaginative aggressive childhood tendencies. This assumption supports our speculation that her proclivity for traumatic visions could have been derived from the powerful, innate aggressive drive (we shall deal with this topic in subchapter 9.4). The violent deeds of wounding heads (scalping) and eyes, as acts of traumatization, are interchangeable in their latent meaning.

The above hypothesis found further indirect clarification in the following related associations. We had mentioned her father's artistic designs integrating the doll bust into the images of his photographs. Susanne mistakenly recollected this photo substituting the miniature bust with the doll's eye. We assume that the artist's amnesia is determined by the unconscious ground on which her horror visions came to thrive. It could hint at repressed aggressive fantasies concerning the eyes, originating in her early childhood. In the prior subchapter, we analyzed the image of "dragon wings" with their typical configuration of ridges, sickle shapes, and serrated contours, which was recognized as a symbolic representation of aggression. It is worth pointing out again the episode in which the red circular marks on the wings in Uccello's painting, *St. George and the Dragon*, were suppressed from Susanne's memory as she was trying to recall its details (Figs. 9.12 and 9.36). Moreover, in spite of the numerous visits Susanne made to the National Gallery in London to see its collection of paintings, including Uccello's, she never came to recognize that St. George's lance was piercing the dragon's eye in the painting. Only during our analysis, in which the artist was repeatedly exposed to the painting, did she become aware of this important detail in the image—the sight of an eye being pierced by a sharp instrument (the lance in the painting).

We have presented much oblique evidence that could bring us closer to the primary scenes and might permit us to partially reconstruct them, thus affording us a better understanding of the roots of Susanne's phobias. The verification of our premises concerning the origins is curtailed by the well-known phenomenon of amnesia.

Susanne's ommetaphobia is one such case, in which we arrived at the supposition that her intense fear has its origin in the metamorphosis of the aggressive drive in her early childhood. This conclusion is in accordance with the Freudian approach as well as with its further development, especially the discoveries made by Melanie Klein in the psychoanalysis of children.

The artist's aggressive tendencies, which were brought to her conscious attention through our analysis, led to her partial acceptance of the existence of such a previously unacknowledged innate proclivity. The potent presence of this inner reality could be one of the determinants of Susanne's idiosyncratic perception and multiple phobias. The analyzed aggressive drive finds embodiment in the visual images in her art.

9.3.7 Mandala Symbolism

With the examples discussed in subchapter 7.3 (the globules in Fanning Everything's image), we have demonstrated how over the years, the artist's psyche has developed different symbolic visualizations of the circular shape, conveying multiple meanings. Through their application, Susanne metaphorically represents different aspects of human existence. In the following, we will analyze, in the context of various shapes, how mandala symbolism has found expression in Susanne's art. The artist became vaguely familiar with a mandala in 1999 when a friend, who studied East Asian art history, sent her a photocopy of a detail of a 4,500-year-old Sri Yantra[51] from India, a mystical diagram embedded with concentric circles which circumscribe numerous overlapping triangles that are symmetrically arranged.

On close inspection, the artist perceived that these triangles displayed subtle differences, as no two were alike, which captivated her. Susanne knew that this design had something to do with meditation, but did not pursue the matter any further. She kept the picture in a drawer and looked at it once in a while, fascinated by its intricacy, but otherwise she did not try to use it.

In 2006, she had a philosophical discussion with a religious friend, which centered on the "Tree of Knowledge" and "man's eviction from paradise," as described in Genesis, and how in

51 The friend sent her only the center part of the Sri Yantra: the circle with the arranged triangles inside. The image Susanne saw did not include the two concentric rings of lotus petals, the multiple outer circles, and the bounding square frame with a T-shaped "gate" at each side.

this biblical narrative the fundamental human problem about the nature of existence was allegorized. Trying to emphasize the point, her friend scribbled a rather chaotic zigzag pattern of what he called, "Mankind's wanderings and errors after the Fall." To show her interlocutor how she might represent the "human existence in God's universe," Susanne drew freehand concentric shapes (circles and triangles).[52] A month later, she transformed this impromptu sketch into a watercolor and soon after into an oil painting, which she named *Sri Yantra* (Fig. 9.41), in reference to the ancient sacred Indian diagram that had inspired her.[53] With this title, she related the design directly to mandala symbolism, although, at that time, Susanne had no specific knowledge about its connection to religion, art, and psychology (it was extensively explored by C. G. Jung.[54])

The analysis of the circle shapes in *Give Me Wings!* brought the researchers' attention to mandala symbolism, and we assume that the abstract metaphors contained in the artist's *Sri Yantra* have direct and indirect connections with some unconscious meaning, which will be the subject of the following investigation. The examination and decoding of the meaning of the *Sri Yantra*'s circular shapes extends our understanding and sheds new light on the symbolism behind the rings of Touchless Misty. Susanne encoded various metaphorical implications about the existence of the human being in the universe into the concentrically nesting circles, triangles, and polygons. By these shapes, she tried to express, in a highly abstract way, her personal concepts concerning the essential facets of human life, especially its fundamental component—spirituality.

The "fallen" human condition was characterized by Susanne's friend as "mankind's wanderings and errors." Out of this existential circumstance, each person must find a way to the appropriate meaning of life. She compares this wayfaring to the nested pathways of a typical medieval labyrinth, frequently arranged in a concentric pattern, which was usually incorporated into the design of the tiled floors in major cathedrals. These labyrinths (mostly in a circular design) could be construed as embedding the quintessential aspect of mandala symbolism, particularly in view of their placement in religious buildings.

Pondering a way to illustrate her friend's concept about the origin of the creation and the meandering of mankind through the various predicaments[55] that ensued after the original paradise was lost, the artist settled on a set of concentric circles, triangles, and polygons. Through them, she symbolically represented the scope of the cosmos, from the unimaginably small to the endlessly large, to epitomize her own essential idea about existence in visual metaphors.

In *Sri Yantra,* Susanne touched various enigmas of existence that she anticipated a human being would be likely to encounter in searching for the meaning of life. This is a quest, in which the person would seek the answers to such perennial questions as, "Where did I come from?," "Who am I?," "Where do I go from here?" Throughout history, prophets and philosophers have attempted to give solutions to such riddles. With the lack of satisfactory answers to these and other related questions, Susanne was thrown into a maze of confusion and doubt. When she contemplated the course of humankind's journey and her own experience, the symbolism of labyrinths came to her mind. It had a marked influence on her first sketch of *Sri Yantra,* which she unknowingly endowed with mandala symbolism.[56]

As she worked on the design, she deliberately avoided any reference to a preferred viewing orientation. The image (like a wheel) is intended to be seen at any rotated position. The artist composed her *Sri Yantra* with variations in shapes (rings, regular polygons, and irregular forms) in a multitude of colors. She employed gold to symbolically represent

---

52 Next to the date marked on the piece of paper that she used for this sketch, the artist also wrote "Creation" as its title.

53 This painting was primarily executed from her sketch, which might have been influenced by her recollection of the millennia-old meditation image that was sent to her by her friend. The artist liked the name Sri Yantra for this painting but this shall not imply that Susanne followed the standard plan that is required to properly construct a traditional Sri Yantra.

54 Jung 1972

55 The artist was thinking of spiritual, social, historical, mental, and physical parameters.

56 As mentioned above, Susanne could not have made a conscious correlation between a classical labyrinth and the essential characteristic of a mandala, although their symbolical similarities are obvious to her now.

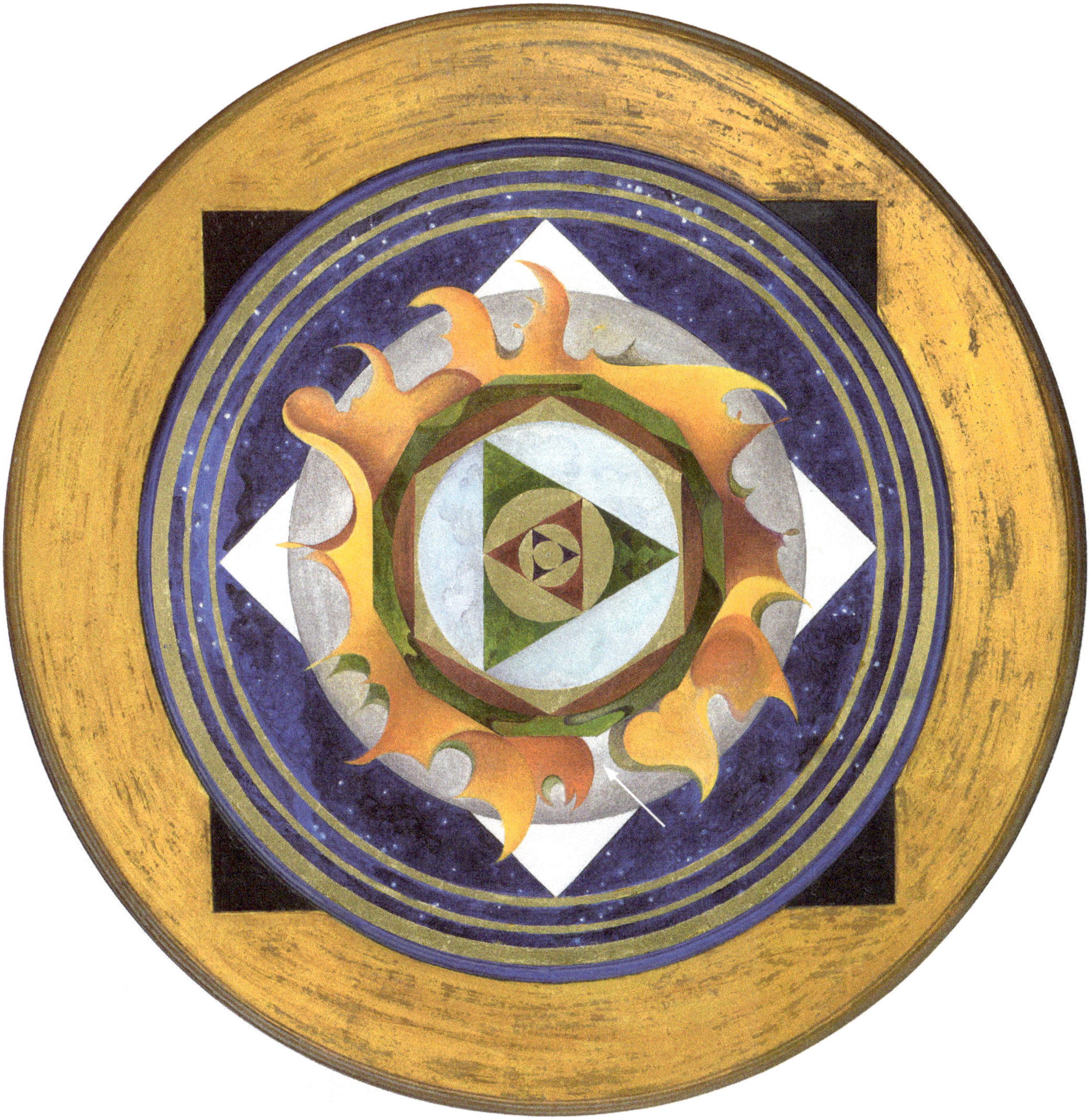

Fig. 9.41. Susanne Schuenke, *Sri Yantra*, 2006. Oil and gold leaf on a circular canvas and wood, diameter 33 in (83 cm). Private collection, Washington, D.C.
The choice of orientation is optional, and the white arrow added to indicate the gap in the "ring of fire."

some of her cherished beliefs. The central position was designated for spirituality as one of the main meanings of existence that will enable humans to live in peace, in harmony, and without fear. The multiple golden circles are not only symbols of perfection and completeness, but also reflect the stages of spiritual development. They weave the red thread of human destiny through the design, symbolizing for the artist the paramount importance of the process that is the final destination of our never-ending inward[57] journey, which we can reach through spiritual growth.

The concentric circles continuously grow in size from the central point, serving as a analogy for the spiritual presence that permeates all aspects of existence. From the furthest circle of the cosmic diagram, the focus of contemplation is anchored to the center. Susanne explains that because of the emphasis on the concentric design of the composition, the eyes of the observer will return again and again to the center. Furthermore, the singular point acts as a reference for all the individual shapes, as well as their relation to each other. This visual scheme works like a vortex spiraling back to the epicenter, forming a metaphorical representation of the genesis of the world. The exact center of the painting is a minute hole (Fig. 9.42 (A)),[58] which Susanne refers to as "zero dimension" or "emptiness." To explain why she thought of "emptiness," Susanne recalled a book, *Tao Te Ching*,[59] the primary text of Taoism that she read more than 30 years earlier, which had left a lasting impression on her. The legendary author of the book, Lao Tzu (or Laozi in Pinyin), speaks of the usefulness and the central importance of "emptiness" in one of the book's chapters. He affirms that an authentic, natural being must somehow be related to the "nothing" that lies at the core of reality.

Susanne pointed to Lao Tzu's use of the metaphor of a wheel with many spokes whose hollow center (i.e., the hub—through which an axle is inserted) fulfills its task work because of the emptiness. Susanne read this book at age 18, while still in high school. At that time, she was inundated with a multitude of associations, ambivalent tendencies, and questions about existence and its meaning. These contemplations had begun to obsess her since adolescence, and she could not untangle her mind from these preoccupations. One of the core teachings of Taoism that fascinated her is *wu wei*, translated into German as *ohne Tun* (English literally: "without action"), generally known in English as "doing without doing" or "action without action."

During the discussion of Lao Tzu's concept, the artist spontaneously arrived at an association: "The hub of the universe," that due to her archeological studies, she connected with omphalos. The ancient Greek religious artifact is a stone purported to mark the center, the "navel" (*omphalos* in Greek) of the world in Greek mythology. In antiquity, the omphalos bowl was a round, shallow dish with a domed bulge at the inside center, which may have had religious as well as secular uses. What gives this ware the name "omphalos" is the bowl's raised, round middle, which resembles the shape of the navel. The central bulge was made by depressing the bottom side of the soft clay vessel upward before it was fired, which probably had the practical purpose of allowing a person drinking from it to place a finger into the hollow to hold the dish more securely. Following this knowledge, she unexpectedly connected the hole made by the compass needle on her "Sri Yantra" diagram with the navel.

Susanne despises any literary reference to the omphalos, and its visual representations and

57 Australian Aborigines speak of "seven directions: north, south, east, west, above, below, and within" (see Morgan, 1994, page 141). Susanne had never heard of the "within" orientation in describing space and was immediately taken with the concept, correlating it with a "spiritual course." Reading Morgan's book years after creating *Sri Yantra*, she recognized that the essence of her painting revolved around this "inside" direction.

58 The "point" in question is in the center of the circle marked (A) in the illustration. Technically, this hole was caused by the piercing needle of the compass during the process of drawing the concentric circles. The artist had a choice to fill this hole but left it in place when she recognized its appropriate metaphorical role, indicating the infinity inside.
In a traditional Sri Yantra, there is a dot in the center of the nested triangles. It is called the Bindu, the power point from which the Cosmos emerges and unites. This center point is a symbol, often compared with the hub of a wheel. Looking at the hole in the location of a Bindu, during the process of painting of *Sri Yantra*, Susanne all of sudden had difficulties inserting the compass needle in the center, which was for a moment triggered by two of her phobias of the navel and of needle penetration.

59 Lao Tzu, *Tao Te Ching*, chapter 11, first paragraph.

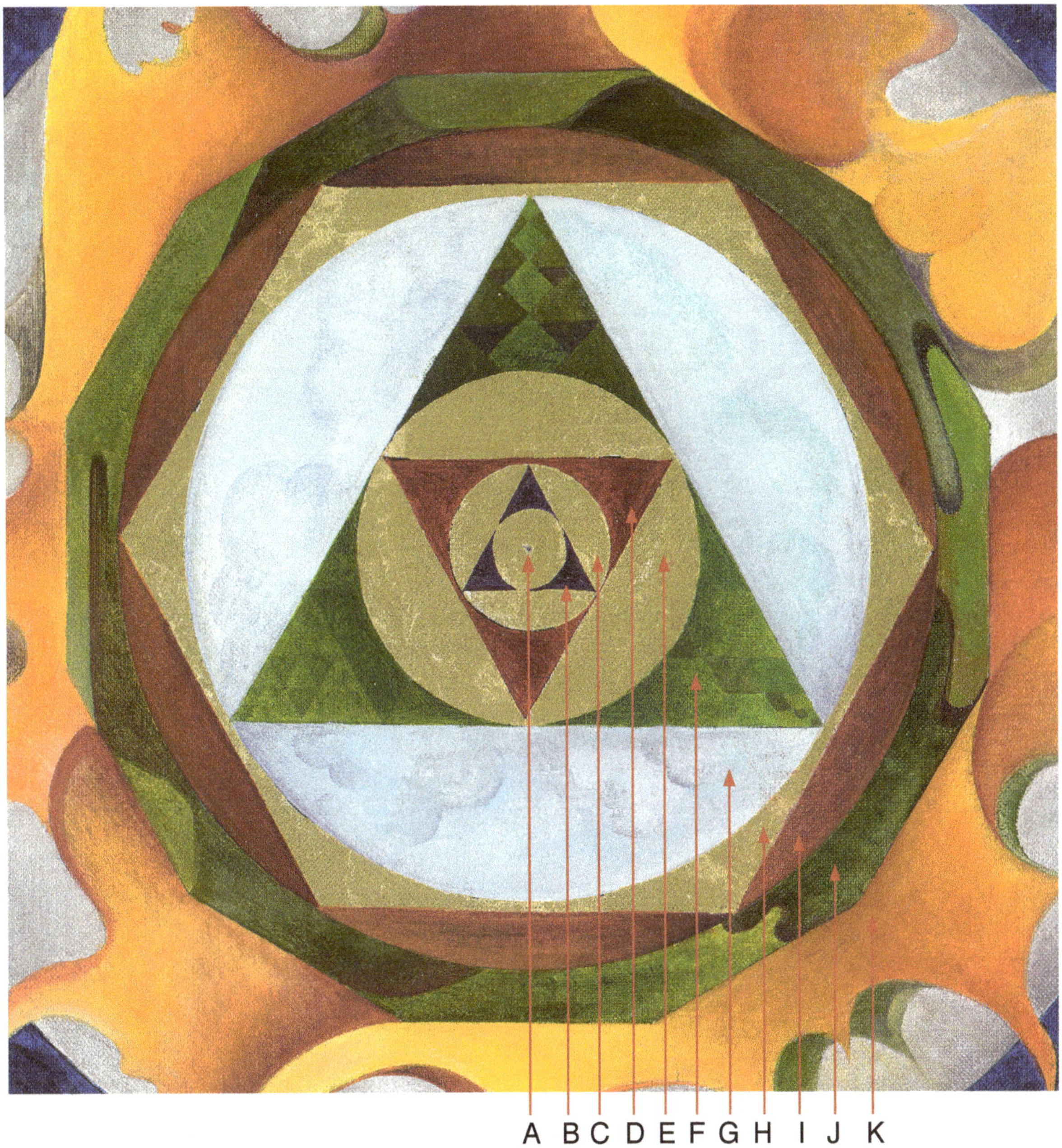

Fig. 9.42. A close-up of Fig. 9.41, with the following details:
(Nomenclature by the artist)

- A Golden circle: spiritual existence (including a minute hole in the center of A).
- B Dark triangle: counter force.
- C Golden circle: spiritual existence.
- D Red triangle: energy of life.
- E Golden circle: spiritual existence.
- F Green triangle: physical existence.
- G Circle with sky and clouds: planetary existence.
- H Golden hexagonal: spiritual existence.
- I Brown circle: surface of earth (land).
- J Green dodecagon: vegetation.
- K Ring of fire: struggles and existential suffering (see also Fig. 9.41).

meanings. Mentioned dormant knowledge was accentuated during the course of analyzing her omphalophobia. Keywords, such as "omphalos," "navel," "emptiness," "hole," usually determine her idiosyncratic neurotic reactions. The terms evoke different associations and perceptions that painfully relate to various episodes from her life, becoming metaphorical signs filled with emotionally charged significance. Those words can refer to the center of *Sri Yantra,* which is of paramount importance to this painting as a metaphor that signifies a specific latent meaning for Susanne. We assume that they are a condensation of various significant emotional experiences, transitory perceptions, and even primary situations that may lie at the origin of her phobic reaction to the navel itself.

For Susanne, all the concentric circles in the painting express outward-flowing energy, like the ripples on a pond's surface spreading radially after a stone toss. Using the same analogy, we can envision such outward movement of the affective feelings, whose psychic energies flow outward like the wavelets caused by the initiating source. With the borderless, concentric design, Susanne metaphorically and unwearyingly expresses the powerful force that emanates from the unconscious like nuclear radiation.

It could be argued that the unconscious had nothing to do with the creation of the hole made by the compass needle, since it was an inevitable byproduct of making concentric circles. Furthermore, we note that the artist had the initial intention to fill the hole caused by the compass, which she had done numerous times for other paintings. Yet this was abandoned, as she apprehended almost intuitively that the hole could be a very fitting symbol with multiple meanings. For example, we speculate that this hole could serve as a symbolic portal for discharging unconscious affects. The hole in *Sri Yantra* can also represent an imaginary entrance to the inner infinity. This metaphorical interpretation of her action (deciding to keep the hole uncovered) manifested as a leap of imagination in Susanne's mind. The whole imagery of *Sri Yantra* is based on the metaphorical way of thinking that is typical of unconscious processes.

In the following, we will present a relevant selection of particular features of various geometrical formations, such as equilateral triangles, polygons, squares, and the tongues of flame shapes found in the circular arrangements in *Sri Yantra*.

Having been initially inspired by the philosophical conversation she had in 2006, in this painting, the artist intended to introduce a dark triangle that stands in stark contrast to the golden circles, as "counter-forces." They are antipodal opposites that could be interpreted widely in meanings ranging from "evil" to "goodness" (Fig. 9.42 (B)). On the unconscious level, the black triangle could be a representation of the inner "dark" forces (the so-called "reverse side" revealed through our analysis): Aggression, violence, egocentric desires, fantasies with taboo content. This supposition could be confirmed by a detail that deserves a closer look. The dark triangle is hollowed out by the inner, golden circle that interrupts the triangle's contour at three spots (Fig. 9.42 (B)). This effect weakens the dark shape, breaking it up into three reduced elements resembling arrowheads. In the watercolor preceding the oil version, this triangle was painted as one uninterrupted shape. But during the oil painting process, the artist spontaneously changed the design and was pleased to take advantage of the golden circle to dampen the otherwise intense appearance of the dark triangle. It is possible that this detail (i.e., the broken lines of the triangle) was unconsciously determined as a defense mechanism to disempower the wild, uncontrollable inner forces that the dark triangle represents.

The second circle of gold (Fig. 9.42 (C)) surrounds the dark triangle completely. This encompassing golden circle acts as a buffer against the dark triangle, metaphorically indicating the continuing process of the persistent attempt to suppress the negative inner forces. By setting the vertexes of each of the three nested triangles (black (B), red (D), and green (F)) in opposite directions from the preceding one, Susanne emphasized the different tendencies: The negative (evil—black triangle (B) in Fig. 9.42), the life energy (red—triangle (D) in Fig. 9.42), and the material (green for all kinds of living organisms—triangle (F) in Fig. 9.42). Because this painting is designed purposely to have countless viewing orientations,[60] the triangles can point to any direction. Nevertheless, by having the triangles all share a common center, the artist symbolically implied the possibility for

60 The painting is mounted to be hung so that it can be turned at any desired viewing angle.

reconciliation among these contrary tendencies through the unifying aspect of the central point on which everything else hinges.

Although Susanne does not like the equilateral triangle much, she made use of it in *Sri Yantra* because she wanted all the shapes to nest within one another, stressing the singular source of their origin and equality, signifying the interconnection of all aspects of existence united in one image.[61]

The circles, according to Susanne's personal symbolic hierarchy, are positive and powerful shapes, superior to triangles. The latter she senses in the majority of cases as negative, because their apexes can be seen as needle-sharp. Consequently, all the triangles in *Sri Yantra* are encased inside circles, by which she metaphorically wants to negate the uncomfortable associations they cause her.

Through the confinement of the triangles in her superior circles, the artist makes the triangles in this painting "the prisoners of the circles." The pairing of the triangles and circles is followed by a sequence of four shapes with specific symbolic meanings that are intended: Clouded blue sky circle—Earth's atmosphere ((G) in Fig. 9.42); brown circle—the planet's ground, the lithosphere ((I) in Fig. 9.42); a green dodecagon—the Earth's biosphere ((J) in Fig. 9.42); and a golden hexagon placed between sky and earth—a reference to the spiritual aspect of our existence ((H) in Fig. 9.42); same as the golden circles (A), (C), and (E) already indicated (see Fig. 9.42).

Those above parameters (A to J) are surrounded by a ring-shaped, geometrically chaotic formation of blazing flames (Fig. 9.41), by which she consciously alludes to the suffering of mankind. Susanne here uses fire as a synonym for human conflicts, where every clash results in pain and destruction. It is noteworthy that the flames, in an irregular pattern of curvilinear triangular forms, are warped into sickle-shaped tongues. Their threatening, elongated peaks bear a resemblance to a food blender's blade. Painted in glowing red and orange hues, they underscore the message of extreme danger. The sickle shapes in this image are similar to comparable features in a number of Susanne's paintings, including the wing contours of Touchless Misty (see subchapter, 9.3.4). This observation confirms our earlier assumption that this detail is the artist's personal symbol of aggression.

Following the traces of fire as it appears with its symbolical meaning in *Sri Yantra*, Susanne thought immediately of a painting, which she created 20 years earlier, titled *Revolution* (1985, Fig. 9.43(b); see also subchapter 13.2, page 379). In this work, she personifies a violent revolt in an oppressive society as a portrait bust rising from a sea of blood. Above this, the blue sky at the right turns swiftly into absolute darkness at the left of the painting. A bright glow behind the head indicates the reflection of fire flaring up from the cracks in the back of the bust's skull and getting ready to blaze into a firestorm.

A closer look at the bust reveals a fatal cut that slices across its neck, through which blood oozes out and drips over the shoulder, dooming this metaphoric figure, *Revolution*, to its eventual demise. These specific details of the painting allegorically express Susanne's thought that a violent uprising is like an out-of-control wildfire that will inevitably end in total destruction. The rebellion that started with lofty optimism and ideals will lapse into the dark night, when "the revolution devours its own children."[62] The blazing sickle shapes in these two paintings, *Sri Yantra* and *Revolution*, give us additional support for our interpretation of this configuration, which was first proposed in the analysis of the serrated wing contours of Touchless Misty as a symbol of aggression and horror in Susanne's iconography (see subchapter 9.3.4).

We observe that Susanne used various grayish shades of pink, white, and blue for the back of the head in *Revolution*, and, in *Sri Yantra*, for the background of the ring of flames, the artist intentionally chose gray.

This particular coloration in both paintings hints at the human brain's "gray matter" which Susanne associates with the development of our consciousness, cognition, and mindfulness, and considers as the epitome of the evolution of humankind. Previously, we have remarked that for Susanne, the depiction of flames is a visual metaphor for the ongoing conflicts and violence

61 One could see this in correlation with the well-known traditional symbol for the Christian Trinity made of an equilateral triangle. (Murray 1998, page 542, "Triangle"; page 543, "Trinity.")

62 The original quote is "Die Revolution frißt ihre eigenen Kinder" from Georg Büchner's 1835 play, *Dantons Tod* (Danton's Death) (Act 1, scene 5), which was spoken by Danton.

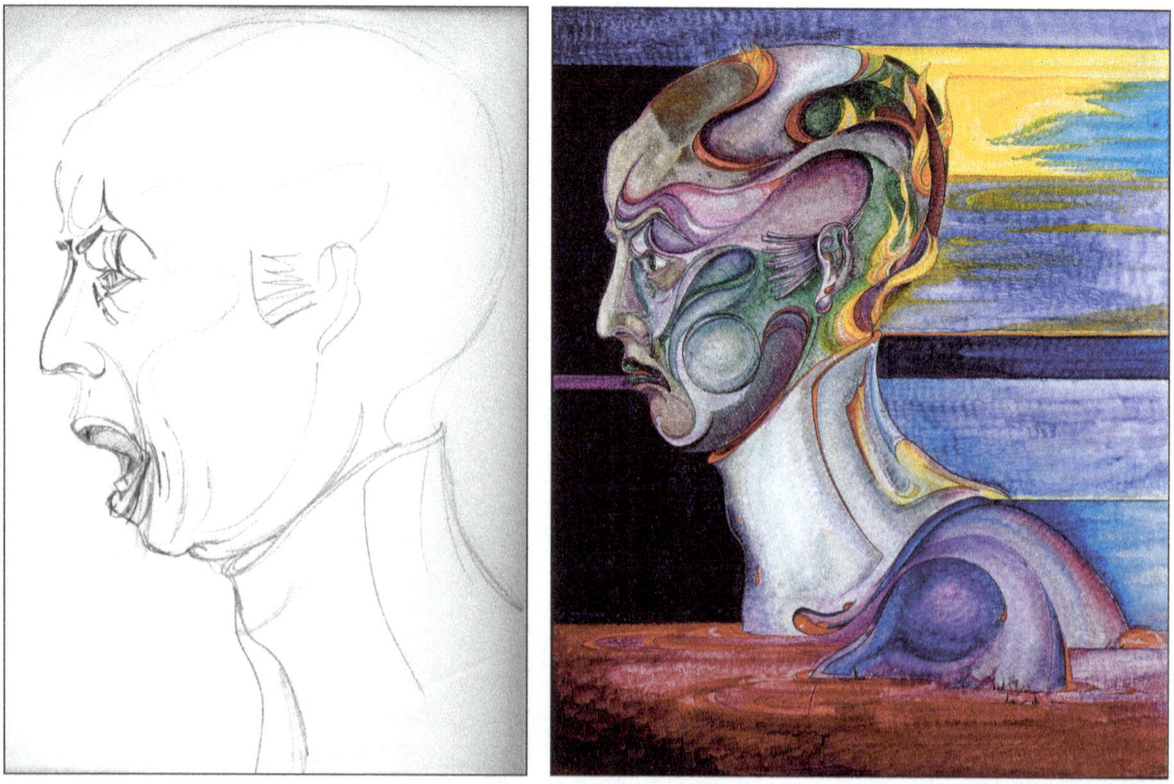

Fig. 9.43 a-b. Susanne Schuenke, *Revolution*,1985.
(a) Detail from preliminary drawing, pencil on paper, 11.7" x 16.2" (29.7 x 41.2 cm) Collection of the artist.
(b) Fig. 9.43. Susanne Schuenke, *Revolution*,1985. Oil and silver leaf on board, 24 x 20 in (60 x 50 cm). Collection of the artist.

smoldering beneath the conscious mind. We assume that the gray background metaphorically mirrors the mentioned progress of evolution, but in spite of this, flames of human conflict leap up to the sky. In reference to this, Susanne's circular shapes, constructed by her conscious mind but guided by her unconscious, can be understood as protective barriers against the conflicting inner tendencies.

In regard to *Revolution*, Susanne was willing to share the following information which opened up a Pandora's box: She herself was the model for the portrait in *Revolution*. As a student working one evening in 1985, she was sitting in front of a double window with the inner pane opened into the room; the pane mirrored her head, which was illuminated by a desk lamp. As she looked straight at the outer window pane against the night background, she discovered that her head's left profile was reflected back onto the outer glass from the inner one. This gave her a rare opportunity to study her own profile and draw the image of it with a variation of the facial expression, including a scream (9.43(a)). The drawing was soon used in the design of *Revolution*. Looking at the painting for our study, it is amazing to discover, even for Susanne, how much undisguised cruelty (the sea of blood, cut throat, blood in the ear, cracking head, etc.) she was able to inflict on the image that was literally her own portrait, and how much sadness marked this imagery. (We return in subchapter 13.2. once more to this painting.)

As mentioned above, in *Sri Yantra*, the ring of flames metaphorically expresses human violence and, at first impression, it seems there is no way out. Yet, in the ring of fire there is a small gap where the wall of flames does not fully close its devouring grip (Fig. 9.40), thereby offering a glimpse of hope in a stream of humanity's sorrow. The artist sees this opening as a passageway, a window to another dominion, where human life can be engaged in shaping and developing a new realm, in which humankind reaches an advanced state of existence—an enlightened one.[63]

63 For this desired positive state of existence, Susanne uses the word "there" in an abstract sense (like "the beyond") in contradistinction to "here" (i.e. our day-to-day reality). These terms are explained in detail in chapter 12.4 (golden background).

9.3.8 Colors: White, Gray, and Reddish Tints

Susanne always makes preliminary drawings for her paintings, and using these first designs, we try to understand through analysis what her conscious intentions were and to what degree they reflected such factors as her experiences and memories, thoughts and preferences, and past and present emotions. The artist makes premeditated as well as intuitive decisions about colors to emphasize the peculiarities she has already invested in the lines and forms. We have repeatedly shown that the unconscious participates significantly in this process. Her spontaneous selection of the main color(s) and her choice of additional hues are mostly guided by her feelings. These instances we have already enumerated throughout this study.

In this subsection, we shall delve into color selection as it pertains to Touchless Misty, whom Susanne considers to be the most beautiful of the seven butterflies. In the poetic commentary, she describes his chromatic qualities with expressions such as "fragile daintiness," "elegant polished white surface," and "pleasant luster." For the artist, the reference to "luster" is evocative of the softly shimmering surface of pearls, which intrigues with its play of light and reflection. In this spontaneous verbal commendation, ingrained parental guidelines surface. The father always used the term "clean" to express his admiration of a young female, which included an unspoken connotation for "not having been sexually active." Another parental motto, instilled in the daughters, was the definition of "elegance and class" in appearance and demeanor. In compliance with this precept, both the true lady and true gentleman must be "striking in their unobtrusiveness." Furthermore, meeting social expectations due to this parental maxim was taught to be the foundation for a successful, "pleasant and elegant" interaction with others. These guidelines resound in the artist's comment on Touchless Misty (Susanne's personification). The "*fragile daintiness*" alludes to femininity, while "*polished white*" reflects the parental efforts aimed at instilling an unblemished state of solid, idealistic values in their daughters' mindset by following the father's program, which the artist metaphorically compares with the process of polishing silverware.[64] She considers herself a result of such constant "polishing" by her parents, so that she not only shines for her own self through her achievements but also for them by living up to her father's ambitions and expectations. Thus, she has become her father's "polished" personal trophy. In consequence, these subtle values for individual distinction and elegance underpinned the family's catechism, and we assume that they surfaced metaphorically in Touchless Misty's coloration.

The color white is rich in symbolism and associations. In general and, for Susanne as well, white is connected with cleanliness and purity, and its unadulterated nature makes it the ideal color to represent an unpolluted state in human thoughts and affairs. This is especially apparent in such traditional symbolic items as the white altar cloth, the Easter lily, or the virginal bridal dress in Western culture. The German saying "Eine weiße Weste haben" ("having a white vest") signifies the possession of a clear conscience. This implication of the idiomatic expression about the color white underscores moral virtue and purity of heart. In many Asian cultures, the symbolic significance of white extends to include the color's use in the funeral customs and as a sign of mourning. This practice had been mostly lost to the West after the Middle Ages.

Using the symbolism of white, Susanne heightens the all-desired characteristics of elegance, superiority, and beauty that were bestowed on Touchless Misty. As mentioned before, a subtle yellowish glow in the wings leads to the illusion of the golden background shimmering through which alludes to a spiritual domain (see chapters 10 and 12).

The gauze-like translucency of the wings, together with the innocent white of the butterfly, promotes the impression of a delicate, vulnerable, and mysterious creature. This characterization contradicts the other tendencies that have metaphorically been coded in the dragon wings of Touchless Misty. Those aspects were described previously as the "reverse side" of this butterfly, representing aggression and strength, antithetical to the daintiness and fragility symbolized by the white hue.

64 Susanne is familiar with this laborious and recurrent process because it was taught to her when she was young so as to keep the family silver in good condition.

The choice of colors for at least three butterflies[65] in the painting originated from a living model in nature, the blue morpho with its scintillating blue on its top side.

For the coloration of Touchless Misty, a personification of Susanne, the artist's mind picked the appropriate hues from the same model again, but this time the choice was made from the blue morpho's less colorful underside,[66] usually beige and whitish hues, marked with brownish eyespots (Figs. 9.34 and 9.35).

Furthermore, the artist enhances the original, muted beige-whitish tone of the blue morpho to an alabaster white as the base color for butterfly No. 4. We assume that Susanne made this modification to unconsciously beautify her self-image. She associates this coloration with the appearance of the full moon at its zenith. The shift in the color nuance could also be determined by the artist's metaphorical identification with the moon. (See subchapter 8.1.3.)

Touchless Misty, however, is far from being flawless snow-white. On a closer look, we see that the majority of the butterfly's surface is actually painted in nuances of gray. The artist consciously applied the shades of gray to introduce an illusion of three-dimensionality, while maintaining the impression of an all-white butterfly. At the butterfly conservatory in New York, Susanne observed species of blue morpho displaying some dark, almost black areas on their outer wings, often concentrated at the wing tips, accentuating the fringes (Fig. 9.14). The recurrence of these striking details in the wings of other butterfly species are well known to Susanne, and in her earlier painting, *The Connoisseur* (1988), a single blue morpho butterfly (Fig. 5.15) is realistically painted with the characteristic dark marks on the edges of its wings. In contrast, Touchless Misty has no dark periphery area on the wings, and when this fact was pointed out to her, the artist replied that she wanted "a beautiful white butterfly." According to her, black applied to the whiteness of Touchless Misty would dim his "noble image." Therefore, she consciously chose the less threatening color gray for the modulating shades, arguing that "on a bright sunny day, shadows can cause remarkable nuances of darkened hues on the clean, white snow without having it judged as 'soiled.'"

It can be observed that Susanne avoided the use of solid black not only in Touchless Misty but also in all the other butterflies. In this context, we might recall that black was forbidden in her family, especially in clothing, due to her father's superstition in regard to this hue. The color was considered a symbolic representation for dying or the harbinger of the dreaded end, and this apprehension by her father could have influenced Susanne's avoidance of pure black. The closing phrase describing Touchless Misty in the poetic commentary is "wherever his shadows dare to fall." This reference to "shadows" conveys a looming feeling of danger, metaphorically expressed in this image. It is plausible that the artist might be associating the expectation of threat with the black markings on blue morpho's wings. In this schema, the use of gray for the shadows could find an appropriate interpretation. The gray was intentionally employed to create the appearance of three-dimensionality for the butterfly. The presence of this shade in Touchless Misty's otherwise white coloration might indicate the substitute of the threatening black. In this way, black sneaks in through the back door.

When the artist had nearly finished coloring Touchless Misty for the watercolor study, she was faced with the decision to select the hue for the butterfly's ring shapes. She recalled that her first inclination was to use a striking red as the suitable choice because of her love for intense reds, especially crimson, as her favorite color. As was pointed out before, for Susanne, this chroma symbolizes life, positive energy, joy, strength, power, and dynamism. However, she is aware that red is also often associated with danger, sexuality, and life-threatening circumstances, all of which have a negative connotation for her. As soon as the idea came up, she recognized that she could not realize it, because assigning such a color to the ring patterns would have significant consequences for the composition (for a demonstration of this, see Fig. 9.44). The artist was concerned with preserving the delicate equilibrium which existed among the

65 Butterflies No. 2, True Blue; No. 3, Pale Moonlight; and No. 6, Fanning Everything.

66 The underside of blue morpho's wings features a variety of brown and whitish hues, and it is marked with several spots of varying sizes that imitate the looks of large avian predators' eyes, each with white at the center, dark "pupil" and brownish "iris." Those large birds prey on small insect-eating birds, which are in turn the butterfly's main predators, and the eyespots' mimicry effect frightens them off.

seven butterflies, and the implementation of her idea would have made Touchless Misty appear unbearably gaudy. Such overwhelming attention to him in the assembly of the butterflies would cause the loss of the painting's aesthetic balance. For that reason, she did not paint the circles in lush red. Yet, it is conceivable that her avoidance of striking red was also motivated by a subliminal determination that this coloration announce a blunt signal of sexuality, flaring up like a provocative neon sign in a red-light district. The introduction of such "vulgarity" would have ruined Touchless Misty's elegance. This act could be tantamount to the daughter violating her fealty to the parental moral codes and maxims, which exhorted her to be tasteful and modest. She did not go forward with this lively shade for the rings and postponed the solution for the time being.

After having established the dominant orange color for Firebird (butterfly No. 5), which rose like an exclamation mark next to the white of Touchless Misty, Susanne took a fresh look at the overall chromatic balance of the watercolor study and worked out a compromise: She chose a very thin, diluted orange hue for the rings. However, she could not overcome her dislike of orange even in such an weakened appearance, and in the oil painting, she developed the color in varying shades, ranging from very light to slightly saturated reddish-brown in gentle nuances—a very faint echo of her beloved red. In the following, we shall probe deeper into the genesis of this tone, as it has an important interpretive significance.

As noted previously, the prototype for this circular design originates from the wing marks on the underside of the blue morpho, which are colored in variations of dull white and beige-brown and lack any red connotation. By some inner impetus, the artist changed the coloration of the rings from the blue morpho's original brownish-beige to a weakened orange in the watercolor and then modified it again to a faint reddish-brown in the oil painting. Although the light orange in the watercolor was consciously introduced for compositional balance, the artist's unconscious imparted another scenario through which it manifested its own agenda through Susanne's artwork.

Our analysis suggests that, besides the explicit reason for the selection of the orange nuance for the rings in the watercolor, there is also an implicit basis for choosing this color, prominently displayed for the image of Firebird (representation of the father), which was driven by unconscious self-identification with him. We also find a tendency for camouflage in the choice. Orange, created by mixing red and yellow, is already a diversion from pure red. It is our supposition that by applying the subdued reddish-brown on the butterfly's rings, the artist may have been unconsciously coding an allusion to red in the guise of a less striking hue. By coloring the rings in this manner, Susanne unconsciously manifested her desire to make Touchless Misty more alluring for Firebird. This accords well with our previous observation in regard to the red underpainting used in True Blue as a possible intimation of sexuality (see chapter 5).

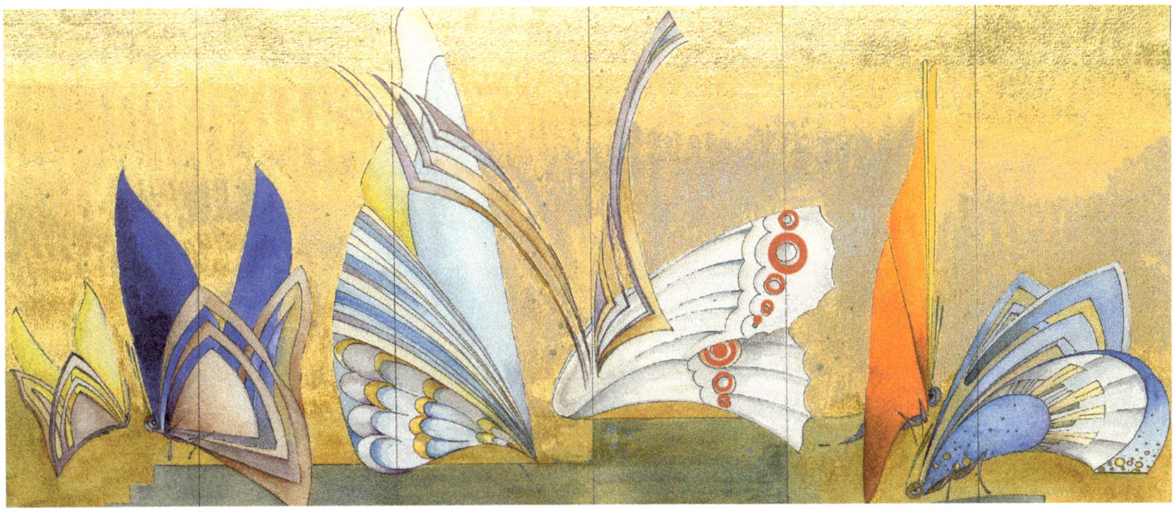

Fig. 9.44. Illustration highlighting the rings in Touchless Misty. The rings accentuated with an overlay of red colored circles (applied to the watercolor study of *Give Me Wings!* (Fig. 2.12)).

9.4 Optical Illusions — Faces

Cognitive optical illusions are a well-known phenomena in the perception of nature as well as in the visual arts. Our world provides us with many natural forms that have for centuries inspired people to see an old man's profile in the outline of a mountain, a man's face in the moon, an animal shape in a cloud formation, a horse's head in a dark, interstellar, molecular cloud (the Horsehead Nebula in the constellation Orion), and so on. These natural configurations are thought to be the accidental results of various physical processes, not guided by any intentional motive or design. In some cases, these kinds of simulacra are more subjective than others, because their interpretation depends on each viewer's perception and cultural background, not necessarily shared by everyone. Visual artists often have a heightened sensitivity for this kind of "creative seeing." For example, Leonardo da Vinci (1452–1519), in his *Treatise on Paintings,* remarked about the human tendency to recognize certain familiar objects and patterns, including facial expressions in random natural configurations, even as accidental as stains on the wall.[67]

There are various types of optical illusions, but the one that is relevant to our discussion is known as an "ambiguous illusion," in which the appearance of a design can be interpreted as having two images (usually seen alternatively) by the observer. One famous example of an ambiguous illusion was first introduced by the Danish psychologist, Edgar Rubin, around 1915. It is a pair of patterns sharing a common boundary, which causes a visual effect that alternates between two possibilities, only one of which can be seen as a distinct object at any given instance of perception. The illusion, now known as Rubin's vase or the figure-ground vase, emerges when the negative space ("ground")[68] around the vase ("figure") forms the silhouettes of two human profiles facing each other. Rubin defined this phenomenon as a "figure-ground reversal," but he was not the first to make use of this type of man-made cognitive illusion. For example, over one hundred years earlier (circa 1793), the royalist survivors who supported the monarchy during the French Revolution used the figure-ground illusion in an engraving (Fig. 9.45) as a camouflage to covertly depict the profiles of King Louis XVI and Queen Marie-Antoinette ("ground") through the adroit manipulation of the contours of an urn ("figure").

Ambiguous illusions can also be created by skillful arrangement of familiar items that are combined to form an aggregate object of an entirely different nature. In the 16th century, the Italian painter, Giuseppe Arcimboldo (1526 or '27–1593), specialized in creating artworks based on this type of optical illusion, in which a painting could be seen as an unusual still life, as a portrait, or as both, composed entirely of plants, seashells, books, or other objects.[69] With striking artistry, Arcimboldo arranged these familiar items in a way that beguiled the viewer to perceive the image as a bust-portrait of a human being. However, the peculiarity of the image would force the observer to pay closer attention to the strange facial features. To the onlooker's surprise, the "portrait" would actually turn out to be made up of these individual objects.

There are two other intentional optical illusions in art we will mention before we analyze ambiguous configurations in Susanne's works. The Dutch artist Maurits Cornelis Escher (1898–1972) designed intriguing optical illusions using the contrasts between "negative space" and "positive space." His woodcut, *Sky and Water I* (1938)[70], depicts a formation of black geese flying in a white background at the top of the composition. Underneath, a school of white fish swims in black water. The fascination of the image lies in the seamless transformation of the

---

67 "Look at certain walls dirtied with various stains or with a mixture of different kinds of stones...you will be able to see in them a resemblance to various landscapes adorned with mountains, rivers, rocks, trees, plains, wide valleys and hills. You will also be able to see various battles and figures in quick movements, and strange expressions on faces, and costumes, and an infinite number of things" (Leonardo da Vinci as quoted in English translation in Moorhouse, 1990, page 19).

68 "Negative space" will be understood throughout this text as the "empty" space (also called the "ground") around the figure. The shape of the negative space is defined by the contours of the figure(s) depicted.

69 Some of Arcimboldo's famous "illusionistic portraits" can be seen in Norbert Schneider, *Still Life* (Taschen Verlag, Cologne: 1999): *Summer* (1573), page 130; *Autumn* (1573), page 131; and *The Librarian* (c.1566), page 191.

70 Ernst 1986, page 24, Fig. 31.

birds (starting from the topmost goose) into the fish (starting from the bottommost fish) or vice versa. The enchanting surprise is that the fish ("figure") ascending out of the water transform themselves into the "ground" (white sky) for the birds, and the same can be said for the birds ("figure") descending into the water to turn into the "ground" for the fish below. The negative space becomes positive space and vice versa, as the birds and fish alternate as "figure" and "ground." This example of figure-ground reversal is a superb demonstration of the impossibility of determining what is the positive or the negative space unless the observer only pays attention to one set of figures (birds or fish) by ignoring the other.

Another 20th century artist, Salvador Dalí (1904-1989), intrigued by ambiguous illusions, called them "double images." In his painting, *Slave Market with the Disappearing Bust of Voltaire* (1940),[71] a head-and-shoulders image of the French philosopher, Voltaire, transforms into a pair of Dutch burger women dressed in black and white with ruff collars, or conversely they turn into the philosopher's bust. For most observers, the two perceptions switch back and forth, and they can only see one image or the other at any given moment. Dalí called this technique to induce the perception of two alternating images in the same space the "paranoiac-critical method." Thus, these optical illusions were created on purpose by artists to beguile the viewer's mind.

Ambiguous illusions are of great interest to our study, as we have located a few instances of them in Susanne's paintings, all created unintentionally and most of them not recognized by the artist's conscious mind before the analysis. These unconsciously created ambiguous images were mostly discovered accidentally by the analyst or other onlookers in accordance with some marks, ranging from the whole design of the objects to a small detail of them. The identification of these revealed optical illusions has been validated on the basis of particular data from the artist's life and artwork. We had the advantage of obtaining a suitable array of personal information from the artist firsthand, and this became the foundation for arriving at reasonable assumptions and interpretations concerning Susanne's involuntarily created ambiguous illusions. We will discuss certain optical illusions that appear in Susanne's works which will present us with the opportunity to further clarify the involvement of the unconscious in their creation.

A convincing case of unconscious symbolism was revealed in an ambiguous illusion, which we uncovered in one of Susanne's early paintings titled *Das Meer der Zeit* (*The Sea of Time*), 1982 (Fig. 9.1). The analysis of an unintended image in this work became a key event for the authors of this research, as it led to a reliable foundation to substantiate the influential role of the unconscious processes in creativity. We surprisingly found a hitherto hidden figure in this painting: One can see a surprisingly clear image in negative space, that closely resembles a female torso seen from behind (Fig. 9.46). Further analysis of this finding convinced us that this image is not accidental. This specific optical illusion was brought to light 26 years after the artist had involuntarily created it, and, through our discovery, she became aware of the ambiguous image.

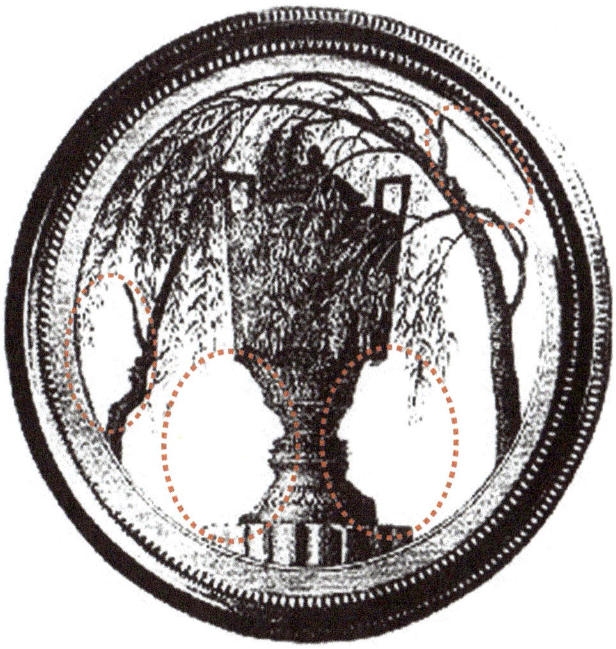

Fig. 9.45. Anonymous Engraving, circa 1793, showing the profiles of King Louis XVI and Queen Marie Antoinette of France and others in the figure-ground reversal (areas marked by red ellipses) through the contours of the urn and tree (the work was created to embed several profiles of the French royal family members to covertly convey monarchist sentiment). After Gombrich (1985).

71 Moorhouse, 1990, page 15; also, Descharnes and Néret, 1993, p. 340–341. For a discussion of Dalí's use of ambiguous illusions, see pp. 311–317 of Descharnes and Néret.

At first, Susanne declined to acknowledge the shape's presence, but her heavy doubt about the existence of a female trunk in this painting was eventually erased, when she had a spontaneous association that recalled a long-forgotten sketch. This prompted a surprising chain of discoveries, which presented us with proof that this torso was identical with a nude study that she had drawn two years before creating *The Sea of Time*. The old drawing corresponded so closely with the torso defined by the negative space in this painting that the resemblance could be mathematically measured to confirm their congruity (see Figs. 9.49 (b) and 9.50 (b)). This changed the attitude of the artist. Up to this point, she had been skeptical of this kind of perception in the negative space. After that she became convinced of the presence of an unintended meaningful image in this painting.

In the following, we will retrace the steps involved in arriving at the discovery.[72]

1.) On a leisurely beach walk, the analyst remarked about the choppy waves of the ocean, saying, "This is nature, wild nature." The artist commented in her own peculiar way, "No, this is much more," referring to a fantasy, which she had always correlated with the sea, without divulging any further. After returning home, she pulled out her first oil painting created in 1982, *The Sea of Time*, to clarify her cryptic remark at the beach. She explained its allegorical meaning: "Water equals time."[73] In the painting, she tried to illustrate this analogy, which came to her mind a year earlier while she was crossing the English Channel on a hovercraft. Watching the waves and splashes of the sea, she ruminated whether each drop could metaphorically represent a human life span, and that the waves' swelling and rolling could stand for the passing of immeasurable ages.

2.) The analyst examined the painting carefully, and suddenly, on the right side of the painting, he perceived an image of a female torso embedded in the negative space between the figure's face-and-neck contour and the dark night sky. The right side of the torso appeared to be shaded by numerous dark horizontal bars, representing the encroaching night sky (Fig. 9.46). Without revealing his discovery, he encouraged the artist to look closely and tell him what she saw in that area. Susanne had trouble recognizing any shape in the space he pointed out, but finally, with great hesitation, she asked if he meant a female torso seen from behind.

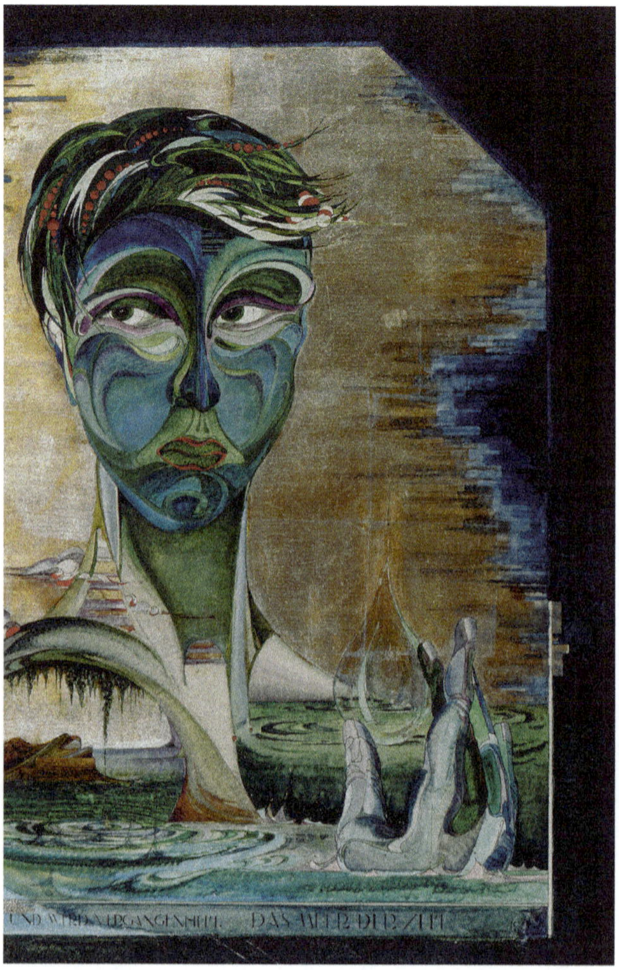

Fig. 9.46.
Detail from Fig. 9.1. The right part of *The Sea of Time*, where the shape of a female torso seen from behind is found in the negative space.

72 The sequence of steps in the artist's realization was written down immediately after the discovery of the image in the negative space.

73 This idea is also incorporated into the artwork in the writing at the bottom of the painting, where Susanne, ahead of her own title, quoted two lines from one of her favorite Chinese poems (which she read in a German translation), because the verses matched her musing perfectly when she was crossing the Channel: "*In wilden Wogen wälzt sich her die Zeit . Die Gegenwart verschäumt und wird Vergangenheit. Das Meer der Zeit*" (in Susanne's English translation: "Time rolls forward in wild waves. The Present foams up and becomes Past. The Sea of Time."). The poem is "Praise of Laughter" by Feng Weimin (circa 1511–1590), found in Ernst Schwarz (editor/translator), *Chrysanthemen im Spiegel—Klassische chinesische Dichtungen* (Berlin: 1969).

After the analyst confirmed her observation, she immediately expressed her doubt that any significance could be ascribed to this shape, declaring defensively that since it had never been her intention to depict such a form, it could not be a meaningful part of the painting.

3.) Nevertheless, during that discussion Susanne had a vague feeling of "something familiar in this torso-formation," and she decided to look through her catalogue of paintings and drawings to see, just in case, if she could find a comparable female form. However, the search was unsuccessful.

4.) Hours later, alone in her kitchen washing dishes, she kept thinking of "the slightly twisted nude figure from behind" which the analyst pointed out, as it continued to trouble her that the image somehow felt familiar. Therefore, she went looking through the archives of her life-class study drawings. Between 1980 and 1984, she had attended several intensive four-week training sessions to learn to draw the human body from nude models. Those classes resulted in hundreds of studies, and in 2001, she selected her "most interesting" ones for photocopying in a reduced size, which she catalogued and filed according to the body postures. When she searched her archives under the category, "female—sitting, seen from back," she quickly found the photocopy of a head-to-waist sketch of a female model, seen from behind in a slightly twisted posture (in Fig. 9.47 marked as (1)). Although the twist of that figure seemed to match the torso in the negative space found in *The Sea of Time*, the sketch showed only a part of the body down to the waist. Therefore, the outline failed to correspond sufficiently to the female shape in the painting's negative space.

5.) The study (Fig. 9.47 (1)), referred to henceforth as (1), was not a match, but a fragment of another drawing in the upper right corner on the same photocopy caught her eye (Fig. 9.47 (2)), which turned out to be a truncated copy of a full sketch that was drawn from life on the same sheet from her sketch pad. Since the photocopy of the sketch was dated (encircled in red in Fig. 9.47), she was able to locate the original drawing in her archives and discovered that the actual sheet from the sketch pad contained three sketches of the backside of the same female model in a squatting pose (Fig. 9.48 (1), (2), and (3)).

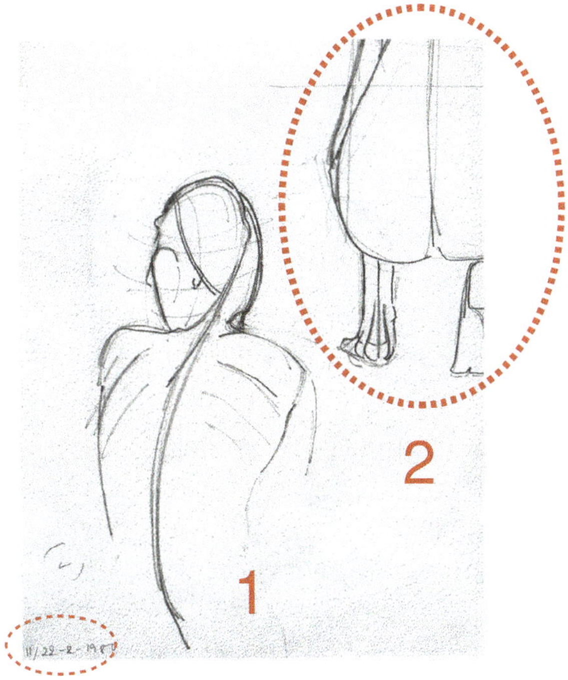

Fig. 9.47. A photocopy showing part of a work sheet from a life class with sketch of a female torso (see Fig. 9.48 for the full sheet). Red numbers and circles added to facilitate understanding.

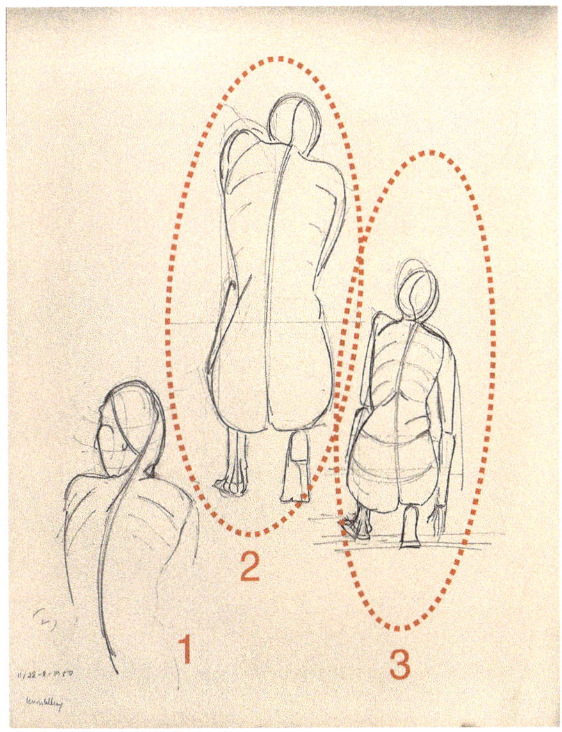

Fig. 9.48. Susanne Schuenke, "life class sketches," February 22, 1980. Pencil on paper, 22 x 16 in (56 x 40 cm). Artist's collection. The original work sheet from the life class with sketches of a female model (red numbers and circles added to facilitate understanding).

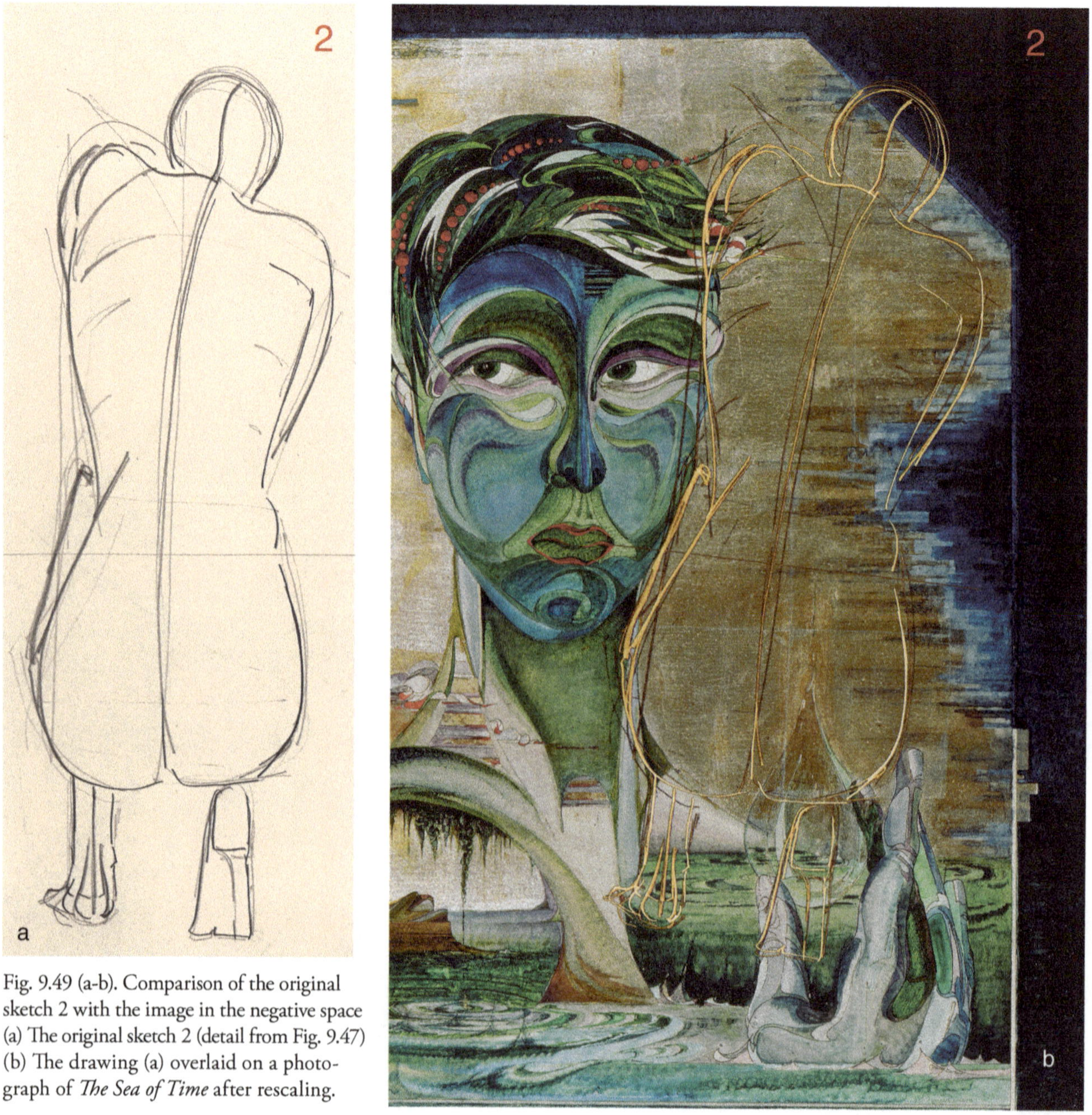

Fig. 9.49 (a-b). Comparison of the original sketch 2 with the image in the negative space (a) The original sketch 2 (detail from Fig. 9.47) (b) The drawing (a) overlaid on a photograph of *The Sea of Time* after rescaling.

The sketches (2) and (3)[74] found on the original sheet appeared similar to the figuration observed by the analyst in the negative space toward the right margin of *The Sea of Time.* For purposes of comparison, Susanne laid the outlines of the two figures (2 and 3) in a contrasting color on a clear foil and overlaid them individually on two photographic copies of the oil painting, carefully adjusting for scale (Figs. 9.49(a–b) and 9.50(a–b)). The match was striking, and it shocked her. (Figs. 9.49 and 9.50 show the overlays generated by a phototechnical process, preventing potential subjective alteration from the original sketch drawings.)

6.) Of the three sketches found from the original sheet, the third sketch (3) was the most convincing match, which dissolved her initial disbelief and made her wonder what else she

74 When Susanne made the photocopy of this sheet, she did not consider the studies (2) and (3) as interesting enough to be catalogued for reference. The only reason the truncated copy of the study (2) appeared in the photocopy was due to not cropping the sketch by masking it during the photocopying process.

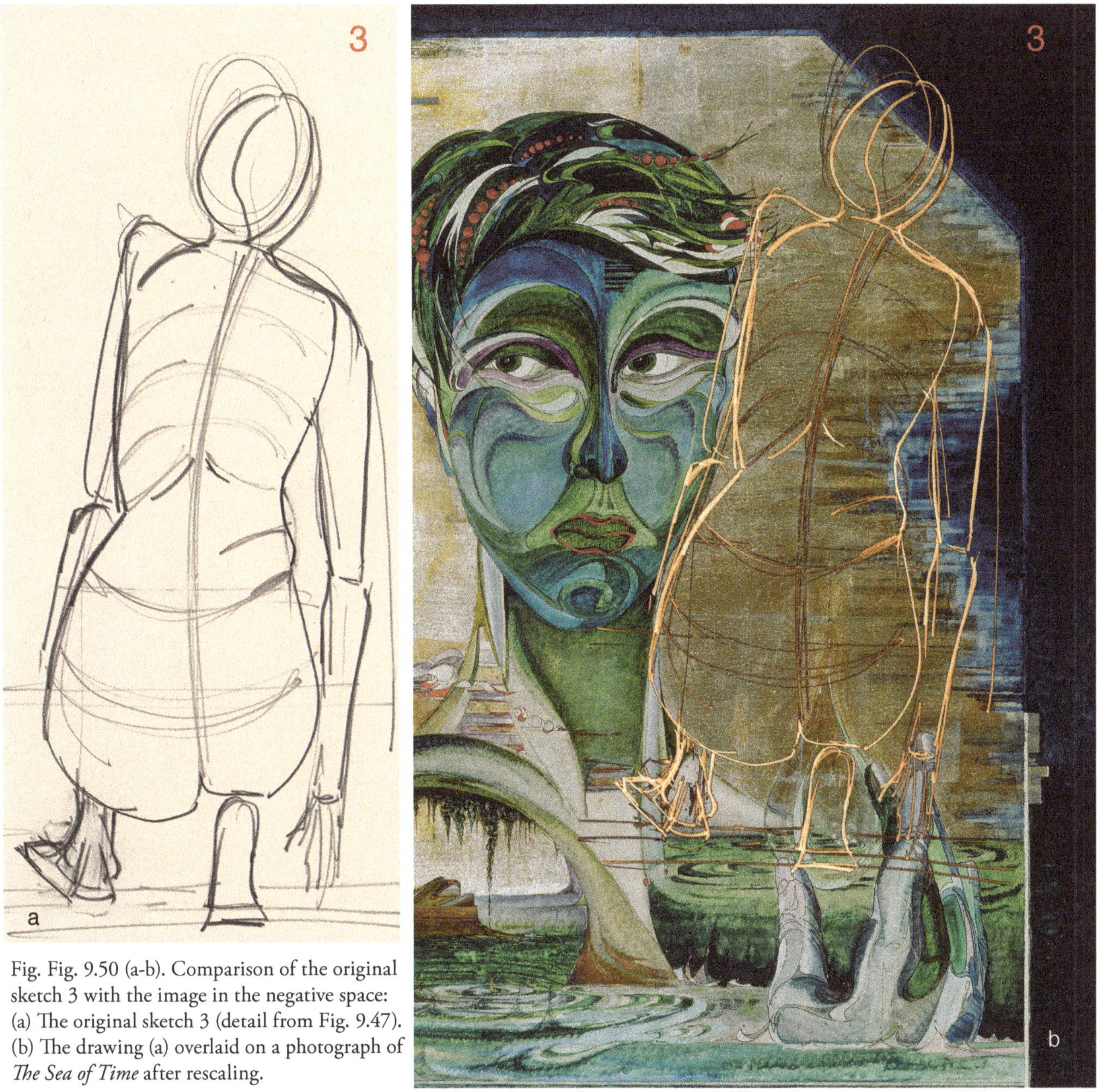

Fig. Fig. 9.50 (a-b). Comparison of the original sketch 3 with the image in the negative space: (a) The original sketch 3 (detail from Fig. 9.47). (b) The drawing (a) overlaid on a photograph of *The Sea of Time* after rescaling.

would unconsciously register, recast, and cause to reemerge unexpectedly in her paintings without her intention. In tracing these steps, we want to stress that her intuition played a fundamental role in retrieving the original source for the image of the female torso in the painting. The power of the "something" that led her to the discovery still astounds her to this day, as it possibly constitutes the most convincing part in this "doubting Thomas" episode.

7.) Another detail of importance to our interpretation emerged when we tried to ascertain the significance of the date on the sketch sheet. The notation we found was marked "11–22.2.1980," meaning it was the 11th drawing made on February 22, 1980, which happened to coincide with Susanne's second day of life class drawing.[75] Coming from a family who frowned upon human sensuality, she had not encountered an undressed person before. Susanne must have been deeply

75 Susanne entered the program offering life class studies for the first time in her life on Feb. 21, 1980. This date was recorded by her on the cover sheet of the sketch pad she used for the class.

moved by these sessions on the first week of the drawing class. We assume that under the influence of this sensitive experience[76] the images of the life classes were firmly engraved in her mind, which then could have resurfaced two years later, and unconsciously incorporated into *The Sea of Time.* The drawing with the matching torso was made during such an emotionally impressive situation, which adds weight to the supposition that this image of a "woman from behind" in the negative space carries a significant message.

8.) One more additional consideration gives further support to the assumption of the unconscious' involvement in the creation of the torso in *The Sea of Time.* Susanne remembers that at first she painted the figure's bust and a hand, both rising out of the water. The thumb and middle finger hold a huge water drop with a pronounced tapering tip. Originally she had no intention for the background aside from rendering it in silver leaf with a few clouds brushed in (Fig. 9.51). Later in the painting process, however, she changed her mind and introduced a starry night sky on the left side of the painting which blended with the darkly painted frame. She intended the stars to refer to "the past,"[77] metaphorically illustrating the theme of the painting. Additionally, she augmented the subject with a text from a Chinese poem, which she incorporated at the bottom of the painting. Only then she felt the need to introduce some starless dark sky into the scene from the right edge of the painting that would symbolize "the future" (Fig. 9.52 (right)).[78] She accomplished this by shading the area with spontaneous strokes of dark blue color. This step turned out to be essential in unconsciously forming and defining the shape of a female torso in the negative space between the bust on the left and the night sky on the right. As a consequence of this, the preexisting water drop, which was painted intentionally, combined perfectly with the bottom portion of the torso (the buttocks), fitting like the key in a lock (Fig. 9.53).

This configuration (the buttocks and the drop), once perceived, is hard to disregard. It is reasonable to suppose that the artist unconsciously, with phenomenal precision, expressed a specific message through the figure-ground phenomenon. The crucial detail in this combination is the position of the water drop's pointed tip, which leads to two possible interpretations: a) the drop is either penetrating the space between the buttocks or b) being excreted from the body. Both could reflect the repressed fantasies and desires from the artist's early childhood. The first view could account for the image's unconscious symbolism as indicative of the anal stage of sexual development. The second view could attribute the symbolic figuration to the young Susanne's speculations concerning the secret of "where babies came from" (cloacal theory of birth[79] or cloacal fantasy[80]).

For our second example, we return to the optical illusion of the hand/fish figuration in *The First Hour of Full Moon* previously introduced in subchapter 8.1.3 (and Fig. 8.8). We recapitulate our earlier discussion. In this work, Susanne depicted a lively night-sky scene around the disk of the full moon. She intentionally manipulated the swirling lines of the clouds and their colors, to let the observer discern the head, bust, and arms of an imaginary "moon goddess" in profile, hovering over the landscape and hoisting the lunar disc to its zenith. We had called attention to a specific detail of this painting: the left hand of the goddess holding the lunar disc (Fig. 8.8; see blue arrows), which Susanne consciously designed. However, the hand, for many years since the painting's completion, was perceived by nearly all viewers as a "fish" (Fig. 8.8, see red arrows). The artist did not recognize the shape as resembling a fish at all, and it was only through analysis that she was finally able to visualize the "wrist" of the hand and the nearby swirling patterns as the gills and eye of a fish. When this realization came, she was highly astonished that she could have missed it for well over a decade.

76 Nudity was not allowed by Susanne's parents as they considered it "not appropriate behavior" and, as a consequence, she never experienced it in the family. Notwithstanding this attitude, there were plenty of artworks displaying nudity on the walls of the family home and in the art books available to the children.

77 It takes a long time for the light of the stars to reach the earth.

78 The artist explains that in this context the night sky without stars could symbolize the future because the light of the stars has not arrived yet.

79 Sigmund Freud, *On the Sexual Theories of Children*, Pelican Freud Library, 7:187–204.

80 Auchincloss and Samberg 2012

Fig. 9.51. Photocopy of a detail from *The Sea of Time* made early in the painting process, showing the hand and teardrop clearly outlined in ink. In this view, there is no sky formation planned in the space to the right. Also note the beginning of the first layer of oil paint visible in the neck and hand.

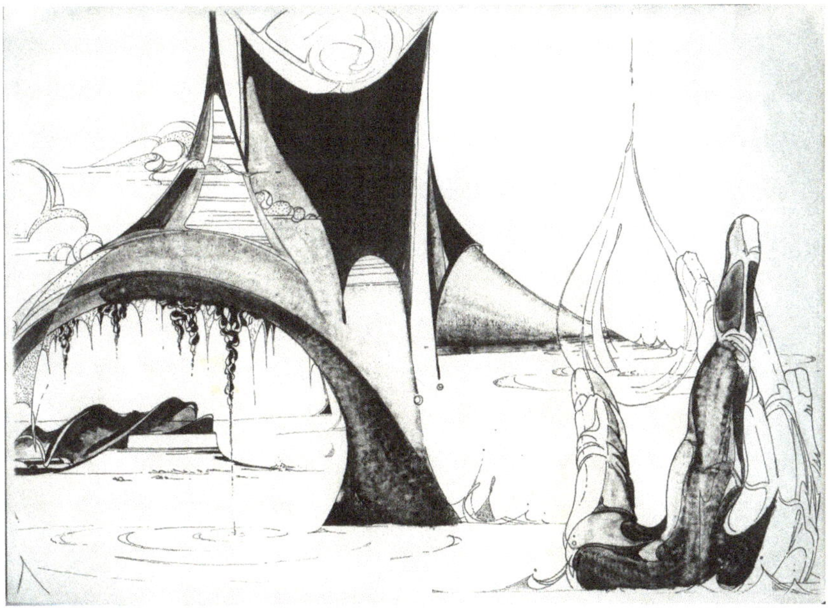

The double image of hand/fish here is an example in which the intended image (hand) was transmuted involuntarily into another image (fish). The mechanism of unconscious condensation could be behind this optical illusion. We suppose that such transfiguration reflects latent content that manifests in the imagery. We had already assumed (chapter 8, page 156 ff) that the same meaning, authoritarian power, underlies the instances of two similar configurations that were identified as the hand of the Moon goddess and as the "finger of the father" in Susanne's watercolor, *The Letter of the Law* (Fig. 8.7; also mentioned in chapter 4). Since the moon goddess Selene could be interpreted as Susanne's implicit self-identification as well as that of her parent, we posit that she unconsciously incorporated symbolical representations of herself and her father in this image through the ambiguous illusion of the hand/fish configuration.

Returning to the discussion on butterfly Touchless Misty, we present three images as optical illusions, which we refer to henceforth as "Native American Face," "Big Face," and "Third Face," all created unconsciously (for the purpose of identification consult Figs. 9.54 (1–2) and 9.62.) During the painting process, the artist suddenly recognized in the white butterfly's hind wing an image that she had not consciously designed, which reminded her of a Native American face in left profile. The area spreads from the bottom midsection of Touchless Misty and extends to the

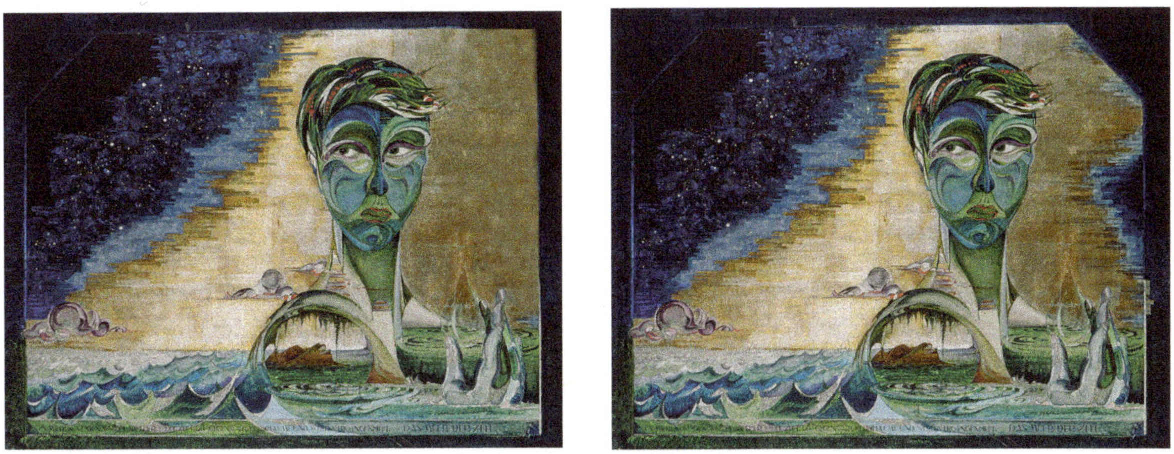

Fig. 9.52. Simulated reconstruction made for this study illustrating the painting *The Sea of Time* before adding the night sky at the right margin and after. (Some oxidation over the years has changed the silver into a yellowish hue.)
Left: Before—note the smooth silver leaf area between the bust and the right edge of the painting.
Right: After—note the filled sky with the optical illusion in the negative space.

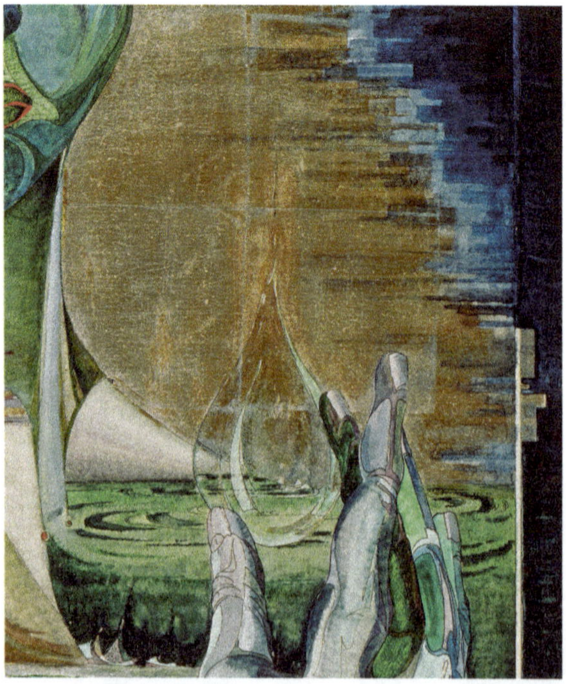

Fig. 9.53. Detail from Fig. 9.1. Right side of *The Sea of Time*, showing a huge teardrop with a tapering tip.

edge of the hind wing, covering nearly a quarter of the butterfly's profile. The largest ring, which we have already discussed in subchapter 9.3.5, served as an eye with the front wing covering its upper part mimicking an eyelid. The two smaller rings were imagined as dangling earrings and the ridges of the hind wing as feathers' shafts on a Native American paramount chief's war bonnet. Susanne came to treasure this serendipitous creation, calling it furtively her "Little Indian" without revealing its existence to anyone until our study.[81] The face reminds her persistently of images of pre-Columbian artworks (see Fig. 9.55 for a typical example).[82]

The illustration depicts the typical Mayan facial profile involving heavy eyelids (which Susanne calls a "sleepy look"), a receding forehead flowing directly from the nose, and the pronounced curvature of the lower lip and chin, all of which appear to find their match in Susanne's unintentionally created image (Fig. 9.54). She has always been attracted to such ethnically unique artistic styles. However, despite her interest, for many years she avoided learning more about pre-Columbian cultures for fear of being exposed to the grisly artifacts of their rituals involving human sacrifice.

Our research shows that the different imagery of the painting *Give Me Wings!* is connected with the artist's significant emotional experiences. The creation of the "Little Indian" image could be a fit example in accordance with her childhood perception of this foreign culture. We began to probe this possibility by starting with a proposition that the facial profile found in the butterfly might be correlated with that of Susanne's father. A silhouette portrait of the father existed, which was made when he was in his early twenties. A comparison between the portrait and "Little Indian" did not establish a correlation that was convincing in resemblance. Susanne also tried to match her own profile to see if there were some similarities between them, but this result, too, was negative. However, there is one exception, which could be a sign of her identification with the "Little Indian." The following fact confirms this assumption. As mentioned before, Susanne had suffered a lifelong perception of her profile as lacking a well-defined chin line, which finally prompted her to have such skillful cosmetic surgery that even her own family failed to recognize the result of the operation. While she was editing the manuscript for this chapter, she suddenly associated the shape of her pre-surgery chin and the receding chin line that she happened to see in the unconsciously created "Little Indian" face. We have included in this subchapter a comparison of the receding chin line between "Little Indian" and Susanne before the surgery (Fig. 9.56), and it is fairly easy to see why she made this association. Furthermore, the compositional drawing, where this "Little Indian" face can already be noted, was made during the recovery period after the chin augmentation operation. From this perspective, it is significant that, during the analysis, she saw in the "receding chin" of "Little Indian" the same segment of the facial contour she herself previously

81 Growing up in Germany, her earliest association with Native Americans had been a carnival or Mardi Gras costume for children playing cowboys and Indians which was quite popular, as the affinity for Native Americans has always been strong in Germany. As an adult, she came to know through reading about the cultures of the native peoples in the Americas and their disappearing traditions and wisdom.

82 A typical example of Susanne's knowledge about pre-Columbian artwork is a relief from the sarcophagus lid of King Pakal of the ancient Mayan city of Palenque, portraying the seated king surrounded by the intricately shaped objects and structures. His face has the characteristics of the typical Mayan style, in which the flattened forehead flows into the nose smoothly without any break in contour; and a pronounced eye completes the image.

possessed. Accordingly, we suppose that the artist harbored a certain degree of self-identification with this unconsciously created image.

While discussing the above associations, Susanne recalled that her father had several different sets of 19th and early 20th century miniature tin toy soldiers that were between two and four inches tall. One of these sets contained Native Americans dressed in their stereotypical costumes, including the feather headdress. The parents did not readily allow the children to handle these fragile metal figurines, but Susanne managed to do so sometimes. This gave her the sense of being privileged to play with her father's collection, since permission was seldom granted. Those rare occasions might have given her the thrill of being in a cowboys and Indians game that the neighborhood boys would engage in from time to time. It was Susanne's deep-rooted desire to join the boys instead of being consigned to the typical pastimes for girls.

The serrated contours of the butterfly's dragon wings (see subchapter 9.3.4) happen to define the profile of the "Little Indian" figure. Susanne associates both images with violence. While we discussed their linkage, she was tracing the profile of the "Little Indian" with her finger. When she reached its receding forehead, she touched her own head and spontaneously said, "Scalping." Immediately thereafter, she refused to talk about it further. However, after overcoming her resistance to delve into the matter, a window of opportunity opened. We sensed another possible angle to

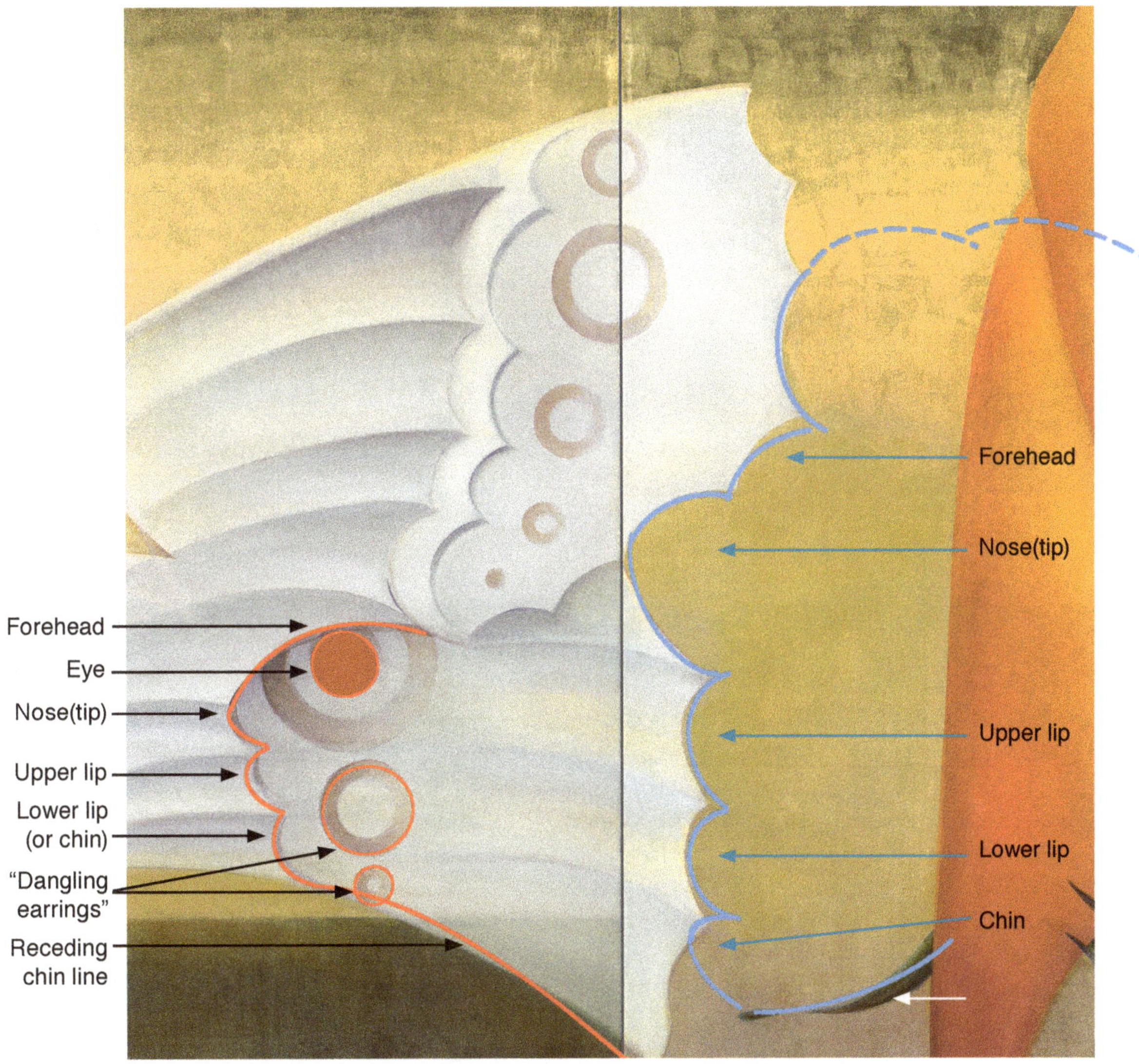

Fig. 9.54. Two faces that are identified in the contours of Touchless Misty's wings:
(1) "Little Indian" (outlined in red); (2) "Big Face" (outlined in blue).
White arrow points to tail end of Firebird.

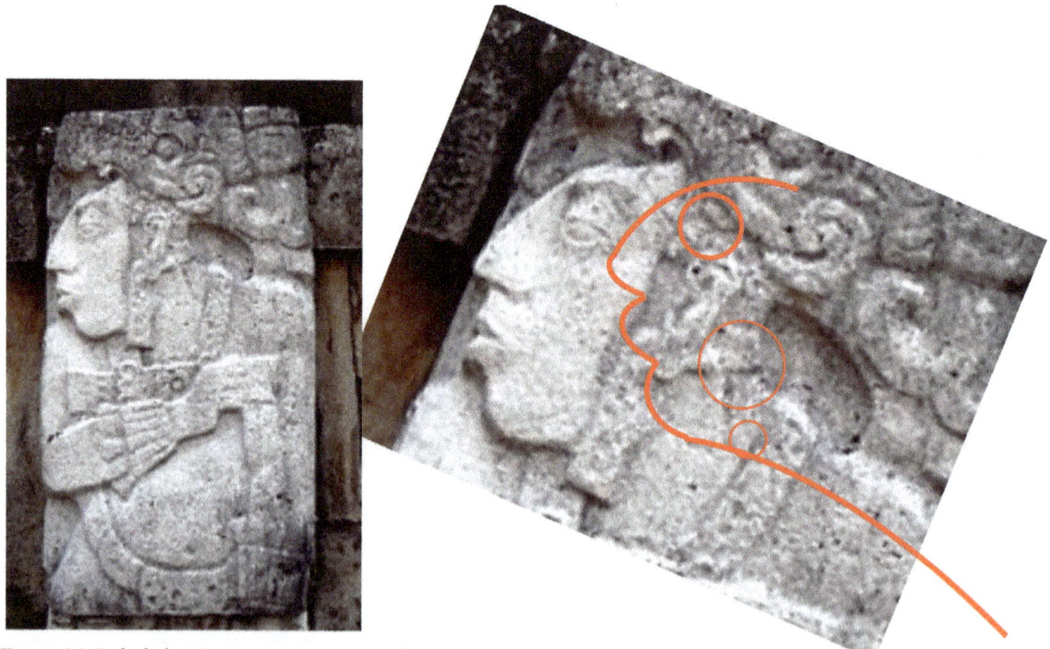

Fig. 9.55. Pakal the Great. Stone carving from the ancient Mayan site of Palenque, Mexico. Right: Detail overlaid with a red contour of the "Native American face" from the image of Touchless Misty for comparison.

interpret the unconscious creation of "Little Indian," in accordance with cruel rituals. This is the same connotation revealed in the symbolism of aggression of the dragon-like wings.

Under the influence of books about pre-Columbian cultures that Susanne read during her adolescent years in Germany, she formed a certain idea about some specific cruelties that were practiced by the indigenous peoples of the Americas before the Europeans arrived. These unappealing aspects instilled in her mind visions of the Native American warriors scalping their defeated enemies and the Mayan priests tearing the hearts out of sacrificial victims. These actions mingled with reports made by the European colonists of other gruesome rituals and customs. This information contributed to Susanne's partial view of pre-Columbian cultures, and, in her mind, reflected the West's attitude toward Native Americans as notoriously brutal, aggressive, and barbarous.[83] The Hollywood movies and the mass media of the era (circa 1960s and later) cultivated the perception of savagery associated with Native Americans. Such representations were steeped in an ethnocentric bias that often neglected the historical facts of the colonists cruelties. The process that embedded the unconscious symbolism of danger and aggressiveness in the dragon wings was most likely at work, when Susanne's mental images of Native Americans were metaphorically planted in the shape of "Little Indian" with the same symbolic association. As remarked before, the dragon and the Native American in Touchless Misty share the same potential for threat. With this understanding in mind, we were able to trace and analyze the presence of the aggressive drive in the artist's psyche through the mechanism of projection. Her mind transferred those tendencies, which haunted her with a sense of dread and uncertainty, into a variety of representative symbolic shapes and images. Likely, there is unconscious self-identification of the artist with a Native American who incorporates such stereotypical images that express forcefulness, courage, assertiveness, aggression, and combativeness. The image of the native warriors, representing those tendencies possibly manifests the artist's unconscious aggressive drive.

Another optical illusion, a second "face" in left profile can be seen in the negative space between Touchless Misty and Firebird (see Fig. 9.54 for detail). We have coined this unintended image "Big Face." The point where the outlines of Touchless Misty's two wings overlap could be perceived as the tip of a bulbous nose and the contour below as big lips and a round chin, whereas the two

83 During her twenties, through her academic studies, Susanne learned about the positive heritage of the native peoples of the Americas which mitigated her former one-sided image of them, as a consequence of taking up anthropology/ethnology as her second minor.

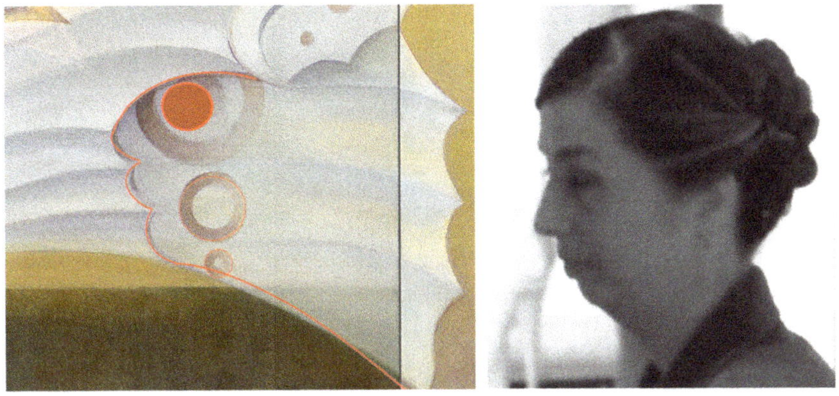

Fig. 9.56.
Outline of the "Little Indian" in comparison with the profile of the artist's face before 2003. (Note the receding chin lines in both figures.)

convex curves above the nose could be interpreted as a forehead (Fig. 9.54 (2), outlined in blue). "Big Face," positioned between the two butterflies, leads us to contemplate the relationship once desired by her. By observing that the lips of "Big Face" are actually kissing Touchless Misty, we suggest that there is a certain intimate bond between the butterflies due to their representations. Moreover, the bulbous nose, probing the "cleft" between the wings of Touchless Misty, could hint at the incestuous fantasies that the artist used to have in her childhood. This observation, however, should not come as a surprise, since we have already amassed enough analytic evidence to assert that Touchless Misty and Firebird are personifications, respectively, of Susanne and her father, and her transferential attitude toward him (multiple expressions of father complex). The inventiveness of the unconscious in constructing visual metaphors to encode its tendencies is amazing.

Contemplating the origin of the specifically shaped nose, Susanne recalled some particularities in her father's art, which we assume could have had significant influence on the emergence of this prominent feature associated with Touchless Misty and Firebird. When Susanne was 21 years old, her father painted *The Weightlifter* (Fig. 4.5), and while it was taking shape, she observed the painting process and participated in family discussions about it. She still vividly remembers many of the painting's intricate details, two of which we will now turn our attention to. The first item is a minute side scene (Fig. 9.57) in which Susanne's father depicted a small carriage being pulled by a horse. The driver's tiny face displays a strikingly bulbous nose (Fig. 9.58).

Regarding this figure, Susanne recalled that during one of the family's usual coffee talks, which happened to be held in front of the painting, her mother remarked to her husband that he had truly portrayed himself in the carriage driver. At that time, Susanne still unquestioningly accepted her parents' words. Therefore, her mind accepted that her father executed a self-portrait in side profile in the coachman's facial features. This image was modeled after one of the windup toys from the early 20th century in her father's toy collection (Fig. 9.59 a–b), and Susanne watched him copying the small toy carriage in his painting.

Comparing the actual toy against its painted counterpart, the overall similarity is compelling, but not in the detail of the nose, which exhibits a striking difference. The portrayal of the coachman shows a bulbous nose, unusually large and protruding, hinting at a phallic metaphor. There is the obvious, unconscious sexual innuendo. It is plausible that Susanne unconsciously processed this characteristic with a further development in its symbolism. It had been already intimated by the shape of Touchless Misty's front, which we have remarked previously as resembling the phallus. The rounded front of butterfly No. 4 is comparable by its size and shape with the nose of "Big Face," fitting closely into the space where it penetrates the indention of the wing contour (Fig. 9.60). Furthermore, the contour that forms the rear edge of the "Little Indian" configuration also traces the "lips" of "Big Face" (considered as a signifier[84] of her father in our analysis), giving the impression of him kissing the back of the butterfly.

84 Jacques Lacan, *Écrits: A selection*. Translated from French by Alan Sheridan (New York: 1977), chapter 3: "The Function and Field of Speech and Language in Psychoanalysis," page 30.

Our evaluation of the symbolism of the bulbous nose gains greater validity, especially when seen together with the sexually charged vignette scene on the barbell's hub depicted in *The Weightlifter*. Four images surrounding the nude bride appear to symbolically illustrate various male attitudes toward the young female figure. The hub's shape reminds Susanne of a mandorla,[85] and inside this form her father created an enigmatic assembly of symbolic images (Fig. 9.61). They range from highly idealized figures to those with obvious sexual tendencies. Her father named a single eye surrounded by rays in the top left, the "Eye of Providence" (Fig. 9.61 (2)). The descriptive names of the four faces listed in the following were given by Susanne. Beneath, a central figure, a young nude bride (Fig. 9.61 (1)), identified as such by the wreath and long, translucent veil, is surrounded by four faces. On the right side, the largest of them is seen in side profile with a hood (Fig. 9.61 (3)), whose large nose and open lips nearly touch the bride, hinting that she is the object

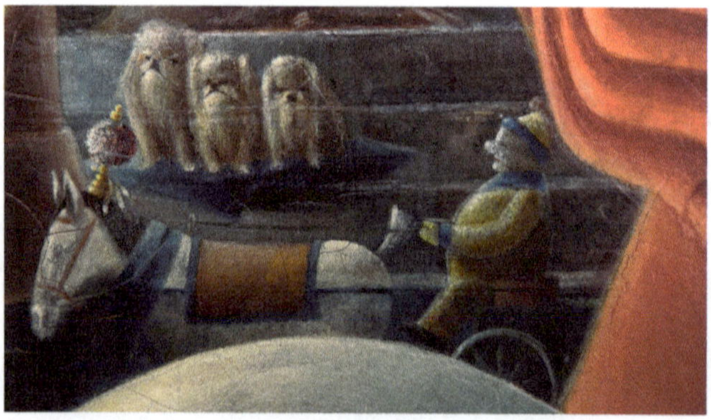

Fig. 9.57. Heinz-Günter Schünke, *The Weightlifter* (detail from Fig. 4.5), showing the carriage driver (located above the left weight disc).

Fig. 9.58. (Below)
Detail from Fig. 9.57, showing the enlarged view of the head of the carriage driver; which was then overlaid with a contour drawing of the "Big Face" for comparison.

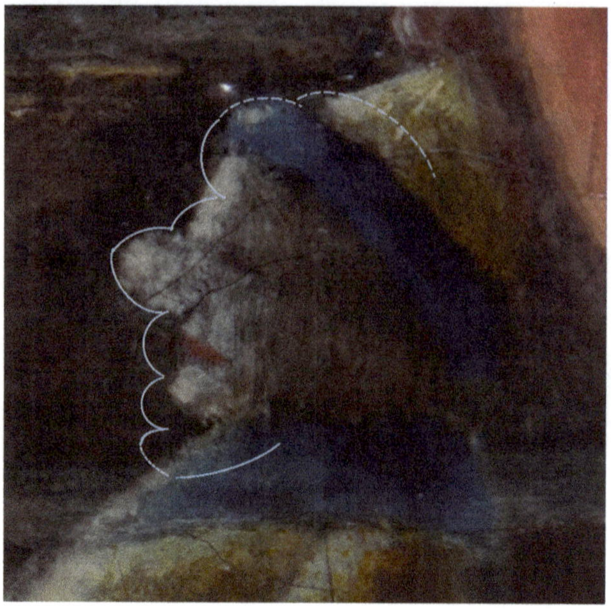

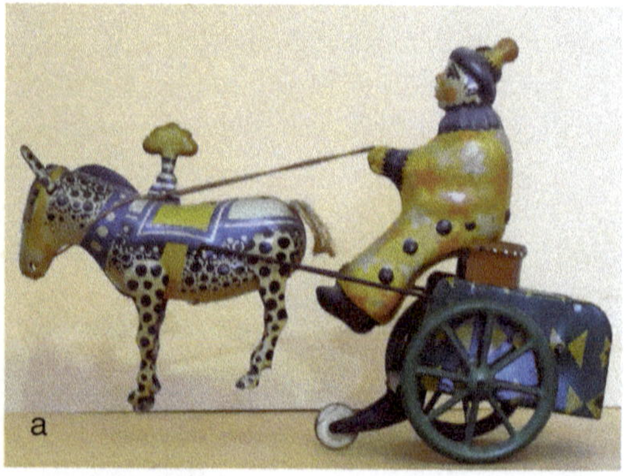

Fig. 9.59 (a-b).
(a) A tin toy from the collection of the artist's father, 7½ long, 2¾ wide, 5 inches tall (19 x 7 x 13 cm), first half 20th century.
(b) An enlarged detail: head of the carriage driver.

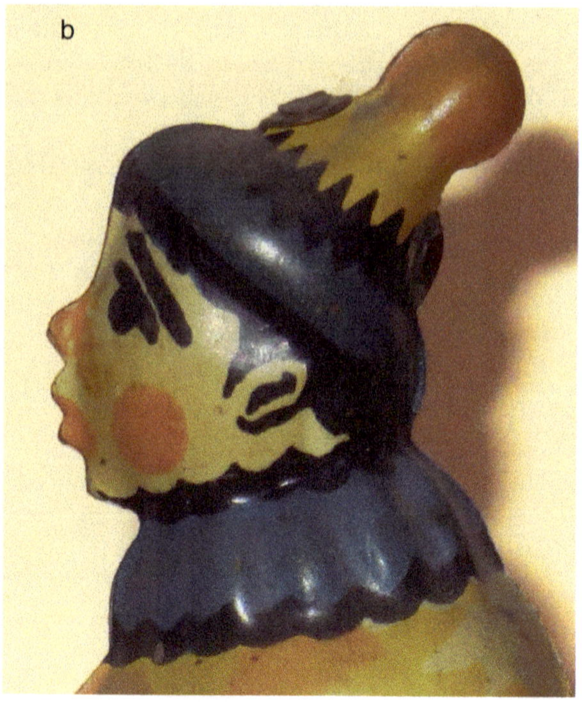

85 "Mandorla" (literally, "almond" in Italian) is an almond-shaped frame for a sacred figure—in Christian artworks, usually depicting Christ or the Virgin Mary.

of desire. Below this, another face appears in profile, characterized by a dominant gaze, which passes beyond the nude body into infinity (Fig. 9.61 (4)). Susanne associated this face with a wise philosopher like Confucius.[86] A rotund, bald-headed face, with its mouth wide open, gawks at the bride from the lower left. Susanne identified this specific likeness as typifying the lustful "Old Silenus" (Fig. 9.61 (5)), a fat and often drunken mythological follower of Dionysus. He was immortalized over the centuries as Western art's depiction of the base animalistic drives.[87] Above him, an elderly face bears, according to Susanne, an expression of disapproval (Fig. 9.61 (6)). The soubriquets she gave represent her perception of the personages surrounding the bride with their ambiguity and conflicting desires. We also assume, as well, her identification with the nude female figure (bride) in accordance with the mechanism of projection.

Susanne watched the progress of the painting during the many months of its creation. She vaguely remembers the feeling of embarrassment in seeing the bridal figure standing passively with closed eyes while being exposed to the ogling eyes of the men, waiting to be garnished for their feast. Susanne perceives the bride's nudity as alluding to the consummation of the marriage and what will follow inevitably: being forced to play the traditional female role in a patriarchal society which restricts women's potential. The image of the hooded figure with the open lips ready to kiss the bride could be the equivalent to the image of "Big Face," which was discovered in the negative space to the right of the diaphanous, veil-thin, white wing of Touchless Misty. Both images triggered in Susanne mixed emotions of discomfort and shame. The emotional response to certain details in the father's painting could have remained strong in her mind. Thus, this could be one of the unconscious sources for the creation of the visual metaphor, "Big Face," hidden in the negative space and caressing the butterfly, reflecting Susanne's desire for intimacy which stemmed from her childhood fantasies.

Recalling the previously discussed works by her father, *The Bar Scene* and *The Street*, we can state that the topic of sexuality was one of the dominant themes in his art. There is a seething, sensual passion that finds its expression in her father's creativity. In the home environment, numerous paintings and sculptures with erotically-charged topics by various artists were displayed. We have analyzed Susanne's perception of some of those artworks in context with her idiosyncratic reaction to sexual issues. This can give us important background information concerning the influence of artwork on Susanne's psychosexual development. It should be noted that, regardless of the apparent manifestations of sexuality in his art, Susanne does not recall detecting any cues in his looks, gestures, or body movements that alluded to sexual attitudes demonstrated by him toward her mother, or, for that matter, anyone else. As remarked before, he did make, on various occasions, comments in which sexuality was always denigrated to the "animalistic" or vulgar level. Only in the field of art did he consider the unmistakable visual expression of sexuality to be acceptable without any bias.

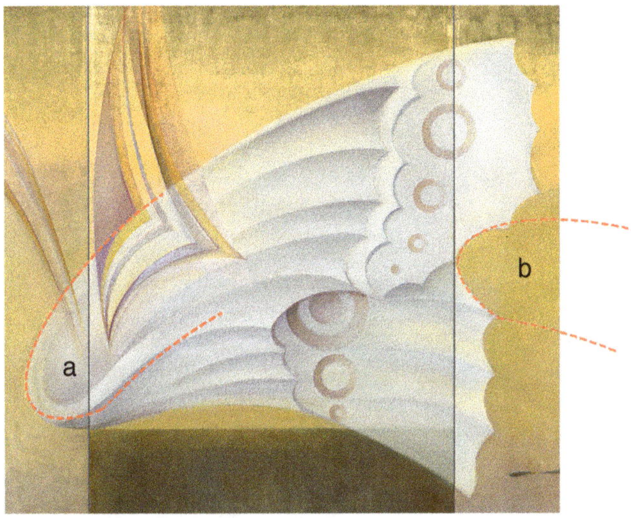

Fig. 9.60.
Shapes of possible phallic symbolism in Touchless Misty; outlined in dotted red.
(a) The rounded front.
(b) The same shape and size as (a) fit into the "nose" of the optical illusion (as outlined in blue in Fig. 9.54).

86 All associations to this vignette were given by Susanne during the analysis. To her knowledge, her father never explained or named these figures.

87 Susanne remembers some of these representations from Arnold Böcklin's paintings, which she and her father saw at an exhibition. "Old Silenus" was also frequently represented in ancient Greek art: Susanne cites an antique Greek vase, a pelike (a ceramic container with two open handles, often painted with mythological scenes), believed to be by Kleophon—as an example. (For the exact plate, see Erika Simon, *Die Griechischen Vasen* (Munich, 1976), plate 209).

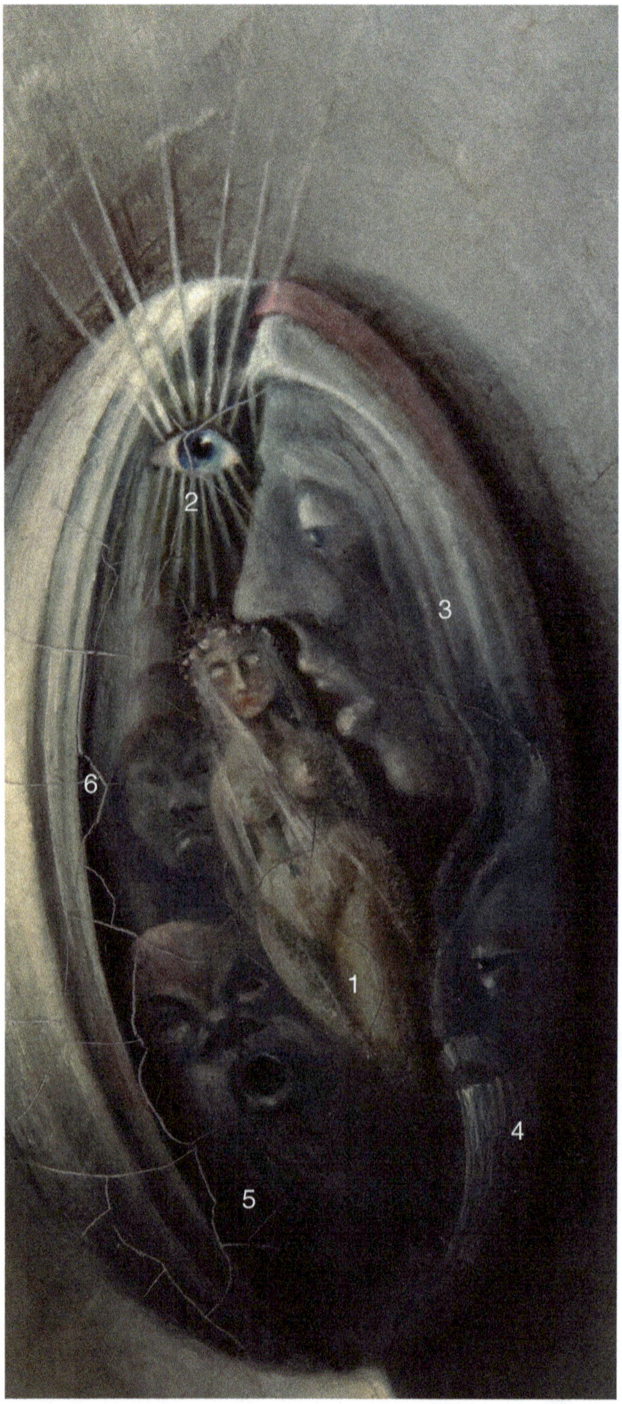

Fig. 9.61
Heinz-Günter Schünke, *The Weightlifte* (detail from Fig. 4.5). Detail of the center piece (hub) from the left weight disc (numbers added to identify the elements in the illustration. The names for the items were given by Susanne).

(1) Bride
(2) "Eye of Providence"
(3) Hooded face
(4) "Confucius" in profile
(5) "Old Silenus" en face
(6) A disapproving face en face

In this line of thought, we recall the engraving after Boilly that hung in her parents' bedroom (*La Douce Resistance*, see chapter 8), in which the male lover is seen eagerly kissing his paramour on her neck, while she appears to be feigning her resistance to his advance (Fig. 8.34). "Big Face" could serve as a metaphoric visualization of Susanne's suppressed childhood longing to be the object of her father's love. In this context, the depiction of the pristine white butterfly named "Touchless" is suggestive of being a bride, confirming the above assumption. This goes along with Susanne's account of her grievance and suffering due to the lack of desired physical contact while she was growing up in her teens. In turn, this finds metaphorical confirmation by the towering profile of Firebird, a personification of her father, standing next to Touchless Misty, but turning his back on the white butterfly. We emphasize our observation of the arrangement of these two butterflies placed in close proximity with such significant features as the "nose penetration" and the tail-like extrusion coming out of Firebird's abdomen (interpreted as a penile projection) that nearly comes in contact with Touchless Misty's hind part (Fig. 9.54, the white arrow). This leads us to the assumption that Susanne's incestuous fantasies played an essential role in the emergence of the optical illusion in the negative space. After all these years, the repressed tendencies still retain their potency as a latent force.

We recognized the coachman's nose as a specific detail from *The Weightlifter* and as a signifier of her father's unconscious symbolism in his art. It could have determined the congruent message in Touchless Misty's "Big Face" with its "nose" penetrating the rear profile of the butterfly (Fig. 9.60) and possibly even be an echo of the scenario from *The Weightlifter's* vignette (Fig. 9.61; the prominent nose of (3) hovering over (1)). The above presupposition could find confirmation of the latent meaning of noses in Susanne's artwork. Throughout her childhood and adolescence, Susanne consistently refused to endow the human faces in her drawings with a nose (for example, see Figs. 6.1 and 6.18). She remembers her parents asking her why she left out the nose, and her answer was, "I do not like it." The phenomenon of suppression and its reflection in her art have already been repeatedly stated in this research. The absence of one of the crucial facial features in her drawings and paintings over many years could be interpreted in this light. In the previous chapters, the shapes and meanings suspected of incorporating phallic symbolism were recurrently discussed (Figs. 4.8 and 8.24 (a–c)). A bulbous nose penetrating the cleft in the butterfly's wings is a new addition to our previous assumption of phallic symbolism (see subchapter 4.4.1, page 43). In this contex, once more we mention Susanne's early work *Silberhochzeit*, (1976, Fig. 6.17), celebrating her parents' silver anniversary. In this canvas, we can observe a rare depiction of noses, portrayed merging together, as if to "penetrate" one another.

There is yet another possible optical illusion in Touchless Misty's wings, which we choose to refer as "Third Face" (Fig. 9.62). In the butterfly's front wing (above the "Little Indian" face) there is a contour consisting of a series of concave curves that parallels the five circular patterns (rings and dot) to the right, which can be envisioned as a facial profile looking to the left. The first curvature at the top can be thought of as the forehead, followed by the longest of the curves (adjacent to the largest ring in the front wing), which may be viewed as a nose. The next two curves continue as the upper and lower lips, and, finally at the bottom, a chin follows. The top ring that abuts the "facial" contour could be regarded as the "eye" of this illusory "face."

It is conceivable that this formation might have accidentally come into existence, because the curve that could define the "nose" is rather indistinct compared to the ones that we observed in "Little Indian" and "Big Face." Therefore, the acceptance of this configuration as a third "face" could be discounted. Nevertheless, we would like to consider a hypothetical interpretation for this image because the great majority of conspicuous features and formations that we have found in the images of the seven butterflies in *Give Me Wings!* show the hand of the artist's unconscious. Certainly, the features shaping the "Third Face" form a discernible pattern on Touchless Misty's image. Accordingly, we feel obliged to explore the possibility of this "Third Face" as a formation manifesting some traces of

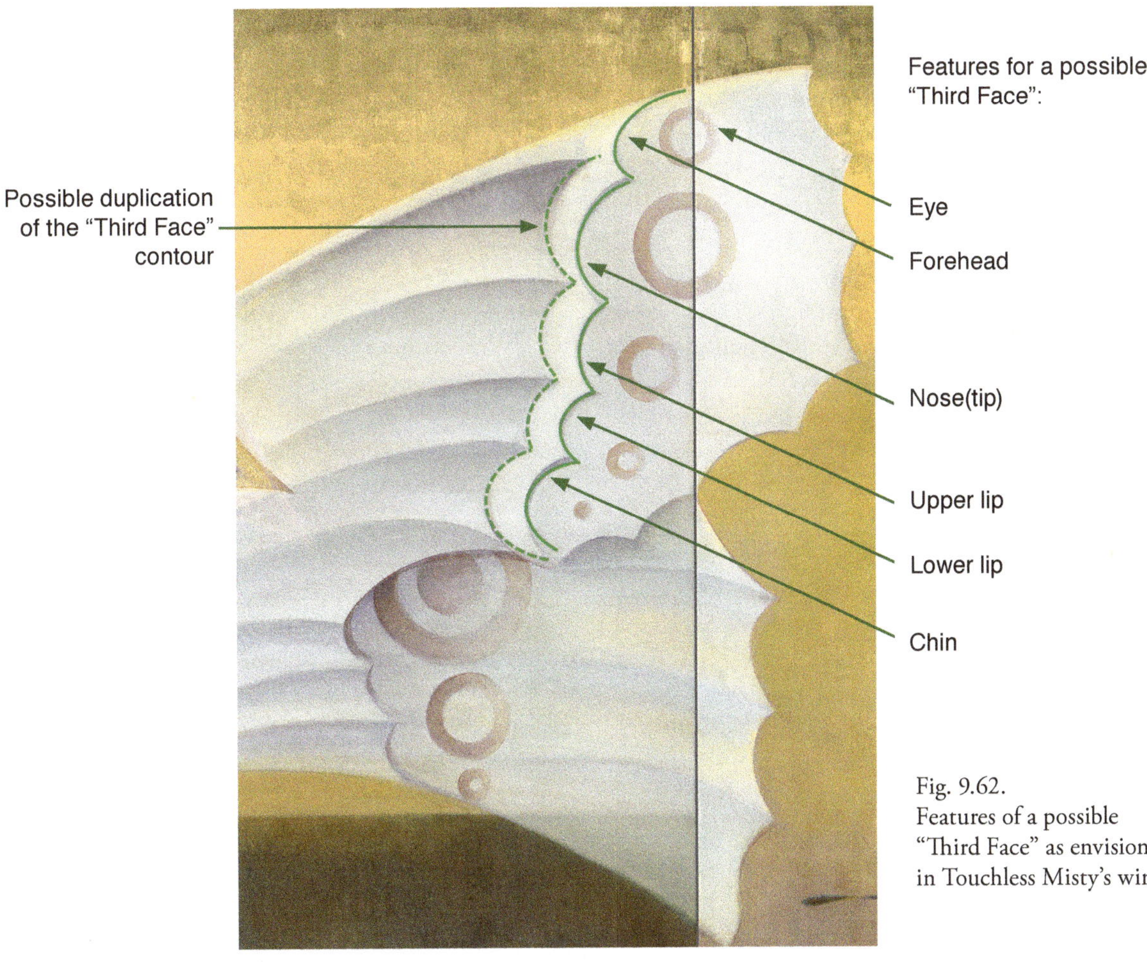

Fig. 9.62.
Features of a possible "Third Face" as envisioned in Touchless Misty's wings

the unconscious. Having recognized the butterfly Touchless Misty as the personification of Susanne, along with her partial identification with the "Little Indian" and her father's representation in the "Big Face," we have come to envision the possibility of Susanne's mother as being implicitly embodied in the "Third Face."

The association of scalping in context with the recognition of the "Little Indian" (see page 268) suddenly brought back a very painful memory in Susanne's mind. She recalled her mother sharing her experience of an accident she had in her youth, when her long hair was caught in an electric drill, which caused a severe wound to her scalp. The thought of this immediately made Susanne wince. Could the "wounded scalp (of the mother)" and the "Little Indian" image have a possible connection? This junction of intertwining contemplations could give us some insight in answering the above question affirmatively.

Initially, Susanne could not correlate her mother with an overt instance of cruelty, but with the cliché of scalping, the artist's unconscious could also metaphorically partially represent her mother in this image in accordance with the secondary association of her head wound in the past. In this line, the recollection of the mother's violent act of castration of a doll (see subchapter 7.1) might establish another link. To this chain of circumstantial evidence, we could refer the feminine castration complex (see page 223).

Additionally, bearing in mind the mother's accident causing her head wound, Susanne found a rare photograph of her mother as a young adult, which shows her face being framed by long black hair and dominated by deep, dark eyes (Fig. 9.63).

Susanne was familiar with this picture during her years of growing up, and while she was talking about this photograph, she examined the upper ring on the front wing (the possible "eye" for the "Third Face") and the target-like formation which she saw as the "eye" of the "Little Indian" figure. Suddenly, her mind was stirred by a strong association that both conspicuous "eyes" could be somehow connected with mother's expressive face in the photograph. Furthermore, Susanne remembers that her mother once explained that her first name, "Ruth," means "cow-eyed" in old Hebrew—with the understanding of having beautiful, large dark eyes.[88] It is worth mentioning in this context Susanne's suffering from ommetaphobia that, as we assumed, reflects repressed aggressive tendencies in her childhood (subchapter 9.3.6).

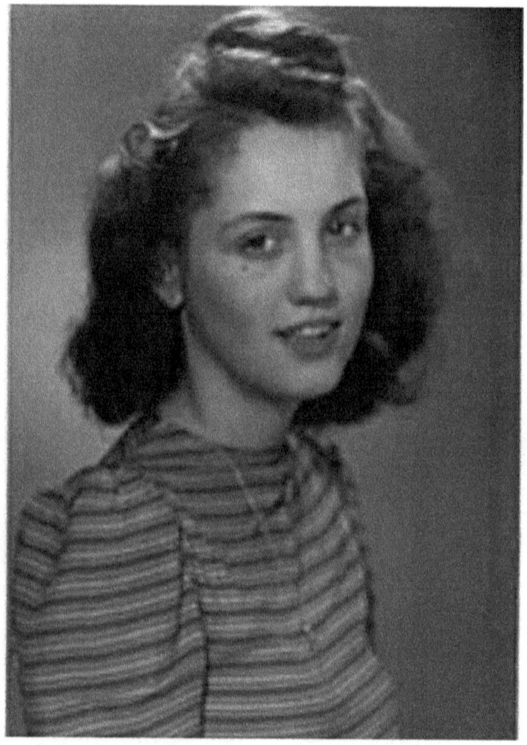

Fig. 9.63. A youthful photograph of the artist's mother Ruth-Eva Fietze (about age 14).

Moreover, one might contemplate how the unconscious mind determined to place metaphoric faces in such density (Susanne, the father, and the mother) in the wings of Touchless Misty. We could even attempt to read yet another "face" in this crowded assembly, a duplication or repetition of the "Third Face" in the white margin between the gray lines of the "Third Face" and the rear edge of the "dragon wing" defined by five ridges (Fig. 9.62). This formation might appear like two overlapping profiles, like the traditional double profiles on coins or cameos[89] representing different persons. Such repetition opens up another

88 The mother's father was a scholar in ancient languages and knew Hebrew, so it is supposed she got this information about the meaning of the name from him.

89 As an example of a double-portrait in profile: The Gonzaga Cameo, carved of Indian sardonyx in the Hermitage Museum, St. Petersburg, Russia (the two portraits in profile belong to different personages).

possibility for interpretation: The double profile, defined by the borders of the "dragon wings" in the image of Touchless Misty (personification of Susanne), could metaphorically represent Susanne and her mother.

To sum up, we discovered four "faces" as optical illusions populating the wings of Touchless Misty. First, we came to the awareness that the serrated contours of the butterfly's wings were structures comparable with those of the dragon as a symbol of aggression. The analysis of the image of the "Little Indian" disclosed the same latent meaning. The dual profile of the "Third Face" we supposed as personification of Susanne and her mother. This coupled contour could reveal the daughter's identification with her mother. Additionally, the father's face ("Big Face"), pressing tightly against Touchless Misty (personification of Susanne), brings all the protagonists of this unconsciously painted "drama" together into a singular focus. This would complete the family triad in the imagery of this butterfly, consisting of the personifications of Susanne and her parents, which we were able to identify through our analysis of *Give Me Wings!*.

According to the mentioned assumption, it is conceivable that a strong interconnection exists among all four images discussed above, which ultimately points to the artist's instinctual drives, such as aggression and sexuality in the framework of the well-known Elektra complex.

Some of our above suppositions are just hypotheses, but we have the courage to introduce them, considering that the truth is born in argument.

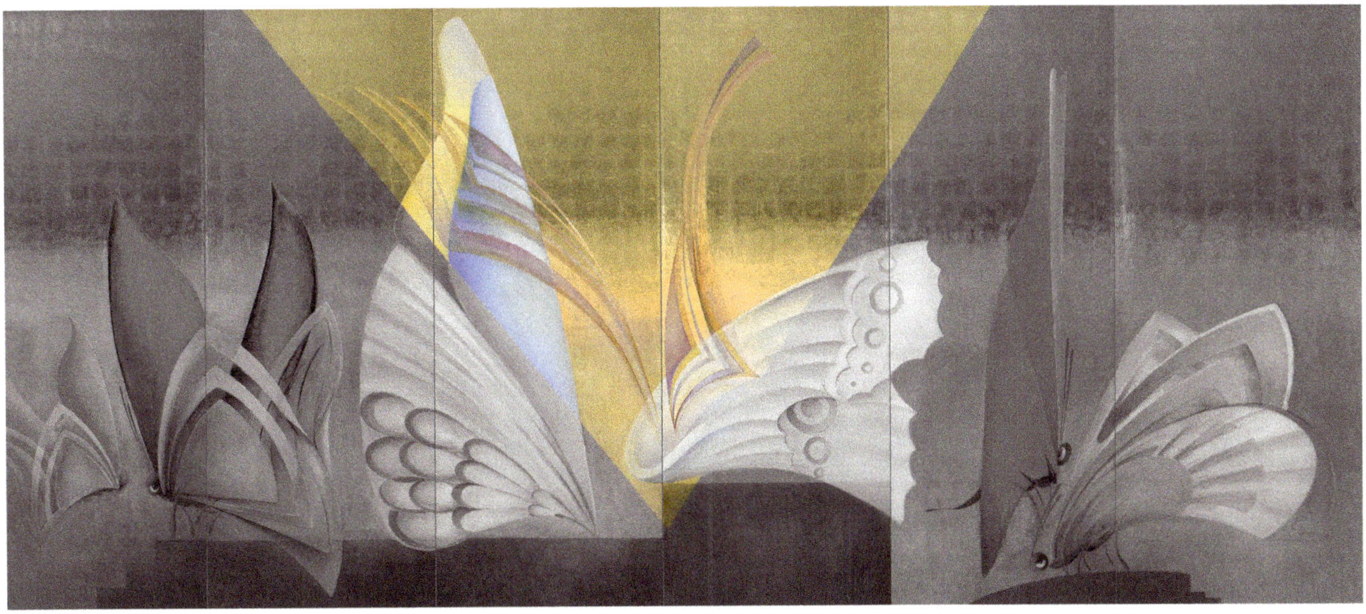

Fig. 10.0. *Give Me Wings!* with butterfly No. 7, Air, highlighted.

In the absence of true understanding the one in the middle was nicknamed "Air," and the others couldn't even decide on a gender so it stayed an "it." "Air" is bridging between them, it is with them, but not of them, just visiting, hovering in an ephemeral moment before its unpredictable disappearance. With the light mirroring on its wings, "Air's" iridescent qualities will charm you away.

—From the artist's poetic commentary, 2004

Chapter 10

In Search of Spirituality: Butterfly No. 7 — Air

Liftoff

The manifestations of the phenomenon of personification, as revealed in the other six butterflies, remained a puzzle for a long time in our analysis regarding butterfly No. 7, Air. To recapitulate, first we discovered Firebird and True Blue as personifications of the artist's father. Then, we recognized this phenomenon in the other butterflies as well. Fanning Everything stands for her mother, including partly Aunt Hella and Susanne. Little Why, Pale Moonlight, and Touchless Misty personify Susanne. After having identified these six butterflies as representing Susanne and her parents, we were left with the seventh butterfly which was inconspicuously positioned at the center of the painting. The analyst asked the artist: "Who do you think could be personified by this image?" Her immediate, although hesitatingly worded, response was a surprise. Instead of assuming another member of her family or a close friend, she said: "It is different, it is like an idea of something ... a subject of great importance." This answer did not come out of the blue, but was most likely determined by something embedded in this image of fundamental significance to Susanne.

The latent meaning encapsulated in the image of butterfly Air turned out to be the most entangled issue in our case study. To understand the message behind this entity, we started with the artist's poetic commentary which gave us the first clues: the image named "Air"; being "with them not of them"; "hovering in an ephemeral moment." On that basis, we gradually accumulated the indicators that the artist had bestowed on this enigmatic image. In the following subchapters, we will introduce this butterfly's peculiar attributes, which reveal its essential difference in comparison to the others.

10.1 Description

Butterfly No. 7, Air, rules the center of the composition, hovering above the podium in front of butterflies No. 3 and No. 4. The span of Air's open wings occupies the widest space in the group. While the others are depicted by their side profiles at various angles, this creature is presumably seen straight from the back in a rear profile and envisioned as moving toward the golden background. There is a canyon-like gap between the wings, and the canvas panel line which also marks the middle of the six-panel painting runs precisely through this interspace.

The artist always comprehended this butterfly as "flying away," and this perception can be found in her initial sketch, which captures the creature's torso, the head, and a pair of antennae in a manner that clearly depicts the butterfly from its rear (Fig. 10.1). In creative drawing I, the artist dispensed with these corporeal markers for a butterfly. Therefore, the forerunner of Air no longer has any recognizable anatomical parts, except for a pair of abstract wings, and is perceivable as a butterfly only by the context (Fig. 2.2 (A) and 10.2). As mentioned in chapter 2, the images of all the butterflies in creative drawing I (A, B, and C; Fig. 2.2) were mirror-reversed to obtain their final positions in the compositional drawing (Fig. 2.11). Consequently, the topside of butterfly A's right wing (in its upper part) became the topside of butterfly Air's left wing (in its upper part). The topside of butterfly A's left wing (in its bottom part) became the topside of butterfly Air's right wing (in its bottom part) (Fig. 10.2). Air's right wing is twisted around its middle and reveals its underside at the top (Fig. 10.3). The forerunner of this shape can be traced back to butterfly A's left wing in creative drawing I. A comparable configuration was observed in True Blue's wings, and it was defined by the artist as the "flip-over effect" in chapter 5 (Fig. 5.1 (m)).

The structure of the wings was rendered as strips of gossamer membrane alternating with matching open space between them. The artist explains her intention to create an illusion of oscillation of the wings between visibility and invisibility. A lack of a unified, coherent material structure gives the impression that the entity is flickering in and out of our sight. This indicates Air's transcendent state of existence in space and time.

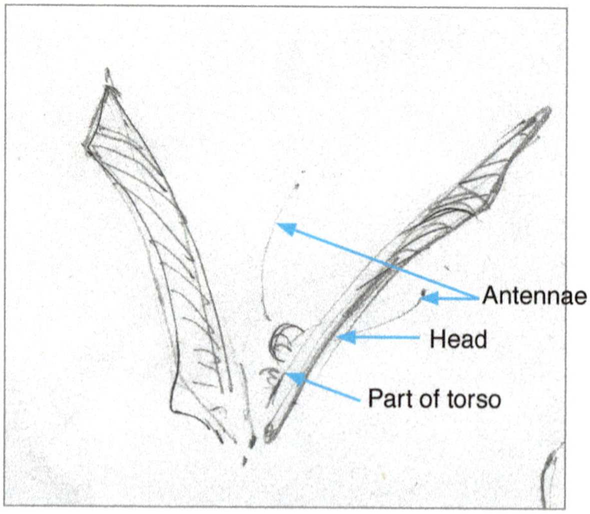

Fig. 10.1. Detail from Fig. 2.1 b, taken from a page sketched in the butterfly conservatory (top left).

This image might be interpreted by some observers as a part of a multiple-exposure effect found in photography or the dissolving appearance one perceives when a design on a trivision billboard is being flipped to another one, the sight of which Susanne found fascinating. Furthermore, through her admiration for traditional Japanese folding screens, she appreciates the various viewing perspectives that such three-dimensional artworks can present. It is similar to the varying perspectives from the multiple image reflections that she used to experience in front of a tall trifold mirror in her childhood.[1]

The above perceptual experience could have influenced Susanne's creation of the "oscillating" impression of butterfly Air. The ethereal appearance, peculiar to this butterfly, anticipates the description from her poetic commentary, where Air is portrayed as "just visiting, hovering in an ephemeral moment before the unpredictable disappearance." She may well ask whether the wings are even partly corporeal, because the visible elements are drawn alternating with empty space. This creates the impression of a shifting, mirage-like phenomenon. The image is unlike the depiction of any other butterfly in the painting. This design could be construed as a surrealistic visualization of an essence which is invisible to the material world.

1 These multiple-image perspectives brought the artist back to a memory, which we have mentioned before (subchapter 7.2.3, page 130). As a small child, she loved to sit in the center of a large trifold mirror, which she closed around her to observe every movement she made being reflected countless times on the left and right panels of the mirror. This could well have been the primary source for the "multiple-exposure" appearance of the image of Air.

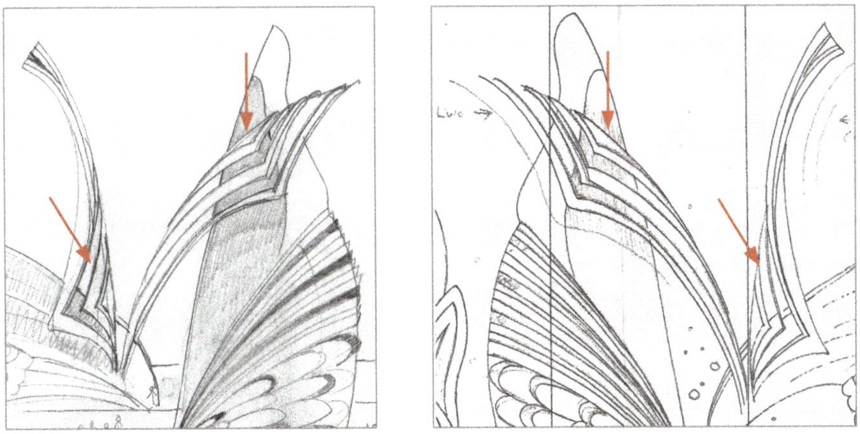

Fig.10.2.
Left:
Detail from Fig. 2.2 (creative drawing I), butterfly –A–.

Right:
Detail from Fig 2.11 (compositional drawing), butterfly Air.

Comparison for clarification; arrows point to the top sides of the wings.

On the compositional drawing, Susanne wrote down three pencil notations as a reminder for later consideration. The first remark, in German and English, "*Echo Linien*? (white in white),"[2] is written with an arrow which points to the two curves that partly repeat the central butterfly's right wing contour (Fig.10.4, red overlay). In subchapter 10.4, we will return to this annotation "echo lines?" for further contemplation concerning the latent meaning of butterfly Air's configuration. A second note, "*Echo Linie?*" (English: echo line?) with an arrow directs to a single repetition of the outer wing contour. For Susanne, these three tracing lines that surround and mimic the contours of the wings were an indication of the vibrational nature of the whole structure. This is similar in symbolism to a series of concentric semicircular lines drawn to visually represent the propagating

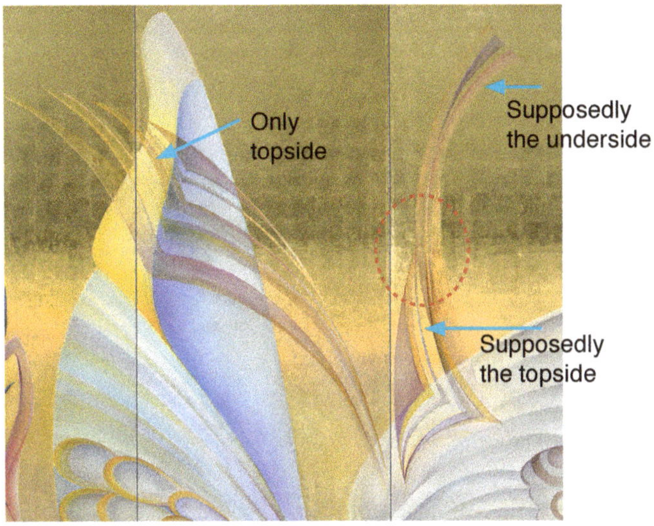

Fig. 10.3. Detail of butterfly Air from Fig. 1.0. The red oval shape highlights the flip-over effect in the top of the right wing.

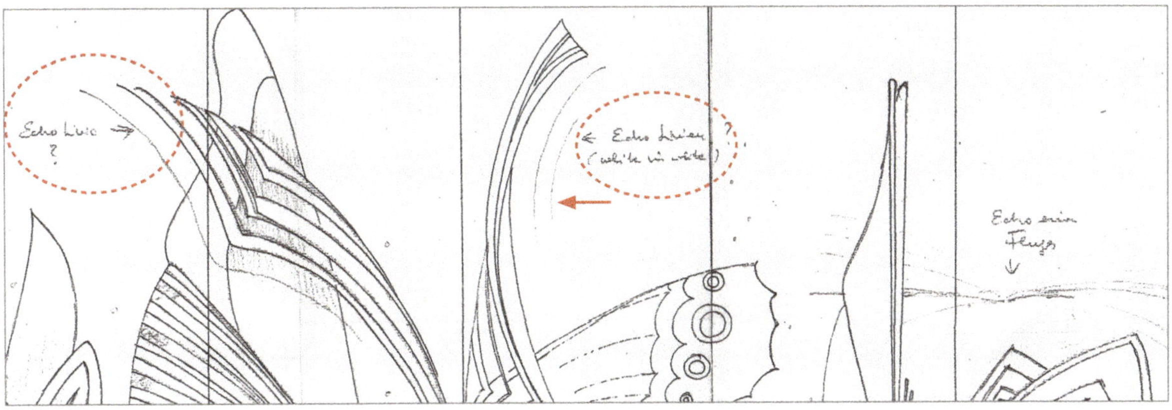

Fig. 10.4. Detail from Fig. 2.11 (the compositional drawing for *Give Me Wings!*). Butterfly No. 7 with the artist's commentaries in pencil: "Echo Linie" and "Echo Linien ? (white in white)" (German for "echo line" and "echo lines" respectively) encircled in red. Also towards the right margin: "Echo eines Fluges" (German for "echo of a flight"). In addition, note the repeated lines next to the wing (indicated with arrow).

2 Echo Linien (English: echo lines). Susanne used the term "echo" as "repetition or reflection" of something in the nature of waves. It is also conceivable that the question mark in her pencil annotation could be a cue for another possible meaning.

vibratory sound or radio waves often used by radio stations for their logos. It is also possible that the artist was unconsciously attempting to represent something that is insubstantial, metaphysical, or ethereal, which accords well with Susanne's concept of spirituality (see subchapter 10.4.1). The third notation also has an arrow, and is pointing to a faintly drawn butterfly close to the right margin of the drawing; the note states, "echo of a flight." This image was eventually dropped from the final painting, and its disappearance will be analyzed in chapter 11.

We have found that Air's two wing-like shapes are, except for the slight difference in size and perspective, nearly congruent under rotational transformation. If the left wing is rotated at its center by approximately 210° to the right, the transformation would essentially produce the shape and orientation of the right wing. The existence of this rotational symmetry between both wings was totally unknown to the artist until the analysis revealed its existence (Fig. 10.5). Therefore, the right wing's configuration could be considered to be an "upside-down" shape in relation to the left one, nearly an inverted version of the left wing. This leads us to ask why rotational symmetry was introduced by the artist instead of the expected reflective symmetry along a vertical axis. We will provide an appropriate explanation for this after determining some specific unconscious symbolism as the original source of this butterfly's image (see subchapter 10.4.2).

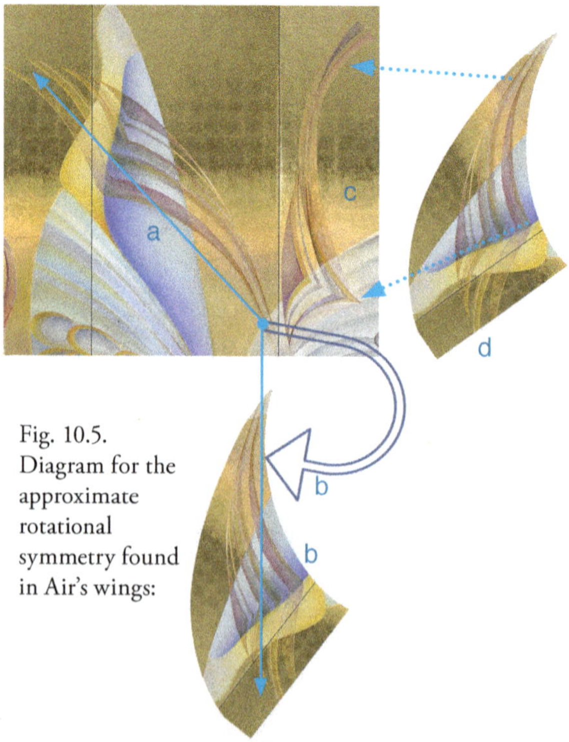

Fig. 10.5.
Diagram for the approximate rotational symmetry found in Air's wings:

(a) Detail from *Give Me Wings!* The left wing is aligned with the axis in an eleven o'clock position (solid arrow).

(b) The position of the left wing is rotated clockwise to a six o'clock position (solid arrow).

(c) The right wing.

(d) For comparison, (b) is set next to the right wing, demonstrating the similarity between both wings.

10.2 In the Absence of True Understanding ...

Before delving into the interpretation of the unconscious symbolism associated with the peculiarities of the seventh butterfly, we will present some general contemplation which must be taken into consideration as we probe into the artist's creation of this enigmatic image. Mulling over the unknown has always occupied Susanne's mind. When the senior researcher suggested working together on comprehending the role of the unconscious in her creativity, Susanne's interest was immediately aroused to realize the project, although at first the proposed approach sounded unusual to her. Her involvement as a co-author in this investigation is an instance of her curiosity to understand the roots of creation of her images.

Psychoanalytic studies have uncovered the significant role that the unconscious plays in human creativity. Our research for the traces of the unconscious in art has shown that the essence of its modus operandi manifests in a symbolic language, which reflects an interconnected network of the artist's significant emotional experiences. The inner workings of the unconscious follow a peculiar "logic" that is quite different from the traditional logical systems in hard science and philosophy. The unconscious processes reveal their presence through symbols, metaphors, and allegories that whimsically encode the latent meanings in a complex and multifaceted manner. It requires much detective work to track and evaluate the copious amount of information collected, in order to decode the unconscious messages that are embedded in the visual manifestations. Deciphering the artist's imaginative visual language has provided valuable insight concerning the workings of the creative unconscious.

The "translation work" that we had to undertake to achieve our objective included identifying branching passageways and their interconnections, which are usually hidden and become revealed through the artist's free associations. Recognizing the significance of the various details of past emotional experiences helps us solve the puzzle of their unconscious representations in the manifest content of dreams or, in our case, in the creative imagery of the artist. The ever-shifting metamorphosis of the unconscious that we observe in dreamwork and artwork appears to present us with a bewildering array of riddles too convoluted for the human intellect to grasp if based only on our traditional logic. Once we bring the unconscious to the conscious awareness through the proven praxis of analysis, much progress can be made toward a better comprehension of the mystery of the creative mind.

In her life, Susanne has repeatedly encountered paradoxes, and when she came to an insight that resolved a particular impasse, she experienced a sensation of instant peace flooding her troubled mind. Since Susanne learned to talk, she wanted to know and understand everything, from petty childish things to grand inquiries about life.

Susanne cherishes the feeling of tranquility when she finds a gratifying answer to a challenging question. For instance, around the age of 11 or 12, she could not accept the rule of arithmetic that stated, "You must not divide by zero," without being given the reason why it must be so. Luckily, she got an acceptable explanation from a mathematician whose pedagogic experience corresponded with her searching mind. From him, she learned some special aspects of zero, which the school curriculum did not teach at Susanne's grade level. He told her that "instead of being 'nothing,' zero could be a value for something infinitely small, and therefore, any number divided by such a 'zero' results in infinity." The legitimate mathematical operation would be $\lim 1/x = \infty$, where x approaches 0. The soothing power of this idea, which is essentially a philosophical perspective, has never left her since.

By her early twenties, after searching in vain for the answers to the foundational question of the meaning of life, the task left her with an ever-increasing unsettling and unbearable feeling of "absence of true understanding." A decade later, driven by insatiable curiosity for the unknown and doubts about the known, she managed to muster enough bits and pieces of knowledge and cues from diverse sources, sometimes even contradictory, to begin to form a meaningful weltanschauung about various aspects of existence in this world. It is of importance to her that she should develop her own viewpoints.

Above, we have touched upon Susanne's idiosyncratic way of thinking in the case of division by zero, and certainly other examples could be commented upon. These range from economic issues, politics, and religion to scientific topics such as fractals, infinity, and the dimensional structure of space. In each of these areas, her intuitive, imaginative, and often contrarian worldview is different from the normative views that are accepted by the great majority of people. Discussions frequently create situations where she becomes quite saddened or even exasperated by the interlocutor's inability to understand her ideas and perspectives.

The artist's phrase, "In absence of true understanding" in the poetic commentary, which we touched upon previously, could well illustrate her frustration on the conscious level. This arises from the reactions of others to her views, attitude, and creative ideation. They have responded to some of her standpoints by judging them as neither true nor realistic.

In Susanne's view, there are many subjects, topics, and issues, to which people have access only by way of emotional experience and imagination, but not by scientific knowledge, theoretical explanations, or formal logic. Such topics involve religious subject matters, parapsychological phenomena, spiritual states, ecstatic sensation, and more. The recognition of these experiences is mostly based on beliefs but not on rational aspects that could prove their existence.

The poetic commentary introduces the seventh butterfly as follows: "In absence of true understanding, the one in the middle was nicknamed 'Air' ..." This statement about the creation of the sobriquet carries some clues that might help us decipher the unconscious symbolism of the peculiarity of the manifested image. The passage, quoted above, at first glance contains a paralogical reasoning in the determination of the moniker, which makes us wonder what kind of connection existed between the words "Air" and the "absence of true understanding" that led to the butterfly's appellation. Could the interconnection hold a specific metaphoric significance for the artist?

Her puzzlement over this creature is unparalleled among the portrayed butterflies. She expresses this in the poetic commentary: "the others could not even decide on a gender so it stayed an 'it.'"[3] Moreover, Susanne in the guise of the third-person voice in the commentary says that "the others" notice that the butterfly "is with them, but not of them." It is implied that this entity has fundamentally different qualities and belongs to a dimension that is other than that of the group of six butterflies, as it hovers over them and leads into the golden background.

Butterfly Air's enigmatic configuration eludes a clear definition. What looks like a pair of trimmed down, translucent, and abstract multi-layered wings can be interpreted as an imaginative, surrealistic rendition of a vibrational source. With this, butterfly No. 7 reveals its existence only indirectly through traces of oscillation in the air, and the image, which reminds us of a silhouette of wings is unveiled by the disturbance in the medium. The artist's mind might have construed the seventh butterfly as an energy, which can be "seen" as a vibratory phenomenon. Therefore, Susanne, in search of the adequate moniker for the butterfly, felt it was something significant, yet she was unable to define and articulate this in words. For a short time, she had even considered changing this ambiguous creature's nickname to "Enigma." Nevertheless, she decided to stick with "Air," which was the first name that came to mind in a spontaneous association.

Susanne intuitively sensed some mystery in this creation but could not figure out anything certain. In her recollection, at the beginning of her design work she wanted to express the intricacies of the wing movements of a flying butterfly that the naked eye is unable to resolve in detail. Her aim was to find something that would identify the nature of this image.[4] The search for "the true understanding" of what butterfly No. 7's imagery signified became more complicated by the cryptic annotation "echo lines?" penciled in next to the butterfly, as mentioned in our description above. In our prior footnote 2, we speculated on some possible sources for the phrase associated with waves, but we have yet to uncover the latent meaning behind the question mark after the words.

At the time of drawing this butterfly, Susanne thought the lines and annotations represented vibrations in the air of an energetically charged source that she could not specify further. Later, in the process of this research, the artist contemplated that the puzzle of the "echo of the line?" might connect to some feelings she visualized in the image but could not comprehensively qualify. The statement "in the absence of true understanding" reflects these circumstances.

In regard to her assumption, Susanne perceives the medium of air as a transmitter for different kinds of information. These are received through her hyper-sensitivity toward her scent-filled surroundings. The aromas have included Father's hand soap, Mother's perfume, the exciting smell of the father's car, and the cigarette smoke from the parents, to mention a few. All these sensations were highly desirable stimuli. The artist, using the subject of air as a metaphor, conveys a variety of contents that manifest in her imagery. In our study, we have observed a considerable number of her paintings that dealt with such topics.

For example, three years before *Give Me Wings!*, the artist created a five-panel artwork, *The Elements of the World*, (2001) (Fig. 10.6),

3 We will come back to this important remark later in the chapter, but here it will be mentioned that this wording reflects Susanne's decades-long experience with her family discussions, in which she was accepted by the others as an intellectually potent partaker—a role that was traditionally associated with men at the time she was growing up. Susanne was once told by a friend of the family: "You really are the son of your father."

4 Here we might observe possible parallels to certain drawing techniques that are found in comic strips and comic books. Although the artist's parents strictly banned comic strips at home, she was not a total stranger to the universally renowned Mickey Mouse that was introduced to her by her friends, and to the daily or weekly humorous cartoons that were printed in the newspapers. In this medium, certain established conventions, such as speech balloons, motion or streaks lines, multiple images, and quiver lines (a series of stacked lines outlining around an object to indicate its quiver or vibration), are employed to facilitate visualization of sequential actions. Susanne's casual knowledge in this art medium might have played a factor in her eventual portrayal of the butterfly Air, although she was not consciously employing the above-mentioned technique. Thus her notation, "echo lines," next to the image of the butterfly No. 7 could possibly have been her way of saying motion or quiver lines.

representing six "classical" elements.[5] The fifth panel is dedicated to the element air. On a shiny, silver ground made of palladium leaves, Susanne created a series of horizontal streaks, indicating the overall movement of air across the sky and swirling clouds unfolding in abstract shapes, by which she visualized the currents of air. In two such whimsical cloud formations (see the oval areas labeled 1 and 2 in Fig. 10.7), we can identify certain similarities in shape with the wings of butterfly Air (for a detailed comparison, refer to Figs. 10.7 and 10.8). The resemblance between these two sets of forms is remarkable, yet at the time butterfly No. 7's wings were being drawn, the artist had absolutely no idea that she was essentially reproducing the patterns from another of her paintings several years prior.

Susanne might have unconsciously rekindled the imagery from *The Elements of the World* and transplanted it to another image, the central butterfly in *Give Me Wings!*, which was named "Air" through a spontaneous association. Shapes similar to those mentioned curly patterns can also be seen in a painting from 2005, *Golden Nectar* (Fig. 8.47). The latter canvas presents a butterfly on a blossom which is intentionally used as camouflage to hide a strongly sensual meaning embedded in the image. The presence of burnt orange with its sexual symbolism reinforces our assumption (see chapter 8). Moreover, we observe a pattern of the swirling configurations reminiscent of those in a painting executed 30 years earlier, *Silver Anniversary* (1976), which was dedicated to the anniversary of her parents' marriage (chapter 6, Fig. 6.17). Here the curly configurations in the parents' cheeks, painted in orange and including some traces of burnt orange, are comparable with the wafting swirls in *Golden Nectar*. In both paintings, it is evident that these forms convey sensual meanings. It is worth mentioning that the cloud shapes in *The Elements of the World* are similar to *Silver Anniversary* and *Golden Nectar*. We assume the swirling airflow as expressed in all three works symbolizes intimacy. Moreover, in *Silver Anniversary*, the smoke rising in curls and loops from a cigarette that Susanne's mother holds, and paint brushes in the father's hand metaphorically indicate the closeness between her parents.

Since Susanne grew up with chain-smoking parents, the image of curling vapor and the smell of tobacco were always delightful for the artist, quite inseparable from her memories of the parents themselves. Although never a smoker herself, she is strongly attracted to the first fume of a freshly lit cigarette to this day, while not even aware of how deeply these reactions are rooted in her early years. As mentioned previously, Susanne's olfactory faculties have played an important role in her impression of people and her immediate environment, dominating her visual and auditory sensations and exerting

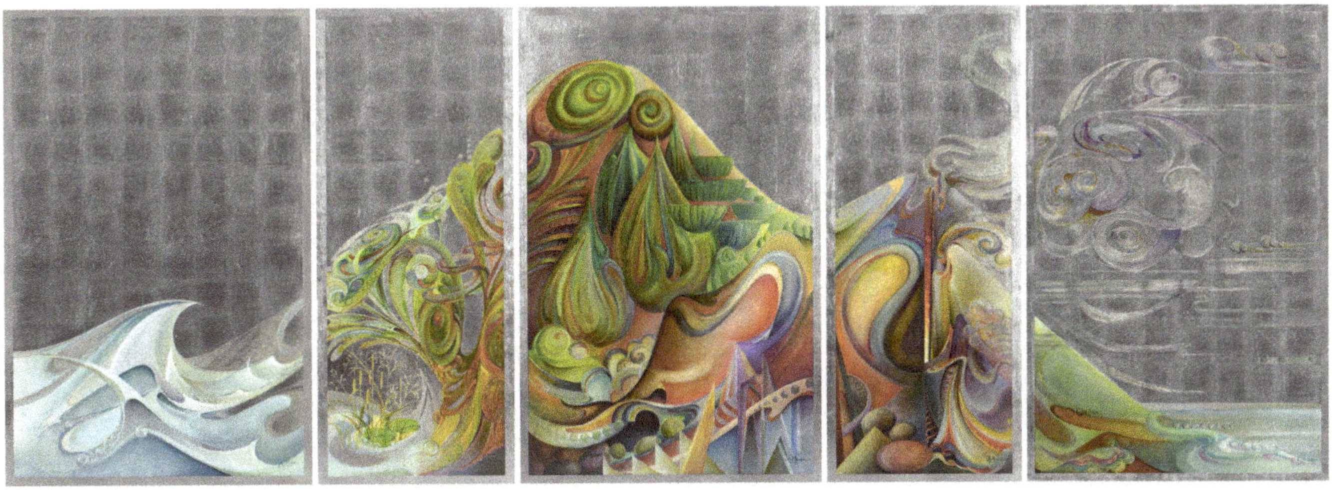

Fig. 10.6. Susanne Schuenke, *The Elements of the World*, 2001. Oil and palladium on canvas, overall dimension of the five-panel painting: 39½ x 107 in (100 cm x 270 cm). Collection of the artist.

5 The artist adopted the four Aristotelian elements: water, earth, fire, and air, to which she then added two more (wood and metal) from the five Asian elements—water, wood, earth, metal, and fire—to create her own unique six "classical" elements.

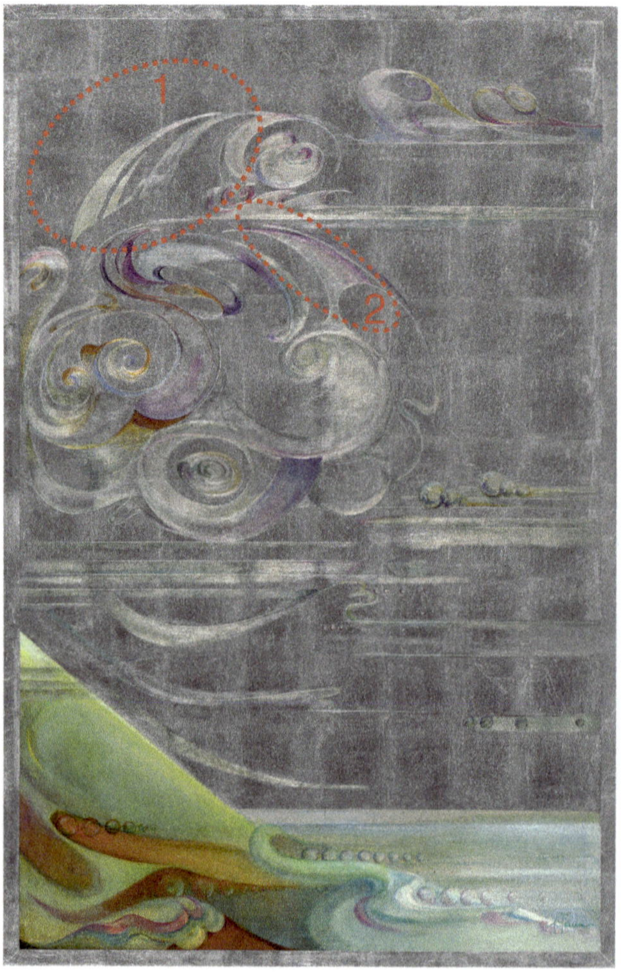

Fig. 10.7.
Detail from Fig. 10.6: the *Air* panel,
39½ x 25½ in (100 x 64 cm).
Encircled in red: whimsical cloud formations for comparison in Fig. 10.8.

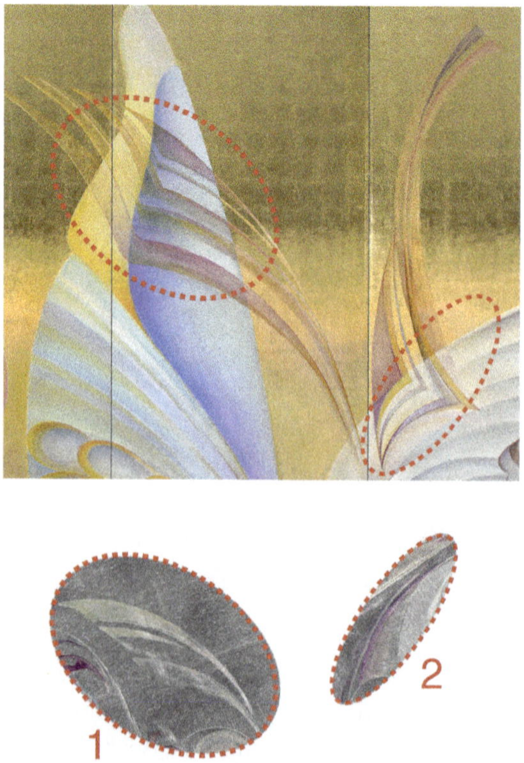

Fig. 10.8.
Collage for comparison.

Top: Butterfly Air with areas marked for comparison.

Bottom: Appropriate areas from the clouds of the panel *Air* (details from Fig. 10.7).

(1) Turned clockwise.
(2) Turned counterclockwise, in addition to being side-reversed (with the neighboring area faded out for emphasis).

a strong influence on her sensory perception. Furthermore, the rising rings of cigarette smoke could be meaningful among a cluster of metaphors, for example, in the monumental painting *Seventeen Legs*, (2005) (Fig. 10.9), [6] that figuratively illustrates colonial power in its self-glorification. It is expressed by physical size (the canvas is 9 feet tall), stomping heel, diamond and gold, fashionable attributes, and alcohol. The cigarette joins the ranks of luxury goods, and the wisp of smoke performs its ephemeral dance, free from all restrictions.

We continue our contemplation about the medium air as a source of delivering specific information through metaphorical expressions. The artist has an interesting experience in making something "invisible" visible involving air, as the following episode reveals. In 1988, she received a commission to paint a landscape on a piece of highly polished chrome mounted on wood, to be installed as part of an interior design. After drawing the compositional sketch, she wanted to project it onto the metallic surface before starting the painting process. For this, Susanne used an apparatus similar to a slide projector, which in a darkened setting projected an image on any given flat area, normally a white canvas in her work. However, the polished chrome acted like a mirror, which caused an unexpected challenge for the artist. On the metallic surface,

6 The earlier version of *Seventeen Legs* is a smaller canvas painted in 1991, and Susanne reworked it (with its sides reversed) in a monumental size in 2005. The figure illustrated in this book is the later version.

she could only see the reflection of the projector's blindingly bright light bulb, while the drawing remained invisible.

The story of a medical doctor in Africa prompted her to come up with an ingenuous solution to her problem.[7] She placed her mouth close to the chrome surface and breathed on it, causing condensation to form for a couple of seconds, which was long enough for her to see a segment from the drawing on the fogged surface. Susanne quickly traced the lines with an ink pen, but the short time span of the condensation required her to repeat the process numerous times. What fascinated her so much was that her exhaling air made the invisible lines visible. When telling this story, the artist drew an analogy between the ephemerality of breath's traces on the chrome surface and that of the perception of the short-lived, pleasurable scent of her parents wafting in the air, which evoked in her the joyous emotion of intimacy and a desire for its constant recurrence.

In her art, Susanne developed specific formations that manifest moving air and speed. Previously, we noted that the series of horizontal streaks painted in *The Elements of the World* might have been employed by the artist to indicate the motion of air. Something akin to this design schema has been applied and extended to a number of her paintings, for example, in depicting racing horses (Figs. 10.12, 10.13 and 10.14 (pages 293-4)). In those canvases, the path of the moving subjects is traced by colorful, horizontal streaks which repeat the colors of the horses. The artist points out that she associates her design of horizontal streaks with her habit of twirling her body rapidly while keeping her eyes open. This exercise gives her the perception of the surroundings as numerous bands of changing colors streaming in front of her eyes, accompanied by the pleasant sensation of the movement of air on her arms.[8]

Susanne, in creating butterfly No. 7 and afterward naming it Air, expressed metaphorically motion whose traces are recognizable in the peculiarities of the image. She did not aim to render the real wings of a butterfly, but rather the clues of their movements. Her impression of what they leave in the air is sketched by the spreading "echo lines." The artist attempted to portray the butterfly's presence by its vibrational "tracks" to picture some quintessence. This puzzling image of butterfly Air could be comparable with dreams or reveries that contain, in coded form, messages of the unconscious, which then can be uncovered and analyzed. We have already presented a partial explanation of the latent meaning by hypothesizing

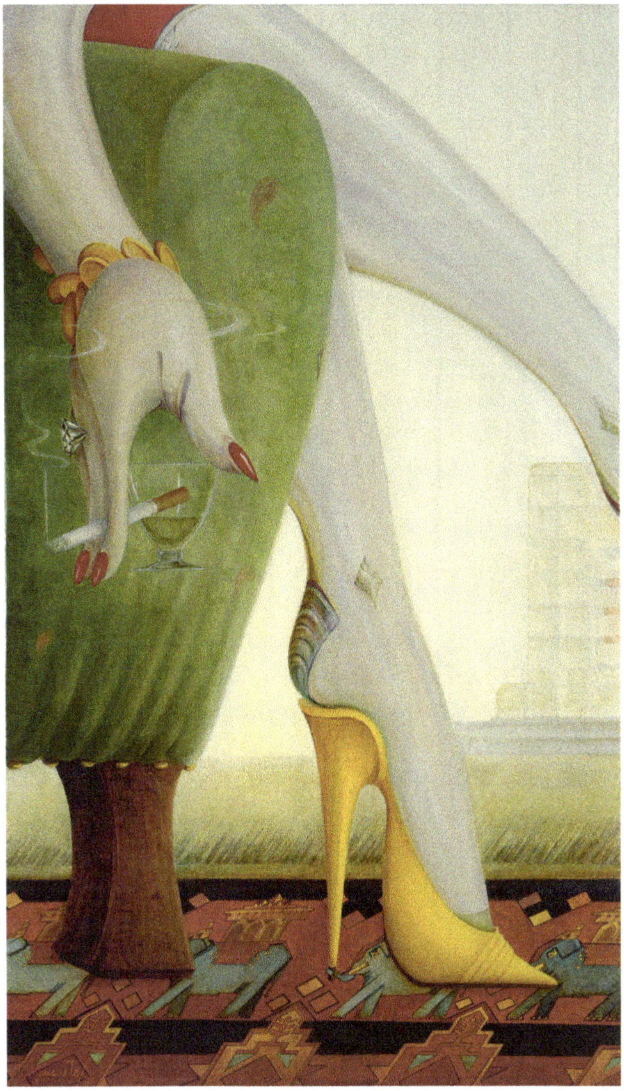

Fig. 10.9. Susanne Schuenke, *Seventeen Legs*, 2005. Oil on canvas. 108 x 64 in (275 x 163 cm). Collection of the artist.

7 In her youth, Susanne read a story about a Western doctor working in the African hinterland who had to convince a tribal people that their chieftain lying in a coma was not dead. To prove this, he took out a pocket mirror and held it in front of his mouth, allowing his breath to fog it. After showing it to the people gathered, the doctor cleared the mirror and repeated the action on the tribal chief which yielded the same result, proving that the man was still breathing and thus alive.

8 In this context, we could conceivably speculate that the rotational symmetry in the image of Air is also somehow a symbolic reflection of her twirling motion.

the imagery of Air as the reflection of idiosyncratic unconscious symbolism, which emanates from the incorporation of the artist's biological as well as spiritual proclivities.

Before proceeding further, we emphasize once more that the assessments of the butterflies in the poetic commentary are de facto free associations. They pertain to the created images and express in highly condensed wording the message originating from the artist's unconscious. The latent meanings have been wrapped implicitly in metaphorical language in a surprisingly informative way. Susanne wondered about the mysterious essence of this butterfly, which she characterized with the phrase "in absence of true understanding."

The expression gives us one more sign of the perplexity and confusion that accompanied the naming of butterfly No. 7. Its nature remained unrecognized to the artist at that time, which is further emphasized in the poetic commentary by the remark that "it is with them, but not of them." When Susanne wrote this, she was not aware that any of the butterflies depicted in her painting represented a personification of anyone that she knew, including herself. She was far from figuring out what Air represented. We assume that the above remark from the poetic commentary was driven by the unconscious reflecting her intuitive feeling about the otherness of this butterfly, and, on that account, she probably hesitated to give it a nickname. Moreover, this quote presents a strong link to a well-known passage from the Gospel of John in the New Testament (see subchapter 10.4.2). The reference led us to associate the image with spirituality and initiated our eventual acceptance of an unexpected interpretation concerning the cryptic meaning of butterfly Air.

The disclosure of the visual expression of the artist's perceptions and specific childhood tendencies during our research, and the consequently evolving understanding of the unconscious influences on the creation of her images, have enabled us to lift the veil from Air's enigmatic configuration. This includes the selectiveness of significant emotional experiences and their transformation into unconscious symbols by the phenomena of condensation, displacement, and the means of representation and their further elaboration. This statement, based on the praxis of dream interpretation, could shed light on the puzzle of this image that was nicknamed "Air." In the following subchapter, we will describe the multiple associations we found that might point to the circumstances that have affected the naming of this central butterfly "Air." The discussion will substantiate our presupposition about the spiritual nature of this complex image.

10.3 The Name and Possible Influences on Its Creation

As shown in the previous chapters, we repeatedly found different traces of the unconscious that underpinned the formation of the butterflies' individual names. Different experiences, forgotten perceptions, latent memories, and suppressed tendencies came together and contributed to the creation of a specific moniker for each butterfly. In certain cases, the resulting sobriquet was due to a singular way of combining English words, but all the names sheltered multiple meanings, which were already manifest in the painting. The nicknames metaphorically encoded a plethora of significant, emotionally charged events in a dense amalgam, which had influenced the artist in creating the images. In investigating possible sources of the seventh butterfly's appellation, we assembled various associations, which offer some conscious and unconscious bases for the artist's choice of the name "Air."

Searching further for early emotional experiences with regard to the word "air," it might be useful to mention (according to her family's recollections) that among the first words young Susanne tried to articulate was *Flugzeug*, the German word for airplane, which she mispronounced as "Fluchlauch." It was an exciting experience for her as a little child discovering moving objects high up in the sky and attempting to trace them with her finger while being taught by her parents what they were and their name. Then, she would imagine herself as an airplane by running around the garden with her arms stretched out like a pair of wings. Therefore, Susanne's imitation of flying came early in her life.

Although the artist perceived butterfly Air as flying away from the viewer's perspective, she described its state with the word "hovering" in the poetic commentary. This might reflect her dream of floating above the ground independent from

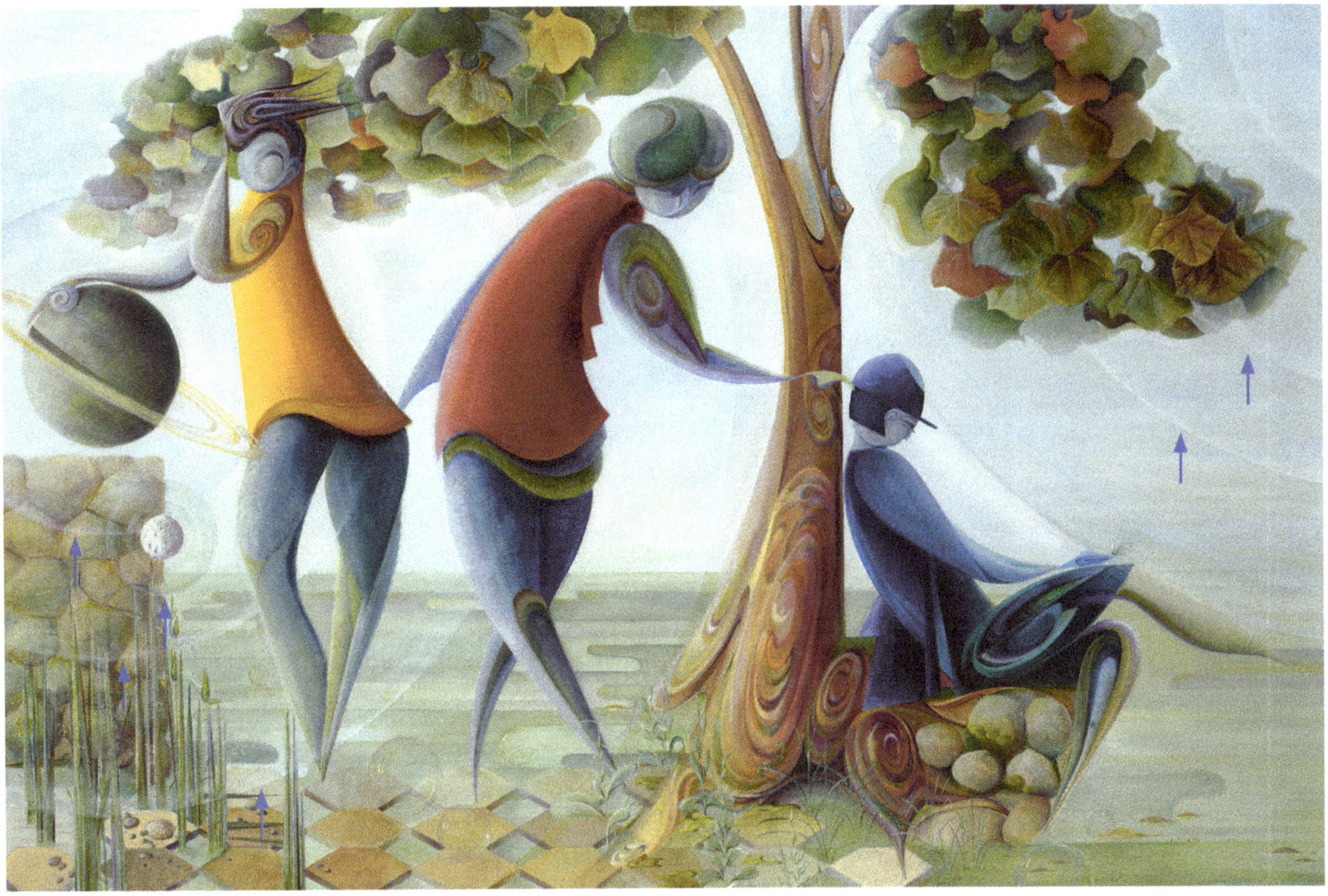

Fig. 10.10. Susanne Schuenke, *Ethereal Spirits*, 2002.
Oil on canvas, 47 x 64 in (110 x 170 cm). Collection of the artist.
Arrows point to the "lines of gravity" in the right half of the painting as well as to the left margin around "Saturn's moon."

gravity. This universal force has been one of the great enigmas of physics, and, in her adolescence, she read much about it in the context of astronomy. In her teens, on TV, she watched astronauts floating in zero-gravity conditions inside their space ship and jumping effortlessly on the lunar surface due to the considerably weaker gravity found on the moon.

Susanne's figurative way of thinking could have made the topic of gravitation a signifier for various aspects of freedom. She accepts the possibility that numerous forces, including those emanating from spiritual energies, exert influences that are invisible to our sensory perception but affect us in a way analogous to the effects of gravity. (See subchapter 10.4.1.) She has tried to express these invisible forces that surround us in her painting *Ethereal Spirits*, 2002, (Fig. 10.10). The initial impression of the painting is of three figures relaxing under a tree by a lake, but a closer look reveals certain subtle features that point to another theme—invisible forces of nature.

We can observe that Susanne depicted barely visible concentric circles around gravitating objects to indicate the presence of attractive forces. The "lines" of gravitational pull can be traced in faint but clearly distinguishable color nuances radiating from a planet with a ring and its accompanying moon, which were imaginatively depicted by the artist as a garden sculpture (see the left margin area of Fig. 10.10). Additionally, several arcs can be observed at the right side of the painting, signifying that there is another, far greater source of gravitation that emanates from beyond the edge of the painted space. The artist intended to signify the all-permeating presence of gravity with those arcs. Another enigmatic phenomenon is observable in the outer leaves of the tree. Its foliage displays

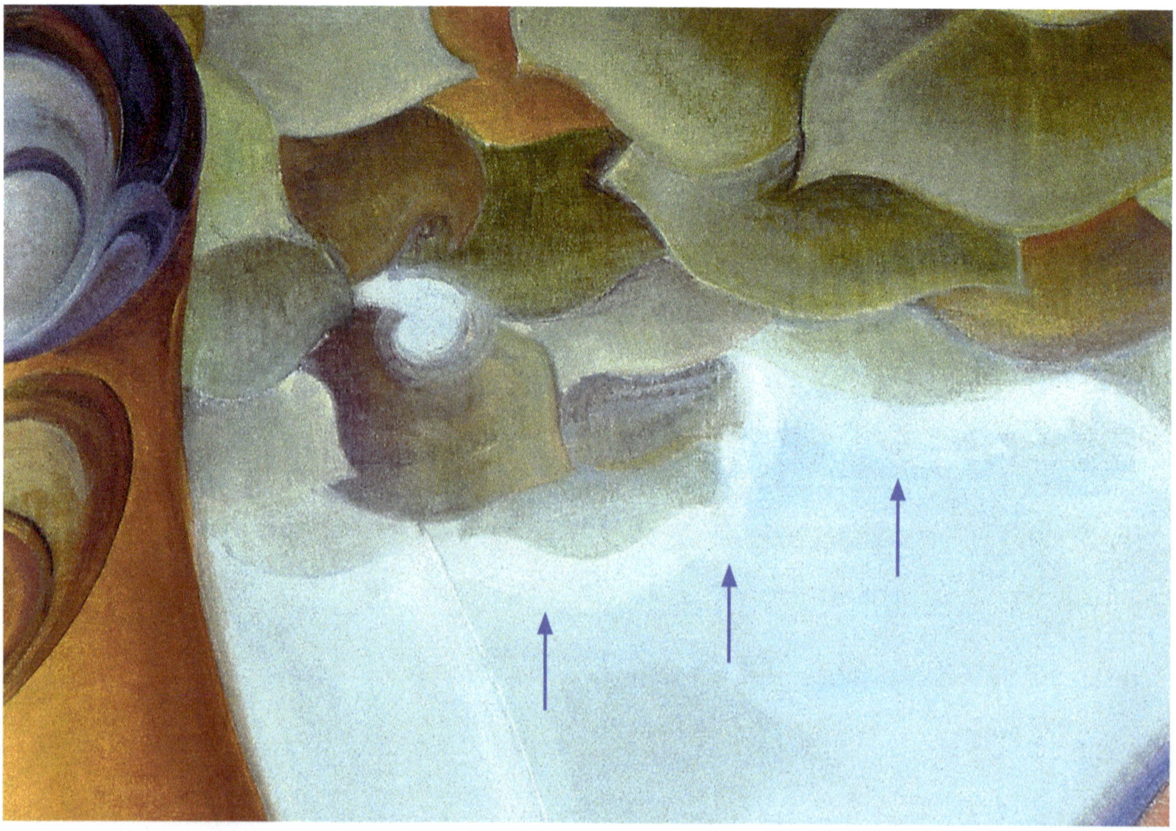

10.11. Detail from Fig. 10.10: An aura around the tree leaves. (contrast heightened for visibility).

an aura (Fig. 10.11) that can be recognized by a hue lighter than the background color. These emanations could be likened to the Kirlian photographs of living organisms.

The title of the painting presents a puzzle to some of her friends, who point out the discrepancy between its name and what they perceive as the main subject of the work. They suggest changing the title to something more apt. However, Susanne stands by its original appellation, because she explicitly hints with it at a specific meaning so important to her. By the title, *Ethereal Spirits,* the artist has intended to convey her belief in the existence of many forms of unknown energy in the cosmos. Susanne imagines that among those energies are immeasurable spiritual forces that permeate our universe.

In choosing the expression, *Ethereal Spirits,* the artist might have associated "ethereal" with the word "ether" which she came across in her extracurricular study in the past and which greatly stirred her curiosity, leaving a lasting impression on her mind. This now-outdated concept of ether entered Susanne's vocabulary in her teenage years through reading about Einstein's theory of relativity.

The appeal of the enigmatic ether was enhanced by the frequent appearance of its derivative word *ethereal* in literature describing incorporeal beings. For example, in Shakespeare's play, *The Tempest,* one of the characters is the airy spirit Ariel. This ethereal being inspired the English Pre-Raphaelite artist John Everett Millais (1829–1896) to paint *Ferdinand Lured by Ariel,* (1849-50),[9] a work Susanne came to know through her art studies. In this painting, Ariel, covered with a gossamer veil and surrounded by green bats, hovers above the ground. He whispers an alluring song into Ferdinand's ear, who listens and stares in Ariel's direction without being able to see the invisible creature.

Through Millais' Ariel, Susanne came to envision the spiritual nature of this imaginary being. The linguistic relation between the two

9 The painting is in a private collection in the UK. For image and details see: The Tate Gallery: *The Pre-Raphaelites,* Exhibition Catalogue 1984. Tate Gallery Publications Department, London, UK, 1984. Catalogue number 24, pages 74-75.

words, "ether" and "ethereal," the homophonic association between the words *Ariel* and *aerial,* as well as Millais' imagery of the spirit "Ariel" with his diaphanous wings might have lain dormant in Susanne's memory. It could have exerted a strong influence on the creation of the image and name of butterfly No. 7, presumably as a representation of a spiritual entity.

The artist had another association with the word "air." She attended a concert with a friend where a composition by J.S. Bach titled, "Air,"[10] was performed. The friend, as she explained to her later, had a strong emotional bond to this piece, and during the performance she burst out in tears. Susanne responded to her with sympathy, although not really understanding what was going on. Since this event, the word "air," when mentioned in context with music, brings back to her the memory of this experience. Such a passionate response to music by the listener was not a novelty to Susanne. She was used to seeing her father crying when listening to his favorite classical composers, especially Beethoven. From this, we can assume that the friend's reaction had familiar elements for Susanne. It might have been one of the multiple sources that could have determined the creation of the name "Air" for butterfly No. 7, in which the reactivation of her empathy was involved.

In the above-described responses to music, Susanne witnessed ecstatic feelings that arose out of the emotion of bliss, which is a transcendent, spiritual experience. The highly sensitive response to music, as one of the epitomes of harmony and beauty,[11] could be identified as manifesting a spiritual aspect of human beings. Subsequently, this experience is also a possible source out of which the name "Air" was unconsciously designated as a matching metaphor that represented spirituality.

There could be objections that spirituality could belong to the phenomenology of the unconscious. This is perhaps a controversial attribution for many, but in accordance with contemporary scientific data and our research, we begin to consider spirituality as a construct of the cultural development[12] of the universal unconscious. We explore further contemplation of this matter in subchapter 10.7.

Spirituality has played a significant role in the artist's personal development. It can be regarded as an important driving force in her life. Thus, it has found persistent symbolic manifestations in her creativity.[13] We feel justified, through our analysis, in deducing that the butterfly named "Air" stands symbolically for an abstract spiritual essence.

There is the possibility that the makeup of the wings of butterfly Air was influenced by the appearance of the gossamer wings[14] of the spiritual entity Ariel in Millais' painting. Air's structure could reflect the otherworldly, transparent, and vapor-like semblance of Ariel's wings. We assume that this surrealistic arrangement of alternating wave-like lines and empty space was unconsciously developed. The artist was not aware of exactly what she was trying to articulate while progressing from creative drawing I to the final oil painting. Nevertheless, while creating the image, Susanne had an inkling that she was portraying something that was essential. She had the intuitive apprehension of an important meaning associated with this butterfly.

During her visit to the butterfly conservatory, the artist observed the insects' flight in fascination, and in her sketches (Fig. 2.1 a–g) she attempted to transform her impression of the butterflies' captivating wing movements and condense their elusive sequences. While talking about those rapid motions, the artist remembered a photo

10 *Air on the G String* by Johann Sebastian Bach (1685–1750) from the second movement of his *Overture* (or *Orchestral Suite) No. 3 in D major*, BWV 1068. Reading the program, Susanne understood "Air" initially as an English word, but her friend explained that Bach's title was the 18th century term for a short composition, an "aria" with or without vocal part.

11 It should be mentioned that Susanne attended numerous concerts with another friend, Tanja, featuring Bach in the Roman basilica of Trier, where yearly organ festivals were held. About the highly influential role that Tanja played in the development of Susanne's concept of spirituality, see subchapter 10.4.5: "Meaning of Life."

12 Damasio 2012, page 29: "There is growing evidence that, over multiple generations, cultural developments lead to changes in the genome."

13 Topics with spirituality in Susanne's oil paintings can be traced back to the 1980s (for example, *Destiny, Collector of Souls, Elysian Fields*, etc.).

14 There is another association involving a compelling gossamer texture: Susanne remembers how she admired a marble bust of a young veiled girl in a museum and marveled at the sculptor's skill at creating the illusion of the thinnest textile enveloping the head. A comparable example of this would be *The Veiled Virgin Mary* (around early 1850s) by Giovanni Strazzi (1815–1878), Presentation Convent, Cathedral Square, St. John's, Newfoundland, Canada.

documentary she saw many years earlier about the hummingbird's amazing wing movement. The pictures were made with a camera of extraordinary shutter speed. They showed for the first time the astonishingly complex sequence of wing angles and postures, revealing the secret of this miniature bird's ability to hover in midair. Susanne found it quite captivating and somehow mysterious. This surprising perception must have left in her mind traces of a positive emotional impression. Each time she refers to the movement of the hummingbird's wings, her hands automatically mimic the characteristic twisting turns the bird makes.

The artist's imagination may have fused those memories about the hummingbirds with her perception of the wing movements of the butterflies which caught her eye, were then stored in her mental archive, and were eventually recreated in her images. In particular, the hummingbird's wings may have unconsciously played a significant role in Susanne's design of the first butterfly she drew in creative drawing I, A that became the predecessor of "Air," (Figs. 2.2 and 10.2). The left wing of A demonstrated notable flip-over effect, which was also incorporated later into Air's right wing. This design from the creative drawing became side-reversed during the process of creating the compositional drawing (Figs. 10.2).

Susanne demonstrated the peculiarities of the hummingbird's flight pattern showing the alternation of the palm and back of the hands, indicating their side reversal (drawing a horizontal figure of eight: ∞). We have presented in chapter 5 (pages 71-72) the analogy between the complex rotational wing pattern of the bird and the graceful hand movements of Spanish flamenco[15] dancers or of the performers of temple dances in Thailand and Bali, which Susanne admires for their elegance. Moreover, in her sensitive perception of the rotational pattern (hummingbird and dancers' hands), she realized the connection between them and certain hand movements of her mother. Susanne showed the sequence of her parent's smoking routine, including a specific twist of her wrist. During the demonstration, the similarity between the mother's rotating hand gesture and those of the dancers was quite a revelation to the artist.

Susanne's fascination with the elegant hand gestures also includes the visual arts. Among her favorites are the paintings of George de LaTour (1593–1652).[16] Similarly, she admires numerous portraits painted by Anthony Van Dyck (1599–1641), which were held in high esteem by his contemporaries, especially for the elegance of the depicted hands.[17]

Returning to the topic of air as the medium of transmission in relation to Susanne's extraordinary sense of smell, the following associations could give us an example of her specific olfactory perception. We have already mentioned that the child Susanne often slept in her parents' bed, where she sensed their movements through the wafts in the air. In the darkness, she could identify Mother and Father by their scents, either from their bodies, clothes, or pillows, which prompted her to utter: "I receive information through air." Kissing her parents, touching their warm, soft skin and inhaling their scents quickly gave Susanne a degree of lasting, delightful pleasure, but unfortunately, due to the parents' discouraging response to her attempts, this was always a short-lived and ephemeral affair (see also subchapter 10.5). The parents' desirable scents became for Susanne comparatively significant sensory markers, and this olfactory information has been stored in her mind and continues to be an important part of her perceptions and attitudes. A number of sensory preferences that were established in her childhood still hold sway. They are particularly reflected in aspects concerning her partnership, in which the scent of the other person influences his attractiveness to her.

15 It might be of interest to note that Susanne saw the movie, *Blood Wedding* (1982) in London in 1982, which she liked so much that she viewed the performance twice more. She later bought a video edition and watched it repeatedly. The movie was a flamenco style dance interpretation of a drama (*Bodas de sangre,* 1932) by the Spanish poet Federico García Lorca (1898–1936), which revolves around a love triangle scenario, in which the bride's husband and her lover kill each other in a knife duel.

16 For Susanne, two of the most representative works by George de la Tour that show exceptionally elegant hand gestures are *The Dream of Saint Joseph* (approximately 1628–1645; Musée des Beaux-Arts de Nantes, Nantes, France) and *Job Mocked by His Wife* (approximately 1625–1650; Epinal, Musée Departemental des Vosges, France). The hand gesture in question belongs in both works to the left hand of the female figure portrayed.

17 For example, *Portrait of George Gage with Two Attendants* (probably 1622–3) by Anthony van Dyck (1599–1641), National Gallery, London.

Her susceptible olfactory sense perhaps could have influenced her childhood drawings, in which the hundreds of human faces she rendered had one conspicuous characteristic: the lack of the nose, as mentioned before. Only in her later teens did this facial feature make its appearance in her artwork (for example, Fig. 5.7, drawn at age 18). Since then, she sometimes renders a nose in frontal view.[18] Often she prefers a design with the division of the face with an irregular, curved vertical line, which delivers two very different facial expressions. In this way, she avoids the depiction of a three-dimensional nose (Figs. 4.7. and 8.52). The information that Susanne has been able to provide from her early childhood substantiates the following interpretation of her unique way of designing the human physiognomy in her art. Her acute sense of smell and the omission of the nose in her portrayals of people in those years may point to the possibility of the repression of desires and fantasies that pertain to her olfactory perception.

Given the artist's extraordinarily sensitive reactions to scent, it is worth mentioning Susanne's repugnance to excrement since early youth, which often would cause her immediate nausea. She remembers that she always left the room immediately whenever her mother changed the baby sister's diapers. Her distinctive olfactory responses have also extended to specific food odors. She has a strong aversion to the aromas of visceral organs (kidney, liver, etc.) being cooked, and the same can be said of fermented dairy products (cheese, sour cream, or yogurt, which she did not eat until her mid-twenties). The intense flavor of mature cheese remains beyond her tolerance. After the above contemplations, we assume that the wave-like configuration of the image of the butterfly Air could also reflect Susanne's unconscious intention to portray the idiosyncratic olfactory perceptions in visual metaphor.

Delving further into the possible sources for the moniker "Air," the researchers present the following associations, which might shed light on the matter. In the 1980s, Susanne received the CD version of *The Photographer*, a theatrical music and dance piece written and composed by Philip Glass[19] as a gift from her younger sister. She played it over the years, and she liked the rhythm and soaring dynamism in it.[20] Through this composition, she became familiar with the life and work of Eadweard Muybridge (1830–1904), a photographer well-known for "his pioneering work in photographic studies of motion and in motion-picture projection."[21]

Before the advent of photography, people had speculated for a long time whether it could be proven "that during a particular moment in a trotting horse's gait all four legs are off the ground simultaneously," and Muybridge decided in 1872 to take the challenge by developing a camera with "a special shutter … that gave an exposure of 2/1,000 of a second," which made it possible for the first time to capture a sequential motion of a running horse on film. Muybridge's photographs showed what the human eye could not observe; they delivered the proof that a galloping horse momentarily "flew" in the air. A few frames from those famous sequential photographs are featured on the album cover of Glass's *The Photographer*. The lyrics from the first act of the opera include the following lines:

Horses in the air
Feet on the ground
Never seen
This picture before

And this is artificial moonlight
An artificial sky

Horses in the air
"Whose baby is this …"[22]

18 There are a few examples of a fully developed (i.e. three-dimensional) nose in Susanne's works created in her adulthood portraying faces in frontal views (Figs. 9.1, 9.2, 10.28, 12.8, and 12.12). It should be noted also that she had no problem rendering noses for faces in side profile (Figs. 9.43; 12.11).

19 Philip Glass (born 1937), *The Photographer*, CBS Records Masterworks MK 37849. The premiere of the dance piece and music took place in 1982 at the Holland Festival, Amsterdam.

20 This music has inspired Susanne to twirl for a lengthy time on countless occasions, trying to synchronize her rotation speed and arm movements with the hammering rhythm. Asked about why the sound attracted her so much which others might characterize as "monotonous," her reply was: "I stop thinking and that is great."

21 New Encyclopedia Britannica, 1987, vol.8, p. 459; the same source used for the next two quotes.

22 The line, "Whose baby is this?" from the first act is pronounced rather than sung unexpectedly in the middle of the singing, which momentarily interrupts the melodic progression of the music. The bold contrast disturbs the harmony

Repeatedly reading the line, "horses in the air," in the lyrics, Susanne had a spontaneous association that those words might have implicitly inspired the creation of the sentence, "Air is bridging between them," in the poetic commentary on butterfly No. 7. Furthermore, during a discussion with the analyst she thought that this association could have been based on her involvement with the topic of racing and flying horses which occupied her mind for a few months before starting to work on *Give Me Wings!* (December 2003). Reviewing the records of the artist's creativity revealed the following useful information for the study.

In the large canvas, *The Big Race*, (2002) (Fig. 10.12), she metaphorically represents the spirit of human competition by the imagery of racing horses. She embeds many symbolic references to mathematical, philosophical, and scientific aspects into the design as indicators of the far-reaching consequences of competition. A year later, she felt inspired to place the horses high in the air, which she accomplished in a new painting, *Flying Horses*, (2003) (Fig. 10.13). In the first sketch for this design, which she made in August 2003, she wrote a comment for herself above the spiral shape, the centerpiece of the new composition:

> "Floating in the air, whirling centers between their feet,
> growing/transgressing into their bodies,
> horses integrated into air color."

Reading the lines above, the phrase, "*horses in the air*," from the opera *The Photographer* could well have been in her mind when she wrote the comment.[23] Working on her *Flying Horses,* Susanne searched for the specific gait of the horse when its four feet were not touching the ground in a book of animal anatomy. Once she had studied the configuration in detail, she could stylize and find more abstract shapes for the legs to be fused with the whirling curves in the air of *Flying Horses*. After finishing the painting in spring 2003, she described the horses depicted as follows:

> "Their hooves run on air, never touching the ground ... The racing horses feed each other with their energy, and their delirious joy of speed overrides the idea of competition. ... They are all running in focus of the finishing line, meanwhile during the journey, they are enjoying the flight."

She repeated the design, choosing the central white horse and painted it in her favorite crimson (*The Red Horse*, 2005; Fig. 10.14). As she wrote, the motif of "horses in the air" might well have been still on her mind, and it could have influenced the naming of butterfly Air and its description, "Air is bridging between them," in the poetic commentary for Air.

During a discussion about Muybridge and his work, Susanne had some spontaneous associations that pointed to a possible link between the details of Muybridge's life and her own emotionally significant experiences:

1) The hypothetical connections may have been established in Susanne's mind because both Muybridge and her father were photographers who experimented with their cameras, resulting in unique images.

2) Susanne read the commentary of Philip Glass in the album booklet, which explained that Muybridge killed his wife's lover when he became convinced that his rival might have been the real father of the son who was recently born. Susanne's hypersensitive reaction to the utterance, "*Whose baby is this,*"[24] during the playing of the opera based on Muybridge's life, could well be rooted in her youthful incestuous fantasies.

3) We suppose that autobiographical episodes in the life of Muybridge (love affair, killing of the competitor) became unconsciously linked to Susanne's repressed sexual and aggressive tendencies, described in previous chapters.

4) Philip Glass's lyric, "Horses in the air," taken in the whole context, could have a particular relevance to naming butterfly No, 7—"Air."

At first glance, an interconnection of the above associations might appear quite speculative. However, the unconscious functions in its specific way, incorporating impressions, experiences, and

of the music, stirs up the listener's attention, but Susanne reacts with annoyance each time she listens.

23 The *Flying Horses* also incorporates her knowledge of the English phrase "white horses" for the foaming white crests of sea waves. She is familiar with the famous painting, *Neptune's Horses* (1892), by the English artist Walter Crane (1845–1915), in which sea waves are imaginatively metamorphosed into a row of white horses galloping through the churning water.

24 When speaking about the topic, Susanne's involuntary touched her nose and ears, and took a deep breath.

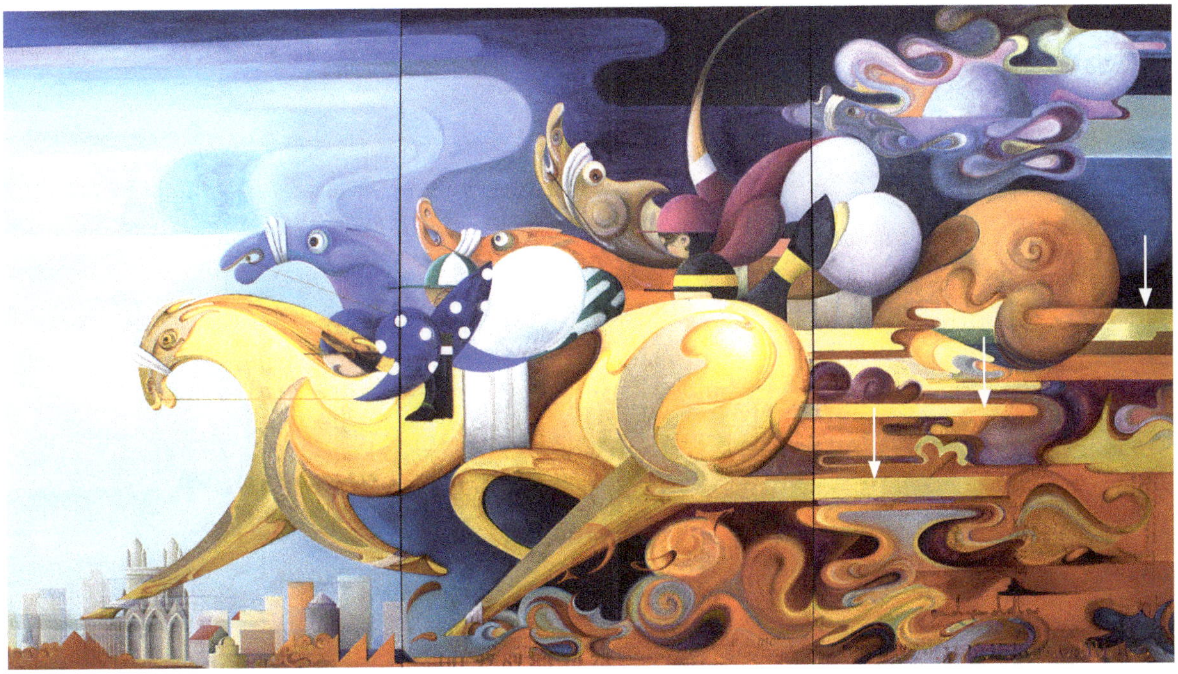

Fig. 10.12. Susanne Schuenke, *The Big Race,* 2002. Oil and gold leaf on canvas (triptych), 79 x 149 in (200 x 356 cm). Collection of the artist. The arrows point to streams of air.

information with eccentric and puzzling priorities that are contrary to our logic-based intellection. The keywords "air" and "baby" have became distinct markers of the modus operandi of the unconscious, which weaves multiple repressed sensual associations from various stages of Susanne's life, particularly from her early childhood experiences.

The above account indicates that accumulated significant emotional experiences have had various associative connections with the subject of air. Through condensation, they were bundled to express specific latent meanings in the imagery of butterfly No. 7. In the image of this butterfly, all the mentioned experiences gradually conflated into a representation of spirituality, while at the same time exhibiting the presence of symbolic signs for sexuality.

An unfathomable amount of information is stored in different strata of the archives of memory. We can infer that various related data in assorted

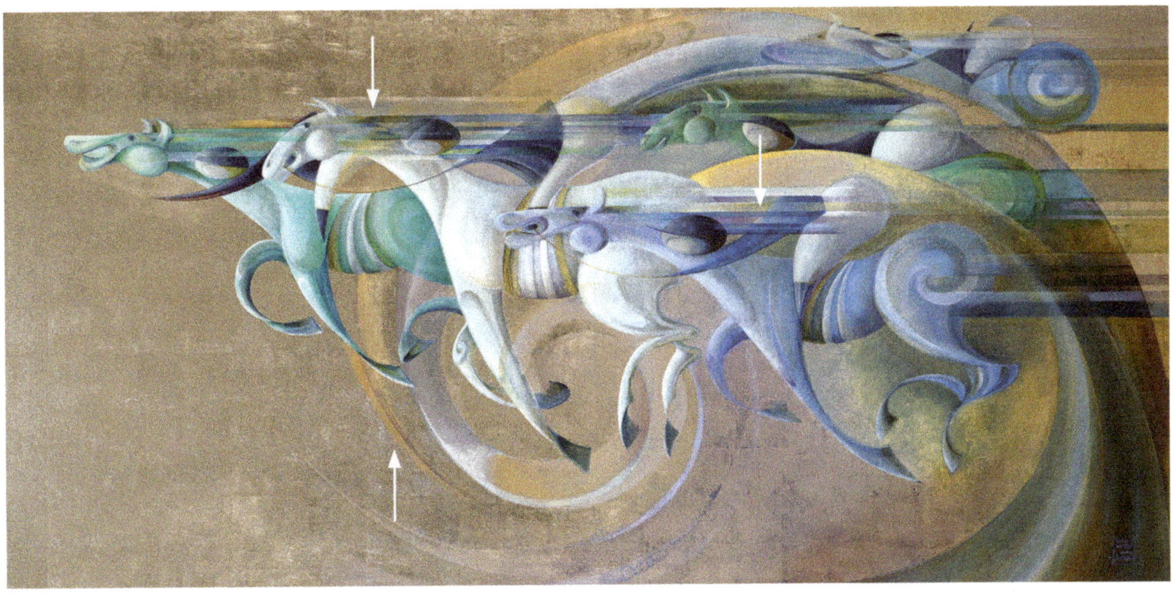

Fig. 10.13. Susanne Schuenke, *Flying Horses,* 2003. Oil and gold leaf on canvas, 40 x 84 in (100 x 212 cm). Private Collection. The arrows point to streams of air.

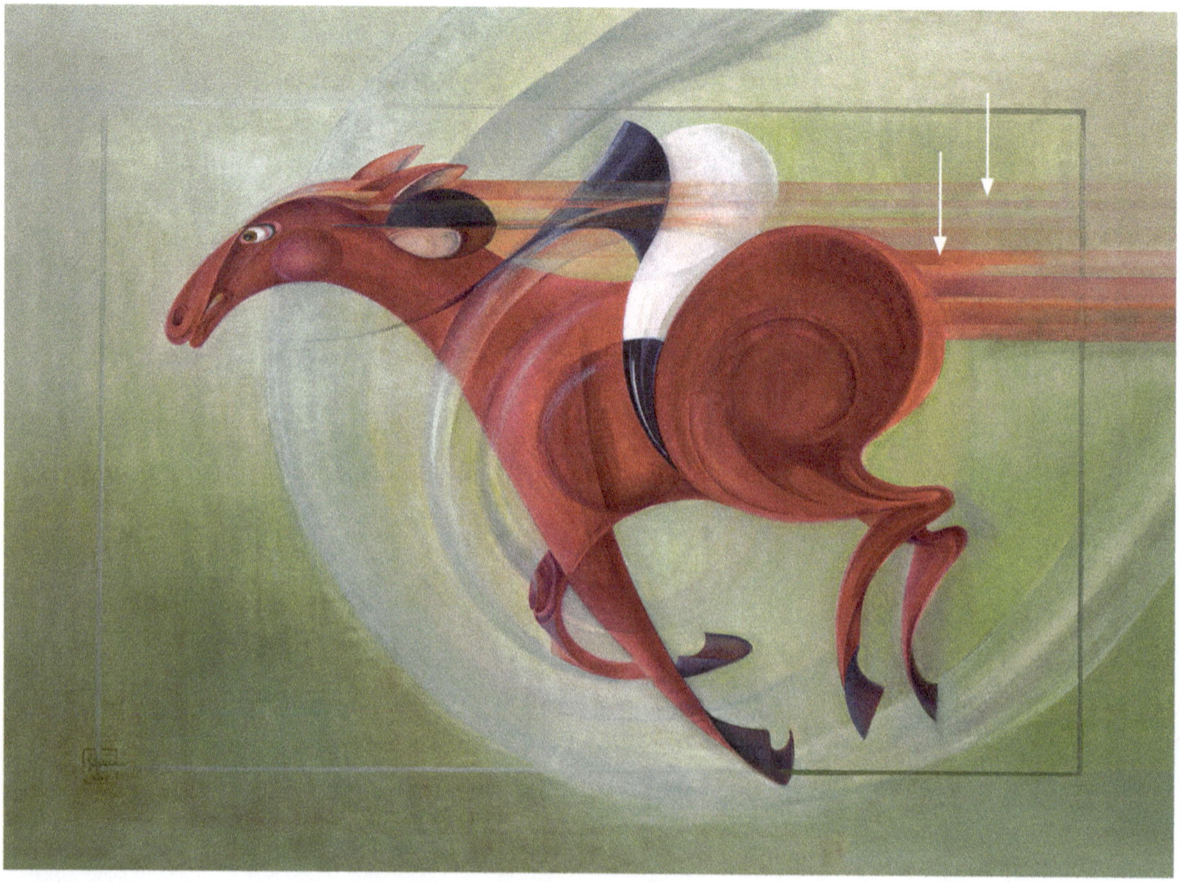

Fig. 10.14. Susanne Schuenke, *The Red Horse,* 2005. Oil on canvas, 35 x 51in (90 x 130 cm). Private collection, Virginia. The arrows point to streams of air.

combinations are selected and utilized by the unconscious in the process of creativity. The result is the transformation of thoughts and emotional experiences in visual images which include symbols, allegories, metaphors, and other semiotic signifiers. These reflect the artist's experiences, coded in one cohesive whole.

10.4 Spirituality

10.4.1 Susanne's Spiritual Concept and Its Development

Insofar as we assume that butterfly Air represents some aspects of Susanne's concept of spirituality, our search for the origins of this imagery impels us to probe further into the artist's appropriate ideas and attitudes in order to interpret the specific details of the butterfly's image.

Before proceeding, it is necessary to clarify the meaning of spirituality for the artist. Driven by the human urge to discover the origin and essence of our existence, there have been countless individual paths to spirituality throughout human history. Susanne's vision of spirituality mostly aligns with its contemporary holistic definition, which seeks certain common threads among mankind's traditions, while not relying on any particular formulation. For her, spirituality encompasses harmonious personal growth by the cultivation of compassion, kindness, moral and ethical qualities, such as tolerance, responsibility, integrity, concern for others (altruism), non-violence, and reverence for nature. To this list, she adds the prerequisite to be a devotee of the transcendental aspects of our mental existence and to search for a higher meaning of life beyond being caught up in a never-ending pursuit of sensual gratification. As an artist, Susanne emphasizes the perception of universal beauty and human creativity as fundamental aspects of spirituality. She believes it includes peaceful co-existence with respect for those who follow various other spiritual paths. The above concept, as generally used, is associated with established religions, with some of their rituals and belief systems.

It should be kept in mind that revealing personal beliefs is a highly sensitive matter for her, especially in reference to such contentious subjects as divine domain, the universal mind, the existence of the soul, spiritual energy, parapsychological phenomena, speculation about otherworldly dimensions, etc., most of which are disparaged in the traditional scientific disciplines. Susanne has spent many years reading about spiritual topics, as well as discussing, contemplating, and speculating about these issues in hopes of finding convincing explanations for them, which she feels is of critical importance to her. She has delved into traditional and contemporary expositions on the subjects elucidated by theologians, philosophers, and practitioners of various spiritual disciplines from both East and West.

Her curiosity has always been eclectic and open-minded, ranging from the latest findings and theories in particle physics and cosmology to various spiritual practices and psychical research. Susanne's search for "the Truth" remains somewhat stagnated in the "absence of true understanding," which is perhaps a rather common situation for many other believers, thinkers, and researchers on this path. Nevertheless, she is not discouraged and takes comfort in the fact that the great developers of mankind's knowledge went beyond the limits of established paradigms. One such contemporary pioneer exploring the perimeters of some of the mentioned phenomena was the Australian neurophysiologist and philosopher, John Eccles (1903–1997). His conviction of the continuing existence of spiritual energy beyond death made a deep impression on Susanne when she read about it in the 1980s.[25] This significantly influenced the evolution of her spiritual concept.

During our search for traces of the unconscious in Susanne's paintings, it had become apparent that her attitudes toward the controversial topics that we have delineated above could not be excluded. This information is indispensable for a comprehensive interpretation of various metaphorical meanings embedded in butterfly Air. With the shared data, the latent content of the image can be appropriately decoded.

The personal information concerning Susanne's significant emotional experiences and her beliefs has been essential in our investigation of the images of the butterflies. The episodes from her life and coincidental circumstances related to them could have been condensed by the unconscious into messages and embedded in forms, lines, colors, and composition of the painting's imagery. We anticipated a similar process to be in effect for the butterfly Air.

For this reason, the artist was asked to share her private beliefs and ideas without hesitation or prevarication, regardless of their appropriateness or inappropriateness, public approval or disapproval. Her reticence to openly talk about her beliefs concerning supernatural topics such as the soul, afterlife, and ultimate reality started early, for her family had been a source of harsh criticism and a constant hindrance when it came to these matters. In this regard, Susanne experienced the same negative attitude in the world outside her home.

From the artist's wide-ranging search for knowledge, she has selectively chosen ideas from various spiritual traditions that appear to her to be reasonable, so as to form an individual vision of spiritual existence. Her private beliefs have become a treasure that sustains her whenever she finds herself struggling with worldly demands, like a water canteen on a long trek through a desert. She is reluctant to share her thoughts on the spiritual aspects of existence, for fear of having them attacked, mutilated, or ridiculed, and, therefore, even in her art, she consciously and unconsciously employs camouflage and coding techniques to protect them.

In regard to the meaning of life, death, and the hereafter, Susanne has clandestinely developed her metaphysical convictions from her family, while treading carefully to avoid conflict with their agnostic worldview. She allowed "her spirit to fly free" as an urge to leave behind the restrictions that her parents had set. She metaphorically expressed this in the image of butterfly Air.

Over the years, she has placed spiritual dimensions at the highest level in her personal hierarchy of values, which contrasts markedly with

25 John Eccles in Popper and Eccles, 1985: dialogue XI, page 557. "John Eccles: 'Thus there may be some central core, the inmost self, that survives the death of the brain to achieve some other existence which is quite beyond anything we can imagine.' " For more about this, see chapters 3.6, 3.10, 3.11, 10.8, and 10.9 in John C. Eccles, *Wie das Selbst sein Gehirn steuert*, 2nd German edition (Munich: Piper, 1997). The title for the English original is *How the Self Controls Its Brain* (Berlin: Springer-Verlag, 1994).

a single-minded, obsessive focus on the physical body and material surroundings. She believes that something essential enables the human being to function harmoniously. She speculates that this "something" is a form of energy that is invisible and transcendent, infinite in its capacity and extent. In attempting to verbalize this "energy," she uses terms such as "spiritual realm" and "the higher existence."

For Susanne, the term "God" was tainted from her childhood onward by her parents, especially her father, who professed an outspoken antireligious opinion. He dominated the family with his vigorous polemics against theological teachings and traditions. He was firmly convinced that the doctrinal faiths backed by the authority of organized religions and churches was part of the societal mechanisms by which the elites in power for millenia usurped the freedom and rights of the individual and controlled the whole population in the name of God and divine prerogatives. For Susanne's father, there was little difference between totalitarian and religious institutions, all of which predicated virtuous benefits, while hiding a controlling intention behind a mask of benevolence. This disapproving stance also found its way into his artworks. This was his private conviction, whereas in real life situations, Susanne found her parents to be very tolerant and accommodating toward individuals of various statuses and religious affiliations. For instance, one of the family's neighbors was a Catholic priest, whom the parents warmly welcomed into their home on several occasions as an honored guest. In spite of the parents' depreciative view of religion, the children grew up to always be respectful of other people's beliefs and not to ridicule their attitudes and practices.

It took Susanne decades in secrecy from her family to search for and find her own stepping stones for her spiritual path independent of any established religions. She began her search by reading about numerous approaches to spirituality. In her thirties, she started yoga practice and tried meditation to activate her potential.

For many years, she longed for a spiritual experience. It happened when she was meditating on her mother's imminent death, and she had an overwhelming vision (see chapter 11). This convinced her of the possibility of exchanging information through spiritual channels extending beyond our physical realm. She has yet to find an adequate explanation of the true nature of this state. Her view on this experience is still evolving, but she believes it is connected with spirituality, which she calls "spiritual dimension."

She has expressed this concept in her oeuvre over the span of more than three decades. Susanne intentionally presents the idea of a cosmic spiritual entity as a human nude, over life-sized and in surrealistic colors. The artist renders this figure commonly in green or blue hues and places it in a golden surrounding. When she creates the background in her paintings with gold leaf, she indicates an iconic meaning for something mysterious, transcendent, and spiritual.

We will present a few such paintings, in which Susanne depicts a superior entity caring for human beings. In *Destiny*, (1988) (Fig. 9.21), a green goddess holds a human puppet on strings. She keeps the figure somehow above the turbulent water below, so that it will not be drowned (detail in Fig. 9.21).

Watching Us, (1996) (Fig. 7.6) pictures a blue female divinity leaning on air[26] and gently watching mankind. Susanne imagined this divine figure being invisible to humanity below, observing the earth from her cosmic setting. The artist added gold to the segmented regions of the sky above the deity, metaphorically emphasizing that the spiritual presence permeates the universe.

In *The Portal of Surprise*, (1994) (Fig. 10.15), a green male figure, an entity from higher dimensions, sits in front of a golden background guarding the portal. He allows the small human stick figures pass through to enter a new state. We note an enigmatic detail in the head of the divinity: the shape of his skull is reduced to a series of ribbed arches spanning a golden inner space. The artist intended to symbolically present the otherworldly, non-material nature of the divinity, who remains unfathomable to human beings' sophisticated reason. We also observe a comparable structure in Air's wings (Fig. 10.16), and such a resemblance could reflect Susanne's conceptualization of a spiritual entity.

In a much earlier work, *Nation*, (1986) (Fig. 10.17), Susanne depicted a bust portrait, in which the upper part of the solid skull alternates with

26 Asked several times, how someone can be leaning on air, the artist is astonished by that doubt. She believes a deity can do anything, and she painted this in *Epochs of Mankind* and also in *Watching Us*.

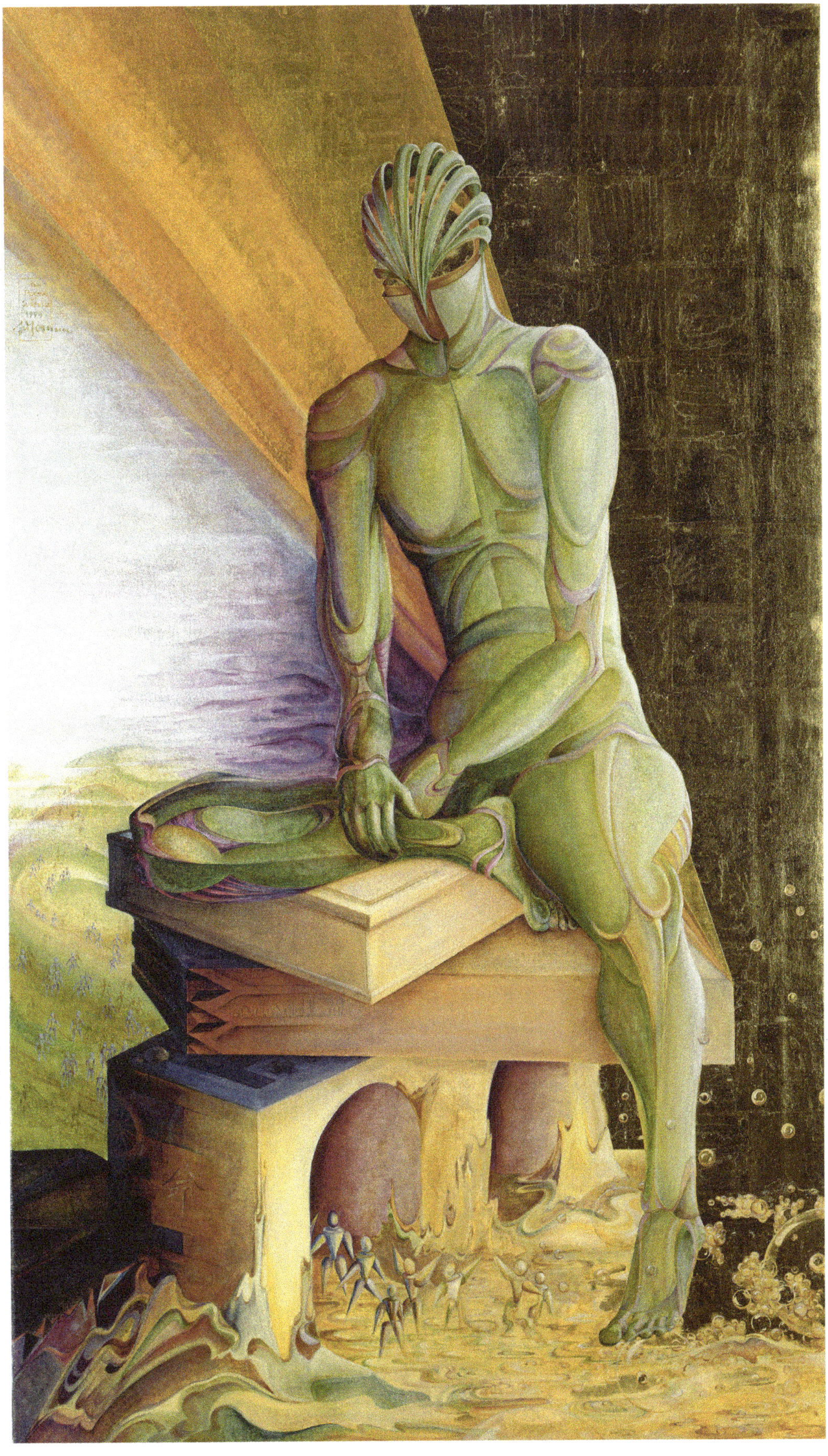

Fig. 10.15.
Susanne Schuenke,
The Portal of Surprise,
1994. Oil and
gold leaf on canvas,
53 x 32 in (135 x 85 cm).
Collection of the artist.

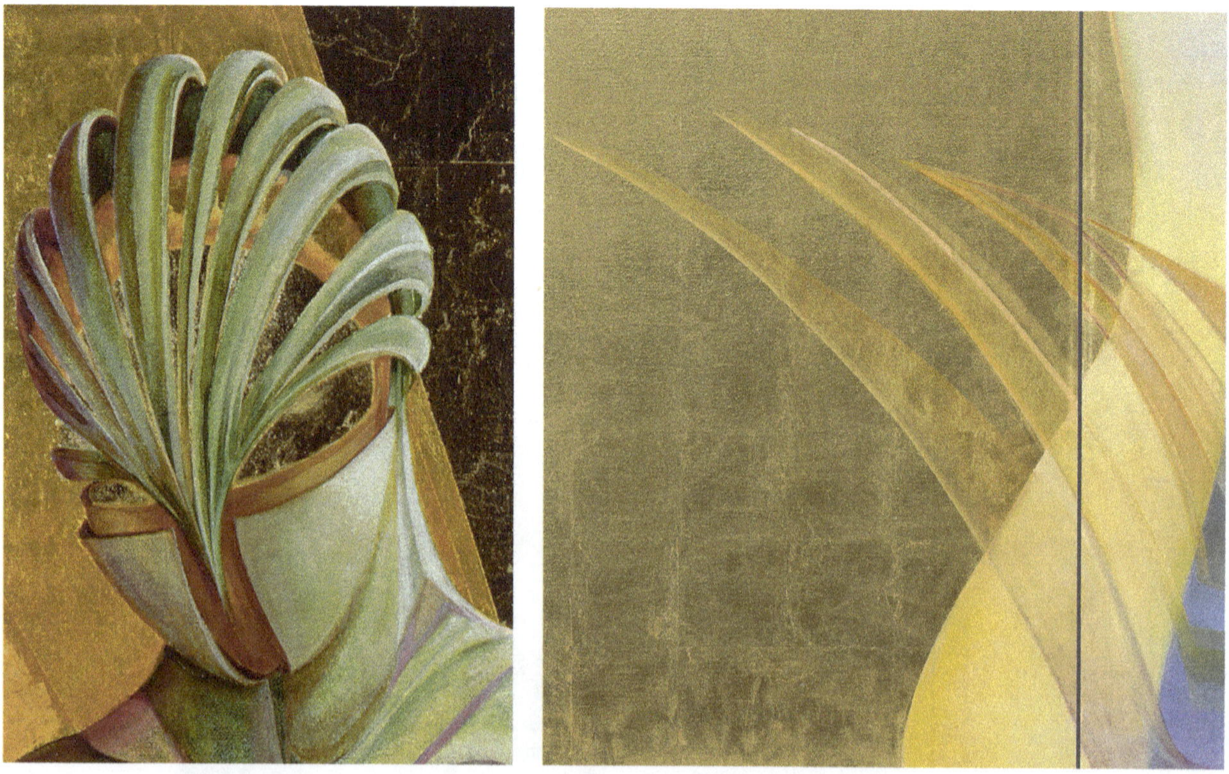

Fig. 10.16.
Left: Detail from Fig.10.15.
Right: Detail from Fig. 1.0. Left wing from butterfly Air for comparison.

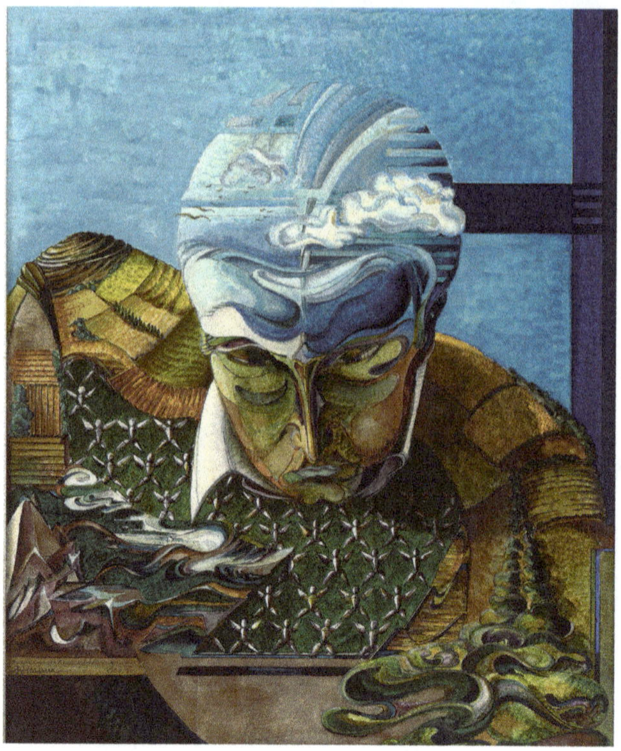

Fig. 10.17.
Susanne Schuenke, *Nation*, 1986.
Oil and silver leaf on board, 24 x 20 in (60 x 50 cm).
Collection of the artist.

"empty space," analogous to the wings of butterfly Air. There is no clear boundary between the inner and outer spaces, as sky and brain fuse together (Fig. 10.19). The cloud-like shapes, floating inside and outside, are vaguely similar to the brain's gray matter. In this way, the artist wanted to figuratively represent thoughts and imagination, drifting like clouds. In the right hemisphere of the figure's cranium, a flock of birds is flying. In the 1990s, the artist wrote down a remark about those birds depicted in *Nation*: "Only the spirit is free to transcend the clouds to higher levels," signifying the bird as a symbol for the spirit. As remarked earlier, a stack of gently curved, wide-open V-shapes in the structure of butterfly Air's left wing prompted us to associate the shapes with the silhouettes of a flock of birds flying away (Fig. 10.18). We assume that these features of Air in *Give Me Wings!* and the birds depicted in the figure's head in *Nation* (Fig. 10.19) carry the same allusion of striving toward spiritual freedom. This analogy could be considered to metaphorically represent the related meaning.

The spiritual essence in Susanne's works could also symbolically be expressed by a tear-shaped drop. For example, in *Elysian Fields*, (1990)

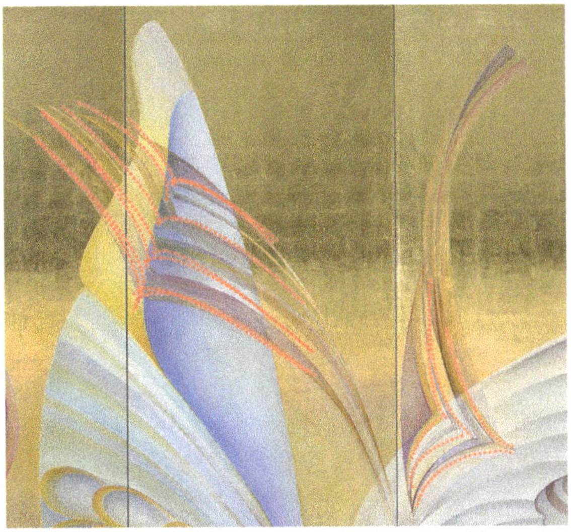

Fig. 10.18. Detail from Fig. 1.0. The wings of butterfly Air enhanced with red overlay to reveal a row of bird-like shapes in silhouette seemingly flying away.

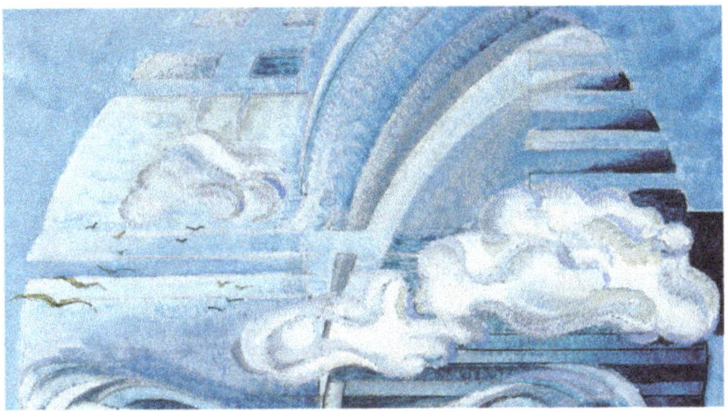

Fig. 10.19. Detail from Fig. 10.17. Upper part of the head "dissolving" and the flock of flying birds.

(Fig. 10.20, a detail from Fig. 12.8), the goddess bestows the "*gutta vitae*" (the drop of life), which endows the new human being with a spark of life.

In *Intermission*, (2001) (Fig. 10.21), created three years prior to *Give Me Wings!*, Susanne expresses the immaterial essence by two signs—a drop and fleeting vapors. The latter configuration has some astonishing similarities to the shape of butterfly Air (Fig. 10.22). Therefore, we will explore this painting in more detail.

Intermission depicts a celebrated actress who is surrounded by her admirers.[27] Her art briefly enchants the audience, but when it is over, all that remains is memory and the emotional response to the experience. Some details from *Intermission* help the viewer understand the painter's

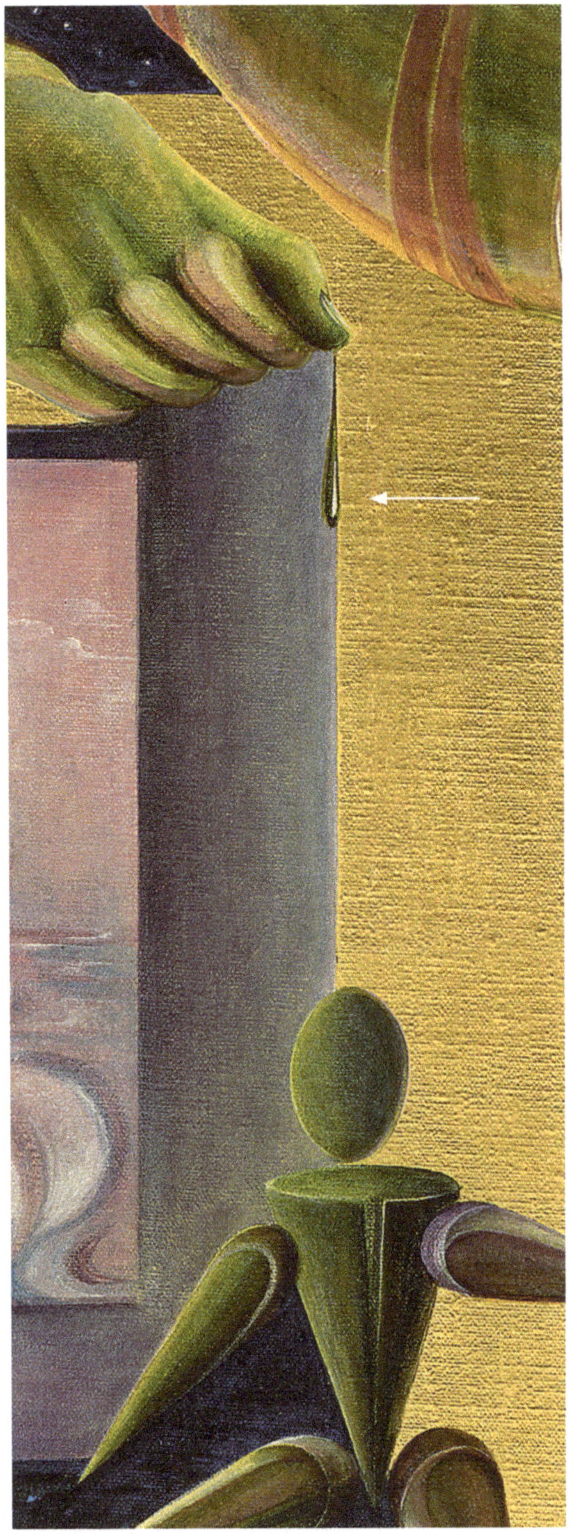

Fig. 10.20. Detail from Fig. 12.8. The arrow points to *gutta vita*.

27 The following is an excerpt from Susanne's description written in 2001: "Encircled by her admirers, honored with a bouquet, the diva is the star of the evening. The air hums with animated talk, the guests celebrate with champagne and hors d'oeuvres. Some members of the audience are privileged to step onto the stage during this short intermission to chat with the leading lady. There are an ambitious and fashionable beauty, an intellectually dominant personality, and a high ranking member of the military. Tonight they all came to recognize her art. The listeners gravitate around this diva who gathers them under her emotional spell."

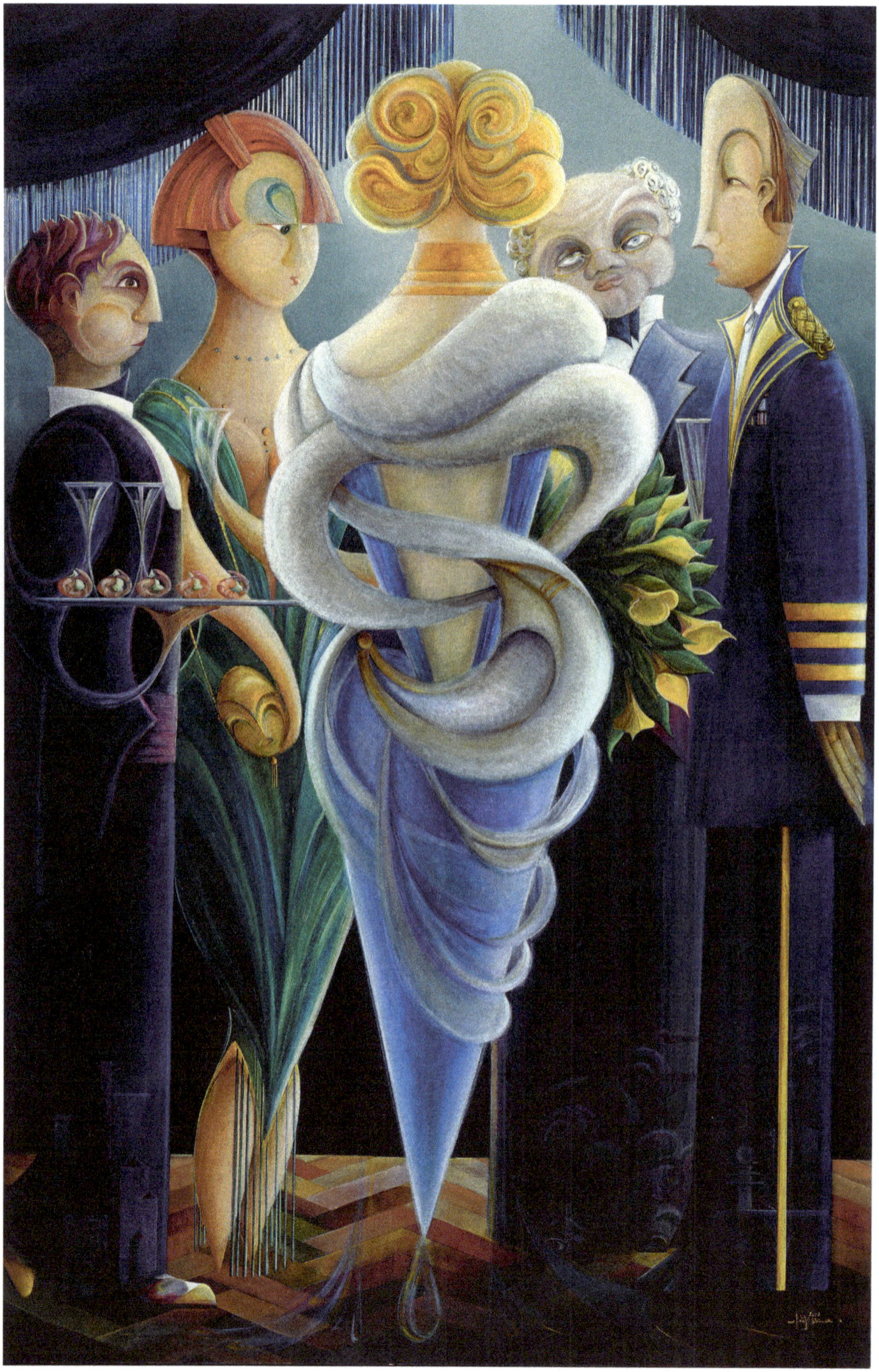

Fig. 10.21. Susanne Schuenke, *Intermission,* 2001. Oil on canvas, 71 x 55 in (180 x 120 cm). Private collection.

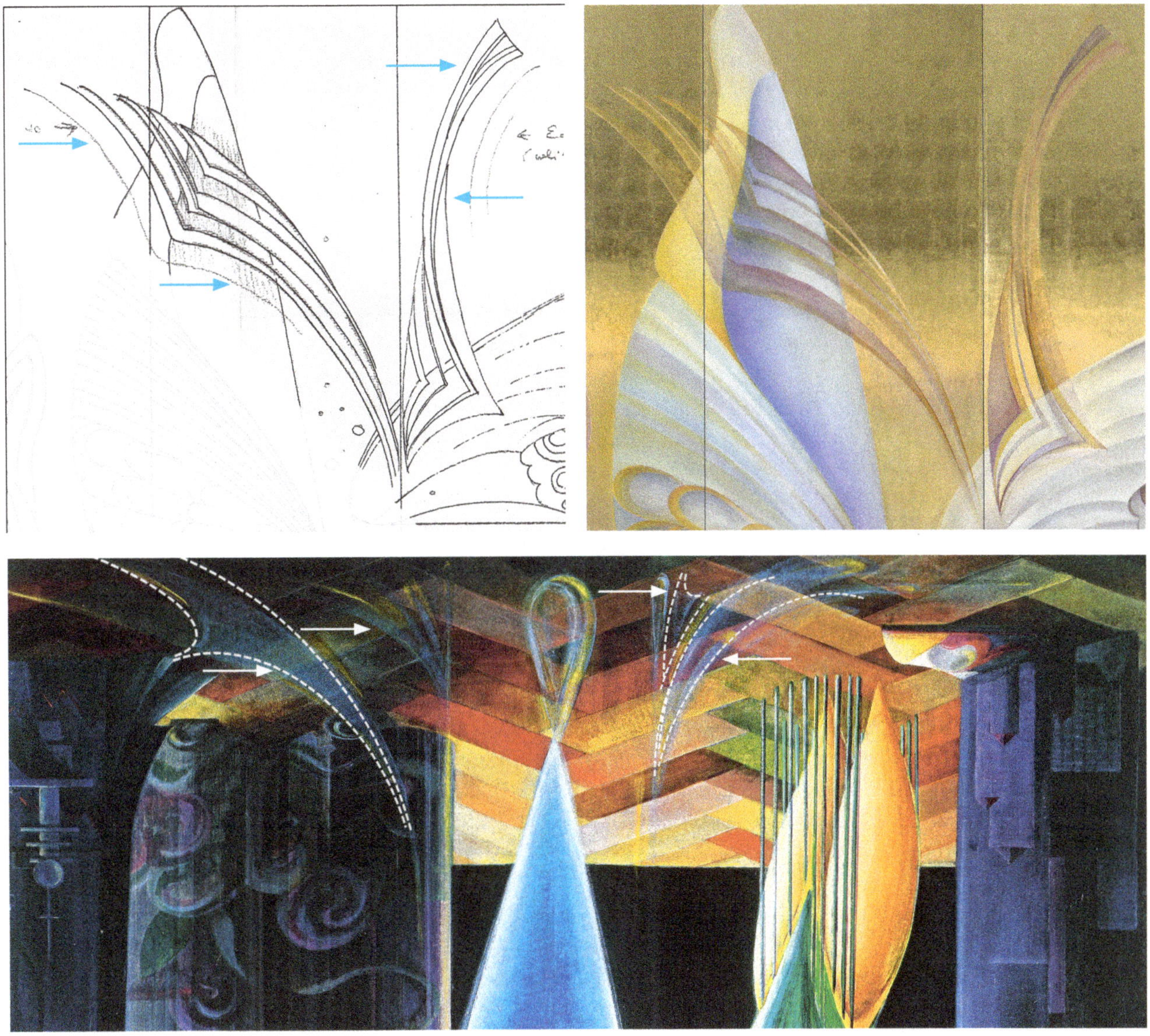

Fig. 10.22. A collage for comparison:
Top left: Butterfly Air. The detail of butterfly No. 7 taken from Fig. 2.11 (compositional drawing); the bottom half faded for clarity.
Top right: Detail from *Give Me Wings!* (Fig. 1.0).
Bottom: Detail from Fig. 10.21 (inverted and adjusted for a higher contrast for clarity). Dotted lines emphasize vapor shapes.

symbolic message. First, the diva's gown tapers surrealistically into a single point, from which a large drop emanates. Susanne developed this shape spontaneously during the painting process and found it suitable to express the essence of the performer's art, showing the innate greatness of art and its ability to touch the human mind in the most concentrated form. In this case, the drop is the symbolic quintessence of the performer's art. We see here "the spark of art," which reminds us of the "gutta vitae" granted by the goddess to the human. Second, the telltale signs of the status of the admirers are symbolically depicted on their legs as representing certain social groups.[28] The naval officer stands for the military, and the waiter represents the working class. The impresario, as the catalyst belonging to the intelligentsia, brings the inner spirit of the art to realization, and the

28 The artist points out certain representative details for identification: The aircraft carrier on the Naval officer's legs; the inner city high-rises above the waiter's sneakers; the socialite's prison-bar like fringes on a green dress with the most risqué décolleté; the dreamlike curling forms on the impresario's tuxedo alluding to presenting exquisite arts. The curling forms mentioned are favorites in Susanne's repertoire, and it does not come as a surprise that she applies them here as an abstract icon for the beauty of the arts. (Three of these details can be seen in Fig. 10.22, presented upside down.)

wealthy socialite is wrapped up in her emphasis on sensuality and materialism. Third, near the imaginative foot of the diva, in the form of a drop, there are the traces of diaphanous, bluish-white formations, which appear like veils detached from the dress and trailing on the floor to the left and the right.[29] These veils are of great interest in light of our interpretation. Turning those spherical triangles shapes by 180 degrees (Fig. 10.22), we can observe a striking similarity to the wings of Air.

Does this similarity between the shape of the veils (2001) and the wings (2003) point to the same symbolism? As mentioned before, the wings are traces left by the flight ("echo of a flight"). The vapor veils at the sides of the diva's drop were intentionally introduced by the artist to visualize the ephemerality of the experience of the performing arts. In Susanne's perception, the emotionally-charged impressions will be cherished in memory in the times to come. The artist created this surrealistic, misty evaporation as an allusion that the diva's performance touches the audience. This figuration is a metaphorical sign of the spiritual influences of art, like the already mentioned drop, which symbolizes the quintessence of her creativity. We assume that the similar shapes found in the veil from *Intermission* and Air's wings are unconscious symbolism that confirms the spiritual nature of what both images represent. It is fascinating to see how the artist unconsciously expresses related spiritual messages by images (vibration of wings/evaporating veil) that represent ephemeral experiences.

10.4.2 Butterfly Air as a Metaphorical Expression of Spirituality

In this subsection, we examine how Susanne's spiritual concept finds its metaphorical expression in the image of butterfly No. 7. From the earliest stage of its creation, Susanne perceived this butterfly as a strikingly singular creature. We pointed out in chapter 2 that eleven days after her visit to the museum in New York the artist made three creative drawings, and the very first figure[30] she rendered in creative drawing I was butterfly A, the predecessor of butterfly Air. In its image, she encapsulated and condensed her most intense impression of her experience in the butterfly conservatory—the effortless flight, so light, so fast, so free, which her eyes could barely catch.

The image turned out to be something incorporeal, as it was portrayed without head, body, or legs. The lines she drew appeared to trace only the wings' contours, but they were so unusual that she was not even sure how to define it. The artist wrote the cryptic annotation "echo lines?" on both sides of this butterfly in the compositional drawing for the watercolor. This notation was a reminder to herself to depict the traces of the flight and the essence of its movement that she experienced with fascination at the conservatory with this image. She was in awe, arising from the electrifying sensations of the butterflies flying close by.[31] The captivating patterns of the flight, the ever-altering shapes of their wings as they flew, and the admiration she felt for the oscillating colors made lasting impressions on the artist. The experience was so strong and specific that it must have determined the creation of butterfly A's image as the first one. Its enigmatic configuration, rendered in the manner of automatic drawing, became a puzzle for Susanne, and her attempt to understand its essence was clearly noted in the poetic commentary written nine months later. The outlandishness of butterfly A gains more significance when compared with the other six butterflies, which are all depicted with clearly defined wing structures.

In the oil painting, three butterflies are in the air, Nos. 1, 5, and 7, but for different aims.

29 Susanne explicitly indicates the fleeting presence of something of very short duration with this imagery. This is her version of the wisp of smoke from the snuffed-out candle in the traditional *vanitas* still-life paintings (see, for example, Murray 1998, page 553, "Vanitas still-life"). A good illustration of this is the candle at the center of David Bailly's *Self-Portrait with Vanitas Symbols* (1651), Stedelijk Museum De Lakenhal, Leiden (Netherlands).

30 Searching for the sequence in which the artist had rendered the three butterflies of creative drawing I, we inspected closely the pencil lines on the actual drawing paper. This revealed that the central butterfly A's lines ran continuously without any interruptions and that the artist had avoided touching or crossing the lines belonging to butterfly A when she drew the contour lines of the second and third butterflies (B and C). This indicated that from the earliest stage of drawing the artist intended to create the illusion of A being in front of and above the other two butterflies (which later became butterflies Pale Moonlight and Touchless Misty).

31 Susanne felt more than once that their wings nearly brushed her cheeks. She also had the incredible experience of one butterfly even landing and resting on her.

Butterfly No. 1, Little Why, jumps up and down with childlike joy and eagerness, which is all she can manage. Meanwhile, butterfly No. 5, Firebird, has risen up in triumph over No. 6, Fanning Everything. In contrast, butterfly No. 7 Air hovers majestically above the podium, ready to head toward the golden background. It is all flight, free of bodily mass and gravity, which in this case also metaphorically means to be liberated from the weighty conditions of the material world. Thus, this central butterfly is set apart from all the others. The artist drew and painted this image according to her intuition without explication about its true nature. However, in the poetic commentary, she had the inkling to write: "it is with them, but not of them," which she picked up from a religious context.[32] By this, Susanne hints at the exclusiveness of this butterfly and expresses her deep respect for its yet-unknown, intrinsic meaning. She senses the butterfly's otherness as to be something exceptional, valuable, and immaterial, and in the painting, this is metaphorically encoded in the peculiarities of the image.

In *Give Me Wings!*, Pale Moonlight is given the largest size. The most striking colors are featured in True Blue and Firebird. The highest step on the podium is conquered by Touchless Misty. The richest embellishment of forms and details is assigned to Fanning Everything, and the most active, most eager one to receive her place under the sun is the sprightly Little Why. In such competitive comparison, it might appear at first glance that Air is less dominant, less colorful, and less striking.[33]

Nonetheless, there are several aspects we have discovered that put butterfly No. 7 in an exceptional position: Levitating in the air; moving toward the golden background; being placed in the center of the painting; embodying the pivotal role in the composition. In this way, the artist has assigned a superior value and rank to the core of this image. Susanne thinks its inner qualities are metaphorically so obvious and powerful to discerning eyes that it does not need any other markers to signify its nature. The intrinsic transparency of the wings and their alternating elements of material structures with empty space become increasingly estranged from an expected anatomy of the "normal" butterflies, linking it with something that is beyond our everyday world. This goes hand in hand with butterfly No. 7's apparent submersion into the golden background, which symbolizes spiritual dimensions (see chapters 11 and 12), suggesting butterfly Air's entrance into a transcendental domain. An additional, indirect proof for its special importance can be observed in the artist's idiosyncratic numbering, intentionally assigning the mystical number "seven" to Air, thereby expressing Susanne's highest esteem for this butterfly.[34]

The butterfly's image points to an immaterial nature, and the accompanying symbolic meaning brings Air in proximity of a spiritual dimension, which Susanne gives the most important rank in her philosophy. Her ideas, speculations, and hopes about existence are condensed into the image of this central butterfly which constitutes a metaphorical expression of her spiritual concept transformed into a visual language.

The peculiarities that symbolize the spiritual nature of butterfly Air could be summarized in the following particulars:

1. The butterfly is moving toward the golden background, which symbolizes spirituality, and merging into it (the golden background will be discussed in chapter 12).

2. The description in the poetic commentary, "with them but not of them," points to the image being given a transcendental quality by this characterization.

---

32 Specifically, the Gospel of John, chapter 17, verses 11 and 16 from the New Testament inspired Susanne's paraphrase.

33 Quite a number of first-time observers, when asked how many butterflies are in the painting, count only six. Being placed between the most beautiful duo, Pale Moonlight and Touchless Misty, it is easy to overlook Air at first glance.

34 Seven is an important and revered number in mythology, religions, and society. See, for example, Brian Bunch, *The Kingdom of Infinite Number: A Field Guide* (New York, NY: W. H. Freeman and Company, 2000, page 82). Originating from the earliest known history of civilization, all of the seven moving (observable) celestial bodies were deified, and the number became sacred and mystical. Also, it should be noted that the seventh chakra in yoga philosophy is the crown chakra, through which the prana (life force) connects to the higher spheres of the cosmos. In addition, in the Abrahamic religions, the ordinal number *seventh* has a significant spiritual connotation, since the Divine dwells in the seventh heaven. Susanne ended up painting seven butterflies in her oil painting after abandoning the eighth from her design.

3. The visible wing elements (translucent by themselves) alternate with empty space, alluding to the ethereal nature of the entity.

4. The central position of Air and its widely spanning wings, free of the ground below, symbolically reflect the artist's spiritual aspiration.

5. There is an unobtrusive coloration of this butterfly. This visual appearance could be interpreted as camouflage, which might have been deployed due to the artist's tendency to hide her tightly-held ideas, many of which are spiritual in nature.

In addition to the above points, we pay closer attention to the rotational symmetry that was observed as Air's configuration (see subchapter 10.1). This enigmatic development deserves a further examination. Could this specific symmetry in the imagery of the butterfly contain some latent message? Our analysis of the image of Air indicates that it is loaded with metaphors, often with multiple meanings. This imagery was free of conscious premeditation as stated by the artist, and it could reflect a modus operandi of the unconscious processes that transmute memories of emotionally charged life situations into various symbolic signs and manifestations, using a variety of coding schemes. Accordingly, we assume that the rotational symmetry was not a groundless, accidental arrangement, but possibly another playful twist of the creative unconscious expressed from the very onset of the creation of butterfly Air. In this light, the rotational symmetry could be an expression of different latent meanings.

The rotational symmetry could contain a metaphor for a significant development of the artist's relationship with her parents. Starting in her late teenage years, as we have narrated in detail previously, an ever-widening rift slowly evolved between Susanne and her parents, a change which could be metaphorically equated with the flip-over effect. The daughter began increasingly to question the thoughts and attitudes of her parents toward various important topics concerning life and its meaning. There was an active effort, mostly by her father and sisters, to categorically suppress the subject of parapsychology. They immediately correlated any interest in this with illegal influences of sects. Also, as we mentioned before, the parents tried to suppress any tendencies connected with the sexual drive. Susanne's father considered sexuality, when unbridled and outside of the conventional mores, would jeopardize the traditional family structure and values. Both parents put much stress on the importance of education, cultural and artistic refinement, and social success, which would bring about an elevated status in society. However, they were unwilling to accept various, specific needs that each of their growing daughters had (contact with their peers, participating in the social life of their age group, dating, etc.). In reference to the latter points, Susanne came to reject her parents' conservative views on these issues. The rotational symmetry through a 180 degree turn could metaphorically represent the reversal in Susanne's thinking from that of her parents. All the essential features delineated above, and their interconnection with her individual experiences, substantiate the ground for decoding the imagery of rotational symmetry and its inner meaning.

Beyond the above presupposition, we could even speculate about the rotational symmetry as a metaphor for a universal development of bio-spiritual unity in the function of BrainMind. In the following, we will analyze these aspects, manifesting in the image of Air. First of all, we will pay attention to spirituality. We assume that an innate proclivity for spiritual matters was an important constituent of the artist's imagery. We will present further confirmations in support of these assertions in the following subchapters titled "Soul," "Ephemerality," "Colors and Camouflage," and "Spiritual Need." Furthermore, the continuing search will reveal other aspects of Air's intrinsic spiritual meaning which are pressing for their recognition.

10.4.3 The Soul

The image of Air reflects the artist's thoughts about the existence of spiritual dimensions, which also include the topic of the soul. We will outline her contemplations in order to follow how her ideas found their visual expression in her paintings. We would like to emphasize that this is not, by any stretch of the imagination, a scientific discussion on the matter, since the current state of science does not recognize any such entity as the soul or spirit. The following is based on the artist's personal philosophy, which she has assembled out of various influences and insights gained through many years of study and searching for the meaning of life.

Susanne believes in the existence of the soul, which she imagines as composed of a specific kind of energy and coded information, connected with other dimensions unknown to our matter-based perception. For her, the soul energy is linked with realms, which are deemed unverifiable at the current state of human knowledge, mostly because our senses and instruments cannot measure and confirm them yet. Nevertheless, she has the conviction that spiritual energy exists in spite of our inability to perceive and quantify it and should be a subject for exploration, although for many that might be an unconvincing topic.

The artist has never been able to find satisfactory answers to her probing questions concerning spiritual existence in any particular system of belief. She has accepted diverse ideas and explanations that made some sense to her. On this basis, she has built a personal spiritual concept. The framework she has constructed gives her certain satisfaction, and she hopes that in the future the advance of science will have widened its scope to include these subjects as part of its serious and respected concerns. For example, she believes that the Chinese concept of yin and yang and the associated vital force "*qi*" (or *ch'i*), which is still controversial in the Western science, would be a good candidate for further scientific inquiries.

Susanne feels hard-pressed to describe "the soul" and "spiritual energy," as they are beyond our sensory perception. In accordance with her readings,[35] she accepts that this phenomena includes information from past existences and that could possibly predispose us to certain personal characteristics and strong emotional tendencies which we display in our present lives. In agreement with the traditional idea concerning the destiny of the soul, she affirms that during the lifetime of a human being, the soul is bound to the body, but upon death, it is set free from the physical confines.

Susanne's concepts about spiritual existence and the soul have been gathered from scores of sources over many years and developed over two decades into her present creed. From her late sister-in-law, whom she respected for her advanced knowledge of Buddhism and yoga practices, Susanne received various reading and listening materials, which impressed her deeply and shaped her thoughts from her thirties onwards, adding more valuable information to form her convictions. Her spiritual development was shaped mostly by reading about related topics of interest being dealt with by different religions, especially Buddhism[36] and Hinduism. We mention also the conversations with her mother, as well as discussions with friends representing various belief systems.

Over the course of years, she came to believe, based on these Eastern religions, in the idea of the soul, which exists before, during, and after our life on Earth. The soul concept and its relationship to spiritual dimensions became for her an acceptable worldview. This finally could give her a basis for the meaning of existence. As we have remarked before, Susanne's fear of criticism and ridicule had conditioned her to keep her ideas concerning spiritual matters private, forcing her to rarely voice them outside the circle of her trusted friends. This group did not include her family, as both parents were outspoken in their dislike of religious institutions, and they certainly did not foster their children to be interested in topics they considered as religious delusions. Philosophically speaking, her father was a pure materialist, i.e., he was of the opinion that when the body dies, the cells dissolve and nothing remains of the person in any form. He rejected any speculations and discussions about any kind of existence after death. Late in his life, on a few occasions, he began to ask Susanne such questions as, "What is there after the end of the cosmos?", or "What do you think happens afterwards?" However, when the daughter explained her ideas, they were always rejected with dismissive responses, declaring that after death, "There is nothing."

Her mother was more tolerant of Susanne's speculations. Sometimes she made cryptic allusions, such as, "There are many things between heaven and earth we do not understand." Her comments about parapsychological phenomena were based on reading relevant books about the subjects which she shared with her daughter. Her ambiguous attitude was more supportive of Susanne, although she would not discuss her daughter's speculative thoughts. When Susanne was reaching her early adulthood and wanted to talk about spiritual and transcendental aspects of existence openly, the

35 Among the most influential of the books were those of Myss 1966; Tolle 1999; Chopra 1994; Newton 1994; and Weiss 1988.

36 Rinpoche 1992: *The Tibetan Book of Life and Death*, which she read in her thirties.

parents became alarmed that their daughter had fallen victim to a religious cult, and they warned her to stay away from those esoteric contemplations.

In her thirties, she became more assured of the existence of the soul and the spiritual aspects of human life. She began to carefully mention one or another of the topics relating to the matter, which was immediately met with a wall of resistance. She was confronted with skeptical questions and disdainful comments from her family members, such as: "Susanne, you fell in the hands of a cult" (Father, younger sister), "Who influenced you?" (Father), "Who has proven this?" (Father), "Be reasonable, come back on your feet" (younger sister), "You have to live in this world" (parents), "You think too much" (younger sister), and "How can you think like that? That's horrible, I cannot hear it" (older sister).

Obviously, the ever-deprecating remarks of the parents and siblings conditioned her to be extremely careful as to whom she could trust in exchanging her thoughts, speculations, theories, and questions about the nature of the soul, spiritual realms, afterlife, and the ultimate reality. This negative emotional experience was the crucial component for the development of Susanne's fear of disclosure. She became very vulnerable with regard to sharing her concepts, even for this research. She feels this is akin to being stripped naked in public. Subsequently, she would only discuss them within a circle of close friends who held a similar view.

Accordingly, the assumption could be made that the artist unconsciously applied camouflage to butterfly No. 7. She dressed it up in unfavorable colors to implicitly divert any attention from the signs of spiritual meanings that are harbored in this image (for more details, see subchapter 10.6). The concealment is accomplished unconsciously through the metaphorical peculiarities of the butterfly's configuration and coloration. Nevertheless, when she chromatically fuses the image into the golden background, the symbol for spirituality in the artist's iconography, she discloses the true nature of butterfly Air as an unconscious messenger of this realm. This presupposition will be further explored and given more supporting observations in the analysis below.

10.4.4 Images of the Soul in Some of Susanne's Paintings

Through her studies in art history, Susanne knew that there were some traditions for visually representing the soul. Since antiquity, birds with their ability to fly could symbolize the soul[37] in the arts. Since the Middle Ages, it has been customary in Western Christian art to depict human souls as naked bodies in the scenes of Heaven, the Last Judgment, and the Resurrection of the Dead.[38] Starting with the Hellenistic period, the soul (Greek: psyche) was sometimes personified as a female that was either equipped with butterfly wings[39] or shown with the butterfly as her companion.[40]

As the senior researcher became aware of Susanne's belief in the existence of the soul, he began to look for the symbols and metaphors she had been creating to represent her conceptualization of this issue in her art. The earliest painting that can be considered to embody the topic of the soul is a watercolor from July 1980, titled *Seller of Souls*. Its design developed over the years, and Susanne reworked the topic twice in her oil paintings, *Collector of Souls*, (1988), and *The Rise of Karma*, (2002).

In the *Seller of Souls*, we observe a female nude from behind, surrealistically colored green, who is about to ascend a spiral staircase carrying three rings, each enclosing a stick figure marionette[41] dangling on strings in her left hand

37 Murray, 1998, page 58.

38 Two examples as representative of such iconographic depictions: Hans Memling, *The Last Judgment*, 1467–71, Muzeum Narodowe, Gedansk. Michelangelo Buonarroti, *Last Judgment*, 1536–41, Sistine Chapel, Vatican, Rome.

39 Bertel Thorvaldsen, *Psyche*, 1844, Alte Nationalgalerie, Berlin. Psyche is equipped with butterfly wings.

40 François Gérard, *Psyche and Amor* (also known as *Psyche Receiving Cupid's First Kiss*), 1789, Louvre Museum, Paris. In the painting, a butterfly is seen symbolically hovering over Psyche's head. This painting was executed to illustrate the story of the love between Psyche and Cupid (or Amor) as narrated by Lucius Apuleius (2nd century CE) in his *Metamorphoses.*

41 Twenty-five years later, the artist took up the same idea of expressing the superiority of an entity (i.e., she juxtaposed the subject with miniature stick figures). In creative drawing I, she added stickfigures to the three butterflies (C, A, and B), changing them into monumental super-beings (see Fig. 2.2). This thematic representation can be observed throughout the artist's creative life, for example in such works as *The Portal of Surprise* (1994; see Fig. 10.15), *Watching Us* (1996; see Fig. 7.6), *The Takeover* (1997; see Fig. 4.14), and one shortly before designing *Give Me Wings!, Marianne* (2003, not illustrated).

like a shopping bag (Fig. 10.23). The gigantic superior entity ferries the souls of humans to another dimension.

The name *Seller of Souls* (German title: *Seelenverkäufer*) sprang spontaneously into the artist's mind. It is surprising to find the artist using the word "soul" in the title (*Seele* in German), since at the time of the creation of this watercolor the development of Susanne's concept of spiritual existence was still in an embryonic state. The title could indicate a metaphoric manifestation of her mental condition of deep depression with obstinate thoughts of death. At the time, she was caught in the clutches of a desperate inner darkness without a positive outlook on her future, despite her well-managed and successful academic studies, and she tried in anguish to grasp the meaning of life. Thus, the idea of "selling the soul" might have reflected her feelings of lost integrity in those years of doubt and misery. The German compound noun "*Seelenverkäufer*" might have become a metaphor for her mental state. The expression is also a German idiom used to describe an unseaworthy ship, i.e., a "floating wreck." The sad reason for nicknaming such a vessel "seller of souls" is the high probability of sinking, taking the lives of the passengers and crew. The artist was aware of this implication. We assume she intuitively used this title as a metaphor for her suicidal thoughts which nearly overwhelmed her at that time.

Eight years later, in 1988, she picked up the image and content from the above-mentioned watercolor and expanded it into a new, life-size oil painting that she named *Collector of Souls* (1988, Figs. 10.24). Her situation had changed; she had successfully completed her studies, and they were now behind her. Moreover, she was living near London, UK, with her future husband and was finally able to paint on large-size canvases. The improved circumstances could have determined the change in the title from *Seller* to the more benevolent sounding *Collector*. In this painting, the central figure is ascending on the winding golden stairs that lead into the dark, starry sky over the clouds. The right hand touches the top of the newel, which is rendered as a moonlike

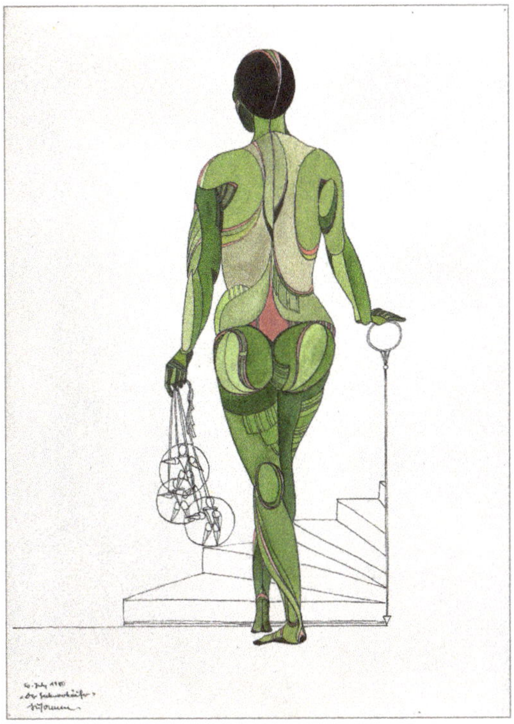

Fig. 10.23. Susanne Schuenke, *Seelenverkäufer (Seller of Souls)*, 1980. Watercolor, 19 x 14 in (48 x 36 cm). Collection of the artist.

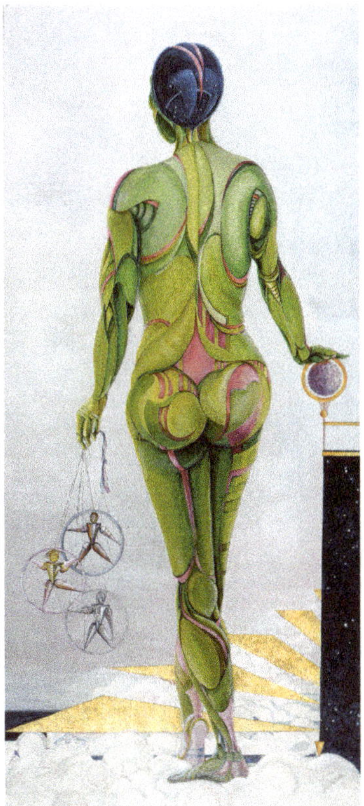

Fig. 10.24. Susanne Schuenke, *Collector of Souls*, 1988. Oil with gold leaf on canvas, 67 x 32 in (172 x 81 cm). Corporate collection, Berlin, Germany.

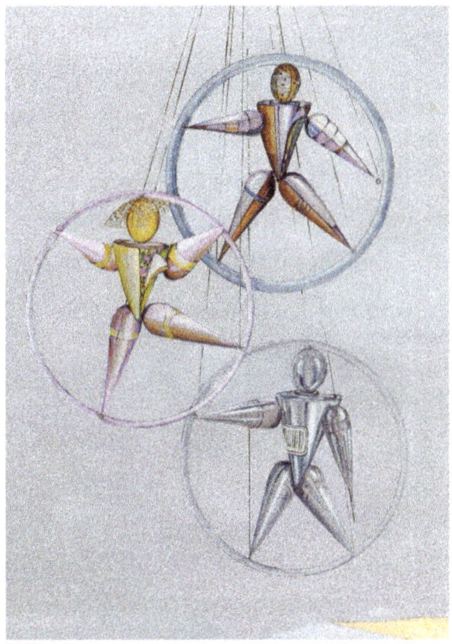

Fig. 10.25. Detail from Fig. 10.24. Three general characterizations of people collected and carried in the rings.
Top ring: the "individualist."
Middle ring: the "artist."
Bottom ring: the "mass person."

orb. These details were metaphorically intended to indicate the heavenly realm. The souls are carried by "the collector," a superior being, to a spiritual abode. The featureless marionettes from the 1980 watercolor have evolved into three distinct types—"individualist," "artist,"[42] and "mass-person." The painting's new title points to Susanne's conscious intention, through the use of an assortment of human types that she identified, to represent some primary characteristics of individual souls. With this work, the image of the highly stylized puppets, colorful and three-dimensional, was firmly established in Susanne's art as a symbolic representation of human souls (Fig. 10.25).

With the creation of *The Rise of Karma* (later renamed[43] *Tat II*; Fig. 10.26) 12 years later in 2002, Susanne returned to the topic of the transition from this life to another realm, and the title for the new painting was derived from her evolving spiritual concept, which also incorporated the term "karma." The development of her idea is based on her reading and elaboration of this ancient Eastern belief. According to Susanne's explanation, she used the title, *Rise of Karma*, to emphasize the process of the transformation of the soul.

In this second oil painting, the artist changed the coloration, tinting the divinity in a wide range of blues and merged the figure gradually with the blue strata of atmosphere. The staircase-to-heaven scenery is abandoned, and the human figures that were carried in the rings in *Collector of Souls* are replaced with bubbles. The deity escorts a loosely floating cluster of six bubbles with her left hand. At her right side, a row of bubbles ascends along a vertical axis from the ground upwards. The artist has transformed the stick figures from the predecessors of this painting into her favorite bubbles, with their subtle connotation of the soul as a beautiful, free-floating perfect essence after a short physical existence in this world.

The seed of this transformation was already planted in the *Seller of Souls*, where, for the first time, the artist expressed her idea of the human soul as a stylized stick figure encapsulated in a circular enclosure which became a recurring symbol in

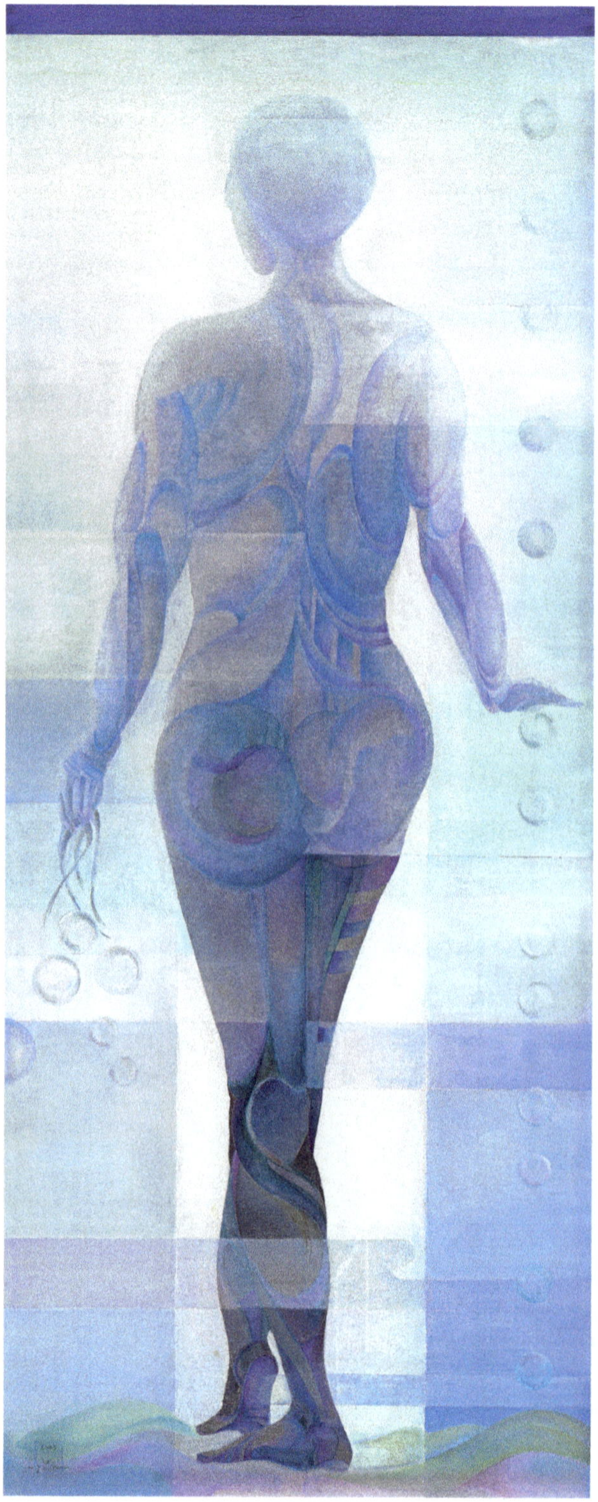

Fig. 10.26. Susanne Schuenke, *The Rise of Karma* (renamed to *Tat II*), 2002. Oil with palladium leaf on canvas, 67 x 28½ in (170 x 70 cm). Corporate collection, Florida.

42 Susanne has always identified herself with the "artist" marionette among the three types of humans carried in the rings by the "collector." The "artist" figure is the only one of the three puppets which shares the same reddish and greenish palette as the "collector."

43 The later renaming of the painting came from outsiders for commercial purposes and does not reflect the artist's intentions.

her personal iconographic repertoire. The two-dimensional circle, as a constituent of Susanne's icon for the soul, derived from her positive emotional attachment to this shape (see chapter 7.3) and her optimistic outlook connected with it. These symbolic configurations developed into the imagery of three-dimensional spheres—bubbles—signifying the spiritual core of the human being, the soul. The artist intended to represent the soul abstractly by the sphere, for she considers it to be the most perfect object in nature. She imagines that the souls, depicted as bubbles, continue to rise higher and eventually reach liberation from karma. *The Rise of Karma* scenario reflects a concept of existence that is enriched with hope for growth and a positive outcome.

The bubble as a symbol of the soul had already emerged some years earlier in another painting, *The Portal of Surprise*, (1994) (Fig.10.15). Susanne depicted stick figures representing the newly dead passing through a portal and, to their great surprise, finding themselves in a brightly illumined scene, contrary to their fearful expectation. Under the watchful gaze of a supreme being, the stick figures in the luminous region undergo a rapid transformation into bubbles that are rising upward. It is worth mentioning that there are additional paintings in which the topic of the soul is also presented either with stick figures or with bubbles: for example, *Destiny* (1988; Fig. 9.21, 9.22), *The Four Elements* (1990; Fig. 9.26), *Elysian Fields* (1990; Figs. 10.20 and 12.8), *Watching Us* (1996; Fig. 7.6), *Destiny II* (1997; Fig. 12.10), and *Heaven and Earth* (1998; Fig. 9.32).

Just before the creation of Air in *Give Me Wings!*, Susanne painted *Freedom* (2003; described in detail in subchapter 11.3.4; see Fig. 11.5) as a direct consequence of her experience after her mother's death. In this work, a stylized, colorful human figure representing a person's spiritual essence is depicted walking away from earthly life. The artist paired it with a ghostlike figure to the right that is nearly identical in contour to the left figure but side reversed and bare of clothes (Fig. 10.27), in pale blues. Its yellowish details reflect the golden sparkles from the surroundings and give the impression of a swirling spiritual energy field. Through this image, Susanne intended to express some aspects of the soul in its purer state as a representative of the spiritual realm.

10.4.5 The Foundation of Susanne's Quest for the Meaning of Life

From her teenage years onward, Susanne was entangled in a Gordian knot of inner conflicts and anguish, for which she could not find any resolution. As noted previously, in her late childhood she lost the assurance of being loved by her parents when they began to deny her physical intimacy involving kissing, caressing, and hugging, despite her continuous desire for such closeness that gave her much-needed attention (attention-seeking emotions), comfort, and security. Her mother, who tried to minimize the number of kisses that Susanne tried to give her, would declare: "You are too old for that!" The statement made no sense to the daughter, who had grown up used to getting her desires for comforting and soothing touches met by the parents. Her mother refused to directly answer Susanne's plea: "Do you love me?" The mother would only impatiently reply, "You know that," without ever clearly saying, "Yes."

From age 13 on, Susanne became increasingly isolated socially from her peers. She lost her childhood playmate, the girl who lived next door, as Susanne's family moved away to a neighboring town. Due to the long hospital stays that occurred in her fifth, seventh, and ninth grades, Susanne had to repeat them. She was assigned to classes with increasingly younger classmates. She continued to attend an all-girls high school in the previous city, because she liked and admired the teachers. The long, daily commute that she had to make to the school by bus and train gave her no time or location to cultivate personal relationships with her classmates. She had no peers, and only her parents, two sisters, an aunt, and the parents' friends constituted Susanne's environment for social interaction. The parents' friends integrated her in their discussions as an equally respected participant, which was, for that time, a positive substitute for her.

There were some other significant experiences influencing Susanne's attitude toward life during her adolescence. Always a voracious reader, somewhere at age 12, she stumbled upon a world atlas with a section called "World Population," which caused her to fall into a fit of deep despair. The atlas contained a striking diagram illustrating how the extrapolated number of the people in the world had grown over the centuries from the year of Christ's birth until 1965, including

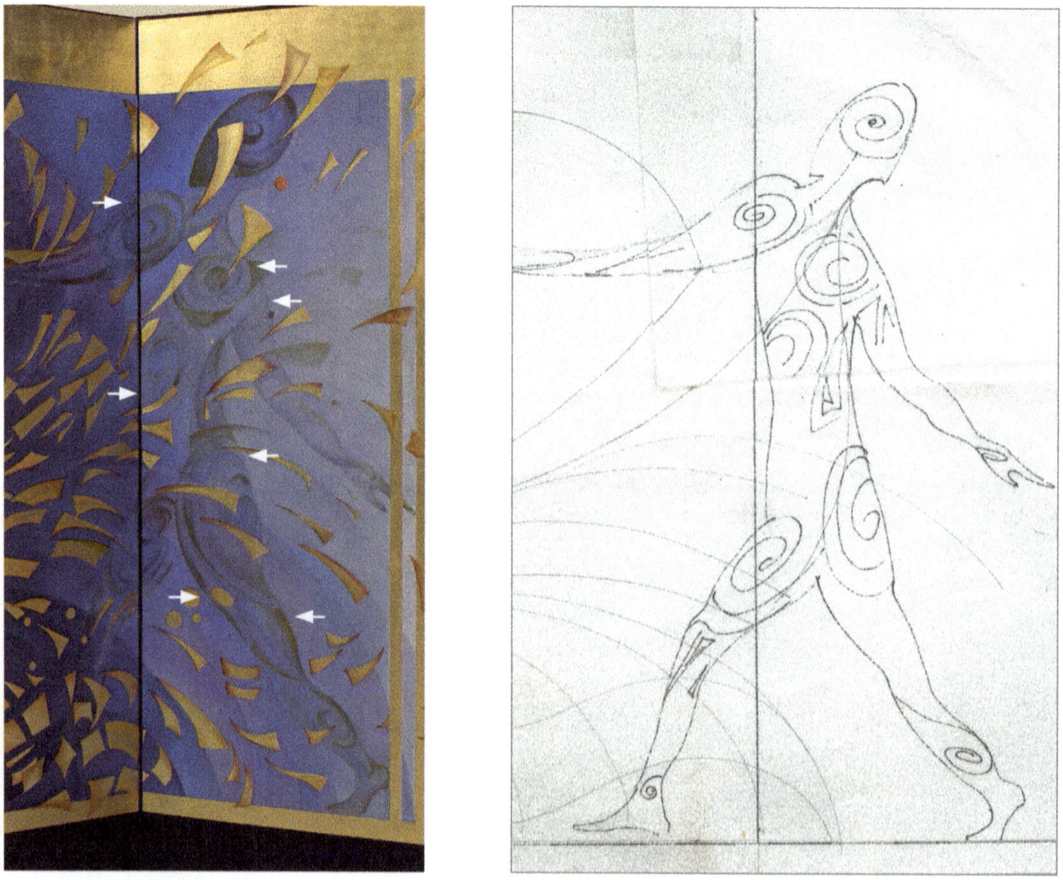

Fig.10.27. Detail from Fig. 11.5 (*Freedom*). The arrows point to the representation of the "soul" figure; and for better visibility, the same figure is shown in the drawing stage (the detail number 2 from Fig. 11.3).

a population projection to the year 2000. This population explosion gave her the shock of her life, as she was immediately horrified by the realization of its potentially grim consequences. The only remedy, she concluded, was a drastic reduction in the birth rate and, therefore, she would not add to the skyrocketing growth of the world population with her own offspring.

In the early 1970s, when Susanne was around age 15, the world was still in the midst of the Cold War between the superpowers. The threat of a sudden mass extinction of mankind by a nuclear war was in the minds of many people. Such a scenario was widely disseminated by the mass media and academic studies, as well as by private and public discussions. Being on the frontline of the fragile political balance between East and West, the people of West Germany were keenly aware that the future existence of Central Europe, or even the whole world, was utterly dependent on the sanity of the key political players. Susanne imagined that should anyone in charge of the government and its nuclear arsenal lose his mind and press the "red button," nuclear catastrophe would take its unstoppable course. This prospect was deeply troubling to her, as she had ruminated on the possibility of all living organisms being killed at any given moment by a person's decision far away and out of control.

Also, during those years, learning in her history classes about so many wars, cruelties, tortures, persecutions, and genocides heightened her anxiety concerning the unpredictability and volatility of human existence. In the decade of the 1970s, the world witnessed the continuation of the Vietnam War, which the news media critically reported on with graphic images of destruction and carnage shown on the newspaper pages and television screens. Ireland and West Germany were shaken by a decade-long series of terrorist acts involving bombings and killings.

Susanne's perception that the earth had become a very frightening place to live, and her despair of the situation in the world was kindled even more by the news of catastrophic starvation in Africa that was caused by the by the Nigerian Civil War. She was particularly affected by the pictures of children dying of starvation that were widely circulated by the mass media at that time and were forever ingrained in her mind.

As mentioned above, Susanne had a number of long hospitalizations that began at the age of 11. Chronic health issues with her ears demanded a series of surgeries. This period of her life lasted for the next ten years. The fear of the hospital stay, of the next operation, and especially of being exposed to dreaded syringes, the frequent use of which grew with each subsequent stay in the clinic, facilitated the outbreak of her trypanophobia.[44]

At age 16, her ongoing health problems reached their nadir when she was diagnosed with Ménière's disease. This demanded an emergency hospitalization, during which she was given a daily intravenous infusion over a two-week period.[45] That was the last straw, beyond her capacity for endurance. Coming home, she bandaged her wrists and hands for several days to protect herself from any more attempts to insert needles into her body. Over the next two years, she persistently rejected any ear operations suggested by the doctors to alleviate the condition. Moreover, in spite of severe dental problems, she refused outright to go to the dentist for years. This resistance had a regrettable outcome, when one day she had to undergo dental surgery to remove eight decayed teeth.

Susanne's open rejection was of all doctors, dentists, and any kind of medical personnel who handled syringes, injections, vaccinations, and blood tests. For her, these procedures became the embodiment of horror, making her life quite miserable. She began to contemplate that the best way to escape from this would be death, and she thought of it as a beautiful thing, since it would relieve her of such unbearable sufferings.

The strain of despair grew, and over a decade her fantasies about death came to occupy her mind with imaginations for its realization, which she kept well-hidden from everyone. What stopped her from a rash act was her need to substantiate her decision with the philosophical and ethical legitimization to choose death over life.

She delved deeply into her reading and discovered the works of the Norwegian dramatist, Henrik Ibsen. She eagerly devoured his social and psychological dramas written between 1877 and 1899. Her ongoing pessimistic perception of life obviously colored her subjective interpretation significantly, especially of some of Ibsen's plots. Her worsening depression during those years intensified an identification with Ibsen's characters, who committed suicide as the way out of their tragic dilemma.[46] However, because death was an absolutely taboo topic in the family, she could never discuss those specific decisions made by Ibsen's protagonists with any member of her family.

She was convinced from her solitary, secret contemplation that the only logical way out of living in darkness without having any meaning had to be death. She projected the various outcomes from Ibsen's plays onto her situation to find a legitimate ground for this conclusion. Among the plays, Susanne highly cherished *The Lady from the Sea*, which delivered a positive message that impressed her deeply. In a crucial life circumstance in the play,[47] the heroine, Ellida, was able to make her own decision once she had gained the freedom to choose between two irreconcilable outcomes, and she took full responsibility for her choice.

This existential contemplation of Ibsen's heroine became a pivotal point for Susanne, which ultimately guided her out of her personal conundrum. The recognition of having the freedom to decide for herself, nevertheless, did not give her the ultimate ground to overcome the allure of an early death. Accordingly, she continued searching for the meaning of existence. It took her nearly 30 years before she came to an agreement to accept her life.

On this matter, despite the generally supportive attitudes of her parents, and especially her mother's great patience, they were of little help, for they repudiated any faith-based perspective on existence for their daughters. This was due to negative experiences in their youth, when they were forced to go through the "confirmation" process,

44 Trypanophobia: the extreme fear of medically related shots and injections (American Psychiatric Association Diagnostics and Statistical Manual of Mental Health Disorders, 4th Edition (DSM-IV)).

45 By Susanne's account, 14 painful intrusions.

46 Henrik Ibsen (1828–1906): *Ghosts* (1881), *Wild Duck* (1884), *Rosmersholm* (1886), *Hedda Gabler* (1890), and others.

47 *The Lady from the Sea* (1888), last act and scene, dialogue between Ellida, Wangel, and the Stranger.

a prolonged period of religious indoctrination that the German Protestant church required of its members, usually starting in the early teens. The parents' traumatic personal experiences in the Second World War also played a critical role in their loss of faith, as they felt that the horror of the war and the existence of a benevolent deity could not be reconciled. They turned away from any religious concept and belief. Nevertheless, they brought their children up with the declared intention of fostering in them the freedom to choose a faith once they are capable of making decisions on their own.

Her parents put a great emphasis on education, creativity, the arts, responsibility, social and ethical values, and self-discipline. These values, including devotion to family and children, were the fundamental reasons for their existence. However, they did not anticipate the peculiarities of the psychic development of their daughter. Susanne significantly deviated from their way of thinking and perception. She needed an individual approach, especially to address her existential questions.

10.4.6 Developing a Concept for the Meaning of Life.

Susanne seriously started to question the meaning of life early in her teenage years. Her search involved asking her parents and friends for their perspectives as well as delving extensively into the accounts of philosophers, scientists, historians, artists, and literary authors in an attempt to find the right direction in her life, to fulfill her potentials, and to reach harmony with herself and the world.

Susanne began to walk along the thorny path of her quest for answers. She encountered different perspectives, some contradictory, others unsatisfactory. As a consequence, for many years, she meandered before she came out of the deadlock. She tried to find some prospects, so as to set the course for the future to overcome various life difficulties.

A fateful event happened at the age of 21 that irreparably broke Susanne's trust in the wisdom of her father. After she had just passed the last of her high school graduation exams and was waiting for university enrollment, she asked an existential question of her father: "Why do I live? What is the sense of life?" In response, her father exploded in an instant like a volcano, spewing out a torrent of tirades and screams, berating Susanne.

His loss of control and sudden outburst was completely unexpected and shocking to her, and she was utterly at a loss as to what had happened. She never asked him the question again and repeated it only to her mother in the night conversations they had separately from her father. Her mother believed that having a sense of duty to others was a sufficient reason to live, but this was not an adequate answer for the daughter. Moreover, Susanne questioned her sisters concerning the meaning of life but was met with evasive responses.

Susanne fell into a deep pessimism and remained there in a permanent state of despair to the end of her twenties. Her studies, including learning three foreign languages on the side, and long travel hours to the university, were so time-consuming that there was no chance to socialize with her peers and exchange personal perceptions about life and its challenges.

When she was 24, during her summer break from the University of Cologne, Susanne took classes at the European Summer Academy at Trier, Germany. There she met Tanja,[48] 25 years her senior, who talked about certain aspects of God in such a loving way that greatly impressed Susanne (Fig. 10.28). They became the closest of friends for years to come. Tanja, being tolerant and patient, did not react with any alarm, reproach, or moralizing when her young friend spoke of her desire to die. Instead, she remained calm, kind, and sympathetic, and gave Susanne confidential, soothing answers. She did not fully understand, but absorbed the advice because intuitively she sensed the trustworthiness of her mentor.

One of Tanja's cryptic comments was, "God gives you exactly as much burden as He knows you can carry." And another: "But, Susanne, you have chosen your parents, you know that!"[49] The last statement, controversial with regards to the religious catechism, showed how the liberal Catholic[50] had outgrown the limits of age-old

48 Tanja Binsfeld (1930–1993).

49 This implicitly suggests the preexistence of the soul and the choice of the circumstance of one's birth is not solely determined biologically, but by the individual soul as well.

50 Tanja was open-minded and tolerant toward other faiths, accepting freedom of belief, and she was much disappointed by the animosities and intolerance that have been promulgated by the dogmatic believers of various religions throughout

dogmas. Tanja interpreted life and faith from her own mature and idiosyncratic point of view, which was enormously beneficial to Susanne in her search for a path through life. The positive emotional experience with Tanja outweighed the accumulation of distrust against established religions that was instilled in Susanne's mind by her atheistic parents.

Tanja's statements, paradoxical and not entirely clear to Susanne at the time, resonated in her mind because they plucked the string of the power of free choice. She was affirming what Susanne had found and admired a decade earlier in Ellida's solution to her predicament in Ibsen's *The Lady from the Sea.* With this insight, Susanne began to look at the challenging question of the meaning of life in a different light. The new perspective gave her the confidence to cope with her ambivalent emotions and to trust in her power to overcome her existing problems.

Another pivotal response from Tanja came when Susanne asked her if a certain decision might be a mistake, and she replied: "If it is a mistake, maybe it is good to make a mistake." Nobody in Susanne's family would ever have accepted such a statement. After all, everything the three daughters were taught was geared to avoid making mistakes and the consequent "punishment from life," according to her father's pronouncement. Therefore, Tanja's assertion stood in sharp contrast to the guidance given by Susanne's father, and the wisdom behind it gave her a completely unexpected perspective and a new outlook.

The implication of Tanja's statement planted a seed in Susanne's mind that would eventually grow to increase her self-confidence and instill in her the courage to walk some unexplored paths. Through her friendship, Susanne experienced the feeling of being appreciated, loved, and accepted, and she has never forgotten the human warmth and spiritual wisdom of Tanja. Susanne believes that her identification with her friend set in place one of the most important foundational blocks, on which her understanding of the meaning of life could gradually develop at its own pace. The artist continued to keep in touch with her friend through letters after she left Germany for London and then later for the United States, sharing her thoughts, reveries, plans, as well as ideas about her art. Many of Tanja's remarks stayed with her, often giving her a lifeline in a sea of sadness and loneliness.

In 2004, just before she began to work on *Give Me Wings!*, Susanne painted the symbolic portrait *Tanja* in honor of her (Fig. 10.28). The monumental version is based on a much smaller one Susanne had designed just before her friend lost her battle with cancer in 1993 at age 63. In 2003, the artist returned to paint her personal memorial to Tanja, who continued to exert guiding influence on Susanne long after her passing. In this larger than life portrait, the artist pays homage, in her own words, to "the preciousness and beauty of Tanja's humanity." She remembers how she admired Tanja's kindness which had an intrinsic spiritual quality in the way her friend approached everybody. Tanja did not preach to do good; she simply did it in many ways, small and large.

In this portrait, Susanne expressed her emotional attitude toward Tanja's essence. The face is timeless, formed by harmonious flows of lines, and, together with the captivating eyes, radiates a loving expression. The artist adorns the eyelids and brows with green coloration. The hair fans out as gingko leaves that crown the head. The green spreads with the foliage caressing the neck and shoulder on the side where Tanja's cancer was located. We can see how the dominant green in this portrait functions not only as the symbolic color of nature per se but also as an expression of her friend's passion for beauty, art, and life. She was an embodiment of an attitude that was opposite to Susanne's pessimistic perception of life. She was drawn to her friend's feelings and outlook, and gradually integrated them as a new perspective. Susanne's veneration for her friend underpins the specific symbolism of this portrait. She first learned the properties and evolutionary history of the gingko tree[51]

history. Susanne remembers that Tanja treasured a piece of silver jewelry, "the Hand of Fatima," named after a daughter of the Prophet Muhammad, which was given to Tanja by her husband, who brought it home from one of his archaeological field trips to the Middle East.

51 The gingko tree (gingko biloba) is a rare species, considered a living fossil, the only surviving member of its ancient genus from the Permian period of the earth's history (approximately 270 million years ago). The gingko is classified as a broadleaf tree as well as a coniferous one, which makes it extraordinarily important for Susanne. Gingko is dioecious i.e., it comes as male and female individual plants. In autumn, the leaves' color changes to a highly praised, glorious saffron yellow.

from Tanja's rich botanical knowledge. Susanne is especially attracted to the irregular indentures in the leaves that cause each of them to appear unique.[52] All of the tree's outstanding distinction could be symbolically applied to her friend—the rarity of her being; the positive, pure, and archaic features of her soul shining from the leaves.

In a comparison of Air's configuration with the structure of the gingko leaves, some similarities can be discerned (see collage at Fig.10.29). With our mindfulness of Tanja's enormous influence on Susanne's spiritual development, we assume a common denominator behind both formations representing spirituality. The peculiarities of Tanja's personality, and of her portrait's design, might have implicitly inspired the creation of the image of butterfly Air. The above-mentioned metaphorical correlation could demonstrate how unconscious processes choose, connect, and compress information and its details to create symbolic meanings.

Susanne absorbed Tanja's wisdom, but years would have to elapse before it was processed and slowly resurfaced in her life. Despite Tanja's influence, Susanne continued to be disheartened as she experienced days and years passing by, utterly devoid of meaning. The habit of living, instead of the will to live, kept her going. When she was 25, Susanne decided to proceed with her education at a college in London, and for the first time, she was separated from home, parents, language, and familiar location. During that year abroad, her depression hit rock bottom to the point that she would fantasize daily about running into a fast moving bus or stepping in front of an underground train. Regardless of her mental condition, she was academically successful in college.

After she returned from England, she moved from her parents' home to a student house close to the university and worked on her master thesis, which she completed a year later. Then, under the encouragement of her parents, she focused on a doctorate in art history for the following four years. All this time, she continued to suffer and her psychological state did not improve. She was overwhelmed with feelings of being completely lost without having any meaningful perspective. Only the goal of completing her doctorate kept her holding onto life.

One day, while doing research for her dissertation, she came across an isolated quote in an architectural periodical from the 17th century French philosopher, mathematician, and mystic, Blaise Pascal: "You would not search for me, if you had not found me already."[53] Without knowing the context in which this statement by Pascal appeared in his *Pensées*, it might appear to some readers as a paradox.[54] However, for Susanne, who was still struggling with her search for the meaning of life, it was instantly perceived as a revelation. She felt that this uncanny message was the long-lost key to unlock her deeply tangled problems. Always being attracted by paradoxical contradictions, the chance discovery of this enigmatic sentence inexplicably gave her highly-needed certainty and assurance, a lifeboat in the ocean of doubts and despair in which she still was aimlessly floating.

Susanne still remembers, decades later, how powerfully that sentence instantly overwhelmed and dispelled any other thought, and it has never lost its impact on her since then. She took the statement literally and was smitten with the surprising twist in the message, which she interpreted at that time as follows: You (Susanne) would not search for me (the meaning of life), if you (Susanne) had not found me (the meaning of life) already. Susanne understood Pascal's words to mean that someone higher than herself was assuring her that she had already found the meaning of life by herself.

Susanne's encounter with Pascal's saying left an unexpected impact on her, for the words resonated in her mind as if they were being addressed directly to her. The statement struck her quite powerfully,

52 The fascination was so strong that Susanne convinced her parents to buy two gingko trees from a nursery and plant them in their garden.

53 Blaise Pascal (1623–1662), quoted in French from his *Penseés* (Brunschvicg 553, 1897 edition): "*Console-toi. Tu ne me chercherais pas si tu ne m'avais trouvé.*" Susanne read the quote in German: "*Du würdest nicht nach mir suchen, wenn Du mich nicht schon gefunden hättest.*" She photocopied it and still has it with her to this day. The quote is translated and interpreted from this version in our analysis. Up to that time, Susanne knew Pascal only as a mathematician and that one of the earliest computer languages was named in his honor. She found him to be highly intellectual, and only learned much later about the mystical aspect of his writings.

54 The author of the essay in the periodical had taken the quote out of context, for the sentence was part of a sequence of short remarks that Pascal wrote about the Passion of Jesus Christ.

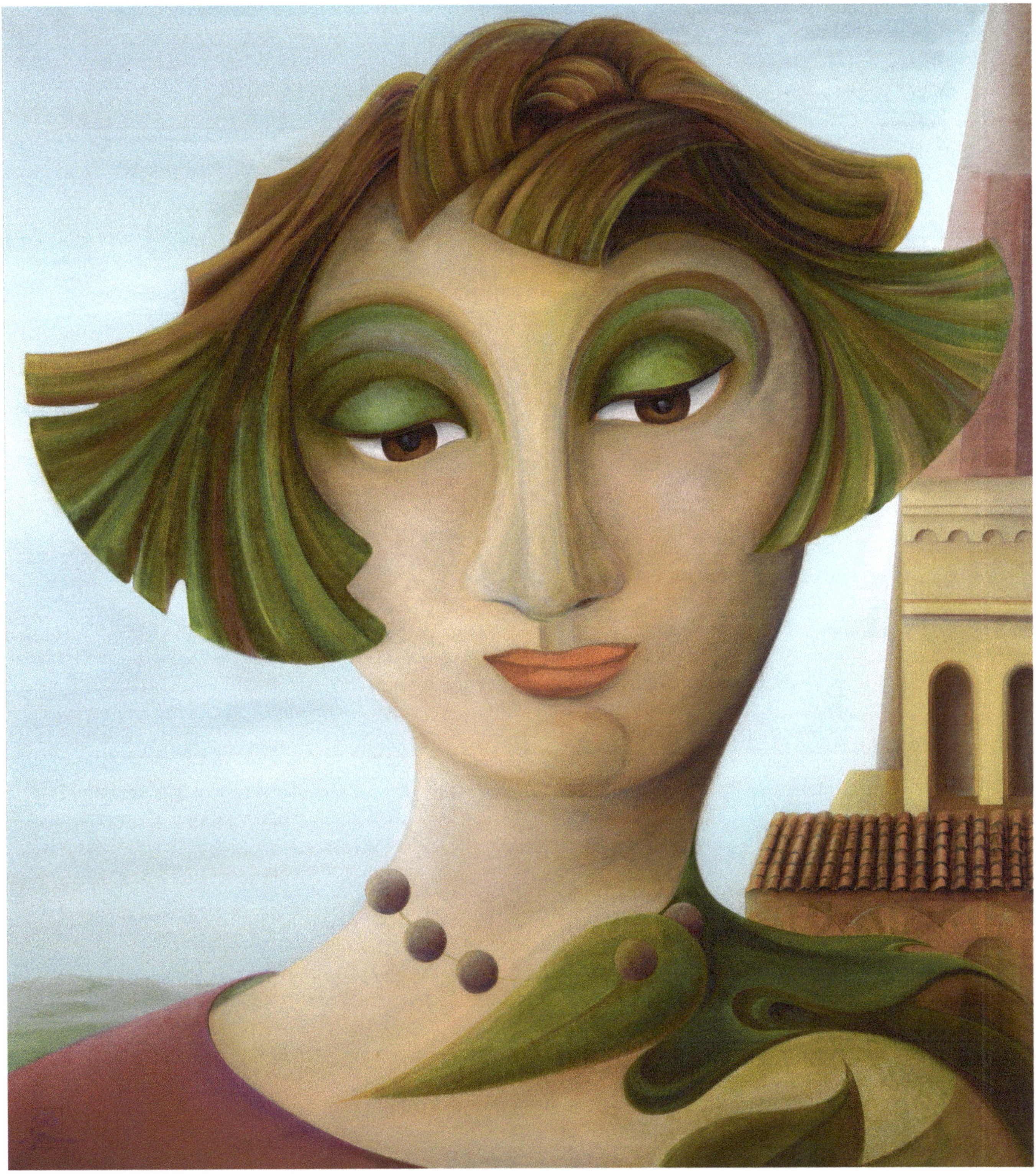

Fig. 10.28. Susanne Schuenke, *Tanja,* 2004. Oil on canvas, 82 x 75 in (208x 190 cm). Collection of the artist.

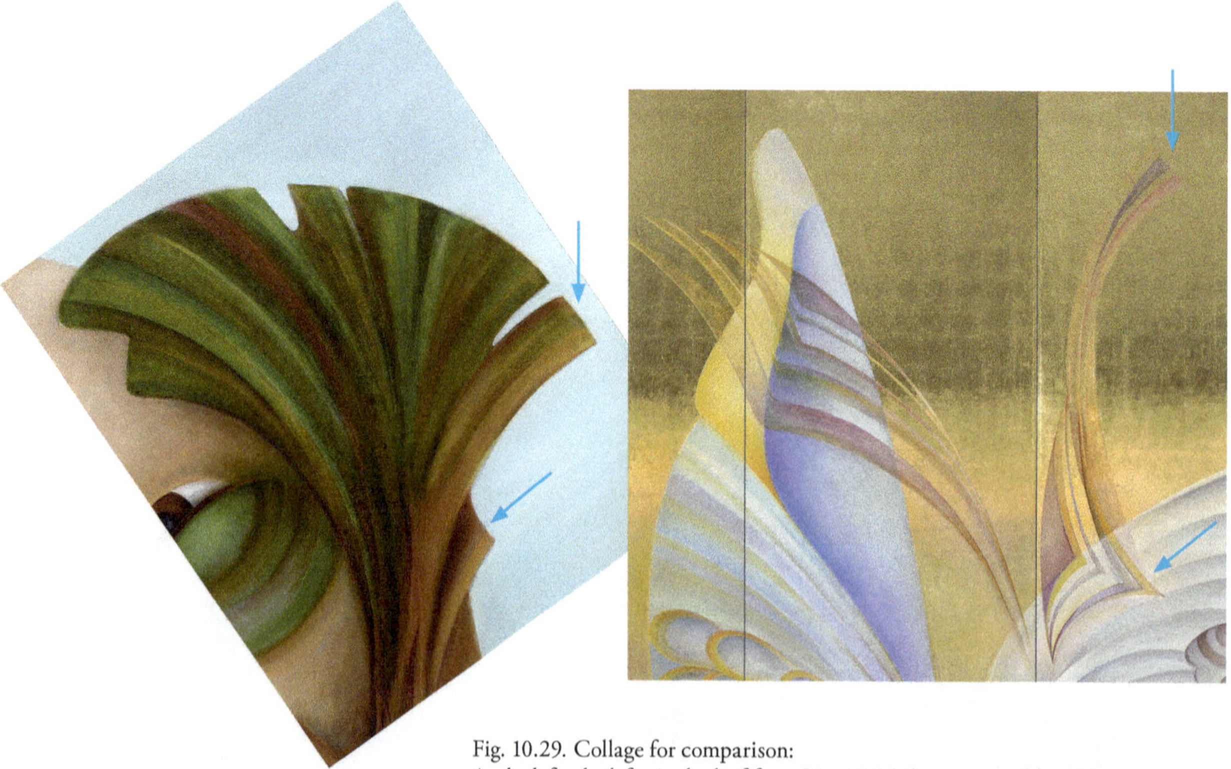

Fig. 10.29. Collage for comparison:
At the left: the left gingko leaf from Fig. 10.28 shown turned by 180°.
At the right: butterfly Air from Fig.10.0.
Arrows point to shared characteristics of the configurations.

as Pascal's authority in essence substituted for that of her father, who still held dominating influence on her. The experience might have even come as a sort of wish fulfillment, since Susanne had been dreaming of receiving such an enormously reassuring statement from her father which could have given her a definitive answer that she was so desperately seeking.

In this regard, Pascal acted, on one side, as a proxy for the "good" father whom she had been wishing would "believe in her." On the other side, the replacement allowed her to develop an optimistic outlook and trust in herself. Pascal's assuring words gave her the hope and strength to hold on through the dark times of her life, during which much of her mind was preoccupied with the desire to leave this world behind. We believe that the wisdom she found in Pascal's saying significantly relieved Susanne from her dependency on her father, which she had since early childhood.

Two significant emotional events in Susanne's twenties, Tanja's friendship with her wisdom and the enlightening statement by Pascal, became the turning points that opened her mind to a perspective of seeing life in a way unknown to her through her upbringing. The gentle guidance of her mature friend together with the French philosopher's enigmatic reassurance supplied a constant stream of positive life energy for her. Under the above influence, Susanne could slowly begin to form an answer to her existential question about the meaning of life which could counterbalance the weight of her pessimistic perception of the world. Furthermore, she developed friendships with some fellow students who greatly enriched her life. Susanne began to understand that "Life isn't about waiting for the storm to pass… it's about learning to dance in the rain."[55] This quote contains a truth, which Susanne has tried to follow.

The wisdom of this attitude, free of dogmatic confines, was bequeathed initially by Tanja and Pascal. They laid the first cornerstones upon which she has steadily added her own thoughts to form the spiritual basis of existence that has guided her through life. Her affinity for spirituality and other related concepts, such as the belief in the existence

55 Anonymous, possibly by Vivian Greene.

of spiritual energy, the soul, eternal existence, transmigration of the soul, etc., are continuously expressed consciously and unconsciously through her creative works. Looking at Susanne's development, we can see that Tanja's and Pascal's sage knowledge exerted an essential influence in her emergence from deep depression and made life worth living.

A metaphorical confirmation of the radical change that came to Susanne's life found an expression in a small watercolor *Träume an einem Freitagnachmittag* (English: *Dreams on a Friday Afternoon*), 1986 (Fig. 10.30), in which Susanne spontaneously painted a daydream. The work can be understood as her positive evaluation of her actual situation, which was symbolically expressed in the design. The details of the scenery indicate items from her daily life, while she was intensively working on her doctorate. There are a few handwritten manuscript pages from Susanne's thesis paper, part of a floor plan of an English medieval cathedral, books from the library, a cup of tea, and more.

One of the important details of this design is a torn violet ribbon. The artist remembers that this detail came during the drawing without any premeditation. Once it was created, she immediately understood its metaphorical meaning as a sign of her freedom: the chain that was holding her was now broken. Another item in this watercolor that sparked our attention through analysis was the chestnut tree in bloom, which we recognized as symbolizing her approaching the conferring of her academic degree, the beginning of the realization of her creative life in painting, and the anticipation of a budding relationship with a new friend. Thus, *Dreams on a Friday Afternoon* illustrates that, instead of persisting in doubt as to how and why to live, she now felt that she was finally on the right track.

In the image of the butterfly Air, we see the expression of the artist's contemplation on the nature of spiritual existence through visual metaphors that were encoded through the butterfly's shape, lines, colors, composition, and other factors discussed in this chapter. Butterfly Air, rising out of the fog into the golden background, metaphorically illustrates how the artist, after having been lost, wandering blindly through the wilderness of deep depression, and fighting a vortex of despair, came to enlightenment (see also chapter 12.2). The dark and massive appearance of the podium signifies the gravity-like force of her past perception of life, which no longer possesses the power to keep her earthbound. The image of Air, floating freely above the dull, brown podium, is the metaphoric expression of Susanne's achievement in overcoming the gloom of the past.

10.5 Ephemerality

In the poetic commentary, the artist described butterfly Air as "just visiting, hovering in an ephemeral moment before the unpredictable disappearance." She recognized it as an enigma, which could be a metaphorical representation of something that is "fluctuating" in and out of our perception. One can only speculate about this butterfly's intrinsic qualities, which Susanne sensed as being of a transcendental nature. The imagery of Air contains visual traces that signal the existence of some dormant meaning that we unveiled during our research as the spiritual aspect of this surrealistic image.

In the depiction of butterfly No. 7 in flight and the corresponding statement in the poetic commentary, Susanne captured her observation of ever-changing shapes, colors, and positions of the living butterflies as they impressed her at the Museum of Natural History. She might have also unintentionally incorporated certain memories from her experiences from earlier times. Her artistic imagination could be the manifestation of pleasant transient events that only lasted for a fleeting moment (ephemerality) and then disappeared unpredictably, to her disappointment, thereby prompting her to long for their return.

Sudden thoughts, intuitive feelings, daydreams, contradictory tendencies, desires, and other mental activities arise as ephemeral moments in the conscious mind. The control over their appearance or disappearance often causes a great deal of difficulty. These temporary phenomena leave memory traces that influence different aspects of existence, and they can resurface as coded images in works of art.

Susanne's choice of the word "visiting" in the commentary might indicate that too often in her life the positive emotions had turned out to be only momentary, vanishing rapidly and leaving her behind, alone and deprived of attention. When Susanne visits her family home in Germany, she

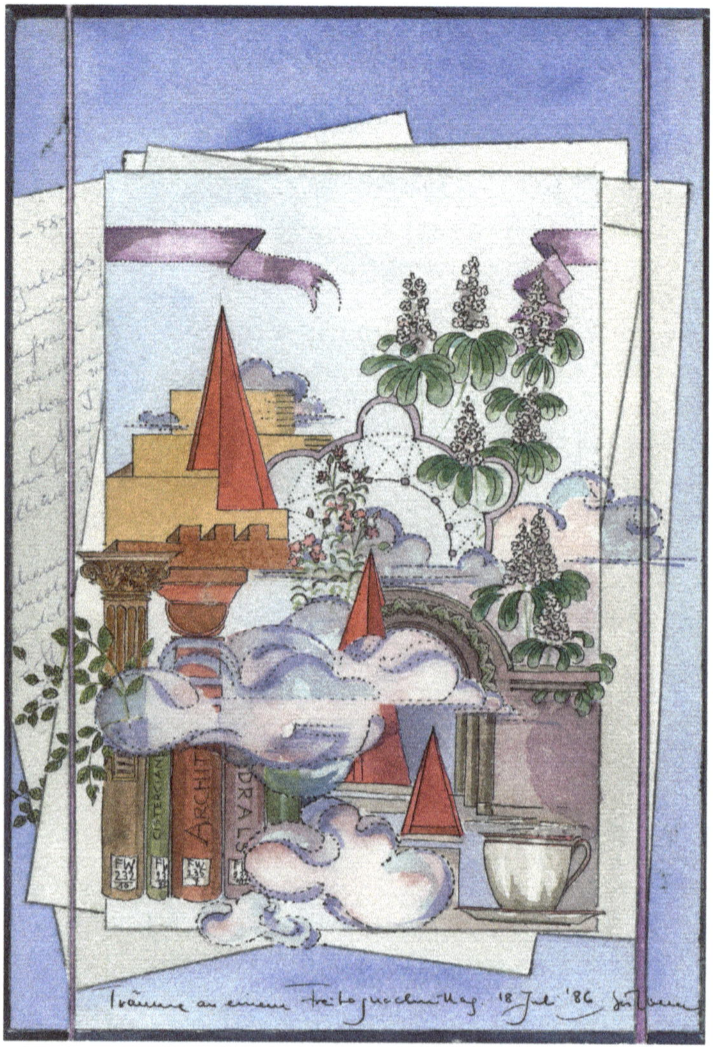

Fig. 10.30. Susanne Schuenke, *räume an einem Freitagnachmittag* (Dreams on a Friday Afternoon) 1986. watercolor, 9½ x 6¾ in (24 x 17 cm). Collection of the artist.

has many associations about different events and significant emotional experiences connected with her past.

Many delightful emotions are connected with antique treasures in her family home, which are much more than only objects to Susanne, as those pieces evoke the cherished sentiments linked with her childhood and youth. A specific glass or dish can give her a flashback of the family celebrating the holidays. Sometimes a favorite painting revives the memory of the time when she was with her parents at an art fair discussing the artwork before deciding to acquire it. In an instant, a certain item treasured by the family can trigger a cascade of thoughts and feelings about the captivating moments from the past in Susanne's mind. Her admiration for her parents includes their interest and knowledge, their paintings, their keen involvement in creating beauty and sharing the excitement of it, their smiles and tone of voice, the allure of the transitory smells of cigarettes and coffee they enjoyed, and the comforting feeling of being together as a close-knit family sharing precious, intimate moments.

From her earliest years, she had an intense need to observe her mother and father, which made Susanne highly acute in scrutinizing any smell, tone, movement, or change in the parents' behavior. Susanne's perceptions are a basis for idiosyncratic reactions, indicating the emotionally significant experiences of the past. We emphasize some additional concrete information: In her childhood, she was strongly attracted to specific desirable smells, such as the fragrance of her parents' skin, the mother's perfume lingering in clothes, and the aroma on Susanne's hands after washing them with her father's favorite soap. The waft of scent accompanying a kiss and a quick retreat, stolen from her mother's cheek before she could protest, made the girl long for more such kisses. Even today, when she catches a whiff of a freshly lit cigarette, the scent that she was accustomed to in her parents' home, her mind is immediately flooded with memories of those pleasant times.

Her receptivity also applies to such coincidental events as a wisp of a gentle breeze, a caressing ray of sunlight, a quick movement of a bird just flying by, or specific sounds. To all this, Susanne often reacts in a highly affected manner. These transitory sensations evoke emotional pleasure that she desires to prolong.

Ephemerality is also relevant to ideas. Her parents emphasized the fleeting aspect of thoughts and inspirations in their statement: "An idea never comes twice." This sentence is ingrained in Susanne's mind. From age 11 on, she made a habit of writing down or sketching her transient ideas immediately before they would evaporate for good. She has acted since then accordingly, keeping a record of her creative work, such as annotating, dating, signing, and archiving.

Perhaps it is from this perspective that we might have a better understanding of the annotations "echo lines?" that Susanne wrote down next to the image of butterfly No. 7 in the compositional drawing. It could be a sign of the hasty attempt to capture her spontaneous association: the volatile impression of the essence of the image that she had just redrawn. This reference is accompanied by the question marks, which might signify her hesitation about the latent meaning she intuitively felt but could not adequately articulate.

Returning once more to the experience of scents, it is necessary to mention that the artist's mother was traumatized by the firebombing of her hometown Berlin in World War II. As a result, whenever she smelled smoke in the house, she was in panic, and everyone in the family had to immediately search for the source of the potential threat. It is informative that during the analysis of the phrase "ephemeral moment" in the poetic commentary, the following spontaneous fantasy came to Susanne's mind. In her imagination, a pile of paper on a desk situated in front of her suddenly emitted a small flame, which quickly grew into a substantial fire threatening to engulf the entire house. In this imaginary burning house, her mind was consumed by running through various feasible scenarios to extinguish the fire and save her home. This fantasy illustrates how strong empathetic identification exists in Susanne's psyche. Her reverie indicates the connection with her mother's obsession that has become a quintessential symbolic expression associated with threatening situations, concerning her parents' past. Many years ago, there was a real situation when a small fire broke out in the parents' home and was extinguished by the fire department before major damage occurred.

We have previously pointed out in chapter 4 that fire and its associations were somehow connected with the image of Firebird as the personification of her father, and with significant facets of his behavior and personality as well. In her childhood and much of her adolescence, Susanne idolized her father, and during those periods, as far as she can recall, she did not notice any severe and prolonged outbreak of his hot, volcanic temper. Her father's painfully caustic and berating conduct started when Susanne was in her late teens. This behavior dominated the family life for the subsequent decades, and was no longer congruent with the daughter's idealization of him as the "good father."

These unpredictable eruptions of the father's anger increased in frequency and were followed by hours and even days in which everyone was wrapped in a gloomy mood.[56] Peace and harmony in the family had become a series of short-lived, ephemeral periods that were regularly broken. Due to those uncertainties, she developed the apprehension that happiness could be lost at any moment. Her mother had once remarked about it, "When you become aware that you are happy, then the happiness has already passed." This confirmed Susanne's concerns that nothing lasts permanently in this world.

With the father's choleric temper which caused stressful situations in the family, the task of adjusting to his increasingly unsettling behavior became steadily more challenging. Susanne's

56 While discussing and describing this topic during the analysis, Susanne was stricken with sudden fatigue accompanied by a nearly irresistible desire to sleep. This reaction could well be one of her defense mechanisms to avoid the unpleasant memories and the ambivalent emotions associated with her father.

emotional state alternated significantly depending on his conditions. Her mother demanded from her daughters that they accommodate his irrational mood swings for the sake of peace. The family later came to realize that the father's out-of-control anger was a side effect of his advancing diabetes.

The features of ephemerality could be traced in the metaphorical expressions found in some peculiar details of the image of butterfly Air. For instance, there are empty spaces in both wings that can be considered as a non-coherent structure, which might be a symbolic expression of distinct alternation in Susanne's condition in accordance with various circumstances. The shape of the right wing appears reversed and upside down in comparison with the left one, and the clear gap between the two halves of the butterfly could also be construed to mirror the dissonance related to the artist's family situation and different way of thinking.

As noted previously (see subchapter 10.4.2), the ethereal structure of the wings of butterfly No. 7 and its immersion into the golden background, which represent spirituality, share the same symbolization. This supports our assumption that butterfly Air is a metaphor for encapsulating the artist's lifelong aspiration to find her spiritual identity, which would change the feelings of ephemerality into a perception of a positive lasting perspective in the future.

The representation of an ephemeral condition, as depicted in Air, is not new in Susanne's art. Over the decades, she has presented some other varieties of images in which she symbolized and visualized such short-lived moments. The well-established traditional metaphor of the bubble as representing the transitory nature of existence repeatedly finds employment in the artist's paintings, delivering a fundamental symbol for human perception of the ephemeral condition. The bubbles might disappear in the next moment, and with this visual symbolism, Susanne conveys the idea that human life is only a moment in the eternity of the universe. She expresses this meaning in a number of paintings. In *Epochs of Mankind* (Fig. 7.5), bubbles represent various eras of time, condensing centuries into fleeting instants. In *Rise of Karma* (Fig. 10.26), the same translucent spheres visualize souls that are supposed to be eternal. In *Intelligence* (Fig. 7.26), these fragile globules stand for ideas and thoughts that are, transitory for Susanne.

The artist's closing remark about butterfly No. 7 in the poetic commentary, "Air's iridescent qualities will charm you away," connotes her strong, positive emotional perception of this mysterious image. She remarks that the excitement of encountering something inexplicably beautiful is like a spiritual experience for her. One such instance is her fascination with objects that display striking scintillation. Susanne is familiar with the remarkable iridescence of the highly polished surfaces of mother-of-pearl. Certain seashells, specially buffed and prepared as objets d'art, display a lustrous surface, and they were treasured in her family's collection. A nautilus shell was the model from which her father skillfully depicted the pearlescent head of an athlete in his painting *The Weightlifter* (Fig. 4.5). We have also already noted in chapter 5 that Susanne expressed her admiration for the iridescent colors of the blue morpho species, when she was creating the image of butterfly True Blue, a personification of her father. In the same chapter, we have recounted Susanne's and her father's praise for a painting by Arnold Böcklin in an exhibition which displayed the play of light and colors on the shimmering mermaids' tails in masterful strokes.

A few more of her delightful experiences with shimmering objects come to mind from her childhood. For example, Susanne blew soap bubbles and followed the changing play of colors on the thin surface as the translucent spheres floated in the air. She also remembers being enchanted by the surprising appearance of iridescent colors on the plumage of the peacocks in her parents' garden, on a film patch of motor oil in a puddle, and on the bodies of some flies and beetles.

The expression "iridescent" could also bring to mind the captivating, magical appearance of the rainbow,[57] an ephemeral celestial arc in the sky. All that playful mystery of the light "charm[s] you away," and this poetical articulation might also be metaphorically expressed in the magnificent and fascinating colors of True Blue and Firebird

57 The word *iridescence*, which was coined in the late 18th century, has its ultimate root in the Greek word "Iris" (rainbow). In Greek mythology Iris is also the name of a messenger-goddess, the personification of the rainbow, who travels between the Olympian world and human world on the rainbow (after Konrat Ziegler and Walther Sontheimer, *Der Kleine Pauly: Lexikon der Antike in fünf Bänden*, (New York: Deutscher Taschenbuch Verlag, 1979), Volume 2, column 1452).

(see chapters 4 and 5), reflecting the memory of ephemeral moments associated with iridescence, signifying positive emotions.

10.6 Colors and Camouflage

As noted above, one of the peculiarities of butterfly Air is its coloration. While the other butterflies can be easily defined as "blue," "white," etc., butterfly No. 7's color scheme requires a closer look before concluding that it is a combination of many pale nuances of violet, purple, brown, ochre, yellow, and even of burnt orange, all executed in transparent paints. Due to their transparency, the extremely thin layers of colors on top of the gold leaf display a variety of iridescent hues.

As discussed in chapter 6 (Little Why), for a long time, yellow and violet, alone or together, have been colors that the artist dislikes. For Susanne, most yellows are very cold tints. She has a personal appraisal about violet: "It is an unclear tone for me. Maybe it takes away my favorite color red." However, her views did not stop her from using yellow and violet in her paintings. Usually, she employs them to characterize negative contexts.[58] Yet, this not the case in *Give Me Wings!*, where these tones are present in the butterflies Little Why (see chapter 6) and Air. The latter symbolizes spirituality and, therefore, possesses a high value for the artist. It seems to be a contradiction to use "negative" colors for this entity, but we can find clarification in the following considerations.

We recall the sequence in which Susanne assigned the colors to each butterfly in the watercolor. Butterfly No. 7 was the last one to receive its hues. In this situation, the artist pondered a number of reasons. Her choice of color had to comply with several conditions, which are as follows:

1.) The coloration for No. 7 had to avoid a high saturation because such "strong color" would "cut" the painting visually in half. Consequently, any color must be pale.

2.) The color choice should avoid a new hue, even the artist's favorites, reds or greens, because this would draw the focus exclusively to the center. She remembers having contemplated the alternative of cladding No. 7 in a white veil, but she abandoned this because it would be too similar to Touchless Misty and take away the individuality of both butterflies (Nos. 4 and 7).

3.) The main point for her was that the colors must preserve an overall harmony among all major chromatic components of the painting. She looked to the hues of all the butterflies and decided on pale violet, with deviations into purple, together with yellow and brown. The mentioned nuances match some hues from all the other butterflies. In this way, on the unconscious level, these color choices might symbolically imply the acceptance of and reconciliation with all other personifications that are represented in the painting.

These conscious and unconscious influences could have determined the gentle chromatic appearance of this butterfly. When seen in conjunction with the enigmatic shape and the transparency of the openwork wings, it may point to a specific, hidden meaning. The coloration imitates the golden background and conveys the illusion of fusing with it, especially through the use of translucent glazes. Layers of yellow and violet glazes on top of each other result in brownish hues. With this, butterfly Air gives the impression of a golden appearance, becoming a part of the background. The aim was to endow the butterfly with a comparable effect as the fluctuating nuances of the gold leaf's reflective surface under different illuminating conditions. This would give Air the illusion of merging optically into the golden background. Moreover, applying the coloration in a technique of transparent layers allowed the golden background to shine through the colors, which emphasized the specifically different nature of Air in comparison with the other butterflies, promoting the perception of its materiality fading away. These additional details and observations allude to butterfly Air sharing the same spiritual meaning as the golden background. This is one of the basic points of our assumption about Air's immaterial nature, which we were able to decipher after wandering "in absence of true understanding" for some time. When Susanne painted butterfly No. 7, she was convinced that its specific appearance and coloration was based completely on her conscious decision to avoid making this butterfly dominate the others, although she had already implicitly placed Air in the center of the composition.

58 For example: *Connoisseur* (the vulnerability and dependency of artists in the art world; Fig. 6.6), *Greed* (exposing the ugly face of human avarice; Fig. 6.14), *Change in the Weather* (commenting on political ambition; Fig. 6.12), and *Born to Starve* (calling attention to the tragedy of overpopulation; Fig. 6.13). For more details, see chapter 6.

Could there be any other interpretation to account for the creation of the chromatic appearance of Air? What could have caused the selection of a hue so obviously inconsistent with the artist's individual chromatic preferences? We also wonder if the unattractive colors of butterfly Air, the combination of pale violet and a muddy yellow-ochre (which the artist considers ugly) unconsciously serves as a cloak for this butterfly's inner meaning. Therefore, its appearance is a diversion that prevents something extremely precious underneath from being revealed. To elevate Air as something of the highest value, Susanne could have painted this butterfly in any striking and beautiful color that she usually reserves for such an occasion. For example, she could have used sparkling white and gold, as one of the annotations in her first drawing indicates (Fig. 2.2), or perhaps, her most favorite hue of spectacular crimson red. In this case, the butterfly would have undeniably become the central focus of the composition and openly exhibited the artist's favoring this entity. However, by principally employing the disliked combination of violet and yellow, which she modified in pale hues, she downplayed the image's appearance and inadvertently furnished the butterfly with a disguise.[59]

Susanne neither had the conscious intention nor was aware of her procedure of concealment when she used a combination of those colors. Did she unconsciously create this deceptive effect? Our answer is "yes." Air, as the representation of spirituality, could be vulnerable to attacks in accordance with this topic, particularly with its parapsychological content. By adding violet as a tint of negativeness to yellow for the appearance of Air, she made the butterfly less attractive.[60] Consequently, her psyche employed protective camouflage as a defense mechanism against the detection of the highly valued concepts.

As mentioned above, Air's coloration of pale yellow and ochre inconspicuously imitates the golden background, so that the butterfly can pass unnoticed. In essence, the colors of Air are repeating the neighboring hues like a chameleon. This camouflage is also present in the curved lines of the lower part of Air's right wing. They overlap with the corresponding ridge-lines of Touchless Misty's front wing (Fig. 10.29, right part), which conceal the lower part of Air in the dragon wings of Touchless Misty. Therefore, Air fuses by shapes and colors into its surroundings, which disguise the butterfly's existence. This might explain the initial difficulty many observers experience, when looking at the painting for the first time, in noticing the presence of the seventh butterfly. Deciphering the latent meaning residing within the peculiarities of colors and configuration of the image of Air as representing spirituality supports our assumption of a protective camouflage.

By blending and partly submerging this butterfly into its golden surroundings, the artist signifies their spiritual unity. This choice allows the golden background which represents the spiritual realm (see chapter 12) in the painting to shine through, by which Air and the background are intrinsically linked. Additional support for this interpretation comes from the poetic commentary where Susanne describes the appearance of butterfly No. 7: "With the lights mirroring on its wings, Air's iridescent qualities will charm you away," in which the butterfly's qualities that she speaks of are actually determined by the optical properties of the golden background (see chapter 12, note 27).

59 In the discussion of this context with Susanne, she drew the comparison with "éminence grise," a term familiar to her, as an expression for the low-key appearance of a person with extraordinarily powerful influence. She knows this phrase especially from a painting by Jean-Léon Gérôme (1824–1904) titled, *L'Eminence Grise* (oil on canvas, Museum of Fine Arts, Boston). This painting portrays François Leclerc du Tremblay, a Capuchin friar who was a confidant and confederate of Cardinal Richelieu, the Prime Minister of the French King Louis XIII. In Gérôme's work, the friar's humble and unobtrusive appearance is deceptive, as his association with Richelieu empowers him with much authority and influence, and those who happened to be in his presence are seen compelled to acknowledge it by paying him their respects with postures of reverence and subservience. The same situation applies to the image of Air which is of great importance to Susanne. Butterfly Air, in spite of its abstract and plain appearance, holds the center of the composition and is framed by butterflies Nos. 3 and 4, both turned toward it.

60 Writing this reminded Susanne of what she read about a custom in the Chinese culture of the past: The parents, hoping to protect their newborn children from harm, believed that by referring to them with derogative and disparaging names, it would make their most precious babies "unattractive" to evil spirits, who would otherwise in jealousy whisk away the children. She considers this a kind of verbal subterfuge in a specific mental environment, perhaps foreign to our present time, to defend against the high infant mortality rate that former societies suffered before the advent of medical science.

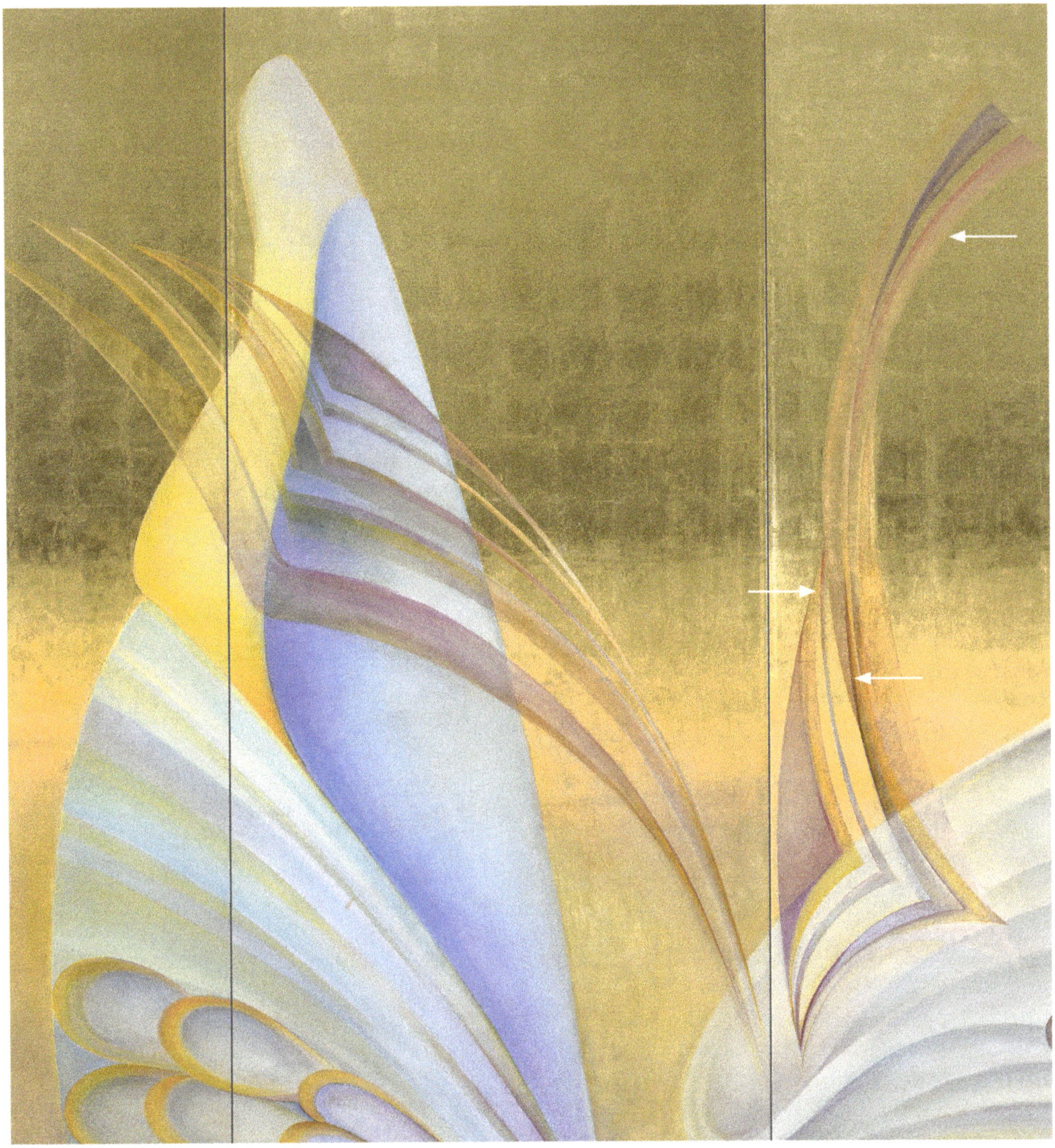

Fig. 10.31. Arrows point to traces of burnt orange in the right wing of butterfly No. 7, Air.

In the course of analyzing this particular aspect of their interconnection, Susanne had a spontaneous association that offered a new perspective, presenting us with a different facet of metaphorical meaning in the merging of the image and the background. As an art historian, she was well aware of the medieval vision of sacred architecture in which the Divine light emanating from the sun passes through the colorful stained glass windows of a gothic cathedral and illuminates their pious scenes so that God's presence, by the means of the light, fills the interior of the church and enlightens the minds of the believers.[61] The medieval visitors in the church perceived the sunlight shining through the colorful glass pictures as a spiritual experience. Following this thought, Susanne might have created the golden background as an unconscious representation of the "spiritual light" which passes

61 The French Gothic cathedral was one of Susanne's oral PhD examination topics, for which she had spent a considerable time studying. For the metaphysical experiences of observers in the 12th century, see for example: Otto von Simson, *Die Gotische Kathedrale* (Darmstadt: Wissenschaftliche Buchgesellschaft (WBG), 1979, pp.77–82 and 169–174).

through Air's wing structure, and permeates the entire painting. Using light as a sign for the sacred and the transcendent is a universal theme in art and myths. Therefore, the metaphoric link between light and the divine becomes relevant in analyzing the artist's painting.

There is another significant observation in Air's coloration. Among the nuances of orange, we can clearly identify several small slivers of burnt orange embedded in the yellow-violet hues of the image of Air (Fig. 10.31). The color burnt orange was analyzed in detail in butterfly No. 3, Pale Moonlight, and recognized as an unconsciously developed personal symbol signifying sexual tendencies (see chapter 8.3.2). Areas in burnt orange can be found in four other butterflies (Nos. 1, 3, 5, and 6), signaling the same meaning. We came to the premise that butterfly No. 7 simultaneously signifies not only the existence of spiritual essence but also the corporeal basis. The identification of the signs of the sexual drive even in this spiritual image could be found in the traces of burnt orange color that are present in Air as unconscious symbolism (see the following subchapter 10.6). Considering the coloration in question as a sign of biological drives, we might recognize it as a marker of these imperatives in butterfly Air.

In spite of Susanne's suppression of the biological drives to a level of remote significance, they press themselves into pronounced presence, manifesting not only in her fantasies, dreams, and different neurotic reactions, but also in her paintings.

In the case of butterfly Air, the instinctual drives are metaphorically disguised underneath a wrap of spirituality. As we have repeatedly mentioned, the mechanism of camouflage works to cover up the appearance of biological forces in the images of all the butterflies, and the same principle is present in the image of Air. Furthermore, the interpretation of the image of Air could suggest that the biological drives and spirituality are integral constituents of the modus operandi of the unconscious.

10.7 Spiritual Need

Butterfly No. 7, as a metaphorical, visual expression of spirituality, reflects the artist's pathways of her personal development. Many signs in the structure and coloration of this singular creature could be of paramount importance in understanding the influence of the unconscious from the perspective of social evolution,[62] constituting "a 'social me' and a 'spiritual me'."

Susanne regards the various phenomena of spirituality as her private concern, in view of the skeptical attitude that pervades contemporary technological societies to this matter. While growing up, she learned that talks of spiritual and transcendental experiences will often be met with incredulity and ridicule, particularly when they are outside the bounds of the traditional faiths. As a consequence, she has been reluctant to freely discuss these topics even with relatives and friends. In effect, she has been keeping her self-imposed silence because of her prior experience with others, in which they expressed an unsympathetic, if not outright hostile attitude toward her thoughts and vision.

In subchapter 10.4.5, we explored Susanne's quest for the meaning of life, which was driven by various ongoing circumstances and inner demands for an answer. This situation persisted for many years. Her search for a solution brought her to a path of spirituality that was introduced to her by her friend Tanja and solidified by a specific quote of the philosopher Pascal. Their wisdom resonated powerfully in her mind. The precepts of Tanja and Pascal gradually became the quintessence of the artist's further development.

In general perspective, Susanne's inner growth and maturation reflects the process of socialization in the evolution of a human being. Spirituality as an innate need, by compulsive perseveration, and its psychological dynamics, could be regarded as a powerful, modifying psychic force that lies dormant in the human mind. Her preoccupation with spiritual contemplations could be comparable to the tension and ambivalence that accompany the fulfillment of the biological drives.

Susanne's spiritual needs were disclosed not only from her life history but also through her art, which was significantly determined by her unconscious, as we have discovered numerous symbolic references to it, revealing an assortment of information in the details of her paintings during our analysis. Her insatiable desire for a higher meaning indicates the strength of this

62 Damasio 2010, page 24.

psychic force and its innate nature, analogous to biological drives. This assumption finds confirmation in Michael Graziano's research in which he states: "We are all spiritual. ... It is built into our social machinery"[63] in the process of the evolution of the BrainMind. Regarding spirituality as a phenomenon of biological and social evolution, he wrote: "The spirit world exists but only as information instantiated on the hardware of the brain." His view is that spirituality provides a survival advantage to the individuals united in a group for adjustment to the environment.

The image of butterfly Air, as a transmitter of the artist's thoughts about the nature of existence and her significant emotional experiences related to it, could be recognized as unconscious visualization of spiritual essence. On the one hand, spirituality, as a distinctive aspect of humankind, could be considered one of the important attributes that indicates the progress of the gradual development of human consciousness. It has always been promoted and serves as a marker of a society's level of civilization. On the other hand, human history shows that at certain times, because of the intolerance of the dominant faith, particular spiritual beliefs had to be hidden in order for them to survive. Traditionally, at least in the West, spirituality has usually been considered a derivative of the conscious mind. However, could spirituality only be recognized as a particular construct of it?

We consider that, in the long process of psychic evolution of the human BrainMind, spirituality has become an intrinsic need that longs to be fulfilled in the same manner as other instinctual drives do. The image of Air, as the metaphorical visualization of spiritual existence, integrates not only the artist's personal experiences (see also chapters 11 and 12), but it also symbolically reflects the essentially spiritual nature of the human being as viewed from the perspective of the social evolutionary process.

We have argued throughout this chapter that many of the symbolic expressions that we found in the image of Air have their origins in the artist's personal unconscious. Nevertheless, we also assumed that some of the building material of the butterfly's image came from phylogenetic memory. The biological and social aspects are integrated through their interactions and connectedness via various psychic processes of transformation, such as sublimation, replacement, camouflage, condensation, symbolic visual representation, creativity, fantasies, dreams, various pathological expressions, secondary elaboration, and so forth. In this context, we could surmise that a spiritual need, embedded in unconscious processes, may exist as significant a force to be reckoned with as any other instinctual drives, whose appropriate fulfillment could be critical in constituting the mind.

The acceptance of the co-existence of biological drives and spiritual needs would distance us from a tendentious, confined, one-sided point of view. On this basis, an integral approach could be created for the interpretation of the numerous conjunctions between the traditional biological drives and spiritual needs, properly accounting for their combined influences and multifarious manifestations.

Thus, we are prompted to ask the fundamental question: Did the unconscious manifest the spiritual in the imagery as an innate need? Is there a natural urge for this within the artist's psyche in order to realize a wish-fulfilling function? Or, is it an attribute of the censorship of the superego, with the aim to strive for a socially respectable human ideal? The significance of the issue posed in this interpretation cannot be overestimated. We believe the valid answer to these questions does not lie in a unilateral solution but in a multilateral, impartial approach. In our assessment, the image of Air signifies the co-existence of the biological forces and the social and spiritual reality standing together as a symbol of wholeness: a bio-psycho-socio-spiritual integral.

63 Graziano, 2013, (page 212; the next quote: page 227).

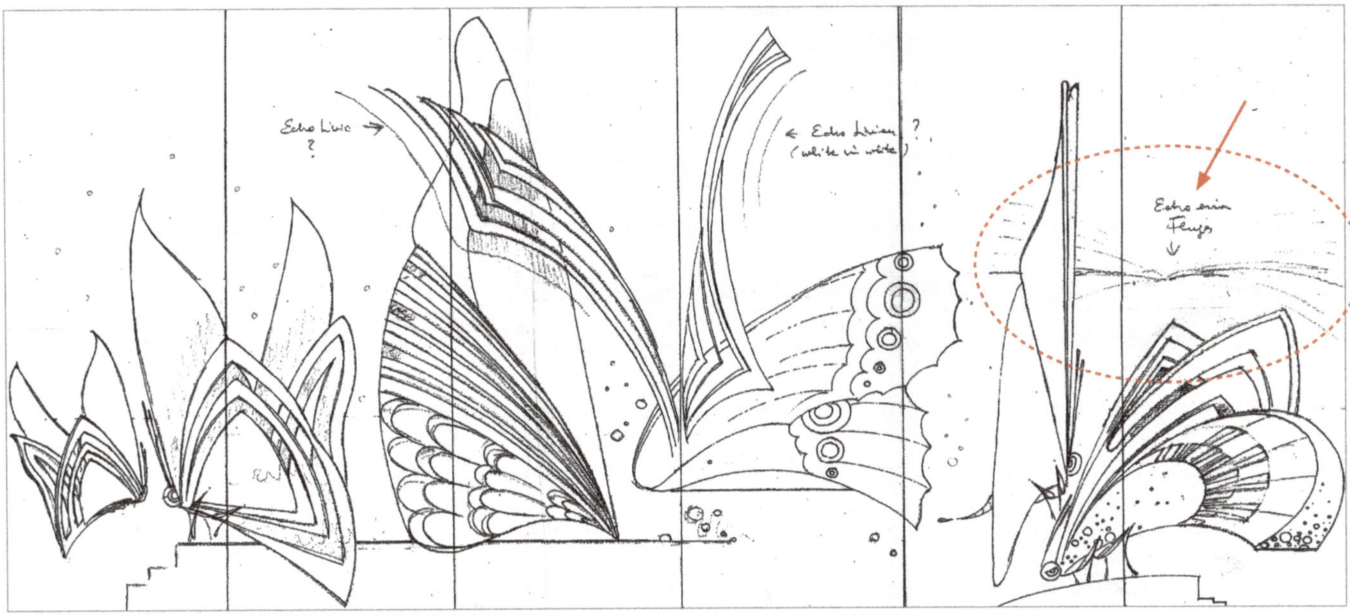

Fig. 11.0. The compositional drawing (the drawing used for the watercolor), Dec. 23 2003. Encircled in red: the "Eighth Butterfly." The arrow pointing to the artist's note.

Chapter 11

The Eighth Butterfly — Echo of a Flight

She is gone

11.1 Discovery of Butterfly No. 8: Image and Annotation

While analyzing the development of the images in *Give Me Wings!* from the first sketches through the different stages to the finished oil painting, an additional butterfly, whose existence Susanne had forgotten, was serendipitously recognized. This discovery was made above the butterfly Fanning Everything. Upon closer inspection of the photocopy of the compositional drawing for the watercolor (Fig. 2.11), the analyst paid attention to the rightmost German annotation in this drawing, *Echo eines Fluges* ("Echo of a flight"). The writing appears above a couple of strong lines and nearly a dozen very faint ones originating at a common point and fanning out (Fig. 11.0). This enigmatic line configuration, which for the purpose of identification we have named "Butterfly No. 8," could be thought of as a representation of fluttering wings wide open in flight.

The image was never developed beyond this drawing. The butterfly spans from approximately the middle of the fifth section of the drawing to the right edge of the sixth section. It is positioned behind Firebird's front wings and above butterfly No. 6. The configuration of faint outspread lines suggests a winged creature flying away from those two butterflies and receding into the background.

Due to the thin pencil strokes, the butterfly appears to be depicted only in one dimension, for neither the surface of the wings nor the depth of its body can be discerned. These details will become significant for our interpretation of butterfly No. 8 and its meaning. Looking up the specific sketches from the American Museum of Natural History Butterfly Conservatory (Fig. 11.1), the artist recalled the amazement she experienced watching those ever-moving butterflies. She was musing on how exuberantly the life force manifested the essence of their existence in the vigor of their flight.

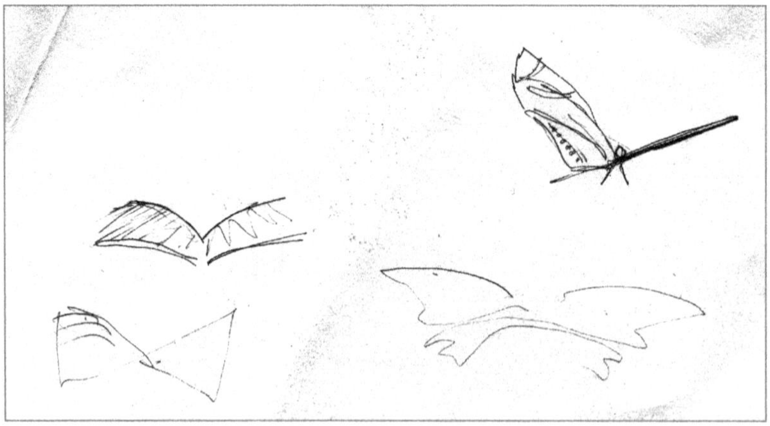

Fig. 11.1. Detail from Fig. 2.1(d). A sketch from the butterfly conservatory.

The same sketches also elicited regretful nostalgia because of her vain desire to freeze the butterflies' alluring, transient movements.

Susanne remembers her frustration at failing to capture the nuances of the fast-moving shapes and colors dancing in front of her eyes, while the insects flew about in a frenzy. Innumerable fascinating movements eluded her sight, and she experienced their disappearance with a sigh. She had the feeling of disappointment at not being able to hold on to the ephemeral moment. The artist spontaneously coined the term "echo of a flight" to express her impression. During the analysis, we became aware of some significant meaning encapsulated in this annotation that she had written to herself.

11.2 Metaphorical Meaning of Image and Annotation

We can expect that implicit reasons exist for the expression "echo of a flight," as well as why this image of butterfly No. 8 vanished in the subsequent watercolor and oil painting. Presumably, the artist's mind unconsciously imparted important metaphorical meanings to the image, to the accompanying words, and even to the butterfly's eventual disappearance.

As our study progressed, Susanne was asked about the possible meaning of these faint lines in conjunction with the metaphorical notation "echo of a flight." She replied that the figure could symbolize the memory and emotions of the bereaved, regarding a person who has passed away, or it could be equivalent to a departed person's spiritual essence or energy. She added that her philosophical view concerning the impermanence of earthly life and its eventual dissolution is embodied in the image of butterfly No. 8 flying away into the background. Moreover, she continued, this "may be the unknown dimension of a deceased one, meaning that person's soul," which was unconsciously encoded in the drawn image.

11.3 Influences on the Creation of the Image

The artist's notation, "echo of a flight," and her speculative comment about this butterfly indicate possible meaningful sources of the creation of this peculiar image. In this section, we examine those factors that may have contributed to the portrayal of the butterfly. First of all, we will outline the artist's thoughts about death and the soul that were possibly expressed in the imagery of butterfly No. 8. Furthermore, we will examine images from the artist's painting, *Freedom*, which she created in direct connection with her mother's death, and analyze the relevant, emotional experiences.

11.3.1 The Artist's Concept of Death

In Susanne's family, as already mentioned in previous chapters, the topic of death was taboo because her father prohibited the use of the word "dead" in Hochdeutsch (High German or Standard German).[1] He had a superstition that pronouncing the word could bring about the dreaded fate. Father also forbade any member of the family to wear black, a sign of death for him. His vehement rejection of this inevitable human destiny did not influence Susanne the same way. Moreover,

1 The Standard or High German pronunciation for *Tod* (death) and *tot* (dead) is identical (pronounced tōt). However, Susanne's father, although a Standard German speaker, switched to a dialectal ("Low" or Low Saxon) German, where the *t* in these words were pronounced with a soft *d* instead of the standard sharp *t*, whenever he had to use those words in a conversation, perhaps thinking that by intentionally mispronouncing these words he could cheat Death.

her attitude developed in the opposite direction. During her teens, she became attracted to the topic of suicide and reading Henrik Ibsen's plays, as mentioned in chapter 10, made her curious to explore this subject. Over the decades, her personal thoughts about death have evolved due to her spiritual development. The artist considers death as a mere steppingstone in a continuing cycle of existence. For her, it is neither the beginning nor the end, but simply a transition from life on earth with its singular possibilities to another phase of existence that offers its own new opportunities for spiritual unfolding and realization.

With this understanding, she no longer feels the seductive appeal of self-inflicted death as a solution for a desperate situation in life. Suicide would, in essence, cut short whatever potential with which one might have been endowed, particularly in regard to certain allotted talents and spiritual tasks that she feels all individuals come into this world to fulfill. Thus, a self-perpetrated death would interfere with their life's natural development.[2]

In this context, it becomes a tragic and premature solution for someone who has given up because the individual's mind has become paralyzed by despair. Now, for Susanne, death will be the logical outcome only when a life has either achieved its objective or exhausted all its chances and capacities to reach further fulfillment in a life cycle. From this point of view, dying could be celebrated as the liberation of the soul from the demands and restrictions of earthly existence.

Virtually all major religions of the world teach that after death the soul enters into other realms of existence. The merits or demerits that have been acquired throughout the life, from which it has just departed, have different developments. Some religions do not allow any further evolution for the soul and declare one is either eternally rewarded or punished. Other faiths consider the soul's continual spiritual growth as the very purpose of its coming into this world.

For Susanne, the concept of reincarnation holds an acceptable explanation for the mystery of eternal existence and the soul's aspiration to reach spiritual maturity. This belief is featured in Eastern religions, such as Hinduism and Buddhism, but also in pre-Christian European cults. To attain the sacred, the soul must be given repeated opportunities. The barely recognizable "echo" traces of butterfly No. 8, still lingering in an enigmatic linear arrangement in the air, might be indicative of such a transcendental journey.

11.3.2 Spiritual Entity and Soul

As we may recall from chapter 10, the artist's belief in the existence of parapsychological phenomena and soul had a significant influence on the creation of the image of butterfly No. 7, Air, as a metaphorical representation of spirituality. Susanne's attitude toward death and the afterlife, we can expect, had an impact on the appearance and disappearance of butterfly No. 8.

Comparing the "lost butterfly" No. 8 with No. 7, we can observe noticeable correspondences of their wispy linear shapes; their interspaces, which present the imagery resembling a multiple-exposure view; and their wings spread open, giving the impression that they are moving away. The artist calls these specific configurations "my surreal impression of oscillation." Overall, there is a palpable sense of the two images presenting an attempt at portraying something ethereal and invisible. The short comments written above the images of butterflies No. 7 and No. 8 are similar in their wording and suggest a common underlying definition. The features shared by both butterflies could contain related symbolic meanings.

The artist previously hinted that this vanished butterfly may have symbolized a departed person's spiritual essence or energy. Even so, she did not make the connection between this perception and the possibility that the imagery of butterfly No. 8 in her drawing might be an unconscious representation of her mother's soul until the intriguing positioning of this butterfly above Fanning Everything was pointed out during the analysis. This assumption was accepted by the artist due to the fact that butterfly No. 8 spans over Fanning Everything, a personification of her mother.

Having gained this insight, she suddenly felt a very strong urge to check the date of the compositional drawing, wondering if it had anything to do with a certain significant date

2 Committing suicide would only be an interruption of this process. Hypothetically, the problematic situation, without the appropriate solution to resolve the difficulty, will be presented again in one of the next life cycles in an even more challenging circumstance. Therefore, nothing would be gained through the premature, self-inflicted death; indeed, much will be made worse by it. Later, Susanne found confirmation of this in the works by Weiss 1988, Newton 1996, and Rankin 2007.

pertaining to her mother. The drawing is extant only as a photocopy made during the work process and, as such, has neither the date nor signature on it. However, the artist clearly remembers her excitement when the copy of the compositional drawing was made. Then, she transformed the drawing into a watercolor. Susanne worked until its completion that evening, and she experienced a feeling of being totally exhausted. Therefore, the artist concludes that the date on the watercolor, which was recorded on the work, is also valid for the compositional drawing.

To her amazement, she found that the watercolor is dated December 23, 2003 and titled "Before the Flight" (Fig. 2.12). This date is the day and month when, one year earlier in 2002, her mother underwent heart surgery in Germany, from which she died five days later without regaining consciousness.[3] Since then, December 23 has taken on an extraordinary significance for Susanne as a day of remembrance. Obviously, on that day in 2003, during the long hours of working with the compositional drawing, when butterfly No. 8 and the accompanying comment entered the design, the artist was under the influence of this painful event, which had happened the year before.

11.3.3 A Singular Vision

From December 23, 2002 onward, Susanne, who had been living in the United States, received daily news from her family about the mother's worsening condition. Around 1 a.m. on December 28, she was informed by a phone call that her father and sisters were hurrying back to the hospital, as the mother's death was expected within a few hours. After the call, she sat in a meditative state with her eyes closed, in a dark room. She was trying to concentrate on sending some supportive energy in the form of white light to her mother and appealing to Providence repeatedly to grant "the best for Mommy."

After remaining in that state for some time, Susanne suddenly had a vision entirely inside her mind. A group of neatly arranged, shining rectangles appeared in precise alignment, one above another. As she continued to focus on the vision with fascination, the shape began to change. She explains: "Imagine the rectangles were printed on a fabric, like a flag; then a breeze started to blow, gently at first, then stronger." The entire formation began to undulate. As the rippling intensified, the rectangles suddenly transformed into shining triangles, which flew in all directions toward the periphery of her sight. While the triangular shapes were rushing away, small circles of various colors began to stream out from the center of her vision, heading outward. The whole sequence of changing colors and configurations reminded Susanne of a fireworks display.

With this visually stunning episode came an overwhelming sense of joy, euphoria, and bliss akin to a state about which the mystics of many cultures have spoken. The ecstasy was so powerful that tears of joy rolled down her cheeks. Susanne has never encountered such intense and positive emotions in her life, before or since, and they stay fresh and vivid in her memory to this day. What happened exactly to her on the night of her mother's death remains a mystery to Susanne. She has interpreted it as a confirmation of her spiritual beliefs. She narrates: "My mother had always been curious about what may come after death. Being without any religious framework, we both discussed once, many years ago, 'What if … ,' and I asked her, when the event would happen, if it were possible, to get in contact with me, at least one time, and let me know."

This conversation, as a dormant expectation, might have been one of the constituents for the remarkable spiritual experience, which Susanne considers to be the fulfillment of the mother's promise.

11.3.4 The Painting *Freedom*

The above vision made a deep impression on the artist, and, in the morning, she drew it from her memory in a small watercolor sketch (Fig. 11.2).[4]

One month later, after returning from the funeral in Germany, guided by this sketch, she expanded the scene with the addition of a pair of human figures, creating two preliminary drawings (Figs. 11.3 and 11.4) for the oil painting titled

3 Even more unmistakable and significant for this date is that Dec. 23 has a specific meaning in Susanne's family. This is the day before Christmas Eve, when her parents together with the children decorated the Christmas tree in the evening. The unexpected coma and subsequent death of the mother during the time of Christmas was particularly traumatic for the family.

4 The watercolor sketch depicts the sequence of the scenes from Susanne's vision progressively from left to right.

Freedom (2003, Fig. 11.5).[5] The changes, including the coloration, in the later painting indicate that she intended to create a symbolic work based not only on her visionary experience but also on her thoughts and imaginings about the transformative process from the earthly state of being to another realm beyond the physical. After the completion of *Freedom* in the summer of 2003, she wrote a commentary,[6] quoted in part below:

"On the left, out of pitch-black darkness appears a grating structure of unflinching rigidity (like a prison window). The strictness gets broken, starts vibrating and floating—the first step to liberation. The energy grows, the waves undulate, the colors oscillate—and sparkles explode from an unfathomable center.

Darkness changes from purple to glowing ultramarine, climbing up toward a celestial light—translucent hues of azure—setting the stage for the flight of the sparkles, each with their individual shape and course, toward another reality inside an apparent chaos, which holds its structure beyond our understanding.

From the left, a human finally walks away from the earthly rigidity. His hand rests for a passing moment on that cage, as his head turns back for a last look, but he strides forward in full awareness of his progress toward a totally new existence. Unhampered, he passes through the center of an exploding creation encouraged and assisted by someone (a second figure at the right) who appears like a mirage—a reflection of that first human figure. The second—'ghost'—figure possesses a strange translucent quality and represents a dimension of man, which you can neither pin down in the material realm, nor find through surgery or autopsy. It cannot be caged or killed. It is eternal."

The metaphorical description quoted above correlates directly with specific elements of the painting, *Freedom*, and it clarifies some of the artist's personal symbolism that she has employed. Furthermore, her deviations from the original vision, introducing additional elements, aided us significantly in arriving at our interpretations.

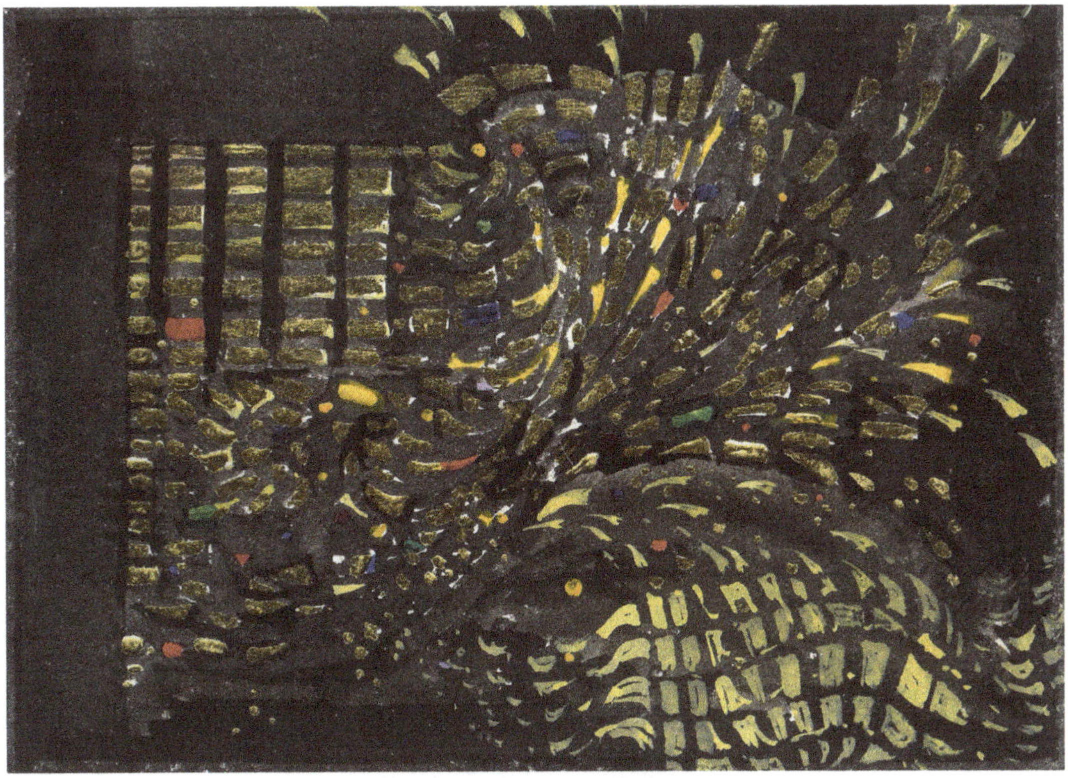

Fig. 11.2. Susanne Schuenke, *Sketch of the vision,* Dec. 28, 2002.
Watercolor, 4 x 5¾ in (10.3 x 14.7 cm). Collection of the artist's family, Germany.

5 The oil painting *Freedom* consists of four panels hinged together to form a folding screen to enable varying viewing perspectives. The work was completed a few months before the artist began to work on the design for *Give Me Wings!*.

6 We quote here the original without editing.

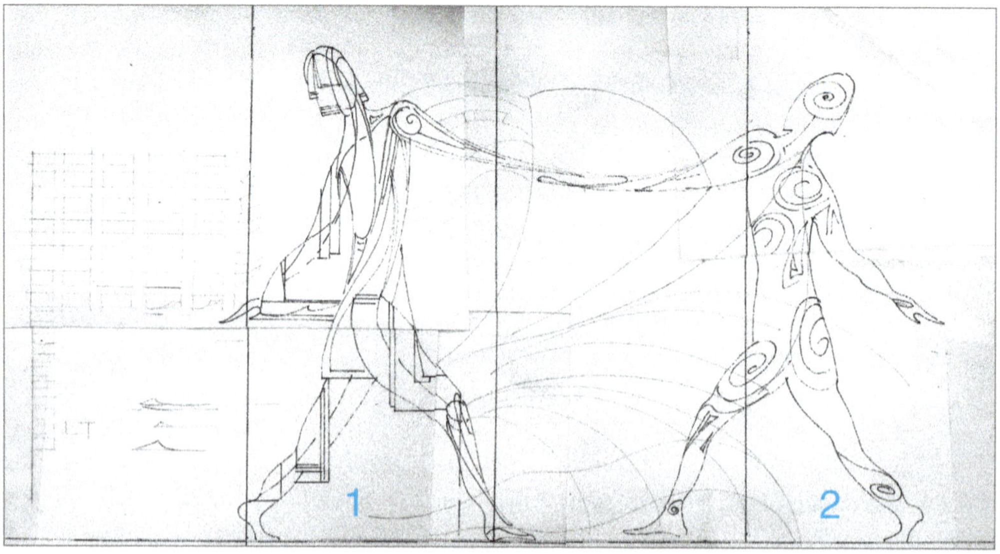

Fig. 11.3. Susanne Schuenke, Drawing figures for *Freedom*.

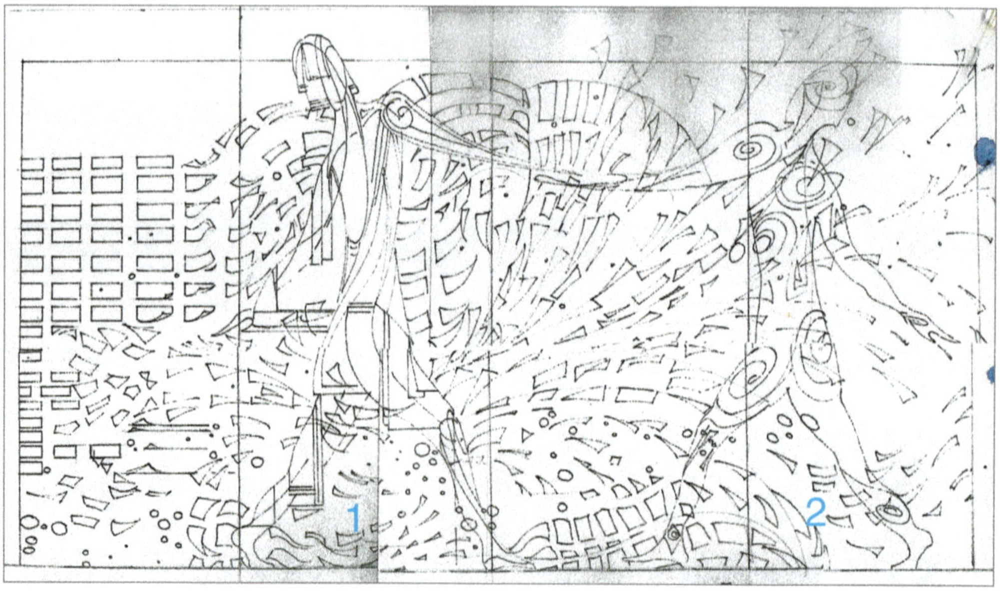

Fig. 11.4. Susanne Schuenke, Drawing for the oil painting.

The rigid grid pattern formed by the black ground might hint at demands and restrictions. These could be, for example, imposed by one's family and society, as well as by self-inflicted limitations, such as personal problems and complexes, or even universal imperatives, which hinder someone from achieving personal freedom and full creative potential. The grid configuration can, therefore, be inferred to symbolize imprisonment. The bright light[7] streaming through the rectangles gives the illusion of seeing the "openings between the bars of a prison cell."[8] To increase this perception, Susanne intentionally chose gold as the best medium to illustrate the incomparable luminosity that she experienced in the vision. Following the sequence of development in the vision, the restricting bars break down and tumble into disorder, giving way to the light, toward which golden triangles in various curvilinear configurations stream out. All this allegorically expresses the eruptive and inexorable transition toward freedom, once the prison walls have come down.

7 The light Susanne saw in her vision was such an incredibly bright white that it might be comparable with looking at the sun. It was the most intense light that she has ever seen; yet it was gentle and not blinding.

8 Technically, the painter achieved this effect by applying tapes over all the elements in her drawing that were to be gilded later before starting to paint. After this, she painted the canvas with black background, starting at the left edge and continuing with gradually lightening hues of blue to the right edge. Then she gilded the assigned areas after removing the adhesives.

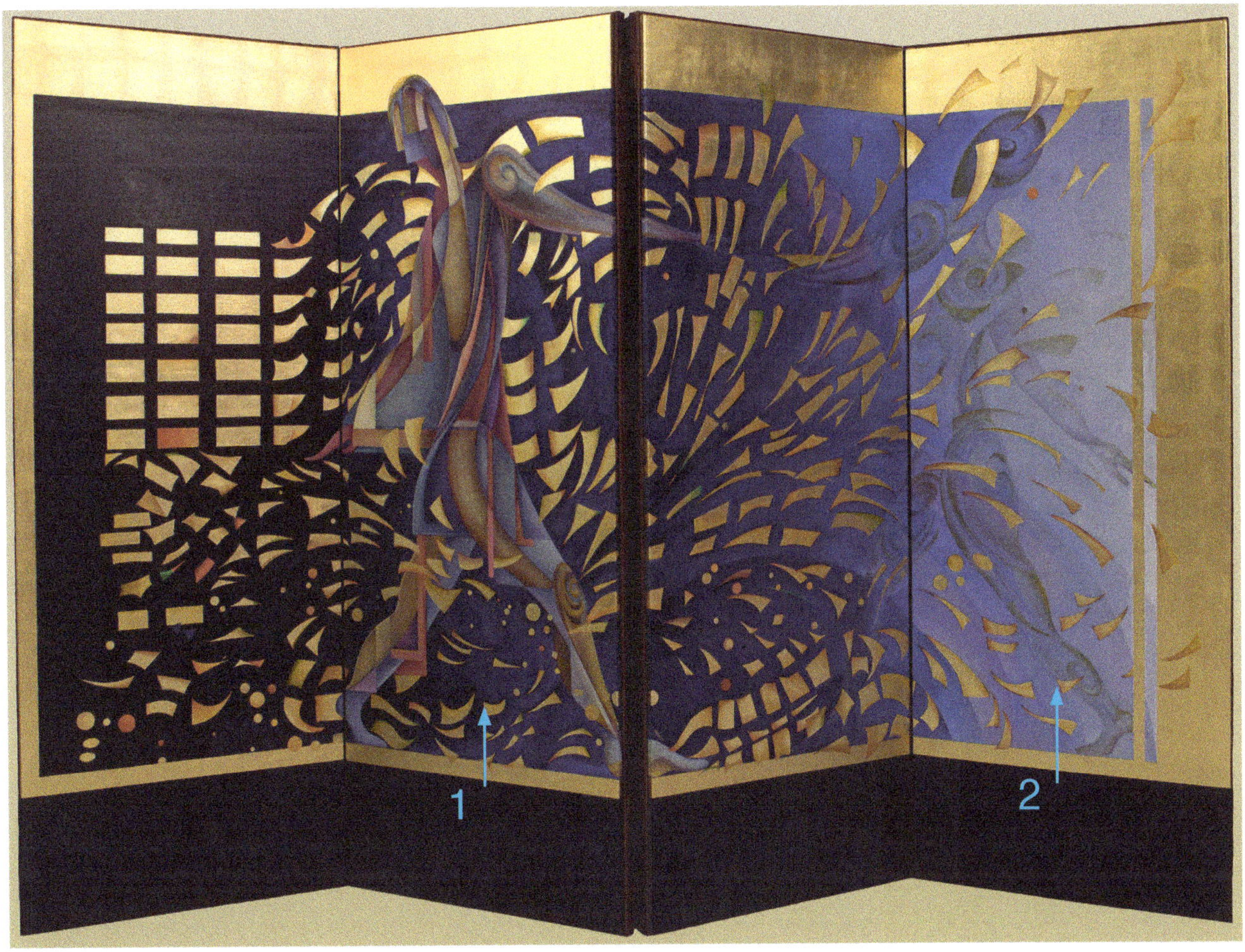

Fig. 11.5. Susanne Schuenke, *Freedom*, 2003.
Oil and gold leaf on canvas, 67 x 104 in (170 x 260 cm). Private collection, Florida.
The four-panel piece shown in folded-screen display. Arrows point to two figures.

We might wonder if this theme of the luminous light streaming out of the background has laid the foundation for the development of the symbolic, golden background in the painting *Give Me Wings!* a few months later. We will examine this further in the next chapter.

As mentioned above, when Susanne transferred her vision into a painting, she intentionally added two figures. Furthermore, she transformed the background from stark darkness into gradually lightening ultramarine, which is a color with strong spiritual associations for her. This coloration was not part of what she saw in her meditative state.

The first figure, (Figs. 11.3, 11.4 ("1"), and 11.5 ("1")), detaching his left hand and breaking his last contact with the confining environment, is leaving the rigidity of the physically-bound life. The figure is walking on the pathway from darkness into the light, attracted by the irresistible beauty and freedom of the illuminated, spiritual dimension that lies ahead.

The second figure (Figs. 11.3, 11.4 ("2"), 11.5 ("2")), a side-reversed counterpart of the first one, steps into the scene from the golden border on the right and reaches out a helping hand to assist the first figure with his passage to the higher domain.[9] This second figure is a representative of the positive

9 In the context of "passage" and the "spirit" guiding the human figure, Susanne suddenly had an association and recalled a scene from the performance of Mozart's *The Magic Flute* by the Metropolitan Opera in the 1990s. She was impressed by the visual image of the hero, Tamino, leading his beloved heroine, Pamina, on a path through a chamber of fire to test their courage, reaching out his hand to help her (in Act 2, scene 7). This scenario might have influenced this part of the design.

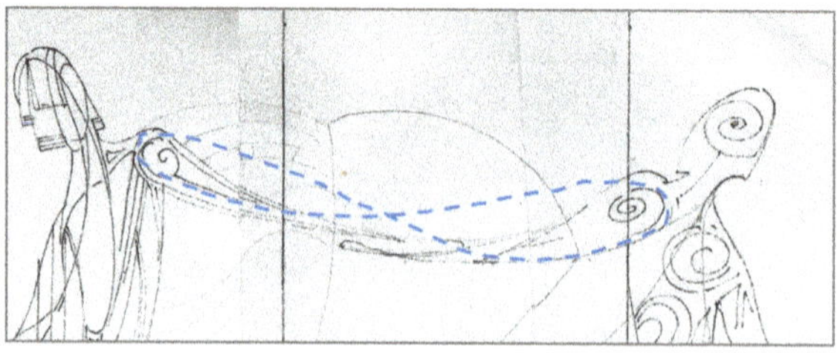

Fig.11.6. Detail from Fig. 11.3. The arms of both figures forming the symbol of infinity (indicated with overlay of a blue dotted line).

forces connected with the spiritual realm, which for Susanne epitomize the idea of a soul companion who leads the first one toward the golden zone.

The painting was designed as a four-part folded screen. The whole scene is surrounded by a continuous golden border, narrow at the bottom and left side, wide at the top and right side. This framing design can also be interpreted as the visible part of a golden ground behind the scene. The flying elements are reflecting the light from this "zone beyond." The artist understands this imagery as a metaphor for spirituality: "embracing all levels of existence."

The extended arms of each figure join in the middle of the third panel, thereby forming an elongated, horizontally laid figure eight, the symbol for infinity, "∞"[10] (Fig. 11.6). The artist intentionally embedded this mathematical symbol in the design to underscore the interconnectedness between the figures and to allude to the eternal process of transmutation from the earthly realm to the spiritual dimension and vice versa.

11.3.5 The Origin of the Figures

The figures in *Freedom* originated from an older pencil drawing that was connected with the topic of liberation. In London, 21 years before the creation of *Freedom*, the artist drew a human being who is attempting to break out of an unbearable situation—a scenario with which she identified herself (*Breaking Bondage*, 1982, Fig. 11.7).[11] This was the time when Susanne, a postgraduate student, suffered through the nadir of depression. Her persistent daily desire was to leave this life, and she longed for liberation from all the pressures that she was enduring.

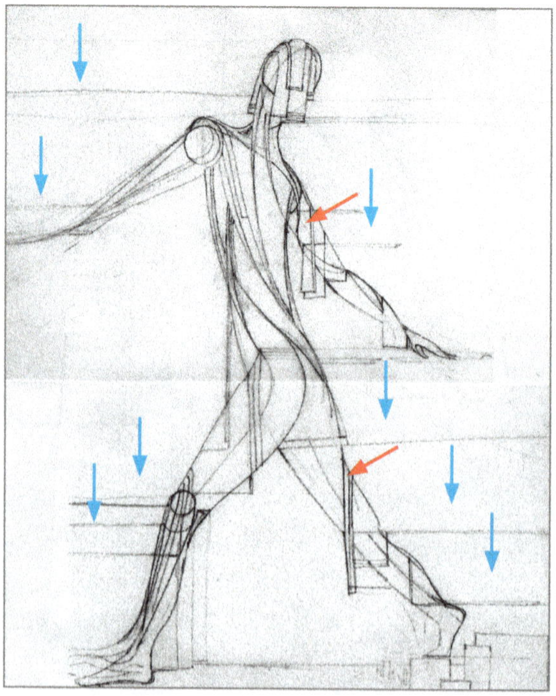

Fig. 11.7. Susanne Schuenke, *Breaking Bondage*, 1982. Pencil drawing (extant only in a photocopy), 8 x 7 in (20.5 x 17.8 cm). Collection of the artist.
Blue arrows show the horizontal lines of the "bondage." Red arrows point to loosely hanging, torn ribbons.

In this frame of mind, she depicted a person fettered by numerous constraining strips attached to various parts of the body, who tries to break loose from the bondage. The work shows some bonds are torn and hang loosely from the body (see red arrows in Fig. 11.7) as the person begins to move with an open stride. In 2003, the artist transposed this figure as side-reversed image (Fig. 11.3 ("1")) into the design of her vision, intending to symbolize liberation from oppressive earthen conditions. The second figure in the same drawing (Fig. 11.3 ("2")) was also created based on *Breaking Bondage*, but it repeats only the outline of the physique of the person, to which she added spiral configurations that she calls "swirling vortices of energy."

11.3.6 A Significant Emotional Experience from Childhood

The figures depicted in *Freedom* are surrounded by sharp, pointed objects. In reference to the latter, the artist had an association that the creation

10 This infinity symbol can be traced by following the contour of the two arms that are joined in the middle of the third canvas panel, where the intersecting point between the two loops of the symbol represents the entry/departure junction between the two realms.

11 See also Fig. 10.30 (watercolor *Dreams on a Friday Afternoon*,1986) where the same torn ribbon indicates a comparable desire of becoming free.

of these potentially dangerous configurations could have its roots in an episode from her early childhood. Susanne had been told by her mother more than once about the incident as a reminder of how difficult it was for the parent to deal with her daughter's behavior when she was a small child.

According to the story, one day, the toddler had strained Mother's nerves beyond what she was able to tolerate. She finally lost her self-control and threw a doll at the child in anger. Flung too high, the toy hit an antique reverse glass painting hanging on the wall, shattering the valuable artwork into smithereens. Luckily nobody was hurt, but the mother dreaded the moment she would have to explain to her husband the destruction of a 17th century Dutch painting.[12] The growing wrath of her mother, the shock of the crash, the splintering glass, and the remorseful anguish of the parent must have been a traumatic event for the child. Susanne has no memory of this episode apart from what she was told much later by her mother. Any recollection of the original incident obviously was suppressed but could have surfaced in a specific detail of the vision—the flying shards in the dark. It could be assumed that the emotionally-charged scene from early childhood, noted above, presents a possible source of her visionary experience in the meditative state. The colorful fragments of the smashed glass painting might be thought of as a counterpart to those flying pieces in her vision.

11.3.7 The Greatest Gift

Through the chain of association, the artist suddenly recognized that the line configuration of butterfly No. 8 looked quite similar to a special gift she received from her mother in 1999. The present was a pair of miniature books sculpted from clay, which her mother created at Susanne's specific request when her parent was undergoing art therapy as part of her rehabilitation program following a stroke that she had suffered in 1996. Susanne's mother treasured books, and she constantly read to the children for many years until they were able to do so fluently for themselves. Therefore, Mother and books were inseparable[13] in Susanne's memory.

The stroke had left her mother blind, and Susanne patiently trained her to learn to see again. After several months, she was finally able to see and read anew. To this day, Susanne considers her greatest victory was helping her mother overcome this stroke-caused blindness against all odds, including the pessimistic prognosis of the mother's neurologists. As a consequence, her mother's ceramic books, especially created for Susanne in those difficult years of recovery, represent the most precious gift imaginable for her. The arrangement of pencil strokes, which render butterfly No. 8, strongly reminds the artist of the front edge profiles of those book sculptures (Figs.11.8 a, b, and c).

In this context, we can also remark that Susanne created *The Flight of Wisdom* (2005; Fig. 8.13) depicting a heap of books, some of which are

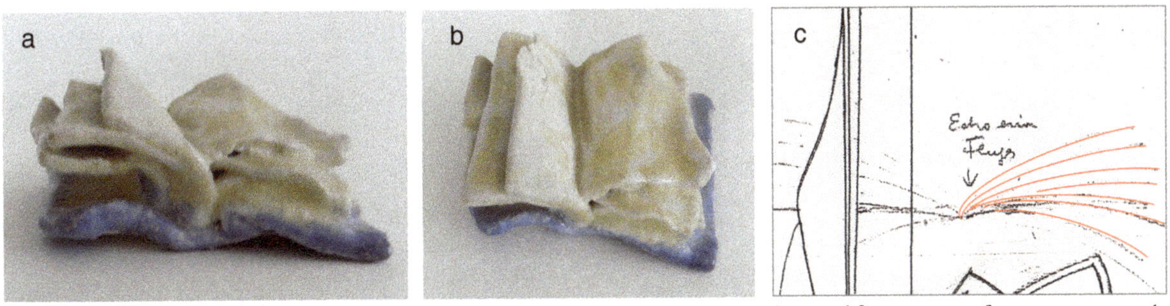

(a) Side view. (b) Top view

Fig. 11.8 (a-b). Ruth-Eva Schünke-Fietze, *Open Book,* 1999.
Glazed clay, approx 2¼ x 1¼ x 2 in (6 x 3 x 5 cm). Collection of the artist.

(c) Detail from Fig. 11.0 for comparison, with red overlay to enhance faded pencil lines.

12 Susanne was later told that this painting depicted a typical kitchen scene, where a woman is seen shelling mussels in a dark background.

13 Many years earlier, when Susanne rode a red bicycle to the university, the mother, skilled in miniature art, made a gift for the daughter—a five-inch-tall metal bicycle with a pile of library books strapped on the bike rack. Her mother handcrafted those miniature books from cardboard and leather with tiny title labels affixed to their spines. Today, the cherished gift sits on Susanne's bookcase near her work desk.

flying away from the planet, where they have been abandoned. She intended this design as an allegory of the disappearance of wisdom (i.e., books), which will have painful consequences, as the earth will then regress to a moonlike barrenness. The tomes are shown in various configurations, untidily thrown together. The arrangement, especially of the left half of the open book, on which the figure bows her head in grief, bears a remarkable resemblance to the line configuration of butterfly No. 8, as well as to the mother's ceramic books (Fig. 11.8). The volumes, representing knowledge, could metaphorically allude to her late mother's love for books, which nourished the artist's inquisitiveness. By the figure grieving over the flying-away tomes, Susanne could unconsciously express bereavement for her mother.

11.3.8 The Dream of Flying

Susanne's mother once told her that, in her own youth, in her sleep, she had beautiful dreams, in which she ran very quickly, suddenly lifted off, and flew over the hedges—a tale that greatly fascinated the daughter. Such dreams are not uncommon because the wish to fly like a bird and glide freely on the currents of the air is as old as mankind. Susanne shares this universal aspiration and considers the dreams of soaring up into the sky a metaphorical expression of the innate tendencies of human beings to ascend to a higher level of existence and spiritual freedom. This longing was symbolically expressed by the central butterfly Air in all stages of the painting's process and butterfly No. 8 in the compositional drawing. Moreover, the artist had given her watercolor design the suggestive title, *Before the Flight*, which later was changed into *Give Me Wings!*. Both titles metaphorically reflect the dream of flying.[14]

11.4 Disappearance into the Golden Background

The information presented above concerning Susanne's mother, the daughter's perception of her death, and the metaphorical meaning expressed in analyzed artworks strengthened our assumption that the line drawing of butterfly No. 8, whose existence was forgotten by the artist, represents a visual signifier[15] for her deceased parent at the unconscious level. The photocopy of the compositional drawing clearly shows the lines that make up this butterfly, but those lines were gilded over at the watercolor stage and never reappeared in the oil painting. In particular, during the process of gilding the background in the watercolor version, the artist covered the thin lines of butterfly No. 8 with the full intention of redrawing them on top of the gold-leafed ground. That was a conscious decision, because it was technically easier to spread the viscous sizing liquid for the gold leaf over the whole area than applying it around each individual line of the butterfly. However, she never "revived" (i.e., redrew) this linear imagery on the gold leaf. One of the puzzling circumstances for this butterfly is its disappearance.

The artist explained the butterfly's disappearance by compositional reason to avoid crowding the painting's rightmost panel. Factually, she automatically "buried" this butterfly along with its accompanying annotation "echo of a flight" under the golden surface. Could the suppression of the array of associated emotions toward the mother have something to do with this? In the disappearance of butterfly No. 8, we could assume the involvement of a latent, unconscious determination. To underpin this assumption, we have availed ourselves of the analysis of butterfly No. 6, Fanning Everything, in chapter 7. In this previous chapter, we identified this butterfly as an unconscious personification of the artist's mother and analyzed in particular the contradictory hostile attitude to the mother in the context of Elektra- and castration complexes. In addition, we used the multitude of data accumulated during the research in the previous chapters concerning Susanne's complex relationship with her parents, which manifested symbolically in the images of other butterflies.

The received information encapsulates the deeply-rooted aspects of Susanne's psyche, concerning sexual and aggressive instinctual drives. We have pointed out Susanne's repressed

14 As mentioned before, Susanne titled her watercolor design in December 2003, *Before the Flight*. The title, *Give Me Wings!* for the oil painting was coined by the philanthropist who commissioned the artwork in 2004.

15 Nasio 1998, page 147: "One should add that this condensation, or erasure of one signifier over another which vanishes, produces another signifier, which I had elsewhere called the *metaphorical signifier*, that is to say, the additional signifier [*le signifiant en plus*], the plus-*One*. This is the way what occurs is not just substitution, but substitution and condensation."

tendencies toward her parents, which were often ambivalent. They included hostile, frustrated desires of biological drives. In her youth, her father was her idol and the model to be emulated (father complex). Susanne placed him on the highest pedestal of the family hierarchy and competed with other members of her family for his attention and love. Correspondingly, she relegated her mother to a secondary role (Elektra complex). The lingering effects of these repressions and complexes could well have been at the root of the disappearance of butterfly No. 8 and its entombment into a beautiful golden surrounding.

In the following chapter, the meaning of the golden background will be further elaborated as representation of the spiritual realm. Susanne, in her grateful remembrance of her mother's praiseworthy sacrifices and virtues, could have wished that Mother's soul would be liberated and would fly to a higher realm. This attitude was articulated in the eulogy that Susanne wrote for her mother's funeral. She expressed her bona fide appreciation for her mother's devotion to the family, which was evident through her caring, loving, and self-sacrificing actions. Susanne praises her parent's inner strength and will to survive, with her surprising endurance of suffering. She emphasizes her mother's calm self-assurance and dignity, and her ethical, moral, and philosophical convictions, which were held with open-mindedness imbued with much passion for rejecting injustice. The speech ends with her tribute to the remarkable attention and support her mother gave the daughter, who was troubled with her medical and emotional problems. All of this motivates Susanne's respect, sense of duty, allegiance, and deep gratitude to the mother. On this basis, covering butterfly No. 8 with the golden background could be interpreted as a symbolic act by the artist to fulfill the wish for a permanent paradisiacal dwelling for her mother.

We also consider the possibility that the eventual entombment under the golden surface of butterfly No. 8 was unconsciously motivated by the urge to perform a mourning ritual, a universal custom found in human societies. We have previously pointed out that on December 23, 2002, the artist's mother went into surgery, during which she entered into a coma, and died on December 28. The day Susanne's mother lost her mental presence became, in essence, a memorial day for her family, and precisely one year later on December 23, 2003, Susanne lit a candle in her home in memory of her mother. That was also the day when the artist was creating the compositional drawing and watercolor, where the image of butterfly No. 8 was first sketched and then covered up with gold leaf. However, while she was engaged in these activities, she did not consciously connect this design in any way with her mother's passing. From the circumstances noted above, we could construe that a mourning ritual was performed on the anniversary of her mother's death. Susanne's ritual was unconsciously[16] expressed by an act of a symbolic entombment. The image of butterfly No. 8 (representation of the mother's soul) was covered by the gold leaf, the medium which in Susanne's iconography signifies a higher, purer realm of existence—the world of spirituality, peace, and tranquility. Such an interment and creation of a dignified memorial was an unconscious expression of confession, atonement, and purification to resolve her longstanding repressed tendencies. This rite of mourning may be construed as a symbolic act of reconciliation with her mother to liberate the artist from the sense of guilt she had suffered from all her life.

Figuratively, the artist implicitly manifested the realization of her mother's dream "to leave this vale of tears"[17] in the imagery. The fulfillment of her mother's wish might be called a metaphorical grace, asking for a blessing on her mother on account of her goodness and pleading for her harmonious afterlife existence in the spiritual realm, where she will be immersed in its beauty and find rest. The artist's creative imagery could be her unconscious equivalent to an invocation.

---

16 Freud (1917) considered mourning "a conscious and apparent process." Robert Bocock, concerning mourning rituals, accepts the importance of the unconscious component. He states "mourning rituals express both affection and love toward the dead and handle the unconscious hostility too" (Bocock 2003, page 62).

17 The artist remembers her mother using this expression once when Susanne was a teen having a conversation with her about death, in which the mother said: "*Ich werde froh sein wenn ich dieses Jammertal verlasse*" (I will be glad when I leave this vale of tears). Susanne inquired what she meant, and her answer was "*Dieses Leben*" (This life). Then, her mother continued, saying that she was curious about what would happen after death. Susanne asked, as we have noted previously (see subchapter 11.3.2), for her mother to send her a sign, if possible, after her passing, and the mother agreed to try.

In this context, the feeling of bliss that overwhelmed Susanne in the vision could have been a cathartic release from latent affects reflecting aggression and sexuality, which could be a source of self-condemnation that she has never been able to successfully resolve. The metaphorical aspect of the artist's visionary experience with its rich imagery, as noted in subchapter 11.3.3, substantiates this interpretation of the latent meaning of the disappearance of butterfly No. 8. Moreover, the "ritual" Susanne carried out with this butterfly likely had the same functional aim as the mourning rituals traditionally performed in various cultures.[18] In a religious or spiritual context, this pays homage to the deceased and prays for their continual existence and well-being. By this, the mourners release their psychic tensions which have accumulated as a consequence of the trauma of bereavement.

18 Many religious traditions prescribe certain fixed periods of time for the mourning of the dead, some lasting as short as a few days and others, as long as a year or more. The observed mourning period is essentially a ritual performance that must be executed successfully, after which the mourners can return to the routines of their lives.

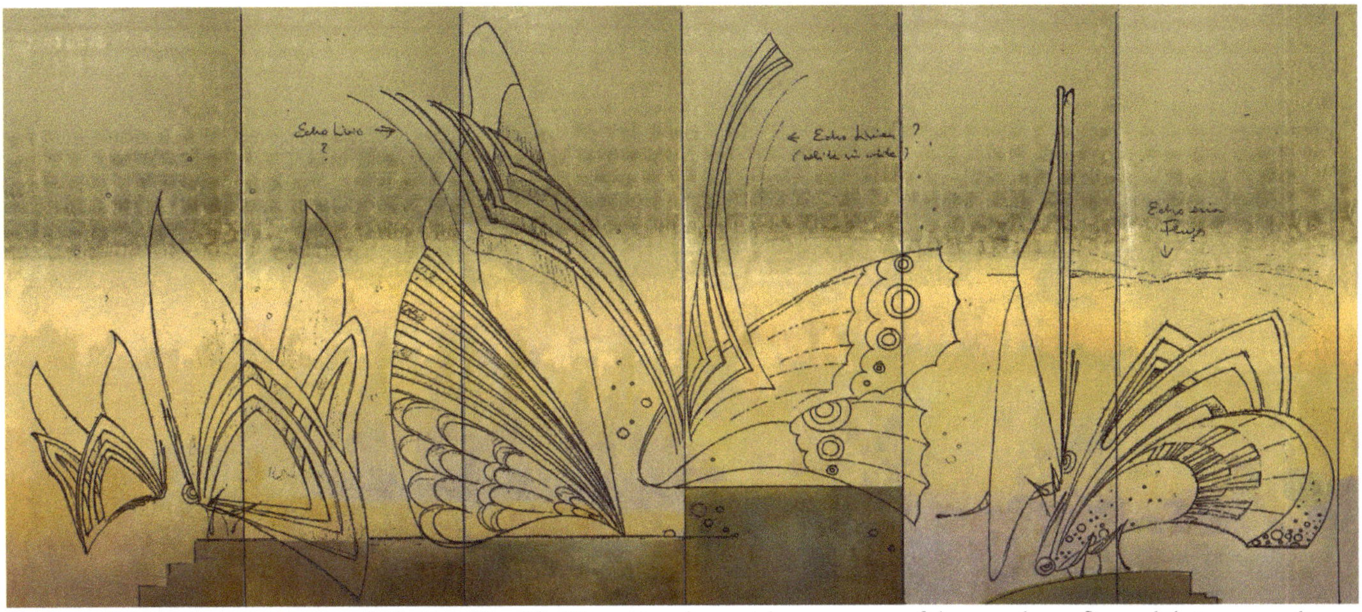

Fig. 12.0. Schematic representation of *Give Me Wings!* for illustrating the spatial arrangement of the seven butterflies and their surroundings.

Chapter 12

The Setting — Podium, Fog, and Golden Background

The butterflies in *Give Me Wings!* are placed in a symbolic setting which can supply valuable information for the analysis of traces of the unconscious in the painting. Our findings, in the context of the butterflies' surroundings, further support some conjectures we have already made in deciphering the metaphorical meanings behind the images of individual butterflies. The elements of the setting that we will consider are a dull brown podium, a light yellow fog, and a gold leaf background.

The lower part of the painting is composed of a podium structure in two parts with stairs on both sides that provides most of the butterflies with a location on which to rest. The middle and upper third of the canvas is covered with gold leaf. The fog fills the lower and middle part of the painting and partially blocks the view of the golden background, which shines unobstructed in its upper part. (Fig. 12.0).

The artist unconsciously infused latent meanings in these three components encoded through appropriate symbolism, just as is the case with the images of the butterflies.

12.1 The Podium

12.1.1 The Podium as Hierarchical Structure

The podium begins with a set of three steps in the middle of the first left-hand panel of the painting. The platform extends until the end of the third panel. The fourth stair continues over the entire width of the fourth panel. At the far right end of this stair, the podium abruptly ends with a vertical drop into a narrow gap at the bottom of the fifth panel. It reemerges with a shallow curved slope, which terminates around the middle of the last panel with two small steps.

The butterflies occupy meaningful places on this multilevel structure. Entering from the left, butterfly No. 1, Little Why (a personification of Susanne as a child), full of ambition to claim a spot on the podium, jumps up eagerly in the air to reach it. Butterfly No. 2, True Blue (a personification of her father), guards the edge of the extended third stair, like a gatekeeper blocking access to the platform. On the same level, closer to the center, butterfly

No. 3, Pale Moonlight (another personification of Susanne), with her back turned to True Blue, commands a substantial space on this platform to the edge of the fourth stair. Butterfly No. 4, Touchless Misty (the third personification of Susanne), monopolizes the highest stage, even overstepping its boundaries at both ends of the pedestal.

Butterfly No. 5, Firebird (a personification of Susanne's father), separated by a gap from the loftiest part of the podium, takes up a narrow space above the left edge of the shallow outlying extension of the podium. He is in a position above butterfly No. 6, Fanning Everything (a personification of the artist's mother), demonstrating his dominance. Fanning Everything, despite her submissive posture, holds most of the low-lying hill—the second part of the podium structure. In the center of the painting, delicate, gossamer-like butterfly No. 7 (a representation of spirituality) hovers supremely over the podium, not bound by the ground, free of the grip of hierarchical order and rivalry below.

Why did the artist place and rank these butterflies in such a way on the podium? We have previously noted that in the first creative drawing (Fig. 2.2) the ground area, indicated by lines, was populated by stick figures representing people who, by their tiny proportions, bestowed monumental dimensions on the butterflies. Working on the compositional drawing, as the artist remembers, she first positioned the butterflies at varying heights in the design. Then, she drew two horizontal parallels and one curved line, including sets of steps, adjusted to their different height positions (Fig. 2.11),[1] providing them with a base to sit on. When watercolor was added to this outlined structure, it became a multileveled podium that gained the symbolic meaning of a certain hierarchical order loaded with significant literal and figurative implications.

The butterflies are engaged in rivalry for a spot on the podium. On the stage, the space is crowded and their positions are exclusive. In Western culture, our directional preference for explicative visual materials that have story lines (cartoons, charts, graphs, etc.) generally follows the pattern established by reading and writing direction, which is from left to right. This principle could also be partially applied to *Give Me Wings!*.

In this way, the three steps at the far left might mark the beginning. The direction of the little butterfly's forward and upward movement also gives a hint at the rightward flow of the composition. The "story line," orchestrated by the unconscious, however, is not about the progressive movement of Susanne's life starting from the far left and ending at the far right, where the metaphoric representations of her parents, Firebird and Fanning Everything, are located. Using the term "story line," we mean the complex relationship in the family, including the hierarchical order and different dynamic factors, in regards to influences on Susanne's psychic development. However, once we understand that the butterfly at the far left (Little Why) is a personification of young Susanne, the symbolism of "the beginning" becomes apparent, since Little Why represents the artist in her childhood.

The placement on the podium, as previously stated, symbolizes appropriate status and achievements as judged by society, the family, and Susanne herself. The analysis revealed that the artist unconsciously embedded a multi-faceted allegorical meaning in the figurative images of the butterflies, their positions, and the setting. The specific compositional sequence of the images on the pedestal echoes the hierarchical order in the family. The podium by itself metaphorically represents the biological basis of life. The vertical arrangement of fog and background stands for gradation of the principles and ideals in her upbringing, where greater emphasis was placed by her parents on socio-cultural standards.

The analysis of the structure of the podium, the discovery of some aspects of the symbolism of the stairs (see subchapter 12.1.2), and the peculiarities of the coloration (see 12.1.3) brings us not only to the mentioned-above familial and social hierarchical dispositions but also to the domain of biological drives. The latter ones in their unconscious metaphorical manifestation in the imagery of the podium's design reflect the powerful presence of such forces in Susanne's psyche.

---

1 The first horizontal line starts close to the right margin of the first panel of the painting and runs through panel 2 and 3, ending in the left part of panel 4. This line provides the butterflies Nos. 2 and 3 with a base. The second horizontal line, positioned higher, begins at the front of butterfly No. 4 and becomes its base. The line runs only through panel 4. The curved line rises from the bottom, close to the middle of panel 5, stretching into the middle of panel 6, where it terminates in the shape of steps.

Instinctual drives and bodily functions were routinely associated by Susanne's parents with vulgarity, which must have greatly influenced her negative conceptualization of the appropriate physiological basis of human existence. In the artist's family, the topic of sexuality became increasingly unavoidable with the girls' coming of age. The parents were steadfast in their strong opposition to the contemporaneously attuned standpoints of their children concerning partnership and marriage. In this context, the father had a judgmental attitude toward the materialistic motivation of future mates.[2] This caused discord between the parents and their three adult daughters which grew into an ever-widening rift as the years went by. Such a divisive situation could be recognized in the gap between the two parts of the podium structure (a large, stepped formation to the left and a small, shallower one to the right) that could be the unconscious signifier for the divergence and split between Susanne and her parents.

There are two podium segments: a small one for Firebird and Fanning Everything (personifications of the father/mother), and a large one for the other butterflies (personifications of Susanne and the "good" father). The lower height of the parents' podium could metaphorically indicate the superior hierarchical importance that the artist assigned to the larger platform. It could underscore the developed polarization of standpoints of parents and daughters, described above. However, all the multiple facts gained by the analysis in the previous chapters give us reason to think that Susanne stayed bound to her parents, unable to break free of their pervasive psychological presence (emotional attachment). This substantiates that the two platforms, where all the butterflies are situated, constitute one unified podium structure. The interconnection of the two podium segments below the viewed area might also be inferred from the fact that the color for both platforms is of the same earthen tone, which points to their common origin.

Although the second, smaller part of the podium does not show a visible connection to the first one in the painting, it is an inseparable part of the common structure. This is confirmed by Susanne's recollection concerning her intent at the time the design was executed. According to her, she created the podium primarily as a "service structure," just to supply a ground for the figures. She has never doubted that it extends beyond the sides and bottom of what can be seen on the canvas, just as she imagines that the golden background spreads endlessly in all directions above the podium level. The artist took the unity of the podium structure to be so self-evident that for a while she had difficulty grasping that some observers did not share her perception. The above arguments support an assumption of the existence of a joined podium structure. The gap between the segments might be a visual indicator that reflects a significant discord that developed during the years in the relationship between Susanne and her father (for details see chapters 4, 5, and 9).

Susanne's long-held desire was to emulate and eventually even reach a higher level than her father in artistic and academic accomplishments. On both accounts she succeeded, as she completed her doctorate program and became an artist able to support herself through her art. At the same time, she managed to achieve far greater personal freedom than her father ever had. On this matter, it could be taken into consideration that her father accepted his responsibility to support the family. The highest position that Touchless Misty occupies on the podium, in accordance with Susanne's personification, might unconsciously express the self-evaluation of her achievements and potential.

This position on the elevated structure reflects a special honor, being in the spotlight, rising above others. In this view, the steps represent levels of accomplishment, in contrast to the curved surface of the far right side, where butterflies Nos. 5 and 6, as personification of father and mother, reside. Such metaphorical arrangement might unconsciously indicate the precarious footing that poses the threat of slipping away from the position of honor and respect in challenging personal or social situations, especially in accordance with their worsening health (father's diabetes and mother's stroke). This could have determined Susanne's fear in the past that her parents could become unable to realize their creativity in art and, consequently, could not maintain their upper-middle class status. The placement on the isolated and precarious segment of the podium substantiates this assumption.

2 The parents were highly critical of their eldest daughter's choice of her husband. Similarly, they refused to meet Susanne's partner even after her marriage to him, and Susanne's younger sister married only after both parents had passed on.

Susanne's parents' well-respected status in society was the result of their hard work backed by a high motivation as well as their education and culture, which they treasured as their most valuable capital. Within the post-war reconstruction era of West Germany, they managed to achieve an affluent income and a corresponding upper-middle class lifestyle, which was then imprinted, along with its social ethics, on their children's minds as their desirable goal to be emulated. They were very mindful in teaching their daughters to show fundamental respect for all fellow human beings, regardless of religious beliefs, cultures, and customs. Furthermore, they set an admirable example by acting according to their principles in personal encounters with others. Nevertheless, it was not difficult to sense in their decorum a certain sense of class distinction based on their own origin, rooted in their middle and upper-middle class backgrounds, with even a modest aristocratic title among their great-grandparents.[3]

In line with his emphasis on social status, her father always asked his daughters about the professions of their playmates' parents to judge the families accordingly. This obsessive concern with social positions has haunted Susanne and her sisters all their lives. Although the artist's parents continued to stress the fundamental equality of all people regardless of their social station, there were numerous instances in which various exemptions and restrictions were used to justify their social bias.[4] For example, when her parents commented with negative undertones that someone had a "Bergmann" (German for "miner")[5] as a father, they alluded to the lack of education, culture, or small chance of social rise. The coal miner was used as a strawman by her father in his frequent catchphrase: "Well, my father was not a miner!" and by her mother saying, "I did not grow up in a coal scuttle!" By these and other similarly snide remarks, they hoped to protect their children from the bad language, poor manners, crudeness, and vulgarity that they thought were rife among working class people. Thereby, the parents demonstrated a certain contradiction to their professed, high-minded egalitarian principles. It was puzzling to the children to witness how their mother and father exaggerated the merits and demerits of each other's family ancestry during heated discussions between them.

As the children became more mature and perceptive, a discrepancy became painfully clear to them. The parents had pride in following certain aspects of the upper-middle class standards like high culture, comfortable income, and freedom from the routine and menial. However, they neglected the accepted norms of social life in the community: engagement with various communal activities, such as social clubs, church membership, simple sociable gatherings, and networking among their equals. The parents led a family life that was rather peculiar and isolated, almost hermetic. In regard to social integration, the teenage daughters did not participate in community life. Only the remarks of their schoolmates made them aware of what they missed. An incredible number of deviations from the social norms caused increasing disorder within the household. Susanne and her sisters were actually growing up in an artist's home with a bohemian lifestyle. The mother spent an enormous amount of energy trying to uphold a bourgeois appearance.

In spite of these occasional lapses, the parents acted in concert to ensure that their daughters would come to identify themselves with the family's values and heritage. They stressed the need for honoring past, positive traditions, striving for personal excellence, cultivating a solid work ethic, and attaining a respectable social status. Furthermore, they emphasized to the children the importance of culture and education which, once obtained, could never be taken away from them.

The parents were part of the *Wirtschaftswunder* (German economic miracle)[6] that eventually allowed them with their professional success to attain a comfortable living standard and material wealth. In relation to his financial

3 In fact, Susanne's father was so enamored with the idea of giving his last name the intimation of aristocratic family origins that he proceeded to combine his and his wife's family names upon their marriage into a hyphenated surname to give it the appearance of a significant family history, in imitation of the past practice of some European noble families.

4 The concept of a stratified society was conveyed by the parents. Susanne also learned about this in her studies of history and social sciences.

5 A stock code word used by her father to denote poorly-educated people.

6 The German economic miracle took place in the 1950s in West Germany.

prowess, the father often commented with a smug understatement: "After all, it had cost a few marks," expressing his satisfaction at being able to afford the high quality of their lifestyle. He considered his daughters' clothing to be of special importance by saying that a connoisseur would recognize such clothes and jewelry for their exquisite level of quality and sophistication. Therefore, the observer would respect the wearer as a representative of a high standard of culture. Susanne perceived her father's remarks as implying that dressing elegantly was primarily to gain recognition that the daughters came "from a good family" (German: "*aus gutem Hause stammen*").

This distinction between the display of refinement and the parading of wealth was the key to how her father viewed others who were also prosperous beneficiaries of the *Wirtschaftswunder*. The parents sharply distanced themselves from these nouveau riches, whom he and his wife considered arrogant, pretentious, crude, and, inevitably, devoid of culture, tradition, education, and taste.

Her upbringing was focused on looking "respectable" not only in attire but also in manners, language, taste, and education to underscore a high level of cultural refinement. This was in line with the father's social ambition for a suitable status that went with estimable financial holdings. It was not enough that he should look respectable to society; his whole family should as well.

Reminiscing about her parents' insistence on looking respectable, Susanne made a rather sad remark, that she could not remember ever being told by her parents that she looked beautiful—a positive comment, which she might have secretly longed for. The daughters could not express such a desire openly because it would have immediately elicited disdainful responses from their parents. Their father would especially impute undignified motives to them.[7] Susanne's wish for such praise only came to be unexpectedly realized one day, years later in her mid-twenties, when she was told by a girlfriend how beautiful and attractive she looked when she laughed. Her friend's remark came as a complete shock to her because she had been so indoctrinated to think solely of looking respectable, and not physically attractive.

Furthermore, the father drilled the girls into believing that any future sons-in-law were likely to be more interested in the family wealth, which would eventually be inherited by the daughters, than in their personal appeal. This cynical prediction of the daughters' future marital prospects contributed nothing positive to the development of their self-confidence, if material possessions were of higher significance than other merits when it came to attracting a partner. However, the parents, in the upbringing of their children, focused on the development of personal qualities and virtues. From her father's canon of honorable behavior, Susanne learned integrity, incorruptibility, and civic courage (German: *Zivilcourage*), the last of which stands for the bravery to speak up and stand one's ground to defend the principles and rights that one holds against the abuse of power. He valued this virtue highly, and he often expressed it by his favorite statement: "I am politically and economically independent!" Other virtues she assimilated from her father include the importance of giving one's best and delivering results of the highest quality.

From her mother, Susanne learned to be perceptive and responsive to others' suffering and hardships, to have a strong sense of responsibility, accompanied by an equally strong commitment to fulfilling her duty, which the mother often remarked on as having been inherited from her own parents' staunch Prussian Protestant work ethic. The mother craved a life of peace in beautifully embellished surroundings without conflicts and stress.

Susanne tried to realize these virtues that were essentially set forth by her parents. As she matured, she slowly found her own priorities, some of which were undeniably based on the parental foundations, but Susanne claims others as her "personal conquests." She has come to uphold a strong belief in a spiritual basis for life that finds realization in her creativity. Many of her concerns, ideas, and hopes have found metaphorical manifestations in her paintings.

7 The parents persistently admonished the daughters to dress and to behave in a way that they would not to be perceived as wishing to attract inappropriate attention from men. One of her father's typical suggestive statements of dissuasion would be "… or do you want to look like a wee-wee girl?" by which he alluded that a specific way of dressing would be comparable with the provocative attire of a prostitute; thus intentionally creating the feeling of shame in his daughters' minds.

To sum up this subchapter, the podium (with its elevations and stairs and the specific placements of the images of the personified butterflies on it) allegorically reflects many aspects of the artist's upbringing.

12.1.2 The Symbolism of Stairs

The artist grew up with steps and stairs in her childhood home, which was a townhouse with the bedrooms and the workshop located on the second floor. The staircase was set at the back of the living room, integrated into its space. Its steps were covered with a crimson red stair runner all the way up and its wall was lined with bookcases. Susanne always liked stairs; she loved to sit on the steps, to run up and bounce down, preferably with a lot of noise. In the children's room, a bunk bed provided the sleeping quarters for the older sister and her. From toddler age onward, Susanne commandeered the top bunk, to which she climbed on a ladder. When she could not sleep after going to bed, which was often, she would walk over to the workshop, where she was allowed to paint or play while her parents worked. At the far corner of the workshop was a small, windowless attic closet, which was accessed through a short set of stairs from the workshop. This place was the most treasured area where little Susanne entertained herself. Here, on the highest possible spot (in relation to the workshop), she could be the master and owner in all of her imaginary role-playing. In the family garden, there was another favorite place: an old hawthorn tree, as we mentioned before. It had grown crooked and low-lying over the years, which made it easy for a child to climb the trunk up to the branches. Susanne spent countless hours there pretending it was a tree house, an airplane, or an explorer's ship.

Susanne's relish for ascending to a high place stayed with her into adulthood. In her twenties, as a postgraduate student conducting research on medieval architecture, while visiting Gothic cathedrals, she was able to climb to the highest level of the nave wall of some of the cathedrals. At the clerestory level, she could walk along the small and rather dangerous pathway in front of the windows, or inside the attic space above the vault. The artist remembers the joy and excitement she felt, secured only by a thin, steel rope railing, while looking down into the nave from a height of 100 feet or more.[8] Being high up definitely provided an exhilarating experience for her.

Steps, stairs, and other similar formations[9] frequently appear in the artist's designs. In some cases, she uses stair-like configurations to break the smooth flow of a line whose straight course has become too tedious for her aesthetic sensibility. In other instances, they are used to add a little more detail, often as a "just-three-steps" configuration creeping into the composition. Drawing curves sometimes results in a similar, unexpected outcome. Whenever she feels that something inside her urges a change in the shape or direction of the flow, it could end up in a complete reversal, a transformation into steps, loops, spirals, or even a sudden interruption by what the artist calls a "breaking point." She realizes the inner need by redirecting the energy of the movement through a counterbalancing or contrasting element in the design, to prevent it from becoming clichéd. We have been able to identify over 30 instances of the artist's use of stair-like structures in her paintings.

In 1984, the artist created a watercolor titled *-A- like Ambition,*[10] which depicts a nude figure prostrated on a set of steps with a monumental letter –A– towering over the figure (Fig. 12.1).

8 For example, Susanne had the opportunity to do a close-up study of Ely Cathedral, with the nave height of 72 ft (22 meters) and the lantern at the crossing with a height of 170 ft (52 m).

9 Beside the conventionally known "steps" and "stairs," in buildings, in her designs Susanne uses formations composed from a regular/irregular sequence of rectangles or blocks piled on top of each other, representing risers (in different heights) and treads (in varying depths) and names them accordingly with the same terms. We will follow her terminology in this analysis.

10 The original German title *A wie Anspruch* (literally, *A as in Demand* (or *Claim, Requirement*)) cannot be translated into English without losing the reason for the artist's choice of the letter *A*, since there is no appropriate word in English that begins with a letter *A* denoting for demand, claim, or requirement (*Anspruch* in German). The closest English word that would retain the artist's intent would be *Authority*, since individuals and their uniqueness are often crushed under the weight of those who claim authority over them. The word *Ambition* is another possibility, which the artist chose, since it is her own ambition that is the ultimate source of the hardships that she has had to endure in order to fulfill it. Somehow Susanne identified her father's ambition to be the source of the powerful "claim" ("Anspruch"), which she feared to fail, thereby not fulfilling his demands and losing his respect and love that she so desperately sought.

Susanne was aware of a strong self-identification with the reclining female suffering under the merciless, authoritarian dominion symbolically represented by the looming capital letter standing astride an apparently lifeless body. The letter that the artist considers as "cold and devoid of all sympathy" is executed in oxidized silver leaf. Its metaphorical meaning is the artist's bold, visual abstraction of the life-suffocating requirements and expectations of parents, academic institutions, society, and Susanne's own ambitions, all of which she felt compelled to fulfill. It should be remarked that *-A- like Ambition* was created while the artist was working on her doctorate, a difficult period of her life when she was under enormous pressure.

A dramatic color change in the body is depicted from lively green (lower torso and legs) to pale whitish-gray (head, upper torso and arm). A green liquid drips from the hand. With this coloration, the artist intended to signal that vitality (represented in green) is dangerously ebbing away.[11] The stairs in this image are irregular, and the next steps appear decidedly too steep, leading to the impression that the challenge to climb the stairs to the top was too difficult for the figure. The painting metaphorically reflects the artist's despair under the unbearable pressure of all the expectations forced on her, and her contemplation of the only possible way out of the life's impasse, death, which she felt was her only realistic choice.

Five years later, after having successfully completed her studies, Susanne painted an alternative version of this painting in oil, *Sleeper*, (1989) (Fig. 12.2). In this work, she removed the lethal threat that was encapsulated in the overwhelming authority of –A– from the design, which stood above the prone figure surrounded by murky clouds signifying uncertainty and loss of vision. In the new version, there appears a starry night sky, and the recumbent woman, now placed on a golden step, is no longer ashen in her appearance, as she recovers her vitality. Toward the horizon, the sky seems to brighten as if the sun were about to rise and a hopeful day soon to dawn. *Sleeper*, unlike the unremittingly pessimistic *-A- like Ambition*, presents a new perception that looks toward life rather than its demise, and the person depicted is no longer perishing under the oppressive

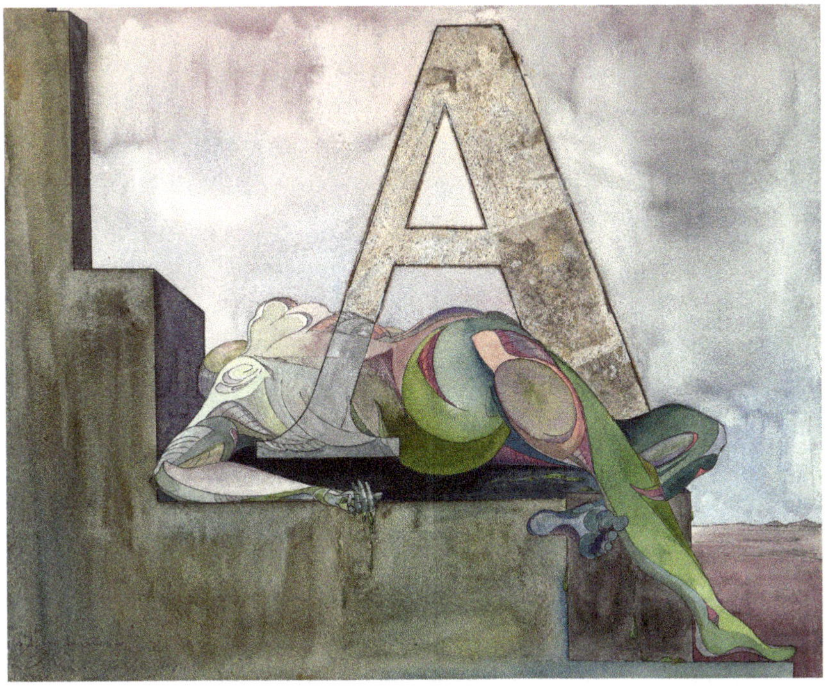

Fig. 12.1. Susanne Schuenke, *-A- like Ambition*, 1984. Watercolor with silver leaf, 16 x 20 in (40.5 x 51 cm). Collection of the artist.

11 In reference to the pale whitish-gray coloration of the upper half the body, we have already mentioned two paintings that had influence on Susanne (see subchapter 8.1.2), both of which depicted dead bodies: *The Death of Chatterton* (by Henry Wallis) and *Dead Soldier* (Anonymous, Italian School).

circumstances. Instead, she slumbers,[12] regaining her strength and tranquility in order to face the oncoming challenges, indicated by the continuing upward steps. The hopeful signs around her, such as golden steps, starry sky, and approaching sunrise, emphasize this positive outlook. The small tortoise to the left in the painting might signify the need to walk slowly, urging her to be patient—a virtue that the fast-paced Susanne so far has not acquired.

The analysis of these two paintings shows that they reflect her life situations and experiences. The artist always thought that the image of stairs stands for obstacles that must be overcome to find the pathway out of life's predicaments. This could especially be in circumstances where she has had to face crucial decisions that she was fearful of making. This includes the use of ascending stairs as a metaphor for achieving something desirable, such as personal growth, a higher level of knowledge, professional success, or even an insight into a higher spiritual realm. Susanne employs her stairs iconography in these contexts. In *-A- like Ambition*, the stairs stand for challenges that might result in a desperate condition. In *Sleeper*, they are used as a symbol for a hopeful outcome. Hence, the same stairs can stand as symbols for existing challenges and their unfolding, with the potential for either a negative (failing) or positive (thriving) consequence. Subsequently, Susanne has believed for many years that stairs are her artistic abstraction for different pathways to overcoming difficulties and obstacles to achieve success. However, one may ask if there is another symbolism manifested in the image of stairs in both paintings.

12.1.3 Another Approach to Interpreting the Symbolism of Stairs

In the previous chapters, we have analyzed numerous determinants for the formation of personal symbols and their embodiment in the imagery of the artist's paintings, and in many cases we found their origins to be rooted in her instinctual drives. We have considered these discoveries in accordance with the psychoanalytic framework dealing with the unconscious symbolic expressions of biological drives. Therefore, in order to spotlight such additional possible metaphorical and symbolic meanings coded in steps and stairs, we now return to the two paintings mentioned above and focus on details that could give the basis for further interpretation. Regarding the watercolor *-A- like Ambition*, we consider the following details to be meaningful to our analysis (refer to Fig. 12.3 for the numbered items below):

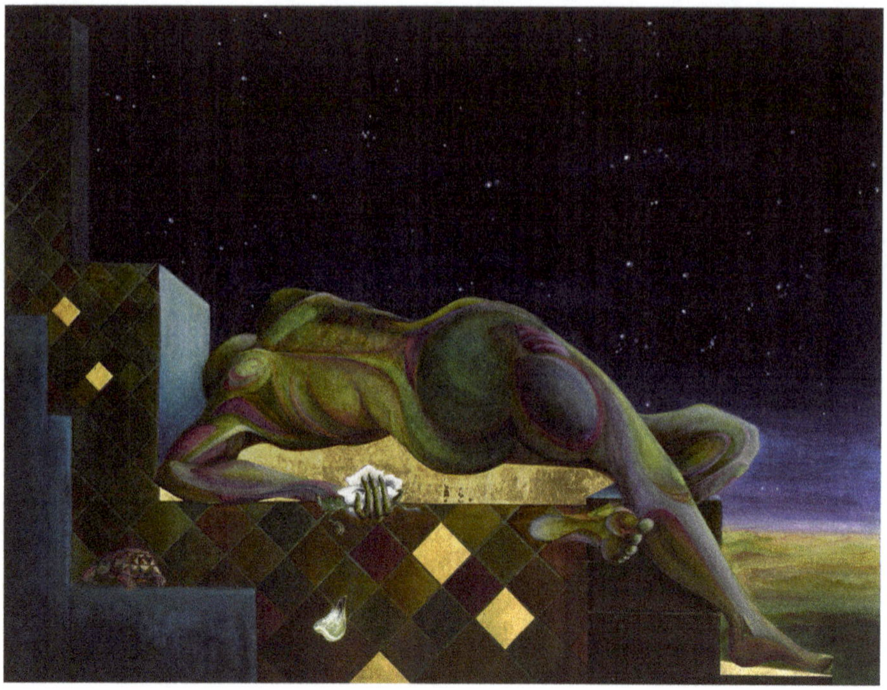

Fig. 12.2. Susanne Schuenke, *Sleeper,* 1989. Oil and gold leaf on canvas, 30 x 40 in (76 x 101 cm). Collection of the artist.

12 The figure holds a poppy blossom, which is the iconographic symbol for sleep.

(1) The exposed buttocks of the reclining female nude.

(2) The construction of the letter –A–, forming a huge triangle and standing astride the figure, encasing it, and emphasizing the difference in coloration between the upper and the lower body.

(3) The green liquid, mostly dripping down from the "vessel" formed by the hand, but also found splattered on the stairs.

(4) Significantly prolonged, vertically-orientated and horizontally-orientated rectangle shapes make up the stair structure. The bluish gray stair risers (the vertical part of a stair) to the left emphasize the ominous verticality. The sidewall of the stairs has a dirty, greenish gray color, and looks like a monolithic, concrete block.

(5) The stair's tread in dark indigo appears nearly black.

(6) The variation in the intensity of the body's color—between a noticeable paleness in its upper part of the body and contrasting deep hues of green throughout the lower one (marked in Fig. 12.3.(6) as "color discrepancy").

(7) Curved triangular forms in hues of purplish red, often ending with sharp points, appearing adjacent to the green areas of buttocks, knee, and ankle.

The features of specific interest in *Sleeper*, painted five years later, are enumerated below. This painting features the reclining female nude depicted in an identical posture and perspective on a comparable stair-setting as in *-A- like Ambition*. However, there are considerable alterations and modifications between *-A- like Ambition* and *Sleeper* (see Fig. 12.4, which highlights the differences with corresponding numbers 1–9):

(1) The exposed buttocks are nearly identically postured, but the chroma is darker, and more saturated.

(2) The letter –A– is absent, and the figure's contour is framed by a dark, starry night sky.

(3) The hand clasps a white poppy blossom with a dark center (partially hidden under the fingers). A long stem ends in a seedpod. A single petal falls toward the bottom.

(4) The stairs in the two paintings are nearly identical only in shape. The sidewall of *Sleeper*'s stairs is tiled in a diamond checker pattern, with some in golden color. The stair risers now reflect the light of the morning glow.

(5) The stair's tread on which the figure reclines is gilded.

(6) The color saturation is strong and harmonious throughout the figure (no drastic difference between upper and lower body).

(7) A purple shape resembling a hand on the hip is visible in the upper thigh of the slumbering figure.

(8) The primary stair structure is repeated in a smaller scale: secondary stair structure.

(9) A small tortoise walks on the lowest step of the smaller stair. Its carapace is decorated with triangles, some of whose hues repeat those of the tiles.

In analyzing those pronounced features of the two paintings, we utilized the psychoanalytic technique used in the interpretation of dreams (method of free association, as mentioned in the introduction). Particular attention is paid to any peculiarities of the manifest content that act as an outlet of the unconscious in delivering its messages. Accordingly, we were able to unmask the latent content in the imagery symbolically expressed in specific details of the painting. We came to the understanding that the messages embedded by the unconscious in dreams could also manifest in artworks with comparable symbolic content, as was the case with the two paintings mentioned above (see 12.1.1).

We previously established in interpreting both paintings that the reclining figure represented the artist. She was aware that the image of *-A- like Ambition*[13] visualized the pressure of the *Anspruch* (demand) under the strain of her actual circumstances: tension in the relationship with the father, existential problems (meaning of life),

13 *-A- like Ambition* will be referred to as *Ambition* also in the following analysis.

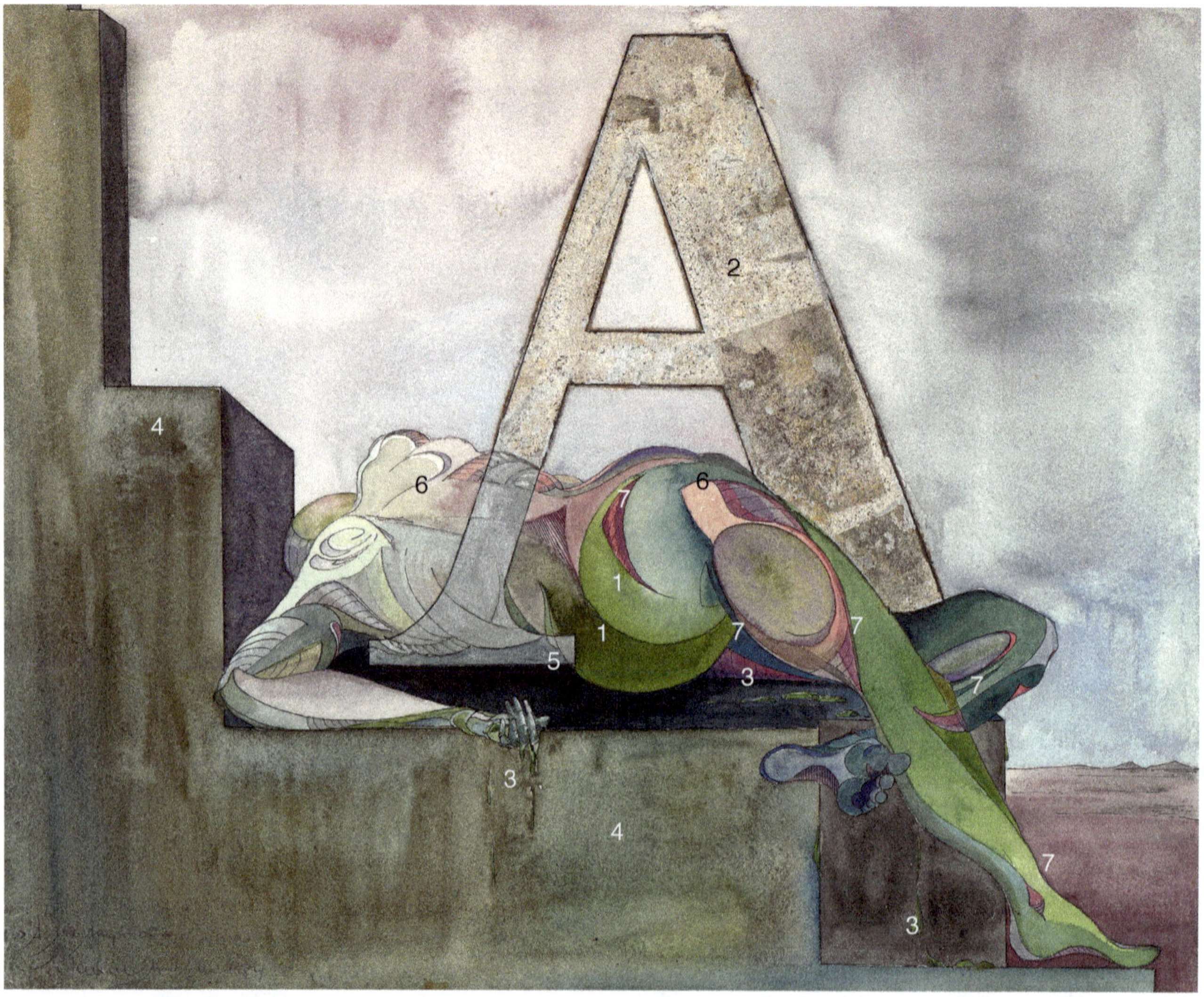

Fig. 12.3. Annotation for Fig. 12.1 (*-A- like Ambition"*). The numbers refer to the corresponding ones in the text.

(1) Exposed buttocks.
(2) The letter –A–.
(3) Green liquid.
(4) Vertical and horizontal rectangles (steps).
(5) Stair tread in indigo.
(6) Color discrepancy.
(7) Purplish-red triangle shapes.

working on the doctoral thesis, living away from the family home, and having a relatively isolated personal life. In our analysis, we were able to shed light also on unconscious influences that significantly contributed to the formation of this watercolor's imagery beyond the mentioned factors at the time.

During our analysis of the butterflies, especially True Blue and Firebird, Susanne's father complex was recognized. We can assume that this transferential attitude had powerful and lasting influences on the unconscious expression of numerous details of *Ambition* and *Sleeper*, created 20 and 15 years, respectively, before *Give Me Wings!*. The following discussion offers a set of interpretations for the selected features of the paintings in the sequence of the lists above.

We pay attention to the exposure of the female nude with her buttocks facing the viewer at the center of the painting—a topic laden with much sexual content (Fig. 12.3 (1) and Fig. 12.4 (1)). In *Ambition,* the abstract shape of the letter –A– can be interpreted as a personification of a human being standing victoriously astride the defeated body (Fig.12.3 (2)). The metallic silver appearance of the letter and its straight, unbending lines can

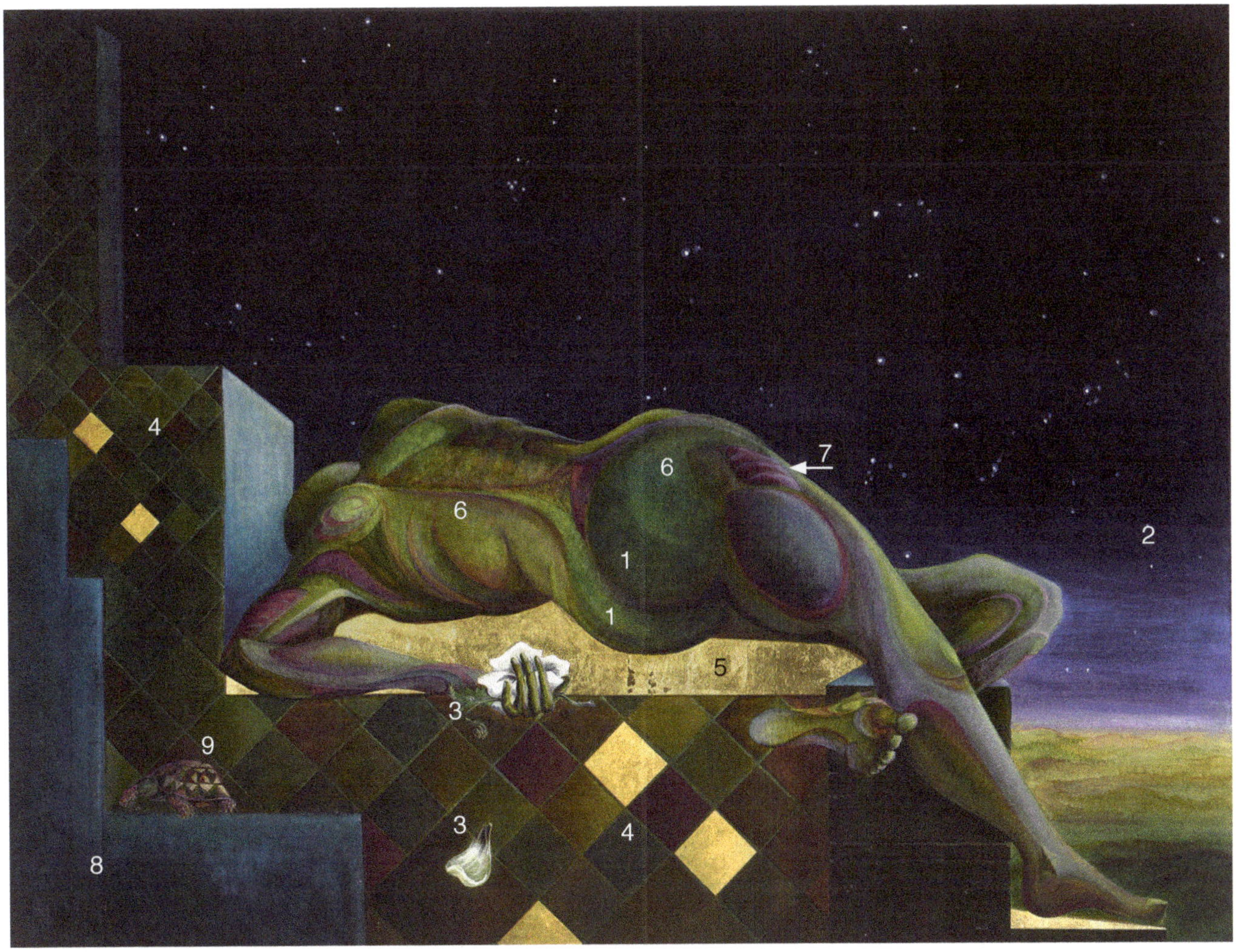

12.4. Annotation for Fig. 12.2 (*Sleeper*). The numbers refer to the corresponding ones in the text.

(1) Exposed buttocks.
(2) Starry night sky and approaching morning.
(3) Poppy blossom, capsule, and petal.
(4) Primary stair structure with golden tiles.
(5) Golden surface.
(6) Color saturation.
(7) Shape of the hand.
(8) Secondary stair structure.
(9) Tortoise.

metaphorically convey an impression of the unwavering strength of uncompromising authority. The supremacy of this monumentalized letter over the prone woman underneath is apparent, as in her portrayal there is no sign of resistance, but only of resignation. The power of –A– is unchallengeable, just as her father was. The female nude's posture could metaphorically reflect Susanne's perceptions of herself under the dominating influence of her father. It could replay the pertinent fantasies that she harbored as a child and young woman toward him.

In contrast, *Sleeper* was created at a time when the artist had already been living in an established relationship with her future husband for two years. The painting eventually became a gift to him.[14] As we compare the metaphorical meanings of the two paintings, the difference between the life circumstances in the times of the creation of *Ambition* and *Sleeper* will be discernible. In *Sleeper*, we can observe that the composition of *Ambition* has undergone drastic change. The artist has consciously abandoned the symbol of oppression, –A–, and, doing so, unknowingly dethroned the

14 Her partner liked the painting from the beginning; thus, Susanne promised it as a gift for him after completion.

father from his absolute dominance over her. In place of the tarnished silver letter, a dark-blue, starry night sky, with a hint of approaching morning, arcs over the reclining figure (Fig. 12.4 (2)) as a metaphorical expression of the artist's optimistic expectations. In both paintings, the items in the woman's hand are packed with metaphoric signs hinting at the plausible presence of sexual and reproductive drives beneath the imagery, which are difficult to ignore. In *Ambition*, green viscous liquid drips from the hand, and the deposit of it is also found in several spots on the stairs, giving the impression of body fluid being discharged (Fig. 12.3 (3)). In *Sleeper*, the hand no longer drips with liquid but holds a white poppy blossom with a dark center. The choice of flower, including a stem with the seed capsule (Fig. 12.4 (3)), was determined by the artist's intention to denote the state of sleep.[15] Flowers are universally used as a symbolic reference to femininity,[16] and in this context, the single fallen petal in the painting may very well hint at the loss of virginity.[17] In this contest, the depiction of the seed capsule on the long stem next to the flower can allude to fertility, which further confirms the presence of unconscious symbolism in this painting pertaining to the topic of reproduction. The same coded meaning had already appeared in *Ambition*, in the portrayal of the fluid leaking from the hand, as mentioned.

The stair structure in *Ambition* is composed of bland and bleak concrete blocks (Fig. 12.3 (4)), with a gray, nondescript façade conveying the ambience of a harsh setting with threatening undertones. Perhaps, this manifests the dictates of familial patriarchy under which the artist suffered. In contrast, a similar stair in *Sleeper* is decorated with multi-colored tiles, including golden ones (Fig. 12.4 (4)). Furthermore, the tread of the larger stairway, nearly black in *Ambition* (Fig. 12.3 (5)), is gilded like a royal dais in *Sleeper* (Fig.12.4 (5)), on which the figure reclines. This could evoke the impression of a matrimonial bed, unconsciously symbolizing the celebration of a state of intimacy that has been consummated with a partner. We discovered another metaphoric signifier for the painting's sexual content. It is a shape resembling a hand lying on the buttock (Fig. 12.4 (7))—an image completely unintended and unrecognized by Susanne when it was painted.

In *Sleeper*, the artist embellished the composition by adding a smaller, parallel, dark blue simulacrum of the primary stair structure, (Fig. 12.4 (8)). The lowest tread of the secondary stairs is occupied by a slow moving tortoise (Fig. 12.4 (9)), comparable in its positioning to the woman on the main stairway. The artist recalled that she wanted to break the dead silence of the night scene with something moving—a bird would be too fast, a crawling insect off-putting, but a small tortoise, she felt, was just right. In her artistic imagination, she modeled the carapace with many colorful triangles whose hues are similar to the tiles of the stairs. The diminutive tortoise could be an unconscious reference to the artist's childhood, when Susanne and her older sister kept such a pet in the garden. Thus, the tortoise[18] could also symbolize an early golden age of happiness and togetherness with her parents and siblings. Metaphorically, its presence in the painting could allude to her life circumstances at the time the work was created, which might have signified Susanne's hope again for recreating a golden age in her life with the new partner. The tortoise could also symbolize

15 It was very important for the artist to assure the viewer of this painting (*Sleeper*) that the figure is asleep and not dying (unlike in *Ambition*). That prompted her to choose the poppy flower including the seed capsule as an obvious symbolic association with sleep, because, through the archaeology study, she knows about this connection since antiquity from the ancient Greek myth of Morpheus and Hypnos—the minor Greek deities associated with sleep. Morpheus is symbolically associated with the poppy.

16 This is in accordance also with the Freudian interpretation: "*Blossoms* and *flowers* represent the female genitals, or more particularly, virginity. Do not forget that the blossoms are really the genitals of the plants." (From Sigmund Freud, *A General Introduction to Psychoanalysis* (New York: 1920), Part Two: The Dream, X. Symbolism in the Dream.) For example, many paintings of flowers by the American artist, Georgia O'Keefe, are often cited as a good demonstration of Freud's statement.

17 The presumed symbolism in our case is in accordance with its common metaphorical meaning. Susanne met her future husband at the age of 29, and she did not have any sexual relationship before age 30.

18 This tortoise, which Susanne thought was introduced for the purpose of compositional necessity, later gave her the inspiration to create a major work (*The Long Journey*, 1995; see Fig. 8.9), in which the tortoise symbolically embodied mankind's remarkable scientific and artistic achievements through its millennia of history.

longevity in this painting, since Susanne knew that this unassuming animal could live for more than 120 years. In this context, it could be construed that the artist was metaphorically intimating that the newfound relationship would be a long-lived one.

Susanne, after ten years of intense academic studies, was trying to establish a life away from her parents as an independent artist in London, and her husband provided the necessary support toward that goal (see chapter 5). He organized the practical aspects of living in a foreign country and backed her in promoting her art. She appreciated his positive attitude toward her, which was in stark contrast to a decade of growing tension and conflict with her father. Susanne's husband, 20 years her senior, was a substitute in some aspects for her guiding father, who gave her security and comfort in her childhood. Subsequently, she transferred the paternal power that was in accordance with her ideal of the soothing and assuring fatherly role for a man in her life to her spouse. This statement finds confirmation in the two relationships she has had following the dissolution of her marriage of 17 years, as the subsequent partners have been 15 or more years older. One of them was a "good father" figure who bestowed on Susanne the freedom to be herself, helped her toward that goal, participated in the activities of her social life, and basked in her artistic success. The other partner gave her the long sought-after understanding of her personality and the roots of the painful difficulties with her parents, helping to distance herself from the negative experiences of the past and build a more optimistic perspective for the future. In those relationships, Susanne replayed the role of a powerless child whose life is under the authoritarian control of her parent.

Returning to the two paintings in question, in *Ambition,* the curved triangular shapes in purplish-red coloration with pointed endings (some of them sickle shaped) embedded in the curvy, green parts of the body, might appear, in accordance to the artist's iconography, as if they were hostile objects (Fig. 12.3 (7)). The purplish forms in the nude figure are still present in *Sleeper*, but they are more integrated into the body in mellower green hues, less alien, and more like a part of the musculature. These clandestine triangles could function like highlights of the pleasant feelings coming from the before mentioned touch-sensitive points of contact with the parents when she was allowed to share the bed with them.

The coloration of the reclining body in *Ambition* is mostly in saturated greens in its lower half, but features extreme paleness in its upper part, with the –A– marking the boundary line (Fig. 12.3 (6)). With this change of color, the artist metaphorically projected the enormous pressure of the circumstances she was facing which consequently depleted her life energy. The peculiarities of the intense hues concentrated in the extruding buttocks and even the leg muscles, which call for attention, led us to the following interpretation. This coloration could confirm the sexual significance of those anatomical areas of Susanne's body (buttocks and legs).

As mentioned before, her situation five years later had drastically changed. In *Sleeper*, the reclining figure is presented with high chroma throughout the body, and there is no more division in the intensity of colors between the upper and lower torso (Fig. 12.4 (6)). This might be symbolically indicative of having an intimate relationship that was hitherto unknown to her. The positive changes in her mental state could be the consequence of satisfaction not only in reference to her sexual drive but also to a wider scope of her individual existential needs.

The artist implicitly "celebrates" with *Sleeper* (with the use of visual metaphors such as vivid colors, gold, and flowers) the long-sought freedom to realize an independent life away from the family's "silken straightjacket" and the opportunity to be involved full-time in painting and creating, which would lead to successful exhibitions of her works and a rewarding artistic career. All this replenished her life forces that had been exhausted during the previous decade. Positive expectations and the experience of self-realization fulfill the homeostatic function necessary for a harmonious existence.

The stair motif, analyzed in two of Susanne's works, finds certain analogies in her dreams. The artist recollects that she began to experience dreams with a recurring scenario of climbing stairs with a foreboding of approaching danger and development of fear. These dreams appeared in her adolescence[19] and continued with increasing frequency well into

19 The dreams began years before the stair motif appears in her paintings and were still recurring in the period when *Ambition* (1984) and *Sleeper* (begun in 1989) were created.

her twenties. We shall describe the relevant details as they appeared in the dreams. We do this in order to juxtapose the manifest content of the dreams and paintings and gain a better understanding of some possibly shared latent meanings.

In a typical setting for such "stair" nightmares, she felt required to walk along a "stair passage" (as she named this) that was difficult to finish. Sometimes there was a corridor, which became so low that she had to crawl. She became fearful of the passageway narrowing to the point where she would get stuck in the space, unable to move. In most cases, the dreams included stairs. Susanne usually found herself alone inside a nondescript, windowless, and dimly lit contemporary building, facing a large, gray or dull-colored stairway without any features and being prompted by an inexplicable urge to climb the stairs. They ran along the tall walls without any railing, and as the climbing progressed to a considerable height, the danger of an abysmal fall with a single misstep would rapidly increase. Initially, the steps would be easy to take, but, as the height increased, difficulties set in. Either the steps became irregular, too tall, obstructed, or there would appear the most frightening of possibilities—the stairs broke off in midair, revealing a deep, wide gap. In such a dream scenario, she could risk a dangerous jump over the frightening gap, with the full realization of the consequence of failure, which would plunge her into the depths below with an unimaginably horrifying outcome. Occasionally, she would jump, but more often she abruptly awoke in the midst of the situation with mixed feelings of fear, anxiety, frustration, and emotional exhaustion.

These nightmares haunted her from around the age of 15 up to her early thirties when they eventually faded out. It could be assumed that Susanne's liberation from the frightening dreams of stairs[20] was brought about by the drastic change in the circumstances of her life, which effectuated the cathartic release of various factors, including sexual ones, that were the sources of her frustration, anxiety, and fear.

Over such a distance of years, the artist is not able to recollect the immediate, specific circumstances in her life just prior to the first occurrence of these stair nightmares. Without that critical information, it is difficult to reconstruct the sources and triggers for this specific dreamwork. We assume that the dreams reflected particular life situations, which found means of expression in the two relevant paintings we have analyzed above (*Ambition / Sleeper*). The recurrent dreams and the artworks imply that the artist's life circumstances continue to be dormant in her memory. In accordance with our discussion of the parallel content of the above two works and her "stair" dreams, we conclude that the artist's unconscious processes employ the same stairway symbolism for encoding their messages in her dreams and paintings.

12.1.4 The Symbolism of Color

In an attempt to understand the symbolism of the color chosen for the podium, it is necessary to take into account the importance of seeing the unity of the podium's shape and color, since they enforce each other in delivering the metaphorical message embedded in their combination. The watercolor, done in preparation for the final work, shows the podium in cold, bluish-gray tones, as if made of stones, which was the artist's intention in presenting the pedestal in a neutral hue to avoid giving any competing contrast to the colorful display of the butterflies. The man-made appearance of the podium, and its artificial, angular, configuration combined with this particular choice of color (monotonous gray) metaphorically expresses Susanne's ambivalent evaluation of modern society and its impact. With all its hard edges and straight lines, it seems as if it were manufactured with precision machinery. The contour reminds Susanne of a contemporary cityscape, the symbol of civilization. She facetiously characterizes the appearance of the pedestal by stating, "It breathes with the flexibility of concrete." Thus, the platform reflects the estranged, dehumanizing aspects of urban life.

During the oil painting process, the concrete gray of the podium, as in the watercolor, was gradually and consciously modified by Susanne. After having applied gold leaf in the background, she decided to alter the podium's coloration to an "earthen tone" (opaque brown hues, ranging from medium

20 Freud stated: "Staircases, ladders, and flights of stairs, or climbing of these, either upwards or downwards, are symbolic representations of the sexual act." Freud, 1921: chapter V. Sex in Dreams, paragraph 19.

to dark), reasoning that this would create a more congruous chromatic combination. As we have come to realize through our analysis, this change conceivably reflects the unconscious' expression of specific symbolic meaning. With the shift to brown, which generally symbolizes "Mother Earth,"[21] she expressed unconscious longing for an authentic natural existence. This nuance of the pedestal, on which the drama of the seven butterflies plays out, no longer recalls the hard, bare pavement of the metropolis (gray) but rather a stylized, countryside landscape (brownish). This might be corroborated by the fact that when she was 13 years old, her family moved from the city into the nearby suburbs, where she spent her teen years and young adulthood. Accordingly, in the final painting, the earthen brown color of the podium could well allude to the rural setting where the interfamilial dynamics were enacted.

We also have to consider that the earthen hue of the podium might unconsciously signify the instinctual drives. This could be an instance of the polysemous nature of the manifestation of unconscious messages.

12.2 The Fog

A milky, misty veil rises behind the podium and partially obscures the view of the golden background. Susanne has always called this whitish-yellow layer, "fog." On the ground level of the podium, the fog is the densest, but higher up it begins slowly to dissipate, although still dulling the shimmer of the gold. Finally, about three-fifths of the way up the painting, the haze dissolves, and, above it, the golden background shines unobstructed.

Susanne is familiar with different metaphorical meanings of fog that exist in the visual, performing, and literary arts. She uses this atmospheric phenomenon in her painting to visualize different psychological states. For instance, with the fog, she has symbolically expressed perplexing situations, the confusion of "not being able to see clearly" (as she formulates it) in solving pressing problems, and being lost "in search of the truth," trying to find the appropriate answers. As such, fog has developed in her creativity as a synonym for something unknown and opaque that has become a source of bewilderment. Susanne has incorporated these meanings into her personal iconography which reflects the multitude of experiences over her lifetime. This includes inspirations from the symbolic perceptions of fog by other artists.

One such source came from the description of the fog in the Chinese poet, Huang Zunxian's poem, *The Great London Fog*[22] in her late adolescence, which resonated with her frame of mind so closely in those days that she even learned the entire poem by heart. In the following excerpts from the poem, Zunxian characterizes the weather in London:

The blue sky has died, a yellow sky reigns;

The ocean staggers, clouds tumble,
and dark spirits assemble.

Heaven is groggy from wine, and
God dreams in a stupor;

The country sinks into confusion
at the loss of its sun.

All England lies lethargic in a
boundless sea of fog —

Benighted and hazy, like the dark
kingdom of sweet dreams

The poet expresses his dismay about lack of sunlight in the fourth line of the first stanza:

The country sinks into confusion
at the loss of its sun.[23]

In his desperation for a reprieve from living in such squalor and decay, Huang Zunxian writes (stanza 2, line 2):

[*I*] *worship my wall's lamp like an idol of Buddha.*

21 Neumann 1963

22 Huang Zunxian (1848–1904). Susanne read a German translation, but the translation quoted above is from *Within the Human Realm* by J. D. Schmidt (1994, pp. 268-9). The German version has 27 lines.

23 The poem was written between 1890–1892, when the cumulative effects of the nearly two centuries of industrial revolution and the use of low-grade coal for heat, coupled with the maritime climate of London, would blanket the city with massive smog, which has come to be proverbially and romantically known as the London fog.

We also find such remarks as,

...*even the dusk gets dirty!)* (stanza 3, line 3),

...*But the air has become ink* (stanza 3, line 4),

...*Our eyes and noses are plugged up with corks* (stanza 3, line 6), and

...*the air just stinks* (stanza 4, line 4).

In 1981, Susanne came to England as a student. In preparation for her stay, using watercolor, she painted a personal book cover titled London for a travel guidebook she had bought (Fig. 12.5). The choice of a yellow sky for the city's air pollution was directly influenced by Zunxian's poem and Susanne's negative perception of this color. During her year in the metropolis, she experienced the famed fog of London and remembered it as "restricting the sight, changing the colors, swallowing the sound, and making it heavy to breathe." Such an impression of the phenomenon of fog was remarkably reinforced through an episode that happened during an excursion to the Cornish countryside in southwest England. On a sunny spring day, as she walked along the high cliffs of the Cornwall coastline, suddenly a very dense cloud formed into a white wall and came rolling in from the sea. Initially, she did not understand what was happening. Then she recognized it as fog, which was engulfing her so rapidly that she could barely see anything. For a time, she felt panic, being "embedded and trapped" in the densest fog that she had ever experienced. Susanne became enveloped in oncoming stupor and, not knowing how long it would last, she sat down and decided to wait it out. To her surprise, not too long after, the fog completely dissipated, as if the danger had never existed. She returned home with a sense of wonderment that she had successfully handled the stressful situation which had caused her anxiety.

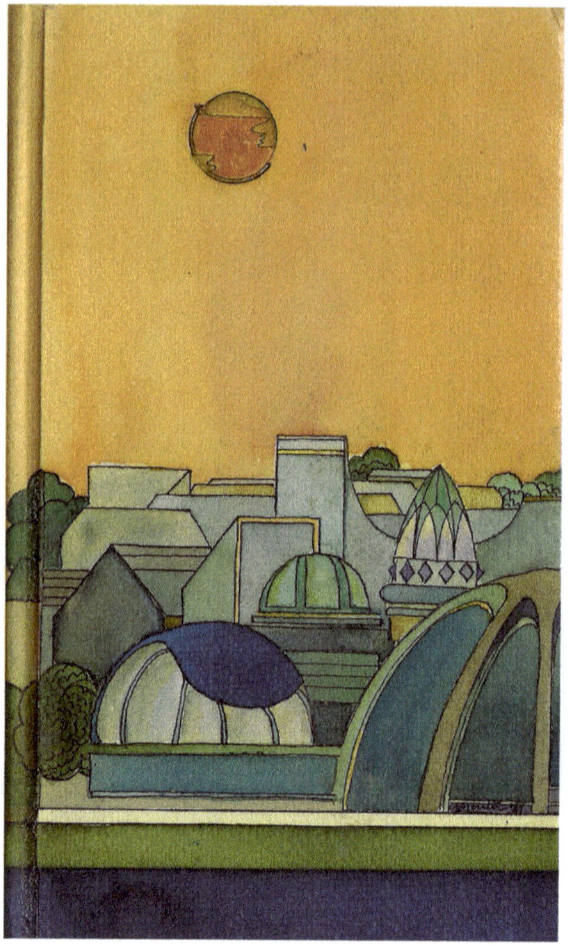

Fig. 12.5. Susanne Schuenke, *London*, 1981.
Watercolor for a book cover,
7.2 x 4.3 in (18.5 x 11cm).
Collection of the artist.

In the above examples from Susanne's life, fog is characterized as a rather negative, frightening phenomenon. She explains, in the fog one cannot see perspective, one has no outlook, no future, no hope and, thus, experiences a state of restless warning. For her, encounters with difficulties were like moving in the fog. They could be emotional, interpersonal, financial, or perhaps trying to adjust to a new and unfamiliar situation or recovering from failure or rejection. In the past, Susanne's fears, despair, depression, sadness, and phobias, like a sort of mental fog bank, became conditional states for her, signaling existing and potential instability. Therefore, the appearance of fog in her painting could symbolically manifest anticipation of coming difficulties in her personal life and to find a perspective in the future.

She would rather not "live down in the fog but higher up, where the air is clear and pure." The butterfly Air lifting off for the golden background could be allegorically understood as striving to reach the light of the sun that must lie beyond the fog. The golden background is obscured by the opaque haze at the level of the pedestal, and all the butterflies are mostly immersed in it. Only Air is ready to ascend above it. In the image of this butterfly, Susanne, to all appearances, conveys her desire for reaching higher spiritual awareness

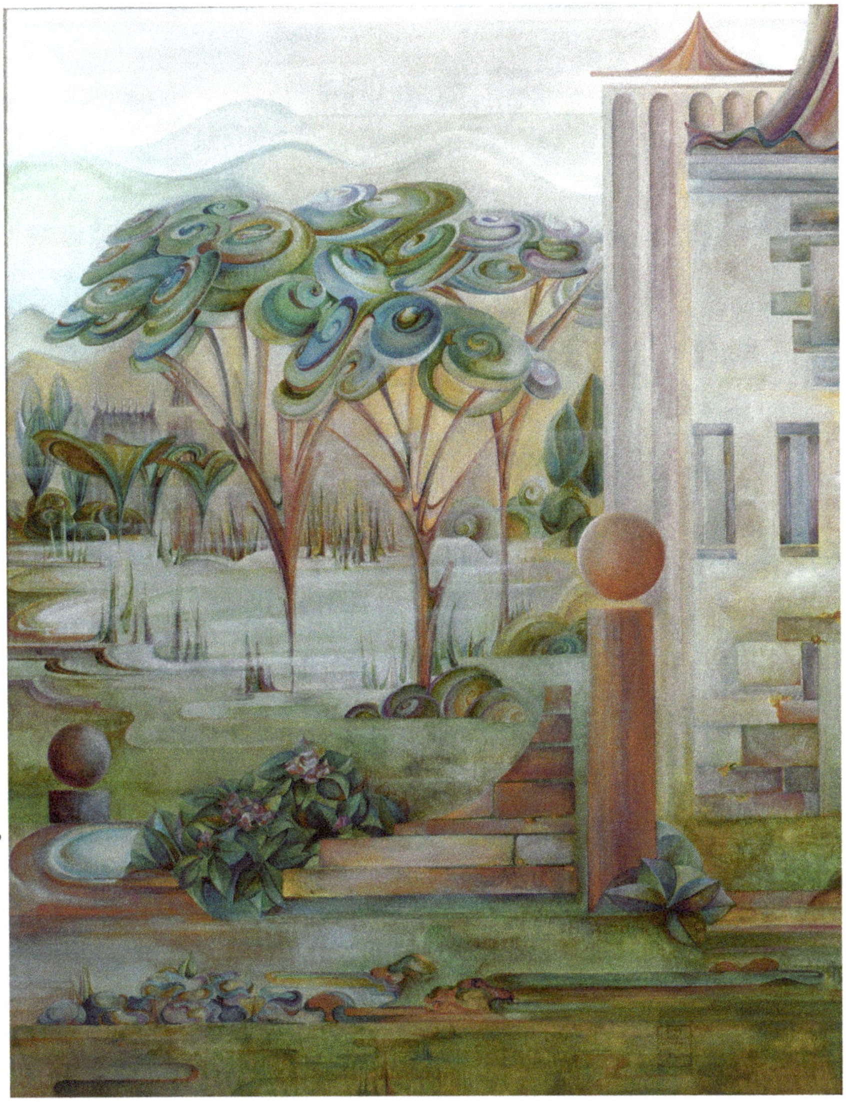

Fig. 12.6. Susanne Schuenke, *On the Way to Compiègne,* 1994. Oil on canvas, 60 x 44 in (150 x 120 cm). Collection of the artist.

and enlightenment. The idea of rising above the fog and clouds is so dear to her that whenever she flies, it gives her great pleasure when the aircraft ascends above them into the bright sunshine. Her immediate response when it happens is that of wonder and joy in seeing the disappearance of what seems like an impenetrable barrier.

She recalls that similar feelings of joy and freedom were expressed by Reinhard Mey in his popular German song in the 1970s, *Über den Wolken* (Above the Clouds), whose refrain is as follows:

Über den Wolken muß die Freiheit wohl grenzenlos sein.
Alle Ängste, alle Sorgen, sagt man,
Blieben darunter verborgen und dann
Würde, was uns groß und wichtig erscheint,
Plötzlich nichtig und klein.[24]

Above the clouds, freedom must be limitless.
All fears, all sorrows, so one says,
Remained hidden beneath, and then,
What seemed to us great and important,
Would suddenly be trivial and small.[25]

A semi-transparent fog can also be a favorable signifier in Susanne's artwork. In her 1994 painting, *On the Way to Compiègne* (Fig. 12.6), the topic, as the artist describes, is a magical walk to the lake in the park. There, the observer enters an oasis surrounded by the hovering layers of a mystical fog, which separates him from the present world. Silence and peace inspire the visitor's imagination to sense an otherworldly harmony. In this context, in *Give Me Wings!,* the golden background appears through the dense fog as the harbinger of approach of the glowing spiritual realms.

24 Reinhard Mey, *Über den Wolken* (*Above the clouds*) (Intercord, 1984).

25 The artist's translation.

12.3 The Golden Background

12.3.1 The Intended Meaning and Influences

The decision to gild the background was made by Susanne to achieve a sense of "calm and purity, as well as powerful and beautiful surroundings for those extraordinary butterflies." She felt that using genuine gold leaf would be perfect for creating this desired effect. Gold is a precious metal,[26] not a paint color, and it has no hue variation in its pure, unalloyed state. Different conditions can significantly change the observer's impression of the gold's appearance. These factors encompass both objective and subjective aspects. On the objective side, they constitute the source of light, the surroundings, and the position of the onlooker relative to the metal, due to the highly reflective nature of gold.[27] On the subjective side, those factors are the peculiarities of the observer's personality, culture, education, sensibility, way of thinking, imagination, fantasies, experiences, emotions, memories, etc.

For millennia, in the religious sphere, gold has been acknowledged as the most valuable metal for the embellishment of devotional objects and images, ritual accessories, and buildings dedicated to venerating the divine. In contemporary times, gold retains its mystery, enchantment, and unchallenged worth in both sacred and secular environments. In the iconography of the world religions, divinities and saints are often depicted with golden haloes surrounding their heads, where the shining disc symbolically combines gold and the sun to represent the spiritual energy and power that these holy beings possess. In Europe, during the Middle Ages and Renaissance, gold was employed in the manufacturing and decorating of countless religious objects, and, in paintings, it was applied as highlights (such as nimbi[28]) or as a flat background representing sacred space.

While living in England, Susanne saw some beautiful examples of the use of a solid golden background in such works as *The Wilton Diptych* (unknown artist, c. 1395–1399) and Masaccio's *Virgin and Child* (Italian, 1401–27) at the National Gallery in London. She was also familiar with the extensive use of golden background in Byzantine and late medieval Italian paintings. With the advent of the Renaissance, European painters began to adopt elaborate systems of perspective to enrich their paintings with a palpable illusion of spatial depth, thus removing the rationale for the existence of a flat background, particularly that of gold. This trend continued well into the later nineteenth century. Pre-Raphaelites and Art Nouveau artists (most notably Gustav Klimt), re-introduced gold into European painting. All this was known to Susanne even before she started her formal studies of art history, as her father experimented with gold leaf in one of his paintings and suggested that she should incorporate this material into her palette.

An additional encouragement for using precious metals in her paintings came from her admiration for Asian paintings, particularly those from Japan. Unlike in Europe, the sumptuous use of gold has never abated since Japan's medieval era. It has continued to be freely employed in both secular and religious paintings. Susanne is familiar with traditional Japanese folding screens, palatial sliding doors, and innumerable lacquerware objects. She admires how the integration of gold leaf into the artworks gives aesthetic satisfaction for the beholder on both visual and meditative levels. A prime, relevant example is a pair of six-panel screens with the topic of *The Plain of Musashi, Mount Fuji and the Moon*, (Fig. 12.7).[29] The painter of the screens presented a naturalistic plain with grasses in the low part and a solid gold leaf background, bare of any individual details in the upper part of the composition. On the left

26 As early as the 4th millennium BCE, gold was universally admired by mankind as the material symbol of power, wealth, refinement, and beauty, as well as of divine omnipotence and the purity of spiritual existence. To this day, mankind's fascination and admiration for gold continues unabated in these regards. In ancient Egypt, the royal tomb chamber was called the "Golden House," (Breitling 1975, pages 10 and 226-7), and was frequently filled with golden artifacts. Grave goods throughout the world since prehistoric times often include various objects made of gold, both sacred and mundane, giving archeologists and historians valuable information about the social status of the deceased.

27 Gold strongly reflects the color of its surroundings, particularly red and yellow. For example, when an observer is dressed in red, the gold object the person sees will have a reddish shine. It is likely, however, the onlooker will not be aware that the color of one's clothing causes the observed tint.

28 Murray 1998, page 224 "halo."

29 For another example see: Munroe 1983, catalogue number 2.

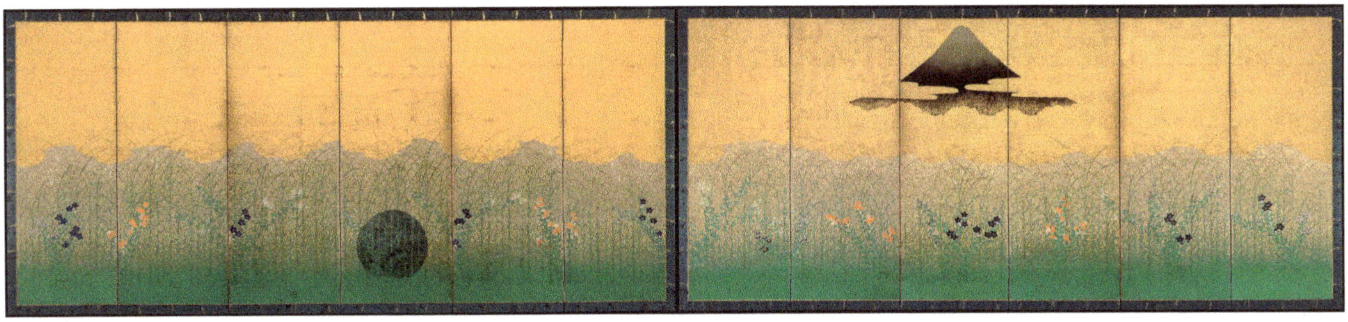

(a) Screen with full moon (b) Screen with Mount Fuji

Fig. 12.7. Anonymous, *The Plain of Musashi, Mount Fuji and the Moon*, with the full moon over the horizon. Japanese, Art Gallery of South Australia, Adelaide, Australia. A pair of screens.

screen, the artist depicted the moon disc behind the plants (Fig. 12.7 (a) or Fig. 8.3) and, on the right screen, the summit of Fujisan emerges out of the golden clouds near the top like a mystical sanctuary (Fig. 12.7 b). This kind of Japanese artwork evokes Susanne's emotional response to beauty and the harmony of nature and her inspiration to transcendental imagination.

For many years, she had developed her own iconography in her art to represent spiritual realms. Eventually, she settled on gold as the most appropriate material to visually represent this essence. By creating the upper portion of the background for *Give Me Wings!* in gold leaf, the artist fully implemented her desire to use gold as a metaphorical representation of the spiritual dimensions. Moreover, by laying down the gold leaf squares uniformly and aligning them vertically and horizontally, she created an orderly background pattern. This arrangement can be construed as a symbolic representation of the orderly realms of the Universe as the artist envisages it.

The golden background encompasses the podium, the fog, and the butterflies. As we have pointed out, she was unaware of the unconscious encoding of latent meanings in the imagery, to which she spontaneously added a monochromatic golden background. She modified the latter by adding the fog which dampens the lower part of the golden backdrop. However, the gold shines through, and it does not appear as a merely sterile, decorative foil behind the scene. The gold, symbolizing a powerful spiritual background, can be perceived as a layer behind the physical world represented by the "earthly," atmospheric mist, just as clouds drift before the infinite blue of the sky.

12.3.2 Golden Areas in Susanne's Paintings

Long before *Give Me Wings!*, Susanne had frequently employed gold leaf in her paintings. She uses this element as an expression of an abstract background, an embellishment of various constituents of the design, or an area that springs up in the composition as a place singled out to emphasize its spiritual significance. The artist regards the precious metal as much more than merely "a beautiful extra color." As mentioned above, she intends to indicate a sphere of spirituality with it. The realm represented by gold could be the divine dominion itself or traces of the spiritual essence in the human world. With the use of gold, she epitomizes the state of harmony and beauty.

In the following discussion, we present a sample selection of her works to substantiate how the artist uses gold to metaphorically represent the presence of the divine or transcendent dimensions that lie beyond the world of everyday human experience. In Susanne's first oil painting with gold leaf, *Destiny*, (1988) (Fig. 9.21), a green female nude is seen casually playing with a puppet on string over churning water while reclining on a golden platform (Fig. 9.22). Her surrealistic skin color, combined with the golden terrace signifying the supernatural essence of this being, catapults the naturalistically depicted figure out of the human world. Following the millennia-long tradition of allegorization, the artist intended to transpose the abstract idea of Fate into a visual image. Susanne's goddess of destiny nonchalantly toys with the dangling, blindfolded human marionette who is unaware of its predicament over the abyss.

This canvas set a course for other artworks involving related philosophical topics that Susanne has painted over the subsequent years. She consciously employs the precious gold to define a sacred domain superior to the sphere of human existence. For instance, in *Elysian Fields*, (1990) (Fig. 12.8) a life-giving deity reposes on a golden plateau above the stars. She dispenses a drop of divine essence, a spark of her spiritual nature, onto a stylized human figure who is ready to enter the earthly world below (Fig. 10.20).

In 1992, Susanne created the six-panel screen titled, *The Land of Iro-Ha* (Fig. 12.9), as an imaginative mountainscape inspired by the well-known thousand-year-old Japanese poem *Iro-Ha*. The poem, included below, was the source of her imagination.

Though the scent may linger
After the flower scatters,
For whom the world stays unchanged?
Today we cross the deep mountains
Of shifting fortunes,
Neither seeing fugitive dreams
Nor intoxicated by them.[30]

Susanne depicts the blooming mountain idyll floating in a golden setting, with which she signifies a superior aesthetic and reality. She bestows an enchanting beauty and harmony on nature for which humanity longs. Meditative immersion evokes thoughts about impermanent fate and eternal existence. The artist returns to the topic of fate ten years later with *Destiny II*, (1997) (Fig. 12.10), in

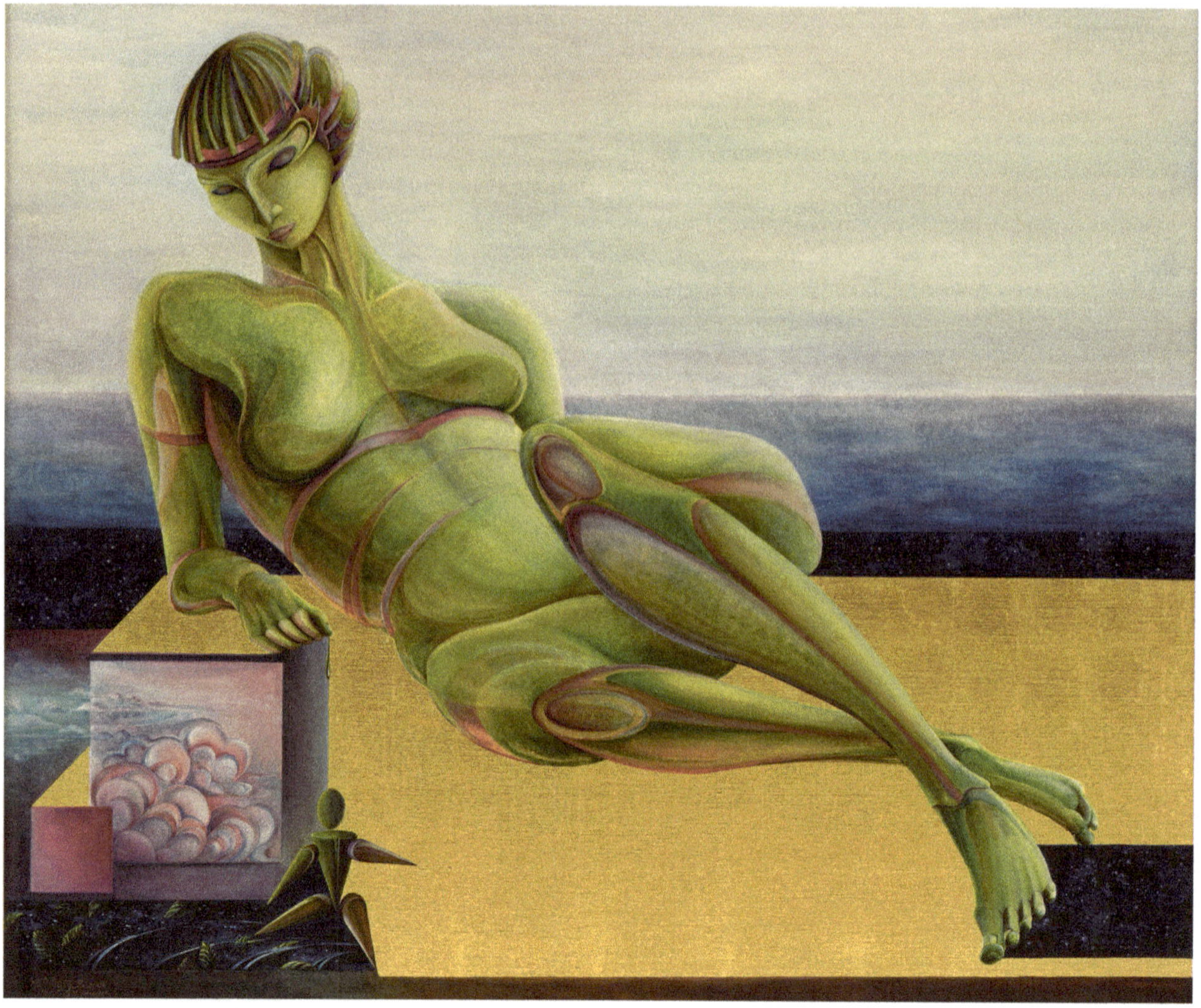

Fig. 12.8. Susanne Schuenke, *Elysian Fields*, 1990. Oil and gold leaf on canvas, 60 x 44 in (150 x 120 cm). Corporate collection, Essen, Germany.

30 A private English translation commissioned for this work.

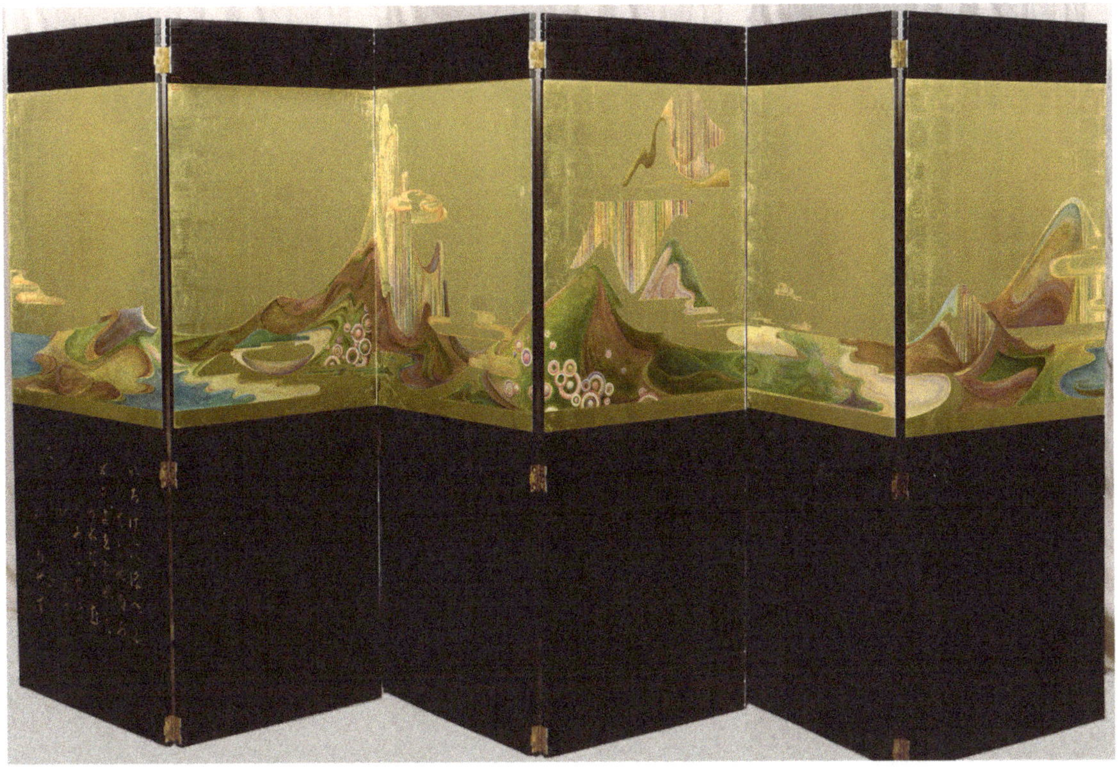

Fig. 12.9. Susanne Schuenke, *The Land of Iro-Ha,* 1992. Oil and gold leaf on lacquered wood, a six-part folding screen, 67 x 150 in (170 x 384 cm). Collection of the artist.

which she portrays a stylized human figure taking center stage and preparing to enter the physical world that is represented by the cloud-covered ground beneath. Despite an uncertain future, the blindfolded figure is courageously parting the golden curtain which separates the temporal earthly abode from eternal heaven, his true spiritual home. He steps onto the ground below for his sojourn, endowed with a plan, spiritual gifts, and universal values to fulfill his mission. To visually indicate this idea, Susanne adorns various details of the figure's body in gold, and other parts in earthly hues, indicating his dual nature—spiritual and material.

A few years later, in 2000, Susanne painted *The Native* (Fig. 12.11), a human portrait in left profile.[31] The rigid, mathematical structures signify the steadfast and methodical patterns of rational thought. The triangular sliding doors open onto the space to the left that is filled with the light of a golden background. This symbolizes the transcendent realm of spirituality, where everything that constitutes the worldly mind loses its framework and instead new values unfold. In her 2001 canvas, *The Dream of Peace* (Fig. 12.12), Susanne rendered a seated person contemplating peace in the world. She surrounded this figure with forms and symbols belonging to a variety of cultures, civilizations, and philosophies, all searching for the magic formula for peace. Because the artist considers peace to be an exalted spiritual state, she bathed the allegorical scene in a golden illumination casting a brilliant light that symbolizes her dream for humanity's better future.

In *Buddha,* (2002) (Fig. 6.16), Susanne interpreted the stages of a person's spiritual development as a journey on a vertical pathway that starts from the darkened area on the bottom of the canvas, signifying the gloom of spiritual ignorance. The path gradually moves upward through the region of mellow golden brown, until it finally reaches the brilliant realm of golden light at the top—the state of enlightenment. Susanne creates this visual metaphor of an individual's spiritual evolution from darkness to light. With its remarkable gradation of colors, *Buddha* foreshadows the three elements which comprise the overall setting of *Give Me Wings!* two years later: The dark podium at the bottom, the fog above, and the pure gold of the golden background at the top, each standing for a different stage of evolving spiritual awareness.

31 The artist titled the canvas originally as *Auftritt* (English: *Entrance*) with the intention to express the transition from an existence based on rationality to that of intuition and imagination. The title *Native* was suggested by a friend.

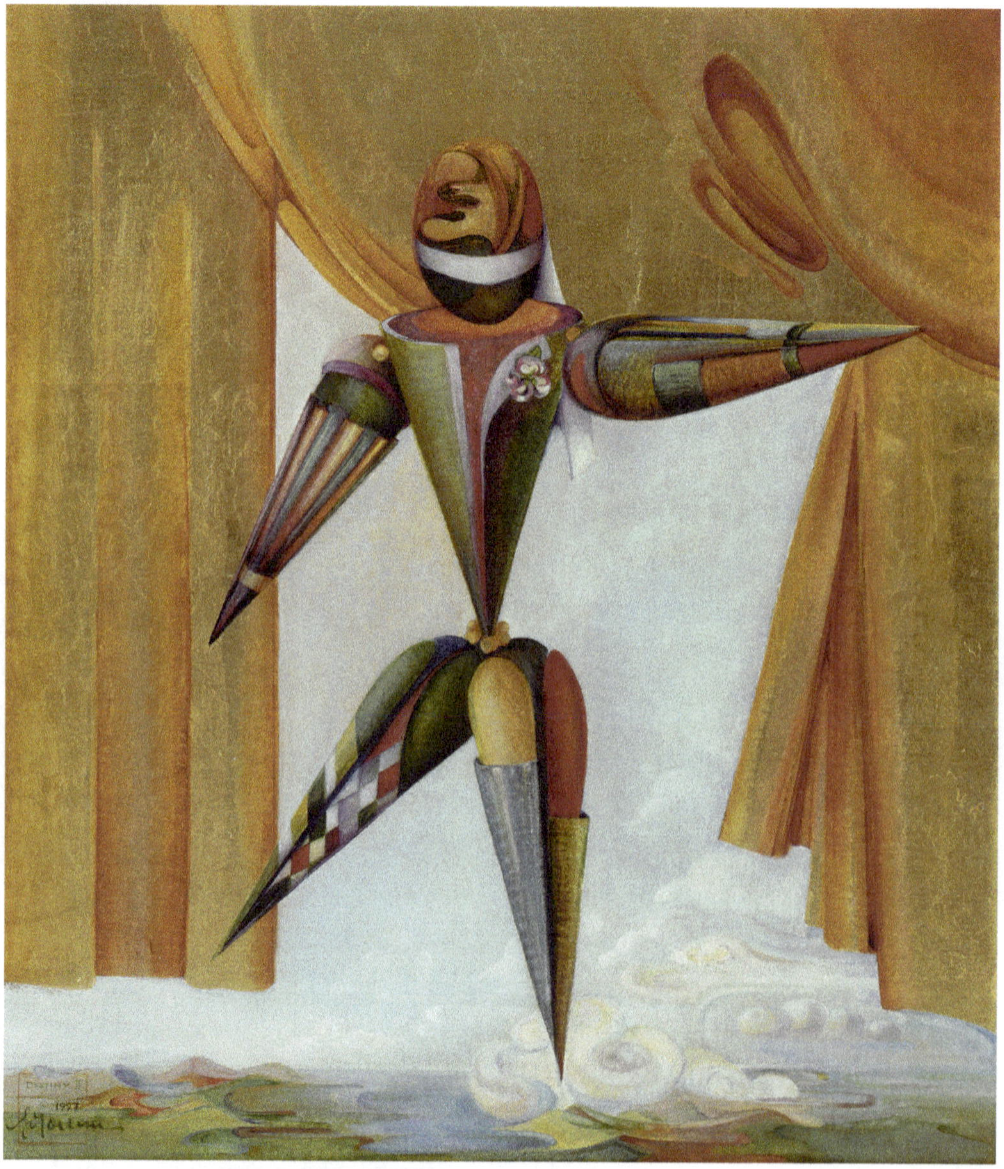

Fig. 12.10. Susanne Schuenke, *Destiny II*, 1997. Oil and gold leaf on canvas, 20 x 18 in (50 x 45 cm). Private collection, Florida.

12.4 The Artist's Concept of "Here and There"

The artist's concept of "here and there" has briefly been touched on (chapter 8), and in this section we examine it in *Give Me Wings!*'s imagery as allegorical representations of different states of an individual's existence. The term appears in the poetic commentary regarding Pale Moonlight: "Her essence ... radiates in spiraling loops or in graceful bends, sharply marking the division between 'here' and 'there,'." In chapter 8, we identified this division as referring to the separation between the front and hind wings, and coined it the "breaking point." It came as a revelation that this point coincided with the boundary of the fog, above which the golden background rose free. This separation reflects different aspects of human life: biological, psychological, social, and spiritual. We came to this assumption by analyzing the peculiarities of Pale Moonlight's wings. The hind one, fully immersed in the fog, metaphorically encodes a worldly life that embraces sensual and material objectives ("here"). In contrast, the front wing, rising above the dense haze (part of "here"), stretches high up as a symbolic visualization of the ascent to spiritual realms ("there") represented by the golden background.

It is worthwhile to give a short description of the artist's concept of "here" and "there." These terms are the artist's personal nomenclature articulating her comprehension of different individual meanings of existence.

For her, "here" stands for what most people would describe as the everyday existence defined by the physical body, its senses, and the material world. For Susanne, "here" also includes her habits, conditioned by the family's and society's demands. These determine her behavior and interrelationships, following appropriate customs and rules. She likes to say, of the existence in "here": "It ranges from learning to brush the teeth,[32] to the legal code of society." In the world of "here," Susanne cannot escape from many negative sensory influences that cause obnoxious intrusions into her mind, such as the noise of incessant vehicular traffic and mindless mass media commercials, the visual onslaught of moving neon lights, the smell of synthetic scents etc. The most disquieting and frantic issue for her is an unexpected encounter with information about the acts of atrocity and inhumanity that appear to inhabit every other page of history books and news reports. Susanne observes that, with each new generation, the lessons of the past appear to be forgotten, and injustice and violence are relentlessly repeated. There is a deficit of compassion and moral responsibility, and, in their place, a surfeit of incorrigible prejudice and the defensiveness of political and religious ideologies. Such situations make it painful for her to tolerate this sort of "here" on earth. Thus, the "here" as it presently persists gives her the reason to search beyond "here" for "there" to find spiritual awakening and enlightenment.

Susanne defines "there" as essentially the opposite of "here." Spiritual aspects predominate in her speculation about "there." She considers this state as being free from the spatiotemporal considerations and limitations of the physical world, allowing her to travel "there" in the present and the future in her imagination.

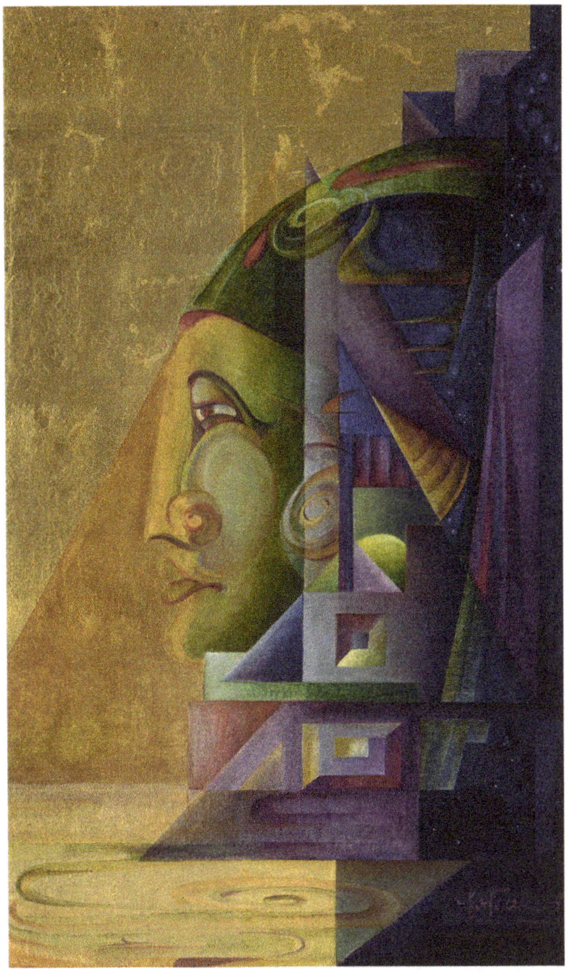

Fig. 12.11. Susanne Schuenke, *The Native*, 2000. Oil and gold leaf on canvas, 25 x 16 in (62 x 40 cm). Private collection, Florida.

Her concept of "there" developed slowly and has become more significant over the years. Whenever she sank into a deep state of melancholy, the thought of it has given her a way out of a mentally suffocating cycle of despair. "There" has been a beacon to help her navigate through the often turbulent and turbid waters of "here."

Susanne envisages that in the future, "there" could be integrated with "here." "There" for her is a metaphor for spiritual awareness and realization, out of which a better existence arises for all. "There" is not a singular invention of the artist's

32 The following anecdotal incident from Susanne's childhood might be able to shed light on how sensitive and imaginative her psyche can be. She has never liked to brush her teeth. Only during analysis did she become aware of the root of this aversion. In her pre-school years, she had a children's book by Thorbjorn Egner titled, *Karius und Bactus* (*Karius and Bactus*. English translation. 1986). The main characters of the book are two young "tooth trolls" living a good life inside a boy's mouth, building a house in his tooth cavities until one day a dentist destroys the house and flushes them out of the boy's mouth. The fate of the two young dental rascals horrified young Susanne, believing that she also had such "friends" living inside her mouth. She thus internalized her positive identification with the two "troll" boys and did not want to harm them with the toothbrush.

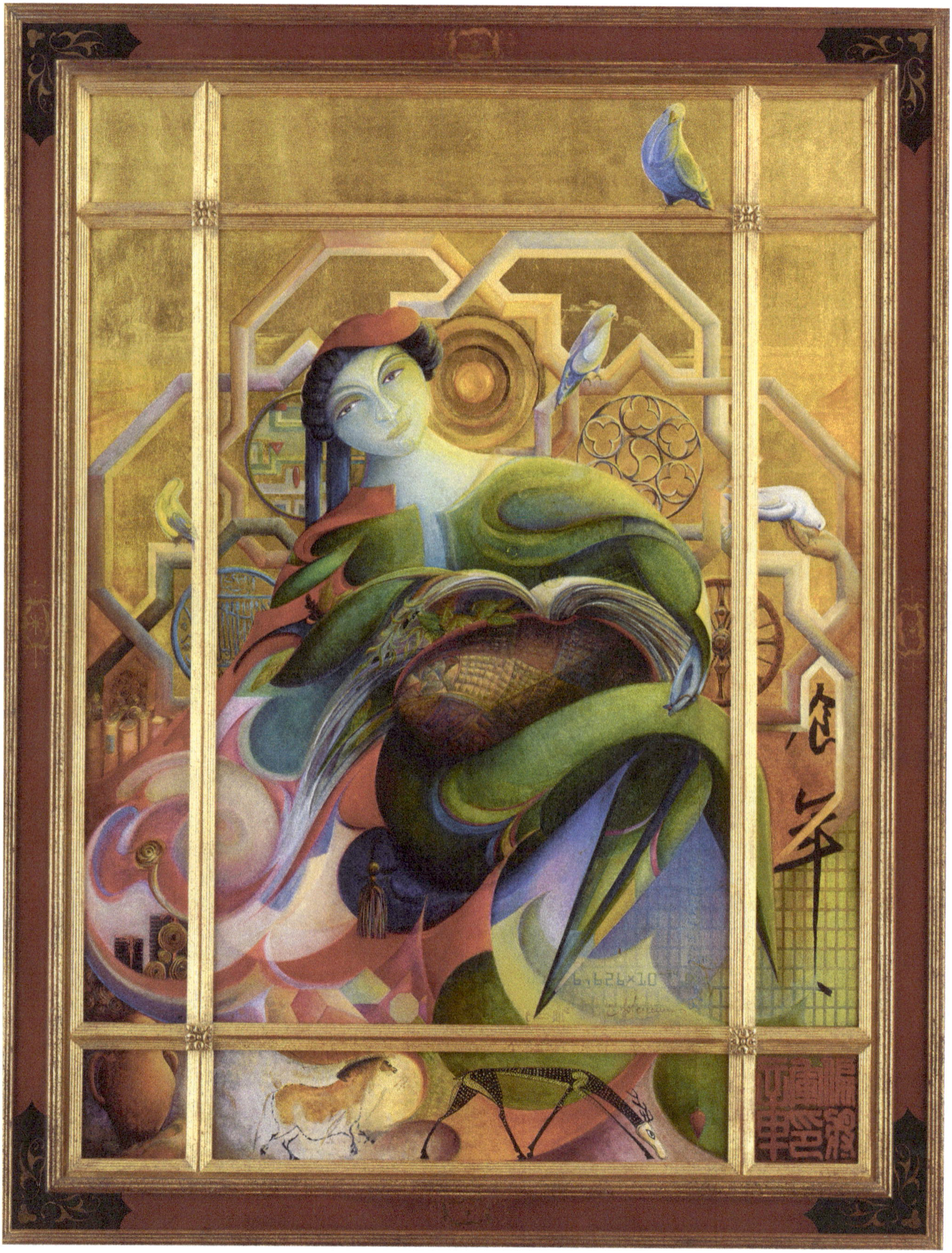

Fig. 12.12. Susanne Schuenke, *The Dream of Peace*, 2001.
Oil and gold leaf on canvas, 50 x 40 in (125 x 100 cm). Private collection, Florida.

mind. Rather, it is another name for all sorts of terms and designations that have been brought forward by humankind to denote that superlative state of existence. "There" has never been precisely defined, but always intuitively longed for. The notion in its many variations has been progressively nourished by cultural and religious traditions from generation to generation and modified by individual and collective experiences.

We can trace the artist's attempt to visualize her general idea of "there" back to as early as 1988 in a group of oil paintings consisting of *Destiny* (Fig. 9.21), *Waiting For Tomorrow* (Fig. 8.28), and *Collector of Souls* (Fig. 10.24). In these canvases, she already expressed her contemplation of "there" in a symbolic way, using the forms, colors (including precious metals), and composition, as signifiers for the visualization of this concept.

In *Destiny*, the goddess of Fate reclines on a golden plateau and benevolently guides the fortune of a human puppet, holding the strings to prevent it from falling haplessly into the abyss. Susanne metaphorically projects that this superior being from "there" protects the human from the perils of "here," keeping him connected with her realm.

In *Waiting For Tomorrow*, two colossal figures, stationed on mountainous islands in a silvery sea, are looking out toward the infinite depth of the night sky and contemplating the perspectives of the future (Fig. 8.28). The scale of the landscape indicates the monumental size of the figures, transposed into a cosmic realm ("there") far away from our "here." The artist envisions that all their attention is focused on the awe-inspiring starry sky,[33] searching the distant horizon in anticipation of the dawn of a new era. The last painting mentioned above, *Collector of Souls* (Fig. 10.24; see chapters 7 and 10 for more details), depicts a divine messenger climbing golden steps above the clouds and stars toward a higher spiritual realm, "there," to deliver three human souls.

She expects the domain of "there," as a more desirable realm of existence than the "here" of today, will increasingly dominate perspectives toward the future. As a consequence, she believes it is possible to gradually bring some aspect of "there" to our life "here," thereby reaching the desired state of convergence between the two. Her imagery in *Longing* (see Fig. 7.18) metaphorically reflects her desire for the synthesis of "here" and "there."

Moreover, she anticipated this perspective long before creating *Give Me Wings!*. It was quite a surprise for the artist to understand, in the context of this research, that her watercolor, *About the Noise and Silence in this World* from 1982 (see chapter 8 and Fig. 8.2 (a)) contains exactly this prospect of evoking qualities from "there" to experience them "here." This painting presumably constitutes the artist's first attempt to express this wishful realm through her imagery. She delights in the experiences of glimpses of "there" through her creative life and by some rare moments of spiritual insight through meditation and imagination, as well as by interactions with friends.

In particular, Susanne has developed her personal way to step out from "here." For instance, when the artist deeply immerses herself in her creativity, she is full of feelings of timeless joy and peacefulness that inspire her limitless imagination. In this state, she is able to travel away from the world of "here" into "there." Susanne craves such a transformation as an imperative of spiritual need, deriving from her inner state. Thus, Susanne likes to let "pen and brush take control," by which the transition to a special condition of mindfulness is often realized. This could be considered equal to an ethereal experience of "there."

Being fully absorbed in the creation of the seven butterflies for hours, Susanne integrated herself into the imagery. The artist and butterflies became interchangeable, when the reality of the material world and the hoped-for higher spiritual existence commingled. The golden background appears as the pathway leading from the heavy base of earthly reality to spiritual heights. In *Give Me Wings!*, the butterfly Air metaphorically plays the role of a mediator between the two domains. It is ready to ascend beyond the bounds of the podium and the fog ("here"), leaving the ground, overcoming its gravity, and flying toward a higher freedom. This leads to liberation from earthly restrictions and materialism into the realm of spirituality and enlightenment ("there").

As we have pointed out, it has taken many years for Susanne to see the significance of "there" in her life and to accept "here" as worthy of living, in spite of its many shortcomings and wrongs. In *Longing* (Fig. 7.18), painted just before *Give Me Wings!*, a man looks out through a magical window located in the upper half of the painting

33 The constellations depicted in the painting are identifiable as Taurus, Gemini, Orion, Pleiades, and so forth.

into a realm of silvery, ethereal swirls as signs for transcendental domain. With this, the artist intended to depict a spiritual existence ("there"), which the onlooking human figure yearns for. In the lower half of the canvas, at the feet of the sitter, the world of technology and commerce, of objects and money, of hierarchy and class, of desire and accumulation enfolds in daily human affairs ("here"). "Here" and "there" begin to share the same stage, and with this, the artist appeals to people to strive for a harmonious symbiosis of both realms.

A year later, in *Give Me Wings!*, the artist's perception of the interaction between earthly reality and a spiritual dimension has become more comprehensively expressed. The visual metaphors and allegories that we found in the images of the butterflies and the setting—podium, fog, golden background—manifest the here-and-there concept of her personal Weltanschauung.

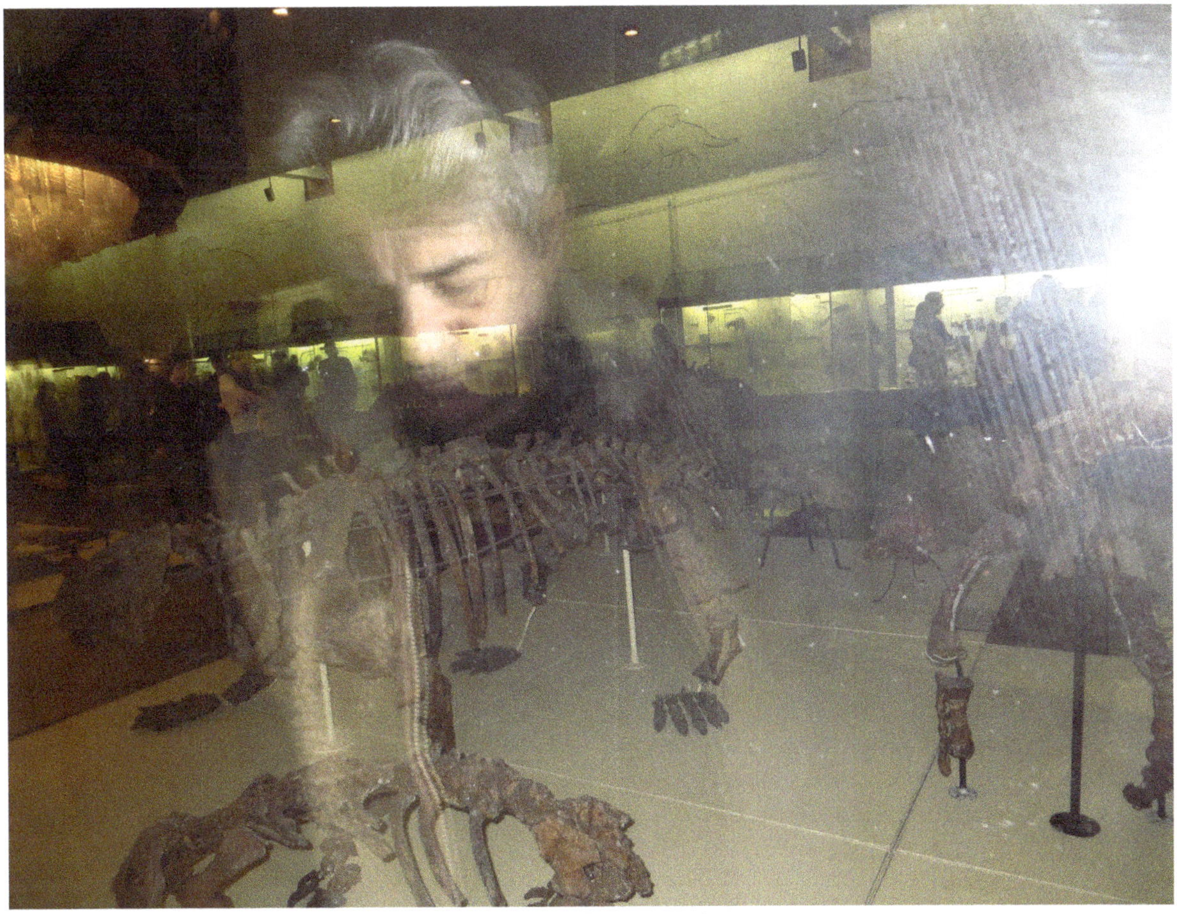

Fig. 13.0. Naum G. Itkin at the Orlov Museum for Paleontology, Moscow, Russia, 2013

Chapter 13

Pathways of Creativity

Contemplations, Comparisons, and Correlations

by Naum G. Itkin

13.1 Discovery of Traces of the Unconscious in Painting

Uncovering the sources of artists' inspirations and of the conscious as well as the unconscious influences on the pathways of their creativity has long been a focal point of discussions and contentions among art scholars and critics. We focused on these issues during a twelve-year research project in analyzing the traces of the unconscious manifesting in symbolic, metaphorical, and allegorical visual expressions in the surrealist paintings of Susanne Schuenke. The psychoanalytic approach employed in our quest, as originally used by Freud in the interpretation of dreams, has turned out to be fruitful in the analysis of her artwork, revealing a dominant role of the unconscious in the creation of her images. This statement is also supported by similar studies of surrealist and expressionist paintings created by various artists.[1] Our investigation has substantiated the prominent role of emotions, motivations, and

1 Lomas 2000; Kandel 2012

memories in the development of the imaginative process. Such unconscious elements are encrypted in symbolic and metaphorical visual imagery. Artworks of surrealist painters can present a worthwhile subject for the scientific study of the origins of the images' creation, analogous to dreams. The analysis of the symbolism of stairs in Susanne's recurrent dreams and two of her paintings revealed a comparable latent content that reflected her existential situations and metaphorical representations of biological drives (subchapters 12.1.2 and 12.1.3). In the course of our research, we were able to uncover many instances of such homogenous unconscious manifestations in the imagery of artworks[2] and dreams. These may indicate a common source for their genesis. Consequently, research on artworks may constitute a significant addition and complement to the study of dreams and their unconscious roots.

In our quest, we were walking into a barely known territory of creativity. Our crossing of this unpredictable topography, exploring meandering waterways back to their source, and recognizing a pathway through surprising discoveries were quite rewarding. The analysis of the visual arts essentially became another "royal road to the unconscious" besides the dream analysis to which Freud was referring. Our exploration has allowed us to form assumptions based on consistent and correlated evidence that not only confirms existing psychoanalytic concepts but also extends them with further observations and perspectives. The discoveries of the symbolic, metaphorical, and allegorical meanings of created images through the scrutiny of their specific configurations, forms, colorations, and compositions significantly deepen the understanding of the modus operandi of the unconscious, shedding light on their intrinsic roots. Therefore, the possibility of studying unconscious processes through different channels, such as the analysis of artworks, could verify and extend our knowledge about the topic in question. In this context, the interpretation of an artist's subjective experiences, as coded in the imagery, can be a reliable foundation to understand how the complex interaction of biological, psychological, and spiritual variables result in the emergence of the artist's personal iconography and unconscious symbolism.

We have shown repeatedly through the analysis of the artist's paintings, particularly *Give Me Wings!,* that in spite of her assumption that her images were determined by her conscious mind, her unconscious was fully involved in the creative process and cloaked its voice into details of the images. Her narrative paintings turned out to be brimming with implicit messages, of which she had no awareness until this study was completed. The artist's free associations and references to her past experiences revealed a kaleidoscope of her inner reality—emotions, motivations, and memories—that led us to the decipherment of the hitherto unknown meanings of her images. Many traces of the unconscious, which were stealthily subverting her conscious intentions during the painting process, came to the surface through the analysis. The latent content of the messages, embedded in her paintings, became accessible for her deliberation.

The vast majority of the psychological studies of painters from the past, which has been published until now, lacks sufficient records of the psychophysiological states of artists. Such detailed information, especially concerning the artists' personal lives and their significant emotional experiences, was not available to the researchers. This had been a major drawback. Rarely do the investigators have direct access to the artist's private life through a substantial and ongoing dialogue. The data obtained directly from intimate and revealing conversations with the artist are invaluable and of great scientific interest. Any information uncovered will have varying degrees of usefulness for the analysis, which could bring to light many puzzling phenomena of creativity. For this reason, it was of inestimable advantage to this study that Susanne, from 2007 onwards, recognizing the value of such an endeavor, agreed to provide her private data without any attempt to conceal. The information gathered from her memories, commentaries, and associations has allowed us to connect particular details of her paintings with some of her life experiences. Moreover, our research has clearly shown the importance of the seemingly trivial and offhand remarks of the artist that on many occasions led to significant breakthroughs in our analysis. We are not aware of any published

2 This idea was used by André Breton in his *Manifeste du surrealism* (1924), in which he defined surrealism as "pure psychic automatism" (see chapter 1).

casework in the field of psychoanalytic research, in which a similar instance of close and sustained corroboration with the painter was available as the basis of an extended study.

While we were engaged in the research, we tried to distance ourselves from all-embracing general concepts, considering that every hypothesis could be speculation based on biases and private persuasions. This might predetermine the entire trajectory of the interpretation of innumerable events and emotional experiences, which have influenced the formation of the individual's psyche. The unconscious is an inexhaustible fountain that originates from an immense reservoir fed by the emotional systems with their universal and personal sensory essence,[3] reflecting negative and positive valence compelled by biological and socio-cultural imperatives recorded in the genome. The significant emotional experiences manifest in apparently unceasing streams of symbolic images conveying multifarious messages. Their meanings are mostly unnoticed by the conscious mind except for their registration as feelings, first impressions, intuitions, or sudden novel ideas.

The case study has been a fascinating journey into the maze of artistic creativity to trace the latent content of Susanne's images in her artwork. This is possible due to the sui generis nature of the unconscious that converts significant emotional experiences, coding them into the imagery. Through analysis, we could decipher the unconscious messages. The mechanism is analogous to the phenomena of dreamwork. It was a great surprise for both authors to discover the far-reaching extent to which the unconscious exercised its power to influence, interfere, or even overrule the conscious design and deliberation of a well-trained and experienced artist. We came to recognize that the artist's unconscious clandestinely guided Susanne's creative output. Nevertheless, how the artistic capacity transforms and weaves conscious and unconscious influences into a narrative painting that tells "a visible story," continues in many aspects to be an enigma. In our work, we offer some plausible keys to unlocking "a mysterious book with seven seals."

One of the most significant findings in our research has been derived from the analysis of *Give Me Wings!* which became the focus of our case study. We discovered the phenomenon of unconscious personification embedded in the images of the butterflies. Butterflies Nos. 1, 3, and 4 personify the artist herself; butterflies Nos. 2 and 5—her father; butterfly No. 6—her mother, and also Susanne and her aunt; butterfly No. 7—spirituality; and butterfly No. 8—the deceased mother. This is quite remarkable, but it should not be a surprise since this phenomenon is one of the typical aspects of dreamwork. The image of each butterfly contains specific details that are metaphorical messages about a personified individual. This information can be deciphered through analysis. Also, the community of seven butterflies symbolizes succinctly the interrelationships in the artist's family. Thus, the latent content of the painting is the saga of the family and its struggling heroine, Susanne, and she had not the faintest inkling of this when she created *Give Me Wings!*.

Creating the assembly of seven butterflies, the artist unconsciously assigned certain hierarchical relationships governing them. Rank, ambition, competition, dominance, and submission are displayed on the "stage" of this painting. All those aspects turned out to be derived from verified life situations in the artist's past. We have come to this insight through the analysis of the images' compositional arrangement, position, relative size, posture, structural details, coloration, and directional orientation. The creation of her imagery can be considered a symbolic replica and chronicle of her family based on the unconsciously coded significant emotional experiences from Susanne's past. We could even posit that the messages conveyed in the painting extend to social implications beyond the artist's family circle. For example, we can observe a certain patriarchal hierarchy metaphorically expressed in the painting, which reflects this social order that still pervades the world and that Susanne has opposed all her life.

In *Give Me Wings!* and other works of the artist, we could correlate a number of specific formations with related underlying metaphorical information. The images of the fan and sun in Susanne's artwork were associated with her mother, who collected antique fans, and whose love and support were sunshine to everybody in the family. The mother repeatedly depicted an anthropomorphic face of sun in her artwork (subchapter 7.2.2). A stretched-out index finger or

3 Peil 2014. We mean also sensory-cognitive context.

resembling configurations remind her of father's authoritative directives. Bubbles and spheres, the artist's cherished objects, signify an abundance of symbolism in her art. They refer to such diverse topics as enlightenment, mental energy, hope, brevity of personal existence, and the soul (subchapter 7.3). Similarly, circles and rings carry manifold meanings in the artist's personal iconography, and they can symbolize perfection, totality, eternity, harmony, and the state of being embraced and protected (subchapter 9.3.5). The same spherical and circular configurations can have highly negative qualities for Susanne when they represent eyeballs and navels, since those are major sources of her phobic reactions. Another motif in her artwork is the metaphor of the craters on the moon. They are caused by meteorite impacts, and the artist identifies them with scars, applying those shapes intentionally to indicate pain and suffering.

Moreover, in the hind wing of butterfly No. 3, the images of oversized oval scales, which Susanne associates with the Ephesian Artemis, the mother goddess of fertility, could be the embodiment of the artist's suppressed reproductive drive (subchapter 8.2.4).

Sickle shapes, ridges, serrated contours, spiky configurations, pointed and elongated objects, sharp tips, a stretched-out index finger, and oblong, rounded formations carry unconscious latent meaning, concealing sexual and aggressive tendencies that lurk underneath peaceful façades in some of her paintings. We came to recognize that these objects and configurations were the signifiers of original circumstances from the artist's past and the emotions associated with them, which exerted a considerable influence on the creation of the images. The combination of raised ridges, sickle shapes, and serrated contour of butterfly No. 4. reminded the artist spontaneously of dragon wings, which we decoded as symbolic traces of the aggressive drive concealed underneath the beautiful surface of this butterfly—a personification of Susanne (chapter 9). Such unconscious imagery could be at the root of the artist's manifold recurring fantasies of horror and violence that have haunted her for many decades.

Freud interpreted sharp, prolonged configurations as unconscious phallic symbols through analysis of dreams. This point of view was always the target of sharp criticism by his opponents. Following Freud, Anton Ehrenzweig[4] extended the same interpretation of these shapes on works of art. He considered "the artistic creation ... of inarticulate form elements ... as the main receptacle of art's unconscious symbolism."[5] These details of the images conceal the significant content of primary mental processes, reflecting the imperatives of biological drives.

Through our analysis of Susanne's imagery, the configurations mentioned-above may be regarded as Ehrenzweig's inarticulate forms. We came to the assumption that these inarticulate structures are typical coding signs of an archaic matrix, in which the innate program of the realization of generative masculine power is embedded in accordance with the evolutionary phylogenetic development of biological drives and behavioral imperatives as a result of socialization and culture. This matrix, modified in the process of ontogenesis by absorbing conscious perceptions of reality (secondary mental processes, personal unconscious, repression), is the basis for the creation of unconscious symbolism that manifests in personal iconography. The symbolism of inarticulate forms in art is characteristic of all unconsciously created images.

In the imagery, we uncovered various coded signs that revealed multiple facets of Susanne's attitude toward her parents. On one side, her identification with her father and mother determined the absorption and integration of their precepts. On the other side, there were ambivalent tendencies, including hostile ones, as results of frustrated desires of instinctual drives, repressed in various periods of her life. For instance, the latter aspects could be at the root of the disappearance and entombment of butterfly No. 8 (personification of her deceased mother; see chapter 11). We infer that perhaps the golden background covering butterfly No. 8 could signify the unconscious symbolic act of consecrating the memories of Susanne's mother as a means of reconciling with her, thereby liberating her mind from the sense of guilt that Susanne has suffered from all her adult life.

4 Ehrenzweig 1953 and 1967

5 Ehrenzweig 1953, Preface and Introduction, page ix.

One of the remarkable discoveries of our research was the recognition of optical illusions created unknowingly by the artist in the negative spaces of her paintings. In one of them, we identified a silhouette resembling a female torso seen from the back. Following her intuitive inkling, the artist searched for and found a nude study drawing from her student years that portrayed a comparable female figure, which matched the one in the oil painting in almost the exact mathematical proportion (subchapter 9.4; Fig. 9.49). In this composition, Susanne had intentionally depicted a magnified water drop as a visualization of her fantasy that every drop of water could symbolically be equivalent to an individual human lifespan. This drop shape was part of the preparatory drawing and remained in all stages of the painting. In the finished oil painting, its position is nested precisely between the buttocks of the truncated figure. This effect was not intended by the artist. The observation led to the presumption that she unconsciously introduced a symbolic representation of her childhood speculations about cloacal birth into the image (subchapter 9.4, page 264).

Another optical illusion, a facial profile, was discovered in the negative space between the butterfly Touchless Misty (a personification of Susanne) and Firebird (personification of the father) in *Give Me Wings!* (see Fig. 9.54). The face profile plausibly correlates with her father in accordance with multiple details and associations. This optical illusion shares its outlines with the right contour of Touchless Misty, giving the impression that the "nose" of that profile is apparently penetrating the rear of the white butterfly. Again, this was an unintended effect, but we came to recognize that this optical illusion was yet another signifier for the original circumstances from the artist's past and the emotions associated with them, which in this instance correlated with her latent incestuous childhood fantasies. These findings evince the power and persistence of memories and their associated emotions that stem from events of the distant past and continue to affect and shape the present. Also in Touchless Misty, the butterfly with so-called dragon wings, there is an implicitly created optical illusion with another hidden reference to cruelty and violence: a profile that, upon recognizing it, Susanne privately named "Little Indian," which she associated with aggression in accordance with a socially created cliché (subchapter 9.4 and Fig. 9.54). We recognized the unconscious self-identification of the artist with this image.

In addition to shapes and optical illusions, we have also collected concrete indications that particular colors, certain hues of red and orange (subchapter 8.3.2), may represent the sexual and aggressive drives in Susanne's psyche. The analysis of the burnt orange rudimental scale in the butterfly Pale Moonlight allows us to hypothesize unconscious sexual significance of this hue for Susanne (subchapter 8.3). We suppose those color preferences can be correlated with specific artworks that surrounded her since childhood. Their influence is presumably due to their suggestive sexual content, such as her father's works *Bar Scene* and *The Street* and the copperplate etchings after Louis Leopold Boilly in her parents' bedroom (Figs. 8.34–36 and 8.38).

It can be proposed that these artworks have formed the basis of Susanne's personal unconscious color symbolism, which ranges from orange to red, denoting sexuality for her. These discoveries confirm the existence of the unconscious determination for color preferences and their selection in the process of creativity in line with specific symbolic and metaphoric meanings. Due to the sparsity of the existing studies about the roots behind a painter's choice of colors, the recognition of unconscious determination of the color selection is another significant outcome of our investigation.

The mentioned formations and colorations in Susanne Schuenke's artworks became idiomatic markers of instinctual drives, disguised in specific details of the imagery. Through those indicators, the unconscious revealed its meanings. The appropriate symbolism was established in the artist's mind through significant emotional experiences from her early childhood onward.

We found that in Susanne's paintings virtually all nuances in the images and composition carry particular meanings, reflecting the sui generis nature of the unconscious. Emotionally laden experiences from the past or present are converted into painted images, constituting the manifest content, whose latent messages are encoded in specific details. Even the setting carries significant intimate, metaphorical value. The podium stands as a metaphor for various levels of personal accomplishment or instinctual drives. The fog could be an allegory for the state of confusion or uncertainty, often metaphorically revealing the ongoing difficulties and turmoil in her personal life. The golden background represents spirituality.

Spirituality became one of the dominant topics that found repeated visualizations in her art in various disguises, and we recognize this in the case of the enigmatic image of butterfly Air (chapter 10) and the golden background in the setting (chapter 12). The signs of spiritual needs permeated her creativity, and their perseveration and psychological dynamics might be comparable with any other of the instinctual drives and their imperatives as conscious and unconscious modifiers of behavior (see subchapter 10.7). Spiritual needs, like an innate psychic force, may have evolved as an additional means for the human species' survival. The acceptance of the coexistence of biological drives and spiritual needs in their correlation would distance us from the often overstated, one-sided interpretation of the causation of different mental phenomena.

After the introduction of the concrete data that were revealed during the research and their subsequent interpretation, we will share with the reader some concluding remarks. Our work reiterates the psychoanalytic methodology for the interpretation of dreams that became equally valid in the analysis of the modus operandi of the unconscious in the genesis of different visual expressions in Susanne's paintings. This case study demonstrates that the messages of the unconscious are resonating and traceable in human creativity.

The revelation of the unconscious imperatives in a painting has the advantage of this process in comparison with the analysis of a dream as the latter usually remains incomplete due to the amnesia after awakening. Moreover, the manifest content as expressed in the design is tangible and unaltered since the moment it has been transpired in the artwork. Therefore, we have an unvarying picture for the uncovering of the latent content that was covertly materialized in metaphorical, symbolical, and allegorical images with their peculiarities of form, color, and composition.

As in the interpretation of dreams, in the analysis of the painting, we took into account the extensive amount of firsthand data, associations, and recollections of significant emotional experiences from Susanne's past that became available to us in accordance with the psychoanalytic approach. On this basis, we were able to decode the unique visual imagery as it was shaped by the unconscious. We found out that its presence was so pervasive that nearly the entirety of Susanne's artistic creativity contained implicit meanings.

In this regard, our investigation has shown that such aspects as different forms, deviation from realistic depiction, various imaginative distortions, the peculiar choice of colors and their unexpected combination, differentiation, abstraction, surrealistic stylization, and specific compositional organization became, by their metaphorical meanings and symbolization, messengers of the dynamic functioning of the BrainMind system. The imagery could signify the painter's feelings, emotions, motivation, memory, instinctual drives as well as psychological and spiritual needs.

In our case study, the artist initially thought that all her artistic creations were the result of her conscious consideration through the exercise of her free will. However, based on our analysis of many of the artist's works, we gradually came to the understanding that her belief turned out to be incorrect. As we progressively uncovered the hidden sources of various visual expressions, we found strong support that the overwhelming majority of the peculiarities of her artwork were determined by the unconscious. The images and their details echo the artist's emotional and perceptual realities. Significant emotional experiences underlay almost every aspect of Susanne's imagery in her paintings. Hence, we have tangible, unchangeable objects for analysis, representing the impact of the instinctual affective system of the brain.

Our analysis shows that the unconscious affective tendencies could be expressed in the peculiarities of the creative works of a visual artist as the traces of her memories of the emotionally charged events from the past, including early childhood. Most of our findings in this study have identified that those memories constituted the underpinnings for the images in her paintings. We were able to link peculiarities of her creative works with those past events by interpreting the metaphorical meaning of the images. Aggressive and sexual impulses, needs and desires, sensory stimuli, and feelings pertaining to the emotionally-charged events of the past and present undergo transformation into diverse and unpredictable metaphors expressed in assorted forms, colors, and spatial positions.

The strenuous, often painful experiences are linked mainly with the parents and also associated with repressed sexual and aggressive instinctual drives. The energy of these imprints does not disappear and continues to reside within the mind as latent tendencies with a high level of sensitivity, which can be reinforced throughout a person's life. This stressful reactivity has its background in the phylogenetic evolution of the individual's ancestors and in the dynamics of the ontogenetic development. In the evolutionary process, the chronic sensitization by the milieu constitutes the foundation of the susceptibility which finds expression in the personal psyche with various idiosyncratic reactions.

During our exploration, we became aware that even drawings from nature, made at the spur of a moment, at the butterfly conservatory, presumably through "pure psychic automatism," expressed particular latent content. The resulting sketches of the living models show displacement, omission, suppression, and invention of features. For example, the artist avoided depicting the veins in the wings and replaced them with a fan-like structure (chapter 2), and she painted eyes in her own distinctive way (chapter 9). Both designs are significant departures from the characteristics of a real butterfly. Moreover, the artist partially skipped drawing the insects' legs (see chapter 2). We could connect these deviations with specific unconscious meaning in accordance with her aichmophobia, ommetaphobia, and arachnophobia.[6] These peculiarities were interpreted to mean that she was processing the visual information under the influence of phobias, which illustrates how the top-down modulating system of prefrontal cortical networks exert cognitive control over perception and action.

The designs of her images have been nourished by Susanne's attitudes, concepts, beliefs, personality issues, complexes, and repressed tendencies. All of these constituents are transmuted implicitly into her imagery where every part and detail, twist and turn, and shade and shape turned out to carry pertinent unconscious symbolic implications.

The painter verbally recapitulated her visual depiction of the butterflies in the poetic commentary that became the definitive foundation for the interpretation of latent content. She had condensed spontaneously her perception of the personified butterflies into specific verbal characterizations and created appropriate monikers, including their gender assignment. Both channels of information (visual and verbal) were complementary to each other, reflecting the same specified unconscious meanings, which were revealed in the course of our analysis.

The artist's participation as a co-author in this study, discovering the roots of her imagery and writing the manuscript, turned out to have a beneficial therapeutic effect on her numerous phobias from which she has suffered since her youth.

Susanne noticed in astonishment that over time the frequency and intensity of experiencing imaginary visions of being harmed by cutting or piercing objects had drastically decreased. By her estimation, the incidents of these horror visions have been reduced by about 90% of the level from the beginning of the study. Her omphalophobia and arachnophobia have become milder. The medical procedures, especially intrusions of the veins, are relatively acceptable with doctors and staff whom she positively trusts. However, seeing sharp blades, shards, and needles continues to be upsetting to her. The same is true after hearing the names of the phobia-sensitive body areas, such as the navel, eyes, and veins.

Besides devoting much energy and time to the work on this project, Susanne leads an active social life, creates new paintings, displays art in her studio gallery, and organizes a couple of exhibitions of her works every year. Her creativity continues to flourish unbridled, and her painting, *A Room Full of Guests* (2012), brought her artistic expression to a new level of recognition with its inclusion in a comprehensive compilation of the representative works of outstanding female artists.[7] This development was unanticipated at the beginning of our research. It testifies to the soundness of the psychoanalytic approach to healing.

---

6 Aichmophobia, extreme fears of sharp things; ommetaphobia extreme fears of injury of the eyes; arachnophobia extreme fears of spiders.

7 Fuchs, Reinhard. *Women in Art: The Great Female Artists from the Middle Ages to the Modern Era.* Vienna: Edition Fuchs, 2013. Page 392.

When the messages from the various layers of the mind are decoded properly through the careful application of the psychoanalytic approach based on free associations, intuition, imagery, and their correlation, the result could be as cogent as derived by the scientific method. For instance, the close correspondence of visual attributes of images in *Give Me Wings!* with their verbal characteristics in the poetic commentary shows how the same meanings are carried through different channels which can be considered as scientifically persuasive. The positive effect of the research on Susanne's mental state and the activation of her creative potentials support our following assumptions. We suggest that her neurotic reactions originate from the same unconscious base that urged the artist to create her images. Due to the above consideration, we can state that the discovery of the unconscious roots of Susanne's creativity has brought appropriate beneficial consequences. It is in congruency with the positive results of psychoanalytic treatment.

As was remarked before, in discovering the traces of the unconscious in visual art as exemplified in Susanne Schuenke's paintings, particularly in her *Give Me Wings!*, we focused our attention on the peculiarities of creative expressions and their metaphorical meanings. During our investigation, we made numerous assumptions concerning how each symbolic image was born in the artist's mind based mostly on her personal experiences which were unearthed through free association and brought to her awareness. We have discovered significant correlations between the images examined and her perceptions and feelings from the past. We touched much indirect evidence that permitted us to presume some components of the primary scenes and even partially reconstruct them, which brought some likely origins of Susanne's phobias to light. As noted prior, we arrived at the supposition that her fears connected with the navel, sharp objects, and eyes have their roots in the metamorphosis of sexual and aggressive drives in her early childhood. This finding is in accordance with Freudian discoveries as well as the conclusions reached by Melanie Klein in her psychoanalytic study of children.

It has become apparent from our study that the metaphorical meanings of Susanne's creativity are not only specific to the artist's personal circumstances, but they are also broad enough in their implications to address the universal, biological, and social processes of evolution, out of which humans' psychical life arises and continues to evolve.

New discoveries are being added constantly to our knowledge of the complex interactions of the brain-mind-body-environment. Even so, a large number of unanswered questions remain, and one of them is the understanding of the interconnection among biological, psychological, and spiritual aspects of the human mind. Our case study adds a few missing pieces of the mosaic to make some useful contributions to the whole picture.

13.2. Art in Research of the Unconscious Processes

The synthesis of our discoveries confirms that the artworks of surrealist painters could be a significant addendum for scientific research into the creation of the images, and an understanding of their conscious and unconscious genesis. The art historians Ernst Kris and Ernst Gombrich[8] were interpreting the works of art as a mirror of the artists' conscious and unconscious mind. Artists have the singular ability to represent the inner and outer world through creativity, which allows them to express their vision of reality to the audience. Thus, they fulfill a very important social function, opening up innovative viewpoints to the observer to contemplate the biological, psychological, and spiritual aspects of human nature and their multi-dimensional interactions. Art signifies one of the most characteristic traits of the human species, making us distinct from other animals. The human mind is capable of imagination and creation, which has enabled the emergence of civilization and its attributes—art, music, religion, science, and technology. Art in its various guises, as a universal product of the human being, constitutes a viable gateway for understanding the phenomenology and functions of the BrainMind.

In this context, it is worth mentioning the remarkable contemplation of neuroscientist Vilayanur S. Ramachandran[9] about universal principles of art. He regards that the psychological, spiritual, and socio-cultural means, expressed in art by metaphorical, symbolical, and allegorical

8 Gombrich and Eribon 1991

9 Ramachandran 2011

images, have a neural foundation. Also, Antonio Damasio hypothesizes that "the mental events correspond to certain states of brain circuits."[10] Stanislas Dehaene has shown, based on EEG (electroencephalography) and fMRI (functional magnetic resonance imaging) studies, the "correlation between brain activation and mental states."[11] The "artful brain"[12] creates the mind, processing the sensory inputs and coding the information into various symbolic representations of the images. Therefore, the wealth of information which can be obtained through analysis of artwork is valuable to future attempts at the integral understanding of the neuropsychological processes of the BrainMind system. By incorporating the analysis of art in cross-disciplinary approaches, science will be capable of giving additional reliable explanations that will illuminate many issues such as consciousness, unconscious processes, reciprocal transformations, the interrelationship between objectivity and subjectivity, the whole and the parts, interplay of the brain structures and their functions, basic instincts and their "confederation,"[13] psychological and spiritual needs.

Penetration into the essence of the above-mentioned rainbow of issues might open new points of view to take into consideration numerous vectors that construct our minds and behavior. It is reasonable to expect more experimental research to correlate the subjective experiences of artists with objective data obtained through contemporary technologies, even including monitoring the brain's neuronal activities while engaged in creative action. This could provide a foundation for uncovering the specific influences of unconscious processes as the roots of creativity. Such an approach could become a fruitful source that brings further insight into the interconnections in the BrainMind. The convergence of art with neuropsychoanalysis can add new perspectives to our understanding of how the brain brings forth the mind.

13.3 Selective Comparison of Personal Iconographies

The increased cross-disciplinary collaboration between science and art has ushered new insights into the understanding of the mystery of artistic creativity. In this context, current scientific studies of works of the painters associated with the Surrealist movement (Dalí, Duchamp, Ernst, Masson, Miró, etc.), and the symbolists and expressionists with elements of surrealism in their works (for example, Klimt, Kokoschka, and Schiele) have greatly enriched our knowledge of how the creativity of an artist transforms different conscious and unconscious influences into painted images. From the numerous publications available on the topic dealing with the oeuvre of those artists, we selected *The Haunted Self: Surrealism, Psychoanalysis, Subjectivity* by David Lomas,[14] *Marcel Duchamp* by Dawn Ades, Neil Cox, and David Hopkins,[15] and *The Age of Insight*[16] by Eric Kandel. Lomas and Kandel incorporate a number of psychoanalytic interpretations that are in congruency with our approach. In exploring the artworks of Susanne Schuenke, we have made findings that are comparable in importance and complementary to the discoveries of the aforementioned authors.[17] From these three books, we selected artworks, according to their topics and connotations, and juxtaposed them with some in Susanne's paintings. This comparison shows the similarities as well as differences in the artistic expressions through the specifics of the images articulated by the artists' personal iconography.

The book by David Lomas is one of the notable works in psychoanalytic research on art. Following a Freudian approach, Lomas offers a broad spectrum of discoveries, unraveling the complex web of manifestations of the unconscious in numerous paintings by the surrealists. Analyzing Salvador Dalí's *Metamorphosis of Narcissus*, a painting to which the artist wrote

10 Damasio 2012, pages 16-17.
11 Dehaene 2014, page 15.
12 Ramachandran 2005
13 Gazzaniga 2018, page 233.
14 David Lomas 2000
15 Ades, Hopkins, and Cox 1999
16 Kandel 2012
17 We came upon these books after the majority of our discoveries were made independently.

an accompanying poem and a prologue with the selfsame title, Lomas emphasizes the "close reciprocity in Dalí's work between writing and painting."[18] On the basis of these two primary sources, Lomas presents a coherent clarification of the various mental problems that continued to haunt Dalí throughout his life. He presents a convincing argument that the image of Narcissus in this painting is a reference to the artist himself (i.e., identification and projection). Lomas recognizes that Dalí, using this mythological allegory, revealed an unconscious message under a surrealist banner about his personal life situation. Dalí visualizes the metamorphosis of Narcissus with two parallel images. The first depicts the mythological character in self-reflection in the water. In the second image, as a result of the transformation, the head is replaced by a white, cracked egg, from which a white narcissus flower springs. This imagery is Dalí's metaphorical illustration of the positive changes in his life described in his poem that was written simultaneously to accompany the painting, which ends with the line, "Gala – my narcissus."[19] Dalí had wed Gala three years before the completion of the painting and poem, and they remained married until Gala passed away 45 years later.

As stated before, Susanne's painting, *Give Me Wings!,* and the accompanying poetic commentary also complements each other, delivering the corresponding information through visual and literary representations in her individualistic expression. Comparably, in the images of the analyzed butterflies, we discovered the same phenomena of identification and projection of real-life situations which Lomas noted. As with Dalí, Susanne expressed an optimistic outlook in her painting with her own distinct imagery. For example, the configuration of a butterfly's wing, suggestive of a finger pointing upwards into the golden background, turned out to be her unconscious visual metaphor for an auspicious future which in her case conveyed an expectation of a new partnership (butterfly No. 3, Pale Moonlight; subchapter 8.2.6).

Interpreting Joan Miró's *Self-Portrait I* (1937), Lomas discusses various influences of the artist's favorite painters on this work, and he discerns the specific, symbolically loaded signs that are synthesized in the portrait: flames on the forehead (Blake) and in the hair (Masson), stylized sunflowers, the dominance of yellow, and the turbulent shapes of fire (Van Gogh). The last three features clearly allude to Miró's identification with the Dutch painter, whom he admired as his ego-ideal.

Similarly, our research revealed that Susanne was strongly influenced by the artworks in her family's art collection, including paintings done by her parents. For instance, during the analysis, she suddenly remembered a small glass sculpture called Sabino Butterfly, which was treasured by her family (subchapter 9.2; Fig. 9.5). Butterfly No. 4, one of the personifications of the artist herself in *Give Me Wings!,* shares remarkable similarities with this glass piece. From this, we assumed that it became the source of inspiration and the prototype for the unconscious creation of this butterfly in the painting.

Another example of influences we found in regard to the colors yellow and violet, which Susanne frequently applies to indicate negative content. We traced the formation of such a specific evaluation of this color combination back to one of her father's artworks, *The Procession to Allensbach*. In this painting, these hues dominate a scene depicting discrimination of women (Figs. 6.8-9), which left a lasting impact on her young mind. After that, Susanne involuntarily might have linked yellow and violet with the undertone of diminished value. In *Give Me Wings!,* she portrayed the smallest of the seven butterflies, Little Why, unconsciously in those two hues. Metaphorically, the little butterfly's color and size with the symbolic underpinnings behind them, together with other characteristics (see chapter 6), hint at Susanne's inferiority complex. She was unaware of her self-identification with this diminutive butterfly before analysis.

In analyzing André Masson's paintings, Lomas emphasized that Masson was replaying the frightening scenarios that had their origin in the painter's traumatization in the trenches of the First World War. His art manifests the horrors of violence and death in his often-repeated motifs. Such were the depictions of massacres, atrocities,

18 Lomas 2000, page 172.

19 Lomas 2000, page 184.

and a mysterious cemetery. His obsessive self-expression with these topics can now be considered as post-traumatic stress disorder (PTSD). Masson frequently drew spiral and other circular forms in his works, which Lomas interprets as being the embodiment of the interminable cyclical returns of traumatic war experiences. Human violence is metaphorically illustrated in *Battle of Fishes*, where Masson substitutes the combatants with fish. Similarly, the anthropomorphized rocks in *Dawn at Montserrat* and the hallucinatory vision in *Landscape of Wonders* reflect the frightening experience the artist had when he and his wife were stranded in the mountains of Montserrat at night. This was due to a sudden change in weather which engulfed them in a sea of cloud until nightfall, preventing them from climbing down, and leaving them perched on a precipice, in a state of extreme fear. These feelings of utter vulnerability and abandonment could have been a reactivation of his war experiences in the trenches under artillery fire, when he was seized by sheer terror.

Susanne's memory archive of violent acts was full of the indelible records of wars with their brutal atrocities, particularly World War II, to which her parents' experience attested to. That information was augmented by gruesome scenes from movies she had seen, and this all could have significantly influenced the reactivation of her horror visions. She has suffered from a multitude of terrifying imaginations, in which she has been haunted by threatening cutting devices, needles, and glass shards. These and other pointed shapes resurfaced in various configurations among all the butterflies in the painting as sharp-edged forms, needle-point endings, thorny shapes, and wing contours resembling blades and scissors. These kinds of tools were present in her father's workshop and mother's kitchen. Susanne's violent thoughts and fantasies connected with them could be a projection of her repressed aggressive tendencies in childhood and her traumatization by medical procedures that she had undergone. To this list, we might add the incident of Susanne witnessing the "castration" of a male doll with a hot iron by her mother and aunt. This episode had lasting traumatic consequences, activating her castration complex.

Susanne's emotional fixation of the above-mentioned traumatic events could be compared with Masson's ever-present obsession with violence and cruelties (as analyzed by Lomas). Our study found that Susanne has the same compulsive urge to repeatedly revive her negative experiences from the past, which are unconsciously transformed in the images of her art through symbolic representation. In this context, Susanne had a stressful encounter with natural forces similar to Masson's mountain trip. She was suddenly trapped in a fog from the sea which caused her great confusion, reviving her preexisting phobia of being lost. Since then, the "fog" motif has become part of her personal iconography as a signifier for bewilderment and anxiety.

In his painting *Pieta, or Revolution by Night* (1923), Max Ernst depicts a young man in a white smock, held in the arms of an older, kneeling man with a mustache. The younger man is recognizable by his profile as the painter himself, whereas the kneeling one can be inferred as his father. Lomas interprets that the work is an unconscious manifestation of a dominating father and the artist's feminine self-identification in visual imagery. A plausible explanation for the loose, white shirt in *Pieta*, following Dawn Ades' analysis,[20] might be the gowns worn by the hysteric female patients at the Pitié-Salpêtrière in Paris, which was known to Ernst, who attended Jean-Martin Charcot's lectures and demonstrations of hypnosis at this clinic. The identification of the father is elaborated again in Ernst's canvas titled *Celebes* (1921), where a huge, mechanistic and cumbersome elephant is seen as a metaphorical personification of the painter's father, a "representative of an axis of authority,"[21] whom the artist described as a "petty tyrant, staunchly upholding values as outmoded as his Wilhelmine moustache."

Analogously, in *Give Me Wings!*, Susanne, in her iconography, metaphorically personifies her father in the butterflies No. 2 and No. 5 (see chapters 5 and 4, respectively). This identification was created, we assume, in accordance with real-life situations and is reflected in their prominent features, such as dominating height and color, a posture of superiority, sharp shapes, etc. Butterfly No. 4, as

---

20 Lomas 2000, page 76.

21 This and the following quote are from Lomas 2000, page 78.

the personification of the artist, masquerades in pristine white and parades its polished cleanliness.[22] This coloration can be seen as an unconscious symbolization of Susanne's compliance with the expectations of her father. Moreover, butterfly No. 1 (Little Why), which we regard as the unconscious personification of Susanne as a child, is factually a diminutive, reversed-image replica of butterfly No. 2. Little Why as a symbolic self-identification with her father is obvious in our case.

Lomas' detailed research accumulated a great amount of pertinent information about the painters. However, some questions dealing with the most intimate personal information remain unanswered in his work. If Lomas had had the direct access to the details of the artists' personal lives, he might have been able to gain additional valuable information to further confirm his interpretations.

The second book by Ades, Hopkins, and Cox in this comparative synopsis is dedicated to the analysis of the works of the enigmatic artist Marcel Duchamp. One of the monograph's distinguishing features is uncovering various underlying symbolic meanings through their interpretation of the forms, colors, and compositions in Duchamp's artworks as well as his concepts and comments. The authors' approach turned out to be an adequate way to reveal multiple factors that impacted his imagery. They assembled a great body of information on the influences of various contemporary artists on Duchamp's art. For example, the influence of Matisse and Van Dongen is shown to be evident in *Portrait of Dr. Dumouchel.* Using non-naturalistic colors, Duchamp created the appearance of auras emanating from the doctor's hand, head, and body which are suggestive of the special healing power of Raymond Dumouchel, a student of radiology at the time of this painting. The monograph's authors assumed that Duchamp appropriated the idea of aura, along with blue as the color of peace and spiritual harmony, from popular theosophical writings. Similarly, Susanne depicted an aura emanating from a tree in the painting *Ethereal Spirits,* which was based on her belief in spiritual energy pervading the universe.

One of the characteristics of Duchamp's art is his mordant expression of eroticism that has been his way of unmasking the forbidden topic of human sexuality, suppressed by his Catholic upbringing and the prevailing social norms. The artist's droll and derogative neologisms and parodies point to his conception on this matter. His attitude finds expression in allegories and metaphors, heavily laced with sexual innuendoes. Duchamp created a special vocabulary (e.g., "wasp or sex cylinder," "love gasoline," "butterfly pump," "celibate utensil," etc.) punning on the ubiquitous sexual drive, which could have influenced the creation of certain shapes in Duchamp's works. For example, his drawing from 1912, *The Bride Stripped Bare by the Bachelors,* which was made during a trip to Munich, depicts a "robotic 'Bride' who is apparently menaced by two highly aggressive 'Bachelors' with phallic weapons."[23]

This topic can also be illustrated with the painter's invention of *Rrose Sélavy* as his female alter ego. The alias was written on photographs of the artist, cross-dressed as a fashionable lady. Many of those pictures were taken by Man Ray, a pioneering photographer and Duchamp's fellow artist. The second word in the name is phonetically easy to unmask—it stands for "c'est la vie" ("That's life"). The first word was originally "Rose,"[24] to which he added an extra "r" later to create his pseudonym. When the first "r" is pronounced (in French) distinctly in *Rrose,* the real understanding of the pun stands out, as it sounds like "Eros c'est la vie" (Eros, that's life). This declaration is an apt vignette that evinces the oeuvre of a perplexing artist of the 20th century, who questions, criticizes, and challenges the traditional attitudes toward gender relationships, art, and personal self-identification.

One of Duchamp's major works is *The Bride Stripped Bare by Her Bachelors, Even* (1915-23), a mixed media artwork also referred to as the *Large Glass.* It was accompanied by the artist's written commentaries called "Green Box," in which the notes are indispensable in the overall understanding of the metaphorical and symbolical content of his imagery. Metaphorically, the transparency of the glass box (instead of

22 See subchapter 9.1.2: Susanne's father demanded that his daughters be "clean" in reference to extra-marital behavior.

23 Ades, et al. 1998, page 53.

24 This was used in Duchamp's 1921 sculpture *Why not Sneeze, Rose Sélavy?*

conventional canvas) promotes the perception of the bride as being "encased" and displayed like a zoological specimen, emphasizing her animal qualities. Ades, et al. suggest that Duchamp's cryptic expression "Sex Cylinder" could be related to a funnel-like end of a vertical tube, a dominant element of the bride's design. The bride, being hooked to the top bar, is described by Duchamp as *pendu femelle* ("hanged female"). The French word *femelle* normally describes a female animal, and it is only used pejoratively toward a woman, indicating Duchamp's assessment of the bride as animalistic. Ades at al. assume that the images of certain forms in the work, which the artist referred to as "Draught Pistons" and the "Milky Way," are his metaphors for fecundity. This finds confirmation in his "Green Box," where Duchamp labels the bride as "an 'agricultural machine', or 'apparatus/instrument for farming'."[25]

Susanne's attitude toward the topic of also reproduction finds its specific expression in her art. She applies her own set of visual markers, for example, clusters of scales reminiscent of the rows of breasts in a typical Ephesian statue of the goddess Artemis and yellow globules resembling fish roe within a kidney-shape.

Returning to Duchamp's *Large Glass*, the bachelors (named "Nine Malic Moulds") look similar to Chinese lanterns. The artist could have intended a metaphorical analogy between the lanterns and the bachelors. As the fire in the lanterns shines, Duchamp's bachelor males glow with sensual desire. The metaphor of "glowing" in Susanne's painting has a spiritual meaning. The artist uses the shining golden background to symbolize an all-pervading spirituality. It rises behind and above the images of the seven butterflies and illumines the creatures. It would be desirable to combine Ades, et al.'s interpretation on the basis of the psycho-analytic approach. From the latter point of view, their book leaves unanswered the nature and details of the significant emotional events in Duchamp's life that obviously resurfaced in the unconsciously coded images in his artworks. David Lomas' study incorporates an psychoanalytic interpretation that offers some answers to such a deficit. However, his research was also hampered by the obvious lack of detailed knowledge of the artists' private lives and their significant emotional experiences.

A close work-relationship with Susanne and her active involvement as a co-researcher determined unprecedented access to her private life history. This gave the unique opportunity to gain a broad scope of first-hand personal data, clarifying it with the artist on a continuing basis and verifying their authenticity through different channels. Processing the received information together with the artist herself allowed us to make ongoing adjustments of our working hypotheses and gave us a reliable foundation for decoding the metaphorical meanings of the images. Susanne's poetic commentary to *Give Me Wings!*—as an instance of free association—has contributed an additional angle to the analysis of the unconscious contents of her visual art to our study. In this context, the spontaneously created nicknames for the butterflies have proven to contain unexpected insight into coded meanings. The analysis of the imagery and commentary indicated that each name unfolded into a panoply of inner implications, including certain biological, psychological, and socio-cultural aspects. The latent contents encoded in the metaphorical visual expressions and the verbal comments to her creative works supplement each other and manifest specific messages from the artist's unconscious.

Eric Kandel, in *The Age of Insight: The Quest to Understand the Unconscious in Art, Mind, and Brain, from Vienna 1900 to the Present*,[26] analyzes the artworks of Gustav Klimt, Oskar Kokoschka, and Egon Schiele. By applying the psychoanalytic approach, he interprets the presence of the unconscious instinctual drives as they manifest symbolically in their portraiture paintings. In one of the most popular works by Klimt, *The Kiss*, the artist depicts a couple in an intimate embrace, in which the lovers' clothes are embellished with shapes and patterns of "iconic sexual symbols."[27] Kandel describes the woman's clothes adorned with ovoid and stylized flowers as an indicator of female fertility whereas erected rectangles, ovoids, and spirals on the male figure are recognized as

25 Ibid., page 97.

26 Kandel 2012

27 Ibid., pages 114-115.

symbolism for sperm. The couple is placed on a hill at the edge of a hollow. The rock is carpeted with a plethora of semi-naturalistically rendered blossoming flowers.

Another well-known work by Klimt, the portrait of *Adele Bloch-Bauer I* (1907), likewise displays an abundance of shapes streaming dynamically on and around the figure. She is partly immersed in a golden background with impressive ornamentation. Her dress and surroundings present a busy mosaic of different geometric forms (triangles, rectangles, circles, spirals, etc.) which accentuate sexual connotation with their symbolism, comparable with those in *The Kiss*. Adele's folded hands and the clasped hands of the lovers in *The Kiss* metaphorically hint at their union. In using a golden background, especially in *The Kiss*, Klimt might have emphasized the spiritual fusion of the couple and, in Adele's portrait, her spirituality.

As we analyzed in several chapters, the sexual content of Susanne's paintings was embedded in various metaphorical configurations. In *Golden Nectar* (chapter 8, Fig. 8.47), Susanne intentionally used a blossom, stylized into a circle, to camouflage the form and details of a female breast. She consciously added the surrounding butterflies as a hidden reference to caressing touches to the breast. The appearance of the butterflies in the design could be connected with her positive experience in the butterfly conservatory when one of them landed on her arm. This choice of metaphorical expression for strong sensual experience is a conscious reference to the artist's sensitive erogenous zones.

Another case of camouflaged sexuality in the guise of flowers is *Allegro* (Fig 5.22). Susanne was challenged by the task of painting "sexy legs," the undertaking of which she was not eager to do. She replaced the lower torso by rendering a bouquet of red roses, stylized and combined with an assortment of radiating circles. This substitute could be her unconscious expression for making reference to her father's design which he had created decades earlier for an undergarment advertisement.

Susanne also expressed the sexual symbolism in some unconsciously depicted optical illusions. Implicit double images were found in the moon goddess's hand: the fish formation as phallic and reproductive symbolism in *First Hour of Full Moon* (discussed in chapter 8, Fig. 8.8). Furthermore, the contour of a female torso with a drop penetrating the buttocks, symbolizing the anal stage of sexual development, can be recognized in *Sea of Time* (see subchapter 9.4, Fig. 9.46). These examples show configurations representing sexual meanings that the artist only recognized many years after the creation of the images. Likewise, in *Sleeper* (subchapter 12.1.3), the artist depicted a female nude and on the upper thigh (Fig. 12.4 (7), we discovered a shape that resembles "the hand clasping the buttock." This sexual innuendo was unintended and unidentified by Susanne.

Adding to the above presuppositions, there is another relevant observation in Susanne's painting *Longing* (see subchapter 5.2.4 and Fig. 7.18). In this work, a marginal male nude, in muddy red, squirms in a lasciviously erotic pose at the bottom of the canvas. By Susanne's association, this could be correlated with the elements of twisting and warping postures of the amorous pair in the copperplate prints after Boilly that hung in her parents' bedroom. It might be suggested that the configuration of the curling red figure could be an echo of the position of the couple in the prints. Furthermore, the coloration might be a reference to the hues of red and burnt orange in her father's artwork (*Bar Scene* and *The Street*). It could illustrate how Susanne's various perceptions fuse and manifest in images, reflecting the modus operandi of the unconscious in forming its symbolism. Furthermore, we assume the existence of phallic symbolism in the details of her painted images, such as the finger-like shape of the butterfly Firebird's wings (subchapter 4.4.2), the "scales" of Pale Moonlight, the front part of Touchless Misty, and the blue shape in the hind wing of Fanning Everything (Fig. 8.24). Thus, sexuality finds its expression in a multitude of shapes and colors, which constitute her individual iconography.

Continuing the comparison of artists' symbolic expressions, we will pay attention to Kandel's analysis of traces of aggressive drive in Oskar Kokoschka's works. The Austrian artist was enthralled with the idea of depicting the inner life of his sitters. He aimed to reveal the sexuality and aggression dwelling beneath the surface through their portraitures. For instance, Kokoschka's *Self-Portrait as Warrior* (1909) is a clay sculpture with contorted forms, expressing strong emotional suffering. It was depicted in the physiognomy of "an impassioned cry." With this sculpture, the artist revealed his own inner struggle, which he likened to being thrown into the midst of a battle.[28] His use of tempera paints in finishing the clay surface of his portrait is of particular interest, as he employed strong orange, blue, and red in a non-naturalistic context and even applied the coloring with his own hand instead of brushes to underscore his strong emotional pain and anguish.

Regarding the artistic visualization of the psychic condition of a person in portraiture, a parallel can be drawn between the inner turmoil expressed in Kokoschka's *Self-Portrait as Warrior* and the emotionally charged message in Susanne's *The Warrior* (Fig. 8.16). Kokoschka conveyed his mental state in his sculpted bust, whereas Susanne expressed her thoughts and emotions depicting an imaginary person—a 9-foot canvas portrait of an ancient Chinese warrior.

Susanne's *The Warrior* (2005) was inspired by an exhibition of a selection of statues from the millennia-old terracotta army discovered in the tomb of Qin Shi Huang, the first Chinese Emperor (259 to 210 BCE). Her contemplation and emotional response to the clay soldiers are metaphorically expressed in this painting. The ancient statues lost all their original colors, displaying only a monotonous light gray hue, but Susanne's imagination took flight and created the polychrome color scheme for her own rendition of a Qin dynasty warrior. In her painting, a sickly Phthalo green is framing and accentuating the aged eyes. This non-naturalistic color follows down the nasolabial furrow and fades. The hue is repeated as a faint glow in the white neck scarf, mainly on the warrior's right side. We mentioned before[29] the artist's symbolic use of Phthalo green to signify degeneration, decadence, and devastation. In this context, we assume that Susanne used the specific paint in the portraiture to denote her opposition to aggression and atrocities, which are epitomized in war. The features of his physiognomy include unflinching eyes, an elongated contour of the upper eyelids, a pin-point tapering moustache, and firmly closed lips. They are evocative indicators of the warrior's former powers which were unleashed against his enemies in the past. However, Susanne comments: "He has so much sadness and wisdom in his look." This encapsulates his message—and hers—about the devastating effects of aggression in warfare.

Tellingly enough, the hair, which would be expected to be black for a person of Chinese origin, appears in warm, reddish dark brown. By use of this coloration, she might indicate symbolically her compassion for the soldier's cruel experiences. A wart on his cheek located next to the right nasolabial furrow could associate with Susanne's father, who had an identical facial mark. The artist's father survived the five years of savage fighting in the Eastern Front in World War II and became an outspoken pacifist. His participation in the war was so devastating that it scarred his psyche for the rest of his life. It is possible that this portraiture is a symbolic expression of Susanne's empathy for her father's traumatic experiences.

In his analysis, Kandel emphasizes the anguish and pain of the 23-year-old Kokoschka as it manifested visually in the artist's sculpted self-portrait. A similar expression might be observed in 29-year-old Susanne's work, *Revolution* (which we discussed in subchapter 9.3.7, page 254 and Fig. 9.43). In this work, she unconsciously represented her life-and-death struggle. She rendered a bust portrait that was meant to be a metaphorical personification of political revolutions. It was her intention to visualize the tragic consequences that follow radical changes in society. The high-minded goals of the revolution are often transformed into the outright usurpation of absolute power, which is then maintained through brutal oppression and a reign of terror. The imagery could also be seen to reflect Susanne's inner state of mind at the time of the painting, in which she implicitly revealed her situation.

Her internal conflicts, sufferings, and the desire for death in that period of her life are comparable with Kokoschka's own "war" with his circumstances when he created *Self-Portrait as Warrior*. In the preliminary drawing for *Revolution* (Fig. 9.43a), Susanne rendered the profile of the head with a gaping mouth indicative of screaming, which is akin in its expression of extreme emotional pain to the "impassioned cry" in Kokoschka's sculpture.

---

28 Kandel 2012, page 135. Kandel makes reference to Kokoschka's autobiography which acknowledges the influence of a Polynesian mask he saw in the Museum of Natural History in Vienna.

29 See chapter 8 footnote 76.

Although she drew the personification of political revolutions after her face, she remained unaware of the unconscious portrayal of her inner fight against the allure of death for many years. It is still somewhat unsettling for her to accept this cruel imagery as an outlet of her mental turbulence, including suppressed aggressive tendencies and self-destructive inclination. Those were also revealed in some of Susanne's other paintings we have discussed, most notably in the butterfly Touchless Misty's serrated wing contours and hidden optical illusion of the "Little Indian" in *Give Me Wings!* (subchapters 9.3.4 and 9.4). Susanne, like Kokoschka, in *Revolution*, employs dramatic color contrasts using bright yellow, orange, green, indigo, and darkened reds. She judges these chromatic combinations as disharmonic and unpleasant.

In the comparative discussion of the artworks of various painters, the emphasis was on their perception of themselves, others, and the world expressed in metaphorical, allegorical, and symbolical visual imageries. When we juxtapose the findings of Lomas, Ades, et al., and Kandel with those of our analysis, we see correlations among certain meanings, which each artist conveys with their distinct iconography. The latent contents and ways of the artists' expression point to shared biological drives that manifest their imperatives traversing time and cultural space.

The mentioned researchers meticulously located, accumulated, and processed a wealth of available information about the artists, extracting the relevant data from their biographies, writings and recorded commentaries, interviews, lectures, as well as observations and memoirs of their contemporaries, which formed the foundation for their interpretations. But, when confronted with the paucity of intimate personal information, their analyses could not be as comprehensive as they could have been in the case of revealing significant emotional experiences. Without this, the extent of the engagement of the unconscious in the creation of visual imagery in paintings cannot be comprehensively explained. Thus, the authors had limitations of private data and, therefore, could only speculate about the messages that lay in these circumstances beyond a well-founded analytic evaluation. In this crucial regard, our research has an exceptional advantage due to a plethora of personal information. Furthermore, we have had the exclusive possibility of continuously receiving, correlating, and processing relevant data. These conditions in the research have advanced our interpretation and its validation. The foregoing short comparison indicates the unique self-expression of the artists, conveying certain emotional states that are being reflected in their artworks and coded in their personal iconography.

13.4 Unconscious Processes in the Light of Contemporary Development of Cognitive Neuroscience

Much has happened in the science of the human brain and mind during the last 75 years. Neuroscientists have acquired the ability to use electroencephalography (EEG), functional magnetic resonance imaging (fMRI), nanowire, and other technologies to study the neuronal processes of the functioning human brain. The received information based on objective concrete data enables new levels of comprehension about the working of the BrainMind.[30] For our case study, the discoveries are especially significant in understanding the role of the modus operandi of conscious and unconscious processes and their interactions. In this context, we will touch upon selected achievements of contemporary cognitive neuroscience in accordance to some of Freud's concepts and our related findings.

Antonio Damasio assumes that the "self comes to mind"[31] through the creation of images and offers hypotheses to the question of "how does the brain construct a mind?"[32] Damasio's quest is clarified by his unifying concept of the development of different stages of self and consciousness which he bases on discoveries in evolutionary biology, sociobiology, and neuroscience. From the perspective of the evolutionary past, the developing system of self became more and more complex for dynamic

30 The terms are used here according to Panksepp and Biven 2012, page 7: BrainMind (bottom-up view), MindBrain (top-down view). Both are double capitalized to emphasize the united functional system of brain and mind (monistic perspective).

31 Damasio 2010: *Self Comes to Mind.*

32 Ibid, page 6.

adaptation, in accordance with the imperatives of homeostasis. Environmental and social conditions have been integrated and ingrained in neural networks. Gradually, a unified bio-psycho-social functional system of the BrainMind was formed. The regulation of this system is mostly realized by unconscious processes. As Damasio states, "... the human unconscious literally goes back to early life-forms, deeper and further than Freud or Jung ever dreamed."[33]

Damasio considers three stages in the evolutionary development of the self: the protoself, the core self, and the autobiographical self. The protoself is associated with primordial feelings that are directly related to the body. Body and brain have established a loop through the exchange of signals, sending them in both directions and creating a hot-line of permanent interconnections which maintains the homeostasis. Interruptions of this bond result in disharmony that immediately influences the state of the body, brain, and mind. The "body-brain-mind" acts as a single organismic functional unit. In this context, Damasio states that the spontaneously arisen "*Feeling is the mental aspect of that unity*."[34] (Emphasis according to the original text.)

The protoself originates from the lower and mid brainstem, where all automatic regulations of visceral functions are processed. Primordial feelings are the pivoting point in the development of the emotional systems, the core neural network of which is located in the upper brainstem. The brainstem is evolutionarily the oldest part of the brain, a structure shared by many other species, being the foundation of the evolution of automatic action programs. The protoself co-evolved with the affective systems, generating the core self. Thereafter, the autobiographical self progressively emerged under social and cultural influences. This tri-fold structure of "self" in the form of images manifests in the cerebral cortex.

These regions perform the image-making function by co-operation with subcortical structures, including the lower, middle, and upper brainstem, re-activating primordial feelings, and the affective systems, including the constituents of the core self and the autobiographical self. The inter-coordination of the mentioned structures is realized through mappable neural patterns that developed in the evolutionary process. Different functions of the brain are "represented in the form of maps, thereby contributing images to the mind."[35] Those maps consist of neural circuits that are activated by appropriate stimuli and experienced in our mind as visual, auditory, tactile, olfactory, and gustatory images. The image-making function is induced by multiple factors, such as various particulars of the affective systems, cognition, memory, imagination, and, obviously, language. The essence of the core self finds its realization in action as a response to the "relationship between the organism and the object ... engaging the protoself and modifying"[36] it. The protoself is the bottom strata of a multilayered foundation in the generation of images in the mind. The core self and the autobiographical self transform and specify them in the process of their final creation. These processes, continuously refined through evolution and coded in the genome, are represented throughout the unconsciously working mechanisms of the human BrainMind.

The autobiographical self incorporates social, cultural, and spiritual aspects of "social persona," constituting the "social me" and "spiritual me."[37] The sense of identity is a significant attribute of the autobiographical self. The autobiographical self is based on the factual individual information, memory, and moral principles. It is formed during life experiences in family and society and especially associated with emotionally charged events. The process of how the "self comes to mind" is far from being completely explained, but the hypothesized concept elucidates the horizon for new ideas. Damasio's vantage point offers a well-founded outlook, from which we can begin to understand such complicated phenomena as the creation of the human mind and the unconscious/conscious in their complementary collaboration.

---

33 Damasio 2018, page 22.

34 Damasio 2018, page 126.

35 Damasio 2010, page 21.

36 Ibid, page 24.

37 Ibid, page 24.

Our quest to unravel the image-making creativity of a surrealist painter resulted in many discoveries which could confirm numerous assumptions of Damasio. Psychoanalysis can significantly enrich knowledge about the creation of the images by the MindBrain and contribute to important perspectives on this matter. The synthesis of psychoanalysis, cognitive psychology, neuroscience, evolutionary biology, and socio-biology could become the newly paved royal road to illuminate the BrainMind conundrum on this matter. Damasio's characterization of the evolutionary development of protoself, core self, and autobiographical self is overlapping in some ways with the Freudian classifications of the structure of personality—id, ego, and superego. There are equivalences that could be counted on both sides.

According to our case study, all stages of the development of the self find their expressions in the details of the images created by the artist. Susanne's imagery reflects many things including feelings, emotions, biological drives, influences of family, society and culture, facets of personality, patterns of behavior, problems, complexes, psychological sensitivities, the reaction to different external situations and internal imperatives, existential issues, ideological concepts, and attitudes. The impact of these factors on the artist is unconsciously coded into the painted images—their specific forms, colors, placement in composition, and also in their hierarchical arrangements, orientations, and multi-dimensionality. We have brought the latent content behind those particulars to awareness through our analysis of their metaphorical and symbolic meanings.

Jaak Panksepp and Lucy Biven stressed that human emotions have a biological foundation. They identified "at least seven basic affective systems: ... SEEKING (expectancy), FEAR (anxiety), RAGE (anger), LUST (sexual excitement), CARE (nurturance), PANIC/GRIEF (sadness), and PLAY (social joy)."[38] These emotional systems, reflecting evolutionary development, significantly impact the function of the human mind, generating much of its basic activities. Panksepp's selection of the seven fundamental emotions was based on his animal studies, in which he found that their affects correlate with human emotions. He determined that we share the mentioned emotional systems with animals, especially mammalians, and he has demonstrated that they are creatures capable of emotions and consciousness. Nevertheless, the complexity of human affective processes and consciousness cannot be understood from animal studies alone. The human consciousness is significantly different in its cognitive scope from that of animals. Our emotions are quite likely more complex than those of animals, especially social emotions (for example, embarrassment, guilt, empathy, pride, etc.). Humans exhibit a spectrum of emotional expressions, which is diverse from that of animals. One of the differences is human beings' relative capability of controlling their emotions by their willpower, realizing inhibitory functions. Accepting the special traits of human emotions, one must account for their evolutionary development, based on a neurobiological foundation (anatomical, biochemical, and energetic). The neurons by their function as biological information-processors and the source of inherited instinctual drives are in discord to socially established principles, which could be the etiological foundation of unwholesome consequences.[39]

Many recent studies and theories proposed by neuroscientists validate the critical importance of the role that emotions play in human behavior as Freud exemplified in his emphasis on the repressed memories of emotionally significant past experiences in the individual's life. Numerous experimental inquiries by neuroscientists support the importance of these affective systems on the functioning of the BrainMind. Their pervasive influences manifest as unique, reactive expressions in each individual, frequently resulting in disturbing disorders that constitute the core approach of psychoanalysis. Primary emotional processes (as enumerated by Panksepp) and their transmutation into secondary and tertiary processes are the foundation of the integration of neurobiological circuits of the brain and their appropriate construction of the mind.

In the past, emotional experiences were studied mostly in subjective psychological terms. The objective research of the biology of emotions

38 Panksepp and Biven 2012, page xi.

39 Llinas 2002

is a relatively modern domain of neuroscience. The contemporary findings in neuroscience, concerning the affective systems and the related cognitive processes interconnected with them, lead to a new multi-disciplinary understanding of the function of the BrainMind system. There is significant scientific data about the complicated interactions between the subcortical regions of the brain and various cortical regions, particularly the prefrontal areas associated with cognitive control of emotional reactions and adaptive corrections of behavior. Therefore, researchers in psychology and neuroscience, focusing on the understanding of the modus operandi of unconscious processes, should pay closer attention to the qualitative nature of the affective processes.

It is recognized that emotions are triggered by the subcortical regions of the brain. The affective systems are also in conjunction with humans' cultural and spiritual needs as social beings. These combined aspects are grounded on biological development and shaped by life-experiences and environmental demands, along with the acquisition of languages that evolved in connection with the higher forms of social communication. The large size of the cortical regions of the human brain engaged in socialization, learning, decision-making, and other higher cognitive functions indicate the immense significance of their activities in forming human mental life.

However, the amplification of the role of neocortical processes could essentially not curb the arousal of the affective systems with their imperative stimuli from the subcortical regions. The understanding of the affective dynamics and their evolutionary (phylogenetic) and individual (ontogenetic) development could answer many questions concerning parallel ongoing processes, their transformations, and the adaptive states of human mental life.

Revealing the network of the unconscious should involve the analysis of the consequences of its activities through a multi-disciplinary quest using psychoanalysis, psychiatry, neuroscience, and cognitive psychology. Synthesizing these results could be a reliable way of decoding the hidden programs created by the "great programmer, Mother Nature." This should progressively lead to a more comprehensive understanding of the involvement of the unconscious and conscious pathways in the BrainMind function. Various neuroscientific discoveries that have emerged in the last two decades have already substantiated these aspects.

During Freud's life, no neuroscientific foundation of his concepts was available, but he predicted that there would come a time when his assertions would find confirmation by objective data obtained with sufficiently advanced methodologies. As commented briefly above, Freud's belief in the evolutionary biological foundation of the psyche finds supporting evidence in modern neuroscientific discoveries, which infuse new insights into psychoanalysis and stir its further development, known now as neuro-psychoanalysis. Accordingly, the advancement of psychoanalysis through the incorporation of solid neuroscientific data has become a decisive step toward the validation of Freud's foresight.

Nowadays, there are a number of correspondences between Freud's presuppositions and neuroscientific discoveries of the significant role of the inherited biological affective processes that support his psychoanalytic theories. In spite of that, his concepts of the functions and phenomenology of the human mind continue to either be dismissed outright or hotly contested in regard to their validity and utility. Consequently, more research and data are needed to pave a way to correlate the results of psychoanalysis and neuroscience. Such an approach is worthwhile, and the integration of both the mentioned disciplines will open new perspectives to elucidate the processes of the mind. The positive exchange is mutual as Karen Kaplan-Solms and Mark Solms, in emphasizing the scientific contribution that psychoanalysis has made to neuroscience, write: "Now the time has come for us to re-introduce the fruits of Freud's labors to the neuroscientific field out of which they originally grew."[40]

We should delve into the "logistic" structures of the mind by psychological approaches employing psychoanalytic concepts and other methods, while at the same time taking into account the recent developments in neuroscience. This will be the most rewarding strategy for the future growth of the brain and mind sciences. Under this purview,

40 Mark Solms and Karen Kaplan-Solms 2000, page 66.

classical psychoanalysis also contributes its valuable share to the progress of neuropsychology and neuropsychoanalysis in comprehending the role of emotion, cognition, memory, motivation, and their interconnections in the development of mental processes.

Freud, in his *Project for a Scientific Psychology* (written 1895 and unpublished until 1950),[41] proposed a program of understanding psycho-dynamic processes of the mind in terms of the neuroscientific mechanisms of the brain. He anticipated that the psychological structures of mental processes could be clarified by the discoveries of their neurological representations in the future. But soon after, he abandoned this approach and concentrated his effort on understanding the phenomena of the mind in terms of psychological structures and their psycho-dynamic interactions. It was a fateful decision, which resulted in the creation of psychoanalysis. Freud went on to develop psychological theories concerning sexual and aggressive instincts, the vast power of the unconscious, the complex developmental processes of children and youth, and the persistent influences of emotions, memories, and motivations. All of these ideas were revolutionary in his day. In spite of the continuing controversial reception of his concepts, the main focus on the unconscious, which Freud proposed to the science of mind and the healing process for the troubled human mind, is still highly relevant.

At first glance, the integration of the subjectivity of psychoanalysis with the objectivity of neuroscience is judged by many researchers to be exceedingly difficult and for many scientists questionable. The followers of this standpoint regard the brain as a biological organ and the mind as a psychological and spiritual construct, like two fundamentally different types of entities. They refuse the assumption that the brain and mind are two sides of the same coin, claiming that this analogy is a convenient descriptive device and such "unity" exists only in subjective human mentality. Moreover, they accept that the coin might be a single entity, but each side is made of a different essence so that the mind is not reducible to the brain (matter). Therefore, they notice that the interpretation of neuroscientific findings could be done with a more critical eye. Otherwise, neuroscientists will find the brain but miss the mind.

According to the contemporary concept of wholeness, the brain and mind are one united multidimensional functional system developed in the bio-social evolutionary process. The wholeness could be substantiated by the phenomenon of reciprocal transformations, developed in the biological and social evolution. This phenomenon provides a bridge to unite the seeming separation of the biological and psychological essences of the brain and mind, respectively. From this point of view, we could find the brain and the mind in their integration. David Bohm states, "... Mind and matter are not separate substances. Rather, they are different aspects of ... the whole and unbroken movement." He calls it, "the holomovement." [42] Panksepp and Biven consider the transformation of the neural system's activity into a subjective mental experience as "the most troublesome issue in all neuroscience."[43] In addressing this conundrum, they quote Robert Holt, who said in 1989 that "There is an impenetrable mystery in the fact that subjective experience exists in a physiochemical world."[44] Kandel (2018) supports the above statements: "... when hundreds or thousands of neurons form circuits carrying signals from one part of the brain to another, the end result is perception, movement, thought, and emotion."[45] These neural circuits are the foundation for the creation of mental processes, which integrate information of evolutionary and individual development, coded in the structures of the brain.

Vinod Deshmukh (2012) suggests this issue could be comprehended from the perspective of holons nested in holarchy or the "interactive wholes, as all living organisms [that] are more than the mere sum of their parts. ... It holds, that [a self-organizing] system or an organism, is a coherent unified whole, that cannot be fully explained in

41 Freud, Sigmund: *Project for a Scientific Psychology* (original German: *Entwurf einer Psychologie*), (1895) unpublished manuscript. Available on internet as: users.clas.ufl.edu.

42 Bohm 2002, page 14 and 191.

43 Panksepp and Biven 2012, page 389.

44 Panksepp and Biven 2012, page 389.

45 Kandel 2018, page 20.

terms of individual parts or characteristics."[46] He describes ten functional oscillatory neural networks that generate and regulate complex human behavior, awareness, and different mental activities.

Michael Gazzaniga (2018) considers that through evolution and the process of subtle improvement the conscious became a part of organic life that "links subjective experience with objective processing, which has been around since the first living cell."[47] This ground rule became a common foundation in the development of living organism from simple forms to homo sapiens. The genetic discoveries of the origin of life, recorded in the genotype by the structure of DNA, actually represent a code script of inherited programs. Nature as code-maker ciphers its messages in symbolic form, conveying biological information during the process of evolution, selecting the species with the most successful adaptation to the environment and so determines the survival of the fittest and their reproduction. Gazzaniga emphasizes that scientists began to apply new principles in the explanation of the functions of living organisms based on the theory of relativity, quantum theory, systems theory, etc. This approach brings novel reasoning in the interpretation of different topics in the question of BrainMind. For example, the concept of wave-particle duality, presented by Niels Bohr, stated the simultaneous existence of two realities and one not reducible to the other but unified in a single system: two sides of one coin.

Furthermore, in accordance with R-theory, synthesized by John Kineman[48] of the mathematical biologist Robert Rosen's Systems Theory, there is "an infinite principle of wholeness" [49] in nature. On the contrary, the mechanistic view of nature ("machine metaphor") generally ignores that objective and subjective aspects are parts of the whole and Kineman discusses the existence of their fundamental functional oneness. Therefore, the worldview on systems as a process determined by "cyclic causation" denies the ultimate separation, accentuating the principle of unification. This paradigm could also reasonably be applied to the dynamic system of BrainMind. The traditional attitude toward living organisms like machines cannot explain their complex functions.

Clinical observation of different mental diseases points to the significance of brain structures and their dynamic functional interactions. The numerous clinical cases of changed personality syndrome due to traumatic brain damage attest to this fact. For example, there is the famous case of *Phineas Gage*, whose ventromedial prefrontal cortex and orbitofrontal cortex[50] were partially destroyed by a flying iron rod, which caused observable changes in his personality, especially moral behavior. However, we cannot only attribute the clinical symptoms to organic lesions and brain injuries. There are no singular direct parallels between the observed symptomatology and the localized organic damage in some instances.

The damage to the same brain region of different individuals, even if clearly localized, may exhibit a different clinical picture, depending on the psychophysical integration. Although the specific symptomatology could be rooted in the peculiarities of the brain with its singular milieu and developmental history, the mind may manifest as a novel clinical picture with its own unique functional pattern. The inherited predisposition of the BrainMind system could be the foundation for the formation of such singular clinical manifestations that are, on the one hand, universal and, on the other hand, strongly personal, similar to the fingerprints of each human individual. One of the distinct constituents in this process is the significant emotional experiences integrated into individual development. Accordingly, multiple variables, both universal and individual, contribute to the evolution of the dynamic functional systems of the brain and the mind.[51] The BrainMind continues to evolve constantly with suitable connective pathways, achieving effective adaption to changing circumstances. The developed functional neural networks could be at the foundation of different psychological processes.

---

46 Deshmukh 2012, page 247; in bracket what Prof. Deshmuhk added in personal communication.

47 Gazzaniga 2018, page 236.

48 Kineman 2012

49 Kineman 2017, this and the next two quotes in this paragraph: pages 405-406.

50 Damasio 2005

51 Luria 1973

From the developmental perspective, it is important to consider the neuroanatomical fact of the extension of ventromedial and orbital prefrontal cortical areas in adult humans as compared to children and mammals. These regions are responsible for specific inhibitory control mechanisms in emotional expressions, social behavior, personality formulation, as well as in decision making and other complex cognitive processes. Solms and Turnbull (2002) stress the significance of a highly developed "self" system in humans, as the crucial characteristic that sets us apart from other animals. This system determines the conscious inhibition of desires, impulses, and unacceptable tendencies according to the reality principle. The latter increases its influence through maturation, which depends on significant emotional experiences especially with parents, caregivers, peers, and other important persons. Their influences are introjected into the mind, processed, stored, and later resurfaced as unconscious imprints in the individual's feelings, thoughts, and behavior. This concept is in agreement with the Freudian theory of the ego making decisions based on the reality principle instead of allowing the id to take immediate actions based on the pleasure principle.

The inhibitory functions of the mind have been localized in the prefrontal cortex by neuroscientists, who have found that the increased activation in this region is often accompanied by a decreased level of activity in the amygdala and the hypothalamus. Such top-down modulating tendencies suppress the affective processes linked with this region. Moreover, the higher cognitive activities of the prefrontal cortex may exert controlling influence not only on emotions but also on memories and their recall. These findings, being of neurobiological origin, correlate well with the traditional psychoanalytic concept of repression, one of the significant defense mechanisms discovered by Freud in his development of psychoanalysis.

The observed structural and functional aspects of the BrainMind system could bring many clinical realities to light, revealing Freudian assertions concerning the interactions among the id, ego, and superego. Mark Solms, in his essay *What is "the unconscious," and where is it located in the brain?* (2017),[52] considers that new findings of neuroscience incorporated into psychoanalysis give foundation to correlate with some Freudian assumptions about the content of dynamic workings of consciousness, unconscious, id and repression and their localization. Freud was convinced that consciousness was an intrinsic property of the cortex, but animal experiments in the 1940s already showed that the generation of consciousness emanates from the ERTAS (extended reticulo-thalamic activating system), localized in the upper brainstem. The confirmation of this might be found in the studies of children, who were born without a cerebral cortex (anencephaly) but do express various emotional reactions. This indicates that they are not lacking a conscious mind. This is also supported by cases of adults, who underwent a partial removal of the cerebral cortex due to medical conditions, but continued to have a conscious mind and emotional responses.

Moreover, Solms suggests the view that the id, in accordance with the "pleasure principle," is conscious. This statement is in line with Michael Gazzaniga's book, *The Conscious Instinct* (2018), in which he challenges the established outlook, stating that "we must realize that consciousness is an instinct."[53] Freud thought that the repressed content, turning unconscious, constitutes part of the id. Solms emphasizes that repressions originate from cognitive imperatives according to the "reality principle," which is based on learning, whereas the id is an innate entity. The id and the repressed unconscious are located in different subcortical regions of the brain: the id is situated mainly in the ERTAS and the limbic system, but the repressed unconscious is engrained in the basal ganglia and cerebellum. Obviously, there are multiple dynamic interconnections between the mentioned systems. Furthermore, by Solm's view, "the fundamental stuff of consciousness is not *perception* (as Freud claimed) but rather *arousal*."[54] These novel ideas need further contemplation and verification by objective scientific data. It is possible that there might exist some circuits between those locations in question which determine differentiation in their function.

52 Solms 2017

53 Gazzaniga 2018, page 236.

54 Solms 2017, page 90.

The Freudian paradigm about the imperatives of unconscious processes continues to be contentious in spite of steadily growing scientific evidence that substantiates the influence of unconscious processes on the function of body-brain-mind. Here is a short overview of the research-based verification of this statement.

Contemporary imaging technologies[55] objectively corroborate the activation of certain regions of the brain in the process of imagination. In these cases, the same circuits are operating as of those individuals who are doing similar activities in actuality during experimental research. This illustrates that specific neural patterns are the sources and the correlates of mental activity.

Neuroscientific studies indicate the existence of emotional systems,[56] which could constitute the neurophysiological basis of the unconscious processes that automatically determine the affective responses of human beings. They are genetic programs that have been formed and refined during humankind's evolutionary history to primarily facilitate the behavioral needs to respond quickly to external threats and dangers in order to survive. A classical illustration is William James'[57] insight about unconscious physiological responses in dangerous situations. Automatic reactions emerge immediately after facing the object of fear, which involves appropriate neural circuits. The activation of this network begins in the amygdala, triggering visceral adaptive body responses (heart rate, respiration, sweat glands, muscles). Only after that do the insular cortex, the ventromedial prefrontal cortex, and the dorsal prefrontal cortex transform the unconscious activity into conscious awareness. The secondary feelings create a subjective state of fear.

In accordance with numerous contemporary studies, we cannot deny the hormonal and neurobiological foundations of mental arousal. Aroused psychological states are accompanied by appropriate physiological alterations that can be measured objectively by various means, such as the chemical analysis of oxytocin, prolactin, and vasopressin, and the objective expressions of visceral reactions mediated by the sympathetic and parasympathetic nervous systems. Thus, when analyzing the subjective states of the mind, the physiological indicators must be taken into account as biomarkers of the coexistence of biological processes.

In 1964, the German neuroscientists Kornhuber and Deecke described a phenomenon, which they named "readiness potential" (*Bereitschaftspotential*)[58] or pre-motor potential; they discovered this during experiment by giving the participants the task to fulfill a specific voluntary movement. The researchers registered an activation of the appropriate pre-motor area in the forebrain (200 msec prior to the actual movement by the will, predicting the intended motor action), which is only instrumentally recorded (EEG). This fact led to the assumption that "free will" is just an illusion. Neuroscientist V. S. Ramachandran[59] infers that the "readiness potential" is an immediate unconscious reaction that has developed in the evolutionary process as an automatic action program with great importance for survival in extreme situations.

The discovery of mirror neurons, which fire up unbeknownst to the conscious mind, confirms the existence of unconscious cognitive processes. These mirror neurons are active in the brain of an observer without mimicking the behavior physically. We could assume that this is the neurological foundation of the unconscious ability of human beings to place themselves in similar mental states to understand others (empathy), to predict their actions, and facilitate learning.

Gestalt and cognitive psychologists have developed new concepts to explain how the mind processes sensory information. For example, they consider that visual perception is based on the instant identification of the whole's structure (holistic principle) rather than on the individual elements of the observed object and that this is largely inborn. Thus, cognitive science is beginning to recognize that unconscious processes are largely responsible for action before the conscious mind is able to form its

55 EEG—electroencephalography, MRI—magnetic resonance imaging, PET—positron emission tomography.

56 Panksepp and Biven 2012

57 James (1890), 2007

58 Kornhuber and Deecke 1965

59 Ramachandran 2011

perception of the world from the filtered data. Moreover, there is a connection between the actual perception and the past experience of a person. Accordingly, every image that is formed by the conscious mind is subjective, since the unconscious processes significantly influence the formation of the model of reality in the mind. It is based on the individual's history integrated with genetically coded information. Already in the late 19th century, the German physicist Hermann von Helmholtz[60] conjectured that, in processing the sensory information from the outside world to form a final picture in the conscious mind, the brain needs additional information. For example, in regard to vision, Helmholtz proposed that the brain does not rely solely on the information, which it perceives from the eyes, and as a consequence, an "unconscious inference" is necessary for the final perception by the conscious mind. Therefore, the direct access to the world is an illusion, and what the conscious BrainMind perceives as reality is actually generated through the filters of the brain and mind.

Research in cognitive psychology of visual perception has shown that the mind's images are not the same as the ones on the retina. First, the patterns of photons impinging on the retina are immediately transformed into a special neural code and delivered by electrical signals to the visual association cortex, which processes the information into the final "images" that come to conscious awareness. However, before that happens, there is a determinative participation from the bottom-up and the top-down processes that are integrated into the final mentation.

The perception depends significantly on the phylogenetic and personal memories that manifest some concrete meaning in the visual experiences, which are recorded and stored in the brain in the form of symbols, signifying negative or positive implications from the outer world. Thus, the resultant inner image and its associated significances are one-of-a-kind constructions of the brain and mind, even with regards to forms and colors. Accordingly, the elaborated image as a gestalt perception (an organized whole), constructed on the basis of the individual's inheritance and personal experiences, can be thought of as a symbolic representation of some particular meaning. It is comparable to the function of a word (a verbal command), which conveys a specific message for an appropriate psychological and physiological response by an individual. Insofar as the final image is the result of the latent aspects of the individual's history and inherited tendencies are woven into a particular perceptual experience, our specific sensitive responses could consequently be interpreted as the result of unconscious influences. Therefore, the image's imbedded meaning and significance are specific to each individual, even if a group of people is experiencing the same sensory event or object. This mechanism could explain the various forms of individual idiosyncratic reactions that can be observed in clinical practice. Furthermore, the similar emotional experiences of individuals usually result in specific mental states that could manifest in exclusive representation in artists' creativity. This could provide us with the basis for assuming the existence of an inner personal iconography.

Such customization of the external world by the unconscious into an inner mental reality is a universal process not exclusive to artistic creativity. It is worth mentioning in this context that discoveries in neuroscience and cognitive psychology, including the categorization of the visual stimuli from the external world, are processed unconsciously in subcortical regions before they reach the lateral prefrontal and the inferior temporal cortices, where the final image is realized.

Visual perception can illustrate the influences of unconscious processes on this function. Meanwhile, it has been discovered, that around thirty different regions in the brain participate in creating the final aware image. We will mention, as examples, two clinical observations as discussed by Ramachandran. In the first one,[61] he describes the lack of perception of colors as the result of damage on both sides of the brain in an area called V4 in the temporal lobe. The awareness of coloration was found to be the result of an automatic unconscious, innate program. Confirmation that the brain region V4 is specialized in processing colors was proven by

60 Kandel 2016, pages 21 and 23.

61 Ramachandran 2011, page 61.

fMRI, single-neuron studies, and direct electrical stimulation. The second clinical observation is the phenomenon of "blindsight."[62] Ramachandran refers to the discovery made by Larry Weiskranz and Alan Cowey in the 1970s. A completely blind patient was told to reach and touch a spot of light; even when he could not see it, he was encouraged to guess when he did so. To the surprise of the experimenter, the blind patient hit the spot correctly (in repeated trials with 99% accuracy). Ramachandran explains that visual perception was processed due to the existence of two pathways in the brain ("New Pathway"—visual cortex, and the "Old Pathway"—Superior Colliculus in the parietal lobe). The visual information travels along these pathways from the retina to the brain. Therefore, when the visual cortex ("new pathway") is damaged, the visual perception can still be processed by the "old pathway."

The recent developments of new methods to record neuronal activities, such as the use of intravascular neural interface with nanowire electrodes,[63] have allowed researchers to monitor the functioning of a group of neurons or even a single neuron. This approach appreciably increases the ability of neuroscientific research to understand the working mechanisms of the brain and mind in ever finer detail. The capability to explore the brain from inside should illuminate its various functions, including unconscious and conscious phenomena. The data obtained from the advances in brain mapping technology is of great importance to elucidate many subjective issues of the MindBrain, using objective information.

According to Rodolfo Llinas,[64] feelings and desires are actually reflections of brain-cellular processes. Every neuron possesses an intrinsic, particular oscillation that is coded in the genome. Many signals arise from the properties of a single cell's neuronal activity which can resonate with a distant group of neurons, evoking synchronous responses in different regions of the brain and producing dynamic operating circuits. This could be the neurobiological foundation of different mental activities of the brain (cognition, emotion, memory, etc.), and it may be indirectly related to the alterations of the mind's state with its oscillatory patterns of thoughts, perceptions, dreams, images, and subjectivity. Brain cells have the innate property of sensing objects or events and the quality of plasticity in order to modify their internal environment to adapt to the changing circumstances of the world, maintaining homeostasis, which is pivotal for the proper functioning of the brain and body. The spontaneous oscillatory neuronal and mental activity might confirm the essential role of unconscious processes, constituting different vectors of functional BrainMind dynamics.

The phenomenology of hypnosis, which played a significant role at the dawn of the development of psychoanalysis, gives us clear verification for the influential existence of the unconscious. In particular, due to amnesia, the orders given in the stage of somnambulism to hypnotized individuals remain out of their awareness. Nevertheless, those commands are obeyed after awakening. This confirms the power of the unconscious over behavior in the posthypnotic state.[65]

Clinical psychoanalytic practice illustrates that much of the human memory of the past remains as latent content in the unconscious state, and it can significantly influence our feelings, emotions, perception, and actions. Furthermore, it can cause mental disturbances. In the process of analysis, when certain particulars (data, perceptions, emotionally charged events, etc.) are brought to conscious awareness, then mental health disorders, especially obsessive-compulsive neuroses and phobias, undergo notable resolution and improvement; they can even disappear. This well-known fact in the psychoanalytic therapy is a reliable and repeatable confirmation of the significance of unconscious processes in pathogenesis.

The above factual information selected in this subchapter substantiates the prominent role of the unconscious in the mental processes. Ever

62 Ramachandran 2004, page 28, and 2011, page 61-63.

63 Llinas 2002, pages 70-71.

64 Llinas 2002

65 Experimental research, in regard of influences of suggestion, made in somnambulism stage of hypnosis, on different mental functions in post-hypnotic state, was undertaken by Ovchinnikova, Nasinovskaya, and Itkin, from 1969 until 1989, at Moscow State University, Faculty of Psychology. The results are summarized in their book published in Russian by Moscow State University Press, 1989; (Title in English: *Hypnosis in Experimental Personality Research*).

since Freud proposed his psychoanalytic theory, there have been numerous attempts to discredit his assertions. Some of the criticisms were simply motivated by social as well as personal biases based on religious, cultural, and philosophical attitudes. Others were centered on the theory's general lack of objectivity, experimental evidence and, in these cases, critics claimed that the clinical observations obtained by the psychoanalysts were likely to be subjective in accordance with cognitive biases. Further doubts were cast against psychoanalysis and its effectiveness with the rise of behavioral therapy.

Some neuroscientific studies have begun to experimentally check Freud's insights and discoveries of psychological aspects of dreams. For example, John Allan Hobson and Robert McCarley,[66] from 1975 onward, proposed an influential theory of dreams based on REM sleep.[67] Their experimental research became the basis for a neurochemical explanation for how REM and non-REM periods of sleep are switched on or off by the reciprocal interactions of three neurotransmitters (acetylcholine, noradrenaline, and serotonin). Hobson and McCarley found the secretions of these chemicals in a set of three well-defined nuclei in the pons of the brainstem, which they identified as the source of REM sleep and called them "dream state generator." The theory, developed strictly on objective experiments and physiological reasoning, seemed to contradict the Freudian concept concerning the function and interpretation of dreamwork. Hobson made a presentation at the 1976 annual meeting of the American Psychiatric Association (APA), pointing out that his neurophysiological activation-synthesis theory was sufficient to explain dreams. This led to a vote of no confidence by the APA, considering Freud's dream theory as not "scientifically tenable."[68]

McCarley and Hobson's theory relied on the assumption that the REM sleep and dreaming were strictly correlated, and the latter only occurred during the 90-minute cycles of REM sleep. But accumulated experimental data indicate that dreams also partially exist during the non-REM states that are reasonably similar to REM dreams, except in regard to longevity. Furthermore, contrary to Hobson's conclusion on the indispensable involvement of the pontine brain stem in the activation of the dreams, it was discovered in many clinical cases that in spite of lasting damage to the pons, the patients continued to dream.[69] Therefore, the activation mechanism of dreams is not exclusively located in the pontine brain stem, and the arousal could originate from other regions of the brainstem and brain. In fact, recent brain imaging studies indicate that dreams can be generated by highly specific forebrain mechanisms, and lesions to some cortical regions could cause a global loss of dreaming.[70] Two specific anatomical groups associated with the loss of dreaming are the region of white matter encompassing the ventromedial prefrontal cortex—which is involved in the arousal, emotion, motivation, and memory—and the occipito-temporo-parietal junction, which is involved in various cognitive processes, including space, object, and face recognition, language, working memory, self-referential processing, and abstract thinking. Additionally, these cortical areas with highly specific forebrain mechanisms are active during REM sleep. The subcortical regions (amygdala, periaqueductal gray (PAG), hypothalamus, hippocampus, nucleus accumbens), where the affective system is localized are the same. Consequently, it is highly plausible that both mentioned regions are involved in the generation and formation of dreams. Therefore, the assertion that the pontine brain stem is exclusively responsible for dreams[71] can no longer be endorsed.

To sum up: Although knowledge about the modus operandi of the unconscious is far from complete, the growing comprehension of its role in the workings of our BrainMind system

66 Hobson and McCarley 1975

67 Eugene Aserinsky and Nathaniel Kleitman discovered REM (Rapid Eye Movement) sleep in 1953.

68 We are following here the information as given by Solms and Turnbull (2002, chapter 6) and Solms (2015, part IV).

69 Solms 2000, pages 843–50.

70 In the past, the well-known frontal lobotomy as a treatment for severe psychosis brought about the inability to dream as a side effect of the operation. Contemporary anti-psychotic drugs (used as a chemical lobotomy) seem to have a similar impairing effect in the vast majority of patients' ability to dream.

71 Hobson and McCarley 1977, page 1346.

has progressed significantly, based on objective experimental methodology. As a consequence of the recent advances made in cognitive neuroscience, researchers accept that the imperatives of the unconscious in the function of BrainMind have been found to be even more pronounced than Freud asserted. The contemporary received data indicate that it is of great importance to take into consideration the patterns that originated from simple organisms and their development during evolution to the complex homo sapiens.

The evolved universal regularities markedly determine the foundation of the intrinsic, hardwired working mechanism of the BrainMind system. The growing number of discoveries regarding the unconscious processes in neuroscience, cognitive psychology, and neuropsychoanalysis made by different scientists, and the corroborative efforts among numerous researchers,[72] elucidate many complicated aspects of the BrainMind and their interrelationship. With new insight, scientists are building a reliable foundation to overcome former unfavorable attitudes toward the unconscious per se. These could widen the horizon to unravel the working mechanisms of body-brain-mind (and vice-versa: mind-brain-body) with their circular, intrinsic interrelationship, homeostatic plasticity, and functional wholeness that integrates biological, psychological, social, and spiritual aspects of existence. Usage of this knowledge makes decisive differences in the practice of medical professionals, enhancing their potential ability in the treatment of various diseases. More and more psychologists, psychotherapists, art-therapists, psychiatrists, and other medical professionals concede to the important role unconscious processes play in the function of the BrainMind and widely apply this fundamental approach to their work.

72 We refer to the works of Antonio Damasio, Stanislav Dehaene, Vinod Deshmukh, Michael Gazzaniga, Michael Graziano, Eric Kandel, Rodolfo Llinás, Alexander Luria, Jaak Panksepp, V.S. Ramachandran, and Mark Solms, to name a few.

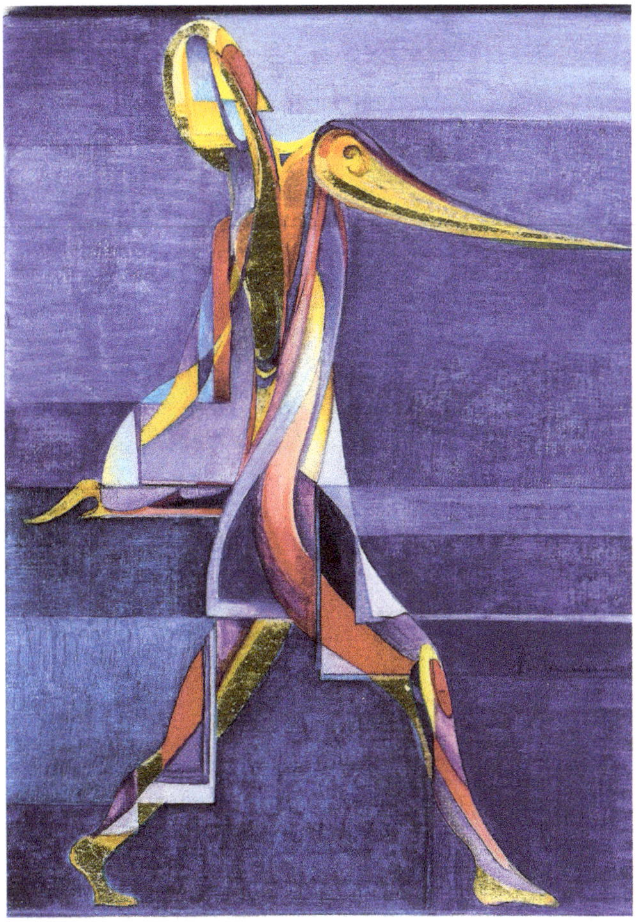

Fig. 13.1. Susanne Schuenke, *Figure from Freedom*, 2003, Oil and gold leaf on board, 7.5 x 5.5 in (19 x 14 cm). Private collection, Essen, Germany.

Note from the Authors

Dear Reader,

In this case study, you have been introduced to our discoveries of the metaphorical, symbolical, and allegorical meanings of the artist's imagery and its unconscious origins which manifest themselves in her artwork.

We avoid declaring these insights as conclusions and express the majority of our revelations as assumptions with a relative level of validity. Therefore, your critique is appreciated in response to this research. As we are open to discussion, reasonable correction, and improvements, outside comments will be taken into consideration in order to that which seems contrary to our inferences. We intend to incorporate your feedback into the next edition of this book because we hope that collective minds will bring a new perspective to our continuing quest.

With great thanks, Naum G. Itkin and Susanne Schuenke

Contact the authors: info@ArtePress.org

Acknowledgments

Having different professional backgrounds (psychiatry/psychology and art) as well as disparate native languages (Russian and German), it was a demanding task for us, the authors, to reach a shared understanding of our findings that validate the pervasive role of unconscious processes in artistic creativity. We faced a great challenge to express the retrieved information, its coordinated interpretation, and our meticulous reasoning in appropriate academic English, so that this complex topic, expanding the frontier of brain and mind science, could become readily accessible to both specialists and interested general readers. Therefore, we are very thankful for the highly qualified support that we have received through the years from the genesis of the manuscript to its final realization as a book.

Our scientific mentor, Vinod Deshmukh (MD, PhD), a retired professor of neuroscience with a broad knowledge beyond his specialty and a researcher with a mind that flies over the scientific landscape with an eagle's eye has provided indispensable aid for us over all these years, especially with his professional advice and continuous flow of input, pointing to relevant scientific literature for our perusal. Moreover, his present personal pursuits as a poet and painter have given us added insights into the topic of this study from the perspective of a man accomplished in both science and art.

Our first editorial mentor, Mary Fletcher Shipp, immensely improved our English while retaining our metaphor-rich style and keeping an eye on the coherent organization of the content. Later in the years, our editor was Theodor Hornoi-Centerwall, a professional library specialist, and a well-trained mind in the humanities and linguistics. We are also truly grateful for Ted Johnson's help in bringing 40 years of experience in publishing and printing to a meticulous proofreading of our manuscript. Our last reader was Anna Bartlett, M.A., instructor of English at UNF and FSCJ, who completed the final copy editing of our text. We are appreciative of the professionals of Raven Images, Inc. in Jacksonville, Florida for preparing carefully calibrated high-resolution scans directly from original artworks to reproduce their true colors for the illustrations used in this book. We would like to express our deep gratitude to our book designer Frances Keiser at Sagaponack Books & Design, who painstakingly laid out our richly illustrated manuscript for publication with great competence and enthusiasm and coped with its multitude of challenges.

We wish to acknowledge our respective outstanding professors, who were instrumental in our journey many years ago through the land of never-ending exploration and learning: Professor Andrei Sergeevich Chistovich (Андрей Сергеевич Чистович, 1897-1981), psychiatry and psychoanalysis, St. Petersburg, Russia; Olga Vasilievna Ovchinnikova (Ольга Васильевна Овчинникова), PhD in Psychology, Faculty of Psychology, Moskow State University; Professor Günter Binding (Dr. Ing., Dr. Phil.), Art History, Architecture, and Urban Conservation, University of Cologne, Germany.

We thank our friends for their unwavering support of our quest and encouragement to bring this book to completion. We remember our parents, who would have been proud of this accomplishment.

Bibliography

Ades, Dawn, Fiona Bradley, and GB Liverpool. *Salvador Dalí: A Mythology*. London: Tate Gallery, 1998.

Ades, Dawn, David Hopkins, and Neil Cox. *Marcel Duchamp*. New York, N.Y.: Thames and Hudson, 1999.

Adler, Alfred. *The Science of Living*. New York: Anchor Books, 1929. (German: *Lebenskenntnis*. Berlin: S. Fischer Taschenbuch Verlag, 1978 (Neuveröffentlichung: republication).

Alley, Rewi. *Selected Poems of the Tang & Song Dynasties*. Hong Kong: Hai Feng Pub., 1981.

Auchincloss, Elizabeth L., Eslee Samberg (ed.), and American Psychoanalytic Association. *Psychoanalytic Terms and Concepts*. 4th rev. ed. New Haven, Conn.: Yale University Press, 2012.

Bammes, Gottfried. *Die Gestalt des Menschen: Lehr- und Handbuch der Künstleranatomie*. Ravensburg: Otto Maier Verlag, 1973.

Beckmann, Petr. *A History of π (pi)*. New York: St. Martin's Press, 1971.

Birren, Faber. *The Power of Color: How It Can Reduce Fatigue, Relieve Monotony, Enhance Sexuality, and More*. Secaucus, N.J.: Carol Publication Group, 1997.

Bocock, Robert. *Sigmund Freud*. 2nd rev. ed. London: Routledge, 2003.

Bode, Sabine. *Die Vergessene Generation: Die Kriegskinder brechen ihr Schweigen*. 2. Aufl. ed. Stuttgart: Klett-Cotta, 2004.

Bohm, David. *Wholeness and Implicate Order*. New York: Routledge, 2002.

Bowlby, John. *Attachment. Attachment and Loss Vol. I. 2nd ed. New York: Basic Books, 1982.*

Braden, Gregg. *Fractal Time: The Secret of 2012 and a New World Age*. Carlsbad, Calif.: Hay House, 2009.

Breitling, Günter, Jean-Paul Divo, and Jense Friedeman, et al. *Das Buch vom Gold*. Frankfurt Am Main: Verlag C.J. Bucher, 1975.

Breton, André. "Max Ernst," in *What Is Surrealism? Selected Writings*, edited by Franklin Rosemont. New York: Pathfinder Press, 1978.

Breton, André. *Entrée Des Mediums, Oeuvres Complètes, Tome 1*. Paris: Gallimard, 1988.

Breton, Andre. *What Is Surrealism?: Selected Writings*, edited by Franklin Rosemont. New York: Pathfinder Press, 1978.

Briggs, John, and F. David Peat. *Turbulent Mirror: An Illustrated Guide to Chaos Theory and the Science of Wholeness*. New York: Harper & Row, 1989.

Britannica, Inc. *The New Encyclopaedia Britannica*. 15th ed. Chicago: Encyclopaedia Britannica, 1987.

Bunch, Bryan. *The Kingdom of Infinite Number: A Field Guide*. New York: W. H. Freeman and Company, 2000.

Carhart-Harris, R.L. and K. J. Friston. "The default-mode, ego-functions and free-energy: a neurological account of Freudian ideas." *BRAIN: A Journal of Neurology*, 133(4) Apr. 2010: 1265–1283.

Chomsky, Noam and Mitsou Ronat. *On Language: Chomsky's Classic Works Language and Responsibility and Reflections on Language in One Volume*. New York: New Press, 1979.

Chopra, Deepak. *The Seven Spiritual Laws of Success: A Practical Guide to the Fulfillment of Your Dreams*. San Rafael, Calif.: Amber-Allen Pub., 1994.

Damasio, Antonio. *Descartes' Error: Emotion, Reason, and the Human Brain*. London: Penguin Books, 2005.

Damasio, Antonio. *Self Comes to Mind: Constructing the Conscious Brain*. New York: Vintage Books (Random House, Inc.), 2010.

Damasio, Antonio. *The Strange Order of Things: Life, Feeling, and the making of Culture*. New York: Pantheon Books, 2018.

Danino, Michael. *The Lost River: On the Trail of the Sarasvatī*. Haryana, India: Penguin Books, 2010.

Dehaene, Stanislas. *Consciousness and the Brain: Deciphering How the Brain Codes Our Thoughts*. New York: Penguin Books, 2014.

Descharnes, Robert, and Gilles Néret. *Salvador Dalí 1904-1989: Das malerische Werk*. Originalausg. ed. Köln: Benedikt Taschen, 1993.

Deshmukh, Vinod D. *The Astonishing Brain and Holistic Consciousness: Neuroscience and Vedanta Perspectives*. New York: Nova Science Publishers, 2012. http://www.novapubishers.org'catalog/product_info.php?products_id=33900

Dor, Joël. *The Clinical Lacan*, edited by Judith Feher Gurewich in collaboration with Susan Fairfield. Northvale, N.J.: J. Aronson, 1997.

Eccles, John C. *How the Self Controls Its Brain*. Berlin: Springer-Verlag, 1994.

Eglash, Ron. *African Fractals: Modern Computing and Indigenous Design*. New Brunswick, N.J.: Rutgers University Press, 1999.

Ehrenzweig, Anton. "Unconscious Form-Creation in Art." *British Journal of Medical Psychology* vol. 22, no. 1-2 (1949): 88-109.

Ehrenzweig, Anton. *The Hidden Order of Art: A Study in the Psychology of a Realistic Imagination.* Berkeley and Los Angeles: University of California Press, 1967.

Ehrenzweig, Anton. *The Psychoanalysis of Artistic Vision and Hearing: An Introduction to a Theory of Unconscious Perception.* New York: The Julian Press, 1953.

Ellenberger, Henri F. *The Discovery of the Unconscious.* New York, N.Y.: Basic Books, 1970.

Ende, Michael. *Jim Knopf und Lukas der Lokomotivführer* (English translation: *Jim Button and Luke the Locomotive Driver*, 1963). Stuttgart: Thienemann, 1960.

Ernst, Bruno. *Der Zauberspiegel des Maurits Cornelis Escher.* Berlin: Taco Verlagsgesellschaft und Agentur, 1986.

Farber, Barry A., Debora C. Brink, and Patricia M. Raskin, eds. *The Psychotherapy of Carl Rogers: Cases and Commentary.* New York: Guilford Press, 1996.

Fassmann, Kurt, ed. *Kindlers Malerei Lexikon in 15 Bänden.* München: Taschenbuch-Verlag, 1982.

Freud, Sigmund. *The Basic Writing of Sigmund Freud*, translated by Abraham A. Brill. New York: Random House, 1995.

Freud, Sigmund. "Creative Writers and Daydreaming" (1908), in *The Standard Edition of the Complete Psychological Works of Sigmund Freud, Volume IX (1906–1908)*, edited and translated by James Strachey. London: The Hogarth Press, 1959.

Freud, Sigmund. *Dream Psychology: Psychoanalysis for Beginners.* New York: The James A. McCann Company, 1921.

Freud, Sigmund, *Inhibitions, Symptoms and Anxiety* (1926), in *The Standard Edition of the Complete Psychological Works of Sigmund Freud, Volume XX (1925–1926)*, edited and translated by James Strachey. London: The Hogarth Press, 1959.

Freud, Sigmund. *The Interpretation of Dreams*, translated by A. A. Brill. New York: Macmillan, 1913.

Freud, Sigmund. *Leonardo Da Vinci: A Psychosexual Study of an Infantile Reminiscence*, translated by Abraham A. Brill. London: Moffat, Yard & Company, 1916.

Freud, Sigmund. "Mourning and Melancholia" (1917), in *The Standard Edition of the Complete Psychological Works of Sigmund Freud, Volume XIV (1914–1916)*, edited and translated by James Strachey, 243-258. London: The Hogarth Press, 1975

Freud, Sigmund. *The Major Works of Sigmund Freud* (*Great Books of the Western World, Vol. 54*). Chicago: Encyclopædia Britannica, 1952.

Freud, Sigmund. "Mourning and Melancholia" (1917), in *The Standard Edition of the Complete Psychological Works of Sigmund Freud, Volume XIV (1914–1916)*, edited and translated by James Strachey, 243-258. London: The Hogarth Press, 1975.

Psychologie), unpublished manuscript of 1895 in *The Standard Edition of the Complete Psychological Works of Sigmund Freud, Volume I (1886–1899)*, edited and translated by James Strachey, 355-445. London: The Hogarth Press, 1966.

Fuchs, Reinhard. *Women in Art: The Great Female Artists from the Middle Ages to the Modern Era.* Vienna: Edition Fuchs, 2013.

Gazzaniga, Michael S. *The Consciousness Instinct: Unraveling the Mystery of How the Brain Makes the Mind.* New York: Farrar, Straus and Giroux, 2018.

Glass, Philip. *The Photographer: A Music-Drama in Three Acts*, conducted by Michael Riesman. Sony Masterworks MK 37849. 1983. CD.

Gombrich, Ernst Hans and Didier Eribon. *Looking for Answers.* New York: Harry N. Abrams, 1991.

Gombrich, Ernst Hans. *Meditation on a Hobby Horse and Other Essays on the Theory of Art: With 140 Illustrations.* Oxford: Phaidon Press, 1985.

Gordon, Dillian. *100 Great Paintings, Duccio to Picasso: European Paintings from the 14th to the 20th Century.* London: Sponsored by Coutts & and Published by Order of the Trustees Publications Dept., National Gallery, 1981.

Graziano, Michael S. A. *Consciousness and the Social Brain.* New York: Oxford University Press, 2013

Greene, Brian. *The Elegant Universe: Superstrings, Hidden Dimensions, and the Quest for the Ultimate Theory.* New York: W.W. Norton, 1999.

Gundert, Wilhelm, Annemarie Schimmel, and Walter Schubbing, eds. *Lyrik des Ostens.* München: Carl Hanser Verlag, 1952.

Hagman, George. *The Artist's Mind: A Psychoanalytic Perspective on Creativity, Modern Art and Modern Artists.* New York: Routledge, 2010.

Hawking, Stephen, and Leonard Mlodinow. *A Briefer History of Time.* New York: Bantam Books, 2005.

Hobson, J. A., R. McCarley, and P. Wyzinki. "Sleep cycle oscillation: reciprocal discharge by two brainstem neuronal groups." *Science* 189, No. 4196 (1975): 55-58.

Hobson, J. A. and R. McCarley. "The brain as a dream state generator: an activation-synthesis hypothesis of the dream process." *The American Journal of Psychiatry* 134, No. 12 (1977):1335-48.

Holt, Robert R. *Freud Reappraised.* New York, NY: The Guilford Press, 1989.

Hornby, Albert Sydney, E.V. Gatenby, and H. Wakefield. *The Advanced Learner's Dictionary of Current English.* 2nd ed. London: Oxford University Press, 1963.

James, William. *The Principles of Psychology Vol.1.* originally published 1890. New York: Cosmo, 2007.

Jantzen, Hans. *Über den gotischen Kirchenraum und andere Aufsätze.* Berlin: Mann, 1951.

Jeismann, Karl Ernst, Gustav Muthmann, eds. *Wort und Sinn: Lesebuch für den Deutschunterricht.* Paderborn: Ferdinand Schöningh, 1974.

Jung, Carl. G. *Mandala Symbolism.* Princeton, N.J.: Princeton University Press, 1972.

Jung, Carl. G. *Dreams*, translated by R. F. C. Hull. Princeton, N.J.: Princeton University Press, 1974.

Jung, Carl G., Marie-Louise von Franz, Aniela Jaffé, Jolande Jacobi, and Joseph L. Henderson, eds. *Man and His Symbols.* Garden City, N.Y.: Doubleday, 1964.

Kandel, Eric R. *Reductionism in Art and in Brain Science: Bridging the Two Cultures.* New York: Columbia University Press, 2016.

Kandel, Eric R. *The Age of Insight: The Quest to Understand the Unconscious in Art, Mind, and Brain: From Vienna 1900 to the Present.* New York: Random House, 2012.

Kandinsky, Wassily. *Concerning the Spiritual in Art*, translated by Michael Sadler. New York: Dover Publications, 1977.

Kaplan-Solms, Karen, and Mark Solms. *Clinical Studies in Neuro-Psychoanalysis: Introduction to a Depth Neuropsychology.* 2nd ed. London: Karnac Books, 2000.

Kineman, John J. "R-Theory: A Synthesis of Robert Rosen's Relational Complexity." *System Research and Behavioral Science* 29, issue 5 (2012): 527-538.

Kineman, John J. "A causal framework for integrating contemporary and Vedic holism." *Progress in Biophysics and Molecular Biology* 131(2017): 402-423.]

Kitzbichler, Manfred G., Marie L. Smith, Søren R. Christensen, Ed Bullmore, and Tim Behrens. "Broadband Criticality of Human Brain Network Synchronization." *PLoS Computational Biology* 5, no. 3 (2009): e1000314.

Klein, Melanie and Joan Riviere. *Love, Hate and Reparation*, with a preface by John Rickman. New York: W. W. Norton, 1964.

Klein, Melanie. *The Collected Writings of Melanie Klein, Volume 1 – Love, Guilt and Reparation and Other Works, 1921-1945.* London: Hogarth Press, 1975.

Klein, Melanie. *The Psycho-Analysis of Children.* The authorized translation by Alix Strachey (revised in collaboration with Alix Strachey by H. A. Thorner). New York: Delacorte Press. 1975.

Koenig, Becky. *Color Workbook.* 3rd ed. Upper Saddle River, N.J.: Prentice Hall, 2009.

Kornhuber, Hans H. and Lüder Deecke. "Hirnpotentialänderungen bei Willkürbewegungen und passiven Bewegungen des Menschen: Bereitschaftspotential und reafferente Potentiale." *Pflügers Archiv für die gesamte Physiologie des Menschen und der Tiere* 284, issue 1 (1965): 1-17.

Lacan, Jacques. *Écrits: A Selection*, translated by Alan Sheridan. New York: Norton, 1977.

LeDoux, Joseph. *The Emotional Brain: The Mysterious Underpinnings of Emotional Life.* London: Weidenfeld & Nicolson, 1996.

Livio, Mario. *The Golden Ratio: The Story of Phi, the World's Most Astonishing Number.* New York: Broadway Books, 2002.

Llinas, Rodolfo. *I of the Vortex: From Neurons to Self.* Cambridge, Mass.: MIT Press, 2002

Lomas, David. *The Haunted Self: Surrealism, Psychoanalysis, Subjectivity.* New Haven, Conn.: Yale University Press, 2000.

Luria, Alexander R. *The Working Brain: An Introduction to Neuropsychology.* Harmondsworth, London: Penguin, 1973.

Mandelbrot, Benoit B. *The Fractal Geometry of Nature.* San Francisco: W. H. Freeman, 1982.

Mayo Clinic. *Art & Healing at Mayo Clinic.* Rochester, Minn.: Mayo Foundation for Medical Education and Research, 2014.

Miller, Alice. *Das Drama des begabten Kindes und die Suche nach dem wahren Selbst.* Frankfurt am Main: Surkamp Verlag, 1979.

Miller, Alice. *The Drama of the Gifted Child: The Search for the True Self*. Rev. ed. New York: Harper Perrenial, 1997. (Translation of *Das Drama des begabten Kindes und die Suche nach dem wahren Selbst.* Frankfurt am Main: Suhrkamp Verlag, 1983.)

Miller, Alice. *The Untouched Key: Tracing Childhood Trauma in Creativity and Destructiveness.* New York: Anchor Books, 1991. (Translation of *Der geschmiedete Schlüssel.* Frankfurt am Main: Suhrkamp Verlag, 1991.)

Miller, Arthur I. *Einstein, Picasso: Space, Time, and Beauty That Causes Havoc.* New York: Basic Books, 2001.

Miller, E. K. and J. D. Cohen. "An integrative theory of prefrontal cortex function." *Annual Review of Neuroscience* 24 (2001):167-202.

Moorhouse, Paul. *Dalí.* San Diego, California: Thunder Bay Press, 1990.

Morgan, Marlo. *Mutant Message Down Under.* New York, N.Y.: HarperCollins Publishers, 1994.

Munroe, Alexandra, ed. *Autumn Grasses and Water: Motifs in Japanese Art: from the Suntory Museum of Art.* New York: Japan House Gallery, 1983.

Murase, Miyeko. *Masterpieces of Japanese Screen Painting: The American Collections.* New York: G. Braziller, 1990.

Murray, Peter, and Linda Murray. *The Oxford Companion to Christian Art and Architecture.* Oxford: Oxford University Press, 1996.

Myss, Caroline M. *Anatomy of the Spirit: The Seven Stages of Power and Healing.* New York: Harmony Books, 1996.

Nasio, Juan-David. *Appendix: The Concept of the Subject of the Unconscious,* translated by Boris Belay in *Disseminating Lacan*. Edited by David Pettigrew and François Raffoul. Albany, N.Y.: State University of New York Press, 1996.

Nasio, Juan-David. *Five Lessons on the Psychoanalytic Theory of Jacques Lacan,* translated by David Pettigrew and François Raffoul. Albany, New York: State University of New York Press, 1998.

Neumann, Erich. *The Great Mother: An Analysis of the Archetype*. 2nd ed. Princeton N.J.: Princeton University Press, 1963.

Newton, Michael. *Journey of Souls: Case Studies of Life between Lives*. St. Paul, Minn.: Llewellyn, 1994.

Ovchinnikova, O. V., E. E. Nasinovskaya, and N. G. Itkin. **Гипноз в экспериментальном исследовании личности** (published in Russian. English: *Hypnosis in Experimental Personality Research*. Moscow: Moscow University Press, 1989.

Panksepp, Jaak, and Lucy Biven. *The Archaeology of Mind: Neuroevolutionary Origins of Human Emotions*. New York: W. W. Norton & Company, 2012.

Panofsky, Erwin. *Meaning in the Visual Arts: Papers in and on Art History*. New York: Doubleday & Company, 1955.

Parrott, E. O. *The Pre-Raphaelites: A Catalogue for the Tate Exhibition*. London: Tate Gallery, 1984.

Pascal, Blaise. *Pascal's Pensées,* translated by A. J. Krailsheimer. Harmondsworth, London: Penguin Books, 1966. A number of other English translations are also available in print and online.

Peil, Katherine T. "Emotion: The Self-regulatory Sense." *Global Advances in Health and Medicine*: Vol. 3, No. 2. March 2014.www.gahmj.com: 80-108 (accessed last May 2018)

Pevsner, Nikolaus, John Fleming, and Hugh Honour. *The Penguin Dictionary of Architecture*. 3rd ed. Harmondsworth, London: Penguin Books, 1980.

Pincus, David. "Fractal Brains: Fractal Thoughts." *Psychology Today*, September 5, 2009. https://www.psychologytoday.com/blog/the-chaotic-life/200909/fractal-brains-fractal-thoughts (last accessed June 5, 2018).

Popper, Karl R., and John C. Eccles. *The Self and Its Brain*. New York: Springer-Verlag, 1981 (Corrected 2nd Printing, 1985).

Ramachandran, V.S. *A Brief Tour of Human Consciousness*. New York: Pi Press, 2004.

Ramachandran, V. S. *The Tell-Tale Brain: A Neuroscientist's Quest for What Makes Us Human*. New York: W.W. Norton & Co., 2011.

Ramachandran, V. S. *The Artful Brain*. London, Great Britain: Fourth Estate, 2005.

Ramachandran, V. S. and Sandra Blakeslee. *Phantoms in the Brain: Probing the Mysteries of the Human Mind*. New York: William Morrow & Co., 1998.

Rankin, Trudy Corry. *Soul Notes of a Composition: In the World Between Two Worlds of Grief from Suicide*. Bloomington, Ind.: AuthorHouse, 2007.

Rinpoche, Sogyal. *The Tibetan Book of Living and Dying,* edited by Patrick Gaffney and Andrew Harvey. San Francisco, California: HarperCollins Publishers, 1992.

Robertson, Jean, and Craig McDaniel. *Painting as a Language: Material, Technique, Form, Content*. Fort Worth: Harcourt College Publishers, 2000.

Rosen, Robert. *Life Itself: A Comprehensive Inquiry Into the Nature, Origin, and Fabrication of Life*. New York: Columbia University Press, 1991.

Rubin, Edgar. *Visuell wahrgenommene Figuren: Studien in psychologischer Analyse*. Kobenhaven: Gyldendalske Boghandel, 1921.

Schmidt, J. D. *Within the Human Realm: The Poetry of Huang Zunxian, 1848-1905*. Cambridge: Cambridge University Press, 1994.

Schultze-Kraft, Matthias, Daniel Birman, Marco Rusconi, Carsten Allefeld, Kai Görgen, Sven Dähne, Benjamin Blankertz, and John-Dylan Haynes. "The point of no return in vetoing self-initiated movements." *Proceedings of the National Academy of Sciences* (PNAS) 113(4): 1080-1085.

Sedlmayr, Hans. *Die Revolution der Modernen Kunst*. Hamburg: Rowohlt Taschenbuch Verlag GmbH, 1955.

Shuman, Sandra G. *Source Imagery: Releasing the Power of Your Creativity*. New York: Doubleday, 1989.

Shlain, Leonard. *Art & Physics: Parallel Visions in Space, Time, and Light*. New York: Morrow, 1991

Simson, Otto von. *Die Gotische Kathedrale: Beiträge zu ihrer Entstehung und Bedeutung*. 3. Aufl. ed. Darmstadt: Wissenschaftliche Buchgesellschaft, 1979. English original: Simson, Otto Von. *The Gothic Cathedral: Origins of Gothic Architecture and the Medieval Concept of Order* (*Bollingen series*). 2nd ed. Princeton, N.J.: Princeton University Press, 1974.

Solms, Mark. "Dreaming and the REM sleep are controlled by different brain mechanisms." *Behavioral and Brain Science* (2000) 23 (6), 843–50

Solms, Mark. *The Feeling Brain: Selected Papers on Neuropsychoanalysis*. London: Karnac Books, 2015

Solms, Mark, and Oliver Turnbull. *Brain and the Inner World: An Introduction to the Neuroscience of Subjective Experience*. New York: Other Press, 2002.

Solms, Mark. "What is 'the unconscious,' and where is it located in the brain? A neuropsychoanalytic perspective." *Annals of the New York Academy of Sciences* 1406, issue 1 (2017): 90-97.

Stachelscheid, Carl August, and Heinz Todtmann. *Geboren im Feuer: Stahl Ein Farbbildbuch*. Stuttgart: Verl. Die Schönen Bücher, 1956.

Tolle, Eckhart. *The Power of Now: A Guide to Spiritual Enlightenment.* Novato, Calif.: New World Library, 1999.

Tolstoy, Leo. *What Men Live By, and Other Tales,* translated by Louise Shanks Maude and Aylmer Maude. Boston: Stratford Company, 1918.

Tresidder, Jack. *Dictionary of Symbols: An Illustrated Guide to Traditional Images, Icons, and Emblems.* San Francisco: Chronicle Books, 1998.

Vos, Dirk De. *Hans Memling: Catalogue.* Antwerp: Ludion, 1994.

Weiss, Brian L. *Many Lives, Many Masters.* New York: Simon & Schuster, 1988.

Wehlte, Kurt. *Werkstoffe und Techniken der Malerei: Mit einem Anhang über Farbenlehre: Ein Fachbuch.* Ravensburg: Otto Mayer Verlag, 1967.

Zelanski, Paul, and Mary Pat Fisher. *Color.* 6th ed. Upper Saddle River, N.J.: Prentice Hall, 2010.

Ziegler, Konrad, and Walter Sontheimer, eds. *Der Kleine Pauly: Lexikon der Antike in fünf Bänden.* München: Taschenbuch-Verl., 1979.

Picture Credits

Nomenclature: the symbol 🅮 indicates that the artwork is in the public domain.
🅭 indicates the artwork is under the Creative Commons license.

Fig. 5.16. Arnold Böcklin: *Mermaids at Play.* Wikimedia Commons 🅮. The original work is located in the Kunstmuseum Basel, Basel, Switzerland.

Figs. 8.3. and 12.8. Wikimedia Commons 🅮. The original work by an unknown 18th century Japanese artist is located in the Art Gallery of South Australia, Adelaide, Australia.

Fig. 8.18. Wikimedia Commons 🅭. The original work is located in the Vatican Museum, Rome, Italy. Artemis of Ephesus. License attribution: anonymous (https://commons.wikimedia.org/wiki/File:Artemis_Ephesiana_Galleria_Candelabri_Inv2505.jpg), „Artemis Ephesiana Galleria Candelabri Inv2505", https://creativecommons.org/licenses/by/3.0/legalcode

Figs. 9.12 and 9.36. Paolo Uccello: *St George and the Dragon.* Wikimedia Commons 🅮. The original work is located in the National Gallery, London, UK.

Fig. 9.13. Jurij Zaninović (1876-1946), *Dragon,* 1900-1901. From the Dragon Bridge in Ljubljana, Slovenia. License: the Creative Commons Zero 🄍 license (accessed on 12-01-2017 from www.maxpixel.net/Dragon-Slovenia-Statue-762166).

Figs 9.14, 9.15, and 9.16: Accessed from Pexels (www.pexels.com) under the Creative Commons Zero 🄍 license (no permission and attribution required) on 05-13-2018.

Fig. 9.55. Palenque, King Pakal. Wikimedia Commons 🅭. License attribution: tato grasso (https://commons.wikimedia.org/wiki/File:0155_Palenque.JPG), „0155 Palenque", https://creativecommons.org/licenses/by-sa/2.5/legalcode

Back cover portrait photos by Jeff H. Nelson

Fig. 13.0 by Susanne Schuenke

Artworks Index

CPSIA information can be obtained
at www.ICGtesting.com
Printed in the USA
LVHW052350261119
638638LV00002B/2

9 781732 220508